Companies Act 1985

CHAPTER 6

A Table showing the derivation of the provisions of this consolidation Act will be found at the end of the Act. The Table has no official status.

ARRANGEMENT OF SECTIONS

PART I

FORMATION AND REGISTRATION OF COMPANIES;
JURIDICAL STATUS AND MEMBERSHIP

CHAPTER I

COMPANY FORMATION

Memorandum of association

A

CHAPTER II

ISSUES BY COMPANIES INCORPORATED, OR TO BE INCORPORATED, OUTSIDE GREAT BRITAIN

PART IV

ALLOTMENT OF SHARES AND DEBENTURES

General provisions as to allotment

Pre-emption rights

Commissions and discounts

Amount to be paid for shares; the means of payment

Chapter III

Share Premiums

Chapter IV

Reduction of Share Capital

Chapter V

Maintenance of Capital

Chapter VI

Financial Assistance by a Company for Acquisition of its Own Shares

Provisions applying to both public and private companies

Private companies

CHAPTER VII

REDEEMABLE SHARES; PURCHASE BY A COMPANY OF
ITS OWN SHARES

Redemption and purchase generally

CHAPTER VIII

MISCELLANEOUS PROVISIONS ABOUT SHARES AND DEBENTURES

Share and debenture certificates, transfers and warrants

A 4

PART VII

ACCOUNTS AND AUDIT

CHAPTER I

PROVISIONS APPLYING TO COMPANIES GENERALLY

Accounting records

PART IX

A COMPANY'S MANAGEMENT; DIRECTORS AND SECRETARIES; THEIR QUALIFICATIONS, DUTIES AND RESPONSIBILITIES

Officers and registered office

Provisions governing appointment of directors

Disqualification

Part XI

Company Administration and Procedure

Chapter I

Company Identification

Chapter II

Register of Members

CHAPTER III

GENERAL

PART XIX

RECEIVERS AND MANAGERS
(ENGLAND AND WALES)

PART XX

WINDING UP OF COMPANIES REGISTERED
UNDER THIS ACT OR THE FORMER COMPANIES ACTS

CHAPTER I

PRELIMINARY

Modes of winding up

Contributories

Chapter II

Winding Up by the Court

Jurisdiction (England and Wales)

Jurisdiction (Scotland)

Grounds and effect of winding-up petition

Commencement of winding up

The official receiver (England and Wales only)

CHAPTER VII

MISCELLANEOUS PROVISIONS ABOUT WINDING UP

PART XXI

WINDING UP OF UNREGISTERED COMPANIES

PART XXII

BODIES CORPORATE SUBJECT, OR BECOMING SUBJECT, TO THIS ACT (OTHERWISE THAN BY ORIGINAL FORMATION UNDER PART I)

CHAPTER I

COMPANIES FORMED OR REGISTERED UNDER FORMER COMPANIES ACTS

Part XXV

Miscellaneous and Supplementary Provisions

Part XXVI

Interpretation

Companies Act 1985

1985 CHAPTER 6

An Act to consolidate the greater part of the Companies
Acts.   [11th March 1985]

B E IT ENACTED by the Queen's most Excellent Majesty, by and
with the advice and consent of the Lords Spiritual and
Temporal, and Commons, in this present Parliament
assembled, and by the authority of the same, as follows:—

PART I

FORMATION AND REGISTRATION OF COMPANIES ;
JURIDICAL STATUS AND MEMBERSHIP

CHAPTER I

COMPANY FORMATION

Memorandum of association

1.—(1) Any two or more persons associated for a lawful
purpose may, by subscribing their names to a memorandum of
association and otherwise complying with the requirements of
this Act in respect of registration, form an incorporated company,
with or without limited liability.

(2) A company so formed may be either—

    (*a*) a company having the liability of its members limited
        by the memorandum to the amount, if any, unpaid on

Mode of
forming
incorporated
company.

the shares respectively held by them ("a company limited by shares ") ;

(b) a company having the liability of its members limited by the memorandum to such amount as the members may respectively thereby undertake to contribute to the assets of the company in the event of its being wound up (" a company limited by guarantee ") ; or

(c) a company not having any limit on the liability of its members (" an unlimited company ").

(3) A " public company " is a company limited by shares or limited by guarantee and having a share capital, being a company—

(a) the memorandum of which states that it is to be a public company, and

(b) in relation to which the provisions of this Act or the former Companies Acts as to the registration or re-registration of a company as a public company have been complied with on or after 22nd December 1980 ;

and a " private company " is a company that is not a public company.

(4) With effect from 22nd December 1980, a company cannot be formed as, or become, a company limited by guarantee with a share capital.

Requirements with respect to memorandum.

2.—(1) The memorandum of every company must state—

(a) the name of the company ;

(b) whether the registered office of the company is to be situated in England and Wales, or in Scotland ;

(c) the objects of the company.

(2) Alternatively to subsection (1)(b), the memorandum may contain a statement that the company's registered office is to be situated in Wales ; and a company whose registered office is situated in Wales may by special resolution alter its memorandum so as to provide that its registered office is to be so situated.

(3) The memorandum of a company limited by shares or by guarantee must also state that the liability of its members is limited.

(4) The memorandum of a company limited by guarantee must also state that each member undertakes to contribute to the assets of the company if it should be wound up while he is a member, or within one year after he ceases to be a member, for payment of the debts and liabilities of the company contracted before he ceases to be a member, and of the costs, charges and expenses of winding up, and for adjustment of the rights of the contributories among themselves, such amount as may be required, not exceeding a specified amount.

(5) In the case of a company having a share capital—

   (a) the memorandum must also (unless it is an unlimited company) state the amount of the share capital with which the company proposes to be registered and the division of the share capital into shares of a fixed amount;

   (b) no subscriber of the memorandum may take less than one share; and

   (c) there must be shown in the memorandum against the name of each subscriber the number of shares he takes.

(6) The memorandum must be signed by each subscriber in the presence of at least one witness, who must attest the signature; and that attestation is sufficient in Scotland as well as in England and Wales.

(7) A company may not alter the conditions contained in its memorandum except in the cases, in the mode and to the extent, for which express provision is made by this Act.

3.—(1) Subject to the provisions of sections 1 and 2, the form of the memorandum of association of—

   (a) a public company, being a company limited by shares,

   (b) a public company, being a company limited by guarantee and having a share capital,

   (c) a private company limited by shares,

   (d) a private company limited by guarantee and not having a share capital,

   (e) a private company limited by guarantee and having a share capital, and

   (f) an unlimited company having a share capital,

shall be as specified respectively for such companies by regulations made by the Secretary of State, or as near to that form as circumstances admit.

Forms of memorandum.

(2) Regulations under this section shall be made by statutory instrument subject to annulment in pursuance of a resolution of either House of Parliament.

4. A company may by special resolution alter its memorandum with respect to the objects of the company, so far as may be required to enable it—

Resolution to alter objects.

   (a) to carry on its business more economically or more efficiently; or

   (b) to attain its main purpose by new or improved means; or

   (c) to enlarge or change the local area of its operations; or (*d*) to carry on some business which under existing circumstances may conveniently or advantageously be combined with the business of the company ; or

(*e*) to restrict or abandon any of the objects specified in the memorandum ; or

(*f*) to sell or dispose of the whole or any part of the undertaking of the company ; or

(*g*) to amalgamate with any other company or body of persons ;

but if an application is made under the following section, the alteration does not have effect except in so far as it is confirmed by the court.

Procedure for objecting to alteration.

5.—(1) Where a company's memorandum has been altered by special resolution under section 4, application may be made to the court for the alteration to be cancelled.

(2) Such an application may be made—

(*a*) by the holders of not less in the aggregate than 15 per cent. in nominal value of the company's issued share capital or any class of it or, if the company is not limited by shares, not less than 15 per cent. of the company's members ; or

(*b*) by the holders of not less than 15 per cent. of the company's debentures entitling the holders to object to an alteration of its objects ;

but an application shall not be made by any person who has consented to or voted in favour of the alteration.

(3) The application must be made within 21 days after the date on which the resolution altering the company's objects was passed, and may be made on behalf of the persons entitled to make the application by such one or more of their number as they may appoint in writing for the purpose.

(4) The court may on such an application make an order confirming the alteration either wholly or in part and on such terms and conditions as it thinks fit, and may—

(*a*) if it thinks fit, adjourn the proceedings in order that an arrangement may be made to its satisfaction for the purchase of the interests of dissentient members, and

(*b*) give such directions and make such orders as it thinks expedient for facilitating or carrying into effect any such arrangement.

(5) The court's order may (if the court thinks fit) provide for the purchase by the company of the shares of any members of the company, and for the reduction accordingly of its capital, and may make such alterations in the company's memorandum and articles as may be required in consequence of that provision.

(6) If the court's order requires the company not to make any, or any specified, alteration in its memorandum or articles, the company does not then have power without the leave of the court to make any such alteration in breach of that requirement.

(7) An alteration in the memorandum or articles of a company made by virtue of an order under this section, other than one made by resolution of the company, is of the same effect as if duly made by resolution ; and this Act applies accordingly to the memorandum or articles as so altered.

(8) The debentures entitling the holders to object to an alteration of a company's objects are any debentures secured by a floating charge which were issued or first issued before 1st December 1947 or form part of the same series as any debentures so issued ; and a special resolution altering a company's objects requires the same notice to the holders of any such debentures as to members of the company.

In the absence of provisions regulating the giving of notice to any such debenture holders, the provisions of the company's articles regulating the giving of notice to members apply.

6.—(1) Where a company passes a resolution altering its objects, then—

    (*a*) if with respect to the resolution no application is made under section 5, the company shall within 15 days from the end of the period for making such an application deliver to the registrar of companies a printed copy of its memorandum as altered ; and

    (*b*) if such an application is made, the company shall—

        (i) forthwith give notice (in the prescribed form) of that fact to the registrar, and

        (ii) within 15 days from the date of any order cancelling or confirming the alteration, deliver to the registrar an office copy of the order and, in the case of an order confirming the alteration, a printed copy of the memorandum as altered.

(2) The court may by order at any time extend the time for the delivery of documents to the registrar under subsection (1)(*b*) for such period as the court may think proper.

(3) If a company makes default in giving notice or delivering any document to the registrar of companies as required by subsection (1), the company and every officer of it who is in default is liable to a fine and, for continued contravention, to a daily default fine.

(4) The validity of an alteration of a company's memorandum with respect to the objects of the company shall not be questioned on the ground that it was not authorised by section 4,

except in proceedings taken for the purpose (whether under section 5 or otherwise) before the expiration of 21 days after the date of the resolution in that behalf.

(5) Where such proceedings are taken otherwise than under section 5, subsections (1) to (3) above apply in relation to the proceedings as if they had been taken under that section, and as if an order declaring the alteration invalid were an order cancelling it, and as if an order dismissing the proceedings were an order confirming the alteration.

Articles of association

Articles
prescribing
regulations for
companies.
7.—(1) There may in the case of a company limited by shares, and there shall in the case of a company limited by guarantee or unlimited, be registered with the memorandum articles of association signed by the subscribers to the memorandum and prescribing regulations for the company.

(2) In the case of an unlimited company having a share capital, the articles must state the amount of share capital with which the company proposes to be registered.

(3) Articles must—

(*a*) be printed,

(*b*) be divided into paragraphs numbered consecutively, and

(*c*) be signed by each subscriber of the memorandum in the presence of at least one witness who must attest the signature (which attestation is sufficient in Scotland as well as in England and Wales).

Tables A, C, D
and E.
8.—(1) Table A is as prescribed by regulations made by the Secretary of State ; and a company may for its articles adopt the whole or any part of that Table.

(2) In the case of a company limited by shares, if articles are not registered or, if articles are registered, in so far as they do not exclude or modify Table A, that Table (so far as applicable, and as in force at the date of the company's registration) constitutes the company's articles, in the same manner and to the same extent as if articles in the form of that Table had been duly registered.

(3) If in consequence of regulations under this section Table A is altered, the alteration does not affect a company registered before the alteration takes effect, or repeal as respects that company any portion of the Table.

(4) The form of the articles of association of—

(*a*) a company limited by guarantee and not having a share capital, (*b*) a company limited by guarantee and having a share capital, and

(*c*) an unlimited company having a share capital,

shall be respectively in accordance with Table C, D or E prescribed by regulations made by the Secretary of State, or as near to that form as circumstances admit.

(5) Regulations under this section shall be made by statutory instrument subject to annulment in pursuance of a resolution of either House of Parliament.

9.—(1) Subject to the provisions of this Act and to the conditions contained in its memorandum, a company may by special resolution alter its articles.

(2) Alterations so made in the articles are (subject to this Act) as valid as if originally contained in them, and are subject in like manner to alteration by special resolution.

Registration and its consequences

10.—(1) The company's memorandum and articles (if any) shall be delivered—

(*a*) to the registrar of companies for England and Wales, if the memorandum states that the registered office of the company is to be situated in England and Wales, or that it is to be situated in Wales ; and

(*b*) to the registrar of companies for Scotland, if the memorandum states that the registered office of the company is to be situated in Scotland.

(2) With the memorandum there shall be delivered a statement in the prescribed form containing the names and requisite particulars of—

(*a*) the person who is, or the persons who are, to be the first director or directors of the company ; and

(*b*) the person who is, or the persons who are, to be the first secretary or joint secretaries of the company ;

and the requisite particulars in each case are those set out in Schedule 1.

(3) The statement shall be signed by or on behalf of the subscribers of the memorandum and shall contain a consent signed by each of the persons named in it as a director, as secretary or as one of joint secretaries, to act in the relevant capacity.

(4) Where a memorandum is delivered by a person as agent for the subscribers, the statement shall specify that fact and the person's name and address.

(5) An appointment by any articles delivered with the memorandum of a person as director or secretary of the company is void unless he is named as a director or secretary in the statement.

(6) There shall in the statement be specified the intended situation of the company's registered office on incorporation.

Minimum
authorised
capital
(public
companies).

11. When a memorandum delivered to the registrar of companies under section 10 states that the association to be registered is to be a public company, the amount of the share capital stated in the memorandum to be that with which the company proposes to be registered must not be less than the authorised minimum (defined in section 118).

Duty of
registrar.

12.—(1) The registrar of companies shall not register a company's memorandum delivered under section 10 unless he is satisfied that all the requirements of this Act in respect of registration and of matters precedent and incidental to it have been complied with.

(2) Subject to this, the registrar shall retain and register the memorandum and articles (if any) delivered to him under that section.

(3) A statutory declaration in the prescribed form by—

(a) a solicitor engaged in the formation of a company, or

(b) a person named as a director or secretary of the company in the statement delivered under section 10(2),

that those requirements have been complied with shall be delivered to the registrar of companies, and the registrar may accept such a declaration as sufficient evidence of compliance.

Effect of
registration.

13.—(1) On the registration of a company's memorandum, the registrar of companies shall give a certificate that the company is incorporated and, in the case of a limited company, that it is limited.

(2) The certificate may be signed by the registrar, or authenticated by his official seal.

(3) From the date of incorporation mentioned in the certificate, the subscribers of the memorandum, together with such other persons as may from time to time become members of the company, shall be a body corporate by the name contained in the memorandum.

(4) That body corporate is then capable forthwith of exercising all the functions of an incorporated company, but with such liability on the part of its members to contribute to its assets in the event of its being wound up as is provided by this Act.

This is subject, in the case of a public company, to section 117 (additional certificate as to amount of allotted share capital).

(5) The persons named in the statement under section 10 as directors, secretary or joint secretaries are, on the company's incorporation, deemed to have been respectively appointed as its first directors, secretary or joint secretaries.

(6) Where the registrar registers an association's memorandum which states that the association is to be a public company, the certificate of incorporation shall contain a statement that the company is a public company.

(7) A certificate of incorporation given in respect of an association is conclusive evidence—

> (*a*) that the requirements of this Act in respect of registration and of matters precedent and incidental to it have been complied with, and that the association is a company authorised to be registered, and is duly registered, under this Act, and

> (*b*) if the certificate contains a statement that the company is a public company, that the company is such a company.

14.—(1) Subject to the provisions of this Act, the memorandum and articles, when registered, bind the company and its members to the same extent as if they respectively had been signed and sealed by each member, and contained covenants on the part of each member to observe all the provisions of the memorandum and of the articles.

Effect of memorandum and articles.

(2) Money payable by a member to the company under the memorandum or articles is a debt due from him to the company, and in England and Wales is of the nature of a specialty debt.

15.—(1) In the case of a company limited by guarantee and not having a share capital, every provision in the memorandum or articles, or in any resolution of the company purporting to give any person a right to participate in the divisible profits of the company otherwise than as a member, is void.

Memorandum and articles of company limited by guarantee.

(2) For purposes of provisions of this Act relating to the memorandum of a company limited by guarantee, and for those of section 1(4) and this section, every provision in the memorandum or articles, or in any resolution, of a company so limited purporting to divide the company's undertaking into shares or interests is to be treated as a provision for a share capital, notwithstanding that the nominal amount or number of the shares or interests is not specified by the provision.

PART I
CHAPTER I
Effect of
alteration on
company's
members.

16.—(1) A member of a company is not bound by an alteration made in the memorandum or articles after the date on which he became a member, if and so far as the alteration—

(a) requires him to take or subscribe for more shares than the number held by him at the date on which the alteration is made ; or

(b) in any way increases his liability as at that date to contribute to the company's share capital or otherwise to pay money to the company.

(2) Subsection (1) operates notwithstanding anything in the memorandum or articles ; but it does not apply in a case where the member agrees in writing, either before or after the alteration is made, to be bound by the alteration.

17.—(1) A condition contained in a company's memorandum which could lawfully have been contained in articles of association instead of in the memorandum may be altered by the company by special resolution ; but if an application is made to the court for the alteration to be cancelled, the alteration does not have effect except in so far as it is confirmed by the court.

(2) This section—

(a) is subject to section 16, and also to Part XVII (court order protecting minority), and

(b) does not apply where the memorandum itself provides for or prohibits the alteration of all or any of the conditions above referred to, and does not authorise any variation or abrogation of the special rights of any class of members.

(3) Section 5 (except subsections (2)(b) and (8)) and section 6(1) to (3) apply in relation to any alteration and to any application made under this section as they apply in relation to alterations and applications under sections 4 to 6.

18.—(1) Where an alteration is made in a company's memorandum or articles by any statutory provision, whether contained in an Act of Parliament or in an instrument made under an Act, a printed copy of the Act or instrument shall, not later than 15 days after that provision comes into force, be forwarded to the registrar of companies and recorded by him.

(2) Where a company is required (by this section or otherwise) to send to the registrar any document making or evidencing an alteration in the company's memorandum or articles (other than a special resolution under section 4), the company shall send with it a printed copy of the memorandum or articles as altered.

(3) If a company fails to comply with this section, the company and any officer of it who is in default is liable to a fine and, for continued contravention, to a daily default fine.

19.—(1) A company shall, on being so required by any member, send to him a copy of the memorandum and of the articles (if any), and a copy of any Act of Parliament which alters the memorandum, subject to payment—

(a) in the case of a copy of the memorandum and of the articles, of 5 pence or such less sum as the company may prescribe, and

(b) in the case of a copy of an Act, of such sum not exceeding its published price as the company may require.

(2) If a company makes default in complying with this section, the company and every officer of it who is in default is liable for each offence to a fine.

20.—(1) Where an alteration is made in a company's memorandum, every copy of the memorandum issued after the date of the alteration shall be in accordance with the alteration.

(2) If, where any such alteration has been made, the company at any time after the date of the alteration issues any copies of the memorandum which are not in accordance with the alteration, it is liable to a fine, and so too is every officer of the company who is in default.

21.—(1) Where a company is to be registered with a memorandum stating that its registered office is to be situated in Wales, the memorandum and articles to be delivered for registration under section 10 may be in Welsh ; but, if they are, they shall be accompanied by a certified translation into English.

(2) Where a company whose registered office is situated in Wales has altered its memorandum as allowed by section 2(2), it may deliver to the registrar of companies for registration a certified translation into Welsh of its memorandum and articles.

(3) A company whose memorandum states that its registered office is to be situated in Wales may comply with any provision of this Act requiring it to deliver any document to the registrar of companies by delivering to him that document in Welsh (or, if it consists of a prescribed form, completed in Welsh), together with a certified translation into English.

But any document making or evidencing an alteration in the company's memorandum or articles, and any copy of a company's memorandum or articles as altered, shall be in the same language as the memorandum and articles originally registered and, if that language is Welsh, shall be accompanied by a certified translation into English.

(4) Where a company has under subsection (2) delivered a translation into Welsh of its memorandum and articles, it may, when delivering to the registrar of companies a document making or evidencing an alteration in the memorandum or articles or a copy of the memorandum or articles as altered, deliver with it a certified translation into Welsh.

(5) In this section " certified translation " means a translation certified in the prescribed manner to be a correct translation ; and a reference to delivering a document includes sending, forwarding, producing or (in the case of a notice) giving it.

A company's membership

Definition
of " member ".
22.—(1) The subscribers of a company's memorandum are deemed to have agreed to become members of the company, and on its registration shall be entered as such in its register of members.

(2) Every other person who agrees to become a member of a company, and whose name is entered in its register of members, is a member of the company.

Membership
of holding
company.
23.—(1) Except in the cases mentioned below in this section, a body corporate cannot be a member of a company which is its holding company ; and any allotment or transfer of shares in a company to its subsidiary is void.

(2) This does not prevent a subsidiary which was, on 1st July 1948, a member of its holding company, from continuing to be a member ; but (subject to subsection (4)) the subsidiary has no right to vote at meetings of the holding company or any class of its members.

(3) Subject as follows, subsections (1) and (2) apply in relation to a nominee for a body corporate which is a subsidiary, as if references to such a body corporate included a nominee for it.

(4) Nothing in this section applies where the subsidiary is concerned as personal representative, or where it is concerned as trustee, unless the holding company or a subsidiary of it is beneficially interested under the trust and is not so interested only by way of security for the purposes of a transaction entered into by it in the ordinary course of a business which includes the lending of money.

Schedule 2 has effect for the interpretation of the reference in this subsection to a company or its subsidiary being beneficially interested.

(5) In relation to a company limited by guarantee or unlimited which is a holding company, the reference in subsection (1) to shares (whether or not the company has a share capital) includes the interest of its members as such, whatever the form of that interest.

24. If a company carries on business without having at least Minimum membership for carrying on business. two members and does so for more than 6 months, a person who, for the whole or any part of the period that it so carries on business after those 6 months—

> (*a*) is a member of the company, and
>
> (*b*) knows that it is carrying on business with only one member,

is liable (jointly and severally with the company) for the payment of the company's debts contracted during the period or, as the case may be, that part of it.

CHAPTER II

COMPANY NAMES

25.—(1) The name of a public company must end with the Name as stated in memorandum. words " public limited company " or, if the memorandum states that the company's registered office is to be situated in Wales, those words or their equivalent in Welsh (" cwmni cyfyngedig cyhoeddus "); and those words or that equivalent may not be preceded by the word " limited " or its equivalent in Welsh (" cyfyngedig ").

(2) In the case of a company limited by shares or by guarantee (not being a public company), the name must have " limited " as its last word, except that—

> (*a*) this is subject to section 30 (exempting, in certain circumstances, a company from the requirement to have " limited " as part of the name), and
>
> (*b*) if the company is to be registered with a memorandum stating that its registered office is to be situated in Wales, the name may have " cyfyngedig " as its last word.

26.—(1) A company shall not be registered under this Act Prohibition on registration of certain names. by a name—

> (*a*) which includes, otherwise than at the end of the name, any of the following words or expressions, that is to say, " limited ", " unlimited " or " public limited company "

or their Welsh equivalents (" cyfyngedig ", " anghyfyn-gedig " and " cwmni cyfyngedig cyhoeddus " respectively) ;

(b) which includes, otherwise than at the end of the name, an abbreviation of any of those words or expressions ;

(c) which is the same as a name appearing in the registrar's index of company names ;

(d) the use of which by the company would in the opinion of the Secretary of State constitute a criminal offence ; or

(e) which in the opinion of the Secretary of State is offensive.

(2) Except with the approval of the Secretary of State, a company shall not be registered under this Act by a name which—

(a) in the opinion of the Secretary of State would be likely to give the impression that the company is connected in any way with Her Majesty's Government or with any local authority ; or

(b) includes any word or expression for the time being specified in regulations under section 29.

" Local authority " means any local authority within the meaning of the Local Government Act 1972 or the Local Government (Scotland) Act 1973, the Common Council of the City of London or the Council of the Isles of Scilly.

(3) In determining for purposes of subsection (1)(c) whether one name is the same as another, there are to be disregarded—

(a) the definite article, where it is the first word of the name ;

(b) the following words and expressions where they appear at the end of the name, that is to say—

" company " or its Welsh equivalent (" cwmni "),

" and company " or its Welsh equivalent (" a'r cwmni "),

" company limited " or its Welsh equivalent (" cwmni cyfyngedig "),

" and company limited " or its Welsh equivalent (" a'r cwmni cyfyngedig "),

" limited " or its Welsh equivalent (" cyfyngedig "),

" unlimited " or its Welsh equivalent (" anghyfyn-gedig "), and

" public limited company " or its Welsh equivalent (" cwmni cyfyngedig cyhoeddus ") ;

(c) abbreviations of any of those words or expressions where they appear at the end of the name ; and (*d*) type and case of letters, accents, spaces between letters and punctuation marks;

and " and " and " & " are to be taken as the same.

27.—(1) A company which by any provision of this Act is either required or entitled to include in its name, as its last part, any of the words specified in subsection (4) below may, instead of those words, include as the last part of the name the abbreviations there specified as alternatives in relation to those words.

(2) A reference in this Act to the name of a company or to the inclusion of any of those words in a company's name includes a reference to the name including (in place of any of the words so specified) the appropriate alternative, or to the inclusion of the appropriate alternative, as the case may be.

(3) A provision of this Act requiring a company not to include any of those words in its name also requires it not to include the abbreviated alternative specified in subsection (4).

(4) For the purposes of this section—

(*a*) the alternative of " limited " is " ltd.";

(*b*) the alternative of " public limited company " is " p.l.c. ";

(*c*) the alternative of " cyfyngedig " is " cyf."; and

(*d*) the alternative of " cwmni cyfyngedig cyhoeddus " is " c.c.c. ".

28.—(1) A company may by special resolution change its name (but subject to section 31 in the case of a company which has received a direction under subsection (2) of that section from the Secretary of State).

(2) Where a company has been registered by a name which—

(*a*) is the same as or, in the opinion of the Secretary of State, too like a name appearing at the time of the registration in the registrar's index of company names, or

(*b*) is the same as or, in the opinion of the Secretary of State, too like a name which should have appeared in that index at that time,

the Secretary of State may within 12 months of that time, in writing, direct the company to change its name within such period as he may specify.

Section 26(3) applies in determining under this subsection whether a name is the same as or too like another.

(3) If it appears to the Secretary of State that misleading information has been given for the purpose of a company's registration with a particular name, or that undertakings or assurances have been given for that purpose and have not been fulfilled, he may within 5 years of the date of its registration with that name in writing direct the company to change its name within such period as he may specify.

(4) Where a direction has been given under subsection (2) or (3), the Secretary of State may by a further direction in writing extend the period within which the company is to change its name, at any time before the end of that period.

(5) A company which fails to comply with a direction under this section, and any officer of it who is in default, is liable to a fine and, for continued contravention, to a daily default fine.

(6) Where a company changes its name under this section, the registrar of companies shall (subject to section 26) enter the new name on the register in place of the former name, and shall issue a certificate of incorporation altered to meet the circumstances of the case ; and the change of name has effect from the date on which the altered certificate is issued.

(7) A change of name by a company under this section does not affect any rights or obligations of the company or render defective any legal proceedings by or against it ; and any legal proceedings that might have been continued or commenced against it by its former name may be continued or commenced against it by its new name.

Regulations about names.
29.—(1) The Secretary of State may by regulations—

(a) specify words or expressions for the registration of which as or as part of a company's corporate name his approval is required under section 26(2)(b), and

(b) in relation to any such word or expression, specify a Government department or other body as the relevant body for purposes of the following subsection.

(2) Where a company proposes to have as, or as part of, its corporate name any such word or expression and a Government department or other body is specified under subsection (1)(b) in relation to that word or expression, a request shall be made (in writing) to the relevant body to indicate whether (and if so why) it has any objections to the proposal ; and the person to make the request is—

(a) in the case of a company seeking to be registered under this Part, the person making the statutory declaration required by section 12(3), (*b*) in the case of a company seeking to be registered under section 680, the persons making the statutory declaration required by section 686(2), and

(*c*) in any other case, a director or secretary of the company concerned.

(3) The person who has made that request to the relevant body shall submit to the registrar of companies a statement that it has been made and a copy of any response received from that body, together with—

(*a*) the requisite statutory declaration, or

(*b*) a copy of the special resolution changing the company's name,

according as the case is one or other of those mentioned in subsection (2).

(4) Sections 709 and 710 (public rights of inspection of documents kept by registrar of companies) do not apply to documents sent under subsection (3) of this section.

(5) Regulations under this section may contain such transitional provisions and savings as the Secretary of State thinks appropriate and may make different provision for different cases or classes of case.

(6) The regulations shall be made by statutory instrument, to be laid before Parliament after it is made ; and the regulations shall cease to have effect at the end of 28 days beginning with the day on which the regulations were made (but without prejudice to anything previously done by virtue of them or to the making of new regulations), unless during that period they are approved by resolution of each House. In reckoning that period, no account is to be taken of any time during which Parliament is dissolved or prorogued or during which both Houses are adjourned for more than 4 days.

30.—(1) Certain companies are exempt from requirements of this Act relating to the use of " limited " as part of the company name.

(2) A private company limited by guarantee is exempt from those requirements, and so too is a company which on 25th February 1982 was a private company limited by shares with a name which, by virtue of a licence under section 19 of the Companies Act 1948, did not include " limited " ; but in either case the company must, to have the exemption, comply with the requirements of the following subsection.

(3) Those requirements are that—

(*a*) the objects of the company are (or, in the case of a company about to be registered, are to be) the promotion of commerce, art, science, education, religion, charity or any profession, and anything incidental or conducive to any of those objects ; and

(*b*) the company's memorandum or articles—

(i) require its profits (if any) or other income to be applied in promoting its objects,

(ii) prohibit the payment of dividends to its members, and

(iii) require all the assets which would otherwise be available to its members generally to be transferred on its winding up either to another body with objects similar to its own or to another body the objects of which are the promotion of charity and anything incidental or conducive thereto (whether or not the body is a member of the company).

(4) A statutory declaration that a company complies with the requirements of subsection (3) may be delivered to the registrar of companies, who may accept the declaration as sufficient evidence of the matters stated in it ; and the registrar may refuse to register a company by a name which does not include the word " limited " unless such a declaration has been delivered to him.

(5) The statutory declaration must be in the prescribed form and be made—

(*a*) in the case of a company to be formed, by a solicitor engaged in its formation or by a person named as director or secretary in the statement delivered under section 10(2) ;

(*b*) in the case of a company to be registered in pursuance of section 680, by two or more directors or other principal officers of the company ; and

(*c*) in the case of a company proposing to change its name so that it ceases to have the word " limited " as part of its name, by a director or secretary of the company.

(6) References in this section to the word " limited " include (in an appropriate case) its Welsh equivalent (" cyfyngedig "), and the appropriate alternative (" ltd." or " cyf.", as the case may be).

(7) A company which is exempt from requirements relating to the use of " limited " and does not include that word as part of its name, is also exempt from the requirements of this Act relating to the publication of its name and the sending of lists of members to the registrar of companies.

31.—(1) A company which is exempt under section 30 and whose name does not include " limited " shall not alter its memorandum or articles of association so that it ceases to comply with the requirements of subsection (3) of that section.

PART I
CHAPTER II
Provisions
applying to
company
exempt under
s. 30.

(2) If it appears to the Secretary of State that such a company—

(a) has carried on any business other than the promotion of any of the objects mentioned in that subsection, or

(b) has applied any of its profits or other income otherwise than in promoting such objects, or

(c) has paid a dividend to any of its members,

he may, in writing, direct the company to change its name by resolution of the directors within such period as may be specified in the direction, so that its name ends with " limited ".

A resolution passed by the directors in compliance with a direction under this subsection is subject to section 380 of this Act (copy to be forwarded to the registrar of companies within 15 days).

(3) A company which has received a direction under subsection (2) shall not thereafter be registered by a name which does not include " limited ", without the approval of the Secretary of State.

(4) References in this section to the word " limited " include (in an appropriate case) its Welsh equivalent (" cyfyngedig "), and the appropriate alternative (" ltd." or " cyf.", as the case may be).

(5) A company which contravenes subsection (1), and any officer of it who is in default, is liable to a fine and, for continued contravention, to a daily default fine.

(6) A company which fails to comply with a direction by the Secretary of State under subsection (2), and any officer of the company who is in default, is liable to a fine and, for continued contravention, to a daily default fine.

32.—(1) If in the Secretary of State's opinion the name by which a company is registered gives so misleading an indication of the nature of its activities as to be likely to cause harm to the public, he may direct it to change its name.

Power to
require
company to
abandon
misleading
name.

(2) The direction must, if not duly made the subject of an application to the court under the following subsection, be complied with within a period of 6 weeks from the date of the direction or such longer period as the Secretary of State may think fit to allow.

(3) The company may, within a period of 3 weeks from the date of the direction, apply to the court to set it aside ; and the court may set the direction aside or confirm it and, if it confirms the direction, shall specify a period within which it must be complied with.

(4) If a company makes default in complying with a direction under this section, it is liable to a fine and, for continued contravention, to a daily default fine.

(5) Where a company changes its name under this section, the registrar shall (subject to section 26) enter the new name on the register in place of the former name, and shall issue a certificate of incorporation altered to meet the circumstances of the case ; and the change of name has effect from the date on which the altered certificate is issued.

(6) A change of name by a company under this section does not affect any of the rights or obligations of the company, or render defective any legal proceedings by or against it ; and any legal proceedings that might have been continued or commenced against it by its former name may be continued or commenced against it by its new name.

Prohibition on trading under misleading name.

33.—(1) A person who is not a public company is guilty of an offence if he carries on any trade, profession or business under a name which includes, as its last part, the words " public limited company " or their equivalent in Welsh (" cwmni cyfyngedig cyhoeddus ").

(2) A public company is guilty of an offence if, in circumstances in which the fact that it is a public company is likely to be material to any person, it uses a name which may reasonably be expected to give the impression that it is a private company.

(3) A person guilty of an offence under subsection (1) or (2) and, if that person is a company, any officer of the company who is in default, is liable to a fine and, for continued contravention, to a daily default fine.

Penalty for improper use of " limited " or " cyfyngedig ".

34. If any person trades or carries on business under a name or title of which " limited " or " cyfyngedig ", or any contraction or imitation of either of those words, is the last word, that person, unless duly incorporated with limited liability, is liable to a fine and, for continued contravention, to a daily default fine.

Chapter III

A Company's Capacity ; Formalities
of Carrying on Business

35.—(1) In favour of a person dealing with a company in good faith, any transaction decided on by the directors is deemed to be one which it is within the capacity of the company to enter into, and the power of the directors to bind the company is deemed to be free of any limitation under the memorandum or articles.

(2) A party to a transaction so decided on is not bound to enquire as to the capacity of the company to enter into it or as to any such limitation on the powers of the directors, and is presumed to have acted in good faith unless the contrary is proved.

Company's capacity: power of directors to bind it.

36.—(1) Contracts on behalf of a company may be made as follows—

(a) a contract which if made between private persons would be by law required to be in writing, and if made according to the law of England and Wales to be under seal, may be made on behalf of the company in writing under the company's common seal ;

(b) a contract which if made between private persons would be by law required to be in writing, signed by the parties to be charged therewith, may be made on behalf of the company in writing signed by any person acting under its authority, express or implied ;

(c) a contract which if made between private persons would by law be valid although made by parol only, and not reduced into writing, may be made by parol on behalf of the company by any person acting under its authority, express or implied.

(2) A contract made according to this section—

(a) is effectual in law, and binds the company and its successors and all other parties to it ;

(b) may be varied or discharged in the same manner in which it is authorised by this section to be made.

(3) A deed to which a company is a party is held to be validly executed according to the law of Scotland on behalf of the company if it is executed in accordance with this Act or is sealed with the company's common seal and subscribed on behalf of the company by two of the directors, or by a director and the secretary ; and such subscription on behalf of the company is binding whether attested by witnesses or not.

Form of company contracts.

PART I
CHAPTER III

(4) Where a contract purports to be made by a company, or by a person as agent for a company, at a time when the company has not been formed, then subject to any agreement to the contrary the contract has effect as one entered into by the person purporting to act for the company or as agent for it, and he is personally liable on the contract accordingly.

Bills of
exchange and
promissory
notes.

37. A bill of exchange or promissory note is deemed to have been made, accepted or endorsed on behalf of a company if made, accepted or endorsed in the name of, or by or on behalf or on account of, the company by a person acting under its authority.

Execution of
deeds abroad.

38.—(1) A company may, by writing under its common seal, empower any person, either generally or in respect of any specified matters, as its attorney, to execute deeds on its behalf in any place elsewhere than in the United Kingdom.

(2) A deed signed by such an attorney on behalf of the company and under his seal binds the company and has the same effect as if it were under the company's common seal.

Power of
company to
have official
seal for use
abroad.

39.—(1) A company whose objects require or comprise the transaction of business in foreign countries may, if authorised by its articles, have for use in any territory, district or place elsewhere than in the United Kingdom, an official seal, which shall be a facsimile of the common seal of the company, with the addition on its face of the name of every territory, district or place where it is to be used.

(2) A deed or other document to which the official seal is duly affixed binds the company as if it had been sealed with the company's common seal.

(3) A company having an official seal for use in any such territory, district or place may, by writing under its common seal, authorise any person appointed for the purpose in that territory, district or place to affix the official seal to any deed or other document to which the company is party in that territory, district or place.

(4) As between the company and a person dealing with such an agent, the agent's authority continues during the period (if any) mentioned in the instrument conferring the authority, or if no period is there mentioned, then until notice of the revocation or determination of the agent's authority has been given to the person dealing with him.

(5) The person affixing the official seal shall certify in writing on the deed or other instrument to which the seal is affixed the date on which and the place at which it is affixed.

40. A company may have, for use for sealing securities Official seal issued by the company and for sealing documents creating or for share evidencing securities so issued, an official seal which is a certificates, etc. facsimile of the company's common seal with the addition on its face of the word " Securities ".

41. A document or proceeding requiring authentication by Authentication a company may be signed by a director, secretary or other of documents. authorised officer of the company, and need not be under the company's common seal.

42.—(1) A company is not entitled to rely against other per- Events sons on the happening of any of the following events— affecting a company's

(a) the making of a winding-up order in respect of the com- status. pany, or the appointment of a liquidator in a voluntary winding up of the company, or

(b) any alteration of the company's memorandum or articles, or

(c) any change among the company's directors, or

(d) (as regards service of any document on the company) any change in the situation of the company's registered office,

if the event had not been officially notified at the material time and is not shown by the company to have been known at that time to the person concerned, or if the material time fell on or before the 15th day after the date of official notification (or, where the 15th day was a non-business day, on or before the next day that was not) and it is shown that the person concerned was unavoidably prevented from knowing of the event at that time.

(2) In subsection (1)—

(a) " official notification " and " officially notified " have the meanings given by section 711(2) (registrar of companies to give public notice of the issue or receipt by him of certain documents), and

(b) " non-business day " means a Saturday or Sunday, Christmas Day, Good Friday and any other day which is a bank holiday in the part of Great Britain where the company is registered.

Part II

Re-registration as a means of altering a company's status

Private company becoming public

Re-registration
of private
company
as public.

43.—(1) Subject to this and the following five sections, a private company (other than a company not having a share capital) may be re-registered as a public company if—

(a) a special resolution that it should be so re-registered is passed ; and

(b) an application for re-registration is delivered to the registrar of companies, together with the necessary documents.

A company cannot be re-registered under this section if it has previously been re-registered as unlimited.

(2) The special resolution must—

(a) alter the company's memorandum so that it states that the company is to be a public company ; and

(b) make such other alterations in the memorandum as are necessary to bring it (in substance and in form) into conformity with the requirements of this Act with respect to the memorandum of a public company (the alterations to include compliance with section 25(1) as regards the company's name) ; and

(c) make such alterations in the company's articles as are requisite in the circumstances.

(3) The application must be in the prescribed form and be signed by a director or secretary of the company ; and the documents to be delivered with it are the following—

(a) a printed copy of the memorandum and articles as altered in pursuance of the resolution ;

(b) a copy of a written statement by the company's auditors that in their opinion the relevant balance sheet shows that at the balance sheet date the amount of the company's net assets (within the meaning given to that expression by section 264(2)) was not less than the aggregate of its called-up share capital and undistributable reserves ;

(c) a copy of the relevant balance sheet, together with a copy of an unqualified report (defined in section 46) by the company's auditors in relation to that balance sheet ;

(d) if section 44 applies, a copy of the valuation report under subsection (2)(b) of that section ; and

(e) a statutory declaration in the prescribed form by a director or secretary of the company—

> (i) that the special resolution required by this section has been passed and that the conditions of the following two sections (so far as applicable) have been satisfied, and

> (ii) that, between the balance sheet date and the application for re-registration, there has been no change in the company's financial position that has resulted in the amount of its net assets becoming less than the aggregate of its called-up share capital and undistributable reserves.

(4) "Relevant balance sheet" means a balance sheet prepared as at a date not more than 7 months before the company's application under this section.

(5) A resolution that a company be re-registered as a public company may change the company name by deleting the word "company" or the words "and company", or its or their equivalent in Welsh ("cwmni", "a'r cwmni"), including any abbreviation of them.

44.—(1) The following applies if shares have been allotted by the company between the date as at which the relevant balance sheet was prepared and the passing of the special resolution under section 43, and those shares were allotted as fully or partly paid up as to their nominal value or any premium on them otherwise than in cash.

Consideration for shares recently allotted to be valued.

(2) Subject to the following provisions, the registrar of companies shall not entertain an application by the company under section 43 unless beforehand—

> (a) the consideration for the allotment has been valued in accordance with section 108, and

> (b) a report with respect to the value of the consideration has been made to the company (in accordance with that section) during the 6 months immediately preceding the allotment of the shares.

(3) Where an amount standing to the credit of any of the company's reserve accounts, or of its profit and loss account, has been applied in paying up (to any extent) any of the shares allotted or any premium on those shares, the amount applied does not count as consideration for the allotment, and accordingly subsection (2) does not apply to it.

(4) Subsection (2) does not apply if the allotment is in connection with an arrangement providing for it to be on terms

that the whole or part of the consideration for the shares allotted is to be provided by the transfer to the company or the cancellation of all or some of the shares, or of all or some of the shares of a particular class, in another company (with or without the issue to the company applying under section 43 of shares, or of shares of any particular class, in that other company).

(5) But subsection (4) does not exclude the application of subsection (2), unless under the arrangement it is open to all the holders of the shares of the other company in question (or, where the arrangement applies only to shares of a particular class, all the holders of the other company's shares of that class) to take part in the arrangement.

In determining whether that is the case, shares held by or by a nominee of the company allotting shares in connection with the arrangement, or by or by a nominee of a company which is that company's holding company or subsidiary or a company which is a subsidiary of its holding company, are to be disregarded.

(6) Subsection (2) does not apply to preclude an application under section 43, if the allotment of the company's shares is in connection with its proposed merger with another company ; that is, where one of the companies concerned proposes to acquire all the assets and liabilities of the other in exchange for the issue of shares or other securities of that one to shareholders of the other, with or without any cash payment to shareholders.

(7) In this section—

    (*a*) "arrangement" means any agreement, scheme or arrangement, including an arrangement sanctioned in accordance with section 425 (company compromise with creditors and members) or section 582 (liquidator in winding up accepting shares as consideration for sale of company's property), and

    (*b*) "another company" includes any body corporate and any body to which letters patent have been issued under the Chartered Companies Act 1837.

1837 c. 73.

Additional requirements relating to share capital.

45.—(1) For a private company to be re-registered under section 43 as a public company, the following conditions with respect to its share capital must be satisfied at the time the special resolution under that section is passed.

(2) Subject to subsections (5) to (7) below—

    (*a*) the nominal value of the company's allotted share

capital must be not less than the authorised minimum, and

   (*b*) each of the company's allotted shares must be paid up at least as to one-quarter of the nominal value of that share and the whole of any premium on it.

(3) Subject to subsection (5), if any shares in the company or any premium on them have been fully or partly paid up by an undertaking given by any person that he or another should do work or perform services (whether for the company or any other person), the undertaking must have been performed or otherwise discharged.

(4) Subject to subsection (5), if shares have been allotted as fully or partly paid up as to their nominal value or any premium on them otherwise than in cash, and the consideration for the allotment consists of or includes an undertaking to the company (other than one to which subsection (3) applies), then either—

   (*a*) the undertaking must have been performed or otherwise discharged, or

   (*b*) there must be a contract between the company and some person pursuant to which the undertaking is to be performed within 5 years from the time the resolution under section 43 is passed.

(5) For the purpose of determining whether subsections (2)(*b*), (3) and (4) are complied with, certain shares in the company may be disregarded ; and these are—

   (*a*) subject to the next subsection, any share which was allotted before 22nd June 1982, and

   (*b*) any share which was allotted in pursuance of an employees' share scheme and by reason of which the company would, but for this subsection, be precluded under subsection (2)(*b*) (but not otherwise) from being re-registered as a public company.

(6) A share is not to be disregarded under subsection (5)(*a*) if the aggregate in nominal value of that share and other shares proposed to be so disregarded is more than one-tenth of the nominal value of the company's allotted share capital ; but for this purpose the allotted share capital is treated as not including any shares disregarded under subsection (5)(*b*).

(7) Any shares disregarded under subsection (5) are treated as not forming part of the allotted share capital for the purposes of subsection (2)(*a*).

46.—(1) The following subsections explain the reference in section 43(3)(*c*) to an unqualified report of the company's auditors on the relevant balance sheet.

(2) If the balance sheet was prepared in respect of an accounting reference period of the company, that reference is to a report made by the auditors and stating without material qualification, that in their opinion the balance sheet—

(*a*) has been properly prepared in accordance with this Act, and

(*b*) gives a true and fair view of the state of the company's affairs as at the balance sheet date.

(3) In any other case the reference is to a report by the auditors stating without material qualification that in their opinion the balance sheet—

(*a*) complies with the applicable accounting provisions, and

(*b*) without prejudice to that (but subject to subsection (4) below), gives a true and fair view of the state of the company's affairs as at the balance sheet date ;

and the accounting provisions referred to in paragraph (*a*) are sections 228 and 238(1) in Chapter I of Part VII and (where applicable) section 258 in Chapter II of that Part.

(4) Where the balance sheet is prepared under Chapter II of Part VII (special category companies), and the company is entitled to avail itself, and has availed itself, of any of the provisions of Part III of Schedule 9, the auditors' report is not required to state that the balance sheet gives a true and fair view of the company's state of affairs as at the balance sheet date.

(5) For purposes of references in this section to the auditors' report, a qualification is not material if, but only if, the auditors in their report state that the thing giving rise to the qualification is not material for the purpose of determining (by reference to the balance sheet) whether at the balance sheet date the amount of the company's net assets was not less than the aggregate of its called up share capital and undistributable reserves.

(6) For the purposes of a report of the auditors falling within subsection (3)—

(*a*) section 228 in Chapter I of Part VII, and Schedule 4 (form and content of company accounts), and

(*b*) (where applicable) section 258 in Chapter II of that Part, and Schedule 9 (the same, in relation to special category companies),

are deemed to have effect in relation to the balance sheet with such modifications as are necessary by reason of the fact that the balance sheet is prepared otherwise than as at the end of an accounting reference period.

47.—(1) If the registrar of companies is satisfied, on an appli- Certificate of re-registration under s. 43.cation under section 43, that a company may be re-registered under that section as a public company, he shall—

    (*a*) retain the application and other documents delivered to him under the section ; and

    (*b*) issue the company with a certificate of incorporation stating that the company is a public company.

(2) The registrar may accept a declaration under section 43 (3)(*e*) as sufficient evidence that the special resolution required by that section has been passed and the other conditions of re-registration satisfied.

(3) The registrar shall not issue the certificate if it appears to him that the court has made an order confirming a reduction of the company's capital which has the effect of bringing the nominal value of the company's allotted share capital below the authorised minimum.

(4) Upon the issue to a company of a certificate of incorporation under this section—

    (*a*) the company by virtue of the issue of that certificate becomes a public company ; and

    (*b*) any alterations in the memorandum and articles set out in the resolution take effect accordingly.

(5) The certificate is conclusive evidence—

    (*a*) that the requirements of this Act in respect of re-registration and of matters precedent and incidental thereto have been complied with ; and

    (*b*) that the company is a public company.

48.—(1) In their application to unlimited companies, sections Modification for unlimited company re-registering.43 to 47 are modified as follows.

(2) The special resolution required by section 43(1) must, in addition to the matters mentioned in subsection (2) of that section—

    (*a*) state that the liability of the members is to be limited by shares, and what the company's share capital is to be; and

    (*b*) make such alterations in the company's memorandum as are necessary to bring it in substance and in form into conformity with the requirements of this Act with respect to the memorandum of a company limited by shares.

(3) The certificate of incorporation issued under section 47(1) shall, in addition to containing the statement required by paragraph (*b*) of that subsection, state that the company has been incorporated as a company limited by shares ; and—

>   (*a*) the company by virtue of the issue of the certificate becomes a public company so limited ; and

>   (*b*) the certificate is conclusive evidence of the fact that it is such a company.

Limited company becoming unlimited

Re-registration of limited company as unlimited.   **49.**—(1) Subject as follows, a company which is registered as limited may be re-registered as unlimited in pursuance of an application in that behalf complying with the requirements of this section.

1967 c. 81.   (2) A company is excluded from re-registering under this section if it is limited by virtue of re-registration under section 44 of the Companies Act 1967 or section 51 of this Act.

(3) A public company cannot be re-registered under this section ; nor can a company which has previously been re-registered as unlimited.

(4) An application under this section must be in the prescribed form and be signed by a director or the secretary of the company, and be lodged with the registrar of companies, together with the documents specified in subsection (8) below.

(5) The application must set out such alterations in the company's memorandum as—

>   (*a*) if it is to have a share capital, are requisite to bring it (in substance and in form) into conformity with the requirements of this Act with respect to the memorandum of a company to be formed as an unlimited company having a share capital ; or

>   (*b*) if it is not to have a share capital, are requisite in the circumstances.

(6) If articles have been registered, the application must set out such alterations in them as—

>   (*a*) if the company is to have a share capital, are requisite to bring the articles (in substance and in form) into conformity with the requirements of this Act with respect to the articles of a company to be formed as an unlimited company having a share capital ; or

>   (*b*) if the company is not to have a share capital, are requisite in the circumstances.

(7) If articles have not been registered, the application must have annexed to it, and request the registration of, printed

articles; and these must, if the company is to have a share capital, comply with the requirements mentioned in subsection (6)(*a*) and, if not, be articles appropriate to the circumstances.

(8) The documents to be lodged with the registrar are—

(*a*) the prescribed form of assent to the company's being registered as unlimited, subscribed by or on behalf of all the members of the company;

(*b*) a statutory declaration made by the directors of the company—

(i) that the persons by whom or on whose behalf the form of assent is subscribed constitute the whole membership of the company, and

(ii) if any of the members have not subscribed that form themselves, that the directors have taken all reasonable steps to satisfy themselves that each person who subscribed it on behalf of a member was lawfully empowered to do so;

(*c*) a printed copy of the memorandum incorporating the alterations in it set out in the application; and

(*d*) if articles have been registered, a printed copy of them incorporating the alterations set out in the application.

(9) For purposes of this section—

(*a*) subscription to a form of assent by the legal personal representative of a deceased member of a company is deemed subscription by him; and

(*b*) a trustee in bankruptcy of a member of a company is, to the exclusion of the latter, deemed a member of the company.

50.—(1) The registrar of companies shall retain the application and other documents lodged with him under section 49 and shall— Certificate of re-registration under s. 49.

(*a*) if articles are annexed to the application, register them; and

(*b*) issue to the company a certificate of incorporation appropriate to the status to be assumed by it by virtue of that section.

(2) On the issue of the certificate—

(*a*) the status of the company, by virtue of the issue, is changed from limited to unlimited; and

(*b*) the alterations in the memorandum set out in the application and (if articles have been previously registered) any alterations to the articles so set out take effect as if duly made by resolution of the company ; and

(c) the provisions of this Act apply accordingly to the memorandum and articles as altered.

(3) The certificate is conclusive evidence that the requirements of section 49 in respect of re-registration and of matters precedent and incidental to it have been complied with, and that the company was authorised to be re-registered under this Act in pursuance of that section and was duly so re-registered.

Unlimited company becoming limited

Re-registration of unlimited company as limited.

51.—(1) Subject as follows, a company which is registered as unlimited may be re-registered as limited if a special resolution that it should be so re-registered is passed, and the requirements of this section are complied with in respect of the resolution and otherwise.

(2) A company cannot under this section be re-registered as a public company ; and a company is excluded from re-registering under it if it is unlimited by virtue of re-registration under section 43 of the Companies Act 1967 or section 49 of this Act.

1967 c. 81.

(3) The special resolution must state whether the company is to be limited by shares or by guarantee and—

(a) if it is to be limited by shares, must state what the share capital is to be and provide for the making of such alterations in the memorandum as are necessary to bring it (in substance and in form) into conformity with the requirements of this Act with respect to the memorandum of a company so limited, and such alterations in the articles as are requisite in the circumstances ;

(b) if it is to be limited by guarantee, must provide for the making of such alterations in its memorandum and articles as are necessary to bring them (in substance and in form) into conformity with the requirements of this Act with respect to the memorandum and articles of a company so limited.

(4) The special resolution is subject to section 380 of this Act (copy to be forwarded to registrar within 15 days) ; and an application for the company to be re-registered as limited, framed in the prescribed form and signed by a director or by the secretary of the company, must be lodged with the registrar of companies, together with the necessary documents, not

earlier than the day on which the copy of the resolution forwarded under section 380 is received by him.

(5) The documents to be lodged with the registrar are—

(*a*) a printed copy of the memorandum as altered in
pursuance of the resolution ; and

(*b*) a printed copy of the articles as so altered.

(6) This section does not apply in relation to the re-registration of an unlimited company as a public company under section
43.

52.—(1) The registrar shall retain the application and other Certification of
documents lodged with him under section 51, and shall issue re-registration
to the company a certificate of incorporation appropriate to the under s. 51.
status to be assumed by the company by virtue of that section.

(2) On the issue of the certificate—

(*a*) the status of the company is, by virtue of the issue,
changed from unlimited to limited ; and

(*b*) the alterations in the memorandum specified in the
resolution and the alterations in, and additions to, the
articles so specified take effect.

(3) The certificate is conclusive evidence that the requirements
of section 51 in respect of re-registration and of matters precedent and incidental to it have been complied with, and that
the company was authorised to be re-registered in pursuance of
that section and was duly so re-registered.

Public company becoming private

53.—(1) A public company may be re-registered as a private Re-registration
company if— of public
company
(*a*) a special resolution complying with subsection (2) below as private.
that it should be so re-registered is passed and has not
been cancelled by the court under the following section ;

(*b*) an application for the purpose in the prescribed form
and signed by a director or the secretary of the company is delivered to the registrar of companies, together with a printed copy of the memorandum and
articles of the company as altered by the resolution ;
and

(*c*) the period during which an application for the cancellation of the resolution under the following section may
be made has expired without any such application
having been made ; or

(*d*) where such an application has been made, the application has been withdrawn or an order has been made under section 54(5) confirming the resolution and a copy of that order has been delivered to the registrar.

(2) The special resolution must alter the company's memorandum so that it no longer states that the company is to be a public company and must make such other alterations in the company's memorandum and articles as are requisite in the circumstances.

(3) A company cannot under this section be re-registered otherwise than as a company limited by shares or by guarantee.

Litigated objection to resolution under s. 53.   **54.**—(1) Where a special resolution by a public company to be re-registered under section 53 as a private company has been passed, an application may be made to the court for the cancellation of that resolution.

(2) The application may be made—

    (*a*) by the holders of not less in the aggregate than 5 per cent. in nominal value of the company's issued share capital or any class thereof ;

    (*b*) if the company is not limited by shares, by not less than 5 per cent. of its members ; or

    (*c*) by not less than 50 of the company's members ;

but not by a person who has consented to or voted in favour of the resolution.

(3) The application must be made within 28 days after the passing of the resolution and may be made on behalf of the persons entitled to make the application by such one or more of their number as they may appoint in writing for the purpose.

(4) If such an application is made, the company shall forthwith give notice in the prescribed form of that fact to the registrar of companies.

(5) On the hearing of the application, the court shall make an order either cancelling or confirming the resolution and—

    (*a*) may make that order on such terms and conditions as it thinks fit, and may (if it thinks fit) adjourn the proceedings in order that an arrangement may be made to the satisfaction of the court for the purchase of the interests of dissentient members ; and

    (*b*) may give such directions and make such orders as it thinks expedient for facilitating or carrying into effect any such arrangement.

(6) The court's order may, if the court thinks fit, provide for the purchase by the company of the shares of any of its members and for the reduction accordingly of the company's capital, and may make such alterations in the company's memorandum and articles as may be required in consequence of that provision.

(7) The company shall, within 15 days from the making of the court's order, or within such longer period as the court may at any time by order direct, deliver to the registrar of companies an office copy of the order.

(8) If the court's order requires the company not to make any, or any specified, alteration in its memorandum or articles, the company has not then power without the leave of the court to make any such alteration in breach of the requirement.

(9) An alteration in the memorandum or articles made by virtue of an order under this section, if not made by resolution of the company, is of the same effect as if duly made by resolution; and this Act applies accordingly to the memorandum or articles as so altered.

(10) A company which fails to comply with subsection (4) or subsection (7), and any officer of it who is in default, is liable to a fine and, for continued contravention, to a daily default fine.

55.—(1) If the registrar of companies is satisfied that a Certificate of company may be re-registered under section 53, he shall— re-registration under s. 53.

    (a) retain the application and other documents delivered to him under that section; and

    (b) issue the company with a certificate of incorporation appropriate to a private company.

(2) On the issue of the certificate—

    (a) the company by virtue of the issue becomes a private company; and

    (b) the alterations in the memorandum and articles set out in the resolution under section 53 take effect accordingly.

(3) The certificate is conclusive evidence—

    (a) that the requirements of section 53 in respect of re-registration and of matters precedent and incidental to it have been complied with; and

    (b) that the company is a private company.

PART III

CAPITAL ISSUES

CHAPTER I

ISSUES BY COMPANIES REGISTERED, OR TO BE REGISTERED, IN GREAT BRITAIN

The prospectus

Matters to be
stated, and
reports to be
set out, in
prospectus.

56.—(1) Every prospectus issued by or on behalf of a company, or by or on behalf of any person who is or has been engaged or interested in the formation of the company, must comply—

> (a) with Part I of Schedule 3 to this Act, as respects the matters to be stated in the prospectus, and
>
> (b) with Part II of that Schedule, as respects the reports to be set out.

(2) It is unlawful to issue any form of application for shares in or debentures of a company unless the form is issued with a prospectus which complies with the requirements of this section.

(3) Subsection (2) does not apply if it is shown that the form of application was issued either—

> (a) in connection with a bona fide invitation to a person to enter into an underwriting agreement with respect to the shares or debentures, or
>
> (b) in relation to shares or debentures which were not offered to the public.

(4) If a person acts in contravention of subsection (2), he is liable to a fine.

(5) This section does not apply—

> (a) to the issue to existing members or debenture holders of a company of a prospectus or form of application relating to shares in or debentures of the company, whether an applicant for shares or debentures will or will not have the right to renounce in favour of other persons, or
>
> (b) to the issue of a prospectus or form of application relating to shares or debentures which are or are to be in all respects uniform with shares or debentures previously issued and for the time being listed on a prescribed stock exchange ;

but subject to this, it applies to a prospectus or a form of application whether issued on or with reference to the formation of a company or subsequently.

57. A condition requiring or binding an applicant for shares in or debentures of a company to waive compliance with any requirement of section 56, or purporting to affect him with notice of any contract, document or matter not specifically referred to in the prospectus, is void.

58.—(1) If a company allots or agrees to allot its shares or debentures with a view to all or any of them being offered for sale to the public, any document by which the offer for sale to the public is made is deemed for all purposes a prospectus issued by the company.

(2) All enactments and rules of law as to the contents of prospectuses, and to liability in respect of statements in and omissions from prospectuses, or otherwise relating to prospectuses, apply and have effect accordingly, as if the shares or debentures had been offered to the public for subscription and as if persons accepting the offer in respect of any shares or debentures were subscribers for those shares or debentures.

This is without prejudice to the liability (if any) of the persons by whom the offer is made, in respect of mis-statements in the document or otherwise in respect of it.

(3) For purposes of this Act it is evidence (unless the contrary is proved) that an allotment of, or an agreement to allot, shares or debentures was made with a view to their being offered for sale to the public if it is shown—

(a) that an offer of the shares or debentures (or of any of them) for sale to the public was made within 6 months after the allotment or agreement to allot, or

(b) that at the date when the offer was made the whole consideration to be received by the company in respect of the shares or debentures had not been so received.

(4) Section 56 as applied by this section has effect as if it required a prospectus to state, in addition to the matters required by that section—

(a) the net amount of the consideration received or to be received by the company in respect of the shares or debentures to which the offer relates, and

(b) the place and time at which the contract under which those shares or debentures have been or are to be allotted may be inspected.

C

PART III
CHAPTER I
Rule governing
what is an
" offer to the
public ".

59.—(1) Subject to the next section, any reference in this Act to offering shares or debentures to the public is to be read (subject to any provision to the contrary) as including a reference to offering them to any section of the public, whether selected as members or debenture holders of the company concerned, or as clients of the person issuing the prospectus, or in any other manner.

(2) The same applies to any reference in this Act, or in a company's articles, to an invitation to the public to subscribe for shares or debentures.

Exceptions
from rule in
s. 59.

60.—(1) Section 59 does not require an offer or invitation to be treated as made to the public if it can properly be regarded, in all the circumstances, as not being calculated to result, directly or indirectly, in the shares or debentures becoming available for subscription or purchase by persons other than those receiving the offer or invitation, or otherwise as being a domestic concern of the persons receiving and making it.

(2) In particular, a provision in a company's articles prohibiting invitations to the public to subscribe for shares or debentures is not to be taken as prohibiting the making to members or debenture holders of an invitation which can properly be regarded as falling within the preceding subsection.

(3) For purposes of that subsection, an offer of shares in or debentures of a private company, or an invitation to subscribe for such shares or debentures, is to be regarded (unless the contrary is proved) as being a domestic concern of the persons making and receiving the offer or invitation if it falls within any of the following descriptions.

(4) It is to be so regarded if it is made to—

    (*a*) an existing member of the company making the offer or invitation,

    (*b*) an existing employee of that company,

    (*c*) a member of the family of such a member or employee, or

    (*d*) an existing debenture holder.

(5) For purposes of subsection (4)(*c*), the members of a person's family are—

    (*a*) the person's husband or wife, widow or widower and children (including stepchildren) and their descendants, and

(b) any trustee (acting in his capacity as such) of a trust the principal beneficiary of which is the person him or herself, or any of those relatives.

(6) The offer or invitation is also to be so regarded if it is to subscribe for shares or debentures to be held under an employees' share scheme.

(7) The offer or invitation is also to be so regarded if it falls within subsection (4) or (6) and it is made on terms which permit the person to whom it is made to renounce his right to the allotment of shares or issue of debentures, but only in favour—

(a) of such a person as is mentioned in any of the paragraphs of subsection (4), or

(b) where there is an employees' share scheme, of a person entitled to hold shares or debentures under the scheme.

(8) Where application has been made to the Council of The Stock Exchange for admission of any securities to the Official List of the Stock Exchange, then an offer of those securities for subscription or sale to a person whose ordinary business it is to buy or sell shares or debentures (whether as principal or agent) is not deemed an offer to the public for purposes of this Part.

61.—(1) A prospectus inviting persons to subscribe for a company's shares or debentures and including a statement purporting to be made by an expert shall not be issued unless—

Prospectus containing statement by expert.

(a) he (the expert) has given and has not, before delivery of a copy of the prospectus for registration, withdrawn his written consent to its issue with the statement included in the form and context in which it is in fact included; and

(b) a statement that he has given and not withdrawn that consent appears in the prospectus.

(2) If a prospectus is issued in contravention of this section, the company and every person who is knowingly a party to the issue of the prospectus is liable to a fine.

62. The expression " expert ", in both Chapters of this Part, includes engineer, valuer, accountant and any other person whose profession gives authority to a statement made by him.

Meaning of " expert ".

C 2

PART III
CHAPTER I
Prospectus to
be dated.

63. A prospectus issued by or on behalf of a company, or in relation to an intended company, shall be dated ; and that date shall, unless the contrary is proved, be taken as its date of publication.

Registration of prospectus

Registration
requirement
applicable in
all cases.

64.—(1) No prospectus shall be issued by or on behalf of a company, or in relation to an intended company, unless on or before the date of its publication there has been delivered to the registrar of companies for registration a copy of the prospectus—

(a) signed by every person who is named in it as a director or proposed director of the company, or by his agent authorised in writing, and

(b) having endorsed on or attached to it any consent to its issue required by section 61 from any person as an expert.

(2) Where the prospectus is such a document as is referred to in section 58, the signatures required by subsection (1) above include those of every person making the offer, or his agent authorised in writing.

Where the offer is made by a company or a firm, it is sufficient for the purposes of this subsection if the document is signed on its behalf by two directors or (as the case may be) not less than half of the partners ; and a director or partner may sign by his agent authorised in writing.

(3) Every prospectus shall on its face—

(a) state that a copy has been delivered for registration as required by this section, and

(b) specify, or refer to statements in the prospectus specifying, any documents required by this or the following section to be endorsed on or attached to the copy delivered.

(4) The registrar shall not register a prospectus unless it is dated and the copy of it signed as required by this section and unless it has endorsed on or attached to it the documents (if any) specified in subsection (3)(b).

(5) If a prospectus is issued without a copy of it being delivered to the registrar as required by this section, or without the copy so delivered having the required documents endorsed on or attached to it, the company and every person who is knowingly a party to the issue of the prospectus is liable to a fine and, for continued contravention, to a daily default fine.

Additional
requirements
in case of
prospectus
issued
generally.

65.—(1) In the case of a prospectus issued generally (that is to persons who are not existing members or debenture holders of the company), the following provisions apply in addition to those of section 64.

(2) The copy of the prospectus delivered to the registrar of companies must also have endorsed on or attached to it a copy of any contract required by paragraph 11 of Schedule 3 to be stated in the prospectus or, in the case of a contract not reduced into writing, a memorandum giving full particulars of it.

(3) In the case of a contract wholly or partly in a foreign language—

(a) the copy required by subsection (2) to be endorsed on or attached to the prospectus must be a copy of a translation of the contract into English or (as the case may be) a copy embodying a translation into English of the parts in a foreign language, and

(b) the translation must be certified in the prescribed manner to be a correct translation.

(4) If the persons making any report required by Part II of Schedule 3 have made in the report, or have (without giving reasons) indicated in it, any such adjustments as are mentioned in paragraph 21 of the Schedule (profits, losses, assets, liabilities), the copy of the prospectus delivered to the registrar must have endorsed on or attached to it a written statement signed by those persons setting out the adjustments and giving the reasons for them.

Liabilities and offences in connection with prospectus

66.—(1) In the event of non-compliance with or contravention of section 56, a director or other person responsible for the prospectus does not incur any liability by reason of that non-compliance or contravention if—

Directors, etc. exempt from liability in certain cases.

(a) as regards any matter not disclosed, he proves that he was not cognisant of it, or

(b) he proves that the non-compliance or contravention arose from an honest mistake of fact on his part, or

(c) the non-compliance or contravention was in respect of matters which, in the opinion of the court dealing with the case, were immaterial or was otherwise such as ought (in the court's opinion, having regard to all the circumstances of the case) reasonably to be excused.

(2) In the event of failure to include in a prospectus a statement with respect to the matters specified in paragraph 13 of Schedule 3 (disclosure of directors' interests), no director or other person incurs any liability in respect of the failure unless it is proved that he had knowledge of the matters not disclosed.

(3) Nothing in section 56 or 57 or this section limits or diminishes any liability which a person may incur under the general law or this Act apart from those provisions.

C 3

PART III
CHAPTER I
Compensation
for subscribers
misled by
statement in
prospectus.

67.—(1) Where a prospectus invites persons to subscribe for a company's shares or debentures, compensation is payable to all those who subscribe for any shares or debentures on the faith of the prospectus for the loss or damage which they may have sustained by reason of any untrue statement included in it.

(2) The persons liable to pay the compensation are—

(*a*) every person who is a director of the company at the time of the issue of the prospectus,

(*b*) every person who authorised himself to be named, and is named, in the prospectus as a director or as having agreed to become a director (either immediately or after an interval of time),

(*c*) every person being a promoter of the company, and

(*d*) every person who has authorised the issue of the prospectus.

(3) The above has effect subject to the two sections next following; and here and in those sections " promoter " means a promoter who was party to the preparation of the prospectus, or of the portion of it containing the untrue statement, but does not include any person by reason of his acting in a professional capacity for persons engaged in procuring the formation of the company.

68.—(1) A person is not liable under section 67 if he proves—

(*a*) that, having consented to become a director of the company, he withdrew his consent before the issue of the prospectus, and that it was issued without his authority or consent, or

(*b*) that the prospectus was issued without his knowledge or consent, and that on becoming aware of its issue he forthwith gave reasonable public notice that it was issued without his knowledge or consent, or

(*c*) that after issue of the prospectus and before allotment under it he, on becoming aware of any untrue statement in it, withdrew his consent to its issue and gave reasonable public notice of the withdrawal and of the reason for it.

(2) A person is not liable under that section if he proves that—

(*a*) as regards every untrue statement not purporting to be made on the authority of an expert or of a public official document or statement, he had reasonable ground to believe, and did up to the time of the allotment of the shares or debentures (as the case may be) believe, that the statement was true ; and

(*b*) as regards every untrue statement purporting to be a statement by an expert or contained in what purports to be a copy of or extract from a report or valuation of an expert, it fairly represented the statement, or was a correct and fair copy of or extract from the report or valuation, and he had reasonable ground to believe and did up to the time of issue of the prospectus believe that the person making the statement was competent to make it and that person had given the consent required by section 61 to the issue of the prospectus and had not withdrawn that consent before delivery of a copy of the prospectus for registration or, to the defendant's knowledge, before allotment under it ; and

(*c*) as regards every untrue statement purporting to be made by an official person or contained in what purports to be a copy of or extract from a public official document, it was a correct and fair representation of the statement or copy of or extract from the document.

(3) Subsections (1) and (2) of this section do not apply in the case of a person liable, by reason of his having given a consent required of him by section 61, as a person who has authorised the issue of the prospectus in respect of an untrue statement purporting to be made by him as an expert.

(4) Where under section 61 the consent of a person is required to the issue of a prospectus and he has given that consent, he is not by reason of his having given it liable under section 67 as a person who has authorised the issue of the prospectus except in respect of an untrue statement purporting to be made by him as an expert.

(5) A person who, apart from this subsection, would under section 67 be liable, by reason of his having given a consent required of him by section 61, as a person who has authorised the issue of a prospectus in respect of an untrue statement purporting to be made by him as an expert is not so liable if he proves—

(*a*) that, having given his consent under the section to the issue of the prospectus, he withdrew it in writing before the delivery of a copy of the prospectus for registration ; or

(*b*) that, after delivery of a copy of the prospectus for registration and before allotment under it, he, on

C 4

becoming aware of the untrue statement, withdrew his consent in writing and gave reasonable public notice of the withdrawal and of the reason for it ; or

(c) that he was competent to make the statement and that he had reasonable ground to believe, and did up to the time of the allotment of the shares or debentures (as the case may be) believe, that the statement was true.

Indemnity for innocent director or expert.

69.—(1) This section applies where—

(a) the prospectus contains the name of a person as a director of the company, or as having agreed to become a director of it, and he has not consented to become a director, or has withdrawn his consent before the issue of the prospectus, and has not authorised or consented to its issue, or

(b) the consent of a person is required under section 61 to the issue of the prospectus and he either has not given that consent or has withdrawn it before the issue of the prospectus.

(2) The directors of the company (except any without whose knowledge or consent the prospectus was issued) and any other person who authorised its issue are liable to indemnify the person named, or whose consent was required under section 61 (as the case may be), against all damages, costs and expenses to which he may be liable by reason of his name having been inserted in the prospectus or of the inclusion in it of a statement purporting to be made by him as an expert (as the case may be), or in defending himself against any action or legal proceeding brought against him in respect of it.

(3) A person is not deemed for purposes of this section to have authorised the issue of a prospectus by reason only of his having given the consent required by section 61 to the inclusion of a statement purporting to be made by him as an expert.

Criminal liability for untrue statements.

70.—(1) If a prospectus is issued with an untrue statement included in it, any person who authorised the issue of the prospectus is guilty of an offence and liable to imprisonment or a fine, or both, unless he proves either—

(a) that the statement was immaterial, or

(b) that he had reasonable ground to believe and did, up to the time of the issue of the prospectus, believe that the statement was true.

(2) A person is not deemed for purposes of this section to have authorised the issue of a prospectus by reason only of his having given the consent required by section 61 to the inclusion in it of a statement purporting to be made by him as an expert.

Supplementary

71. For purposes of sections 56 to 70—

(a) a statement included in a prospectus is deemed to be untrue if it is misleading in the form and context in which it is included, and

(b) a statement is deemed to be included in a prospectus if it is contained in it, or in any report or memorandum appearing on its face, or by reference incorporated in, or issued with, the prospectus.

CHAPTER II

ISSUES BY COMPANIES INCORPORATED, OR TO BE INCORPORATED, OUTSIDE GREAT BRITAIN

72.—(1) It is unlawful for a person to issue, circulate or distribute in Great Britain any prospectus offering for subscription shares in or debentures of a company incorporated or to be incorporated outside Great Britain (whether the company has or has not established, or when formed will or will not establish, a place of business in Great Britain) unless the prospectus complies with the requirements of the next two subsections.

(2) The prospectus must be dated and contain particulars with respect to the following matters—

(a) the instrument constituting or defining the constitution of the company ;

(b) the enactments, or provisions having the force of an enactment, by or under which the incorporation of the company was effected ;

(c) an address in Great Britain where that instrument, and those enactments or provisions, or copies of them (and, if they are in a foreign language, a translation of them certified in the prescribed manner), can be inspected ;

(d) the date on which, and the country in which, the company was incorporated ; and

(e) whether the company has established a place of business in Great Britain and, if so, the address of its principal office in Great Britain.

(3) Subject to the following provisions, the prospectus must comply—

(a) with Part I of Schedule 3, as respects the matters to be stated in the prospectus, and

(b) with Part II of that Schedule, as respects the reports to be set out.

(4) Paragraphs (a) to (c) of subsection (2) do not apply in the case of a prospectus issued more than 2 years after the company is entitled to commence business.

(5) It is unlawful for a person to issue to any person in Great Britain a form of application for shares in or debentures of such a company or intended company as is mentioned in subsection (1) unless the form is issued with a prospectus which complies with this Chapter and the issue of which in Great Britain does not contravene section 74 or 75 below.

This subsection does not apply if it is shown that the form of application was issued in connection with a bona fide invitation to a person to enter into an underwriting agreement with respect to the shares or debentures.

(6) This section—

(a) does not apply to the issue to a company's existing members or debenture holders of a prospectus or form of application relating to shares in or debentures of the company, whether an applicant for shares or debentures will or will not have the right to renounce in favour of other persons ; and

(b) except in so far as it requires a prospectus to be dated, does not apply to the issue of a prospectus relating to shares or debentures which are or are to be in all respects uniform with shares or debentures previously issued and for the time being listed on a prescribed stock exchange ;

but subject to this, it applies to a prospectus or form of application whether issued on or with reference to the formation of a company or subsequently.

73. A condition requiring or binding an applicant for shares or debentures to waive compliance with any requirement imposed—

> (*a*) by subsection (2) of section 72, as regards the particulars to be contained in the prospectus, or
>
> (*b*) by subsection (3) of that section, as regards compliance with Schedule 3,

or purporting to affect an applicant with notice of any contract, document or matter not specifically referred to in the prospectus, is void.

PART III
CHAPTER II
Attempted
evasion of
s. 72 to be
void.

74.—(1) This section applies in the case of a prospectus offering for subscription shares in or debentures of a company incorporated or to be incorporated outside Great Britain (whether it has or has not established, or when formed will or will not establish, a place of business in Great Britain), if the prospectus includes a statement purporting to be made by an expert.

Prospectus
containing
statement by
expert.

(2) It is unlawful for any person to issue, circulate or distribute in Great Britain such a prospectus if—

> (*a*) the expert has not given, or has before delivery of the prospectus for registration withdrawn, his written consent to the issue of the prospectus with the statement included in the form and context in which it is included, or
>
> (*b*) there does not appear in the prospectus a statement that he has given and has not withdrawn his consent as above mentioned.

(3) For purposes of this section, a statement is deemed to be included in a prospectus if it is contained in it, or in any report or memorandum appearing on its face, or by reference incorporated in, or issued with, the prospectus.

75.—(1) It is unlawful for a person to issue, circulate or distribute in Great Britain a prospectus offering for subscription shares in or debentures of a company incorporated or to be incorporated outside Great Britain (whether the company has or has not established, or when formed will or will not establish, a place of business in Great Britain), unless the prospectus complies with the following condition.

Restrictions
on allotment
to be secured
in prospectus.

(2) The prospectus must have the effect, where an application is made in pursuance of it, of rendering all persons concerned bound by all the provisions (other than penal provisions) of sections 82, 86 and 87 (restrictions on allotment), so far as applicable.

PART III
CHAPTER II
Stock exchange
certificate
exempting
from
compliance
with Sch. 3.

76.—(1) The following applies where—

  (*a*) it is proposed to offer to the public by a prospectus issued generally any shares in or debentures of a company incorporated or to be incorporated outside Great Britain (whether the company has or has not established, or when formed will or will not establish, a place of business in Great Britain), and

  (*b*) application is made to a prescribed stock exchange for permission for those shares or debentures to be listed on that stock exchange.

" Issued generally " means issued to persons who are not existing members or debenture holders of the company.

(2) There may on the applicant's request be given by or on behalf of that stock exchange a certificate that, having regard to the proposals (as stated in the request) as to the size and other circumstances of the issue of shares or debentures and as to any limitation on the number and class of persons to whom the offer is to be made, compliance with Schedule 3 would be unduly burdensome.

(3) If a certificate is given under subsection (2), and if the proposals above mentioned are adhered to and the particulars and information required to be published in connection with the application for permission to the stock exchange are so published, then—

  (*a*) a prospectus giving the particulars and information in the form in which they are so required to be published is deemed to comply with Schedule 3, and

  (*b*) except as respects the requirement for the prospectus to be dated, section 72 does not apply to any issue, after the permission applied for is given, of a prospectus or form of application relating to the shares or debentures.

77.—(1) It is unlawful for a person to issue, circulate or distribute in Great Britain a prospectus offering for subscription shares in or debentures of a company incorporated or to be incorporated outside Great Britain (whether the company has or has not established, or when formed will or will not establish, a place of business in Great Britain), unless before the issue, circulation or distribution the requirements of this section have been complied with.

(2) A copy of the prospectus, certified by the chairman and two other directors of the company as having been approved by resolution of the managing body, must have been delivered for registration to the registrar of companies.

(3) The prospectus must state on the face of it that a copy
has been so delivered to the registrar of companies ; and the following must be endorsed on or attached to that copy of the prospectus—

    (*a*) any consent to the issue of the prospectus which is required by section 74 ;

    (*b*) a copy of any contract required by paragraph 11 of Schedule 3 to be stated in the prospectus or, in the case of a contract not reduced into writing, a memorandum giving full particulars of it ; and

    (*c*) where the persons making any report required by Part II of Schedule 3 have made in it or have, without giving the reasons, indicated in it any such adjustments as are mentioned in paragraph 21 of the Schedule, a written statement signed by those persons setting out the adjustments and giving the reasons for them.

(4) If in the case of a prospectus deemed by virtue of a certificate under section 76 to comply with Schedule 3, a contract or a copy of it, or a memorandum of a contract, is required to be available for inspection in connection with application under that section to the stock exchange, a copy or (as the case may be) a memorandum of the contract must be endorsed on or attached to the copy of the prospectus delivered to the registrar for registration.

(5) References in subsections (3)(*b*) and (4) to the copy of a contract are, in the case of a contract wholly or partly in a foreign language, to a copy of a translation of the contract into English, or a copy embodying a translation into English of the parts in a foreign language (as the case may be) ; and—

    (*a*) the translation must in either case be certified in the prescribed manner to be a correct translation, and

    (*b*) the reference in subsection (4) to a copy of a contract required to be available for inspection includes a copy of a translation of it or a copy embodying a translation of parts of it.

78.—(1) A person who is knowingly responsible for the issue, circulation or distribution of a prospectus, or for the issue of a form of application for shares or debentures, in contravention of any of sections 72 to 77 is liable to a fine. Consequences (criminal and civil) of non-compliance with ss. 72–77.

(2) Sections 67, 68 and 69 extend to every prospectus offering for subscription shares in or debentures of a company incorporated or to be incorporated outside Great Britain (whether the company has or has not established, or when formed will

or will not establish, a place of business in Great Britain), substituting for any reference to section 61 a reference to section
74.

(3) In the event of non-compliance with or contravention of
any of the requirements of section 72(2) as regards the particulars to be contained in the prospectus, or section 72(3) as regards
compliance with Schedule 3, a director or other person responsible for the prospectus incurs no liability by reason of the non-
compliance or contravention if—

(a) as regards any matter not disclosed, he proves that he
was not cognisant of it, or

(b) he proves that the non-compliance or contravention
arose from an honest mistake of fact on his part, or

(c) the non-compliance or contravention was in respect of
matters which, in the opinion of the court dealing with
the case, were immaterial or were otherwise such as
ought, in the court's opinion, having regard to all the
circumstances of the case, reasonably to be excused.

(4) In the event of failure to include in a prospectus to which
this Chapter applies a statement with respect to the matters
contained in paragraph 13 of Schedule 3, no director or other
person incurs any liability in respect of the failure unless it
is proved that he had knowledge of the matters not disclosed.

(5) Nothing in section 72 or 73 or this section, limits or diminishes any liability which a person may incur under the general
law or this Act, apart from those provisions.

Supple-
mentary. **79.**—(1) Where a document by which the shares or debentures of a company incorporated outside Great Britain are
offered for sale to the public would, if the company had been
a company incorporated under this Act, have been deemed by
virtue of section 58 to be a prospectus issued by the company,
that document is deemed, for the purposes of this Chapter, a
prospectus so issued.

(2) An offer of shares or debentures for subscription or sale
to a person whose ordinary business it is to buy or sell shares
or debentures (whether as principal or agent) is not deemed an
offer to the public for those purposes.

(3) In this Chapter " shares " and " debentures " have the
same meaning as when those expressions are used, elsewhere in
this Act, in relation to a company incorporated under this Act.

PART IV

ALLOTMENT OF SHARES AND DEBENTURES

General provisions as to allotment

80.—(1) The directors of a company shall not exercise any power of the company to allot relevant securities, unless they are, in accordance with this section, authorised to do so by—

Authority of company required for certain allotments.

(a) the company in general meeting; or

(b) the company's articles.

(2) In this section " relevant securities " means—

(a) shares in the company other than shares shown in the memorandum to have been taken by the subscribers to it or shares allotted in pursuance of an employees' share scheme, and

(b) any right to subscribe for, or to convert any security into, shares in the company (other than shares so allotted) ;

and a reference to the allotment of relevant securities includes the grant of such a right but (subject to subsection (6) below), not the allotment of shares pursuant to such a right.

(3) Authority under this section may be given for a particular exercise of the power or for its exercise generally, and may be unconditional or subject to conditions.

(4) The authority must state the maximum amount of relevant securities that may be allotted under it and the date on which it will expire, which must be not more than 5 years from whichever is relevant of the following dates—

(a) in the case of an authority contained in the company's articles at the time of its original incorporation, the date of that incorporation ; and

(b) in any other case, the date on which the resolution is passed by virtue of which the authority is given ;

but such an authority (including an authority contained in the articles) may be previously revoked or varied by the company in general meeting.

(5) The authority may be renewed or further renewed by the company in general meeting for a further period not exceeding 5 years ; but the resolution must state (or restate) the amount of relevant securities which may be allotted under the authority or, as the case may be, the amount remaining to be allotted under it, and must specify the date on which the renewed authority will expire.

(6) In relation to authority under this section for the grant of such rights as are mentioned in subsection (2)(*b*), the reference in subsection (4) (as also the corresponding reference in subsection (5)) to the maximum amount of relevant securities that may be allotted under the authority is to the maximum amount of shares which may be allotted pursuant to the rights.

(7) The directors may allot relevant securities, notwithstanding that authority under this section has expired, if they are allotted in pursuance of an offer or agreement made by the company before the authority expired and the authority allowed it to make an offer or agreement which would or might require relevant securities to be allotted after the authority expired.

(8) A resolution of a company to give, vary, revoke or renew such an authority may, notwithstanding that it alters the company's articles, be an ordinary resolution ; but it is in any case subject to section 380 of this Act (copy to be forwarded to registrar within 15 days).

(9) A director who knowingly and wilfully contravenes, or permits or authorises a contravention of, this section is liable to a fine.

(10) Nothing in this section affects the validity of any allotment.

(11) This section does not apply to any allotment of relevant securities by a company, other than a public company registered as such on its original incorporation, if it is made in pursuance of an offer or agreement made before the earlier of the following two dates—

>   (*a*) the date of the holding of the first general meeting of the company after its registration or re-registration as a public company, and

>   (*b*) 22nd June 1982 ;

1980 c. 22.

but any resolution to give, vary or revoke an authority for the purposes of section 14 of the Companies Act 1980 or this section has effect for those purposes if passed at any time after the end of April 1980.

Restriction on public offers by private company.

81.—(1) A private limited company (other than a company limited by guarantee and not having a share capital) commits an offence if it—

>   (*a*) offers to the public (whether for cash or otherwise) any shares in or debentures of the company ; or

(*b*) allots or agrees to allot (whether for cash or otherwise) any shares in or debentures of the company with a view to all or any of those shares or debentures being offered for sale to the public (within the meaning given to that expression by sections 58 to 60).

(2) A company guilty of an offence under this section, and any officer of it who is in default, is liable to a fine.

(3) Nothing in this section affects the validity of any allotment or sale of shares or debentures, or of any agreement to allot or sell shares or debentures.

82.—(1) No allotment shall be made of a company's shares or debentures in pursuance of a prospectus issued generally, and no proceedings shall be taken on applications made in pursuance of a prospectus so issued, until the beginning of the third day after that on which the prospectus is first so issued or such later time (if any) as may be specified in the prospectus. Application for, and allotment of, shares and debentures.

(2) The beginning of that third day, or that later time, is " the time of the opening of the subscription lists ".

(3) In subsection (1), the reference to the day on which the prospectus is first issued generally is to the day when it is first so issued as a newspaper advertisement ; and if it is not so issued as a newspaper advertisement before the third day after that on which it is first so issued in any other manner, the reference is to the day on which it is first so issued in any manner.

(4) In reckoning for this purpose the third day after another day—

(*a*) any intervening day which is a Saturday or Sunday, or is a bank holiday in any part of Great Britain, is to be disregarded ; and

(*b*) if the third day (as so reckoned) is itself a Saturday or Sunday, or a bank holiday, there is to be substituted the first day after that which is none of them.

(5) The validity of an allotment is not affected by any contravention of subsections (1) to (4) ; but in the event of contravention, the company and every officer of it who is in default is liable to a fine.

(6) As applying to a prospectus offering shares or debentures for sale, the above provisions are modified as follows—

(*a*) for references to allotment, substitute references to sale ; and

(*b*) for the reference to the company and every officer of it who is in default, substitute a reference to any person by or through whom the offer is made and who knowingly and wilfully authorises or permits the contravention.

(7) An application for shares in or debentures of a company which is made in pursuance of a prospectus issued generally is not revocable until after the expiration of the third day after the time of the opening of the subscription lists, or the giving before the expiration of that day of the appropriate public notice ; and that notice is one given by some person responsible under sections 67 to 69 for the prospectus and having the effect under those sections of excluding or limiting the responsibility of the giver.

No allotment unless minimum subscription received.

83.—(1) No allotment shall be made of any share capital of a company offered to the public for subscription unless—

(a) there has been subscribed the amount stated in the prospectus as the minimum amount which, in the opinion of the directors, must be raised by the issue of share capital in order to provide for the matters specified in paragraph 2 of Schedule 3 (preliminary expenses, purchase of property, working capital, etc.) ; and

(b) the sum payable on application for the amount so stated has been paid to and received by the company.

(2) For purposes of subsection (1)(b), a sum is deemed paid to the company, and received by it, if a cheque for that sum has been received in good faith by the company and the directors have no reason for suspecting that the cheque will not be paid.

(3) The amount so stated in the prospectus is to be reckoned exclusively of any amount payable otherwise than in cash and is known as " the minimum subscription ".

(4) If the above conditions have not been complied with on the expiration of 40 days after the first issue of the prospectus, all money received from applicants for shares shall be forthwith repaid to them without interest.

(5) If any of the money is not repaid within 48 days after the issue of the prospectus, the directors of the company are jointly and severally liable to repay it with interest at the rate of 5 per cent. per annum from the expiration of the 48th day ; except that a director is not so liable if he proves that the default in the repayment of the money was not due to any misconduct or negligence on his part.

(6) Any condition requiring or binding an applicant for shares to waive compliance with any requirement of this section is void.

(7) This section does not apply to an allotment of shares subsequent to the first allotment of shares offered to the public for subscription.

84.—(1) No allotment shall be made of any share capital of a public company offered for subscription unless—

    (*a*) that capital is subscribed for in full ; or

    (*b*) the offer states that, even if the capital is not subscribed for in full, the amount of that capital subscribed for may be allotted in any event or in the event of the conditions specified in the offer being satisfied ;

and, where conditions are so specified, no allotment of the capital shall be made by virtue of paragraph (*b*) unless those conditions are satisfied.

This is without prejudice to section 83.

(2) If shares are prohibited from being allotted by subsection (1) and 40 days have elapsed after the first issue of the prospectus, all money received from applicants for shares shall be forthwith repaid to them without interest.

(3) If any of the money is not repaid within 48 days after the issue of the prospectus, the directors of the company are jointly and severally liable to repay it with interest at the rate of 5 per cent. per annum from the expiration of the 48th day ; except that a director is not so liable if he proves that the default in repayment was not due to any misconduct or negligence on his part.

(4) This section applies in the case of shares offered as wholly or partly payable otherwise than in cash as it applies in the case of shares offered for subscription (the word " subscribed " in subsection (1) being construed accordingly).

(5) In subsections (2) and (3) as they apply to the case of shares offered as wholly or partly payable otherwise than in cash, references to the repayment of money received from applicants for shares include—

    (*a*) the return of any other consideration so received (including, if the case so requires, the release of the applicant from any undertaking), or

    (*b*) if it is not reasonably practicable to return the consideration, the payment of money equal to its value at the time it was so received,

and references to interest apply accordingly.

(6) Any condition requiring or binding an applicant for shares to waive compliance with any requirement of this section is void.

85.—(1) An allotment made by a company to an applicant in contravention of section 83 or 84 is voidable at the instance of the applicant within one month after the date of the allotment, and not later, and is so voidable notwithstanding that the company is in the course of being wound up.

(2) If a director of a company knowingly contravenes, or permits or authorises the contravention of, any provision of either of those sections with respect to allotment, he is liable to compensate the company and the allottee respectively for any loss, damages or costs which the company or the allottee may have sustained or incurred by the contravention.

(3) But proceedings to recover any such loss, damages or costs shall not be commenced after the expiration of 2 years from the date of the allotment.

Allotment of
shares etc. to be
dealt in on
stock
exchange.

86.—(1) The following applies where a prospectus, whether issued generally or not, states that application has been or will be made for permission for the shares or debentures offered by it to be listed on any stock exchange.

(2) An allotment made on an application in pursuance of the prospectus is, whenever made, void if the permission has not been applied for before the third day after the first issue of the prospectus or if the permission has been refused before the expiration of 3 weeks from the date of the closing of the subscription lists or such longer period (not exceeding 6 weeks) as may, within those 3 weeks, be notified to the applicant for permission by or on behalf of the stock exchange.

(3) In reckoning for this purpose the third day after another day—

    (a) any intervening day which is a Saturday or Sunday, or is a bank holiday in any part of Great Britain, is to be disregarded; and

    (b) if the third day (as so reckoned) is itself a Saturday or Sunday, or a bank holiday, there is to be substituted the first day after that which is none of them.

(4) Where permission has not been applied for as above, or has been refused as above, the company shall forthwith repay (without interest) all money received from applicants in pursuance of the prospectus.

(5) If any of the money is not repaid within 8 days after the company becomes liable to repay it, the directors of the company are jointly and severally liable to repay the money with

interest at the rate of 5 per cent. per annum from the expiration of the 8th day, except that a director is not liable if he proves that the default in the repayment of the money was not due to any misconduct or negligence on his part.

(6) All money received from applicants in pursuance of the prospectus shall be kept in a separate bank account so long as the company may become liable to repay it under subsection (4) ; and if default is made in complying with this subsection, the company and every officer of it who is in default is liable to a fine.

(7) Any condition requiring or binding an applicant for shares or debentures to waive compliance with any requirement of this section is void.

(8) For purposes of this section, permission is not deemed to be refused if it is intimated that the application for it, though not at present granted, will be given further consideration.

(9) This section has effect in relation to shares or debentures agreed to be taken by a person underwriting an offer of them by a prospectus as if he had applied for them in pursuance of the prospectus.

87.—(1) The following has effect as regards the operation of section 86 in relation to a prospectus offering shares for sale.

(2) Subsections (1) and (2) of that section apply, but with the substitution for the reference in subsection (2) to allotment of a reference to sale.

(3) Subsections (4) and (5) of that section do not apply ; but—

(a) if the permission referred to in section 86(2) has not been applied for as there mentioned, or has been refused as there mentioned, the offeror of the shares shall forthwith repay (without interest) all money received from applicants in pursuance of the prospectus, and

(b) if any such money is not repaid within 8 days after the offeror becomes liable to repay it, he becomes liable to pay interest on the money due, at the rate of 5 per cent. per annum from the end of the 8th day.

(4) Subsections (6) to (9) apply, except that in subsection (6)—

(a) for the first reference to the company there is substituted a reference to the offeror, and (*b*) for the reference to the company and every officer of the company who is in default there is substituted a reference to any person by or through whom the offer is made and who knowingly and wilfully authorises or permits the default.

Return as to allotments, etc.

88.—(1) This section applies to a company limited by shares and to a company limited by guarantee and having a share capital.

(2) When such a company makes an allotment of its shares, the company shall within one month thereafter deliver to the registrar of companies for registration—

(*a*) a return of the allotments (in the prescribed form) stating the number and nominal amount of the shares comprised in the allotment, the names and addresses of the allottees, and the amount (if any) paid or due and payable on each share, whether on account of the nominal value of the share or by way of premium ; and

(*b*) in the case of shares allotted as fully or partly paid up otherwise than in cash—

(i) a contract in writing constituting the title of the allottee to the allotment together with any contract of sale, or for services or other consideration in respect of which that allotment was made (such contracts being duly stamped), and

(ii) a return stating the number and nominal amount of shares so allotted, the extent to which they are to be treated as paid up, and the consideration for which they have been allotted.

(3) Where such a contract as above mentioned is not reduced to writing, the company shall within one month after the allotment deliver to the registrar of companies for registration the prescribed particulars of the contract stamped with the same stamp duty as would have been payable if the contract had been reduced to writing.

54 & 55 Vict c. 39.

(4) Those particulars are deemed an instrument within the meaning of the Stamp Act 1891 ; and the registrar may, as a condition of filing the particulars, require that the duty payable on them be adjudicated under section 12 of that Act.

(5) If default is made in complying with this section, every officer of the company who is in default is liable to a fine and, for continued contravention, to a daily default fine, but subject as follows.

(6) In the case of default in delivering to the registrar within one month after the allotment any document required by this section to be delivered, the company, or any officer liable for the default, may apply to the court for relief ; and the court, if satisfied that the omission to deliver the document was accidental or due to inadvertence, or that it is just and equitable to grant relief, may make an order extending the time for the delivery of the document for such period as the court thinks proper.

Pre-emption rights

89.—(1) Subject to the provisions of this section and the seven sections next following, a company proposing to allot equity securities (defined in section 94)—

Offers to shareholders to be on pre-emptive basis.

(*a*) shall not allot any of them on any terms to a person unless it has made an offer to each person who holds relevant shares or relevant employee shares to allot to him on the same or more favourable terms a proportion of those securities which is as nearly as practicable equal to the proportion in nominal value held by him of the aggregate of relevant shares and relevant employee shares, and

(*b*) shall not allot any of those securities to a person unless the period during which any such offer may be accepted has expired or the company has received notice of the acceptance or refusal of every offer so made.

(2) Subsection (3) below applies to any provision of a company's memorandum or articles which requires the company, when proposing to allot equity securities consisting of relevant shares of any particular class, not to allot those securities on any terms unless it has complied with the condition that it makes such an offer as is described in subsection (1) to each person who holds relevant shares or relevant employee shares of that class.

(3) If in accordance with a provision to which this subsection applies—

(*a*) a company makes an offer to allot securities to such a holder, and

(*b*) he or anyone in whose favour he has renounced his right to their allotment accepts the offer,

subsection (1) does not apply to the allotment of those securities, and the company may allot them accordingly ; but this is without prejudice to the application of subsection (1) in any other case.

(4) Subsection (1) does not apply to a particular allotment of equity securities if these are, or are to be, wholly or partly paid up otherwise than in cash; and securities which a company has offered to allot to a holder of relevant shares or relevant employee shares may be allotted to him, or anyone in whose favour he has renounced his right to their allotment, without contravening subsection (1)(*b*).

(5) Subsection (1) does not apply to the allotment of securities which would, apart from a renunciation or assignment of the right to their allotment, be held under an employees' share scheme.

Communication of pre-emption offers to shareholders.

90.—(1) This section has effect as to the manner in which offers required by section 89(1), or by a provision to which section 89(3) applies, are to be made to holders of a company's shares.

(2) Subject to the following subsections, an offer shall be in writing and shall be made to a holder of shares either personally or by sending it by post (that is to say, prepaying and posting a letter containing the offer) to him or to his registered address or, if he has no registered address in the United Kingdom, to the address in the United Kingdom supplied by him to the company for the giving of notice to him.

If sent by post, the offer is deemed to be made at the time at which the letter would be delivered in the ordinary course of post.

(3) Where shares are held by two or more persons jointly, the offer may be made to the joint holder first named in the register of members in respect of the shares.

(4) In the case of a holder's death or bankruptcy, the offer may be made—

(*a*) by sending it by post in a prepaid letter addressed to the persons claiming to be entitled to the shares in consequence of the death or bankruptcy by name, or by the title of representatives of the deceased, or trustee of the bankrupt, or by any like description, at the address in the United Kingdom supplied for the purpose by those so claiming, or

(*b*) (until such an address has been so supplied) by giving the notice in any manner in which it might have been given if the death or bankruptcy had not occurred.

(5) If the holder—

(*a*) has no registered address in the United Kingdom and has not given to the company an address in the United Kingdom for the service of notices on him, or

(*b*) is the holder of a share warrant,

the offer may be made by causing it, or a notice specifying where a copy of it can be obtained or inspected, to be published in the Gazette.

(6) The offer must state a period of not less than 21 days during which it may be accepted ; and the offer shall not be withdrawn before the end of that period.

(7) This section does not invalidate a provision to which section 89(3) applies by reason that that provision requires or authorises an offer under it to be made in contravention of any of subsections (1) to (6) above ; but, to the extent that the provision requires or authorises such an offer to be so made, it is of no effect.

91.—(1) Section 89(1), section 90(1) to (5) or section 90(6) may, as applying to allotments by a private company of equity securities or to such allotments of a particular description, be excluded by a provision contained in the memorandum or articles of that company.

(2) A requirement or authority contained in the memorandum or articles of a private company, if it is inconsistent with any of those subsections, has effect as a provision excluding that subsection ; but a provision to which section 89(3) applies is not to be treated as inconsistent with section 89(1).

92.—(1) If there is a contravention of section 89(1), or of section 90(1) to (5) or section 90(6), or of a provision to which section 89(3) applies, the company, and every officer of it who knowingly authorised or permitted the contravention, are jointly and severally liable to compensate any person to whom an offer should have been made under the subsection or provision contravened for any loss, damage, costs or expenses which the person has sustained or incurred by reason of the contravention.

(2) However, no proceedings to recover any such loss, damage, costs or expenses shall be commenced after the expiration of 2 years from the delivery to the registrar of companies of the return of allotments in question or, where equity securities other than shares are granted, from the date of the grant.

93.—(1) Sections 89 to 92 are without prejudice to any enactment by virtue of which a company is prohibited (whether generally or in specified circumstances) from offering or allotting equity securities to any person.

(2) Where a company cannot by virtue of such an enactment offer or allot equity securities to a holder of relevant shares or relevant employee shares, those sections have effect as if the shares held by that holder were not relevant shares or relevant employee shares.

94.—(1) The following subsections apply for the interpretation of sections 89 to 96.

(2) " Equity security ", in relation to a company, means a relevant share in the company (other than a share shown in the memorandum to have been taken by a subscriber to the memorandum or a bonus share), or a right to subscribe for, or to convert securities into, relevant shares in the company.

(3) A reference to the allotment of equity securities or of equity securities consisting of relevant shares of a particular class includes the grant of a right to subscribe for, or to convert any securities into, relevant shares in the company or (as the case may be) relevant shares of a particular class ; but such a reference does not include the allotment of any relevant shares pursuant to such a right.

(4) " Relevant employee shares ", in relation to a company, means shares of the company which would be relevant shares in it but for the fact that they are held by a person who acquired them in pursuance of an employees' share scheme.

(5) " Relevant shares ", in relation to a company, means shares in the company other than—

    (*a*) shares which as respects dividends and capital carry a right to participate only up to a specified amount in a distribution, and

    (*b*) shares which are held by a person who acquired them in pursuance of an employees' share scheme or, in the case of shares which have not been allotted, are to be allotted in pursuance of such a scheme.

(6) A reference to a class of shares is to shares to which the same rights are attached as to voting and as to participation, both as respects dividends and as respects capital, in a distribution.

(7) In relation to an offer to allot securities required by section 89(1) or by any provision to which section 89(3) applies, a reference in sections 89 to 94 (however expressed) to the holder of shares of any description is to whoever was at the close of business on a date, to be specified in the offer and to fall in the period of 28 days immediately before the date of the offer, the holder of shares of that description.

95.—(1) Where the directors of a company are generally authorised for purposes of section 80, they may be given power by the articles, or by a special resolution of the company, to allot equity securities pursuant to that authority as if—

Disapplication of pre-emption rights.

   (*a*) section 89(1) did not apply to the allotment, or

   (*b*) that subsection applied to the allotment with such modifications as the directors may determine ;

and where the directors make an allotment under this subsection, sections 89 to 94 have effect accordingly.

(2) Where the directors of a company are authorised for purposes of section 80 (whether generally or otherwise), the company may by special resolution resolve either—

   (*a*) that section 89(1) shall not apply to a specified allotment of equity securities to be made pursuant to that authority, or

   (*b*) that that subsection shall apply to the allotment with such modifications as may be specified in the resolution ;

and where such a resolution is passed, sections 89 to 94 have effect accordingly.

(3) The power conferred by subsection (1) or a special resolution under subsection (2) ceases to have effect when the authority to which it relates is revoked or would (if not renewed) expire ; but if the authority is renewed, the power or (as the case may be) the resolution may also be renewed, for a period not longer than that for which the authority is renewed, by a special resolution of the company.

(4) Notwithstanding that any such power or resolution has expired, the directors may allot equity securities in pursuance of an offer or agreement previously made by the company, if the power or resolution enabled the company to make an offer or agreement which would or might require equity securities to be allotted after it expired.

(5) A special resolution under subsection (2), or a special resolution to renew such a resolution, shall not be proposed un-

less it is recommended by the directors and there has been circulated, with the notice of the meeting at which the resolution is proposed, to the members entitled to have that notice a written statement by the directors setting out—

    (*a*) their reasons for making the recommendation,

    (*b*) the amount to be paid to the company in respect of the equity securities to be allotted, and

    (*c*) the directors' justification of that amount.

(6) A person who knowingly or recklessly authorises or permits the inclusion in a statement circulated under subsection (5) of any matter which is misleading, false or deceptive in a material particular is liable to imprisonment or a fine, or both.

Saving for
company's
pre-emption
procedure
operative
before 1982.
1980 c. 22.

96.—(1) Where a company which is re-registered or registered as a public company is or, but for the provisions of the Companies Act 1980 and the enactments replacing it, would be subject at the time of re-registration or (as the case may be) registration to a pre-1982 pre-emption requirement, sections 89 to 95 do not apply to an allotment of the equity securities which are subject to that requirement.

(2) A " pre-1982 pre-emption requirement " is a requirement imposed (whether by the company's memorandum or articles, or otherwise) before the relevant date in 1982 by virtue of which the company must, when making an allotment of equity securities, make an offer to allot those securities or some of them in a manner which (otherwise than because involving a contravention of section 90(1) to (5) or 90(6)) is inconsistent with sections 89 to 94 ; and " the relevant date in 1982 " is—

    (*a*) except in a case falling within the following paragraph, 22nd June in that year, and

    (*b*) in the case of a company which was re-registered or registered as a public company on an application made before that date, the date on which the application was made.

(3) A requirement which—

    (*a*) is imposed on a private company (having been so imposed before the relevant date in 1982) otherwise than by the company's memorandum or articles, and

    (*b*) if contained in the company's memorandum or articles, would have effect under section 91 to the exclusion of any provisions of sections 89 to 94,

has effect, so long as the company remains a private company, as if it were contained in the memorandum or articles.

(4) If on the relevant date in 1982 a company, other than a public company registered as such on its original incorporation,

was subject to such a requirement as is mentioned in section
89(2) imposed otherwise than by the memorandum or articles,
the requirement is to be treated for purposes of sections 89 to 94
as if it were contained in the memorandum or articles.

Commissions and discounts

97.—(1) It is lawful for a company to pay a commission to
any person in consideration of his subscribing or agreeing to
subscribe (whether absolutely or conditionally) for any shares
in the company, or procuring or agreeing to procure subscriptions (whether absolute or conditional) for any shares in the
company, if the following conditions are satisfied.

Power of
company
to pay
commissions.

(2) The payment of the commission must be authorised by
the company's articles ; and—

   (*a*) the commission paid or agreed to be paid must not
        exceed 10 per cent. of the price at which the shares
        are issued or the amount or rate authorised by the
        articles, whichever is the less ; and

   (*b*) the amount or rate per cent. of commission paid or
        agreed to be paid, and the number of shares which per-
        sons have agreed for a commission to subscribe abso-
        lutely, must be disclosed in the manner required by the
        following subsection.

(3) Those matters must, in the case of shares offered to the
public for subscription, be disclosed in the prospectus ; and in
the case of shares not so offered—

   (*a*) they must be disclosed in a statement in the prescribed
        form signed by every director of the company or by
        his agent authorised in writing, and delivered (before
        payment of the commission) to the registrar of com-
        panies for registration ; and

   (*b*) where a circular or notice (not being a prospectus)
        inviting subscription for the shares is issued, they must
        also be disclosed in that circular or notice.

(4) If default is made in complying with subsection (3)(*a*)
as regards delivery to the registrar of the statement in prescribed
form, the company and every officer of it who is in default is
liable to a fine.

98.—(1) Except as permitted by section 97, no company shall
apply any of its shares or capital money, either directly or indirectly in payment of any commission, discount or allowance to
any person in consideration of his subscribing or agreeing to
subscribe (whether absolutely or conditionally) for any shares in
the company, or procuring or agreeing to procure subscriptions
(whether absolute or conditional) for any shares in the company.

Apart
from s. 97,
commissions
and discounts
barred.

(2) This applies whether the shares or money be so applied by being added to the purchase money of any property acquired by the company or to the contract price of any work to be executed for the company, or the money be paid out of the nominal purchase money or contract price, or otherwise.

(3) Nothing in section 97 or this section affects the power of a company to pay such brokerage as has previously been lawful.

(4) A vendor to, or promoter of, or other person who receives payment in money or shares from, a company has, and is deemed always to have had, power to apply any part of the money or shares so received in payment of any commission, the payment of which, if made directly by the company, would have been lawful under section 97 and this section.

Amount to be paid for shares; the means of payment

General rules as to payment for shares on allotment.   **99.**—(1) Subject to the following provisions of this Part, shares allotted by a company, and any premium on them, may be paid up in money or money's worth (including goodwill and know-how).

(2) A public company shall not accept at any time, in payment up of its shares or any premium on them, an undertaking given by any person that he or another should do work or perform services for the company or any other person.

(3) If a public company accepts such an undertaking in payment up of its shares or any premium on them, the holder of the shares when they or the premium are treated as paid up (in whole or in part) by the undertaking is liable—

> (a) to pay the company in respect of those shares an amount equal to their nominal value, together with the whole of any premium or, if the case so requires, such proportion of that amount as is treated as paid up by the undertaking; and

> (b) to pay interest at the appropriate rate on the amount payable under paragraph (a) above.

(4) This section does not prevent a company from allotting bonus shares to its members or from paying up, with sums available for the purpose, any amounts for the time being unpaid on any of its shares (whether on account of the nominal value of the shares or by way of premium).

(5) The reference in subsection (3) to the holder of shares includes any person who has an unconditional right to be included in the company's register of members in respect of those shares or to have an instrument of transfer of them executed in his favour.

100.—(1) A company's shares shall not be allotted at a discount.

(2) If shares are allotted in contravention of this section, the allottee is liable to pay the company an amount equal to the amount of the discount, with interest at the appropriate rate.

101.—(1) A public company shall not allot a share except as paid up at least as to one-quarter of its nominal value and the whole of any premium on it.

(2) Subsection (1) does not apply to shares allotted in pursuance of an employees' share scheme.

(3) If a company allots a share in contravention of subsection (1), the share is to be treated as if one-quarter of its nominal value, together with the whole of any premium on it, had been received.

(4) But the allottee is liable to pay the company the minimum amount which should have been received in respect of the share under subsection (1) (less the value of any consideration actually applied in payment up, to any extent, of the share and any premium on it), with interest at the appropriate rate.

(5) Subsections (3) and (4) do not apply to the allotment of bonus shares, unless the allottee knew or ought to have known the shares were allotted in contravention of subsection (1).

Shares to be
allotted as at
least one-
quarter
paid-up.

102.—(1) A public company shall not allot shares as fully or partly paid up (as to their nominal value or any premium on them) otherwise than in cash if the consideration for the allotment is or includes an undertaking which is to be, or may be, performed more than 5 years after the date of the allotment.

(2) If a company allots shares in contravention of subsection (1), the allottee is liable to pay the company an amount equal to the aggregate of their nominal value and the whole of any premium (or, if the case so requires, so much of that aggregate as is treated as paid up by the undertaking), with interest at the appropriate rate.

(3) Where a contract for the allotment of shares does not contravene subsection (1), any variation of the contract which has the effect that the contract would have contravened the subsection, if the terms of the contract as varied had been its original terms, is void.

(4) Subsection (3) applies also to the variation by a public company of the terms of a contract entered into before the company was re-registered as a public company.

(5) The following subsection applies where a public company allots shares for a consideration which consists of or includes (in accordance with subsection (1)) an undertaking which is to be performed within 5 years of the allotment, but the undertaking is not performed within the period allowed by the contract for the allotment of the shares.

(6) The allottee is then liable to pay the company, at the end of the period so allowed, an amount equal to the aggregate of the nominal value of the shares and the whole of any premium (or, if the case so requires, so much of that aggregate as is treated as paid up by the undertaking), with interest at the appropriate rate.

(7) A reference in this section to a contract for the allotment of shares includes an ancillary contract relating to payment in respect of them.

Non-cash consideration to be valued before allotment.

103.—(1) A public company shall not allot shares as fully or partly paid up (as to their nominal value or any premium on them) otherwise than in cash unless—

(a) the consideration for the allotment has been independently valued under section 108; and

(b) a report with respect to its value has been made to the company by a person appointed by the company (in accordance with that section) during the 6 months immediately preceding the allotment of the shares ; and

(c) a copy of the report has been sent to the proposed allottee.

(2) Where an amount standing to the credit of any of a company's reserve accounts, or of its profit and loss account, is applied in paying up (to any extent) any shares allotted to members of the company or any premiums on shares so allotted, the amount applied does not count as consideration for the allotment, and accordingly subsection (1) does not apply in that case.

(3) Subsection (1) does not apply to the allotment of shares by a company in connection with an arrangement providing for the allotment of shares in that company on terms that the whole or part of the consideration for the shares allotted is to be provided by the transfer to that company (or the cancellation) of all or some of the shares, or of all or some of the shares of a particular class, in another company (with or without the issue to that company of shares, or of shares of any particular class, in that other company).

(4) But subsection (3) does not exclude the application of subsection (1) unless under the arrangement it is open to all the holders of the shares in the other company in question (or, where the arrangement applies only to shares of a particular class, to all the holders of shares in that other company, being holders of shares of that class) to take part in the arrangement.

In determining whether that is the case, shares held by or by a nominee of the company proposing to allot the shares in connection with the arrangement, or by or by a nominee of a company which is that company's holding company or subsidiary or a company which is a subsidiary of its holding company, shall be disregarded.

(5) Subsection (1) also does not apply to the allotment of shares by a company in connection with its proposed merger with another company ; that is, where one of the companies proposes to acquire all the assets and liabilities of the other in exchange for the issue of shares or other securities of that one to shareholders of the other, with or without any cash payment to shareholders.

(6) If a company allots shares in contravention of subsection (1) and either—

  (*a*) the allottee has not received the valuer's report required by that subsection to be sent to him ; or

  (*b*) there has been some other contravention of this section or section 108 which the allottee knew or ought to have known amounted to a contravention,

the allottee is liable to pay the company an amount equal to the aggregate of the nominal value of the shares and the whole of any premium (or, if the case so requires, so much of that aggregate as is treated as paid up by the consideration), with interest at the appropriate rate.

(7) In this section—

  (*a*) " arrangement " means any agreement, scheme or arrangement (including an arrangement sanctioned in accordance with section 425 (company compromise with creditors and members) or section 582 (liquidator in winding up accepting shares as consideration for sale of company property)), and

  (*b*) any reference to a company, except where it is or is to be construed as a reference to a public company, includes any body corporate and any body to which letters patent have been issued under the Chartered 1837 c. 73. Companies Act 1837.

D

PART IV
Transfer to
public
company of
non-cash
asset in
initial period.

104.—(1) A public company formed as such shall not, unless the conditions of this section have been complied with, enter into an agreement with a person for the transfer by him during the initial period of one or more non-cash assets to the company or another, if—

    (a) that person is a subscriber to the company's memorandum, and

    (b) the consideration for the transfer to be given by the company is equal in value at the time of the agreement to one-tenth or more of the company's nominal share capital issued at that time.

(2) The " initial period " for this purpose is 2 years beginning with the date of the company being issued with a certificate under section 117 (or the previous corresponding provision) that it was entitled to do business.

(3) This section applies also to a company re-registered as a public company (except one re-registered under section 8 of the Companies Act 1980 or section 2 of the Consequential Provisions Act), or registered under section 685 (joint stock company) or the previous corresponding provision ; but in that case—

1980 c. 22.

    (a) there is substituted a reference in subsection (1)(a) to a person who is a member of the company on the date of registration or re-registration, and

    (b) the initial period is then 2 years beginning with that date.

In this subsection the reference to a company re-registered as a public company includes a private company so re-registered which was a public company before it was a private company.

(4) The conditions of this section are as follows—

    (a) the consideration to be received by the company, and any consideration other than cash to be given by the company, must have been independently valued under section 109 ;

    (b) a report with respect to the consideration to be so received and given must have been made to the company in accordance with that section during the 6 months immediately preceding the date of the agreement ;

    (c) the terms of the agreement must have been approved by an ordinary resolution of the company ; and

    (d) not later than the giving of the notice of the meeting at which the resolution is proposed, copies of the resolution and report must have been circulated to the members of the company entitled to receive the notice and, if the person with whom the agreement in question is proposed to be made is not then a member of the company so entitled, to that person.

(5) In subsection (4)(*a*)—

(*a*) the reference to the consideration to be received by the company is to the asset to be transferred to it or the advantage to the company of the asset's transfer to another person ; and

(*b*) the specified condition is without prejudice to any requirement to value any consideration for purposes of section 103.

(6) In the case of the following agreements, this section does not apply—

(*a*) where it is part of the company's ordinary business to acquire, or arrange for other persons to acquire, assets of a particular description, an agreement entered into by the company in the ordinary course of its business for the transfer of an asset of that description to it or to such a person, as the case may be ;

(*b*) an agreement entered into by the company under the supervision of the court, or of an officer authorised by the court for the purpose, for the transfer of an asset to the company or to another.

105.—(1) The following subsection applies if a public company enters into an agreement contravening section 104, the agreement being made with the person referred to in subsection (1)(*a*) or (as the case may be) subsection (3) of that section, and either— Agreements contravening s. 104.

(*a*) that person has not received the valuer's report required for compliance with the conditions of the section, or

(*b*) there has been some other contravention of the section or of section 108(1), (2) or (5) or section 109, which he knew or ought to have known amounted to a contravention.

(2) The company is then entitled to recover from that person any consideration given by it under the agreement, or an amount equal to the value of the consideration at the time of the agreement ; and the agreement, so far as not carried out, is void.

(3) However, if the agreement is or includes an agreement for the allotment of shares in the company, then—

(*a*) whether or not the agreement also contravenes section 103, subsection (2) above does not apply to it in so far as it is for the allotment of shares ; and

(*b*) the allottee is liable to pay the company an amount equal to the aggregate of the nominal value of the shares and the whole of any premium (or, if the case so requires, so much of that aggregate as is treated as paid up by the consideration), with interest at the appropriate rate.

106. Shares taken by a subscriber to the memorandum of a public company in pursuance of an undertaking of his in the memorandum, and any premium on the shares, shall be paid up in cash.

107. In sections 99 to 105 " the appropriate rate ", in relation to interest, means 5 per cent. per annum or such other rate as may be specified by order made by the Secretary of State by statutory instrument subject to annulment in pursuance of a resolution of either House of Parliament.

Valuation provisions

108.—(1) The valuation and report required by section 103 (or, where applicable, section 44) shall be made by an independent person, that is to say a person qualified at the time of the report to be appointed, or continue to be, an auditor of the company.

(2) However, where it appears to the independent person (from here on referred to as " the valuer ") to be reasonable for the valuation of the consideration, or part of it, to be made (or for him to accept such a valuation) by another person who—

> (*a*) appears to him to have the requisite knowledge and experience to value the consideration or that part of it ; and
>
> (*b*) is not an officer or servant of the company or any other body corporate which is that company's subsidiary or holding company or a subsidiary of that company's holding company or a partner or employee of such an officer or servant,

he may arrange for or accept such a valuation, together with a report which will enable him to make his own report under this section and provide the note required by subsection (6) below.

(3) The reference in subsection (2)(*b*) to an officer or servant does not include an auditor.

(4) The valuer's report shall state—

> (*a*) the nominal value of the shares to be wholly or partly paid for by the consideration in question ;
>
> (*b*) the amount of any premium payable on the shares ;
>
> (*c*) the description of the consideration and, as respects so much of the consideration as he himself has valued, a description of that part of the consideration", the method used to value it and the date of the valuation ;
>
> (*d*) the extent to which the nominal value of the shares and any premium are to be treated as paid up—
>> (i) by the consideration ;
>> (ii) in cash.

(5) Where the consideration or part of it is valued by a person other than the valuer himself, the latter's report shall state that fact and shall also—

(a) state the former's name and what knowledge and experience he has to carry out the valuation, and

(b) describe so much of the consideration as was valued by the other person, and the method used to value it, and specify the date of the valuation.

(6) The valuer's report shall contain or be accompanied by a note by him—

(a) in the case of a valuation made by a person other than himself, that it appeared to himself reasonable to arrange for it to be so made or to accept a valuation so made;

(b) whoever made the valuation, that the method of valuation was reasonable in all the circumstances;

(c) that it appears to the valuer that there has been no material change in the value of the consideration in question since the valuation; and

(d) that on the basis of the valuation the value of the consideration, together with any cash by which the nominal value of the shares or any premium payable on them is to be paid up, is not less than so much of the aggregate of the nominal value and the whole of any such premium as is treated as paid up by the consideration and any such cash.

(7) Where the consideration to be valued is accepted partly in payment up of the nominal value of the shares and any premium and partly for some other consideration given by the company, section 103 (and, where applicable, section 44) and the foregoing provisions of this section apply as if references to the consideration accepted by the company included the proportion of that consideration which is properly attributable to the payment up of that value and any premium; and—

(a) the valuer shall carry out, or arrange for, such other valuations as will enable him to determine that proportion; and

(b) his report shall state what valuations have been made under this subsection and also the reason for, and method and date of, any such valuation and any other matters which may be relevant to that determination.

109.—(1) Subsections (1) to (3) and (5) of section 108 apply also as respects the valuation and report for the purposes of section 104.

Valuation and report (s. 104).

(2) The valuer's report for those purposes shall—

(a) state the consideration to be received by the company,

D 3

describing the asset in question (specifying the amount to be received in cash) and the consideration to be given by the company (specifying the amount to be given in cash) ;

(b) state the method and date of valuation ;

(c) contain or be accompanied by a note as to the matters mentioned in section 108(6)(a) to (c) ; and

(d) contain or be accompanied by a note that on the basis of the valuation the value of the consideration to be received by the company is not less than the value of the consideration to be given by it.

(3) A reference in section 104 or this section to consideration given for the transfer of an asset includes consideration given partly for its transfer ; but—

(a) the value of any consideration partly so given is to be taken as the proportion of the consideration properly attributable to its transfer ;

(b) the valuer shall carry out or arrange for such valuations of anything else as will enable him to determine that proportion ; and

(c) his report for purposes of section 104 shall state what valuation has been made under this subsection and also the reason for and method and date of any such valuation and any other matters which may be relevant to that determination.

Entitlement
of valuer
to full
disclosure.

110.—(1) A person carrying out a valuation or making a report under section 103 or 104, with respect to any consideration proposed to be accepted or given by a company, is entitled to require from the officers of the company such information and explanation as he thinks necessary to enable him to carry out the valuation or make the report and provide a note under section 108(6) or (as the case may be) section 109(2)(c).

(2) A person who knowingly or recklessly makes a statement which—

(a) is misleading, false or deceptive in a material particular, and

(b) is a statement to which this subsection applies,

is guilty of an offence and liable to imprisonment or a fine, or both.

(3) Subsection (2) applies to any statement made (whether orally or in writing) to a person carrying out a valuation or making a report under section 108 or 109, being a statement which conveys or purports to convey any information or explan-

ation which that person requires, or is entitled to require, under
subsection (1) of this section.

111.—(1) A company to which a report is made under section   Matters to be
108 as to the value of any consideration for which, or partly for   communicated
which, it proposes to allot shares shall deliver a copy of the   to registrar.
report to the registrar of companies for registration at the same
time that it files the return of the allotments of those shares
under section 88.

(2) A company which has passed a resolution under section
104 with respect to the transfer of an asset shall, within 15
days of so doing, deliver to the registrar of companies a copy
of the resolution together with the valuer's report required by
that section.

(3) If default is made in complying with subsection (1), every
officer of the company who is in default is liable to a fine and,
for continued contravention, to a daily default fine ; but this is
subject to the same exception as is made by section 88(6) (relief
on application to the court) in the case of default in complying
with that section.

(4) If a company fails to comply with subsection (2), it and
every officer of it who is in default is liable to a fine and, for
continued contravention, to a daily default fine.

Other matters arising out of allotment &c.

112.—(1) If a person becomes a holder of shares in respect   Liability of
of which—   subsequent

> (*a*) there has been a contravention of section 99, 100, 101   holders of
> or 103 ; and   shares
> allotted.

> (*b*) by virtue of that contravention, another is liable to
> pay any amount under the section contravened,

that person is also liable to pay that amount (jointly and severally with any other person so liable), unless he is exempted
from liability by subsection (3) below.

(2) If a company enters into an agreement in contravention
of section 104 and —

> (*a*) the agreement is or includes an agreement for the allot-
> ment of shares in the company ; and

> (*b*) a person becomes a holder of shares allotted under the
> agreement ; and

> (*c*) by virtue of the agreement and allotment under it, an-
> other person is liable to pay any amount under section
> 105,

the person who becomes the holder of the shares is also
liable to pay that amount (jointly and severally with any other

person so liable), unless he is exempted from liability by the following subsection ; and this applies whether or not the agreement also contravenes section 103.

(3) A person otherwise liable under subsection (1) or (2) is exempted from that liability if either—

  (a) he is a purchaser for value and, at the time of the purchase, he did not have actual notice of the contravention concerned ; or

  (b) he derived title to the shares (directly or indirectly) from a person who became a holder of them after the contravention and was not liable under subsection (1) or (as the case may be) subsection (2).

(4) References in this section to a holder, in relation to shares in a company, include any person who has an unconditional right to be included in the company's register of members in respect of those shares or to have an instrument of transfer of the shares executed in his favour.

(5) As subsections (1) and (3) apply in relation to the contraventions there mentioned, they also apply—

  (a) to a contravention of section 102 ; and

  (b) to a failure to carry out a term of a contract as mentioned in subsections (5) and (6) of that section.

Relief in
respect of
certain
liabilities
under
ss. 99 ff. **113.**—(1) Where a person is liable to a company under—

  (a) section 99, 102, 103 or 105 ;

  (b) section 112(1) by reference to a contravention of section 99 or 103 ; or

  (c) section 112(2) or (5),

in relation to payment in respect of any shares in the company, or is liable by virtue of an undertaking given to it in, or in connection with, payment for any such shares, the person so liable may make an application to the court to be exempted in whole or in part from the liability.

(2) If the liability mentioned in subsection (1) arises in relation to payment in respect of any shares, the court may, on an application under that subsection, exempt the applicant from the liability only—

  (a) if and to the extent that it appears to the court just and equitable to do so having regard to the matters mentioned in the following subsection,

  (b) if and to the extent that it appears to the court just and equitable to do so in respect of any interest which he is liable to pay the company under any of the relevant sections.

(3) The matters to be taken into account by the court under subsection (2)(*a*) are—

(*a*) whether the applicant has paid, or is liable to pay, any amount in respect of any other liability arising in relation to those shares under any of the relevant sections, or of any liability arising by virtue of any undertaking given in or in connection with payment for those shares;

(*b*) whether any person other than the applicant has paid or is likely to pay (whether in pursuance of an order of the court or otherwise) any such amount; and

(*c*) whether the applicant or any other person has performed in whole or in part, or is likely so to perform, any such undertaking, or has done or is likely to do any other thing in payment or part payment for the shares.

(4) Where the liability arises by virtue of an undertaking given to the company in, or in connection with, payment for shares in it, the court may, on an application under subsection (1), exempt the applicant from the liability only if and to the extent that it appears to the court just and equitable to do so having regard to—

(*a*) whether the applicant has paid or is liable to pay any amount in respect of liability arising in relation to the shares under any of the provisions mentioned in that subsection; and

(*b*) whether any person other than the applicant has paid or is likely to pay (whether in pursuance of an order of the court or otherwise) any such amount.

(5) In determining whether it should exempt the applicant in whole or in part from any liability, the court shall have regard to the following overriding principles, namely—

(*a*) that a company which has allotted shares should receive money or money's worth at least equal in value to the aggregate of the nominal value of those shares and the whole of any premium or, if the case so requires, so much of that aggregate as is treated as paid up; and

(*b*) subject to this, that where such a company would, if the court did not grant the exemption, have more than one remedy against a particular person, it should be for the company to decide which remedy it should remain entitled to pursue.

(6) If a person brings proceedings against another (" the contributor ") for a contribution in respect of liability to a company arising under any of sections 99 to 105 or 112, and it

appears to the court that the contributor is liable to make such a contribution, the court may exercise the powers of the following subsection.

(7) The court may, if and to the extent that it appears to it, having regard to the respective culpability (in respect of the liability to the company) of the contributor and the person bringing the proceedings, that it is just and equitable to do so—

> (*a*) exempt the contributor in whole or in part from his liability to make such a contribution ; or

> (*b*) order the contributor to make a larger contribution than, but for this subsection, he would be liable to make.

(8) Where a person is liable to a company under section 105 (2), the court may, on application, exempt him in whole or in part from that liability if and to the extent that it appears to the court just and equitable to do so having regard to any benefit accruing to the company by virtue of anything done by him towards the carrying out of the agreement mentioned in that subsection.

Penalty for contravention.
114. If a company contravenes any of the provisions of sections 99 to 104 and 106 the company and any officer of it who is in default is liable to a fine.

Undertakings to do work, etc.
115.—(1) Subject to section 113, an undertaking given by any person, in or in connection with payment for shares in a company, to do work or perform services or to do any other thing, if it is enforceable by the company apart from this Act, is so enforceable notwithstanding that there has been a contravention in relation to it of section 99, 102 or 103.

(2) Where such an undertaking is given in contravention of section 104 in respect of the allotment of shares, it is so enforceable notwithstanding the contravention.

Application of ss. 99 ff to special cases.
1980 c. 22.
116. Except as provided by section 9 of the Consequential Provisions Act (transitional cases dealt with by section 31 of the Companies Act 1980), sections 99, 101 to 103, 106, 108 and 110 to 115 apply—

> (*a*) to a company which has passed and not revoked a resolution to be re-registered under section 43 as a public company, and

> (*b*) to a joint stock company which has passed, and not revoked, a resolution that the company be a public company,

as those sections apply to a public company.

PART V

SHARE CAPITAL, ITS INCREASE, MAINTENANCE AND REDUCTION

CHAPTER I

GENERAL PROVISIONS ABOUT SHARE CAPITAL

117.—(1) A company registered as a public company on its original incorporation shall not do business or exercise any borrowing powers unless the registrar of companies has issued it with a certificate under this section or the company is re-registered as a private company. Public company share capital requirements.

(2) The registrar shall issue a company with such a certificate if, on an application made to him by the company in the prescribed form, he is satisfied that the nominal value of the company's allotted share capital is not less than the authorised minimum, and there is delivered to him a statutory declaration complying with the following subsection.

(3) The statutory declaration must be in the prescribed form and be signed by a director or secretary of the company ; and it must—

(a) state that the nominal value of the company's allotted share capital is not less than the authorised minimum ;

(b) specify the amount paid up, at the time of the application, on the allotted share capital of the company ;

(c) specify the amount, or estimated amount, of the company's preliminary expenses and the persons by whom any of those expenses have been paid or are payable ; and

(d) specify any amount or benefit paid or given, or intended to be paid or given, to any promoter of the company, and the consideration for the payment or benefit.

(4) For the purposes of subsection (2), a share allotted in pursuance of an employees' share scheme may not be taken into account in determining the nominal value of the company's allotted share capital unless it is paid up at least as to one-quarter of the nominal value of the share and the whole of any premium on the share.

(5) The registrar may accept a statutory declaration delivered to him under this section as sufficient evidence of the matters stated in it.

(6) A certificate under this section in respect of a company is conclusive evidence that the company is entitled to do business and exercise any borrowing powers.

(7) If a company does business or exercises borrowing powers in contravention of this section, the company and any officer of it who is in default is liable to a fine.

(8) Nothing in this section affects the validity of any transaction entered into by a company; but, if a company enters into a transaction in contravention of this section and fails to comply with its obligations in that connection within 21 days from being called upon to do so, the directors of the company are jointly and severally liable to indemnify the other party to the transaction in respect of any loss or damage suffered by him by reason of the company's failure to comply with those obligations.

The authorised minimum.

118.—(1) In this Act, "the authorised minimum" means £50,000, or such other sum as the Secretary of State may by order made by statutory instrument specify instead.

(2) An order under this section which increases the authorised minimum may—

(*a*) require any public company having an allotted share capital of which the nominal value is less than the amount specified in the order as the authorised minimum to increase that value to not less than that amount or make application to be re-registered as a private company;

(*b*) make, in connection with any such requirement, provision for any of the matters for which provision is made by this Act relating to a company's registration, re-registration or change of name, to payment for any share comprised in a company's capital and to offers of shares in or debentures of a company to the public, including provision as to the consequences (whether in criminal law or otherwise) of a failure to comply with any requirement of the order; and

(*c*) contain such supplemental and transitional provisions as the Secretary of State thinks appropriate, make different provision for different cases and, in particular, provide for any provision of the order to come into operation on different days for different purposes.

(3) An order shall not be made under this section unless a draft of it has been laid before Parliament and approved by resolution of each House.

Provision for different amounts to be paid on shares.

119. A company, if so authorised by its articles, may do any one or more of the following things—

(*a*) make arrangements on the issue of shares for a difference between the shareholders in the amounts and times of payment of calls on their shares;

(b) accept from any member the whole or a part of the amount remaining unpaid on any shares held by him, although no part of that amount has been called up ;

(c) pay dividend in proportion to the amount paid up on each share where a larger amount is paid up on some shares than on others.

120. A limited company may by special resolution deter- mine that any portion of its share capital which has not been already called up shall not be capable of being called up except in the event and for the purposes of the company being wound up ; and that portion of its share capital is then not capable of being called up except in that event and for those purposes.

Reserve liability of limited company.

121.—(1) A company limited by shares or a company limited by guarantee and having a share capital, if so authorised by its articles, may alter the conditions of its memorandum in any of the following ways.

Alteration of share capital (limited companies).

(2) The company may—

(a) increase its share capital by new shares of such amount as it thinks expedient ;

(b) consolidate and divide all or any of its share capital into shares of larger amount than its existing shares ;

(c) convert all or any of its paid-up shares into stock, and re-convert that stock into paid-up shares of any denomination ;

(d) sub-divide its shares, or any of them, into shares of smaller amount than is fixed by the memorandum (but subject to the following subsection) ;

(e) cancel shares which, at the date of the passing of the resolution to cancel them, have not been taken or agreed to be taken by any person, and diminish the amount of the company's share capital by the amount of the shares so cancelled.

(3) In any sub-division under subsection (2)(d) the proportion between the amount paid and the amount, if any, unpaid on each reduced share must be the same as it was in the case of the share from which the reduced share is derived.

(4) The powers conferred by this section must be exercised by the company in general meeting.

(5) A cancellation of shares under this section does not for purposes of this Act constitute a reduction of share capital.

122.—(1) If a company having a share capital has—

(a) consolidated and divided its share capital into shares of larger amount than its existing shares ; or

(b) converted any shares into stock ; or

(c) re-converted stock into shares ; or

(d) sub-divided its shares or any of them ; or

(e) redeemed any redeemable shares ; or

(f) cancelled any shares (otherwise than in connection with a reduction of share capital under section 135),

it shall within one month after so doing give notice in the prescribed form to the registrar of companies, specifying (as the case may be) the shares consolidated, divided, converted, sub-divided, redeemed or cancelled, or the stock re-converted.

(2) If default is made in complying with this section, the company and every officer of it who is in default is liable to a fine and, for continued contravention, to a daily default fine.

123.—(1) If a company having a share capital (whether or not its shares have been converted into stock) increases its share capital beyond the registered capital, it shall within 15 days after the passing of the resolution authorising the increase, give to the registrar of companies notice of the increase, and the registrar shall record the increase.

(2) The notice must include such particulars as may be prescribed with respect to the classes of shares affected and the conditions subject to which the new shares have been or are to be issued.

(3) There shall be forwarded to the registrar together with the notice a printed copy of the resolution authorising the increase, or a copy of the resolution in some other form approved by the registrar.

(4) If default is made in complying with this section, the company and every officer of it who is in default is liable to a fine and, for continued contravention, to a daily default fine.

124. An unlimited company having a share capital may by its resolution for re-registration as a public company under section 43, or as a limited company under section 51—

(a) increase the nominal amount of its share capital by increasing the nominal amount of each of its shares (but subject to the condition that no part of the increased capital is to be capable of being called up except in the event and for the purpose of the company being wound up), and (*b*) alternatively or in addition, provide that a specified portion of its uncalled share capital is not to be capable of being called up except in that event and for that purpose.

CHAPTER II
CLASS RIGHTS

125.—(1) This section is concerned with the variation of rights attached to any class of shares in a company whose share capital is divided into shares of different classes.

(2) Where the rights are attached to a class of shares otherwise than by the company's memorandum, and the company's articles do not contain provision with respect to the variation of the rights, those rights may be varied if, but only if—

(*a*) the holders of three-quarters in nominal value of the issued shares of that class consent in writing to the variation ; or

(*b*) an extraordinary resolution passed at a separate general meeting of the holders of that class sanctions the variation ;

and any requirement (howsoever imposed) in relation to the variation of those rights is complied with to the extent that it is not comprised in paragraphs (*a*) and (*b*) above.

(3) Where—

(*a*) the rights are attached to a class of shares by the memorandum or otherwise ;

(*b*) the memorandum or articles contain provision for the variation of those rights ; and

(*c*) the variation of those rights is connected with the giving, variation, revocation or renewal of an authority for allotment under section 80 or with a reduction of the company's share capital under section 135 ;

those rights shall not be varied unless—

(i) the condition mentioned in subsection (2)(*a*) or (*b*) above is satisfied ; and

(ii) any requirement of the memorandum or articles in relation to the variation of rights of that class is complied with to the extent that it is not comprised in that condition.

(4) If the rights are attached to a class of shares in the company by the memorandum or otherwise and—

    (*a*) where they are so attached by the memorandum, the articles contain provision with respect to their variation which had been included in the articles at the time of the company's original incorporation; or

    (*b*) where they are so attached otherwise, the articles contain such provision (whenever first so included),

and in either case the variation is not connected as mentioned in subsection (3)(*c*), those rights may only be varied in accordance with that provision of the articles.

(5) If the rights are attached to a class of shares by the memorandum, and the memorandum and articles do not contain provision with respect to the variation of those rights, those rights may be varied if all the members of the company agree to the variation.

(6) The provisions of section 369 (length of notice for calling company meetings), section 370 (general provisions as to meetings and votes), and sections 376 and 377 (circulation of members' resolutions) and the provisions of the articles relating to general meetings shall, so far as applicable, apply in relation to any meeting of shareholders required by this section or otherwise to take place in connection with the variation of the rights attached to a class of shares, and shall so apply with the necessary modifications and subject to the following provisions, namely—

    (*a*) the necessary quorum at any such meeting other than an adjourned meeting shall be two persons holding or representing by proxy at least one-third in nominal value of the issued shares of the class in question and at an adjourned meeting one person holding shares of the class in question or his proxy;

    (*b*) any holder of shares of the class in question present in person or by proxy may demand a poll.

(7) Any alteration of a provision contained in a company's articles for the variation of the rights attached to a class of shares, or the insertion of any such provision into the articles, is itself to be treated as a variation of those rights.

(8) In this section and (except where the context otherwise requires) in any provision for the variation of the rights attached to a class of shares contained in a company's memorandum or articles, references to the variation of those rights are to be read as including references to their abrogation.

126. Nothing in subsections (2) to (5) of section 125 derogates from the powers of the court under the following sections of this Act, namely—

    sections 4 to 6 (company resolution to alter objects),

    section 54 (litigated objection to public company becoming private by re-registration),

    section 425 (court control of company compromising with members and creditors),

    section 427 (company reconstruction or amalgamation),

    sections 459 to 461 (protection of minorities).

127.—(1) This section applies if, in the case of a company whose share capital is divided into different classes of shares—

    (*a*) provision is made by the memorandum or articles for authorising the variation of the rights attached to any class of shares in the company, subject to—

        (i) the consent of any specified proportion of the holders of the issued shares of that class, or

        (ii) the sanction of a resolution passed at a separate meeting of the holders of those shares,

    and in pursuance of that provision the rights attached to any such class of shares are at any time varied ; or

    (*b*) the rights attached to any class of shares in the company are varied under section 125(2).

(2) The holders of not less in the aggregate than 15 per cent. of the issued shares of the class in question (being persons who did not consent to or vote in favour of the resolution for the variation), may apply to the court to have the variation cancelled ; and if such an application is made, the variation has no effect unless and until it is confirmed by the court.

(3) Application to the court must be made within 21 days after the date on which the consent was given or the resolution was passed (as the case may be), and may be made on behalf of the shareholders entitled to make the application by such one or more of their number as they may appoint in writing for the purpose.

(4) The court, after hearing the applicant and any other persons who apply to the court to be heard and appear to the court to be interested in the application, may, if satisfied having regard to all the circumstances of the case, that the variation would unfairly prejudice the shareholders of the class represented by the applicant, disallow the variation and shall, if not so satisfied, confirm it.

The decision of the court on any such application is final.

(5) The company shall within 15 days after the making of an order by the court on such an application forward a copy of the order to the registrar of companies; and, if default is made in complying with this provision, the company and every officer of it who is in default is liable to a fine and, for continued contravention, to a daily default fine.

(6) " Variation ", in this section, includes abrogation; and " varied " is to be construed accordingly.

Registration of particulars of special rights.

128.—(1) If a company allots shares with rights which are not stated in its memorandum or articles, or in any resolution or agreement which is required by section 380 to be sent to the registrar of companies, the company shall deliver to the registrar of companies, within one month from allotting the shares, a statement in the prescribed form containing particulars of those rights.

(2) This does not apply if the shares are in all respects uniform with shares previously allotted; and shares are not for this purpose to be treated as different from shares previously allotted by reason only that the former do not carry the same rights to dividends as the latter during the 12 months immediately following the former's allotment.

(3) Where the rights attached to any shares of a company are varied otherwise than by an amendment of the company's memorandum or articles or by a resolution or agreement subject to section 380, the company shall within one month from the date on which the variation is made deliver to the registrar of companies a statement in the prescribed form containing particulars of the variation.

(4) Where a company (otherwise than by any such amendment, resolution or agreement as is mentioned above) assigns a name or other designation, or a new name or other designation, to any class of its shares, it shall within one month from doing so deliver to the registrar of companies a notice in the prescribed form giving particulars of the name or designation so assigned.

(5) If a company fails to comply with this section, the company and every officer of it who is in default is liable to a fine and, for continued contravention, to a daily default fine.

Registration of newly created class rights.

129.—(1) If a company not having a share capital creates a class of members with rights which are not stated in its memorandum or articles or in a resolution or agreement to which section 380 applies, the company shall deliver to the registrar of companies within one month from the date on which the new class is created a statement in the prescribed form containing particulars of the rights attached to that class.

(2) If the rights of any class of members of the company are varied otherwise than by an amendment of the memorandum or articles or by a resolution or agreement subject to section 380, the company shall within one month from the date on which the variation is made deliver to the registrar a statement in the prescribed form containing particulars of the variation.

(3) If a company (otherwise than by such an amendment, resolution or agreement as is mentioned above) assigns a name or other designation, or a new name or other designation, to any class of its members, it shall within one month from doing so deliver to the registrar a notice in the prescribed form giving particulars of the name or designation so assigned.

(4) If a company fails to comply with this section, the company and every officer of it who is in default is liable to a fine and, for continued contravention, to a daily default fine.

CHAPTER III

SHARE PREMIUMS

130.—(1) If a company issues shares at a premium, whether for cash or otherwise, a sum equal to the aggregate amount or value of the premiums on those shares shall be transferred to an account called " the share premium account ".

Application of share premiums.

(2) The share premium account may be applied by the company in paying up unissued shares to be allotted to members as fully paid bonus shares, or in writing off—

    (a) the company's preliminary expenses ; or

    (b) the expenses of, or the commission paid or discount allowed on, any issue of shares or debentures of the company,

or in providing for the premium payable on redemption of debentures of the company.

(3) Subject to this, the provisions of this Act relating to the reduction of a company's share capital apply as if the share premium account were part of its paid up share capital.

(4) Sections 131 and 132 below give relief from the requirements of this section, and in those sections references to the issuing company are to the company issuing shares as above mentioned.

131.—(1) With the exception made by section 132(4) (group reconstruction) this section applies where the issuing company has secured at least a 90 per cent. equity holding in another company in pursuance of an arrangement providing for the allotment of equity shares in the issuing company on terms that the consideration for the shares allotted is to be provided—

　　(*a*) by the issue or transfer to the issuing company of equity shares in the other company, or

　　(*b*) by the cancellation of any such shares not held by the issuing company.

(2) If the equity shares in the issuing company allotted in pursuance of the arrangement in consideration for the acquisition or cancellation of equity shares in the other company are issued at a premium, section 130 does not apply to the premiums on those shares.

(3) Where the arrangement also provides for the allotment of any shares in the issuing company on terms that the consideration for those shares is to be provided by the issue or transfer to the issuing company of non-equity shares in the other company or by the cancellation of any such shares in that company not held by the issuing company, relief under subsection (2) extends to any shares in the issuing company allotted on those terms in pursuance of the arrangement.

(4) Subject to the next subsection, the issuing company is to be regarded for purposes of this section as having secured at least a 90 per cent. equity holding in another company in pursuance of such an arrangement as is mentioned in subsection (1) if in consequence of an acquisition or cancellation of equity shares in that company (in pursuance of that arrangement) it holds equity shares in that company (whether all or any of those shares were acquired in pursuance of that arrangement, or not) of an aggregate nominal value equal to 90 per cent. or more of the nominal value of that company's equity share capital.

(5) Where the equity share capital of the other company is divided into different classes of shares, this section does not apply unless the requirements of subsection (1) are satisfied in relation to each of those classes of shares taken separately.

(6) Shares held by a company which is the issuing company's holding company or subsidiary, or a subsidiary of the issuing company's holding company, or by its or their nominees, are to be regarded for purposes of this section as held by the issuing company.

(7) In relation to a company and its shares and capital, the following definitions apply for purposes of this section—

  (*a*) " equity shares " means shares comprised in the company's equity share capital ; and

  (*b*) " non-equity shares " means shares (of any class) not so comprised ;

and " arrangement " means any agreement, scheme or arrangement (including an arrangement sanctioned under section 425 (company compromise with members and creditors) or section 582 (liquidator accepting shares etc. as consideration for sale of company property)).

(8) The relief allowed by this section does not apply if the issue of shares took place before 4th February 1981.

132.—(1) This section applies where the issuing company— Relief in respect
of group recon-
structions.

  (*a*) is a wholly-owned subsidiary of another company (" the holding company "), and

  (*b*) allots shares to the holding company or to another wholly-owned subsidiary of the holding company in consideration for the transfer to the issuing company of assets other than cash, being assets of any company (" the transferor company ") which is a member of the group of companies which comprises the holding company and all its wholly-owned subsidiaries.

(2) Where the shares in the issuing company allotted in consideration for the transfer are issued at a premium, the issuing company is not required by section 130 to transfer any amount in excess of the minimum premium value to the share premium account.

(3) In subsection (2), " the minimum premium value " means the amount (if any) by which the base value of the consideration for the shares allotted exceeds the aggregate nominal value of those shares.

(4) For the purposes of subsection (3), the base value of the consideration for the shares allotted is the amount by which the base value of the assets transferred exceeds the base value of any liabilities of the transferor company assumed by the issuing company as part of the consideration for the assets transferred.

(5) For the purposes of subsection (4)—

  (*a*) the base value of the assets transferred is to be taken as—

      (i) the cost of those assets to the transferor company, or

(ii) the amount at which those assets are stated in the transferor company's accounting records immediately before the transfer,

whichever is the less ; and

(b) the base value of the liabilities assumed is to be taken as the amount at which they are stated in the transferor company's accounting records immediately before the transfer.

(6) The relief allowed by this section does not apply (subject to the next subsection) if the issue of shares took place before the date of the coming into force of the Companies (Share Premium S.I. 1984/2007. Account) Regulations 1984 (which were made on 21st December 1984).

(7) To the extent that the relief allowed by this section would
1981 c. 62.   have been allowed by section 38 of the Companies Act 1981 as originally enacted (the text of which section is set out in Schedule 25 to this Act), the relief applies where the issue of shares took place before the date of the coming into force of those Regulations, but not if the issue took place before 4th February 1981.

(8) Section 131 does not apply in a case falling within this section.

Provisions   **133.**—(1) An amount corresponding to one representing the
supplementing premiums or part of the premiums on shares issued by a com-
ss. 131, 132.   pany which by virtue of sections 131 or 132 of this Act, or section 12 of the Consequential Provisions Act, is not included in the company's share premium account may also be disregarded in determining the amount at which any shares or other consideration provided for the shares issued is to be included in the company's balance sheet.

(2) References in this Chapter (however expressed) to—

(a) the acquisition by a company of shares in another company ; and

(b) the issue or allotment of shares to, or the transfer of shares to or by, a company,

include (respectively) the acquisition of any of those shares by, and the issue or allotment or (as the case may be) the transfer of any of those shares to or by, nominees of that company ; and the reference in section 132 to the company transferring the shares is to be construed accordingly.

(3) References in this Chapter to the transfer of shares in a company include the transfer of a right to be included in the company's register of members in respect of those shares.

(4) In sections 131 to 133 " company ", except in references to the issuing company, includes any body corporate.

134.—(1) The Secretary of State may by regulations in a statutory instrument make such provision as appears to him to be appropriate—

(a) for relieving companies from the requirements of section 130 in relation to premiums other than cash premiums, or

(b) for restricting or otherwise modifying any relief from those requirements provided by this Chapter.

(2) Regulations under this section may make different provision for different cases or classes of case and may contain such incidental and supplementary provisions as the Secretary of State thinks fit.

(3) No such regulations shall be made unless a draft of the instrument containing them has been laid before Parliament and approved by a resolution of each House.

CHAPTER IV

REDUCTION OF SHARE CAPITAL

135.—(1) Subject to confirmation by the court, a company limited by shares or a company limited by guarantee and having a share capital may, if so authorised by its articles, by special resolution reduce its share capital in any way.

(2) In particular, and without prejudice to subsection (1), the company may—

(a) extinguish or reduce the liability on any of its shares in respect of share capital not paid up ; or

(b) either with or without extinguishing or reducing liability on any of its shares, cancel any paid-up share capital which is lost or unrepresented by available assets ; or

(c) either with or without extinguishing or reducing liability on any of its shares, pay off any paid-up share capital which is in excess of the company's wants ;

and the company may, if and so far as is necessary, alter its memorandum by reducing the amount of its share capital and of its shares accordingly.

(3) A special resolution under this section is in this Act referred to as " a resolution for reducing share capital ".

Part V
Chapter IV
Application
to court for
order of
confirmation.

136.—(1) Where a company has passed a resolution for reducing share capital, it may apply to the court for an order confirming the reduction.

(2) If the proposed reduction of share capital involves either—

  (*a*) diminution of liability in respect of unpaid share capital ; or

  (*b*) the payment to a shareholder of any paid-up share capital,

and in any other case if the court so directs, the next three subsections have effect, but subject throughout to subsection (6).

(3) Every creditor of the company who at the date fixed by the court is entitled to any debt or claim which, if that date were the commencement of the winding up of the company, would be admissible in proof against the company is entitled to object to the reduction of capital.

(4) The court shall settle a list of creditors entitled to object, and for that purpose—

  (*a*) shall ascertain, as far as possible without requiring an application from any creditor, the names of those creditors and the nature and amount of their debts or claims ; and

  (*b*) may publish notices fixing a day or days within which creditors not entered on the list are to claim to be so entered or are to be excluded from the right of objecting to the reduction of capital.

(5) If a creditor entered on the list whose debt or claim is not discharged or has not determined does not consent to the reduction, the court may, if it thinks fit, dispense with the consent of that creditor, on the company securing payment of his debt or claim by appropriating (as the court may direct) the following amount—

  (*a*) if the company admits the full amount of the debt or claim or, though not admitting it, is willing to provide for it, then the full amount of the debt or claim ;

  (*b*) if the company does not admit, and is not willing to provide for, the full amount of the debt or claim, or if the amount is contingent or not ascertained, then an amount fixed by the court after the like enquiry and adjudication as if the company were being wound up by the court.

(6) If a proposed reduction of share capital involves either the diminution of any liability in respect of unpaid share capital or the payment to any shareholder of any paid-up share

capital, the court may, if having regard to any special circumstances of the case it thinks proper to do so, direct that subsections (3) to (5) of this section shall not apply as regards any class or any classes of creditors.

137.—(1) The court, if satisfied with respect to every creditor of the company who under section 136 is entitled to object to the reduction of capital that either—

Court order confirming reduction.

    (*a*) his consent to the reduction has been obtained ; or

    (*b*) his debt or claim has been discharged or has determined, or has been secured,

may make an order confirming the reduction on such terms and conditions as it thinks fit.

(2) Where the court so orders, it may also—

    (*a*) if for any special reason it thinks proper to do so, make an order directing that the company shall, during such period (commencing on or at any time after the date of the order) as is specified in the order, add to its name as its last words the words " and reduced "; and

    (*b*) make an order requiring the company to publish (as the court directs) the reasons for reduction of capital or such other information in regard to it as the court thinks expedient with a view to giving proper information to the public and (if the court thinks fit) the causes which led to the reduction.

(3) Where a company is ordered to add to its name the words " and reduced ", those words are, until the expiration of the period specified in the order, deemed to be part of the company's name.

138.—(1) The registrar of companies, on production to him of an order of the court confirming the reduction of a company's share capital, and the delivery to him of a copy of the order and of a minute (approved by the court) showing, with respect to the company's share capital as altered by the order—

Registration of order and minute of reduction.

    (*a*) the amount of the share capital;

    (*b*) the number of shares into which it is to be divided, and the amount of each share; and

    (*c*) the amount (if any) at the date of the registration deemed to be paid up on each share,

shall register the order and minute (but subject to section 139).

(2) On the registration of the order and minute, and not before, the resolution for reducing share capital as confirmed by the order so registered takes effect.

(3) Notice of the registration shall be published in such manner as the court may direct.

(4) The registrar shall certify the registration of the order and minute ; and the certificate—

> (a) may be either signed by the registrar, or authenticated by his official seal ;
> (b) is conclusive evidence that all the requirements of this Act with respect to the reduction of share capital have been complied with, and that the company's share capital is as stated in the minute.

(5) The minute when registered is deemed to be substituted for the corresponding part of the company's memorandum, and is valid and alterable as if it had been originally contained therein.

(6) The substitution of such a minute for part of the company's memorandum is deemed an alteration of the memorandum for purposes of section 20.

Public
company
reducing
capital below
authorised
minimum.

139.—(1) This section applies where the court makes an order confirming a reduction of a public company's capital which has the effect of bringing the nominal value of its allotted share capital below the authorised minimum.

(2) The registrar of companies shall not register the order under section 138 unless the court otherwise directs, or the company is first re-registered as a private company.

(3) The court may authorise the company to be so re-registered without its having passed the special resolution required by section 53 ; and where that authority is given, the court shall specify in the order the alterations in the company's memorandum and articles to be made in connection with that re-registration.

(4) The company may then be re-registered as a private company, if an application in the prescribed form and signed by a director or secretary of the company is delivered to the registrar, together with a printed copy of the memorandum and articles as altered by the court's order.

(5) On receipt of such an application, the registrar shall retain it and the other documents delivered with it and issue the company with a certificate of incorporation appropriate to a company that is not a public company ; and—

> (a) the company by virtue of the issue of the certificate becomes a private company, and the alterations in the memorandum and articles set out in the court's order take effect ; and

(*b*) the certificate is conclusive evidence that the requirements of this section in respect of re-registration and of matters precedent and incidental thereto have been complied with, and that the company is a private company.

140.—(1) Where a company's share capital is reduced, a member of the company (past or present) is not liable in respect of any share to any call or contribution exceeding in amount the difference (if any) between the amount of the share as fixed by the minute and the amount paid on the share or the reduced amount (if any), which is deemed to have been paid on it, as the case may be.

Liability of members on reduced shares.

(2) But the following two subsections apply if—

(*a*) a creditor, entitled in respect of a debt or claim to object to the reduction of share capital, by reason of his ignorance of the proceedings for reduction of share capital, or of their nature and effect with respect to his claim, is not entered on the list of creditors; and

(*b*) after the reduction of capital, the company is unable (within the meaning of section 518) to pay the amount of his debt or claim.

(3) Every person who was a member of the company at the date of the registration of the order for reduction and minute is then liable to contribute for the payment of the debt or claim in question an amount not exceeding that which he would have been liable to contribute if the company had commenced to be wound up on the day before that date.

(4) If the company is wound up, the court, on the application of the creditor in question and proof of ignorance referred to in subsection (2)(*a*), may (if it thinks fit) settle accordingly a list of persons so liable to contribute, and make and enforce calls and orders on the contributories settled on the list, as if they were ordinary contributories in a winding up.

(5) Nothing in this section affects the rights of the contributories among themselves.

141. If an officer of the company—

(*a*) wilfully conceals the name of a creditor entitled to object to the reduction of capital; or

(*b*) wilfully misrepresents the nature or amount of the debt or claim of any creditor; or

(*c*) aids, abets or is privy to any such concealment or misrepresentation as is mentioned above,

he is guilty of an offence and liable to a fine.

Penalty for concealing name of creditor, etc.

CHAPTER V

MAINTENANCE OF CAPITAL

Duty of
directors on
serious loss
of capital.

142.—(1) Where the net assets of a public company are half
or less of its called-up share capital, the directors shall, not later
than 28 days from the earliest day on which that fact is known
to a director of the company, duly convene an extraordinary
general meeting of the company for a date not later than 56
days from that day for the purpose of considering whether any,
and if so what, steps should be taken to deal with the situation.

(2) If there is a failure to convene an extraordinary general
meeting as required by subsection (1), each of the directors of
the company who—

> (*a*) knowingly and wilfully authorises or permits the failure,
> or
>
> (*b*) after the expiry of the period during which that meeting
> should have been convened, knowingly and wilfully
> authorises or permits the failure to continue,

is liable to a fine.

(3) Nothing in this section authorises the consideration, at a
meeting convened in pursuance of subsection (1), of any matter
which could not have been considered at that meeting apart
from this section.

General rule
against
company
acquiring own
shares.

143.—(1) Subject to the following provisions, a company
limited by shares or limited by guarantee and having a share
capital shall not acquire its own shares, whether by purchase,
subscription or otherwise.

(2) If a company purports to act in contravention of this
section, the company is liable to a fine, and every officer of the
company who is in default is liable to imprisonment or a fine,
or both ; and the purported acquisition is void.

(3) A company limited by shares may acquire any of its
own fully paid shares otherwise than for valuable consideration ;
and subsection (1) does not apply in relation to—

> (*a*) the redemption or purchase of shares in accordance
> with Chapter VII of this Part,
>
> (*b*) the acquisition of shares in a reduction of capital duly
> made,
>
> (*c*) the purchase of shares in pursuance of an order of the
> court under section 5 (alteration of objects), section 54
> (litigated objection to resolution for company to be re-
> registered as private) or Part XVII (relief to members
> unfairly prejudiced), or
>
> (*d*) the forfeiture of shares, or the acceptance of shares
> surrendered in lieu, in pursuance of the articles, for
> failure to pay any sum payable in respect of the shares.

144.—(1) Subject to section 145, where shares are issued to a
nominee of a company mentioned in section 143(1), or are
acquired by a nominee of such a company from a third person
as partly paid up, then, for all purposes—

PART V
CHAPTER V
Acquisition
of shares by
company's
nominee.

    (*a*) the shares are to be treated as held by the nominee on
his own account ; and

    (*b*) the company is to be regarded as having no beneficial
interest in them.

(2) Subject to that section, if a person is called on to pay
any amount for the purpose of paying up, or paying any
premium on, any shares in such a company which were issued
to him, or which he otherwise acquired, as the company's
nominee and he fails to pay that amount within 21 days from
being called on to do so, then—

    (*a*) if the shares were issued to him as subscriber to the
memorandum by virtue of an undertaking of his in
the memorandum, the other subscribers to the memorandum, or

    (*b*) if the shares were otherwise issued to or acquired by
him, the directors of the company at the time of the
issue or acquisition,

are jointly and severally liable with him to pay that amount.

(3) If in proceedings for the recovery of any such amount
from any such subscriber or director under this section it appears
to the court—

    (*a*) that he is or may be liable to pay that amount, but

    (*b*) that he has acted honestly and reasonably and, having
regard to all the circumstances of the case, he ought
fairly to be excused from liability,

the court may relieve him, either wholly or partly, from his
liability on such terms as the court thinks fit.

(4) Where any such subscriber or director has reason to
apprehend that a claim will or might be made for the recovery
of any such amount from him, he may apply to the court for
relief ; and the court has the same power to relieve him as it
would have had in proceedings for the recovery of that amount.

145.—(1) Section 144(1) does not apply to shares acquired
otherwise than by subscription by a nominee of a public company, where a person acquires shares in the company with
financial assistance given to him directly or indirectly by the
company for the purpose of or in connection with the acquisition,
and the company has a beneficial interest in the shares.

(2) Section 144 (1) and (2) do not apply—

(a) to shares acquired by a nominee of a company when the company has no beneficial interest in those shares, or

(b) to shares issued in consequence of an application made before 22nd December 1980, or transferred in pursuance of an agreement to acquire them made before that date.

(3) Schedule 2 to this Act has effect for the interpretation of references in this section to a company having, or not having, a beneficial interest in shares.

Treatment of shares held by or for public company.

146.—(1) Except as provided by section 148, the following applies to a public company—

(a) where shares in the company are forfeited, or surrendered to the company in lieu, in pursuance of the articles, for failure to pay any sum payable in respect of the shares ;

(b) where shares in the company are acquired by it (otherwise than by any of the methods mentioned in section 143 (3) (a) to (d)) and the company has a beneficial interest in the shares ;

(c) where the nominee of the company acquires shares in the company from a third person without financial assistance being given directly or indirectly by the company and the company has a beneficial interest in the shares ; or

(d) where a person acquires shares in the company with financial assistance given to him directly or indirectly by the company for the purpose of or in connection with the acquisition, and the company has a beneficial interest in the shares.

Schedule 2 to this Act has effect for the interpretation of references in this subsection to the company having a beneficial interest in shares.

(2) Unless the shares or any interest of the company in them are previously disposed of, the company must, not later than the end of the relevant period from their forfeiture or surrender or, in a case within subsection (1)(b), (c) or (d), their acquisition—

(a) cancel them and diminish the amount of the share capital by the nominal value of the shares cancelled, **and**

(b) where the effect of cancelling the shares will be that the nominal value of the company's allotted share capital is brought below the authorised minimum, apply for re-registration as a private company, stating the effect of the cancellation.

(3) For this purpose " the relevant period " is—

(a) 3 years in the case of shares forfeited or surrendered to the company in lieu of forfeiture, or acquired as mentioned in subsection (1)(b) or (c);

(b) one year in the case of shares acquired as mentioned in subsection (1)(d).

(4) The company and, in a case within subsection (1)(c) or (d), the company's nominee or (as the case may be) the other shareholder must not exercise any voting rights in respect of the shares; and any purported exercise of those rights is void.

147.—(1) The directors may take such steps as are requisite to enable the company to carry out its obligations under section 146(2) without complying with sections 135 and 136 (resolution to reduce share capital; application to court for approval).

(2) The steps taken may include the passing of a resolution to alter the company's memorandum so that it no longer states that the company is to be a public company; and the resolution may make such other alterations in the memorandum as are requisite in the circumstances.

Such a resolution is subject to section 380 (copy to be forwarded to registrar within 15 days).

(3) The application for re-registration required by section 146 (2)(b) must be in the prescribed form and be signed by a director or secretary of the company, and must be delivered to the registrar of companies together with a printed copy of the memorandum and articles of the company as altered by the resolution.

(4) If the registrar is satisfied that the company may be re-registered under section 146, he shall retain the application and other documents delivered with it and issue the company with a certificate of incorporation appropriate to a company that is not a public company; and—

(a) the company by virtue of the issue of the certificate becomes a private company, and the alterations in the memorandum and articles set out in the resolution take effect accordingly, and

(b) the certificate is conclusive evidence that the requirements of sections 146 to 148 in respect of re-registration and of matters precedent and incidental to it have been complied with, and that the company is a private company.

PART V
CHAPTER V
Further
provisions
supplementing
ss. 146, 147.

148.—(1) Where, after shares in a private company—

(a) are forfeited in pursuance of the company's articles or are surrendered to the company in lieu of forfeiture, or

(b) are acquired by the company (otherwise than by such surrender or forfeiture, and otherwise than by any of the methods mentioned in section 143(3)), the company having a beneficial interest in the shares, or

(c) are acquired by the nominee of a company in the circumstances mentioned in section 146(1)(c), or

(d) are acquired by any person in the circumstances mentioned in section 146(1)(d),

the company is re-registered as a public company, sections 146 and 147, and also section 149, apply to the company as if it had been a public company at the time of the forfeiture, surrender or acquisition, but with the modification required by the following subsection.

(2) That modification is to treat any reference to the relevant period from the forfeiture, surrender or acquisition as referring to the relevant period from the re-registration of the company as a public company.

(3) Schedule 2 to this Act has effect for the interpretation of the reference in subsection (1)(b) to the company having a beneficial interest in shares.

(4) Where a public company or a nominee of a public company acquires shares in the company or an interest in such shares, and those shares are (or that interest is) shown in a balance sheet of the company as an asset, an amount equal to the value of the shares or (as the case may be) the value to the company of its interest in them shall be transferred out of profits available for dividend to a reserve fund and are not then available for distribution.

Sanctions for
non-
compliance.

149.—(1) If a public company required by section 146(2) to apply to be re-registered as a private company fails to do so before the end of the relevant period referred to in that subsection, section 81 (restriction on public offers) applies to it as if it were a private company such as is mentioned in that section ; but, subject to this, the company continues to be treated for the purpose of this Act as a public company until it is so re-registered.

(2) If a company when required to do so by section 146(2) (including that subsection as applied by section 148(1)) fails to cancel any shares in accordance with paragraph (a) of that subsection or to make an application for re-registration in

accordance with paragraph (*b*) of it, the company and every PART V
officer of it who is in default is liable to a fine and, for continued CHAPTER V
contravention, to a daily default fine.

150.—(1) A lien or other charge of a public company on its Charges
own shares (whether taken expressly or otherwise), except a of public
charge permitted by any of the following subsections, is void. companies
on own shares.

This is subject to section 6 of the Consequential Provisions Act
(saving for charges of old public companies on their own shares).

(2) In the case of any description of company, a charge on
its own shares is permitted if the shares are not fully paid and
the charge is for any amount payable in respect of the shares.

(3) In the case of a company whose ordinary business—

(*a*) includes the lending of money, or

(*b*) consists of the provision of credit or the bailment (in
Scotland, hiring) of goods under a hire purchase agreement, or both,

a charge of the company on its own shares is permitted (whether
the shares are fully paid or not) if it arises in connection with a
transaction entered into by the company in the ordinary course
of its business.

(4) In the case of a company which is re-registered or is
registered under section 680 as a public company, a charge on
its own shares is permitted if the charge was in existence
immediately before the company's application for re-registration
or (as the case may be) registration.

This subsection does not apply in the case of such a company
as is referred to in section 6(3) of the Consequential Provisions
Act (old public company remaining such after 22nd March 1982,
not having applied to be re-registered as public company).

CHAPTER VI

FINANCIAL ASSISTANCE BY A COMPANY FOR ACQUISITION OF ITS OWN SHARES

Provisions applying to both public and private companies

151.—(1) Subject to the following provisions of this Chap- Financial
ter, where a person is acquiring or is proposing to acquire assistance
shares in a company, it is not lawful for the company or any generally
prohibited.
of its subsidiaries to give financial assistance directly or indirectly for the purpose of that acquisition before or at the same
time as the acquisition takes place.

(2) Subject to those provisions, where a person has acquired
shares in a company and any liability has been incurred (by

E

that or any other person), for the purpose of that acquisition, it is not lawful for the company or any of its subsidiaries to give financial assistance directly or indirectly for the purpose of reducing or discharging the liability so incurred.

(3) If a company acts in contravention of this section, it is liable to a fine, and every officer of it who is in default is liable to imprisonment or a fine, or both.

Definitions for this Chapter.
152.—(1) In this Chapter—

    (*a*) " financial assistance " means—

        (i) financial assistance given by way of gift,

        (ii) financial assistance given by way of guarantee, security or indemnity, other than an indemnity in respect of the indemnifier's own neglect or default, or by way of release or waiver,

        (iii) financial assistance given by way of a loan or any other agreement under which any of the obligations of the person giving the assistance are to be fulfilled at a time when in accordance with the agreement any obligation of another party to the agreement remains unfulfilled, or by way of the novation of, or the assignment of rights arising under, a loan or such other agreement, or

        (iv) any other financial assistance given by a company the net assets of which are thereby reduced to a material extent or which has no net assets ;

    (*b*) " distributable profits ", in relation to the giving of any financial assistance—

        (i) means those profits out of which the company could lawfully make a distribution equal in value to that assistance, and

        (ii) includes, in a case where the financial assistance is or includes a non-cash asset, any profit which, if the company were to make a distribution of that asset, would under section 276 (distributions in kind) be available for that purpose,

    and

    (*c*) " distribution " has the meaning given by section 263(2).

(2) In subsection (1)(*a*)(iv), " net assets " means the aggregate of the company's assets, less the aggregate of its liabilities (" liabilities " to include any provision for liabilities or charges within paragraph 89 of Schedule 4).

(3) In this Chapter—

    (*a*) a reference to a person incurring a liability includes his changing his financial position by making an agreement or arrangement (whether enforceable or unenforceable, and whether made on his own account or with any other person) or by any other means, and

(b) a reference to a company giving financial assistance for the purpose of reducing or discharging a liability incurred by a person for the purpose of the acquisition of shares includes its giving such assistance for the purpose of wholly or partly restoring his financial position to what it was before the acquisition took place.

153.—(1) Section 151(1) does not prohibit a company from giving financial assistance for the purpose of an acquisition of shares in it or its holding company if—

(a) the company's principal purpose in giving that assistance is not to give it for the purpose of any such acquisition, or the giving of the assistance for that purpose is but an incidental part of some larger purpose of the company, and

(b) the assistance is given in good faith in the interests of the company.

(2) Section 151(2) does not prohibit a company from giving financial assistance if—

(a) the company's principal purpose in giving the assistance is not to reduce or discharge any liability incurred by a person for the purpose of the acquisition of shares in the company or its holding company, or the reduction or discharge of any such liability is but an incidental part of some larger purpose of the company, and

(b) the assistance is given in good faith in the interests of the company.

(3) Section 151 does not prohibit—

(a) a distribution of a company's assets by way of dividend lawfully made or a distribution made in the course of the company's winding up,

(b) the allotment of bonus shares ,

(c) a reduction of capital confirmed by order of the court under section 137,

(d) a redemption or purchase of shares made in accordance with Chapter VII of this Part,

(e) anything done in pursuance of an order of the court under section 425 (compromises and arrangements with creditors and members),

(f) anything done under an arrangement made in pursuance of section 582 (acceptance of shares by liquidator in winding up as consideration for sale of property), or

(g) anything done under an arrangement made between a company and its creditors which is binding on the creditors by virtue of section 601 (winding up imminent or in progress).

(4) Section 151 does not prohibit—

    (a) where the lending of money is part of the ordinary business of the company, the lending of money by the company in the ordinary course of its business,

    (b) the provision by a company in accordance with an employees' share scheme of money for the acquisition of fully paid shares in the company or its holding company,

    (c) the making by a company of loans to persons (other than directors) employed in good faith by the company with a view to enabling those persons to acquire fully paid shares in the company or its holding company to be held by them by way of beneficial ownership.

Special restriction for public companies.

154.—(1) In the case of a public company, section 153(4) authorises the giving of financial assistance only if the company has net assets which are not thereby reduced or, to the extent that those assets are thereby reduced, if the assistance is provided out of distributable profits.

(2) For this purpose the following definitions apply—

    (a) " net assets " means the amount by which the aggregate of the company's assets exceeds the aggregate of its liabilities (taking the amount of both assets and liabilities to be as stated in the company's accounting records immediately before the financial assistance is given) ;

    (b) " liabilities " includes any amount retained as reasonably necessary for the purpose of providing for any liability or loss which is either likely to be incurred, or certain to be incurred but uncertain as to amount or as to the date on which it will arise.

Private companies

Relaxation of s. 151 for private companies.

155.—(1) Section 151 does not prohibit a private company from giving financial assistance in a case where the acquisition of shares in question is or was an acquisition of shares in the company or, if it is a subsidiary of another private company, in that other company if the following provisions of this section, and sections 156 to 158, are complied with as respects the giving of that assistance.

(2) The financial assistance may only be given if the company has net assets which are not thereby reduced or, to the extent that they are reduced, if the assistance is provided out of distributable profits.

Section 154(2) applies for the interpretation of this sub-section.

(3) This section does not permit financial assistance to be given by a subsidiary, in a case where the acquisition of shares in question is or was an acquisition of shares in its holding company, if it is also a subsidiary of a public company which is itself a subsidiary of that holding company.

(4) Unless the company proposing to give the financial assistance is a wholly-owned subsidiary, the giving of assistance under this section must be approved by special resolution of the company in general meeting.

(5) Where the financial assistance is to be given by the company in a case where the acquisition of shares in question is or was an acquisition of shares in its holding company, that holding company and any other company which is both the company's holding company and a subsidiary of that other holding company (except, in any case, a company which is a wholly-owned subsidiary) shall also approve by special resolution in general meeting the giving of the financial assistance.

(6) The directors of the company proposing to give the financial assistance and, where the shares acquired or to be acquired are shares in its holding company, the directors of that company and of any other company which is both the company's holding company and a subsidiary of that other holding company shall before the financial assistance is given make a statutory declaration in the prescribed form complying with the section next following.

156.—(1) A statutory declaration made by a company's directors under section 155(6) shall contain such particulars of the financial assistance to be given, and of the business of the company of which they are directors, as may be prescribed, and shall identify the person to whom the assistance is to be given.

Statutory declaration under s. 155.

(2) The declaration shall state that the directors have formed the opinion, as regards the company's initial situation immediately following the date on which the assistance is proposed to be given, that there will be no ground on which it could then be found to be unable to pay its debts ; and either—

    (a) if it is intended to commence the winding up of the company within 12 months of that date, that the company will be able to pay its debts in full within 12 months of the commencement of the winding up, or

    (b) in any other case, that the company will be able to pay its debts as they fall due during the year immediately following that date.

E 3

(3) In forming their opinion for purposes of subsection (2), the directors shall take into account the same liabilities (including contingent and prospective liabilities) as would be relevant under section 517 (winding up by the court) to the question whether the company is unable to pay its debts.

(4) The directors' statutory declaration shall have annexed to it a report addressed to them by their company's auditors stating that—

> (a) they have enquired into the state of affairs of the company, and
>
> (b) they are not aware of anything to indicate that the opinion expressed by the directors in the declaration as to any of the matters mentioned in subsection (2) of this section is unreasonable in all the circumstances.

(5) The statutory declaration and auditors' report shall be delivered to the registrar of companies—

> (a) together with a copy of any special resolution passed by the company under section 155 and delivered to the registrar in compliance with section 380, or
>
> (b) where no such resolution is required to be passed, within 15 days after the making of the declaration.

(6) If a company fails to comply with subsection (5), the company and every officer of it who is in default is liable to a fine and, for continued contravention, to a daily default fine.

(7) A director of a company who makes a statutory declaration under section 155 without having reasonable grounds for the opinion expressed in it is liable to imprisonment or a fine, or both.

Special
resolution
under s. 155.
157.—(1) A special resolution required by section 155 to be passed by a company approving the giving of financial assistance must be passed on the date on which the directors of that company make the statutory declaration required by that section in connection with the giving of that assistance, or within the week immediately following that date.

(2) Where such a resolution has been passed, an application may be made to the court for the cancellation of the resolution—

> (a) by the holders of not less in the aggregate than 10 per cent. in nominal value of the company's issued share capital or any class of it, or
>
> (b) if the company is not limited by shares, by not less than 10 per cent. of the company's members ;

but the application shall not be made by a person who has consented to or voted in favour of the resolution.

(3) Subsections (3) to (10) of section 54 (litigation to cancel resolution under section 53) apply to applications under this section as to applications under section 54.

(4) A special resolution passed by a company is not effective for purposes of section 155—

(*a*) unless the declaration made in compliance with subsection (6) of that section by the directors of the company, together with the auditors' report annexed to it, is available for inspection by members of the company at the meeting at which the resolution is passed,

(*b*) if it is cancelled by the court on an application under this section.

158.—(1) This section applies as to the time before and after which financial assistance may not be given by a company in pursuance of section 155.   Time for giving financial assistance under s. 155.

(2) Where a special resolution is required by that section to be passed approving the giving of the assistance, the assistance shall not be given before the expiry of the period of 4 weeks beginning with—

(*a*) the date on which the special resolution is passed, or

(*b*) where more than one such resolution is passed, the date on which the last of them is passed,

unless, as respects that resolution (or, if more than one, each of them), every member of the company which passed the resolution who is entitled to vote at general meetings of the company voted in favour of the resolution.

(3) If application for the cancellation of any such resolution is made under section 157, the financial assistance shall not be given before the final determination of the application unless the court otherwise orders.

(4) The assistance shall not be given after the expiry of the period of 8 weeks beginning with—

(*a*) the date on which the directors of the company proposing to give the assistance made their statutory declaration under section 155, or

(*b*) where that company is a subsidiary and both its directors and the directors of any of its holding companies made such a declaration, the date on which the earliest of the declarations is made,

unless the court, on an application under section 157, otherwise orders.

E 4

CHAPTER VII

REDEEMABLE SHARES ; PURCHASE BY A COMPANY
OF ITS OWN SHARES

Redemption and purchase generally

Power to
issue
redeemable
shares.
159.—(1) Subject to the provisions of this Chapter, a company limited by shares or limited by guarantee and having a share capital may, if authorised to do so by its articles, issue shares which are to be redeemed or are liable to be redeemed at the option of the company or the shareholder.

(2) No redeemable shares may be issued at a time when there are no issued shares of the company which are not redeemable.

(3) Redeemable shares may not be redeemed unless they are fully paid ; and the terms of redemption must provide for payment on redemption.

Financing etc
of redemption.
160.—(1) Subject to the next subsection and to sections 171 (private companies redeeming or purchasing own shares out of capital) and 178(4) (terms of redemption or purchase enforceable in a winding up)—

(a) redeemable shares may only be redeemed out of distributable profits of the company or out of the proceeds of a fresh issue of shares made for the purposes of the redemption ; and

(b) any premium payable on redemption must be paid out of distributable profits of the company.

(2) If the redeemable shares were issued at a premium, any premium payable on their redemption may be paid out of the proceeds of a fresh issue of shares made for the purposes of the redemption, up to an amount equal to—

(a) the aggregate of the premiums received by the company on the issue of the shares redeemed, or

(b) the current amount of the company's share premium account (including any sum transferred to that account in respect of premiums on the new shares),

whichever is the less ; and in that case the amount of the company's share premium account shall be reduced by a sum corresponding (or by sums in the aggregate corresponding) to the amount of any payment made by virtue of this subsection out of the proceeds of the issue of the new shares.

(3) Subject to the following provisions of this Chapter, redemption of shares may be effected on such terms and in such manner as may be provided by the company's articles.

(4) Shares redeemed under this section shall be treated as cancelled on redemption, and the amount of the company's

issued share capital shall be diminished by the nominal value   PART V
of those shares accordingly; but the redemption of shares by a   CHAPTER VII
company is not to be taken as reducing the amount of the
company's authorised share capital.

(5) Without prejudice to subsection (4), where a company is
about to redeem shares, it has power to issue shares up to the
nominal value of the shares to be redeemed as if those shares
had never been issued.

161.—(1) For the purposes of section 47 of the Finance Act   Stamp duty on
1973, the issue of shares by a company in place of shares re-   redemption of
deemed under section 160 constitutes a chargeable transaction   shares.
if, and only if, the actual value of the shares so issued exceeds   1973 c. 51.
the value of the shares redeemed at the date of their redemption.

(2) Where the issue of the shares does constitute a chargeable
transaction for those purposes, the amount on which stamp duty
on the relevant document relating to that transaction is chargeable under section 47(5) of the Finance Act 1973 is the difference
between—

(a) the amount on which that duty would be so chargeable
if the shares had not been issued in place of shares
redeemed under section 160; and

(b) the value of the shares redeemed at the date of their
redemption.

(3) Subject to the following subsection, for the purposes of
subsections (1) and (2) shares issued by a company—

(a) up to the nominal amount of any shares which the
company has redeemed under section 160; or

(b) in pursuance of section 160(5) before the redemption
of shares which the company is about to redeem under
that section,

are to be regarded as issued in place of the shares redeemed or
(as the case may be) about to be redeemed.

(4) Shares issued in pursuance of section 160(5) are not to be
regarded for purposes of subsections (1) and (2) of this section
as issued in place of the shares about to be redeemed, unless
those shares are redeemed within one month after the issue of the
new shares.

162.—(1) Subject to the following provisions of this Chapter,   Power of
a company limited by shares or limited by guarantee and having   company to
a share capital may, if authorised to do so by its articles, pur-   purchase
chase its own shares (including any redeemable shares).   own shares.

(2) Sections 159 to 161 apply to the purchase by a company
under this section of its own shares as they apply to the redemp-

tion of redeemable shares, save that the terms and manner of purchase need not be determined by the articles as required by section 160(3).

(3) A company may not under this section purchase its shares if as a result of the purchase there would no longer be any member of the company holding shares other than redeemable shares.

Definitions of "off-market" and "market" purchase.

163.—(1) A purchase by a company of its own shares is " off-market " if the shares either—

    (a) are purchased otherwise than on a recognised stock exchange, or

    (b) are purchased on a recognised stock exchange but are not subject to a marketing arrangement on that stock exchange.

(2) For this purpose, a company's shares are subject to a marketing arrangement on a recognised stock exchange if either—

    (a) they are listed on that stock exchange ; or

    (b) the company has been afforded facilities for dealings in those shares to take place on that stock exchange without prior permission for individual transactions from the authority governing that stock exchange and without limit as to the time during which those facilities are to be available.

(3) A purchase by a company of its own shares is a " market purchase " if it is a purchase made on a recognised stock exchange, other than a purchase which is an off-market purchase by virtue of subsection (1)(b).

Authority for off-market purchase.

164.—(1) A company may only make an off-market purchase of its own shares in pursuance of a contract approved in advance in accordance with this section or under section 165 below.

(2) The terms of the proposed contract must be authorised by a special resolution of the company before the contract is entered into ; and the following subsections apply with respect to that authority and to resolutions conferring it.

(3) Subject to the next subsection, the authority may be varied, revoked or from time to time renewed by special resolution of the company.

(4) In the case of a public company, the authority conferred by the resolution must specify a date on which the authority is to expire ; and in a resolution conferring or renewing authority that date must not be later than 18 months after that on which the resolution is passed.

(5) A special resolution to confer, vary, revoke or renew
authority is not effective if any member of the company holding
shares to which the resolution relates exercises the voting rights
carried by any of those shares in voting on the resolution and
the resolution would not have been passed if he had not done
so.

For this purpose—

> (*a*) a member who holds shares to which the resolution
> relates is regarded as exercising the voting rights
> carried by those shares not only if he votes in respect
> of them on a poll on the question whether the reso-
> lution shall be passed, but also if he votes on the
> resolution otherwise than on a poll ;
>
> (*b*) notwithstanding anything in the company's articles, any
> member of the company may demand a poll on that
> question ; and
>
> (*c*) a vote and a demand for a poll by a person as proxy
> for a member are the same respectively as a vote and
> a demand by the member.

(6) Such a resolution is not effective for the purposes of this
section unless (if the proposed contract is in writing) a copy of
the contract or (if not) a written memorandum of its terms is
available for inspection by members of the company both—

> (*a*) at the company's registered office for not less than 15
> days ending with the date of the meeting at which the
> resolution is passed, and
>
> (*b*) at the meeting itself.

A memorandum of contract terms so made available must
include the names of any members holding shares to which
the contract relates ; and a copy of the contract so made
available must have annexed to it a written memorandum
specifying any such names which do not appear in the contract
itself.

(7) A company may agree to a variation of an existing
contract so approved, but only if the variation is authorised
by a special resolution of the company before it is agreed
to ; and subsections (3) to (6) above apply to the authority for
a proposed variation as they apply to the authority for a proposed contract, save that a copy of the original contract or (as
the case may require) a memorandum of its terms, together with
any variations previously made, must also be available for
inspection in accordance with subsection (6).

165.—(1) A contingent purchase contract is a contract entered Authority for
into by a company and relating to any of its shares— contingent
purchase
> (*a*) which does not amount to a contract to purchase those contract.
> shares, but

(*b*) under which the company may (subject to any conditions) become entitled or obliged to purchase those shares.

(2) A company may only make a purchase of its own shares in pursuance of a contingent purchase contract if the contract is approved in advance by a special resolution of the company before the contract is entered into; and subsections (3) to (7) of section 164 apply to the contract and its terms.

Authority for
market
purchase.

166.—(1) A company shall not make a market purchase of its own shares unless the purchase has first been authorised by the company in general meeting.

(2) That authority—

(*a*) may be general for that purpose, or limited to the purchase of shares of any particular class or description, and

(*b*) may be unconditional or subject to conditions.

(3) The authority must—

(*a*) specify the maximum number of shares authorised to be acquired,

(*b*) determine both the maximum and the minimum prices which may be paid for the shares, and

(*c*) specify a date on which it is to expire.

(4) The authority may be varied, revoked or from time to time renewed by the company in general meeting, but this is subject to subsection (3) above; and in a resolution to confer or renew authority, the date on which the authority is to expire must not be later than 18 months after that on which the resolution is passed.

(5) A company may under this section make a purchase of its own shares after the expiry of the time limit imposed to comply with subsection (3)(*c*), if the contract of purchase was concluded before the authority expired and the terms of the authority permitted the company to make a contract of purchase which would or might be executed wholly or partly after its expiration.

(6) A resolution to confer or vary authority under this section may determine either or both the maximum and minimum prices for purchase by—

(*a*) specifying a particular sum, or

(*b*) providing a basis or formula for calculating the amount of the price in question without reference to any person's discretion or opinion.

(7) A resolution of a company conferring, varying, revoking or renewing authority under this section is subject to section 380 (resolution to be sent to registrar of companies within 15 days).

167.—(1) The rights of a company under a contract approved under section 164 or 165, or under a contract for a purchase authorised under section 166, are not capable of being assigned.

(2) An agreement by a company to release its rights under a contract approved under section 164 or 165 is void unless the terms of the release agreement are approved in advance by a special resolution of the company before the agreement is entered into ; and subsections (3) to (7) of section 164 apply to approval for a proposed release agreement as to authority for a proposed variation of an existing contract.

168.—(1) A payment made by a company in consideration of—

(a) acquiring any right with respect to the purchase of its own shares in pursuance of a contract approved under section 165, or

(b) the variation of a contract approved under section 164 or 165, or

(c) the release of any of the company's obligations with respect to the purchase of any of its own shares under a contract approved under section 164 or 165 or under a contract for a purchase authorised under section 166,

must be made out of the company's distributable profits.

(2) If the requirements of subsection (1) are not satisfied in relation to a contract—

(a) in a case within paragraph (a) of the subsection, no purchase by the company of its own shares in pursuance of that contract is lawful under this Chapter,

(b) in a case within paragraph (b), no such purchase following the variation is lawful under this Chapter, and

(c) in a case within paragraph (c), the purported release is void.

169.—(1) Within the period of 28 days beginning with the date on which any shares purchased by a company under this Chapter are delivered to it, the company shall deliver to the registrar of companies for registration a return in the prescribed form stating with respect to shares of each class purchased the number and nominal value of those shares and the date on which they were delivered to the company.

(2) In the case of a public company, the return shall also state—

  (a) the aggregate amount paid by the company for the shares ; and

  (b) the maximum and minimum prices paid in respect of shares of each class purchased.

(3) Particulars of shares delivered to the company on different dates and under different contracts may be included in a single return to the registrar ; and in such a case the amount required to be stated under subsection (2)(a) is the aggregate amount paid by the company for all the shares to which the return relates.

(4) Where a company enters into a contract approved under section 164 or 165, or a contract for a purchase authorised under section 166, the company shall keep at its registered office—

  (a) if the contract is in writing, a copy of it ; and

  (b) if not, a memorandum of its terms,

from the conclusion of the contract until the end of the period of 10 years beginning with the date on which the purchase of all the shares in pursuance of the contract is completed or (as the case may be) the date on which the contract otherwise determines.

(5) Every copy and memorandum so required to be kept shall, during business hours (subject to such reasonable restrictions as the company may in general meeting impose, provided that not less than 2 hours in each day are allowed for inspection) be open to inspection without charge—

  (a) by any member of the company, and

  (b) if it is a public company, by any other person.

(6) If default is made in delivering to the registrar any return required by this section, every officer of the company who is in default is liable to a fine and, for continued contravention, to a daily default fine.

(7) If default is made in complying with subsection (4), or if an inspection required under subsection (5) is refused, the company and every officer of it who is in default is liable to a fine and, for continued contravention, to a daily default fine.

(8) In the case of a refusal of an inspection required under subsection (5) of a copy or memorandum, the court may by order compel an immediate inspection of it.

(9) The obligation of a company under subsection (4) to keep a copy of any contract or (as the case may be) a memorandum of its terms applies to any variation of the contract so long as it applies to the contract.

170.—(1) Where under this Chapter shares of a company are redeemed or purchased wholly out of the company's profits, the amount by which the company's issued share capital is diminished in accordance with section 160(4) on cancellation of the shares redeemed or purchased shall be transferred to a reserve, called " the capital redemption reserve ".

(2) If the shares are redeemed or purchased wholly or partly out of the proceeds of a fresh issue and the aggregate amount of those proceeds is less than the aggregate nominal value of the shares redeemed or purchased, the amount of the difference shall be transferred to the capital redemption reserve.

(3) But subsection (2) does not apply if the proceeds of the fresh issue are applied by the company in making a redemption or purchase of its own shares in addition to a payment out of capital under section 171.

(4) The provisions of this Act relating to the reduction of a company's share capital apply as if the capital redemption reserve were paid-up share capital of the company, except that the reserve may be applied by the company in paying up its unissued shares to be allotted to members of the company as fully paid bonus shares.

Redemption or purchase of own shares out of capital
(private companies only)

171.—(1) Subject to the following provisions of this Chapter, a private company limited by shares or limited by guarantee and having a share capital may, if so authorised by its articles, make a payment in respect of the redemption or purchase under section 160 or (as the case may be) section 162, of its own shares otherwise than out of its distributable profits or the proceeds of a fresh issue of shares.

(2) References below in this Chapter to payment out of capital are (subject to subsection (6)) to any payment so made, whether or not it would be regarded apart from this section as a payment out of capital.

(3) The payment which may (if authorised in accordance with the following provisions of this Chapter) be made by a company out of capital in respect of the redemption or purchase of its own shares is such an amount as, taken together with—

(*a*) any available profits of the company, and

(*b*) the proceeds of any fresh issue of shares made for the purposes of the redemption or purchase,

is equal to the price of redemption or purchase ; and the payment permissible under this subsection is referred to below in this Chapter as the permissible capital payment for the shares.

(4) Subject to subsection (6), if the permissible capital payment for shares redeemed or purchased is less than their nominal amount, the amount of the difference shall be transferred to the company's capital redemption reserve.

(5) Subject to subsection (6), if the permissible capital payment is greater than the nominal amount of the shares redeemed or purchased—

(a) the amount of any capital redemption reserve, share premium account or fully paid share capital of the company, and

(b) any amount representing unrealised profits of the company for the time being standing to the credit of any reserve maintained by the company in accordance with paragraph 34 of Schedule 4 (revaluation reserve),

may be reduced by a sum not exceeding (or by sums not in the aggregate exceeding) the amount by which the permissible capital payment exceeds the nominal amount of the shares.

(6) Where the proceeds of a fresh issue are applied by a company in making any redemption or purchase of its own shares in addition to a payment out of capital under this section, the references in subsections (4) and (5) to the permissible capital payment are to be read as referring to the aggregate of that payment and those proceeds.

Availability of profits for purposes of s. 171.

172.—(1) The reference in section 171(3)(a) to available profits of the company is to the company's profits which are available for distribution (within the meaning of Part VIII); but the question whether a company has any profits so available and the amount of any such profits are to be determined for purposes of that section in accordance with the following subsections, instead of sections 270 to 275 in that Part.

(2) Subject to the next subsection, that question is to be determined by reference to—

(a) profits, losses, assets and liabilities,

(b) provisions of any of the kinds mentioned in paragraphs 88 and 89 of Schedule 4 (depreciation, diminution in value of assets, retentions to meet liabilities, etc.), and

(c) share capital and reserves (including undistributable reserves),

as stated in the relevant accounts for determining the permissible capital payment for shares.

(3) The relevant accounts for this purpose are such accounts, prepared as at any date within the period for determining the amount of the permissible capital payment, as are necessary to

enable a reasonable judgment to be made as to the amounts of
any of the items mentioned in subsection (2)(*a*) to (*c*) above.

(4) For purposes of determining the amount of the permissible capital payment for shares, the amount of the company's available profits (if any) determined in accordance with subsections (2) and (3) is treated as reduced by the amount of any distributions lawfully made by the company after the date of the relevant accounts and before the end of the period for determining the amount of that payment.

(5) The reference in subsection (4) to distributions lawfully made by the company includes—

(*a*) financial assistance lawfully given out of distributable profits in a case falling within section 154 or 155,

(*b*) any payment lawfully made by the company in respect of the purchase by it of any shares in the company (except a payment lawfully made otherwise than out of distributable profits), and

(*c*) a payment of any description specified in section 168(1) lawfully made by the company.

(6) References in this section to the period for determining the amount of the permissible capital payment for shares are to the period of 3 months ending with the date on which the statutory declaration of the directors purporting to specify the amount of that payment is made in accordance with subsection (3) of the section next following.

173.—(1) Subject to any order of the court under section 177, a payment out of capital by a private company for the redemption or purchase of its own shares is not lawful unless the requirements of this and the next two sections are satisfied. Conditions for payment out of capital.

(2) The payment out of capital must be approved by a special resolution of the company.

(3) The company's directors must make a statutory declaration specifying the amount of the permissible capital payment for the shares in question and stating that, having made full inquiry into the affairs and prospects of the company, they have formed the opinion—

(*a*) as regards its initial situation immediately following the date on which the payment out of capital is proposed to be made, that there will be no grounds on which the company could then be found unable to pay its debts, and

(*b*) as regards its prospects for the year immediately following that date, that, having regard to their intentions with respect to the management of the company's business during that year and to the amount and character of the financial resources which will in their view be available to the company during that year, the company will be able to continue to carry on business as a going concern (and will accordingly be able to pay its debts as they fall due) throughout that year.

(4) In forming their opinion for purposes of subsection (3)(*a*), the directors shall take into account the same liabilities (including prospective and contingent liabilities) as would be relevant under section 517 (winding up by the court) to the question whether a company is unable to pay its debts.

(5) The directors' statutory declaration must be in the prescribed form and contain such information with respect to the nature of the company's business as may be prescribed, and must in addition have annexed to it a report addressed to the directors by the company's auditors stating that—

    (*a*) they have inquired into the company's state of affairs; and

    (*b*) the amount specified in the declaration as the permissible capital payment for the shares in question is in their view properly determined in accordance with sections 171 and 172; and

    (*c*) they are not aware of anything to indicate that the opinion expressed by the directors in the declaration as to any of the matters mentioned in subsection (3) is unreasonable in all the circumstances.

(6) A director who makes a declaration under this section without having reasonable grounds for the opinion expressed in the declaration is liable to imprisonment or a fine, or both.

Procedure for special resolution under s. 173.

174.—(1) The resolution required by section 173 must be passed on, or within the week immediately following, the date on which the directors make the statutory declaration required by that section; and the payment out of capital must be made no earlier than 5 nor more than 7 weeks after the date of the resolution.

(2) The resolution is ineffective if any member of the company holding shares to which the resolution relates exercises the voting rights carried by any of those shares in voting on the resolution and the resolution would not have been passed if he had not done so.

(3) For purposes of subsection (2), a member who holds such shares is to be regarded as exercising the voting rights carried by

them in voting on the resolution not only if he votes in respect
of them on a poll on the question whether the resolution shall
be passed, but also if he votes on the resolution otherwise than
on a poll ; and, notwithstanding anything in a company's articles,
any member of the company may demand a poll on that question.

(4) The resolution is ineffective unless the statutory declaration
and auditors' report required by the section are available for
inspection by members of the company at the meeting at which
the resolution is passed.

(5) For purposes of this section a vote and a demand for
a poll by a person as proxy for a member are the same (respectively) as a vote and demand by the member.

175.—(1) Within the week immediately following the date
of the resolution for payment out of capital the company must
cause to be published in the Gazette a notice—

PART V
CHAPTER VII

Publicity for
proposed
payment out
of capital.

> (a) stating that the company has approved a payment out
> of capital for the purpose of acquiring its own shares
> by redemption or purchase or both (as the case may
> be) ;
>
> (b) specifying the amount of the permissible capital pay-
> ment for the shares in question and the date of the
> resolution under section 173 ;
>
> (c) stating that the statutory declaration of the directors
> and the auditors' report required by that section are
> available for inspection at the company's registered
> office ; and
>
> (d) stating that any creditor of the company may at any
> time within the 5 weeks immediately following the
> date of the resolution for payment out of capital
> apply to the court under section 176 for an order
> prohibiting the payment.

(2) Within the week immediately following the date of the
resolution the company must also either cause a notice to the
same effect as that required by subsection (1) to be published
in an appropriate national newspaper or give notice in writing
to that effect to each of its creditors.

(3) " An appropriate national newspaper " means a newspaper circulating throughout England and Wales (in the case
of a company registered in England and Wales), and a newspaper circulating throughout Scotland (in the case of a company
registered in Scotland).

(4) References below in this section to the first notice date
are to the day on which the company first publishes the notice
required by subsection (1) or first publishes or gives the notice
required by subsection (2) (whichever is the earlier).

(5) Not later than the first notice date the company must deliver to the registrar of companies a copy of the statutory declaration of the directors and of the auditors' report required by section 173.

(6) The statutory declaration and auditors' report—

    (*a*) shall be kept at the company's registered office through-out the period beginning with the first notice date and ending 5 weeks after the date of the resolution for payment out of capital, and

    (*b*) shall during business hours on any day during that period be open to the inspection of any member or creditor of the company without charge.

(7) If an inspection required under subsection (6) is refused, the company and every officer of it who is in default is liable to a fine and, for continued contravention, to a daily default fine.

(8) In the case of refusal of an inspection required under subsection (6) of a declaration or report, the court may by order compel an immediate inspection of that declaration or report.

Objections by company's members or creditors.
176.—(1) Where a private company passes a special resolution approving for purposes of this Chapter any payment out of capital for the redemption or purchase of any of its shares—

    (*a*) any member of the company other than one who consented to or voted in favour of the resolution ; and

    (*b*) any creditor of the company,

may within 5 weeks of the date on which the resolution was passed apply to the court for cancellation of the resolution.

(2) The application may be made on behalf of the persons entitled to make it by such one or more of their number as they may appoint in writing for the purpose.

(3) If an application is made, the company shall—

    (*a*) forthwith give notice in the prescribed form of that fact to the registrar of companies ; and

    (*b*) within 15 days from the making of any order of the court on the hearing of the application, or such longer period as the court may by order direct, deliver an office copy of the order to the registrar.

(4) A company which fails to comply with subsection (3), and any officer of it who is in default, is liable to a fine and for continued contravention, to a daily default fine.

177.—(1) On the hearing of an application under section 176 the court may, if it thinks fit, adjourn the proceedings in order that an arrangement may be made to the court's satisfaction for the purchase of the interests of dissentient members or for the protection of dissentient creditors (as the case may be) ; and the court may give such directions and make such orders as it thinks expedient for facilitating or carrying into effect any such arrangement.

(2) Without prejudice to its powers under subsection (1), the court shall make an order on such terms and conditions as it thinks fit either confirming or cancelling the resolution ; and, if the court confirms the resolution, it may in particular by order alter or extend any date or period of time specified in the resolution or in any provision in this Chapter which applies to the redemption or purchase of shares to which the resolution refers.

(3) The court's order may, if the court thinks fit, provide for the purchase by the company of the shares of any of its members and for the reduction accordingly of the company's capital, and may make such alterations in the company's memorandum and articles as may be required in consequence of that provision.

(4) If the court's order requires the company not to make any, or any specified, alteration in its memorandum or articles, the company has not then power without leave of the court to make any such alteration in breach of the requirement.

(5) An alteration in the memorandum or articles made by virtue of an order under this section, if not made by resolution of the company, is of the same effect as if duly made by resolution ; and this Act applies accordingly to the memorandum or articles as so altered.

Supplementary

178.—(1) This section has effect where a company has, on or after 15th June 1982,—
  (*a*) issued shares on terms that they are or are liable to be redeemed, or
  (*b*) agreed to purchase any of its own shares.

(2) The company is not liable in damages in respect of any failure on its part to redeem or purchase any of the shares.

(3) Subsection (2) is without prejudice to any right of the holder of the shares other than his right to sue the company for damages in respect of its failure ; but the court shall not grant an order for specific performance of the terms of redemption or purchase if the company shows that it is unable to meet

the costs of redeeming or purchasing the shares in question out of distributable profits.

(4) If the company is wound up and at the commencement of the winding up any of the shares have not been redeemed or purchased, the terms of redemption or purchase may be enforced against the company ; and when shares are redeemed or purchased under this subsection, they are treated as cancelled.

(5) However, subsection (4) does not apply if—

   (a) the terms provided for the redemption or purchase to take place at a date later than that of the commencement of the winding up, or

   (b) during the period beginning with the date on which the redemption or purchase was to have taken place and ending with the commencement of the winding up the company could not at any time have lawfully made a distribution equal in value to the price at which the shares were to have been redeemed or purchased.

(6) There shall be paid in priority to any amount which the company is liable under subsection (4) to pay in respect of any shares—

   (a) all other debts and liabilities of the company (other than any due to members in their character as such),

   (b) if other shares carry rights (whether as to capital or as to income) which are preferred to the rights as to capital attaching to the first-mentioned shares, any amount due in satisfaction of those preferred rights ;

but, subject to that, any such amount shall be paid in priority to any amounts due to members in satisfaction of their rights (whether as to capital or income) as members.

1914 c. 59. (7) Where by virtue of section 66 of the Bankruptcy Act 1914 (payment of interest on debts) as applied by section 612 (application of bankruptcy rules to insolvent companies in England and Wales) a creditor of a company is entitled to payment of any interest only after payment of all other debts of the company, the company's debts and liabilities for purposes of subsection (6) of this section include the liability to pay that interest.

Power for
Secretary of
State to
modify this
Chapter.
179.—(1) The Secretary of State may by regulations made by statutory instrument modify the provisions of this Chapter with respect to any of the following matters—

   (a) the authority required for a purchase by a company of its own shares,

(b) the authority required for the release by a company of PART V
its rights under a contract for the purchase of its own CHAPTER VII
shares or a contract under which the company may
(subject to any conditions) become entitled or obliged
to purchase its own shares,

(c) the information to be included in a return delivered by
a company to the registrar of companies in accordance
with section 169(1),

(d) the matters to be dealt with in the statutory declaration of the directors under section 173 with a view to
indicating their opinion of their company's ability to
make a proposed payment out of capital with due regard to its financial situation and prospects, and

(e) the contents of the auditors' report required by that
section to be annexed to that declaration.

(2) The Secretary of State may also by regulations so made
make such provision (including modification of the provisions
of this Chapter) as appears to him to be appropriate—

(a) for wholly or partly relieving companies from the requirement of section 171(3)(a) that any available
profits must be taken into account in determining the
amount of the permissible capital payment for shares
under that section, or

(b) for permitting a company's share premium account to
be applied, to any extent appearing to the Secretary
of State to be appropriate, in providing for the premiums payable on the redemption or purchase by the
company of any of its own shares.

(3) Regulations under this section—

(a) may make such further modification of any provisions
of this Chapter as appears to the Secretary of State to be
reasonably necessary in consequence of any provision
made under such regulations by virtue of subsection
(1) or (2),

(b) may make different provision for different cases or
classes of case, and

(c) may contain such further consequential provisions, and
such incidental and supplementary provisions, as the
Secretary of State thinks fit.

(4) No regulations shall be made under this section unless a
draft of the instrument containing them has been laid before
Parliament and approved by resolution of each House.

Part V
Chapter VII
Transitional
cases arising
under this
Chapter;
and savings.
1981 c. 62.
1948 c. 38.

180.—(1) Any preference shares issued by a company before 15th June 1982 which could but for the repeal by the Companies Act 1981 of section 58 of the Companies Act 1948 (power to issue redeemable preference shares) have been redeemed under that section are subject to redemption in accordance with the provisions of this Chapter.

(2) In a case to which sections 159 and 160 apply by virtue of this section, any premium payable on redemption may, notwithstanding the repeal by the 1981 Act of any provision of the 1948 Act, be paid out of the share premium account instead of out of profits, or partly out of that account and partly out of profits (but subject to the provisions of this Chapter so far as payment is out of profits).

(3) Any capital redemption reserve fund established before 15th June 1982 by a company for the purposes of section 58 of the Act of 1948 is to be known as the company's capital redemption reserve and be treated as if it had been established for the purposes of section 170 of this Act; and accordingly, a reference in any enactment or in the articles of any company, or in any other instrument, to a company's capital redemption reserve fund is to be construed as a reference to the company's capital redemption reserve.

Definitions
for Chapter
VII.

181. In this Chapter—

    (*a*) " distributable profits ", in relation to the making of any payment by a company, means those profits out of which it could lawfully make a distribution (within the meaning given by section 263(2)) equal in value to the payment, and

    (*b*) " permissible capital payment " means the payment permitted by section 171 ;

and references to payment out of capital are to be construed in accordance with section 171.

Chapter VIII

Miscellaneous Provisions about Shares and Debentures

Share and debenture certificates, transfers and warrants

Nature,
transfer and
numbering of
shares.

182.—(1) The shares or other interest of any member in a company—

    (*a*) are personal estate or, in Scotland, moveable property and are not in the nature of real estate or heritage,

    (*b*) are transferable in manner provided by the company's articles, but subject to the Stock Transfer Act 1963 (which enables securities of certain descriptions to be transferred by a simplified process).

1963 c. 18.

(2) Each share in a company having a share capital shall be distinguished by its appropriate number; except that, if at any time all the issued shares in a company, or all the issued shares in it of a particular class, are fully paid up and rank pari passu for all purposes, none of those shares need thereafter have a distinguishing number so long as it remains fully paid up and ranks pari passu for all purposes with all shares of the same class for the time being issued and fully paid up.

183.—(1) It is not lawful for a company to register a transfer of shares in or debentures of the company unless a proper instrument of transfer has been delivered to it, or the transfer is an exempt transfer within the Stock Transfer Act 1982.

This applies notwithstanding anything in the company's articles.

(2) Subsection (1) does not prejudice any power of the company to register as shareholder or debenture holder a person to whom the right to any shares in or debentures of the company has been transmitted by operation of law.

(3) A transfer of the share or other interest of a deceased member of a company made by his personal representative, although the personal representative is not himself a member of the company, is as valid as if he had been such a member at the time of the execution of the instrument of transfer.

(4) On the application of the transferor of any share or interest in a company, the company shall enter in its register of members the name of the transferee in the same manner and subject to the same conditions as if the application for the entry were made by the transferee.

(5) If a company refuses to register a transfer of shares or debentures, the company shall, within 2 months after the date on which the transfer was lodged with it, send to the transferee notice of the refusal.

(6) If default is made in complying with subsection (5), the company and every officer of it who is in default is liable to a fine and, for continued contravention, to a daily default fine.

184.—(1) The certification by a company of any instrument of transfer of any shares in, or debentures of, the company is to be taken as a representation by the company to any person acting on the faith of the certification that there have been produced to the company such documents as on their face show a prima facie title to the shares or debentures in the transferor named in the instrument.

However, the certification is not to be taken as a representation that the transferor has any title to the shares or debentures.

(2) Where a person acts on the faith of a false certification by a company made negligently, the company is under the same liability to him as if the certification had been made fraudulently.

(3) For purposes of this section—

(a) an instrument of transfer is deemed certificated if it bears the words " certificate lodged " (or words to the like effect) ;

(b) the certification of an instrument of transfer is deemed made by a company if—

(i) the person issuing the instrument is a person authorised to issue certificated instruments of transfer on the company's behalf, and

(ii) the certification is signed by a person authorised to certificate transfers on the company's behalf or by an officer or servant either of the company or of a body corporate so authorised ;

(c) a certification is deemed signed by a person if—

(i) it purports to be authenticated by his signature or initials (whether handwritten or not), and

(ii) it is not shown that the signature or initials was or were placed there neither by himself nor by a person authorised to use the signature or initials for the purpose of certificating transfers on the company's behalf.

Duty of company as to issue of certificates. **185.**—(1) Subject to the following provisions, every company shall—

(a) within 2 months after the allotment of any of its shares, debentures or debenture stock, and

(b) within 2 months after the date on which a transfer of any such shares, debentures or debenture stock is lodged with the company,

complete and have ready for delivery the certificates of all shares, the debentures and the certificates of all debenture stock allotted or transferred (unless the conditions of issue of the shares, debentures or debenture stock otherwise provide).

1982 c. 41. (2) For this purpose, " transfer " means a transfer duly stamped and otherwise valid, or an exempt transfer within the Stock Transfer Act 1982, and does not include such a transfer as the company is for any reason entitled to refuse to register and does not register.

(3) Subsection (1) does not apply in the case of a transfer to any person where, by virtue of regulations under section 3 of the Stock Transfer Act 1982, he is not entitled to a certificate or other document of or evidencing title in respect of the securities transferred ; but if in such a case the transferee—

(a) subsequently becomes entitled to such a certificate or other document by virtue of any provision of those regulations, and

(b) gives notice in writing of that fact to the company,

this section has effect as if the reference in subsection (1)(b) to the date of the lodging of the transfer were a reference to the date of the notice.

(4) A company of which shares or debentures are allotted or debenture stock is allotted to a stock exchange nominee, or with which a transfer is lodged for transferring any shares, debentures or debenture stock of the company to a stock exchange nominee, is not required, in consequence of the allotment or the lodging of the transfer, to comply with subsection (1).

" Stock exchange nominee " means any person whom the Secretary of State designates, by order in a statutory instrument, as a nominee of The Stock Exchange for the purposes of this section.

(5) If default is made in complying with subsection (1), the company and every officer of it who is in default is liable to a fine and, for continued contravention, to a daily default fine.

(6) If a company on which a notice has been served requiring it to make good any default in complying with subsection (1) fails to make good the default within 10 days after service of the notice, the court may, on the application of the person entitled to have the certificates or the debentures delivered to him, exercise the power of the following subsection.

(7) The court may make an order directing the company and any officer of it to make good the default within such time as may be specified in the order ; and the order may provide that all costs of and incidental to the application shall be borne by the company or by an officer of it responsible for the default.

186. A certificate, under the common seal of the company or the seal kept by the company by virtue of section 40, specifying any shares held by a member, is prima facie evidence of his title to the shares.

Certificate to be evidence of title.

187. The production to a company of any document which is by law sufficient evidence of probate of the will, or letters of administration of the estate, or confirmation as executor, of a deceased person having been granted to some person shall be accepted by the company as sufficient evidence of the grant.

Evidence of grant of probate or confirmation as executor.

This has effect notwithstanding anything in the company's articles.

Issue and
effect of
share warrant
to bearer.

188.—(1) A company limited by shares, if so authorised by its articles, may, with respect to any fully paid-up shares, issue under its common seal a warrant stating that the bearer of the warrant is entitled to the shares specified in it, and may provide (by coupons or otherwise) for the payment of the future dividends on the shares included in the warrant.

(2) Such a warrant is termed a " share warrant " and entitles the bearer to the shares specified in it ; and the shares may be transferred by delivery of the warrant.

Offences in
connection
with share
warrants
(Scotland).

189.—(1) If in Scotland a person —

(a) with intent to defraud, forges or alters, or offers, utters, disposes of, or puts off, knowing the same to be forged or altered, any share warrant or coupon, or any document purporting to be a share warrant or coupon, issued in pursuance of this Act ; or

(b) by means of any such forged or altered share warrant, coupon, or document, purporting as aforesaid, demands or endeavours to obtain or receive any share or interest in any company under this Act, or to receive any dividend or money payable in respect thereof, knowing the warrant, coupon, or document to be forged or altered ;

he is on conviction thereof liable to imprisonment or a fine, or both.

(2) If in Scotland a person without lawful authority or excuse (proof whereof lies on him)—

(a) engraves or makes on any plate, wood, stone, or other material, any share warrant or coupon purporting to be—

(i) a share warrant or coupon issued or made by any particular company in pursuance of this Act ; or

(ii) a blank share warrant or coupon so issued or made ; or

(iii) a part of such a share warrant or coupon ; or

(b) uses any such plate, wood, stone, or other material, for the making or printing of any such share warrant or coupon, or of any such blank share warrant or coupon, or any part thereof respectively ; or

(c) knowingly has in his custody or possession any such plate, wood, stone, or other material ;

he is on conviction thereof liable to imprisonment or a fine, or both.

Debentures

190.—(1) A company registered in England and Wales shall not keep in Scotland any register of holders of debentures of the company or any duplicate of any such register or part of any such register which is kept outside Great Britain.

(2) A company registered in Scotland shall not keep in England and Wales any such register or duplicate as above-mentioned.

(3) Neither a register of holders of debentures of a company nor a duplicate of any such register or part of any such register which is kept outside Great Britain shall be kept in England and Wales (in the case of a company registered in England and Wales) or in Scotland (in the case of a company registered in Scotland) elsewhere than—

(a) at the company's registered office ; or

(b) at any office of the company at which the work of making it up is done ; or

(c) if the company arranges with some other person for the making up of the register or duplicate to be undertaken on its behalf by that other person, at the office of that other person at which the work is done.

(4) Where a company keeps (in England and Wales or in Scotland, as the case may be) both such a register and such a duplicate, it shall keep them at the same place.

(5) Every company which keeps any such register or duplicate in England and Wales or Scotland shall send to the registrar of companies notice (in the prescribed form) of the place where the register or duplicate is kept and of any change in that place.

(6) But a company is not bound to send notice under subsection (5) where the register or duplicate has, at all times since it came into existence, been kept at the company's registered office.

191.—(1) Every register of holders of debentures of a company shall, except when duly closed (but subject to such reasonable restrictions as the company may impose in general meeting, so that not less than 2 hours in each day shall be allowed for inspection), be open to the inspection—

(a) of the registered holder of any such debentures or any holder of shares in the company without fee ; and

(b) of any other person on payment of a fee of 5 pence or such less sum as may be prescribed by the company.

(2) Any such registered holder of debentures or holder of shares, or any other person, may require a copy of the register

of the holders of debentures of the company or any part of it, on payment of 10 pence (or such less sum as may be prescribed by the company) for every 100 words, or fractional part of 100 words, required to be copied.

(3) A copy of any trust deed for securing an issue of debentures shall be forwarded to every holder of any such debentures at his request on payment—

(a) in the case of a printed trust deed, of 20 pence (or such less sum as may be prescribed by the company), or

(b) where the trust deed has not been printed, of 10 pence (or such less sum as may be so prescribed), for every 100 words, or fractional part of 100 words, required to be copied.

(4) If inspection is refused, or a copy is refused or not forwarded, the company and every officer of it who is in default is liable to a fine and, for continued contravention, to a daily default fine.

(5) Where a company is in default as above-mentioned, the court may by order compel an immediate inspection of the register or direct that the copies required be sent to the person requiring them.

(6) For purposes of this section, a register is deemed to be duly closed if closed in accordance with provisions contained in the articles or in the debentures or, in the case of debenture stock, in the stock certificates, or in the trust deed or other document securing the debentures or debenture stock, during such period or periods, not exceeding in the whole 30 days in any year, as may be therein specified.

(7) Liability incurred by a company from the making or deletion of an entry in its register of debenture holders, or from a failure to make or delete any such entry, is not enforceable more than 20 years after the date on which the entry was made or deleted or, in the case of any such failure, the failure first occurred.

This is without prejudice to any lesser period of limitation.

Liability of trustees of debentures.

192.—(1) Subject to this section, any provision contained—

(a) in a trust deed for securing an issue of debentures, or

(b) in any contract with the holders of debentures secured by a trust deed,

is void in so far as it would have the effect of exempting a trustee of the deed from, or indemnifying him against, liability for breach of trust where he fails to show the degree of care and diligence required of him as trustee, having regard to the provisions of the trust deed conferring on him any powers, authorities or discretions.

(2) Subsection (1) does not invalidate—

(*a*) a release otherwise validly given in respect of anything done or omitted to be done by a trustee before
the giving of the release ; or

(*b*) any provision enabling such a release to be given—

(i) on the agreement thereto of a majority of not
less than three-fourths in value of the debenture
holders present and voting in person or, where
proxies are permitted, by proxy at a meeting summoned for the purpose, and

(ii) either with respect to specific acts or omissions or on the trustee dying or ceasing to act.

(3) Subsection (1) does not operate—

(*a*) to invalidate any provision in force on 1st July 1948
so long as any person then entitled to the benefit of
that provision or afterwards given the benefit of that
provision under the following subsection remains a
trustee of the deed in question ; or

(*b*) to deprive any person of any exemption or right to be
indemnified in respect of anything done or omitted to
be done by him while any such provision was in
force.

(4) While any trustee of a trust deed remains entitled to the
benefit of a provision saved by subsection (3), the benefit of
that provision may be given either—

(*a*) to all trustees of the deed, present and future ; or

(*b*) to any named trustees or proposed trustees of it,

by a resolution passed by a majority of not less than three-
fourths in value of the debenture holders present in person or,
where proxies are permitted, by proxy at a meeting summoned
for the purpose in accordance with the provisions of the deed or,
if the deed makes no provision for summoning meetings, a meeting summoned for the purpose in any manner approved by the
court.

193. A condition contained in debentures, or in a deed for Perpetual
securing debentures, is not invalid by reason only that the debentures.
debentures are thereby made irredeemable or redeemable only
on the happening of a contingency (however remote), or on the
expiration of a period (however long), any rule of equity to the
contrary notwithstanding.

This applies to debentures whenever issued, and to deeds
whenever executed.

194.—(1) Where (at any time) a company has redeemed Power to
debentures previously issued, then— re-issue
redeemed
(*a*) unless provision to the contrary, whether express or debentures.

implied, is contained in the articles or in any contract entered into by the company ; or

    (*b*) unless the company has, by passing a resolution to that effect or by some other act, manifested its intention that the debentures shall be cancelled,

the company has, and is deemed always to have had, power to re-issue the debentures, either by re-issuing the same debentures or by issuing other debentures in their place.

(2) On a re-issue of redeemed debentures, the person entitled to the debentures has, and is deemed always to have had, the same priorities as if the debentures had never been redeemed.

(3) Where a company has (at any time) deposited any of its debentures to secure advances from time to time on current account or otherwise, the debentures are not deemed to have been redeemed by reason only of the company's account having ceased to be in debit while the debentures remained so deposited.

(4) The re-issue of a debenture or the issue of another debenture in its place under the power which by this section is given to or deemed to be possessed by a company is to be treated as the issue of a new debenture for purposes of stamp duty ; but it is not to be so treated for the purposes of any provision limiting the amount or number of debentures to be issued.

This applies whenever the issue or re-issue was made.

(5) A person lending money on the security of a debenture re-issued under this section which appears to be duly stamped may give the debenture in evidence in any proceedings for enforcing his security without payment of the stamp duty or any penalty in respect of it, unless he had notice (or, but for his negligence, might have discovered) that the debenture was not duly stamped ; but in that case the company is liable to pay the proper stamp duty and penalty.

Contract to subscribe for debentures.

195. A contract with a company to take up and pay for debentures of the company may be enforced by an order for specific performance.

Payment of debts out of assets subject to floating charge (England and Wales).

196.—(1) The following applies, in the case of a company registered in England and Wales, where either a receiver is appointed on behalf of the holders of any debentures of the company secured by a floating charge, or possession is taken by or on behalf of those debenture-holders of any property comprised in or subject to the charge.

(2) If the company is not at the time in course of being wound up, the debts which in a winding up are, under the relevant provisions of Chapter V of Part XX relating to the preferential payments, to be paid in priority to all other debts shall be

paid out of assets coming to the hands of the receiver or other person taking possession, in priority to any claims for principal or interest in respect of the debentures.

(3) In the application of those provisions of Part XX, section 614 and Schedule 19 are to be read as if the provision for payment of accrued holiday remuneration becoming payable on the termination of employment before or by the effect of the winding-up order or resolution were a provision for payment of such remuneration becoming payable on the termination of employment before or by the effect of the appointment of the receiver or possession being taken as mentioned in subsection (1) of this section.

(4) The periods of time mentioned in those provisions of Part XX are to be reckoned from the date of the appointment of the receiver or possession being taken as above mentioned, as the case may be; and in Schedule 19 as it applies for the purposes of this section " the relevant date " means that date.

(5) Payments made under this section shall be recouped as far as may be out of the assets of the company available for payment of general creditors.

197. Notwithstanding anything in the statute of the Scots Parliament of 1696, chapter 25, debentures to bearer issued in Scotland are valid and binding according to their terms.

Debentures to bearer (Scotland).

PART VI

DISCLOSURE OF INTERESTS IN SHARES

Individual and group acquisitions

198.—(1) Where a person either—

(*a*) to his knowledge acquires an interest in shares comprised in a public company's relevant share capital, or ceases to be interested in shares so comprised (whether or not retaining an interest in other shares so comprised), or

(*b*) becomes aware that he has acquired an interest in shares so comprised or that he has ceased to be interested in shares so comprised in which he was previously interested,

then in certain circumstances he comes under an obligation (" the obligation of disclosure ") to make notification to the company of the interests which he has, or had, in its shares.

Obligation of disclosure: the cases in which it may arise and " the relevant time ".

(2) In relation to a public company, " relevant share capital " means the company's issued share capital of a class carrying rights to vote in all circumstances at general meetings of the

F

PART VI   company ; and it is hereby declared for the avoidance of doubt that—

(a) where a company's share capital is divided into different classes of shares, references in this Part to a percentage of the nominal value of its relevant share capital are to a percentage of the nominal value of the issued shares comprised in each of the classes taken separately, and

(b) the temporary suspension of voting rights in respect of shares comprised in issued share capital of a company of any such class does not affect the application of this Part in relation to interests in those or any other shares comprised in that class.

(3) Where, otherwise than in circumstances within subsection (1), a person—

(a) is aware at the time when it occurs of any change of circumstances affecting facts relevant to the application of the next following section to an existing interest of his in shares comprised in a company's share capital of any description, or

(b) otherwise becomes aware of any such facts (whether or not arising from any such change of circumstances), then in certain circumstances he comes under the obligation of disclosure.

(4) The existence of the obligation in a particular case depends (in part) on circumstances obtaining before and after whatever is in that case the relevant time ; and that is—

(a) in a case within subsection (1)(a) or(3)(a), the time of the event or change of circumstances there mentioned, and

(b) in a case within subsection (1)(b) or (3)(b), the time at which the person became aware of the facts in question.

Interests to be disclosed.   **199.**—(1) For purposes of the obligation of disclosure, the interests to be taken into account are those in relevant share capital of the company concerned.

(2) A person has a notifiable interest at any time when he is interested in shares comprised in that share capital of an aggregate nominal value equal to or more than the percentage of the nominal value of that share capital which is for the time being the notifiable percentage.

(3) All facts relevant to determining whether a person has a notifiable interest at any time (or the percentage level of his interest) are taken to be what he knows the facts to be at that time.

(4) The obligation of disclosure arises under section 198(1)
or (3) where the person has a notifiable interest immediately
after the relevant time, but did not have such an interest immediately before that time.

(5) The obligation also arises under section 198(1) where—

    (a) the person had a notifiable interest immediately before
the relevant time, but does not have such an interest
immediately after it, or

    (b) he had a notifiable interest immediately before that
time, and has such an interest immediately after it, but
the percentage levels of his interest immediately before
and immediately after that time are not the same.

200.—(1) Subject to the qualification mentioned below, " per- " Percentage
centage level ", in section 199(5)(b), means the percentage figure level " in
found by expressing the aggregate nominal value of all the shares relation to
comprised in the share capital concerned in which the person interests.
is interested immediately before or (as the case may be) immediately after the relevant time as a percentage of the nominal
value of that share capital and rounding that figure down, if it
is not a whole number, to the next whole number.

(2) Where the nominal value of the share capital is greater
immediately after the relevant time than it was immediately
before, the percentage level of the person's interest immediately
before (as well as immediately after) that time is determined by
reference to the larger amount.

201.—(1) The reference in section 199(2) to the notifiable The notifiable
percentage is to 5 per cent. or such other percentage as may be percentage.
prescribed by regulations under this section.

(2) The Secretary of State may by regulations in a statutory
instrument from time to time prescribe the percentage to apply
in determining whether a person's interest in a company's
shares is notifiable under section 198 ; and different percentages
may be prescribed in relation to companies of different classes
or descriptions.

No regulations shall be made under this section unless a
draft of the instrument containing them has been laid before
Parliament and approved by a resolution of each House.

(3) Where in consequence of a reduction in the percentage
made by such regulations a person's interest in a company's
shares becomes notifiable, he then comes under the obligation
of disclosure in respect of it ; and the obligation must be performed within the period of 10 days next following the day
on which it arises.

F 2

202.—(1) Where notification is required by section 198 with respect to a person's interest (if any) in shares comprised in relevant share capital of a public company, the obligation to make the notification must (except where section 201(3) applies) be performed within the period of 5 days next following the day on which that obligation arises; and the notification must be in writing to the company.

(2) The notification must specify the share capital to which it relates, and must also—

(a) state the number of shares comprised in that share capital in which the person making the notification knows he was interested immediately after the time when the obligation arose, or

(b) in a case where the person no longer has a notifiable interest in shares comprised in that share capital, state that he no longer has that interest.

(3) A notification with respect to a person's interest in a company's relevant share capital (other than one stating that he no longer has a notifiable interest in shares comprised in that share capital) shall include particulars of—

(a) the identity of each registered holder of shares to which the notification relates, and

(b) the number of those shares held by each such registered holder,

so far as known to the person making the notification at the date when the notification is made.

(4) A person who has an interest in shares comprised in a company's relevant share capital, that interest being notifiable, is under obligation to notify the company in writing—

(a) of any particulars in relation to those shares which are specified in subsection (3), and

(b) of any change in those particulars,

of which in either case he becomes aware at any time after any interest notification date and before the first occasion following that date on which he comes under any further obligation of disclosure with respect to his interest in shares comprised in that share capital.

An obligation arising under this subsection must be performed within the period of 5 days next following the day on which it arises.

(5) The reference in subsection (4) to an interest notification date, in relation to a person's interest in shares comprised in a public company's relevant share capital, is to either of the following—

(a) the date of any notification made by him with respect to his interest under this Part, and

(*b*) where he has failed to make a notification, the date
on which the period allowed for making it came to
an end.

(6) A person who at any time has an interest in shares which
is notifiable is to be regarded under subsection (4) as continuing
to have a notifiable interest in them unless and until he comes
under obligation to make a notification stating that he no longer
has such an interest in those shares.

203.—(1) For purposes of sections 198 to 202, a person is Notification
taken to be interested in any shares in which his spouse or any of family and
infant child or step-child of his is interested; and "infant" corporate
means, in relation to Scotland, pupil or minor. interests.

(2) For those purposes, a person is taken to be interested in
shares if a body corporate is interested in them and—
(*a*) that body or its directors are accustomed to act in
accordance with his directions or instructions, or
(*b*) he is entitled to exercise or control the exercise of
one-third or more of the voting power at general meetings of that body corporate.

(3) Where a person is entitled to exercise or control the
exercise of one-third or more of the voting power at general
meetings of a body corporate and that body corporate is entitled
to exercise or control the exercise of any of the voting power
at general meetings of another body corporate (" the effective
voting power ") then, for purposes of subsection (2)(*b*), the effect-
tive voting power is taken as exercisable by that person.

(4) For purposes of subsections (2) and (3), a person is entitled
to exercise or control the exercise of voting power if—
(*a*) he has a right (whether subject to conditions or not)
the exercise of which would make him so entitled, or
(*b*) he is under an obligation (whether or not so subject) the
fulfilment of which would make him so entitled.

204.—(1) In certain circumstances the obligation of disclosure Agreement
may arise from an agreement between two or more persons to acquire
which includes provision for the acquisition by any one or more interests in a
of them of interests in shares of a particular public company company.
(" the target company "), being shares comprised in the relevant
share capital of that company.

(2) This section applies to such an agreement if—
(*a*) the agreement also includes provisions imposing obligations or restrictions on any one or more of the parties
to it with respect to their use, retention or disposal of
their interests in that company's shares acquired in pursuance of the agreement (whether or not together with

F 3

any other interests of theirs in the company's shares to which the agreement relates), and

(*b*) any interest in the company's shares is in fact acquired by any of the parties in pursuance of the agreement ;

and in relation to such an agreement references below in this section, and in sections 205 and 206, to the target company are to the company which is the target company for that agreement in accordance with this and the previous subsection.

(3) The reference in subsection (2)(*a*) to the use of interests in shares in the target company is to the exercise of any rights or of any control or influence arising from those interests (including the right to enter into any agreement for the exercise, or for control of the exercise, of any of those rights by another person).

(4) Once any interest in shares in the target company has been acquired in pursuance of such an agreement as is mentioned above, this section continues to apply to that agreement irrespective of—

(*a*) whether or not any further acquisitions of interests in the company's shares take place in pursuance of the agreement, and

(*b*) any change in the persons who are for the time being parties to it, and

(*c*) any variation of the agreement,

so long as the agreement continues to include provisions of any description mentioned in subsection (2)(*a*).

References in this subsection to the agreement include any agreement having effect (whether directly or indirectly) in substitution for the original agreement.

(5) In this section, and also in references elsewhere in this Part to an agreement to which this section applies, " agreement " includes any agreement or arrangement ; and references in this section to provisions of an agreement—

(*a*) accordingly include undertakings, expectations or understandings operative under any arrangement, and

(*b*) (without prejudice to the above) also include any provisions, whether express or implied and whether absolute or not.

(6) However, this section does not apply to an agreement which is not legally binding unless it involves mutuality in the undertakings, expectations or understandings of the parties to it ; nor does the section apply to an agreement to underwrite or sub-underwrite any offer of shares in a company, provided the agreement is confined to that purpose and any matters incidental to it.

205.—(1) In the case of an agreement to which section 204
applies, each party to the agreement is taken (for purposes of
the obligation of disclosure) to be interested in all shares in
the target company in which any other party to it is interested
apart from the agreement (whether or not the interest of the
other party in question was acquired, or includes any interest
which was acquired, in pursuance of the agreement).

(2) For those purposes, and also for those of the next section,
an interest of a party to such an agreement in shares in the target
company is an interest apart from the agreement if he is interested in those shares otherwise than by virtue of the application
of section 204 and this section in relation to the agreement.

(3) Accordingly, any such interest of the person (apart from
the agreement) includes for those purposes any interest treated
as his under section 203 or by the application of section 204 and
this section in relation to any other agreement with respect to
shares in the target company to which he is a party.

(4) A notification with respect to his interest in shares in the
target company made to that company under this Part by a
person who is for the time being a party to an agreement to
which section 204 applies shall—

> (a) state that the person making the notification is a party
> to such an agreement,
> (b) include the names and (so far as known to him) the
> addresses of the other parties to the agreement, identi-
> fying them as such, and
> (c) state whether or not any of the shares to which the noti-
> fication relates are shares in which he is interested by
> virtue of section 204 and this section and, if so, the
> number of those shares.

(5) Where a person makes a notification to a company under
this Part in consequence of ceasing to be interested in any
shares of that company by virtue of the fact that he or any
other person has ceased to be a party to an agreement to which
section 204 applies, the notification shall include a statement
that he or that other person has ceased to be a party to the
agreement (as the case may require) and also (in the latter case)
the name and (if known to him) the address of that other.

206.—(1) A person who is a party to an agreement to which
section 204 applies is subject to the requirements of this section
at any time when—
> (a) the target company is a public company, and he knows
> it to be so, and

(b) the shares in that company to which the agreement relates consist of or include shares comprised in relevant share capital of the company, and he knows that to be the case ; and

(c) he knows the facts which make the agreement one to which section 204 applies.

(2) Such a person is under obligation to notify every other party to the agreement, in writing, of the relevant particulars of his interest (if any) apart from the agreement in shares comprised in relevant share capital of the target company—

(a) on his first becoming subject to the requirements of this section, and

(b) on each occurrence after that time while he is still subject to those requirements of any event or circumstances within section 198 (1) (as it applies to his case otherwise than by reference to interests treated as his under section 205 as applying to that agreement).

(3) The relevant particulars to be notified under subsection (2) are—

(a) the number of shares (if any) comprised in the target company's relevant share capital in which the person giving the notice would be required to state his interest if he were under the obligation of disclosure with respect to that interest (apart from the agreement) immediately after the time when the obligation to give notice under subsection (2) arose, and

(b) the relevant particulars with respect to the registered ownership of those shares, so far as known to him at the date of the notice.

(4) A person who is for the time being subject to the requirements of this section is also under obligation to notify every other party to the agreement, in writing—

(a) of any relevant particulars with respect to the registered ownership of any shares comprised in relevant share capital of the target company in which he is interested apart from the agreement, and

(b) of any change in those particulars,

of which in either case he becomes aware at any time after any interest notification date and before the first occasion following that date on which he becomes subject to any further obligation to give notice under subsection (2) with respect to his interest in shares comprised in that share capital.

(5) The reference in subsection (4) to an interest notification date, in relation to a person's interest in shares comprised in the

target company's relevant share capital, is to either of the following—

(a) the date of any notice given by him with respect to his interest under subsection (2), and

(b) where he has failed to give that notice, the date on which the period allowed by this section for giving the notice came to an end.

(6) A person who is a party to an agreement to which section 204 applies is under an obligation to notify each other party to the agreement, in writing, of his current address—

(a) on his first becoming subject to the requirements of this section, and

(b) on any change in his address occurring after that time and while he is still subject to those requirements.

(7) A reference to the relevant particulars with respect to the registered ownership of shares is to such particulars in relation to those shares as are mentioned in section 202(3)(a) or (b).

(8) A person's obligation to give any notice required by this section to any other person must be performed within the period of 5 days next following the day on which that obligation arose.

207.—(1) Where section 198 or 199 refers to a person acquiring an interest in shares or ceasing to be interested in shares, that reference in certain cases includes his becoming or ceasing to be interested in those shares by virtue of another person's interest.

(2) Such is the case where he becomes or ceases to be interested by virtue of section 203 or (as the case may be) section 205 whether—

(a) by virtue of the fact that the person who is interested in the shares becomes or ceases to be a person whose interests (if any) fall by virtue of either section to be treated as his, or

(b) in consequence of the fact that such a person has become or ceased to be interested in the shares, or

(c) in consequence of the fact that he himself becomes or ceases to be a party to an agreement to which section 204 applies to which the person interested in the shares is for the time being a party, or

(d) in consequence of the fact that an agreement to which both he and that person are parties becomes or ceases to be one to which that section applies.

(3) The person is then to be treated as knowing he has acquired an interest in the shares or (as the case may be) that he has ceased to be interested in them, if and when he knows both—

    (*a*) the relevant facts with respect to the other person's interest in the shares, and

    (*b*) the relevant facts by virtue of which he himself has become or ceased to be interested in them in accordance with section 203 or 205.

(4) He has the knowledge referred to in subsection (3)(*a*) if he knows (whether contemporaneously or not) either of the subsistence of the other person's interest at any material time or of the fact that the other has become or ceased to be interested in the shares at any such time; and " material time " is any time at which the other's interests (if any) fall or fell to be treated as his under section 203 or 205.

(5) A person is to be regarded as knowing of the subsistence of another's interest in shares or (as the case may be) that another has become or ceased to be interested in shares if he has been notified under section 206 of facts with respect to the other's interest which indicate that he is or has become or ceased to be interested in the shares (whether on his own account or by virtue of a third party's interest in them).

208.—(1) This section applies, subject to the section next following, in determining for purposes of sections 198 to 202 whether a person has a notifiable interest in shares.

(2) A reference to an interest in shares is to be read as including an interest of any kind whatsoever in the shares; and accordingly there are to be disregarded any restraints or restrictions to which the exercise of any right attached to the interest is or may be subject.

(3) Where property is held on trust and an interest in shares is comprised in the property, a beneficiary of the trust who apart from this subsection does not have an interest in the shares is to be taken as having such an interest.

(4) A person is taken to have an interest in shares if—

    (*a*) he enters into a contract for their purchase by him (whether for cash or other consideration), or

    (*b*) not being the registered holder, he is entitled to exercise any right conferred by the holding of the shares or is entitled to control the exercise of any such right.

(5) A person is taken to have an interest in shares if, otherwise than by virtue of having an interest under a trust—

    (*a*) he has a right to call for delivery of the shares to himself or to his order, or

(*b*) he has a right to acquire an interest in shares or is under
an obligation to take an interest in shares,

whether in any case the right or obligation is conditional or absolute.

(6) For purposes of subsection (4)(*b*), a person is entitled to exercise or control the exercise of any right conferred by the holding of shares if he—

(*a*) has a right (whether subject to conditions or not) the exercise of which would make him so entitled, or

(*b*) is under an obligation (whether so subject or not) the fulfilment of which would make him so entitled.

(7) Persons having a joint interest are taken each of them to have that interest.

(8) It is immaterial that shares in which a person has an interest are unidentifiable.

209.—(1) The following interests in shares are disregarded for Interests to be
purposes of sections 198 to 202— disregarded.

(*a*) where property is held on trust according to the law of England and Wales and an interest in shares is comprised in that property, an interest in reversion or remainder or of a bare trustee or a custodian trustee, and any discretionary interest ;

(*b*) where property is held on trust according to the law of Scotland and an interest in shares is comprised in that property, an interest in fee or of a simple trustee and any discretionary interest ;

(*c*) an interest which subsists by virtue of an authorised unit trust scheme within the meaning of the Preven- 1958 c. 45.
tion of Fraud (Investments) Act 1958, a scheme made under section 22 of the Charities Act 1960, section 11 1960 c. 58.
of the Trustee Investments Act 1961 or section 1 of the 1961 c. 62.
Administration of Justice Act 1965 or the scheme set 1965 c. 2.
out in the Schedule to the Church Funds Investment 1958 No. 1.
Measure 1958 ;

(*d*) an interest of the Church of Scotland General Trustees or of the Church of Scotland Trust in shares held by them or of any other person in shares held by those Trustees or that Trust otherwise than as simple trustees ;

(*e*) an interest for the life of himself or another of a person under a settlement in the case of which the property comprised in the settlement consists of or includes shares, and the conditions mentioned in subsection (3) below are satisfied ;

(f) an exempt interest held by a recognised jobber;

(g) an exempt security interest;

(h) an interest of the President of the Family Division of the High Court subsisting by virtue of section 9 of the Administration of Estates Act 1925;

(i) an interest of the Accountant General of the Supreme Court in shares held by him;

(j) such interests, or interests of such a class, as may be prescribed for purposes of this paragraph by regulations made by the Secretary of State by statutory instrument.

(2) A person is not by virtue of section 208(4)(b) taken to be interested in shares by reason only that he has been appointed a proxy to vote at a specified meeting of a company or of any class of its members and at any adjournment of that meeting, or has been appointed by a corporation to act as its representative at any meeting of a company or of any class of its members.

(3) The conditions referred to in subsection (1)(e) are, in relation to a settlement—

(a) that it is irrevocable, and

(b) that the settlor (within the meaning of section 444 of the Income and Corporation Taxes Act 1970) has no interest in any income arising under, or property comprised in, the settlement.

(4) A person is a recognised jobber for purposes of subsection (1)(f) if he is a member of The Stock Exchange recognised by the Council of The Stock Exchange as carrying on the business of a jobber; and an interest of such a person in shares is an exempt interest for those purposes if—

(a) he carries on that business in the United Kingdom, and

(b) he holds the interest for the purposes of that business.

(5) An interest in shares is an exempt security interest for purposes of subsection (1)(g) if—

(a) it is held by a person who is—

(i) a recognised bank or licensed institution within the Banking Act 1979, or an insurance company to which Part II of the Insurance Companies Act 1982 applies, or

(ii) a trustee savings bank (within the Trustee Savings Banks Act 1981), or

(iii) a member of The Stock Exchange carrying on business in the United Kingdom as a stockbroker, and

(*b*) it is held by way of security only for the purposes of a
transaction entered into in the ordinary course of his
business as such a person,

or if it is held by way of security only either by the Bank of
England or by the Post Office for the purposes of a transaction
entered into in the ordinary course of that part of the business
of the Post Office which consists of the provision of banking
services.

210.—(1) Where a person authorises another (" the agent ") Other
to acquire or dispose of, on his behalf, interests in shares provisions
comprised in relevant share capital of a public company, he about
notification
shall secure that the agent notifies him immediately of acquisi- under this
tions or disposals effected by the agent which will or may give Part.
rise to any obligation of disclosure imposed on him by this Part
with respect to his interest in that share capital.

(2) An obligation of disclosure imposed on a person by any
provision of sections 198 to 202 is treated as not being fulfilled
unless the notice by means of which it purports to be fulfilled
identifies him and gives his address and, in a case where he is
a director of the company, is expressed to be given in fulfilment
of that obligation.

(3) A person who—
  (*a*) fails to fulfil, within the proper period, an obligation of
      disclosure imposed on him by this Part, or
  (*b*) in purported fulfilment of any such obligation makes
      to a company a statement which he knows to be false,
      or recklessly makes to a company a statement which
      is false, or
  (*c*) fails to fulfil, within the proper period, an obligation to
      give another person a notice required by section 206,
      or
  (*d*) fails without reasonable excuse to comply with subsec-
      tion (1) of this section,

is guilty of an offence and liable to imprisonment or a fine, or
both.

(4) It is a defence for a person charged with an offence
under subsection (3)(*c*) to prove that it was not possible for him
to give the notice to the other person required by section 206
within the proper period, and either—
  (*a*) that it has not since become possible for him to give
      the notice so required, or
  (*b*) that he gave the notice as soon after the end of that
      period as it became possible for him to do so.

(5) Where a person is convicted of an offence under this section (other than an offence relating to his ceasing to be interested in a company's shares), the Secretary of State may by order direct that the shares in relation to which the offence was committed shall, until further order, be subject to the restrictions of Part XV of this Act; and such an order may be made notwithstanding any power in the company's memorandum or articles enabling the company to impose similar restrictions on those shares.

(6) Sections 732 (restriction on prosecutions) and 733(2) and (3) (liability of directors, etc.) apply to offences under this section.

Registration and investigation of share acquisitions and disposals

Register of interests in shares.

211.—(1) Every public company shall keep a register for purposes of sections 198 to 202, and whenever the company receives information from a person in consequence of the fulfilment of an obligation imposed on him by any of those sections, it is under obligation to inscribe in the register, against that person's name, that information and the date of the inscription.

(2) Without prejudice to subsection (1), where a company receives a notification under this Part which includes a statement that the person making the notification, or any other person, has ceased to be a party to an agreement to which section 204 applies, the company is under obligation to record that information against the name of that person in every place where his name appears in the register as a party to that agreement (including any entry relating to him made against another person's name).

(3) An obligation imposed by subsection (1) or (2) must be fulfilled within the period of 3 days next following the day on which it arises.

(4) The company is not, by virtue of anything done for the purposes of this section, affected with notice of, or put upon enquiry as to, the rights of any person in relation to any shares.

(5) The register must be so made up that the entries against the several names entered in it appear in chronological order.

(6) Unless the register is in such form as to constitute in itself an index, the company shall keep an index of the names entered in the register which shall in respect of each name contain a sufficient indication to enable the information entered against it to be readily found; and the company shall, within 10 days after the date on which a name is entered in the register, make any necessary alteration in the index.

(7) If the company ceases to be a public company it shall continue to keep the register and any associated index until the end of the period of 6 years beginning with the day next following that on which it ceases to be such a company.

(8) The register and any associated index—

(*a*) shall be kept at the place at which the register required to be kept by the company by section 325 (register of directors' interests) is kept, and

(*b*) subject to the next subsection, shall be available for inspection in accordance with section 219 below.

(9) Neither the register nor any associated index shall be available for inspection in accordance with that section in so far as it contains information with respect to a company for the time being entitled to avail itself of the benefit conferred by paragraph 3 or 10 of Schedule 5 (disclosure of shareholdings not required if it would be harmful to company's business).

(10) If default is made in complying with subsection (1) or (2), or with any of subsections (5) to (7), the company and every officer of it who is in default is liable to a fine and, for continued contravention, to a daily default fine.

(11) Any register kept by a company immediately before 15th June 1982 under section 34 of the Companies Act 1967 shall continue to be kept by the company under and for the purposes of this section.

1967 c. 81.

212.—(1) A public company may by notice in writing require a person whom the company knows or has reasonable cause to believe to be or, at any time during the 3 years immediately preceding the date on which the notice is issued, to have been interested in shares comprised in the company's relevant share capital—

Company investigations.

(*a*) to confirm that fact or (as the case may be) to indicate whether or not it is the case, and

(*b*) where he holds or has during that time held an interest in shares so comprised, to give such further information as may be required in accordance with the following subsection.

(2) A notice under this section may require the person to whom it is addressed—

(*a*) to give particulars of his own past or present interest in shares comprised in relevant share capital of the company (held by him at any time during the 3-year period mentioned in subsection (1)),

(*b*) where the interest is a present interest and any other interest in the shares subsists or, in any case, where another interest in the shares subsisted during that 3-year period at any time when his own interest subsisted, to give (so far as lies within his knowledge) such particulars with respect to that other interest as may be required by the notice,

    (c) where his interest is a past interest, to give (so far as lies within his knowledge) particulars of the identity of the person who held that interest immediately upon his ceasing to hold it.

(3) The particulars referred to in subsection (2)(a) and (b) include particulars of the identity of persons interested in the shares in question and of whether persons interested in the same shares are or were parties to any agreement to which section 204 applies or to any agreement or arrangement relating to the exercise of any rights conferred by the holding of the shares.

(4) A notice under this section shall require any information given in response to the notice to be given in writing within such reasonable time as may be specified in the notice.

(5) Sections 203 to 205 and 208 apply for the purpose of construing references in this section to persons interested in shares and to interests in shares respectively, as they apply in relation to sections 198 to 201 (but with the omission of any reference to section 209).

(6) This section applies in relation to a person who has or previously had, or is or was entitled to acquire, a right to subscribe for shares in a public company which would on issue be comprised in relevant share capital of that company as it applies in relation to a person who is or was interested in shares so comprised ; and references above in this section to an interest in shares so comprised and to shares so comprised are to be read accordingly in any such case as including respectively any such right and shares which would on issue be so comprised.

Registration of interests disclosed under s. 212.

213.—(1) Whenever in pursuance of a requirement imposed on a person under section 212 a company receives information to which this section applies relating to shares comprised in its relevant share capital, it is under obligation to enter against the name of the registered holder of those shares, in a separate part of its register of interests in shares—

    (a) the fact that the requirement was imposed and the date on which it was imposed, and

    (b) any information to which this section applies received in pursuance of the requirement.

(2) This section applies to any information received in pursuance of a requirement imposed by section 212 which relates to the present interests held by any persons in shares comprised in relevant share capital of the company in question.

(3) Subsections (3) to (10) of section 211 apply in relation to any part of the register maintained in accordance with subsection (1) of this section as they apply in relation to the remainder of the register, reading references to subsection (1) of that section to include subsection (1) of this.

PART VI

(4) In the case of a register kept by a company immediately before 15th June 1982 under section 34 of the Companies Act 1967, any part of the register so kept for the purposes of section 27 of the Companies Act 1976 shall continue to be kept by the company under and for the purposes of this section.

1967 c. 81.

1976 c. 69.

214.—(1) A company may be required to exercise its powers under section 212 on the requisition of members of the company holding at the date of the deposit of the requisition not less than one-tenth of such of the paid-up capital of the company as carries at that date the right of voting at general meetings of the company.

Company investigation on requisition by members.

(2) The requisition must—

(a) state that the requisitionists are requiring the company to exercise its powers under section 212,

(b) specify the manner in which they require those powers to be exercised, and

(c) give reasonable grounds for requiring the company to exercise those powers in the manner specified,

and must be signed by the requisitionists and deposited at the company's registered office.

(3) The requisition may consist of several documents in like form each signed by one or more requisitionists.

(4) On the deposit of a requisition complying with this section it is the company's duty to exercise its powers under section 212 in the manner specified in the requisition.

(5) If default is made in complying with subsection (4), the company and every officer of it who is in default is liable to a fine.

215.—(1) On the conclusion of an investigation carried out by a company in pursuance of a requisition under section 214, it is the company's duty to cause a report of the information received in pursuance of that investigation to be prepared, and the report shall be made available at the company's registered office within a reasonable period after the conclusion of that investigation.

Company report to members.

(2) Where—

(a) a company undertakes an investigation in pursuance of a requisition under section 214, and

(b) the investigation is not concluded before the end of 3 months beginning with the date immediately following the date of the deposit of the requisition,

PART VI

it is the duty of the company to cause to be prepared, in respect of that period and each successive period of 3 months ending before the conclusion of the investigation, an interim report of the information received during that period in pursuance of the investigation. Each such report shall be made available at the company's registered office within a reasonable period after the end of the period to which it relates.

(3) The period for making any report prepared under this section available as required by subsection (1) or (2) shall not exceed 15 days.

(4) Such a report shall not include any information with respect to a company entitled to avail itself of the benefit conferred by paragraph 3 or 10 of Schedule 5 (disclosure of shareholdings not required if it would be harmful to company's business); but where any such information is omitted, that fact shall be stated in the report.

(5) The company shall, within 3 days of making any report prepared under this section available at its registered office, notify the requisitionists that the report is so available.

(6) An investigation carried out by a company in pursuance of a requisition under section 214 is regarded for purposes of this section as concluded when the company has made all such inquiries as are necessary or expedient for the purposes of the requisition and in the case of each such inquiry, either a response has been received by the company or the time allowed for a response has elapsed.

(7) A report prepared under this section—

> (a) shall be kept at the company's registered office from the day on which it is first available there in accordance with subsection (1) or (2) until the expiration of 6 years beginning with the day next following that day, and
>
> (b) shall be available for inspection in accordance with section 219 below so long as it is so kept.

(8) If default is made in complying with subsection (1), (2), (5) or (7)(a), the company and every officer of it who is in default is liable to a fine.

Penalty for failure to provide information.

216.—(1) Where notice is served by a company under section 212 on a person who is or was interested in shares of the company and that person fails to give the company any information required by the notice within the time specified in it, the company may apply to the court for an order directing that the shares in question be subject to the restrictions of Part XV of this Act.

(2) Such an order may be made by the court notwithstanding any power contained in the applicant company's memorandum or articles enabling the company itself to impose similar restrictions on the shares in question.

(3) Subject to the following subsections, a person who fails to comply with a notice under section 212 or who, in purported compliance with such a notice, makes any statement which he knows to be false in a material particular or recklessly makes any statement which is false in a material particular is guilty of an offence and liable to imprisonment or a fine, or both.

Section 733(2) and (3) of this Act (liability of individuals for corporate default) apply to offences under this subsection.

(4) A person is not guilty of an offence by virtue of failing to comply with a notice under section 212 if he proves that the requirement to give the information was frivolous or vexatious.

(5) A person is not obliged to comply with a notice under section 212 if he is for the time being exempted by the Secretary of State from the operation of that section ; but the Secretary of State shall not grant any such exemption unless—

    (a) he has consulted with the Governor of the Bank of England, and

    (b) he (the Secretary of State) is satisfied that, having regard to any undertaking given by the person in question with respect to any interest held or to be held by him in any shares, there are special reasons why that person should not be subject to the obligations imposed by that section.

217.—(1) A company may remove an entry against a person's name from its register of interests in shares if more than 6 years have elapsed since the date of the entry being made, and either— Removal of entries from register.

    (a) that entry recorded the fact that the person in question had ceased to have an interest notifiable under this Part in relevant share capital of the company, or

    (b) it has been superseded by a later entry made under section 211 against the same person's name ;

and in a case within paragraph (a) the company may also remove that person's name from the register.

(2) If a person in pursuance of an obligation imposed on him by any provision of this Part gives to a company the name and address of another person as being interested in shares in the company, the company shall, within 15 days of the date on which it was given that information, notify the other person that he has been so named and shall include in that notification—

    (a) particulars of any entry relating to him made, in consequence of its being given that information, by the company in its register of interests in shares, and (*b*) a statement informing him of his right to apply to have the entry removed in accordance with the following provisions of this section.

(3) A person who has been notified by a company in pursuance of subsection (2) that an entry relating to him has been made in the company's register of interests in shares may apply in writing to the company for the removal of that entry from the register ; and the company shall remove the entry if satisfied that the information in pursuance of which the entry was made was incorrect.

(4) If a person who is identified in a company's register of interests in shares as being a party to an agreement to which section 204 applies (whether by an entry against his own name or by an entry relating to him made against another person's name as mentioned in subsection (2)(*a*)) ceases to be a party to that agreement, he may apply in writing to the company for the inclusion of that information in the register ; and if the company is satisfied that he has ceased to be a party to the agreement, it shall record that information (if not already recorded) in every place where his name appears as a party to that agreement in the register.

(5) If an application under subsection (3) or (4) is refused (in a case within subsection (4), otherwise than on the ground that the information has already been recorded) the applicant may apply to the court for an order directing the company to remove the entry in question from the register or (as the case may be) to include the information in question in the register ; and the court may, if it thinks fit, make such an order.

(6) Where a name is removed from a company's register of interests in shares in pursuance of subsection (1) or (3) or an order under subsection (5), the company shall within 14 days of the date of that removal make any necessary alteration in any associated index.

(7) If default is made in complying with subsection (2) or (6), the company and every officer of it who is in default is liable to a fine and, for continued contravention, to a daily default fine.

Otherwise, entries not to be removed.   **218.**—(1) Entries in a company's register of interests in shares shall not be deleted except in accordance with section 217.

(2) If an entry is deleted from a company's register of interests in shares in contravention of subsection (1), the company shall restore that entry to the register as soon as is reasonably practicable.

(3) If default is made in complying with subsection (1) or (2), the company and every officer of it who is in default is liable to a fine and, for continued contravention of subsection (2), to a daily default fine.

PART VI

219.—(1) Any register of interests in shares and any report which is required by section 215(7) to be available for inspection in accordance with this section shall, during business hours (subject to such reasonable restrictions as the company may in general meeting impose, but so that not less than 2 hours in each day are allowed for inspection) be open to the inspection of any member of the company or of any other person without charge.

Inspection of register and reports.

(2) Any such member or other person may require a copy of any such register or report, or any part of it, on payment of 10 pence or such less sum as the company may prescribe, for every 100 words or fractional part of 100 words required to be copied ; and the company shall cause any copy so required by a person to be sent to him before the expiration of the period of 10 days beginning with the day next following that on which the requirement is received by the company.

(3) If an inspection required under this section is refused or a copy so required is not sent within the proper period, the company and every officer of it who is in default is liable to a fine and, for continued contravention, to a daily default fine.

(4) In the case of a refusal of an inspection required under this section of any register or report, the court may by order compel an immediate inspection of it ; and in the case of failure to send a copy required under this section, the court may by order direct that the copy required shall be sent to the person requiring it.

(5) The Secretary of State may by regulations made by statutory instrument substitute a sum specified in the regulations for the sum for the time being mentioned in subsection (2).

Supplementary

220.—(1) In this Part of this Act—

Definitions for Part VI.

    " associated index ", in relation to a register, means the index kept in relation to that register in pursuance of section 211(6),

    "register of interests in shares " means the register kept in pursuance of section 211 including, except where the context otherwise requires, that part of the register kept in pursuance of section 213, and

    " relevant share capital " has the meaning given by section 198(2).

(2) Where the period allowed by any provision of this Part for fulfilling an obligation is expressed as a number of days, any day that is a Saturday or Sunday or a bank holiday in any part of Great Britain is to be disregarded in reckoning that period.

Part VII

Accounts and Audit

Chapter I

Provisions Applying to Companies Generally

Accounting records

Companies to keep accounting records.

221.—(1) Every company shall cause accounting records to be kept in accordance with this section.

(2) The accounting records shall be sufficient to show and explain the company's transactions, and shall be such as to—

 (a) disclose with reasonable accuracy, at any time, the financial position of the company at that time, and

 (b) enable the directors to ensure that any balance sheet and profit and loss account prepared under this Part comply with the requirements of this Act as to the form and content of company accounts and otherwise.

(3) The accounting records shall in particular contain—

 (a) entries from day to day of all sums of money received and expended by the company, and the matters in respect of which the receipt and expenditure takes place, and

 (b) a record of the assets and liabilities of the company.

(4) If the company's business involves dealing in goods, the accounting records shall contain—

 (a) statements of stock held by the company at the end of each financial year of the company,

 (b) all statements of stocktakings from which any such statement of stock as is mentioned in paragraph (a) has been or is to be prepared, and

 (c) except in the case of goods sold by way of ordinary retail trade, statements of all goods sold and purchased, showing the goods and the buyers and sellers in sufficient detail to enable all these to be identified.

222.—(1) Subject as follows, a company's accounting records shall be kept at its registered office or such other place as the directors think fit, and shall at all times be open to inspection by the company's officers.

(2) If accounting records are kept at a place outside Great Britain, accounts and returns with respect to the business dealt with in the accounting records so kept shall be sent to, and kept at, a place in Great Britain, and shall at all times be open to such inspection.

(3) The accounts and returns to be sent to Great Britain in accordance with subsection (2) shall be such as to—

(a) disclose with reasonable accuracy the financial position of the business in question at intervals of not more than 6 months, and

(b) enable the directors to ensure that the company's balance sheet and profit and loss account comply with the requirements of this Act as to the form and content of company accounts and otherwise.

(4) Accounting records which a company is required by section 221 to keep shall be preserved by it—

(a) in the case of a private company, for 3 years from the date on which they are made, and

(b) in the case of a public company, for 6 years from that date.

This is subject to any direction with respect to the disposal of records given under winding-up rules under section 663.

223.—(1) If a company fails to comply with any provision of section 221 or 222(1) or (2), every officer of the company who is in default is guilty of an offence unless he shows that he acted honestly and that in the circumstances in which the company's business was carried on the default was excusable.

(2) An officer of a company is guilty of an offence if he fails to take all reasonable steps for securing compliance by the company with section 222(4), or has intentionally caused any default by the company under it.

(3) A person guilty of an offence under this section is liable to imprisonment or a fine, or both.

A company's accounting reference periods and financial year

224.—(1) A company's accounting reference periods are determined according to its accounting reference date.

(2) A company may give notice in the prescribed form to the registrar of companies specifying a date in the calendar year

as being the date on which in each successive calendar year an accounting reference period of the company is to be treated as coming to an end; and the date specified in the notice is then the company's accounting reference date.

(3) However, no such notice has effect unless it is given before the end of 6 months beginning with the date of the company's incorporation; and, failing such notice, the company's accounting reference date is 31st March.

(4) A company's first accounting reference period is such period ending with its accounting reference date as begins on the date of its incorporation and is a period of more than 6 months and not more than 18 months; and each successive period of 12 months beginning after the end of the first accounting reference period and ending with the accounting reference date is also an accounting reference period of the company.

(5) This section is subject to section 225, under which in certain circumstances a company may alter its accounting reference date and accounting reference periods.

Alteration of
accounting
reference
period.

225.—(1) At any time during a period which is an accounting reference period of a company by virtue of section 224 or 226 the company may give notice in the prescribed form to the registrar of companies specifying a date in the calendar year (" the new accounting reference date ") on which that accounting reference period (" the current accounting reference period ") and each subsequent accounting reference period of the company is to be treated as coming to an end or (as the case may require) as having come to an end.

(2) At any time after the end of a period which was an accounting reference period of a company by virtue of section 224 or 226 the company may give notice in the prescribed form to the registrar of companies specifying a date in the calendar year (" the new accounting reference date ") on which that accounting reference period (" the previous accounting reference period ") and each subsequent accounting reference period of the company is to be treated as coming or (as the case may require) as having come to an end.

(3) But a notice under subsection (2)—

    (*a*) has no effect unless the company is a subsidiary or holding company of another company and the new accounting reference date coincides with the accounting reference date of that other company, and

    (*b*) has no effect if the period allowed (under section 242) for laying and delivering accounts in relation to the previous accounting reference period has already expired at the time when the notice is given.

(4) A notice under this section shall state whether the current
or previous accounting reference period of the company—

   (*a*) is to be treated as shortened, so as to come to an end
       or (as the case may require) be treated as having come
       to an end on the new accounting reference date on the
       first occasion on which that date falls or fell after the
       beginning of that accounting reference period, or

   (*b*) is to be treated as extended, so as to come to an end or
       (as the case may require) be treated as having come
       to an end on the new accounting reference date on the
       second occasion on which that date falls or fell after
       the beginning of that accounting reference period.

(5) A notice which states that the current or previous accounting reference period is to be extended has no effect if the current or previous accounting reference period, as extended in accordance with the notice, would exceed 18 months.

(6) Subject to any direction given by the Secretary of State under the next subsection, a notice which states that the current or previous accounting reference period is to be extended has no effect unless—

   (*a*) no earlier accounting reference period of the company
       has been extended by virtue of a previous notice given
       by the company under this section, or

   (*b*) the notice is given not less than 5 years after the date
       on which any earlier accounting reference period of
       the company which was so extended came to an end,
       or

   (*c*) the company is a subsidiary or holding company of
       another company and the new accounting reference
       date coincides with the accounting reference date of
       that other company.

(7) The Secretary of State may, if he thinks fit, direct that subsection (6) shall not apply to a notice already given by a company under this section or (as the case may be) in relation to a notice which may be so given.

226.—(1) Where a company has given notice with effect in Consequence accordance with section 225, and that notice has not been super- of giving seded by a subsequent notice by the company which has such notice under effect, the new date specified in the notice is the company's s. 225. accounting reference date, in substitution for that which, by virtue of section 224 or this section, was its accounting reference date at the time when the notice was given.

(2) Where by virtue of such a notice one date is substituted for another as the accounting reference date of a company—

    (*a*) the current or previous accounting reference period, shortened or extended (as the case may be) in accordance with the notice, and

    (*b*) each successive period of 12 months beginning after the end of that accounting reference period (as so shortened or extended) and ending with the new accounting reference date,

is or (as the case may require) is to be treated as having been an accounting reference period of the company, instead of any period which would be an accounting reference period of the company if the notice had not been given.

(3) Section 225 and this section do not affect any accounting reference period of the company which—

    (*a*) in the case of a notice under section 225(1), is earlier than the current accounting reference period, or

    (*b*) in the case of a notice under section 225(2), is earlier than the previous accounting reference period.

Directors'
duty to
prepare
annual
accounts.

227.—(1) In the case of every company, the directors shall in respect of each accounting reference period of the company prepare a profit and loss account for the financial year or, if it is a company not trading for profit, an income and expenditure account.

(2) Where it is the company's first accounting reference period, the financial year begins with the first day of that period and ends with—

    (*a*) the date on which the accounting reference period ends, or

    (*b*) such other date, not more than 7 days before or more than 7 days after the end of that period, as the directors may determine;

and after that the financial year begins with the day after the date to which the last preceding profit and loss account was made up and ends as mentioned in paragraphs (*a*) and (*b*) above.

(3) The directors shall prepare a balance sheet as at the last day of the financial year.

(4) In the case of a holding company, the directors shall secure that, except where in their opinion there are good reasons against it, the financial year of each of its subsidiaries coincides with the company's own financial year.

Form and content of company individual and group accounts

228.—(1) A company's accounts prepared under section 227 shall comply with the requirements of Schedule 4 (so far as applicable) with respect to the form and content of the balance sheet and profit and loss account and any additional information to be provided by way of notes to the accounts.

(2) The balance sheet shall give a true and fair view of the state of affairs of the company as at the end of the financial year ; and the profit and loss account shall give a true and fair view of the profit or loss of the company for the financial year.

(3) Subsection (2) overrides—

(a) the requirements of Schedule 4, and

(b) all other requirements of this Act as to the matters to be included in a company's accounts or in notes to those accounts ;

and accordingly the following two subsections have effect.

(4) If the balance sheet or profit and loss account drawn up in accordance with those requirements would not provide sufficient information to comply with subsection (2), any necessary additional information must be provided in that balance sheet or profit and loss account, or in a note to the accounts.

(5) If, owing to special circumstances in the case of any company, compliance with any such requirement in relation to the balance sheet or profit and loss account would prevent compliance with subsection (2) (even if additional information were provided in accordance with subsection (4)), the directors shall depart from that requirement in preparing the balance sheet or profit and loss account (so far as necessary in order to comply with subsection (2)).

(6) If the directors depart from any such requirement, particulars of the departure, the reasons for it and its effect shall be given in a note to the accounts.

(7) Subsections (1) to (6) do not apply to group accounts prepared under the next section ; and subsections (1) and (2) do not apply to a company's profit and loss account (or require the notes otherwise required in relation to that account) if—

(a) the company has subsidiaries, and

(b) the profit and loss account is framed as a consolidated account dealing with all or any of the company's subsidiaries as well as the company, and—

(i) complies with the requirements of this Act relating to consolidated profit and loss accounts, and

(ii) shows how much of the consolidated profit or loss for the financial year is dealt with in the company's individual accounts.

If group accounts are prepared, and advantage is taken of this subsection, that fact shall be disclosed in a note to the group accounts.

Group accounts of holding company.

229.—(1) If at the end of its financial year a company has subsidiaries, the directors shall, as well as preparing individual accounts for that year, also prepare group accounts, being accounts or statements which deal with the state of affairs and profit or loss of the company and the subsidiaries.

(2) This does not apply if the company is at the end of the financial year the wholly-owned subsidiary of another body corporate incorporated in Great Britain.

(3) Group accounts need not deal with a subsidiary if the company's directors are of opinion that—

(a) it is impracticable, or would be of no real value to the company's members, in view of the insignificant amounts involved, or

(b) it would involve expense or delay out of proportion to the value to members, or

(c) the result would be misleading, or harmful to the business of the company or any of its subsidiaries, or

(d) the business of the holding company and that of the subsidiary are so different that they cannot reasonably be treated as a single undertaking;

and, if the directors are of that opinion about each of the company's subsidiaries, group accounts are not required.

(4) However, the approval of the Secretary of State is required for not dealing in group accounts with a subsidiary on the ground that the result would be harmful or on the ground of difference between the business of the holding company and that of the subsidiary.

(5) A holding company's group accounts shall be consolidated accounts comprising—

(a) a consolidated balance sheet dealing with the state of affairs of the company and all the subsidiaries to be dealt with in group accounts, and

(b) a consolidated profit and loss account dealing with the profit or loss of the company and those subsidiaries.

(6) However, if the directors are of opinion that it is better for the purpose of presenting the same or equivalent information about the state of affairs and profit or loss of the company and

those subsidiaries, and of so presenting it that it may be readily appreciated by the company's members, the group accounts may be prepared in other than consolidated form, and in particular may consist—

    (*a*) of more than one set of consolidated accounts dealing respectively with the company and one group of subsidiaries and with other groups of subsidiaries, or

    (*b*) of separate accounts dealing with each of the subsidiaries, or

    (*c*) of statements expanding the information about the subsidiaries in the company's individual accounts,

or of any combination of those forms.

(7) The group accounts may be wholly or partly incorporated in the holding company's individual balance sheet and profit and loss account.

230.—(1) A holding company's group accounts shall comply with the requirements of Schedule 4 (so far as applicable to group accounts in the form in which those accounts are prepared) with respect to the form and content of those accounts and any additional information to be provided by way of notes to those accounts. Form and content of group accounts.

(2) Group accounts (together with any notes to them) shall give a true and fair view of the state of affairs and profit or loss of the company and the subsidiaries dealt with by those accounts as a whole, so far as concerns members of the company.

(3) Subsection (2) overrides—

    (*a*) the requirements of Schedule 4, and

    (*b*) all other requirements of this Act as to the matters to be included in group accounts or in notes to those accounts,

and accordingly the following two subsections have effect.

(4) If group accounts drawn up in accordance with those requirements would not provide sufficient information to comply with subsection (2), any necessary additional information must be provided in, or in a note to, the group accounts.

(5) If, owing to special circumstances in the case of any company, compliance with any such requirement in relation to its group accounts would prevent those accounts from complying with subsection (2) (even if additional information were provided in accordance with subsection (4)), the directors shall depart from that requirement in preparing the group accounts (so far as necessary to comply with subsection (2)).

(6) If the directors depart from any such requirement, particulars of that departure, the reason for it and its effect shall be given in a note to the group accounts.

(7) If the financial year of a subsidiary does not coincide with that of the holding company, the group accounts shall (unless the Secretary of State, on the application or with the consent of the holding company's directors, otherwise directs) deal with the subsidiary's state of affairs as at the end of its relevant financial year, that is—

    (*a*) if its financial year ends with that of the holding company, that financial year, and

    (*b*) if not, the subsidiary's financial year ending last before the end of the financial year of the holding company dealt with in the group accounts,

and with the subsidiary's profit or loss for its relevant financial year.

(8) The Secretary of State may, on the application or with the consent of a company's directors, modify the requirements of Schedule 4 as they have effect in relation to that company by virtue of subsection (1), for the purpose of adapting them to the company's circumstances ; and references above in this section to the requirements of Schedule 4 are then to be read in relation to that company as references to those requirements as modified.

Additional
disclosure
required in
notes to
accounts.
    231.—(1) Schedule 5 has effect with respect to additional matters which must be disclosed in company accounts for a financial year ; and in that Schedule, where a thing is required to be stated or shown, or information is required to be given, it means that the thing is to be stated or shown, or the information is to be given, in a note to those accounts.

    (2) In Schedule 5—

    (*a*) Parts I and II are concerned, respectively, with the disclosure of particulars of the company's subsidiaries and of its other shareholdings,

    (*b*) Part III is concerned with the disclosure of financial information relating to subsidiaries,

    (*c*) Part IV requires a company which is itself a subsidiary to disclose its ultimate holding company,

    (*d*) Part V is concerned with the emoluments of directors (including emoluments waived), pensions of directors and past directors and compensation for loss of office to directors and past directors, and

    (*e*) Part VI is concerned with disclosure of the number of the company's employees who are remunerated at higher rates.

(3) Whenever it is stated in Schedule 5 that this subsection applies to certain particulars or information, it means that the particulars or information shall be annexed to the annual return first made by the company after copies of its accounts have been laid before it in general meeting; and if a company fails to satisfy an obligation thus imposed, the company and every officer of it who is in default is liable to a fine and, for continued contravention, to a daily default fine.

(4) It is the duty of any director of a company to give notice to the company of such matters relating to himself as may be necessary for purposes of Part V of Schedule 5; and this applies to persons who are or have at any time in the preceding 5 years been officers, as it applies to directors.

A person who makes default in complying with this subsection is liable to a fine.

232.—(1) A holding company's group accounts for a financial year shall comply with Part I of Schedule 6 (so far as applicable) as regards the disclosure of transactions, arrangements and agreements there mentioned (loans, quasi-loans and other dealings in favour of directors).

(2) In the case of a company other than a holding company, its individual accounts shall comply with Part I of Schedule 6 (so far as applicable) as regards disclosure of those matters.

(3) Particulars which are required by Part I of Schedule 6 to be contained in any accounts shall be given by way of notes to the accounts, and are required in respect of shadow directors as well as directors.

(4) Where by virtue of section 229(2) or (3) a company does not prepare group accounts for a financial year, subsection (1) of this section requires disclosure of such matters in its individual accounts as would have been disclosed in group accounts.

(5) The requirements of this section apply with such exceptions as are mentioned in Part I of Schedule 6 (including in particular exceptions for and in respect of recognised banks).

233.—(1) A holding company's group accounts for a financial year shall comply with Part II of Schedule 6 (so far as applicable) as regards transactions, arrangements and agreements made by the company or a subsidiary of it for persons who at any time during that financial year were officers of the company (but not directors).

(2) In the case of a company other than a holding company, its individual accounts shall comply with Part II of Schedule 6 (so far as applicable) as regards those matters.

(3) Subsections (1) and (2) do not apply in relation to any transaction, arrangement or agreement made by a recognised bank for any of its officers or for any of the officers of its holding company.

(4) Particulars required by Part II of Schedule 6 to be contained in any accounts shall be given by way of notes to the accounts.

(5) Where by virtue of section 229(2) or (3) a company does not prepare group accounts for a financial year, subsection (1) of this section requires such matters to be stated in its individual accounts as would have been stated in group accounts.

Recognised banks: disclosure of dealings with and for directors.

234.—(1) The group accounts of a company which is, or is the holding company of, a recognised bank, and the individual accounts of any other company which is a recognised bank, shall comply with Part III of Schedule 6 (so far as applicable) as regards transactions, arrangements and agreements made by the company preparing the accounts (if it is a recognised bank) and, in the case of a holding company, by any of its subsidiaries which is a recognised bank, for persons who at any time during the financial year were directors of the company or connected with a director of it.

(2) Particulars required by Part III of Schedule 6 to be contained in any accounts shall be given by way of notes to those accounts, and are required in respect of shadow directors as well as directors.

(3) Where by virtue of section 229(2) or (3) a company does not prepare group accounts for a financial year, subsection (1) of this section requires such matters to be stated in its individual accounts as would have been stated in group accounts.

Directors' and auditors' reports

Directors' report.

235.—(1) In the case of every company there shall for each financial year be prepared a report by the directors—

(a) containing a fair review of the development of the business of the company and its subsidiaries during the financial year and of their position at the end of it, and

(b) stating the amount (if any) which they recommend should be paid as dividend and the amount (if any) which they propose to carry to reserves.

(2) The directors' report shall state the names of the persons who, at any time during the financial year, were directors of the company, and the principal activities of the company and its subsidiaries in the course of the year and any significant change in those activities in the year.

(3) The report shall also state the matters, and give the particulars, required by Part I of Schedule 7 (changes in asset values, directors' shareholdings and other interests, contributions for political and charitable purposes, etc.).

(4) Part II of Schedule 7 applies as regards the matters to be stated in the directors' report in the circumstances there specified (company acquiring its own shares or a permitted charge on them).

(5) Parts III, IV and V of Schedule 7 apply respectively as regards the matters to be stated in the directors' report relative to the employment, training and advancement of disabled persons ; the health, safety and welfare at work of the company's employees ; and the involvement of employees in the affairs, policy and performance of the company.

(6) If the company's individual accounts are accompanied by group accounts which are special category, the directors' report shall, in addition to complying with Schedule 7, also comply with paragraphs 2 to 6 of Schedule 10 (turnover and profitability ; size of labour force and wages paid).

(7) In respect of any failure to comply with the requirements of this Act as to the matters to be stated, and the particulars to be given, in the directors' report, every person who was a director of the company immediately before the end of the relevant period (meaning whatever is under section 242 the period for laying and delivering accounts) is guilty of an offence and liable to a fine.

In proceedings for an offence under this subsection, it is a defence for the person to prove that he took all reasonable steps for securing compliance with the requirements in question.

236.—(1) A company's auditors shall make a report to its Auditors' members on the accounts examined by them, and on every report. balance sheet and profit and loss account, and on all group accounts, copies of which are to be laid before the company in general meeting during the auditors' tenure of office.

(2) The auditors' report shall state—

    (a) whether in the auditors' opinion the balance sheet and profit and loss account and (if it is a holding company submitting group accounts) the group accounts have been properly prepared in accordance with this Act ; and

    (b) without prejudice to the foregoing, whether in their opinion a true and fair view is given—

        (i) in the balance sheet, of the state of the company's affairs at the end of the financial year,

G

(ii) in the profit and loss account (if not framed as a consolidated account), of the company's profit or loss for the financial year, and

(iii) in the case of group accounts, of the state of affairs and profit or loss of the company and its subsidiaries dealt with by those accounts, so far as concerns members of the company.

Auditors' duties and powers.

237.—(1) It is the duty of the company's auditors, in preparing their report, to carry out such investigations as will enable them to form an opinion as to the following matters—

(a) whether proper accounting records have been kept by the company and proper returns adequate for their audit have been received from branches not visited by them,

(b) whether the company's balance sheet and (if not consolidated) its profit and loss account are in agreement with the accounting records and returns.

(2) If the auditors are of opinion that proper accounting records have not been kept, or that proper returns adequate for their audit have not been received from branches not visited by them, or if the balance sheet and (if not consolidated) the profit and loss account are not in agreement with the accounting records and returns, the auditors shall state that fact in their report.

(3) Every auditor of a company has a right of access at all times to the company's books, accounts and vouchers, and is entitled to require from the company's officers such information and explanations as he thinks necessary for the performance of the auditor's duties.

(4) If the auditors fail to obtain all the information and explanations which, to the best of their knowledge and belief, are necessary for the purposes of their audit, they shall state that fact in their report.

(5) If the requirements of Parts V and VI of Schedule 5 and Parts I to III of Schedule 6 are not complied with in the accounts, it is the auditors' duty to include in their report, so far as they are reasonably able to do so, a statement giving the required particulars.

(6) It is the auditors' duty to consider whether the information given in the directors' report for the financial year for which the accounts are prepared is consistent with those accounts ; and if they are of opinion that it is not, they shall state that fact in their report.

Procedure on completion of accounts

238.—(1) A company's balance sheet, and every copy of it which is laid before the company in general meeting or delivered to the registrar of companies, shall be signed on behalf of the board by two of the directors of the company or, if there is only one director, by that one.

(2) If a copy of the balance sheet—

(a) is laid before the company or delivered to the registrar without being signed as required by this section, or

(b) not being a copy so laid or delivered, is issued, circulated or published in a case where the balance sheet has not been signed as so required or where (the balance sheet having been so signed) the copy does not include a copy of the signatures or signature, as the case may be,

the company and every officer of it who is in default is liable to a fine.

(3) A company's profit and loss account and, so far as not incorporated in its individual balance sheet or profit and loss account, any group accounts of a holding company shall be annexed to the balance sheet, and the auditors' report shall be attached to it.

(4) Any accounts so annexed shall be approved by the board of directors before the balance sheet is signed on their behalf.

239. For the purposes of this Part, a company's accounts for a financial year are to be taken as comprising the following documents—

(a) the company's profit and loss account and balance sheet,

(b) the directors' report,

(c) the auditors' report, and

(d) where the company has subsidiaries and section 229 applies, the company's group accounts.

240.—(1) In the case of every company, a copy of the company's accounts for the financial year shall, not less than 21 days before the date of the meeting at which they are to be laid in accordance with the next section, be sent to each of the following persons—

(a) every member of the company (whether or not entitled to receive notice of general meetings),

(b) every holder of the company's debentures (whether or not so entitled), and

(c) all persons other than members and debenture holders, being persons so entitled.

(2) In the case of a company not having a share capital, subsection (1) does not require a copy of the accounts to be sent to a member of the company who is not entitled to receive notices of general meetings of the company, or to a holder of the company's debentures who is not so entitled.

(3) Subsection (1) does not require copies of the accounts to be sent—

(a) to a member of the company or a debenture holder, being in either case a person who is not entitled to receive notices of general meetings, and of whose address the company is unaware, or

(b) to more than one of the joint holders of any shares or debentures none of whom are entitled to receive such notices, or

(c) in the case of joint holders of shares or debentures some of whom are, and some not, entitled to receive such notices, to those who are not so entitled.

(4) If copies of the accounts are sent less than 21 days before the date of the meeting, they are, notwithstanding that fact, deemed to have been duly sent if it is so agreed by all the members entitled to attend and vote at the meeting.

(5) If default is made in complying with subsection (1), the company and every officer of it who is in default is liable to a fine.

Directors'
duty to lay
and deliver
accounts.

241.—(1) In respect of each financial year of a company the directors shall lay before the company in general meeting copies of the accounts of the company for that year.

(2) The auditors' report shall be read before the company in general meeting, and be open to the inspection of any member of the company.

(3) In respect of each financial year the directors—

(a) shall deliver to the registrar of companies a copy of the accounts for the year, and

(b) if any document comprised in the accounts is in a language other than English, shall annex to the copy of that document delivered a translation of it into English, certified in the prescribed manner to be a correct translation.

(4) In the case of an unlimited company, the directors are not required by subsection (3) to deliver a copy of the accounts if—

(a) at no time during the accounting reference period has the company been, to its knowledge, the subsidiary of a company that was then limited and at no such time, to its knowledge, have there been held or been exercisable, by or on behalf of two or more companies that were then limited, shares or powers which, if they had been held or been exercisable by one of them, would have made the company its subsidiary, and

(b) at no such time has the company been the holding company of a company which was then limited, and

(c) at no such time has the company been carrying on business as the promoter of a trading stamp scheme within the Trading Stamps Act 1964.

References here to a company that was limited at a particular time are to a body corporate (under whatever law incorporated) the liability of whose members was at that time limited.

242.—(1) The period allowed for laying and delivering a company's accounts for a financial year is as follows in this section, being determined by reference to the end of the relevant accounting reference period (that is, the accounting reference period in respect of which the financial year of the company is ascertained).

(2) Subject to the following subsections, the period allowed is—

(a) for a private company, 10 months after the end of the relevant accounting reference period, and

(b) for a public company, 7 months after the end of that period.

(3) If a company carries on business, or has interests, outside the United Kingdom, the Channel Islands and the Isle of Man and in respect of a financial year the directors (before the end of the period allowed by subsection (2)) give to the registrar of companies notice in the prescribed form—

(a) stating that the company so carries on business or has such interests, and

(b) claiming an extension of the period so allowed by a further 3 months,

the period allowed in relation to that financial year is then so extended.

(4) Where a company's first accounting reference period—

(a) begins on the date of its incorporation, and

(b) is a period of more than 12 months,

the period otherwise allowed for laying and delivering accounts is reduced by the number of days by which the relevant accounting reference period is longer than 12 months.

However, the period allowed is not by this provision reduced to less than 3 months after the end of that accounting reference period.

(5) Where a company's relevant accounting reference period has been shortened under section 226 (in consequence of notice by the company under section 225), the period allowed for laying and delivering accounts is—

(*a*) the period allowed in accordance with subsections (2) to (4) above, or

(*b*) the period of 3 months beginning with the date of the notice under section 225,

whichever of those periods last expires.

(6) If for any special reason the Secretary of State thinks fit to do so, he may by notice in writing to a company extend, by such further period as may be specified in the notice, the period otherwise allowed for laying and delivering accounts for any financial year of the company.

Penalty for non-compliance with s. 241.
243.—(1) If for a financial year of a company any of the requirements of section 241(1) or (3) is not complied with before the end of the period allowed for laying and delivering accounts, every person who immediately before the end of that period was a director of the company is, in respect of each of those subsections which is not so complied with, guilty of an offence and liable to a fine and, for continued contravention, to a daily default fine.

(2) If a person is charged with that offence in respect of any of the requirements of section 241(1) or (3), it is a defence for him to prove that he took all reasonable steps for securing that those requirements would be complied with before the end of the period allowed for laying and delivering accounts.

(3) If in respect of the company's financial year any of the requirements of section 241(3) is not complied with before the end of the period allowed for laying and delivering accounts, the company is liable to a penalty, recoverable in civil proceedings by the Secretary of State.

(4) The amount of the penalty is determined by reference to the length of the period between the end of the accounting reference period and the earliest day by which all those requirements have been complied with, and is—

(*a*) £20 where the period is not more than one month,

(*b*) £50 where the period is more than 1 month but not more than 3 months,

(c) £100 where the period is more than 3 months but not more than 6 months,

(d) £200 where the period is more than 6 months but not more than 12 months, and

(e) £450 where the period is more than 12 months.

(5) In proceedings under this section with respect to a requirement to lay a copy of a document before a company in general meeting, or to deliver a copy of a document to the registrar of companies, it is not a defence to prove that the document in question was not in fact prepared as required by this Part.

(6) Subsections (3) and (4) of this section do not come into force unless and until made to do so by an order of the Secretary of State in a statutory instrument.

244.—(1) If—

(a) in respect of a company's financial year any of the requirements of section 241(3) has not been complied with before the end of the period allowed for laying and delivering accounts, and

(b) the directors of the company fail to make good the default within 14 days after the service of a notice on them requiring compliance,

the court may, on application by any member or creditor of the company, or by the registrar of companies, make an order directing the directors (or any of them) to make good the default within such time as may be specified in the order.

(2) The court's order may provide that all costs of and incidental to the application shall be borne by the directors.

(3) Nothing in this section prejudices section 243.

245.—(1) If any accounts of a company of which a copy is laid before the company in general meeting or delivered to the registrar of companies do not comply with the requirements of this Act as to the matters to be included in, or in a note to, those accounts, every person who at the time when the copy is so laid or delivered is a director of the company is guilty of an offence and, in respect of each offence, liable to a fine.

This subsection does not apply to a company's group accounts.

(2) If any group accounts of which a copy is laid before a company in general meeting or delivered to the registrar of companies do not comply with section 229(5) to (7) or section 230, and with the other requirements of this Act as to the

matters to be included in or in a note to those accounts, every person who at the time when the copy was so laid or delivered was a director of the company is guilty of an offence and liable to a fine.

(3) In proceedings against a person for an offence under this section, it is a defence for him to prove that he took all reasonable steps for securing compliance with the requirements in question.

Shareholders'
right to obtain
copies of
accounts.

246.—(1) Any member of a company, whether or not he is entitled to have sent to him copies of the company's accounts, and any holder of the company's debentures (whether or not so entitled) is entitled to be furnished (on demand and without charge) with a copy of its last accounts.

(2) If, when a person makes a demand for a document with which he is entitled by this section to be furnished, default is made in complying with the demand within 7 days after its making, the company and every officer of it who is in default is liable to a fine and, for continued contravention, to a daily default fine (unless it is proved that the person has already made a demand for, and been furnished with, a copy of the document).

Modified accounts

Entitlement
to deliver
accounts in
modified
form.

247.—(1) In certain cases a company's directors may, in accordance with Part I of Schedule 8, deliver modified accounts in respect of a financial year ; and whether they may do so depends on the company qualifying, in particular financial years, as small or medium-sized.

(2) Modified accounts for a financial year may not be delivered in the case of a company which is, or was at any time in that year—

(a) a public company,

(b) a special category company (Chapter II of this Part), or

(c) subject to the next-but-one subsection, a member of a group which is ineligible for this purpose.

(3) " Group " here means a holding company and its subsidiaries together ; and a group is ineligible if any of its members is—

(a) a public company or a special category company, or

(b) a body corporate (other than a company) which has

power under its constitution to offer its shares or debentures to the public and may lawfully exercise that power, or

(c) a body corporate (other than a company) which is either a recognised bank or licensed institution within the Banking Act 1979 or an insurance company to which Part II of the Insurance Companies Act 1982 applies.

(4) Notwithstanding subsection (2)(c), modified accounts for a financial year may be delivered if the company is exempt under section 252 (dormant companies) from the obligation to appoint auditors and either—

(a) was so exempt throughout that year, or

(b) became so exempt by virtue of a special resolution under that section passed during that year.

(5) For purposes of sections 247 to 250 and Schedule 8, " deliver " means deliver to the registrar of companies under this Chapter; and for purposes of subsection (3)(b), " shares " and " debentures " have the same meaning as when used in relation to a company.

248.—(1) A company qualifies as small in a financial year if for that year two or more of the following conditions are satisfied—

(a) the amount of its turnover for the year is not more than £1·4 million;

(b) its balance sheet total is not more than £700,000;

(c) the average number of persons employed by the company in the year (determined on a weekly basis) does not exceed 50.

(2) A company qualifies as medium-sized in a financial year if for that year two or more of the following conditions are satisfied—

(a) the amount of its turnover for the year is not more than £5·75 million;

(b) its balance sheet total is not more than £2·8 million;

(c) the average number of persons employed by the company in the year (determined on a weekly basis) does not exceed 250.

(3) In subsections (1) and (2), " balance sheet total " means, in relation to a company's financial year—

(a) where in the company's accounts Format 1 of the balance sheet formats set out in Part I of Schedule 4 is adopted, the aggregate of the amounts shown in the balance sheet under the headings corresponding to items A to D in that Format, and

(b) where Format 2 is adopted, the aggregate of the amounts shown under the general heading " Assets ".

(4) The average number of persons employed as mentioned in subsections (1)(c) and (2)(c) is determined by applying the method of calculation prescribed by paragraph 56(2) and (3) of Schedule 4 for determining the number required by sub-paragraph (1)(a) of that paragraph to be stated in a note to the company's accounts.

(5) In applying subsections (1) and (2) to a period which is a company's financial year but not in fact a year, the maximum figures for turnover in paragraph (a) of each subsection are to be proportionately adjusted.

Modified individual accounts.

249.—(1) This section specifies the cases in which a company's directors may (subject to section 250, where the company has subsidiaries) deliver individual accounts modified as for a small or a medium-sized company ; and Part I of Schedule 8 applies with respect to the delivery of accounts so modified.

(2) In respect of the company's first financial year the directors may—

(a) deliver accounts modified as for a small company, if in that year it qualifies as small,

(b) deliver accounts modified as for a medium-sized company, if in that year it qualifies as medium-sized.

(3) The next three subsections are concerned only with a company's financial year subsequent to the first.

(4) The directors may in respect of a financial year—

(a) deliver accounts modified as for a small company if in that year the company qualifies as small and it also so qualified in the preceding year,

(b) deliver accounts modified as for a medium-sized company if in that year the company qualifies as medium-sized and it also so qualified in the preceding year.

(5) The directors may in respect of a financial year—

(a) deliver accounts modified as for a small company (although not qualifying in that year as small), if in the preceding year it so qualified and the directors were entitled to deliver accounts so modified in respect of that year, and

(b) deliver accounts modified as for a medium-sized company (although not qualifying in that year as medium-sized), if in the preceding year it so qualified and the directors were entitled to deliver accounts so modified in respect of that year.

(6) The directors may in respect of a financial year—

(*a*) deliver accounts modified as for a small company, if in that year the company qualifies as small and the directors were entitled under subsection (5)(*a*) to deliver accounts so modified for the preceding year (although the company did not in that year qualify as small), and

(*b*) deliver accounts modified as for a medium-sized company if in that year the company qualifies as medium-sized and the directors were entitled under subsection (5)(*b*) to deliver accounts so modified for the preceding year (although the company did not in that year qualify as medium-sized).

250.—(1) This section applies to a company (" the holding company ") where in respect of a financial year section 229 requires the preparation of group accounts for the company and its subsidiaries.

Modified accounts of holding company.

(2) The directors of the holding company may not under section 249—

(*a*) deliver accounts modified as for a small company, unless the group (meaning the holding company and its subsidiaries together) is in that year a small group,

(*b*) deliver accounts modified as for a medium-sized company, unless in that year the group is medium-sized ;

and the group is small or medium-sized if it would so qualify under section 248 (applying that section as directed by subsections (3) and (4) below), if it were all one company.

(3) The figures to be taken into account in determining whether the group is small or medium-sized (or neither) are the group account figures, that is—

(*a*) where the group accounts are prepared as consolidated accounts, the figures for turnover, balance sheet total and numbers employed which are shown in those accounts, and

(*b*) where not, the corresponding figures given in the group accounts, with such adjustment as would have been made if the accounts had been prepared in consolidated form,

aggregated in either case with the relevant figures for the subsidiaries (if any) omitted from the group accounts (excepting those for any subsidiary omitted under section 229(3)(*a*) on the ground of impracticability).

(4) In the case of each subsidiary omitted from the group accounts, the figures relevant as regards turnover, balance sheet total and numbers employed are those which are included in the accounts of that subsidiary prepared in respect of its relevant financial year (with such adjustment as would have been made if those figures had been included in group accounts prepared in consolidated form).

(5) For the purposes of subsection (4), the relevant financial year of the subsidiary is—
>   (a) if its financial year ends with that of the holding company to which the group accounts relate, that financial year, and
>   (b) if not, the subsidiary's financial year ending last before the end of the financial year of the holding company.

(6) If the directors are entitled to deliver modified accounts (whether as for a small or a medium-sized company), they may also deliver modified group accounts ; and this means that the group accounts—
>   (a) if consolidated, may be in accordance with Part II of Schedule 8 (while otherwise comprising or corresponding with group accounts prepared under section 229), and
>   (b) if not consolidated, may be such as (together with any notes) give the same or equivalent information as required by paragraph (a) above ;

and Part III of the Schedule applies to modified group accounts, whether consolidated or not.

Power of
Secretary of
State to
modify
ss. 247–250
and Sch. 8.

251.—(1) The Secretary of State may by regulations in a statutory instrument modify the provisions of sections 247(1) to (3), 248 to 250 and Schedule 8 ; and those provisions then apply as modified by regulations for the time being in force.

(2) Regulations under this section reducing the classes of companies which have the benefit of those provisions, or rendering the requirements of those provisions more onerous, shall not be made unless a draft of the instrument containing the regulations has been laid before Parliament and approved by a resolution of each House.

(3) Otherwise, a statutory instrument containing such regulations is subject to annulment in pursuance of a resolution of either House.

Dormant companies

252.—(1) In certain circumstances a company may, with a view to the subsequent laying and delivery of unaudited accounts, pass a special resolution making itself exempt from the obligation to appoint auditors as otherwise required by section 384.

(2) Such a resolution may be passed at a general meeting of
the company at which its accounts for a financial year are laid
as required by section 241 (if it is not a year for which the directors are required to lay group accounts); but the following conditions must be satisfied—

> (*a*) the directors must be entitled under section 249 to
> deliver, in respect of that financial year, accounts modi-
> fied as for a small company (or would be so entitled
> but for the company being, or having at any time in
> the financial year been, a member of an ineligible
> group within section 247 (3)), and

> (*b*) the company must have been dormant since the end of
> the financial year.

(3) A company may by such a resolution make itself exempt
from the obligation to appoint auditors if the resolution is passed
at some time before the first general meeting of the company at
which accounts are laid as required by section 241, provided
that the company has been dormant from the time of its formation until the resolution is passed.

(4) A company may not under subsection (3) pass such a resolution if it is a public company or a special category company.

(5) For purposes of this and the next section, a company is
" dormant " during any period in which no transaction occurs
which is for the company a significant accounting transaction;
and—

> (*a*) this means a transaction which is required by section
> 221 to be entered in the company's accounting records
> (disregarding any which arises from the taking of
> shares in the company by a subscriber to the memor-
> andum in pursuance of an undertaking of his in the
> memorandum), and

> (*b*) a company which has been dormant for any period
> ceases to be so on the occurrence of any such trans-
> action.

(6) A company which has under this section made itself exempt
from the obligation to appoint auditors loses that exemption if—

> (*a*) it ceases to be dormant, or

> (*b*) it would no longer qualify (for any other reason) to
> exclude that obligation by passing a resolution under
> this section.

(7) Where the exemption is lost, the directors may, at any time
before the next meeting of the company at which accounts are
to be laid, appoint an auditor or auditors, to hold office until
the conclusion of that meeting; and if they fail to exercise that

PART VII
CHAPTER I
Laying and
delivery of
unaudited
accounts.

power, the company in general meeting may exercise it.

253.—(1) The following applies in respect of a company's accounts for a financial year if the company is exempt under section 252 from the obligation to appoint auditors and either—

  (*a*) was so exempt throughout that year, or

  (*b*) became so exempt by virtue of a special resolution passed during that year, and retained the exemption until the end of that year.

(2) A report by the company's auditors need not be included (as otherwise required by preceding provisions of this Chapter) with the accounts laid before the company in general meeting and delivered to the registrar of companies.

(3) If the auditors' report is omitted from the accounts so delivered, then—

  (*a*) the balance sheet shall contain a statement by the directors (in a position immediately above their signatures to the balance sheet) that the company was dormant throughout the financial year, and

  (*b*) if the accounts delivered to the registrar are modified as permitted by sections 247 to 249—

   (i) the modified balance sheet need not contain the statement otherwise required by paragraph 9 of Schedule 8, and

   (ii) the modified accounts need not include the special report of the auditors otherwise required by paragraph 10 of that Schedule.

Publication of accounts

254.—(1) This section applies to the publication by a company of full individual or group accounts, that is to say the accounts required by section 241 to be laid before the company in general meeting and delivered to the registrar of companies (including the directors' report, unless dispensed with under paragraph 3 of Schedule 8).

(2) If a company publishes individual accounts (modified or other) for a financial year, it shall publish with them the relevant auditors' report.

(3) If a company required by section 229 to prepare group accounts for a financial year publishes individual accounts for that year, it shall also publish with them its group accounts (which may be modified accounts, but only if the individual accounts are modified).

(4) If a company publishes group accounts (modified or other), otherwise than together with its individual accounts, it shall publish with them the relevant auditors' report.

(5) References above to the relevant auditors' report are to the auditors' report under section 236 or, in the case of modified accounts (individual or group), the auditors' special report under paragraph 10 of Schedule 8.

(6) A company which contravenes any provision of this section, and any officer of it who is in default, is liable to a fine.

255.—(1) This section applies to the publication by a company of abridged accounts, that is to say any balance sheet or profit and loss account relating to a financial year of the company or purporting to deal with any such financial year, otherwise than as part of full accounts (individual or group) to which section 254 applies.

(2) The reference above to a balance sheet or profit and loss account, in relation to accounts published by a holding company, includes an account in any form purporting to be a balance sheet or profit and loss account for the group consisting of the holding company and its subsidiaries.

(3) If the company publishes abridged accounts, it shall publish with those accounts a statement indicating—

   (a) that the accounts are not full accounts,

   (b) whether full individual or full group accounts (according as the abridged accounts deal solely with the company's own affairs or with the affairs of the company and any subsidiaries) have been delivered to the registrar of companies or, in the case of an unlimited company exempt under section 241(4) from the requirement to deliver accounts, that the company is so exempt,

   (c) whether the company's auditors have made a report under section 236 on the company's accounts for any financial year with which the abridged accounts purport to deal, and

   (d) whether any report so made was unqualified (meaning that it was a report, without qualification, to the effect that in the opinion of the person making it the company's accounts had been properly prepared).

(4) Where a company publishes abridged accounts, it shall not publish with those accounts any such report of the auditors as is mentioned in subsection (3)(c).

(5) A company which contravenes any provision of this section, and any officer of it who is in default, is liable to a fine.

PART VII
CHAPTER I
Power of
Secretary of
State to alter
accounting
requirements.

Supplementary

256.—(1) The Secretary of State may by regulations in a statutory instrument—

(a) add to the classes of documents—

(i) to be comprised in a company's accounts for a financial year to be laid before the company in general meeting as required by section 241, or

(ii) to be delivered to the registrar of companies under that section,

and make provision as to the matters to be included in any document to be added to either class;

(b) modify the requirements of this Act as to the matters to be stated in a document of any such class;

(c) reduce the classes of documents to be delivered to the registrar of companies under section 241.

(2) In particular, the Secretary of State may by such regulations alter or add to the requirements of Schedule 4 and Schedule 9 (special category companies); and any reference in this Act to a provision of it then refers to that provision as it has effect subject to regulations in force under this section.

(3) Where regulations made under subsection (1)(a) add to either class of documents there mentioned documents dealing with the state of affairs and profit or loss of a company and other bodies, the regulations may also—

(a) extend the provisions of this Act relating to group accounts (or such of those provisions as may be specified) to such documents,

(b) exempt that company from the requirement to prepare group accounts in respect of any period for which it has prepared such a document.

(4) Regulations under this section may make different provision for different cases or classes of case, and may contain such incidental and supplementary provisions as the Secretary of State thinks fit.

(5) Regulations under subsection (1)(a), or extending the classes of company to which any requirement mentioned in subsection (1)(b) applies or rendering those requirements more onerous, shall not be made unless a draft of the instrument containing them has been laid before Parliament and approved by a resolution of each House.

(6) Otherwise, a statutory instrument containing such regulations is subject to annulment in pursuance of a resolution of either House.

CHAPTER II

ACCOUNTS OF BANKING, SHIPPING AND INSURANCE COMPANIES

257.—(1) For purposes of this Act, " special category com- Special
panies " are banking companies, shipping companies and in- category
surance companies ; and— companies
and their

   (*a*) " banking company " means a company which is a accounts.
      recognised bank for the purposes of the Banking Act 1979 c. 37.
      1979 or is a licensed institution within that Act ;

   (*b*) " insurance company " means an insurance company
      to which Part II of the Insurance Companies Act 1982 1982 c. 50.
      applies ; and

   (*c*) " shipping company " means a company which, or a
      subsidiary of which, owns ships or includes among its
      activities the management or operation of ships and
      which satisfies the Secretary of State that it ought in the
      national interest to be treated under this Part of this
      Act as a shipping company.

(2) Except as otherwise provided below, Chapter I of this
Part applies to a special category company and its accounts as it
applies to, and to the accounts of, any other company.

(3) The individual accounts of a special category company,
and the group accounts of a holding company which is, or has
as its subsidiary, a special category company, may be prepared
under this Chapter and not under Chapter I, and contain a
statement that they are so prepared ; and a reference in this Act
to a company's accounts (individual or group) being " special
category " is to their being so prepared and containing that
statement.

(4) Subject as follows, a reference in any enactment or other
document to section 228 or 230 of this Act or to Schedule 4 is,
in relation to special category accounts, to be read as a reference
to section 258 or 259 or Schedule 9 (as the case may require) ;
but this is subject to any contrary context.

258.—(1) Where a company's individual accounts are special Special
category, section 228 and Schedule 4 do not apply, but— category
individual

   (*a*) the balance sheet shall give a true and fair view of the accounts.
      state of affairs of the company as at the end of the
      financial year, and

   (*b*) the profit and loss account shall give a true and fair
      view of the company's profit or loss for the financial
      year.

(2) The balance sheet and profit and loss account shall comply
with the requirements of Schedule 9, so far as applicable.

(3) Except as expressly provided by this section or Part III
of Schedule 9, the requirements of subsection (2) and that

Schedule are without prejudice to the general requirements of sub-section (1) or to any other requirements of this Act.

(4) The Secretary of State may, on the application or with the consent of the company's directors, modify in relation to that company any of the requirements of this Chapter as to the matters to be stated in a company's balance sheet or profit and loss account (except the requirements of subsection (1) above), for the purpose of adapting them to the circumstances of the company.

(5) So much of subsections (1) and (2) as relates to the profit and loss account does not apply if—

> (*a*) the company has subsidiaries, and
> (*b*) the profit and loss account is framed as a consolidated account dealing with all or any of the company's subsidiaries as well as the company and—
>
>> (i) complies with the requirements of this Act relating to consolidated profit and loss accounts (as those requirements apply in the case of special category companies), and
>>
>> (ii) shows how much of the consolidated profit or loss for the financial year is dealt with in the company's accounts.

Special category group accounts.

259.—(1) Where a holding company's group accounts are special category, those accounts shall give a true and fair view of the state of affairs and profit or loss of the company and the subsidiaries dealt with by those accounts as a whole, so far as concerns members of the company.

(2) Where the financial year of a subsidiary does not coincide with that of the holding company, the group accounts shall (unless the Secretary of State on the application or with the consent of the holding company's directors otherwise directs) deal with the subsidiary's state of affairs as at the end of its relevant financial year, that is—

> (*a*) if its financial year ends with that of the holding company, that financial year, and
> (*b*) if not, the subsidiary's financial year ending last before the end of the financial year of the holding company dealt with in the group accounts,

and with the subsidiary's profit or loss for its relevant financial year.

(3) Without prejudice to subsection (1), the group accounts, if prepared as consolidated accounts, shall comply with the requirements of Schedule 9 (so far as applicable), and if not so prepared shall give the same or equivalent information.

(4) However, the Secretary of State may, on the application or with the consent of the holding company's directors, modify

the requirements of Schedule 9 in relation to that company for
the purpose of adapting them to the company's circumstances.

260.—(1) In Schedule 5 (matters to be dealt with in notes Notes to
to accounts)— special

    (*a*) paragraph 8 in Part II (disclosure of shareholdings in category accounts.
        other bodies corporate, not being subsidiaries), and

    (*b*) Part III (financial information about subsidiaries),

do not apply in the case of special category accounts.

(2) Where an item is given in a note to special category
accounts, to comply with Part V or VI of Schedule 5 (directors'
emoluments, pensions etc. ; emoluments of higher-paid employees), the corresponding amount for the immediately preceding financial year shall be included in the note.

(3) If a person, being a director of a company preparing
special category accounts, fails to take all reasonable steps to
secure compliance with subsection (2), he is in respect of each
offence liable to a fine ; but in proceedings against a person
for that offence it is a defence to prove that he had reasonable
ground to believe, and did believe, that a competent and reliable
person was charged with the duty of seeing that subsection (2)
was complied with and was in a position to discharge that
duty.

261.—(1) Where a company's individual accounts are special Directors'
category, the following applies with respect to the directors' report.
report accompanying the accounts.

(2) Paragraphs (*a*) and (*b*) of section 235(1) do not apply as
regards the contents of the report ; but the report shall deal
with the company's state of affairs, the amount (if any) which
the directors recommend should be paid as dividend, and the
amount (if any) which they propose to carry to reserves (within
the meaning of Schedule 9).

(3) Information which is otherwise required to be given in
the accounts, and allowed to be given in a statement annexed,
may be given in the directors' report instead of in the accounts.

If any information is so given, the report is treated as forming
part of the accounts for the purposes of audit, except that the
auditors shall report on it only so far as it gives that information.

(4) Where advantage is taken of subsection (3) to show an
item in the directors' report instead of in the accounts, the
report shall also show the corresponding amount for (or, as
the case may require, as at the end of) the immediately preceding financial year of that item, except where the amount
would not have had to be shown had the item been shown in
the accounts.

(5) Schedule 7 applies to the directors' report only in respect of the matters to be stated, and the information to be given, under paragraphs 1 to 5 (but excluding paragraph 2(3)) and 9, 10 and 11 ; and paragraph 1 of the Schedule does not apply if the company has the benefit of any provision of Part III of Schedule 9.

(6) The report shall, in addition to complying with those paragraphs of Schedule 7, also comply with Schedule 10, where and so far as applicable (disclosure of recent share and debenture issues ; turnover and profitability ; size of labour force and wages paid ; and other general matters) ; but in that Schedule, paragraphs 2 to 4 and 6 do not apply to a directors' report attached to any accounts unless the documents required to be comprised in those accounts include group accounts which are special category.

(7) Section 237(6) does not apply.

Auditors'
report.

262.—(1) The following applies where a company is entitled to avail itself, and has availed itself, of the benefit of any of the provisions of Part III of Schedule 9.

(2) In that case section 236(2) does not apply ; and the auditors' report shall state whether in their opinion the company's balance sheet and profit and loss account and (if it is a holding company submitting group accounts) the group accounts have been properly prepared in accordance with this Act.

PART VIII

DISTRIBUTION OF PROFITS AND ASSETS

Limits of company's power of distribution

Certain
distributions
prohibited.

263.—(1) A company shall not make a distribution except out of profits available for the purpose.

(2) In this Part, " distribution " means every description of distribution of a company's assets to its members, whether in cash or otherwise, except distribution by way of—

    (*a*) an issue of shares as fully or partly paid bonus shares,

    (*b*) the redemption or purchase of any of the company's own shares out of capital (including the proceeds of any fresh issue of shares) or out of unrealised profits in accordance with Chapter VII of Part V,

    (*c*) the reduction of share capital by extinguishing or reducing the liability of any of the members on any of the company's shares in respect of share capital not paid up, or by paying off paid up share capital, and

    (*d*) a distribution of assets to members of the company on its winding up.

(3) For purposes of this Part, a company's profits available for distribution are its accumulated, realised profits, so far as

not previously utilised by distribution or capitalisation, less PART VIII
its accumulated, realised losses, so far as not previously written
off in a reduction or reorganisation of capital duly made.

This is subject to the provision made by sections 265 and 266
for investment and other companies.

(4) A company shall not apply an unrealised profit in paying
up debentures, or any amounts unpaid on its issued shares.

(5) Where the directors of a company are, after making all
reasonable enquiries, unable to determine whether a particular
profit made before 22nd December 1980 is realised or unrealised,
they may treat the profit as realised; and where after making
such enquiries they are unable to determine whether a particular
loss so made is realised or unrealised, they may treat the loss
as unrealised.

264.—(1) A public company may only make a distribution Restriction
at any time— on distribution
of assets.
    (*a*) if at that time the amount of its net assets is not less
        than the aggregate of its called-up share capital and
        undistributable reserves, and
    (*b*) if, and to the extent that, the distribution does not
        reduce the amount of those assets to less than that
        aggregate.

This is subject to the provision made by sections 265 and 266
for investment and other companies.

(2) In subsection (1), " net assets " means the aggregate of the
company's assets less the aggregate of its liabilities (" liabilities "
to include any provision for liabilities or charges within paragraph 89 of Schedule 4).

(3) A company's undistributable reserves are—
    (*a*) the share premium account,
    (*b*) the capital redemption reserve,
    (*c*) the amount by which the company's accumulated, un-
        realised profits, so far as not previously utilised by
        capitalisation of a description to which this paragraph
        applies, exceed its accumulated, unrealised losses (so
        far as not previously written off in a reduction or
        reorganisation of capital duly made), and
    (*d*) any other reserve which the company is prohibited
        from distributing by any enactment (other than one
        contained in this Part) or by its memorandum or
        articles ;

and paragraph (*c*) applies to every description of capitalisation except a transfer of profits of the company to its capital
redemption reserve on or after 22nd December 1980.

(4) A public company shall not include any uncalled share
capital as an asset in any accounts relevant for purposes of
this section.

265.—(1) Subject to the following provisions of this section, an investment company (defined in section 266) may also make a distribution at any time out of its accumulated, realised revenue profits, so far as not previously utilised by distribution or capitalisation, less its accumulated revenue losses (whether realised or unrealised), so far as not previously written off in a reduction or reorganisation of capital duly made—

(a) if at that time the amount of its assets is at least equal to one and a half times the aggregate of its liabilities, and

(b) if, and to the extent that, the distribution does not reduce that amount to less than one and a half times that aggregate.

(2) In subsection (1)(a), " liabilities " includes any provision for liabilities or charges (within the meaning of paragraph 89 of Schedule 4).

(3) The company shall not include any uncalled share capital as an asset in any accounts relevant for purposes of this section.

(4) An investment company may not make a distribution by virtue of subsection (1) unless—

(a) its shares are listed on a recognised stock exchange, and

(b) during the relevant period it has not—

(i) distributed any of its capital profits, or

(ii) applied any unrealised profits or any capital profits (realised or unrealised) in paying up debentures or amounts unpaid on its issued shares.

(5) The " relevant period " under subsection (4) is the period beginning with—

(a) the first day of the accounting reference period immediately preceding that in which the proposed distribution is to be made, or

(b) where the distribution is to be made in the company's first accounting reference period, the first day of that period,

and ending with the date of the distribution.

(6) An investment company may not make a distribution by virtue of subsection (1) unless the company gave to the registrar of companies the requisite notice (that is, notice under section 266(1)) of the company's intention to carry on business as an investment company—

(a) before the beginning of the relevant period under subsection (4), or

(*b*) in the case of a company incorporated on or after 22nd   PART VIII
December 1980, as soon as may have been reasonably
practicable after the date of its incorporation.

266.—(1) In section 265 "investment company" means a   Meaning of
public company which has given notice in the prescribed form   "investment
(which has not been revoked) to the registrar of companies of   company".
its intention to carry on business as an investment company,
and has since the date of that notice complied with the requirements specified below.

(2) Those requirements are—

(*a*) that the business of the company consists of investing
its funds mainly in securities, with the aim of spreading
investment risk and giving members of the company
the benefit of the results of the management of its
funds,

(*b*) that none of the company's holdings in companies
(other than those which are for the time being in investment companies) represents more than 15 per cent. by
value of the investing company's investments,

(*c*) that distribution of the company's capital profits is prohibited by its memorandum or articles of association,

(*d*) that the company has not retained, otherwise than in
compliance with this Part, in respect of any accounting
reference period more than 15 per cent. of the income
it derives from securities.

(3) Notice to the registrar of companies under subsection (1)
may be revoked at any time by the company on giving notice in
the prescribed form to the registrar that it no longer wishes to
be an investment company within the meaning of this section;
and, on giving such notice, the company ceases to be such a
company.

(4) Section 359(2) and (3) of the Income and Corporation   1970 c. 10.
Taxes Act 1970 and section 93(6)(*b*) of the Finance Act 1972   1972 c. 41.
apply for purposes of subsection (2)(*b*) as for those of section
359(1)(*b*) of the Act first mentioned.

267.—(1) The Secretary of State may by regulations in a   Extension of
statutory instrument extend the provisions of sections 265 and   ss. 265, 266
266 (with or without modifications) to companies whose princi-   to other
pal business consists of investing their funds in securities, land or   companies.
other assets with the aim of spreading investment risk and giving
their members the benefit of the results of the management of
the assets.

(2) Regulations under this section—

    (*a*) may make different provision for different classes of companies and may contain such transitional and supplemental provisions as the Secretary of State considers necessary, and

    (*b*) shall not be made unless a draft of the statutory instrument containing them has been laid before Parliament and approved by a resolution of each House.

Realised
profits of
insurance
company with
long term
business.
1982 c. 50.

268.—(1) Where an insurance company to which Part II of the Insurance Companies Act 1982 applies carries on long term business—

    (*a*) any amount properly transferred to the profit and loss account of the company from a surplus in the fund or funds maintained by it in respect of that business, and

    (*b*) any deficit in that fund or those funds,

are to be (respectively) treated, for purposes of this Part, as a realised profit and a realised loss ; and, subject to this, any profit or loss arising in that business is to be left out of account for those purposes.

(2) In subsection (1)—

    (*a*) the reference to a surplus in any fund or funds of an insurance company is to an excess of the assets representing that fund or those funds over the liabilities of the company attributable to its long term business, as shown by an actuarial investigation, and

    (*b*) the reference to a deficit in any such fund or funds is to the excess of those liabilities over those assets, as so shown.

(3) In this section—

    (*a*) " actuarial investigation " means an investigation to which section 18 of the Insurance Companies Act 1982 (periodic actuarial investigation of company with long term business) applies or which is made in pursuance of a requirement imposed by section 42 of that Act (actuarial investigation required by Secretary of State) ; and

    (*b*) " long term business " has the same meaning as in that Act.

Treatment of
development
costs.

269.—(1) Subject as follows, where development costs are shown as an asset in a company's accounts, any amount shown in respect of those costs is to be treated—

    (*a*) under section 263, as a realised loss, and

    (*b*) under section 265, as a realised revenue loss.

(2) This does not apply to any part of that amount representing an unrealised profit made on revaluation of those costs ; nor does it apply if—

> (a) there are special circumstances in the company's case justifying the directors in deciding that the amount there mentioned is not to be treated as required by subsection (1), and

> (b) the note to the accounts required by paragraph 20 of Schedule 4 (reasons for showing development costs as an asset) states that the amount is not to be so treated and explains the circumstances relied upon to justify the decision of the directors to that effect.

Relevant accounts

270.—(1) This section and sections 271 to 276 below are for determining the question whether a distribution may be made by a company without contravening sections 263, 264 or 265.

Distribution to be justified by reference to company's accounts.

(2) The amount of a distribution which may be made is determined by reference to the following items as stated in the company's accounts—

> (a) profits, losses, assets and liabilities,

> (b) provisions of any of the kinds mentioned in paragraphs 88 and 89 of Schedule 4 (depreciation, diminution in value of assets, retentions to meet liabilities, etc.), and

> (c) share capital and reserves (including undistributable reserves).

(3) Except in a case falling within the next subsection, the company's accounts which are relevant for this purpose are its last annual accounts, that is to say those prepared under Part VII which were laid in respect of the last preceding accounting reference period in respect of which accounts so prepared were laid ; and for this purpose accounts are laid if section 241 (1) has been complied with in relation to them.

(4) In the following two cases—

> (a) where the distribution would be found to contravene the relevant section if reference were made only to the company's last annual accounts, or

> (b) where the distribution is proposed to be declared during the company's first accounting reference period, or before any accounts are laid in respect of that period,

the accounts relevant under this section (called "interim accounts" in the first case, and "initial accounts" in the second) are those necessary to enable a reasonable judgment to be made as to the amounts of the items mentioned in subsection (2) above.

(5) The relevant section is treated as contravened in the case of a distribution unless the statutory requirements about the relevant accounts (that is, the requirements of this and the following three sections, as and where applicable) are complied with in relation to that distribution.

Requirements for last annual accounts.

271.—(1) If the company's last annual accounts constitute the only accounts relevant under section 270, the statutory requirements in respect of them are as follows.

(2) The accounts must have been properly prepared in accordance with this Act, or have been so prepared subject only to matters which are not material for determining, by reference to items mentioned in section 270(2), whether the distribution would contravene the relevant section ; and, without prejudice to the foregoing—

> (a) so much of the accounts as consists of a balance sheet must give a true and fair view of the state of the company's affairs as at the balance sheet date, and
>
> (b) so much of the accounts as consists of a profit and loss account must give a true and fair view of the company's profit or loss for the period in respect of which the accounts were prepared.

(3) The auditors must have made their report on the accounts under section 236 ; and the following subsection applies if the report is a qualified report, that is to say, it is not a report without qualification to the effect that in the auditors' opinion the accounts have been properly prepared in accordance with this Act.

(4) The auditors must in that case also have stated in writing (either at the time of their report or subsequently) whether, in their opinion, the matter in respect of which their report is qualified is material for determining, by reference to items mentioned in section 270(2), whether the distribution would contravene the relevant section ; and a copy of the statement must have been laid before the company in general meeting.

(5) A statement under subsection (4) suffices for purposes of a particular distribution not only if it relates to a distribution which has been proposed but also if it relates to distributions of any description which includes that particular distribution, notwithstanding that at the time of the statement it has not been proposed.

Requirements for interim accounts.

272.—(1) The following are the statutory requirements in respect of interim accounts prepared for a proposed distribution by a public company.

(2) The accounts must have been properly prepared, or have been so prepared subject only to matters which are not material

for determining, by reference to items mentioned in section 270(2), whether the proposed distribution would contravene the relevant section.

(3) " Properly prepared " means that the accounts must comply with section 228 (applying that section and Schedule 4 with such modifications as are necessary because the accounts are prepared otherwise than in respect of an accounting reference period) and any balance sheet comprised in the accounts must have been signed in accordance with section 238 ; and, without prejudice to the foregoing—

    (*a*) so much of the accounts as consists of a balance sheet must give a true and fair view of the state of the company's affairs as at the balance sheet date, and

    (*b*) so much of the accounts as consists of a profit and loss account must give a true and fair view of the company's profit or loss for the period in respect of which the accounts were prepared.

(4) A copy of the accounts must have been delivered to the registrar of companies.

(5) If the accounts are in a language other than English and section 241(3)(*b*) (translation) does not apply, a translation into English of the accounts, certified in the prescribed manner to be a correct translation, must also have been delivered to the registrar.

273.—(1) The following are the statutory requirements in respect of initial accounts prepared for a proposed distribution by a public company. *Requirements for initial accounts.*

(2) The accounts must have been properly prepared, or they must have been so prepared subject only to matters which are not material for determining, by reference to items mentioned in section 270(2), whether the proposed distribution would contravene the relevant section.

(3) Section 272(3) applies as respects the meaning of " properly prepared ".

(4) The company's auditors must have made a report stating whether, in their opinion, the accounts have been properly prepared ; and the following subsection applies if their report is a qualified report, that is to say it is not a report without qualification to the effect that in the auditors' opinion the accounts have been so prepared.

(5) The auditors must in that case also have stated in writing whether, in their opinion, the matter in respect of which their report is qualified is material for determining, by reference to

items mentioned in section 270(2), whether the distribution would contravene the relevant section.

(6) A copy of the accounts, of the auditors' report under subsection (4) and of the auditors' statement (if any) under subsection (5) must have been delivered to the registrar of companies.

(7) If the accounts are, or the auditors' report under subsection (4) or their statement (if any) under subsection (5) is, in a language other than English and section 241(3)(b) (translation) does not apply, a translation into English of the accounts, the report or the statement (as the case may be), certified in the prescribed manner to be a correct translation, must also have been delivered to the registrar.

Method of
applying s. 270
to successive
distributions.

274.—(1) For the purpose of determining by reference to particular accounts whether a proposed distribution may be made by a company, section 270 has effect, in a case where one or more distributions have already been made in pursuance of determinations made by reference to those same accounts, as if the amount of the proposed distribution was increased by the amount of the distributions so made.

(2) Subsection (1) of this section applies (if it would not otherwise do so) to—

(a) financial assistance lawfully given by a public company out of its distributable profits in a case where the assistance is required to be so given by section 154,

(b) financial assistance lawfully given by a private company out of its distributable profits in a case where the assistance is required to be so given by section 155(2),

(c) financial assistance given by a company in contravention of section 151, in a case where the giving of that assistance reduces the company's net assets or increases its net liabilities,

(d) a payment made by a company in respect of the purchase by it of shares in the company (except a payment lawfully made otherwise than out of distributable profits), and

(e) a payment of any description specified in section 168 (company's purchase of right to acquire its own shares, etc.),

being financial assistance given or payment made since the relevant accounts were prepared, as if any such financial assistance or payment were a distribution already made in pursuance of a determination made by reference to those accounts.

(3) In this section the following definitions apply—

" financial assistance " means the same as in Chapter VI of Part V ;

" net assets " has the meaning given by section 154(2)(*a*) ;
and

" net liabilities ", in relation to the giving of financial assistance by a company, means the amount by which the
aggregate amount of the company's liabilities (within
the meaning of section 154(2)(*b*)) exceeds the aggregate amount of its assets, taking the amount of the
assets and liabilities to be as stated in the company's
accounting records immediately before the financial
assistance is given.

(4) Subsections (2) and (3) of this section are deemed to be
included in Chapter VII of Part V for purposes of the Secretary
of State's power to make regulations under section 179.

275.—(1) For purposes of sections 263 and 264, a provision
of any kind mentioned in paragraphs 88 and 89 of Schedule 4,
other than one in respect of a diminution in value of a fixed
asset appearing on a revaluation of all the fixed assets of the
company, or of all of its fixed assets other than goodwill, is
treated as a realised loss.

(2) If, on the revaluation of a fixed asset, an unrealised profit
is shown to have been made and, on or after the revaluation, a
sum is written off or retained for depreciation of that asset over
a period, then an amount equal to the amount by which that
sum exceeds the sum which would have been so written off or
retained for the depreciation of that asset over that period, if
that profit had not been made, is treated for purposes of sections
263 and 264 as a realised profit made over that period.

(3) Where there is no record of the original cost of an asset,
or a record cannot be obtained without unreasonable expense
or delay, then for the purpose of determining whether the company has made a profit or loss in respect of that asset, its cost
is taken to be the value ascribed to it in the earliest available
record of its value made on or after its acquisition by the company.

(4) Subject to subsection (6), any consideration by the directors
of the value at a particular time of a fixed asset is treated as a
revaluation of the asset for the purposes of determining whether
any such revaluation of the company's fixed assets as is required
for purposes of the exception from subsection (1) has taken place
at that time.

(5) But where any such assets which have not actually been
revalued are treated as revalued for those purposes under subsection (4), that exception applies only if the directors are
satisfied that their aggregate value at the time in question is

not less than the aggregate amount at which they are for the time being stated in the company's accounts.

(6) Where section 271(2), 272(2) or 273(2) applies to the relevant accounts, subsections (4) and (5) above do not apply for the purpose of determining whether a revaluation of the company's fixed assets affecting the amount of the relevant items (that is, the items mentioned in section 270(2)) as stated in those accounts has taken place, unless it is stated in a note to the accounts—

(*a*) that the directors have considered the value at any time of any fixed assets of the company, without actually revaluing those assets,

(*b*) that they are satisfied that the aggregate value of those assets at the time in question is or was not less than the aggregate amount at which they are or were for the time being stated in the company's accounts, and

(*c*) that the relevant items in question are accordingly stated in the relevant accounts on the basis that a revaluation of the company's fixed assets which by virtue of subsections (4) and (5) included the assets in question took place at that time.

Distributions in kind. **276.** Where a company makes a distribution of or including a non-cash asset, and any part of the amount at which that asset is stated in the accounts relevant for the purposes of the distribution in accordance with sections 270 to 275 represents an unrealised profit, that profit is to be treated as a realised profit—

(*a*) for the purpose of determining the lawfulness of the distribution in accordance with this Part (whether before or after the distribution takes place), and

(*b*) for the purpose of the application of paragraphs 12(*a*) and 34(4)(*b*) of Schedule 4 (only realised profits to be included in or transferred to the profit and loss account) in relation to anything done with a view to or in connection with the making of that distribution.

Supplementary

Consequences of unlawful distribution. **277.**—(1) Where a distribution, or part of one, made by a company to one of its members is made in contravention of this Part and, at the time of the distribution, he knows or has reasonable grounds for believing that it is so made, he is liable to repay it (or that part of it, as the case may be) to the company or (in the case of a distribution made otherwise than in cash) to pay the company a sum equal to the value of the distribution (or part) at that time.

(2) The above is without prejudice to any obligation imposed apart from this section on a member of a company to repay a

distribution unlawfully made to him ; but this section does not apply in relation to—

    (*a*) financial assistance given by a company in contravention of section 151, or

    (*b*) any payment made by a company in respect of the redemption or purchase by the company of shares in itself.

(3) Subsection (2) of this section is deemed included in Chapter VII of Part V for purposes of the Secretary of State's power to make regulations under section 179.

278. Where immediately before 22nd December 1980 a company was authorised by a provision of its articles to apply its unrealised profits in paying up in full or in part unissued shares to be allotted to members of the company as fully or partly paid bonus shares, that provision continues (subject to any alteration of the articles) as authority for those profits to be so applied after that date.

Saving for provision in articles operative before Act of 1980.

279. Where a company's accounts relevant for the purposes of this Part are special category, sections 265 to 275 apply with the modifications shown in Schedule 11.

Distributions by special category companies.

280.—(1) The following has effect for the interpretation of this Part.

Definitions for Part VIII.

(2) " Capitalisation ", in relation to a company's profits, means any of the following operations (whenever carried out)—

    (*a*) applying the profits in wholly or partly paying up unissued shares in the company to be allotted to members of the company as fully or partly paid bonus shares, or

    (*b*) transferring the profits to capital redemption reserve.

(3) References to profits and losses of any description are (respectively) to profits and losses of that description made at any time and, except where the context otherwise requires, are (respectively) to revenue and capital profits and revenue and capital losses.

281. The provisions of this Part are without prejudice to any enactment or rule of law, or any provision of a company's memorandum or articles, restricting the sums out of which, or the cases in which, a distribution may be made.

Saving for other restraints on distribution.

PART IX

A COMPANY'S MANAGEMENT; DIRECTORS AND SECRETARIES; THEIR QUALIFICATIONS, DUTIES AND RESPONSIBILITIES

Officers and registered office

Directors.

282.—(1) Every company registered on or after 1st November 1929 (other than a private company) shall have at least two directors.

(2) Every company registered before that date (other than a private company) shall have at least one director.

(3) Every private company shall have at least one director.

Secretary.

283.—(1) Every company shall have a secretary.

(2) A sole director shall not also be secretary.

(3) Anything required or authorised to be done by or to the secretary may, if the office is vacant or there is for any other reason no secretary capable of acting, be done by or to any assistant or deputy secretary or, if there is no assistant or deputy secretary capable of acting, by or to any officer of the company authorised generally or specially in that behalf by the directors.

(4) No company shall—

    (*a*) have as secretary to the company a corporation the sole director of which is a sole director of the company;

    (*b*) have as sole director of the company a corporation the sole director of which is secretary to the company.

Acts done by person in dual capacity.

284. A provision requiring or authorising a thing to be done by or to a director and the secretary is not satisfied by its being done by or to the same person acting both as director and as, or in place of, the secretary.

Validity of acts of directors.

285. The acts of a director or manager are valid notwithstanding any defect that may afterwards be discovered in his appointment or qualification; and this provision is not excluded by section 292(2) (void resolution to appoint).

Qualifications of company secretaries.

286.—(1) It is the duty of the directors of a public company to take all reasonable steps to secure that the secretary (or each joint secretary) of the company is a person who appears to them to have the requisite knowledge and experience to discharge the functions of secretary of the company and who—

    (*a*) on 22nd December 1980 held the office of secretary or assistant or deputy secretary of the company; or

(b) for at least 3 of the 5 years immediately preceding his appointment as secretary held the office of secretary of a company other than a private company ; or

(c) is a member of any of the bodies specified in the following subsection ; or

(d) is a barrister, advocate or solicitor called or admitted in any part of the United Kingdom ; or

(e) is a person who, by virtue of his holding or having held any other position or his being a member of any other body, appears to the directors to be capable of discharging those functions.

(2) The bodies referred to in subsection (1)(c) are—

(a) the Institute of Chartered Accountants in England and Wales ;

(b) the Institute of Chartered Accountants of Scotland ;

(c) the Chartered Association of Certified Accountants ;

(d) the Institute of Chartered Accountants in Ireland ;

(e) the Institute of Chartered Secretaries and Administrators ;

(f) the Institute of Cost and Management Accountants ;

(g) the Chartered Institute of Public Finance and Accountancy.

287.—(1) A company shall at all times have a registered office Registered to which all communications and notices may be addressed. office.

(2) Notice (in the prescribed form) of any change in the situation of a company's registered office shall be given within 14 days of the change to the registrar of companies, who shall record the new situation.

(3) If default is made in complying with subsection (1) or (2), the company and every officer of it who is in default is liable to a fine and, for continued contravention, to a daily default fine.

288.—(1) Every company shall keep at its registered office a Register of register of its directors and secretaries ; and the register shall, directors and with respect to the particulars to be contained in it of those secretaries. persons, comply with sections 289 and 290 below.

(2) The company shall, within the period of 14 days from the occurrence of—

(a) any change among its directors or in its secretary, or

(b) any change in the particulars contained in the register,

send to the registrar of companies a notification in the prescribed form of the change and of the date on which it occurred ; and a

H

notification of a person having become a director or secretary, or one of joint secretaries, of the company shall contain a consent, signed by that person, to act in the relevant capacity.

(3) The register shall during business hours (subject to such reasonable restrictions as the company may by its articles or in general meeting impose, so that not less than 2 hours in each day be allowed for inspection) be open to the inspection of any member of the company without charge and of any other person on payment of 5 pence or such less sum as the company may prescribe, for each inspection.

(4) If an inspection required under this section is refused, or if default is made in complying with subsection (1) or (2), the company and every officer of it who is in default is liable to a fine and, for continued contravention, to a daily default fine.

(5) In the case of a refusal of inspection of the register, the court may by order compel an immediate inspection of it.

(6) For purposes of this and the next section, a shadow director of a company is deemed a director and officer of it.

Particulars of directors to be registered under s. 288.

289.—(1) Subject to the provisions of this section, the register kept by a company under section 288 shall contain the following particulars with respect to each director—

(*a*) in the case of an individual—

(i) his present Christian name and surname,

(ii) any former Christian name or surname,

(iii) his usual residential address,

(iv) his nationality,

(v) his business occupation (if any),

(vi) particulars of any other directorships held by him or which have been held by him, and

(vii) in the case of a company subject to section 293 (age-limit), the date of his birth ;

(*b*) in the case of a corporation, its corporate name and registered or principal office.

(2) In subsection (1)—

(*a*) " Christian name " includes a forename,

(*b*) " surname ", in the case of a peer or a person usually known by a title different from his surname, means that title, and

(*c*) the reference to a former Christian name or surname does not include—

(i) in the case of a peer or a person usually known by a British title different from his surname, the

name by which he was known previous to the   Part IX
adoption of or succession to the title, or

(ii) in the case of any person, a former Christian
name or surname where that name or surname was
changed or disused before the person bearing the
name attained the age of 18, or has been changed
or disused for a period of not less than 20 years, or

(iii) in the case of a married woman, the name
or surname by which she was known previous to the
marriage.

(3) It is not necessary for the register to contain on any day
particulars of a directorship—

    (a) which has not been held by a director at any time during
the 5 years preceding that day,

    (b) which is held by a director in a company which—

(i) is dormant or grouped with the company keeping the register, and

(ii) if he also held that directorship for any period
during those 5 years, was for the whole of that
period either dormant or so grouped,

    (c) which was held by a director for any period during those
5 years in a company which for the whole of that
period was either dormant or grouped with the company keeping the register.

(4) For purposes of subsection (3), "company" includes any
body corporate incorporated in Great Britain ; and—

    (a) section 252(5) applies as regards whether and when a
company is or has been dormant, and

    (b) a company is to be regarded as being, or having been,
grouped with another at any time if at that time it
is or was a company of which the other is or was
a wholly-owned subsidiary, or if it is or was a wholly-
owned subsidiary of the other or of another company of which that other is or was a wholly-owned
subsidiary.

290.—(1) The register to be kept by a company under sec- Particulars of
tion 288 shall contain the following particulars with respect secretaries to
to the secretary or, where there are joint secretaries, with respect be registered
to each of them— under s. 288.

    (a) in the case of an individual, his present Christian name
and surname, any former Christian name or surname
and his usual residential address, and

    (b) in the case of a corporation or a Scottish firm, its
corporate or firm name and registered or principal
office.

PART IX

(2) Where all the partners in a firm are joint secretaries, the name and principal office of the firm may be stated instead of the particulars specified above.

(3) Section 289(2) applies as regards the meaning of " Christian name ", " surname " and " former Christian name or surname ".

Provisions governing appointment of directors

Share qualification of directors.

291.—(1) It is the duty of every director who is by the company's articles required to hold a specified share qualification, and who is not already qualified, to obtain his qualification within 2 months after his appointment, or such shorter time as may be fixed by the articles.

(2) For the purpose of any provision of the articles requiring a director or manager to hold any specified share qualification, the bearer of a share warrant is not deemed the holder of the shares specified in the warrant.

(3) The office of director of a company is vacated if the director does not within 2 months from the date of his appointment (or within such shorter time as may be fixed by the articles) obtain his qualification, or if after the expiration of that period or shorter time he ceases at any time to hold his qualification.

(4) A person vacating office under this section is incapable of being reappointed to be a director of the company until he has obtained his qualification.

(5) If after the expiration of that period or shorter time any unqualified person acts as a director of the company, he is liable to a fine and, for continued contravention, to a daily default fine.

Appointment of directors to be voted on individually.

292.—(1) At a general meeting of a public company, a motion for the appointment of two or more persons as directors of the company by a single resolution shall not be made, unless a resolution that it shall be so made has first been agreed to by the meeting without any vote being given against it.

(2) A resolution moved in contravention of this section is void, whether or not its being so moved was objected to at the time; but where a resolution so moved is passed, no provision for the automatic reappointment of retiring directors in default of another appointment applies.

(3) For purposes of this section, a motion for approving a person's appointment, or for nominating a person for appointment, is to be treated as a motion for his appointment.

(4) Nothing in this section applies to a resolution altering the company's articles.

293.—(1) A company is subject to this section if— PART IX

   (*a*) it is a public company, or Age limit for
directors.

   (*b*) being a private company, it is a subsidiary of a public company or of a body corporate registered under the law relating to companies for the time being in force in Northern Ireland as a public company.

(2) No person is capable of being appointed a director of a company which is subject to this section if at the time of his appointment he has attained the age of 70.

(3) A director of such a company shall vacate his office at the conclusion of the annual general meeting commencing next after he attains the age of 70 ; but acts done by a person as director are valid notwithstanding that it is afterwards discovered that his appointment had terminated under this subsection.

(4) Where a person retires under subsection (3), no provision for the automatic reappointment of retiring directors in default of another appointment applies ; and if at the meeting at which he retires the vacancy is not filled, it may be filled as a casual vacancy.

(5) Nothing in subsections (2) to (4) prevents the appointment of a director at any age, or requires a director to retire at any time, if his appointment is or was made or approved by the company in general meeting ; but special notice is required of a resolution appointing or approving the appointment of a director for it to have effect under this subsection, and the notice of the resolution given to the company, and by the company to its members, must state, or have stated, the age of the person to whom it relates.

(6) A person reappointed director on retiring under subsection (3), or appointed in place of a director so retiring, is to be treated, for the purpose of determining the time at which he or any other director is to retire, as if he had become director on the day on which the retiring director was last appointed before his retirement.

Subject to this, the retirement of a director out of turn under subsection (3) is to be disregarded in determining when any other directors are to retire.

(7) In the case of a company first registered after the beginning of 1947, this section has effect subject to the provisions of the company's articles ; and in the case of a company first registered before the beginning of that year—

   (*a*) this section has effect subject to any alterations of the company's articles made after the beginning of that year ; and

(b) if at the beginning of that year the company's articles contained provision for retirement of directors under an age limit, or for preventing or restricting appointments of directors over a given age, this section does not apply to directors to whom that provision applies.

Duty of director to disclose his age.
294.—(1) A person who is appointed or to his knowledge proposed to be appointed director of a company subject to section 293 at a time when he has attained any retiring age applicable to him under that section or under the company's articles shall give notice of his age to the company.

(2) For purposes of this section, a company is deemed subject to section 293 notwithstanding that all or any of the section's provisions are excluded or modified by the company's articles.

(3) Subsection (1) does not apply in relation to a person's reappointment on the termination of a previous appointment as director of the company.

(4) A person who—

(a) fails to give notice of his age as required by this section ; or

(b) acts as director under any appointment which is invalid or has terminated by reason of his age,

is liable to a fine and, for continued contravention, to a daily default fine.

(5) For purposes of subsection (4), a person who has acted as director under an appointment which is invalid or has terminated is deemed to have continued so to act throughout the period from the invalid appointment or the date on which the appointment terminated (as the case may be), until the last day on which he is shown to have acted thereunder.

Disqualification

Disqualification orders: introductory.
295.—(1) In the circumstances specified in sections 296 to 300, a court may make against a person a disqualification order, that is to say an order that he shall not, without leave of the court—

(a) be a director of a company, or

(b) be a liquidator of a company, or

(c) be a receiver or manager of a company's property, or

(d) in any way, whether directly or indirectly, be concerned or take part in the promotion, formation or management of a company,

for a specified period beginning with the date of the order.

(2) The maximum period to be so specified is—

(a) in the case of an order made under section 297 or

made by a court of summary jurisdiction, 5 years,
and

(*b*) in any other case, 15 years.

(3) In this section and sections 296 to 300, " company " includes any company which may be wound up under Part XXI.

(4) A disqualification order may be made on grounds which are or include matters other than criminal convictions, notwithstanding that the person in respect of whom it is to be made may be criminally liable in respect of those matters.

(5) In sections 296 to 299, any reference to provisions, or to a particular provision, of this Act or the Consequential Provisions Act includes the corresponding provision or provisions of the former Companies Acts.

(6) Parts I and II of Schedule 12 have effect with regard to the procedure for obtaining a disqualification order, and to applications for leave under such an order ; and Part III of that Schedule has effect—

(*a*) in connection with certain transitional cases arising under sections 93 and 94 of the Companies Act 1981, 1981 c. 62. so as to limit the power to make a disqualification order, or to restrict the duration of an order, by reference to events occurring or things done before those sections came into force, and

(*b*) to preserve orders made under section 28 of the Com- 1976 c. 69. panies Act 1976 (repealed by the Act of 1981).

(7) If a person acts in contravention of a disqualification order, he is in respect of each offence liable to imprisonment or a fine, or both.

296.—(1) The court may make a disqualification order against Disqualifica-
a person where he is convicted of an indictable offence (whether tion on
on indictment or summarily) in connection with the promotion, conviction of
formation, management or liquidation of a company, or with indictable
the receivership or management of a company's property. offence.

(2) " The court " for this purpose means—

(*a*) any court having jurisdiction to wind up the company in relation to which the offence was committed, or

(*b*) the court by or before which the person is convicted of the offence, or

(*c*) in the case of a summary conviction in England and Wales, any other magistrates' court acting for the same petty sessions area ;

and for purposes of this section the definition of " indictable offence " in Schedule 1 to the Interpretation Act 1978 applies 1978 c. 30. in relation to Scotland as it does in relation to England and Wales.

H 4

PART IX
Disqualification
for persistent
default under
Companies
Acts.

297.—(1) The court may make a disqualification order against a person where it appears to it that he has been persistently in default in relation to provisions of this Act or the Consequential Provisions Act requiring any return, account or other document to be filed with, delivered or sent, or notice of any matter to be given, to the registrar of companies.

(2) On an application to the court for an order to be made under this section, the fact that a person has been persistently in default in relation to such provisions as are mentioned above may (without prejudice to its proof in any other manner) be conclusively proved by showing that in the 5 years ending with the date of the application he has been adjudged guilty (whether or not on the same occasion) of three or more defaults in relation to those provisions.

(3) A person is treated under subsection (2) as being adjudged guilty of a default in relation to any such provision if—

(a) he is convicted (whether on indictment or summarily) of an offence consisting in a contravention of or failure to comply with that provision (whether on his own part or on the part of any company), or

(b) a default order is made against him, that is to say an order under—

(i) section 244 (order requiring delivery of company accounts), or

(ii) section 499 (enforcement of receiver's or manager's duty to make returns), or

(iii) section 636 (corresponding provision for liquidator in winding-up), or

(iv) section 713 (enforcement of company's duty to make returns),

in respect of any such contravention of or failure to comply with that provision (whether on his own part or on the part of any company).

(4) In this section " the court " means any court having jurisdiction to wind up any of the companies in relation to which the offence or other default has been or is alleged to have been committed.

Disqualification for fraud,
etc. in
winding up.

298.—(1) The court may make a disqualification order against a person if, in the course of the winding up of a company, it appears that he—

(a) has been guilty of an offence for which he is liable (whether he has been convicted or not) under section 458 (fraudulent trading), or

(b) has otherwise been guilty, while an officer or liquidator of the company or receiver or manager of its property, of any fraud in relation to the company or of any

breach of his duty as such officer, liquidator, receiver PART IX
or manager.

(2) In this section " the court " means the same as in section
297 ; and " officer " includes a shadow director.

299.—(1) An offence counting for the purposes of this section Disqualifica-
is one of which a person is convicted (either on indictment or tion on
summarily) in consequence of a contravention of, or failure to summary
comply with, any provision of this Act or the Consequential conviction.
Provisions Act requiring a return, account or other document
to be filed with, delivered or sent, or notice of any matter to
be given, to the registrar of companies (whether the contravention or failure is on the person's own part or on the part
of any company).

(2) Where a person is convicted of a summary offence counting
for those purposes, the court by which he is convicted (or, in
England and Wales, any other magistrates' court acting for
the same petty sessions area) may make a disqualification order
against him if the circumstances specified in the next subsection
are present.

(3) Those circumstances are that, during the 5 years ending
with the date of the conviction, the person has had made against
him, or has been convicted of, in total not less than 3 default
orders and offences counting for the purposes of this section ;
and those offences may include that of which he is convicted
as mentioned in subsection (2) and any other offence of which
he is convicted on the same occasion.

(4) For the purposes of this section—

(a) the definition of " summary offence " in Schedule 1
    to the Interpretation Act 1978 applies for Scotland 1978 c. 30.
    as for England and Wales, and

(b) " default order " means the same as in section 297
    (3)(b).

300.—(1) The court may make a disqualification order against Disqualifica-
a person where, on an application under this section, it appears tion by
to it that he— reference to
                                                                   association
(a) is or has been a director of a company which has at with insolvent
    any time gone into liquidation (whether while he was companies.
    a director or subsequently) and was insolvent at that
    time, and

(b) is or has been a director of another such company
    which has gone into liquidation within 5 years of the

date on which the first-mentioned company went into liquidation,

and that his conduct as director of any of those companies makes him unfit to be concerned in the management of a company.

(2) In the case of a person who is or has been a director of a company which has gone into liquidation as above-mentioned and is being wound up by the court, " the court " in subsection (1) means the court by which the company is being wound up ; and in any other case it means the High Court or, in Scotland, the Court of Session.

(3) The Secretary of State may require the liquidator or former liquidator of a company—

(a) to furnish him with such information with respect to the company's affairs, and

(b) to produce and permit inspection of such books or documents of or relevant to the company,

as the Secretary of State may reasonably require for the purpose of determining whether to make an application under this section in respect of a person who is or has been a director of that company ; and if a person makes default in complying with such a requirement, the court may, on the Secretary of State's application, make an order requiring that person to make good the default within such time as may be specified.

(4) For purposes of this section, a shadow director of a company is deemed a director of it ; and a company goes into liquidation—

(a) if it is wound up by the court, on the date of the winding-up order, and

(b) in any other case, on the date of the passing of the resolution for voluntary winding up.

Register of disqualification orders.
301.—(1) The Secretary of State may make regulations requiring officers of courts to furnish him with such particulars as the regulations may specify of cases in which—

(a) a disqualification order is made under any of sections 296 to 300, or

(b) any action is taken by a court in consequence of which such an order is varied or ceases to be in force, or

(c) leave is granted by a court for a person subject to such an order to do any thing which otherwise the order prohibits him from doing ;

and the regulations may specify the time within which, and the form and manner in which, such particulars are to be furnished.

(2) The Secretary of State shall, from the particulars so furnished, continue to maintain the register of orders, and of cases in which leave has been granted as mentioned in subsection (1)(*c*), which was set up by him under section 29 of the Com- 1976 c. 69. panies Act 1976.

(3) When an order of which entry is made in the register ceases to be in force, the Secretary of State shall delete the entry from the register and all particulars relating to it which have been furnished to him under this section.

(4) The register shall be open to inspection on payment of such fee as may be specified by the Secretary of State in regulations.

(5) Regulations under this section shall be made by statutory instrument subject to annulment in pursuance of a resolution of either House of Parliament.

302.—(1) If any person being an undischarged bankrupt acts Provision as director or liquidator of, or directly or indirectly takes part in against or is concerned in the promotion, formation or management undischarged of, a company except with the leave of the court, he is liable acting as to imprisonment or a fine, or both. director, etc.

(2) " The court " for this purpose is the court by which the person was adjudged bankrupt or, in Scotland, sequestration of his estates was awarded.

(3) In England and Wales, the leave of the court shall not be given unless notice of intention to apply for it has been served on the official receiver in bankruptcy ; and it is the latter's duty, if he is of opinion that it is contrary to the public interest that the application should be granted, to attend on the hearing of the application and oppose it.

(4) In this section " company " includes an unregistered company and a company incorporated outside Great Britain which has an established place of business in Great Britain.

Removal of directors

303.—(1) A company may by ordinary resolution remove a Resolution director before the expiration of his period of office, notwith- to remove standing anything in its articles or in any agreement between it director. and him.

(2) Special notice is required of a resolution to remove a director under this section or to appoint somebody instead of a director so removed at the meeting at which he is removed.

(3) A vacancy created by the removal of a director under this section, if not filled at the meeting at which he is removed, may be filled as a casual vacancy.

(4) A person appointed director in place of a person removed under this section is treated, for the purpose of determining the time at which he or any other director is to retire, as if he had become director on the day on which the person in whose place he is appointed was last appointed a director.

(5) This section is not to be taken as depriving a person removed under it of compensation or damages payable to him in respect of the termination of his appointment as director or of any appointment terminating with that as director, or as derogating from any power to remove a director which may exist apart from this section.

Director's right to protest removal.

304.—(1) On receipt of notice of an intended resolution to remove a director under section 303, the company shall forthwith send a copy of the notice to the director concerned ; and he (whether or not a member of the company) is entitled to be heard on the resolution at the meeting.

(2) Where notice is given of an intended resolution to remove a director under that section, and the director concerned makes with respect to it representations in writing to the company (not exceeding a reasonable length) and requests their notification to members of the company, the company shall, unless the representations are received by it too late for it to do so—

    (a) in any notice of the resolution given to members of the company state the fact of the representations having been made ; and

    (b) send a copy of the representations to every member of the company to whom notice of the meeting is sent (whether before or after receipt of the representations by the company).

(3) If a copy of the representations is not sent as required by subsection (2) because received too late or because of the company's default, the director may (without prejudice to his right to be heard orally) require that the representations shall be read out at the meeting.

(4) But copies of the representations need not be sent out and the representations need not be read out at the meeting if, on the application either of the company or of any other person who claims to be aggrieved, the court is satisfied that the rights conferred by this section are being abused to secure needless publicity for defamatory matter.

(5) The court may order the company's costs on an application under this section to be paid in whole or in part by the
director, notwithstanding that he is not a party to the application.

Other provisions about directors and officers

305.—(1) A company to which this section applies shall not Directors'
state, in any form, the name of any of its directors (otherwise names on
than in the text or as a signatory) on any business letter on which company
the company's name appears unless it states on the letter in dence, etc.
legible characters the Christian name (or its initials) and surname of every director of the company who is an individual
and the corporate name of every corporate director.

(2) This section applies to—

    (a) every company registered under this Act or under the
        former Companies Acts (except a company registered
        before 23rd November 1916) ; and

    (b) every company incorporated outside Great Britain
        which has an established place of business within Great
        Britain, unless it had established such a place of
        business before that date.

(3) If a company makes default in complying with this section,
every officer of the company who is in default is liable for each
offence to a fine ; and for this purpose, where a corporation is
an officer of the company, any officer of the corporation is
deemed an officer of the company.

(4) For purposes of this section—

    (a) " director " includes shadow director, and " officer " is
        to be construed accordingly ;

    (b) " Christian name " includes a forename ;

    (c) " initials " includes a recognised abbreviation of a Chris-
        tian name ; and

    (d) in the case of a peer or a person usually known by a
        title different from his surname, " surname " means
        that title.

306.—(1) In the case of a limited company the liability of the Limited
directors or managers, or of the managing director, may, if so company may
provided by the memorandum, be unlimited. have directors
with

(2) In the case of a limited company in which the liability of unlimited
a director or manager is unlimited, the directors and any liability.
managers of the company and the member who proposes any
person for election or appointment to the office of director or
manager, shall add to that proposal a statement that the liability
of the person holding that office will be unlimited.

(3) Before the person accepts the office or acts in it, notice in writing that his liability will be unlimited shall be given to him by the following or one of the following persons, namely—

    (*a*) the promoters of the company,

    (*b*) the directors of the company,

    (*c*) any managers of the company,

    (*d*) the company secretary.

(4) If a director, manager or proposer makes default in adding such a statement, or if a promoter, director, manager or secretary makes default in giving the notice required by subsection (3), then—

    (*a*) he is liable to a fine, and

    (*b*) he is also liable for any damage which the person so elected or appointed may sustain from the default ;

but the liability of the person elected or appointed is not affected by the default.

Special resolution making liability of directors unlimited.

307.—(1) A limited company, if so authorised by its articles, may by special resolution alter its memorandum so as to render unlimited the liability of its directors or managers, or of any managing director.

(2) When such a special resolution is passed, its provisions are as valid as if they had been originally contained in the memorandum.

Assignment of office by directors.

308. If provision is made by a company's articles, or by any agreement entered into between any person and the company, for empowering a director or manager of the company to assign his office as such to another person, any assignment of office made in pursuance of that provision is (notwithstanding anything to the contrary contained in the provision) of no effect unless and until it is approved by a special resolution of the company.

Directors to have regard to interests of employees.

309.—(1) The matters to which the directors of a company are to have regard in the performance of their functions include the interests of the company's employees in general, as well as the interests of its members.

(2) Accordingly, the duty imposed by this section on the directors is owed by them to the company (and the company alone) and is enforceable in the same way as any other fiduciary duty owed to a company by its directors.

(3) This section applies to shadow directors as it does to directors.

310.—(1) This section applies to any provision, whether contained in a company's articles or in any contract with the com- Provisions
pany or otherwise, for exempting any officer of the company or exempting
any person (whether an officer or not) employed by the company officers and
as auditor from, or indemnifying him against, any liability which auditors from
by virtue of any rule of law would otherwise attach to him in liability.
respect of any negligence, default, breach of duty or breach
of trust of which he may be guilty in relation to the company.

(2) Except as provided by the following subsection, any such
provision is void.

(3) A company may, in pursuance of such a provision,
indemnify any such officer or auditor against any liability incurred by him in defending any proceedings (whether civil or
criminal) in which judgment is given in his favour or he is acquit-
ted, or in connection with any application under section 144(3)
or (4) (acquisition of shares by innocent nominee) or section
727 (director in default, but not dishonest or unreasonable), in
which relief is granted to him by the court.

PART X

ENFORCEMENT OF FAIR DEALING BY DIRECTORS

Restrictions on directors taking financial advantage

311.—(1) It is not lawful for a company to pay a director Prohibition
remuneration (whether as director or otherwise) free of income on tax-free
tax, or otherwise calculated by reference to or varying with the payments to
amount of his income tax, or to or with any rate of income directors.
tax.

(2) Any provision contained in a company's articles, or
in any contract, or in any resolution of a company or a company's directors, for payment to a director of remuneration as
above mentioned has effect as if it provided for payment, as a
gross sum subject to income tax, of the net sum for which it
actually provides.

312. It is not lawful for a company to make to a director of Payment to
the company any payment by way of compensation for loss of director for
office, or as consideration for or in connection with his retire- loss of office
ment from office, without particulars of the proposed payment etc.
(including its amount) being disclosed to members of the company and the proposal being approved by the company.

313.—(1) It is not lawful, in connection with the transfer of the whole or any part of the undertaking or property of a company, for any payment to be made to a director of the company by way of compensation for loss of office, or as consideration for or in connection with his retirement from office, unless particulars of the proposed payment (including its amount) have been disclosed to members of the company and the proposal approved by the company.

(2) Where a payment unlawful under this section is made to a director, the amount received is deemed to be received by him in trust for the company.

314.—(1) This section applies where, in connection with the transfer to any persons of all or any of the shares in a company, being a transfer resulting from—

    (*a*) an offer made to the general body of shareholders ; or

    (*b*) an offer made by or on behalf of some other body corporate with a view to the company becoming its subsidiary or a subsidiary of its holding company ; or

    (*c*) an offer made by or on behalf of an individual with a view to his obtaining the right to exercise or control the exercise of not less than one-third of the voting power at any general meeting of the company ; or

    (*d*) any other offer which is conditional on acceptance to a given extent,

a payment is to be made to a director of the company by way of compensation for loss of office, or as consideration for or in connection with his retirement from office.

(2) It is in those circumstances the director's duty to take all reasonable steps to secure that particulars of the proposed payment (including its amount) are included in or sent with any notice of the offer made for their shares which is given to any shareholders.

(3) If—

    (*a*) the director fails to take those steps, or

    (*b*) any person who has been properly required by the director to include those particulars in or send them with the notice required by subsection (2) fails to do so,

he is liable to a fine.

315.—(1) If in the case of any such payment to a director as is mentioned in section 314(1)—

    (*a*) his duty under that section is not complied with, or

    (*b*) the making of the proposed payment is not, before the transfer of any shares in pursuance of the offer, approved by a meeting (summoned for the purpose) of the holders of the shares to which the offer relates and of other holders of shares of the same class as any of those shares,

any sum received by the director on account of the payment is deemed to have been received by him in trust for persons who have sold their shares as a result of the offer made; and the expenses incurred by him in distributing that sum amongst those persons shall be borne by him and not retained out of that sum.

(2) Where—

   (a) the shareholders referred to in subsection (1)(b) are not all the members of the company, and

   (b) no provision is made by the articles for summoning or regulating the meeting referred to in that paragraph,

the provisions of this Act and of the company's articles relating to general meetings of the company apply (for that purpose) to the meeting either without modification or with such modifications as the Secretary of State on the application of any person concerned may direct for the purpose of adapting them to the circumstances of the meeting.

(3) If at a meeting summoned for the purpose of approving any payment as required by subsection (1)(b) a quorum is not present and, after the meeting has been adjourned to a later date, a quorum is again not present, the payment is deemed for the purposes of that subsection to have been approved.

316.—(1) Where in proceedings for the recovery of any payment as having, by virtue of section 313(2) or 315(1), been received by any person in trust, it is shown that— Provisions supplementing ss. 312 to 315.

   (a) the payment was made in pursuance of any arrangement entered into as part of the agreement for the transfer in question, or within one year before or two years after that agreement or the offer leading to it; and

   (b) the company or any person to whom the transfer was made was privy to that arrangement,

the payment is deemed, except in so far as the contrary is shown, to be one to which the provisions mentioned above in this subsection apply.

(2) If in connection with any such transfer as is mentioned in any of sections 313 to 315—

   (a) the price to be paid to a director of the company whose office is to be abolished or who is to retire from office for any shares in the company held by him is in excess of the price which could at the time have been obtained by other holders of the like shares ; or

(b) any valuable consideration is given to any such director,

the excess or the money value of the consideration (as the case may be) is deemed for the purposes of that section to have been a payment made to him by way of compensation for loss of office or as consideration for or in connection with his retirement from office.

(3) References in sections 312 to 315 to payments made to a director by way of compensation for loss of office or as consideration for or in connection with his retirement from office, do not include any bona fide payment by way of damages for breach of contract or by way of pension in respect of past services.

" Pension " here includes any superannuation allowance, superannuation gratuity or similar payment.

(4) Nothing in sections 313 to 315 prejudices the operation of any rule of law requiring disclosure to be made with respect to such payments as are there mentioned, or with respect to any other like payments made or to be made to a company's directors.

Directors to disclose interest in contracts.

317.—(1) It is the duty of a director of a company who is in any way, whether directly or indirectly, interested in a contract or proposed contract with the company to declare the nature of his interest at a meeting of the directors of the company.

(2) In the case of a proposed contract, the declaration shall be made—

(a) at the meeting of the directors at which the question of entering into the contract is first taken into consideration ; or

(b) if the director was not at the date of that meeting interested in the proposed contract, at the next meeting of the directors held after he became so interested ;

and, in a case where the director becomes interested in a contract after it is made, the declaration shall be made at the first meeting of the directors held after he becomes so interested.

(3) For purposes of this section, a general notice given to the directors of a company by a director to the effect that—

(a) he is a member of a specified company or firm and is to be regarded as interested in any contract which may, after the date of the notice, be made with that company or firm ; or

(b) he is to be regarded as interested in any contract which may after the date of the notice be made with a specified person who is connected with him (within the meaning of section 346 below),

is deemed a sufficient declaration of interest in relation to any such contract.

(4) However, no such notice is of effect unless either it is given at a meeting of the directors or the director takes reasonable steps to secure that it is brought up and read at the next meeting of the directors after it is given.

(5) A reference in this section to a contract includes any transaction or arrangement (whether or not constituting a contract) made or entered into on or after 22nd December 1980.

(6) For purposes of this section, a transaction or arrangement of a kind described in section 330 (prohibition of loans, quasi-loans etc. to directors) made by a company for a director of the company or a person connected with such a director is treated (if it would not otherwise be so treated, and whether or not it is prohibited by that section) as a transaction or arrangement in which that director is interested.

(7) A director who fails to comply with this section is liable to a fine.

(8) This section applies to a shadow director as it applies to a director, except that a shadow director shall declare his interest, not at a meeting of the directors, but by a notice in writing to the directors which is either—

> (*a*) a specific notice given before the date of the meeting at which, if he had been a director, the declaration would be required by subsection (2) to be made ; or

> (*b*) a notice which under subsection (3) falls to be treated as a sufficient declaration of that interest (or would fall to be so treated apart from subsection (4)).

(9) Nothing in this section prejudices the operation of any rule of law restricting directors of a company from having an interest in contracts with the company.

318.—(1) Subject to the following provisions, every company shall keep at an appropriate place— *Directors' service contracts to be open to inspection.*

> (*a*) in the case of each director whose contract of service with the company is in writing, a copy of that contract ;

> (*b*) in the case of each director whose contract of service with the company is not in writing, a written memorandum setting out its terms ; and

(*c*) in the case of each director who is employed under a contract of service with a subsidiary of the company, a copy of that contract or, if it is not in writing, a written memorandum setting out its terms.

(2) All copies and memoranda kept by a company in pursuance of subsection (1) shall be kept at the same place.

(3) The following are appropriate places for the purposes of subsection (1)—

    (*a*) the company's registered office ;

    (*b*) the place where its register of members is kept (if other than its registered office) ;

    (*c*) its principal place of business, provided that is situated in that part of Great Britain in which the company is registered.

(4) Every company shall send notice in the prescribed form to the registrar of companies of the place where copies and memoranda are kept in compliance with subsection (1), and of any change in that place, save in a case in which they have at all times been kept at the company's registered office.

(5) Subsection (1) does not apply to a director's contract of service with the company or with a subsidiary of it if that contract required him to work wholly or mainly outside the United Kingdom ; but the company shall keep a memorandum—

    (*a*) in the case of a contract of service with the company, giving the director's name and setting out the provisions of the contract relating to its duration ;

    (*b*) in the case of a contract of service with a subsidiary, giving the director's name and the name and place of incorporation of the subsidiary, and setting out the provisions of the contract relating to its duration,

at the same place as copies and memoranda are kept by the company in pursuance of subsection (1).

(6) A shadow director is treated for purposes of this section as a director.

(7) Every copy and memorandum required by subsection (1) or (5) to be kept shall, during business hours (subject to such reasonable restrictions as the company may in general meeting impose, so that not less than 2 hours in each day be allowed for inspection), be open to inspection of any member of the company without charge.

(8) If—

    (*a*) default is made in complying with subsection (1) or (5), or (*b*) an inspection required under subsection (7) is refused, or

(*c*) default is made for 14 days in complying with subsection (4),

the company and every officer of it who is in default is liable to a fine and, for continued contravention, to a daily default fine.

(9) In the case of a refusal of an inspection required under subsection (7) of a copy or memorandum, the court may by order compel an immediate inspection of it.

(10) Subsections (1) and (5) apply to a variation of a director's contract of service as they apply to the contract.

(11) This section does not require that there be kept a copy of, or memorandum setting out the terms of, a contract (or its variation) at a time when the unexpired portion of the term for which the contract is to be in force is less than 12 months, or at a time at which the contract can, within the next ensuing 12 months, be terminated by the company without payment of compensation.

319.—(1) This section applies in respect of any term of an agreement whereby a director's employment with the company of which he is a director or, where he is the director of a holding company, his employment within the group is to continue, or may be continued, otherwise than at the instance of the company (whether under the original agreement or under a new agreement entered into in pursuance of it), for a period of more than 5 years during which the employment— *Director's contract of employment for more than 5 years.*

(*a*) cannot be terminated by the company by notice ; or

(*b*) can be so terminated only in specified circumstances.

(2) In any case where—

(*a*) a person is or is to be employed with a company under an agreement which cannot be terminated by the company by notice or can be so terminated only in specified circumstances ; and

(*b*) more than 6 months before the expiration of the period for which he is or is to be so employed, the company enters into a further agreement (otherwise than in pursuance of a right conferred by or under the original agreement on the other party to it) under which he is to be employed with the company or, where he is a director of a holding company, within the group,

this section applies as if to the period for which he is to be employed under that further agreement there were added a further period equal to the unexpired period of the original agreement.

(3) A company shall not incorporate in an agreement such a term as is mentioned in subsection (1), unless the term is first approved by a resolution of the company in general meeting and, in the case of a director of a holding company, by a resolution of that company in general meeting.

(4) No approval is required to be given under this section by any body corporate unless it is a company within the meaning of this Act, or is registered under section 680, or if it is a wholly-owned subsidiary of any body corporate, wherever incorporated.

(5) A resolution of a company approving such a term as is mentioned in subsection (1) shall not be passed at a general meeting of the company unless a written memorandum setting out the proposed agreement incorporating the term is available for inspection by members of the company both—

> (a) at the company's registered office for not less than 15 days ending with the date of the meeting ;
> and
>
> (b) at the meeting itself.

(6) A term incorporated in an agreement in contravention of this section is, to the extent that it contravenes the section, void ; and that agreement and, in a case where subsection (2) applies, the original agreement are deemed to contain a term entitling the company to terminate it at any time by the giving of reasonable notice.

(7) In this section—

> (a) " employment " includes employment under a contract for services ; and
>
> (b) " group ", in relation to a director of a holding company, means the group which consists of that company and its subsidiaries ;

and for purposes of this section a shadow director is treated as a director.

Substantial property transactions involving directors, etc.

320.—(1) With the exceptions provided by the section next following, a company shall not enter into an arrangement—

> (a) whereby a director of the company or its holding company, or a person connected with such a director, acquires or is to acquire one or more non-cash assets of the requisite value from the company ; or
>
> (b) whereby the company acquires or is to acquire one or

more non-cash assets of the requisite value from such a director or a person so connected,

unless the arrangement is first approved by a resolution of the company in general meeting and, if the director or connected person is a director of its holding company or a person connected with such a director, by a resolution in general meeting of the holding company.

(2) For this purpose a non-cash asset is of the requisite value if at the time the arrangement in question is entered into its value is not less than £1,000 but (subject to that) exceeds £50,000 or 10 per cent. of the company's asset value, that is—

    (*a*) except in a case falling within paragraph (*b*) below, the value of the company's net assets determined by reference to the accounts prepared and laid under Part VII in respect of the last preceding financial year in respect of which such accounts were so laid ; and

    (*b*) where no accounts have been so prepared and laid before that time, the amount of the company's called-up share capital.

(3) For purposes of this section and sections 321 and 322, a shadow director is treated as a director.

321.—(1) No approval is required to be given under section 320 by any body corporate unless it is a company within the meaning of this Act or registered under section 680 or, if it is a wholly-owned subsidiary of any body corporate, wherever incorporated.

(2) Section 320(1) does not apply to an arrangement for the acquisition of a non-cash asset—

    (*a*) if the asset is to be acquired by a holding company from any of its wholly-owned subsidiaries or from a holding company by any of its wholly-owned subsidiaries, or by one wholly-owned subsidiary of a holding company from another wholly-owned subsidiary of that same holding company, or

    (*b*) if the arrangement is entered into by a company which is being wound up, unless the winding up is a members' voluntary winding up.

(3) Section 320(1)(*a*) does not apply to an arrangement whereby a person is to acquire an asset from a company of which he is a member, if the arrangement is made with that person in his character as a member.

322.—(1) An arrangement entered into by a company in contravention of section 320, and any transaction entered into in pursuance of the arrangement (whether by the company or any other person) is voidable at the instance of the company unless one or more of the conditions specified in the next subsection is satisfied.

(2) Those conditions are that—

 (*a*) restitution of any money or other asset which is the subject-matter of the arrangement or transaction is no longer possible or the company has been indemnified in pursuance of this section by any other person for the loss or damage suffered by it ; or

 (*b*) any rights acquired bona fide for value and without actual notice of the contravention by any person who is not a party to the arrangement or transaction would be affected by its avoidance ; or

 (*c*) the arrangement is, within a reasonable period, affirmed by the company in general meeting and, if it is an arrangement for the transfer of an asset to or by a director of its holding company or a person who is connected with such a director, is so affirmed with the approval of the holding company given by a resolution in general meeting.

(3) If an arrangement is entered into with a company by a director of the company or its holding company or a person connected with him in contravention of section 320, that director and the person so connected, and any other director of the company who authorised the arrangement or any transaction entered into in pursuance of such an arrangement, is liable—

 (*a*) to account to the company for any gain which he has made directly or indirectly by the arrangement or transaction, and

 (*b*) (jointly and severally with any other person liable under this subsection) to indemnify the company for any loss or damage resulting from the arrangement or transaction.

(4) Subsection (3) is without prejudice to any liability imposed otherwise than by that subsection, and is subject to the following two subsections ; and the liability under subsection (3) arises whether or not the arrangement or transaction entered into has been avoided in pursuance of subsection (1).

(5) If an arrangement is entered into by a company and a person connected with a director of the company or its holding company in contravention of section 320, that director is not liable

under subsection (3) if he shows that he took all reasonable steps to secure the company's compliance with that section.

(6) In any case, a person so connected and any such other director as is mentioned in subsection (3) is not so liable if he shows that, at the time the arrangement was entered into, he did not know the relevant circumstances constituting the contravention.

Share dealings by directors and their families

323.—(1) It is an offence for a director of a company to buy— Prohibition on directors

(*a*) a right to call for delivery at a specified price and dealing in within a specified time of a specified number of relevant share options. shares or a specified amount of relevant debentures; or

(*b*) a right to make delivery at a specified price and within a specified time of a specified number of relevant shares or a specified amount of relevant debentures; or

(*c*) a right (as he may elect) to call for delivery at a specified price and within a specified time or to make delivery at a specified price and within a specified time of a specified number of relevant shares or a specified amount of relevant debentures.

(2) A person guilty of an offence under subsection (1) is liable to imprisonment or a fine, or both.

(3) In subsection (1)—

(*a*) " relevant shares ", in relation to a director of a company, means shares in the company or in any other body corporate, being the company's subsidiary or holding company, or a subsidiary of the company's holding company, being shares as respects which there has been granted a listing on a stock exchange (whether in Great Britain or elsewhere) ;

(*b*) " relevant debentures ", in relation to a director of a company, means debentures of the company or of any other body corporate, being the company's subsidiary or holding company or a subsidiary of the company's holding company, being debentures as respects which there has been granted such a listing ; and

(*c*) " price " includes any consideration other than money.

(4) This section applies to a shadow director as to a director.

(5) This section is not to be taken as penalising a person who buys a right to subscribe for shares in, or debentures of, a body

corporate or buys debentures of a body corporate that confer upon the holder of them a right to subscribe for, or to convert the debentures (in whole or in part) into, shares of that body.

Duty of
director to
disclose
shareholdings
in own
company.

324.—(1) A person who becomes a director of a company and at the time when he does so is interested in shares in, or debentures of, the company or any other body corporate, being the company's subsidiary or holding company or a subsidiary of the company's holding company, is under obligation to notify the company in writing—

    (*a*) of the subsistence of his interests at that time ; and

    (*b*) of the number of shares of each class in, and the amount of debentures of each class of, the company or other such body corporate in which each interest of his subsists at that time.

(2) A director of a company is under obligation to notify the company in writing of the occurrence, while he is a director, of any of the following events—

    (*a*) any event in consequence of whose occurrence he becomes, or ceases to be, interested in shares in, or debentures of, the company or any other body corporate, being the company's subsidiary or holding company or a subsidiary of the company's holding company ;

    (*b*) the entering into by him of a contract to sell any such shares or debentures ;

    (*c*) the assignment by him of a right granted to him by the company to subscribe for shares in, or debentures of, the company ; and

    (*d*) the grant to him by another body corporate, being the company's subsidiary or holding company or a subsidiary of the company's holding company, of a right to subscribe for shares in, or debentures of, that other body corporate, the exercise of such a right granted to him and the assignment by him of such a right so granted ;

and notification to the company must state the number or amount, and class, of shares or debentures involved.

(3) Schedule 13 has effect in connection with subsections (1) and (2) above ; and of that Schedule—

    (*a*) Part I contains rules for the interpretation of, and otherwise in relation to, those subsections and applies in determining, for purposes of those subsections, whether a person has an interest in shares or debentures ;

(*b*) Part II applies with respect to the periods within which obligations imposed by the subsections must be fulfilled ; and

(*c*) Part III specifies certain circumstances in which obligations arising from subsection (2) are to be treated as not discharged ;

and subsections (1) and (2) are subject to any exceptions for which provision may be made by regulations made by the Secretary of State by statutory instrument.

(4) Subsection (2) does not require the notification by a person of the occurrence of an event whose occurrence comes to his knowledge after he has ceased to be a director.

(5) An obligation imposed by this section is treated as not discharged unless the notice by means of which it purports to be discharged is expressed to be given in fulfilment of that obligation.

(6) This section applies to shadow directors as to directors ; but nothing in it operates so as to impose an obligation with respect to shares in a body corporate which is the wholly-owned subsidiary of another body corporate.

(7) A person who—
(*a*) fails to discharge, within the proper period, an obligation to which he is subject under subsection (1) or (2), or
(*b*) in purported discharge of an obligation to which he is so subject, makes to the company a statement which he knows to be false, or recklessly makes to it a statement which is false,

is guilty of an offence and liable to imprisonment or a fine, or both.

(8) Section 732 (restriction on prosecutions) applies to an offence under this section.

325.—(1) Every company shall keep a register for the purposes of section 324.

(2) Whenever a company receives information from a director given in fulfilment of an obligation imposed on him by that section, it is under obligation to enter in the register, against the director's name, the information received and the date of the entry.

(3) The company is also under obligation, whenever it grants to a director a right to subscribe for shares in, or debentures of, the company to enter in the register against his name—
(*a*) the date on which the right is granted,

(*b*) the period during which, or time at which, it is exercisable,

(*c*) the consideration for the grant (or, if there is no consideration, that fact), and

(*d*) the description of shares or debentures involved and the number or amount of them, and the price to be paid for them (or the consideration, if otherwise than in money).

(4) Whenever such a right as is mentioned above is exercised by a director, the company is under obligation to enter in the register against his name that fact (identifying the right), the number or amount of shares or debentures in respect of which it is exercised and, if they were registered in his name, that fact and, if not, the name or names of the person or persons in whose name or names they were registered, together (if they were registered in the names of two persons or more) with the number or amount of the shares or debentures registered in the name of each of them.

(5) Part IV of Schedule 13 has effect with respect to the register to be kept under this section, to the way in which entries in it are to be made, to the right of inspection, and generally.

(6) For purposes of this section, a shadow director is deemed a director.

Sanctions for non-compliance.

326.—(1) The following applies with respect to defaults in complying with, and to contraventions of, section 325 and Part IV of Schedule 13.

(2) If default is made in complying with any of the following provisions—

(*a*) section 325(1), (2), (3) or (4), or

(*b*) Schedule 13, paragraph 21, 22 or 28,

the company and every officer of it who is in default is liable to a fine and, for continued contravention, to a daily default fine.

(3) If an inspection of the register required under paragraph 25 of the Schedule is refused, or a copy required under paragraph 26 is not sent within the proper period, the company and every officer of it who is in default is liable to a fine and, for continued contravention, to a daily default fine.

(4) If default is made for 14 days in complying with paragraph 27 of the Schedule (notice to registrar of where register is kept), the company and every officer of it who is in default is liable to a fine and, for continued contravention, to a daily default fine.

(5) If default is made in complying with paragraph 29 of the Schedule (register to be produced at annual general meeting), the company and every officer of it who is in default is liable to a fine.

(6) In the case of a refusal of an inspection of the register required under paragraph 25 of the Schedule, the court may by order compel an immediate inspection of it; and in the case of failure to send within the proper period a copy required under paragraph 26, the court may by order direct that the copy be sent to the person requiring it.

327.—(1) Section 323 applies to— Extension of s. 323 to spouses and children.

    (*a*) the wife or husband of a director of a company (not being herself or himself a director of it), and

    (*b*) an infant son or infant daughter of a director (not being himself or herself a director of the company),

as it applies to the director; but it is a defence for a person charged by virtue of this section with an offence under section 323 to prove that he (she) had no reason to believe that his (her) spouse or, as the case may be, parent was a director of the company in question.

(2) For purposes of this section—

    (*a*) " son " includes step-son, and " daughter " includes step-daughter (" parent " being construed accordingly),

    (*b*) " infant " means, in relation to Scotland, pupil or minor, and

    (*c*) a shadow director of a company is deemed a director of it.

328.—(1) For the purposes of section 324— Extension of s. 324 to spouses and children.

    (*a*) an interest of the wife or husband of a director of a company (not being herself or himself a director of it) in shares or debentures is to be treated as the director's interest; and

    (*b*) the same applies to an interest of an infant son or infant daughter of a director of a company (not being himself or herself a director of it) in shares or debentures.

(2) For those purposes—

    (*a*) a contract, assignment or right of subscription entered into, exercised or made by, or a grant made to, the wife or husband of a director of a company (not being herself or himself a director of it) is to be treated as having been entered into, exercised or made by, or (as the case may be) as having been made to, the director; and (*b*) the same applies to a contract, assignment or right of subscription entered into, exercised or made by, or grant made to, an infant son or infant daughter of a director of a company (not being himself or herself a director of it).

(3) A director of a company is under obligation to notify the company in writing of the occurrence while he or she is a director, of either of the following events, namely—

(*a*) the grant by the company to his (her) spouse, or to his or her infant son or infant daughter, of a right to subscribe for shares in, or debentures of, the company ; and

(*b*) the exercise by his (her) spouse or by his or her infant son or infant daughter of such a right granted by the company to the wife, husband, son or daughter.

(4) In a notice given to the company under subsection (3) there shall be stated—

(*a*) in the case of the grant of a right, the like information as is required by section 324 to be stated by the director on the grant to him by another body corporate of a right to subscribe for shares in, or debentures of, that other body corporate ; and

(*b*) in the case of the exercise of a right, the like information as is required by that section to be stated by the director on the exercise of a right granted to him by another body corporate to subscribe for shares in, or debentures of, that other body corporate.

(5) An obligation imposed by subsection (3) on a director must be fulfilled by him before the end of 5 days beginning with the day following that on which the occurrence of the event giving rise to it comes to his knowledge ; but in reckoning that period of days there is disregarded any Saturday or Sunday, and any day which is a bank holiday in any part of Great Britain.

(6) A person who—

(*a*) fails to fulfil, within the proper period, an obligation to which he is subject under subsection (3), or

(*b*) in purported fulfilment of such an obligation, makes to a company a statement which he knows to be false, or recklessly makes to a company a statement which is false,

is guilty of an offence and liable to imprisonment or a fine, or both.

(7) The rules set out in Part I of Schedule 13 have effect for the interpretation of, and otherwise in relation to, subsections (1) and (2) ; and subsections (5), (6) and (8) of section 324 apply with any requisite modification.

(8) In this section, " son " includes step-son, " daughter " includes step-daughter, and " infant " means, in relation to Scotland, pupil or minor.

(9) For purposes of section 325, an obligation imposed on a director by this section is to be treated as if imposed by section 324.

329.—(1) Whenever a company whose shares or debentures Duty to are listed on a recognised stock exchange is notified of any mat- notify stock ter by a director in consequence of the fulfilment of an obligation exchange of imposed by section 324 or 328, and that matter relates to shares notified under or debentures so listed, the company is under obligation to preceding notify that stock exchange of that matter ; and the stock ex- sections. change may publish, in such manner as it may determine, any information received by it under this subsection.

(2) An obligation imposed by subsection (1) must be fulfilled before the end of the day next following that on which it arises ; but there is disregarded for this purpose a day which is a Saturday or a Sunday or a bank holiday in any part of Great Britain.

(3) If default is made in complying with this section, the company and every officer of it who is in default is guilty of an offence and liable to a fine and, for continued contravention, to a daily default fine.

Section 732 (restriction on prosecutions) applies to an offence under this section.

Restrictions on a company's power to make loans, etc., to directors and persons connected with them

330.—(1) The prohibitions listed below in this section are General subject to the exceptions in sections 332 to 338. restriction on loans etc. to
(2) A company shall not— directors and
    (*a*) make a loan to a director of the company or of its persons connected holding company ; with them.
    (*b*) enter into any guarantee or provide any security in connection with a loan made by any person to such a director.

(3) A relevant company shall not—
    (*a*) make a quasi-loan to a director of the company or of its holding company ;
    (*b*) make a loan or a quasi-loan to a person connected with such a director ;
    (*c*) enter into a guarantee or provide any security in connection with a loan or quasi-loan made by any other person for such a director or a person so connected.

(4) A relevant company shall not—

(*a*) enter into a credit transaction as creditor for such a director or a person so connected ;

(*b*) enter into any guarantee or provide any security in connection with a credit transaction made by any other person for such a director or a person so connected.

(5) For purposes of sections 330 to 346, a shadow director is treated as a director.

(6) A company shall not arrange for the assignment to it, or the assumption by it, of any rights, obligations or liabilities under a transaction which, if it had been entered into by the company, would have contravened subsection (2), (3) or (4) ; but for the purposes of sections 330 to 347 the transaction is to be treated as having been entered into on the date of the arrangement.

(7) A company shall not take part in any arrangement whereby—

(*a*) another person enters into a transaction which, if it had been entered into by the company, would have contravened any of subsections (2), (3), (4) or (6) ; and

(*b*) that other person, in pursuance of the arrangement, has obtained or is to obtain any benefit from the company or its holding company or a subsidiary of the company or its holding company.

Definitions for ss. 330 ff.   **331.**—(1) The following subsections apply for the interpretation of sections 330 to 346.

(2) " Guarantee " includes indemnity, and cognate expressions are to be construed accordingly.

(3) A quasi-loan is a transaction under which one party (" the creditor ") agrees to pay, or pays otherwise than in pursuance of an agreement, a sum for another (" the borrower ") or agrees to reimburse, or reimburses otherwise than in pursuance of an agreement, expenditure incurred by another party for another (" the borrower ")—

(*a*) on terms that the borrower (or a person on his behalf) will reimburse the creditor ; or

(*b*) in circumstances giving rise to a liability on the borrower to reimburse the creditor.

(4) Any reference to the person to whom a quasi-loan is made is a reference to the borrower ; and the liabilities of a borrower under a quasi-loan include the liabilities of any person who has agreed to reimburse the creditor on behalf of the borrower.

(5) " Recognised bank " means a company which is recognised as a bank for the purposes of the Banking Act 1979.

(6) " Relevant company " means a company which—

　(a) is a public company, or

　(b) is a subsidiary of a public company, or

　(c) is a subsidiary of a company which has as another
　　　subsidiary a public company, or

　(d) has a subsidiary which is a public company.

(7) A credit transaction is a transaction under which one party
(" the creditor ")—

　(a) supplies any goods or sells any land under a hire-
　　　purchase agreement or a conditional sale agreement;

　(b) leases or hires any land or goods in return for periodical
　　　payments;

　(c) otherwise disposes of land or supplies goods or services
　　　on the understanding that payment (whether in a lump
　　　sum or instalments or by way of periodical payments
　　　or otherwise) is to be deferred.

(8) " Services " means anything other than goods or land.

(9) A transaction or arrangement is made " for " a person if—

　(a) in the case of a loan or quasi-loan, it is made to him;

　(b) in the case of a credit transaction, he is the person to
　　　whom goods or services are supplied, or land is sold
　　　or otherwise disposed of, under the transaction;

　(c) in the case of a guarantee or security, it is entered into
　　　or provided in connection with a loan or quasi-loan
　　　made to him or a credit transaction made for him;

　(d) in the case of an arrangement within subsection (6) or
　　　(7) of section 330, the transaction to which the arrange-
　　　ment relates was made for him; and

　(e) in the case of any other transaction or arrangement for
　　　the supply or transfer of, or of any interest in, goods,
　　　land or services, he is the person to whom the goods,
　　　land or services (or the interest) are supplied or
　　　transferred.

(10) " Conditional sale agreement " means the same as in the
Consumer Credit Act 1974.

332.—(1) Subsection (3) of section 330 does not prohibit a Short-term
company (" the creditor ") from making a quasi-loan to one of quasi-loans.
its directors or to a director of its holding company if—

　(a) the quasi-loan contains a term requiring the director or
　　　a person on his behalf to reimburse the creditor his

I

expenditure within 2 months of its being incurred; and

    (*b*) the aggregate of the amount of that quasi-loan and of the amount outstanding under each relevant quasi-loan does not exceed £1,000.

(2) A quasi-loan is relevant for this purpose if it was made to the director by virtue of this section by the creditor or its subsidiary or, where the director is a director of the creditor's holding company, any other subsidiary of that company; and "the amount outstanding" is the amount of the outstanding liabilities of the person to whom the quasi-loan was made.

Inter-company loans in same group.

333. In the case of a relevant company which is a member of a group of companies (meaning a holding company and its subsidiaries), paragraphs (*b*) and (*c*) of section 330(3) do not prohibit the company from—

    (*a*) making a loan or quasi-loan to another member of that group; or

    (*b*) entering into a guarantee or providing any security in connection with a loan or quasi-loan made by any person to another member of the group,

by reason only that a director of one member of the group is associated with another.

Loans of small amounts.

334. Without prejudice to any other provision of sections 332 to 338, paragraph (*a*) of section 330(2) does not prohibit a company from making a loan to a director of the company or of its holding company if the aggregate of the relevant amounts does not exceed £2,500.

Minor and business transactions.

335.—(1) Section 330(4) does not prohibit a company from entering into a transaction for a person if the aggregate of the relevant amounts does not exceed £5,000.

(2) Section 330(4) does not prohibit a company from entering into a transaction for a person if—

    (*a*) the transaction is entered into by the company in the ordinary course of its business; and

    (*b*) the value of the transaction is not greater, and the terms on which it is entered into are no more favourable, in respect of the person for whom the transaction is made, than that or those which it is reasonable to expect the company to have offered to or in respect of a person of the same financial standing but unconnected with the company.

336. The following transactions are excepted from the prohibitions of section 330—

 (a) a loan or quasi-loan by a company to its holding company, or a company entering into a guarantee or providing any security in connection with a loan or quasi-loan made by any person to its holding company ;

 (b) a company entering into a credit transaction as creditor for its holding company, or entering into a guarantee or providing any security in connection with a credit transaction made by any other person for its holding company.

337.—(1) A company is not prohibited by section 330 from
doing anything to provide a director with funds to meet expenditure incurred or to be incurred by him for the purposes of the company or for the purpose of enabling him properly to perform his duties as an officer of the company.

(2) Nor does the section prohibit a company from doing anything to enable a director to avoid incurring such expenditure.

(3) Subsections (1) and (2) apply only if one of the following conditions is satisfied—

 (a) the thing in question is done with prior approval of the company given at a general meeting at which there are disclosed all the matters mentioned in the next subsection ;

 (b) that thing is done on condition that, if the approval of the company is not so given at or before the next annual general meeting, the loan is to be repaid, or any other liability arising under any such transaction discharged, within 6 months from the conclusion of that meeting ;

but those subsections do not authorise a relevant company to enter into any transaction if the aggregate of the relevant amounts exceeds £10,000.

(4) The matters to be disclosed under subsection (3)(a) are—

 (a) the purpose of the expenditure incurred or to be incurred, or which would otherwise be incurred, by the director,

 (b) the amount of the funds to be provided by the company, and

 (c) the extent of the company's liability under any transaction which is or is connected with the thing in question.

338.—(1) There is excepted from the prohibitions in section 330—

    (*a*) a loan or quasi-loan made by a money-lending company to any person ; or

    (*b*) a money-lending company entering into a guarantee in connection with any other loan or quasi-loan.

(2) " Money-lending company " means a company whose ordinary business includes the making of loans or quasi-loans, or the giving of guarantees in connection with loans or quasi-loans.

(3) Subsection (1) applies only if both the following conditions are satisfied—

    (*a*) the loan or quasi-loan in question is made by the company, or it enters into the guarantee, in the ordinary course of the company's business ; and

    (*b*) the amount of the loan or quasi-loan, or the amount guaranteed, is not greater, and the terms of the loan, quasi-loan or guarantee are not more favourable, in the case of the person to whom the loan or quasi-loan is made or in respect of whom the guarantee is entered into, than that or those which it is reasonable to expect that company to have offered to or in respect of a person of the same financial standing but unconnected with the company.

(4) But subsection (1) does not authorise a relevant company (unless it is a recognised bank) to enter into any transaction if the aggregate of the relevant amounts exceeds £50,000.

(5) In determining that aggregate, a company which a director does not control is deemed not to be connected with him.

(6) The condition specified in subsection (3)(*b*) does not of itself prevent a company from making a loan to one of its directors or a director of its holding company—

    (*a*) for the purpose of facilitating the purchase, for use as that director's only or main residence, of the whole or part of any dwelling-house together with any land to be occupied and enjoyed with it ;

    (*b*) for the purpose of improving a dwelling-house or part of a dwelling-house so used or any land occupied and enjoyed with it ;

    (*c*) in substitution for any loan made by any person and falling within paragraph (*a*) or (*b*) of this subsection,

if loans of that description are ordinarily made by the company
to its employees and on terms no less favourable than those on
which the transaction in question is made, and the aggregate of
the relevant amounts does not exceed £50,000.

339.—(1) This section has effect for defining the "relevant
amounts" to be aggregated under sections 334, 335(1), 337(3)
and 338(4); and in relation to any proposed transaction or arrangement and the question whether it falls within one or other
of the exceptions provided by those sections, "the relevant
exception" is that exception; but where the relevant exception
is the one provided by section 334 (loan of small amount), references in this section to a person connected with a director are to
be disregarded.

(2) Subject as follows, the relevant amounts in relation to a
proposed transaction or arrangement are—

　(*a*) the value of the proposed transaction or arrangement,

　(*b*) the value of any existing arrangement which—

　　　(i) falls within subsection (6) or (7) of section 330,
　　and

　　　(ii) also falls within subsection (3) of this section,
　　and

　　　(iii) was entered into by virtue of the relevant
　　exception by the company or by a subsidiary of the
　　company or, where the proposed transaction or
　　arrangement is to be made for a director of its hold-
　　ing company or a person connected with such a
　　director, by that holding company or any of its
　　subsidiaries;

　(*c*) the amount outstanding under any other transaction—

　　　(i) falling within subsection (3) below, and

　　　(ii) made by virtue of the relevant exception, and

　　　(iii) made by the company or by a subsidiary of
　　the company or, where the proposed transaction or
　　arrangement is to be made for a director of its hold-
　　ing company or a person connected with such a
　　director, by that holding company or any of its sub-
　　sidiaries.

(3) A transaction falls within this subsection if it was made—

　(*a*) for the director for whom the proposed transaction or
　　arrangement is to be made, or for any person con-
　　nected with that director; or

(*b*) where the proposed transaction or arrangement is to be made for a person connected with a director of a company, for that director or any person connected with him ;

and an arrangement also falls within this subsection if it relates to a transaction which does so.

(4) But where the proposed transaction falls within section 338 and is one which a recognised bank proposes to enter into under subsection (6) of that section (housing loans, etc.), any other transaction or arrangement which apart from this subsection would fall within subsection (3) of this section does not do so unless it was entered into in pursuance of section 338(6).

(5) A transaction entered into by a company which is (at the time of that transaction being entered into) a subsidiary of the company which is to make the proposed transaction, or is a subsidiary of that company's holding company, does not fall within subsection (3) if at the time when the question arises (that is to say, the question whether the proposed transaction or arrangement falls within any relevant exception), it no longer is such a subsidiary.

(6) Values for purposes of subsection (2) of this section are to be determined in accordance with the section next following ; and " the amount outstanding " for purposes of subsection (2)(*c*) above is the value of the transaction less any amount by which that value has been reduced.

" Value " of transactions and arrangements.   **340.**—(1) This section has effect for determining the value of a transaction or arrangement for purposes of sections 330 to 339.

(2) The value of a loan is the amount of its principal.

(3) The value of a quasi-loan is the amount, or maximum amount, which the person to whom the quasi-loan is made is liable to reimburse the creditor.

(4) The value of a guarantee or security is the amount guaranteed or secured.

(5) The value of an arrangement to which section 330(6) or (7) applies is the value of the transaction to which the arrangement relates less any amount by which the liabilities under the arrangement or transaction of the person for whom the transaction was made have been reduced.

(6) The value of a transaction or arrangement not falling within subsections (2) to (5) above is the price which it is reasonable to expect could be obtained for the goods, land or services

to which the transaction or arrangement relates if they had been supplied (at the time the transaction or arrangement is entered into) in the ordinary course of business and on the same terms (apart from price) as they have been supplied, or are to be supplied, under the transaction or arrangement in question.

(7) For purposes of this section, the value of a transaction or arrangement which is not capable of being expressed as a specific sum of money (because the amount of any liability arising under the transaction or arrangement is unascertainable, or for any other reason), whether or not any liability under the transaction or arrangement has been reduced, is deemed to exceed £50,000.

341.—(1) If a company enters into a transaction or arrangement in contravention of section 330, the transaction or arrangement is voidable at the instance of the company unless—

> Civil remedies for breach of s. 330.

> (a) restitution of any money or any other asset which is the subject matter of the arrangement or transaction is no longer possible, or the company has been indemnified in pursuance of subsection (2)(b) below for the loss or damage suffered by it, or

> (b) any rights acquired bona fide for value and without actual notice of the contravention by a person other than the person for whom the transaction or arrangement was made would be affected by its avoidance.

(2) Where an arrangement or transaction is made by a company for a director of the company or its holding company or a person connected with such a director in contravention of section 330, that director and the person so connected and any other director of the company who authorised the transaction or arrangement (whether or not it has been avoided in pursuance of subsection (1)) is liable—

> (a) to account to the company for any gain which he has made directly or indirectly by the arrangement or transaction ; and

> (b) (jointly and severally with any other person liable under this subsection) to indemnify the company for any loss or damage resulting from the arrangement or transaction.

(3) Subsection (2) is without prejudice to any liability imposed otherwise than by that subsection, but is subject to the next two subsections.

(4) Where an arrangement or transaction is entered into by a company and a person connected with a director of the company or its holding company in contravention of section 330, that

director is not liable under subsection (2) of this section if he shows that he took all reasonable steps to secure the company's compliance with that section.

(5) In any case, a person so connected and any such other director as is mentioned in subsection (2) is not so liable if he shows that, at the time the arrangement or transaction was entered into, he did not know the relevant circumstances constituting the contravention.

Criminal penalties for breach of s. 330.

342.—(1) A director of a relevant company who authorises or permits the company to enter into a transaction or arrangement knowing or having reasonable cause to believe that the company was thereby contravening section 330 is guilty of an offence.

(2) A relevant company which enters into a transaction or arrangement for one of its directors or for a director of its holding company in contravention of section 330 is guilty of an offence.

(3) A person who procures a relevant company to enter into a transaction or arrangement knowing or having reasonable cause to believe that the company was thereby contravening section 330 is guilty of an offence.

(4) A person guilty of an offence under this section is liable to imprisonment or a fine, or both.

(5) A relevant company is not guilty of an offence under subsection (2) if it shows that, at the time the transaction or arrangement was entered into, it did not know the relevant circumstances.

Record of transactions not disclosed in company accounts.

343.—(1) The following provisions of this section—

    (*a*) apply in the case of a company which is, or is the holding company of, a recognised bank, and

    (*b*) are subject to the exceptions provided by section 344.

(2) Such a company shall maintain a register containing a copy of every transaction, arrangement or agreement of which particulars would, but for paragraph 4 of Schedule 6, be required by section 232 to be disclosed in the company's accounts or group accounts for the current financial year and for each of the preceding 10 financial years.

(3) In the case of a transaction, arrangement or agreement which is not in writing, there shall be contained in the register a written memorandum setting out its terms.

(4) Such a company shall before its annual general meeting make available at its registered office for not less than 15 days ending with the date of the meeting a statement containing

the particulars of transactions, arrangements and agreements which the company would, but for paragraph 4 of Schedule 6, be required by section 232 to disclose in its accounts or group accounts for the last complete financial year preceding that meeting.

(5) The statement shall be so made available for inspection by members of the company; and such a statement shall also be made available for their inspection at the annual general meeting.

(6) It is the duty of the company's auditors to examine the statement before it is made available to members of the company and to make a report to the members on it; and the report shall be annexed to the statement before it is made so available.

(7) The auditors' report shall state whether in their opinion the statement contains the particulars required by subsection (4); and, where their opinion is that it does not, they shall include in the report, so far as they are reasonably able to do so, a statement giving the required particulars.

(8) If a company fails to comply with any provision of subsections (2) to (5), every person who at the time of the failure is a director of it is guilty of an offence and liable to a fine; but—

> (a) it is a defence in proceedings against a person for this offence to prove that he took all reasonable steps for securing compliance with the subsection concerned, and

> (b) a person is not guilty of the offence by virtue only of being a shadow director of the company.

(9) For purposes of the application of this section to loans and quasi-loans made by a company to persons connected with a person who at any time is a director of the company or of its holding company, a company which a person does not control is not connected with him.

344.—(1) Section 343 does not apply in relation to—

> (a) transactions or arrangements made or subsisting during a financial year by a company or by a subsidiary of a company for a person who was at any time during that year a director of the company or of its holding company or was connected with such a director, or

> (b) an agreement made or subsisting during that year to enter into such a transaction or arrangement,

if the aggregate of the values of each transaction or arrangement made for that person, and of each agreement for such a transaction or arrangement, less the amount (if any) by which the value of those transactions, arrangements and agreements has been reduced, did not exceed £1,000 at any time during the financial year.

For purposes of this subsection, values are to be determined as under section 340.

(2) Section 343(4) and (5) do not apply to a recognised bank which is the wholly-owned subsidiary of a company incorporated in the United Kingdom.

Supplementary

Power to increase financial limits.

345.—(1) The Secretary of State may by order in a statutory instrument substitute for any sum of money specified in this Part a larger sum specified in the order.

(2) An order under this section is subject to annulment in pursuance of a resolution of either House of Parliament.

(3) Such an order does not have effect in relation to anything done or not done before its coming into force ; and accordingly, proceedings in respect of any liability (whether civil or criminal) incurred before that time may be continued or instituted as if the order had not been made.

" Connected persons ", etc.

346.—(1) This section has effect with respect to references in this Part to a person being " connected " with a director of a company, and to a director being " associated with " or " controlling " a body corporate.

(2) A person is connected with a director of a company if, but only if, he (not being himself a director of it) is—

(a) that director's spouse, child or step-child ; or

(b) except where the context otherwise requires, a body corporate with which the director is associated ; or

(c) a person acting in his capacity as trustee of any trust the beneficiaries of which include—

(i) the director, his spouse or any children or step-children of his, or

(ii) a body corporate with which he is associated, or of a trust whose terms confer a power on the trustees that may be exercised for the benefit of the director, his spouse, or any children or step-children of his, or any such body corporate ; or

(d) a person acting in his capacity as partner of that director or of any person who, by virtue of paragraph (a), (b) or (c) of this subsection, is connected with that director ; or

(e) a Scottish firm in which—

(i) that director is a partner,

(ii) a partner is a person who, by virtue of paragraph (*a*), (*b*) or (*c*) above, is connected with that director, or

(iii) a partner is a Scottish firm in which that director is a partner or in which there is a partner who, by virtue of paragraph (*a*), (*b*) or (*c*) above, is connected with that director.

(3) In subsection (2)—

(*a*) a reference to the child or step-child of any person includes an illegitimate child of his, but does not include any person who has attained the age of 18 ; and

(*b*) paragraph (*c*) does not apply to a person acting in his capacity as trustee under an employees' share scheme or a pension scheme.

(4) A director of a company is associated with a body corporate if, but only if, he and the persons connected with him, together—

(*a*) are interested in shares comprised in the equity share capital of that body corporate of a nominal value equal to at least one-fifth of that share capital ; or

(*b*) are entitled to exercise or control the exercise of more than one-fifth of the voting power at any general meeting of that body.

(5) A director of a company is deemed to control a body corporate if, but only if—

(*a*) he or any person connected with him is interested in any part of the equity share capital of that body or is entitled to exercise or control the exercise of any part of the voting power at any general meeting of that body ; and

(*b*) that director, the persons connected with him and the other directors of that company, together, are interested in more than one-half of that share capital or are entitled to exercise or control the exercise of more than one-half of that voting power.

(6) For purposes of subsections (4) and (5)—

(*a*) a body corporate with which a director is associated is not to be treated as connected with that director unless it is also connected with him by virtue of subsection (2)(*c*) or (*d*) ; and

(*b*) a trustee of a trust the beneficiaries of which include (or may include) a body corporate with which a director is associated is not to be treated as connected with a director by reason only of that fact.

(7) The rules set out in Part I of Schedule 13 apply for the purposes of subsections (4) and (5).

(8) References in those subsections to voting power the exercise of which is controlled by a director include voting power whose exercise is controlled by a body corporate controlled by him ; but this is without prejudice to other provisions of subsections (4) and (5).

Transactions under foreign law.   **347.** For purposes of sections 319 to 322 and 330 to 343, it is immaterial whether the law which (apart from this Act) governs any arrangement or transaction is the law of the United Kingdom, or of a part of it, or not.

PART XI

COMPANY ADMINISTRATION AND PROCEDURE

CHAPTER I

COMPANY IDENTIFICATION

Company name to appear outside place of business.   **348.**—(1) Every company shall paint or affix, and keep painted or affixed, its name on the outside of every office or place in which its business is carried on, in a conspicuous position and in letters easily legible.

(2) If a company does not paint or affix its name as required above, the company and every officer of it who is in default is liable to a fine ; and if a company does not keep its name painted or affixed as so required, the company and every officer of it who is in default is liable to a fine and, for continued contravention, to a daily default fine.

Company's name to appear in its correspondence, etc.   **349.**—(1) Every company shall have its name mentioned in legible characters—

(a) in all business letters of the company,

(b) in all its notices and other official publications,

(c) in all bills of exchange, promissory notes, endorsements, cheques and orders for money or goods purporting to be signed by or on behalf of the company, and

(d) in all its bills of parcels, invoices, receipts and letters of credit.

(2) If a company fails to comply with subsection (1) it is liable to a fine.

(3) If an officer of a company or a person on its behalf—

(a) issues or authorises the issue of any business letter of the company, or any notice or other official publication of the company, in which the company's name is not mentioned as required by subsection (1), or (*b*) issues or authorises the issue of any bill of parcels, invoice, receipt or letter of credit of the company in which its name is not so mentioned,

he is liable to a fine.

(4) If an officer of a company or a person on its behalf signs or authorises to be signed on behalf of the company any bill of exchange, promissory note, endorsement, cheque or order for money or goods in which the company's name is not mentioned as required by subsection (1), he is liable to a fine ; and he is further personally liable to the holder of the bill of exchange, promissory note, cheque or order for money or goods for the amount of it (unless it is duly paid by the company).

350.—(1) Every company shall have its name engraved in legible characters on its seal ; and if a company fails to comply with this subsection, it is liable to a fine. Company seal.

(2) If an officer of a company or a person on its behalf uses or authorises the use of any seal purporting to be a seal of the company on which its name is not engraved as required by subsection (1), he is liable to a fine.

351.—(1) Every company shall have the following particulars mentioned in legible characters in all business letters and order forms of the company, that is to say— Particulars in correspondence, etc.

(*a*) the company's place of registration and the number with which it is registered,

(*b*) the address of its registered office,

(*c*) in the case of an investment company (as defined in section 266), the fact that it is such a company, and

(*d*) in the case of a limited company exempt from the obligation to use the word " limited " as part of its name, the fact that it is a limited company.

(2) If in the case of a company having a share capital there is on the stationery used for any such letters, or on the company's order forms, a reference to the amount of share capital, the reference must be to paid-up share capital.

(3) Where the name of a public company includes, as its last part, the equivalent in Welsh of the words " public limited company " (" cwmni cyfyngedig cyhoeddus "), the fact that the company is a public limited company shall be stated in English and in legible characters—

(*a*) in all prospectuses, bill-heads, letter paper, notices and other official publications of the company, and

(*b*) in a notice conspicuously displayed in every place in which the company's business is carried on.

(4) Where the name of a limited company has " cyfyngedig " as the last word, the fact that the company is a limited company shall be stated in English and in legible characters—

    (*a*) in all prospectuses, bill-heads, letter paper, notices and other official publications of the company, and

    (*b*) in a notice conspicuously displayed in every place in which the company's business is carried on.

(5) As to contraventions of this section, the following applies—

    (*a*) if a company fails to comply with subsection (1) or (2), it is liable to a fine,

    (*b*) if an officer of a company or a person on its behalf issues or authorises the issue of any business letter or order form not complying with those subsections, he is liable to a fine, and

    (*c*) if subsection (3) or (4) is contravened, the company and every officer of it who is in default is liable to a fine and, in the case of subsection (3), to a daily default fine for continued contravention.

CHAPTER II

REGISTER OF MEMBERS

Obligation to
keep and enter
up register.
352.—(1) Every company shall keep a register of its members and enter in it the particulars required by this section.

(2) There shall be entered in the register—

    (*a*) the names and addresses of the members ;

    (*b*) the date on which each person was registered as a member ; and

    (*c*) the date at which any person ceased to be a member.

(3) The following applies in the case of a company having a share capital—

    (*a*) with the names and addresses of the members there shall be entered a statement—

        (i) of the shares held by each member, distinguishing each share by its number (so long as the share has a number) and, where the company has more than one class of issued shares, by its class, and

        (ii) of the amount paid or agreed to be considered as paid on the shares of each member ;

    (*b*) where the company has converted any of its shares into stock and given notice of the conversion to the rigistrar of companies, the register shall show the amount and class of stock held by each member, instead of the amount of shares and the particulars relating to shares specified in paragraph (*a*).

(4) In the case of a company which does not have a share capital but has more than one class of members, there shall be
entered in the register, with the names and addresses of the
members, the class to which each member belongs.

(5) If a company makes default in complying with this
section, the company and every officer of it who is in default
is liable to a fine and, for continued contravention, to a daily
default fine.

(6) An entry relating to a former member of the company
may be removed from the register after the expiration of 20
years from the date on which he ceased to be a member.

(7) Liability incurred by a company from the making or
deletion of an entry in its register of members, or from a failure
to make or delete any such entry, is not enforceable more than
20 years after the date on which the entry was made or deleted
or, in the case of any such failure, the failure first occurred.

This is without prejudice to any lesser period of limitation.

353.—(1) A company's register of members shall be kept at   Location of
its registered office, except that—   register.

    (*a*) if the work of making it up is done at another office of
        the company, it may be kept there ; and

    (*b*) if the company arranges with some other person for
        the making up of the register to be undertaken on
        its behalf by that other, it may be kept at the office of
        the other at which the work is done ;

but it must not be kept, in the case of a company registered in
England and Wales, at any place elsewhere than in England
and Wales or, in the case of a company registered in Scotland,
at any place elsewhere than in Scotland.

(2) Subject as follows, every company shall send notice
in the prescribed form to the registrar of companies of the
place where its register of members is kept, and of any change
in that place.

(3) The notice need not be sent if the register has, at all
times since it came into existence (or, in the case of a register
in existence on 1st July 1948, at all times since then) been kept
at the company's registered office.

(4) If a company makes default for 14 days in complying with
subsection (2), the company and every officer of it who is in
default is liable to a fine and, for continued contravention, to a
daily default fine.

354.—(1) Every company having more than 50 members shall, unless the register of members is in such a form as to constitute in itself an index, keep an index of the names of the members of the company and shall, within 14 days after the date on which any alteration is made in the register of members, make any necessary alteration in the index.

(2) The index shall in respect of each member contain a sufficient indication to enable the account of that member in the register to be readily found.

(3) The index shall be at all times kept at the same place as the register of members.

(4) If default is made in complying with this section, the company and every officer of it who is in default is liable to a fine and, for continued contravention, to a daily default fine.

355.—(1) On the issue of a share warrant the company shall strike out of its register of members the name of the member then entered in it as holding the shares specified in the warrant as if he had ceased to be a member, and shall enter in the register the following particulars, namely—

    (a) the fact of the issue of the warrant ;

    (b) a statement of the shares included in the warrant, distinguishing each share by its number so long as the share has a number ; and

    (c) the date of the issue of the warrant.

(2) Subject to the company's articles, the bearer of a share warrant is entitled, on surrendering it for cancellation, to have his name entered as a member in the register of members.

(3) The company is responsible for any loss incurred by any person by reason of the company entering in the register the name of a bearer of a share warrant in respect of the shares specified in it without the warrant being surrendered and cancelled.

(4) Until the warrant is surrendered, the particulars specified in subsection (1) are deemed to be those required by this Act to be entered in the register of members ; and, on the surrender, the date of the surrender must be entered.

(5) Except as provided by section 291(2) (director's share qualification), the bearer of a share warrant may, if the articles of the company so provide, be deemed a member of the company within the meaning of this Act, either to the full extent or for any purposes defined in the articles.

356.—(1) Except when the register of members is closed under
the provisions of this Act, the register and the index of members' names shall during business hours be open to the inspection
of any member of the company without charge, and of any
other person on payment of the appropriate charge.

(2) The reference to business hours is subject to such reasonable restrictions as the company in general meeting may impose,
but so that not less than 2 hours in each day is to be allowed
for inspection.

(3) Any member of the company or other person may require
a copy of the register, or of any part of it, on payment of the
appropriate charge; and the company shall cause any copy so
required by a person to be sent to him within 10 days beginning
with the day next following that on which the requirement is
received by the company.

(4) The appropriate charge is—

    (*a*) under subsection (1), 5 pence or such less sum as the
        company may prescribe, for each inspection; and

    (*b*) under subsection (3), 10 pence or such less sum as the
        company may prescribe, for every 100 words (or frac-
        tion of 100 words) required to be copied.

(5) If an inspection required under this section is refused, or if
a copy so required is not sent within the proper period, the
company and every officer of it who is in default is liable in
respect of each offence to a fine.

(6) In the case of such refusal or default, the court may by
order compel an immediate inspection of the register and index,
or direct that the copies required be sent to the persons requiring
them.

PART XI
CHAPTER II
Inspection
of register
and index.

357. Where under section 353(1)(*b*), the register of members
is kept at the office of some person other than the company,
and by reason of any default of his the company fails to comply
with—

    section 353(2) (notice to registrar),

    section 354(3) (index to be kept with register), or

    section 356 (inspection),

or with any requirement of this Act as to the production of the
register, that other person is liable to the same penalties as if
he were an officer of the company who was in default, and the
power of the court under section 356(6) extends to the making
of orders against that other and his officers and servants.

Non-
compliance
with ss. 353,
354, 356;
agent's
default.

PART XI

CHAPTER II
Power to
close register.

358. A company may, on giving notice by advertisement in a newspaper circulating in the district in which the company's registered office is situated, close the register of members for any time or times not exceeding in the whole 30 days in each year.

Power of
court to
rectify
register.

359.—(1) If—

(a) the name of any person is, without sufficient cause, entered in or omitted from a company's register of members, or

(b) default is made or unnecessary delay takes place in entering on the register the fact of any person having ceased to be a member,

the person aggrieved, or any member of the company, or the company, may apply to the court for rectification of the register.

(2) The court may either refuse the application or may order rectification of the register and payment by the company of any damages sustained by any party aggrieved.

(3) On such an application the court may decide any question relating to the title of a person who is a party to the application to have his name entered in or omitted from the register, whether the question arises between members or alleged members, or between members or alleged members on the one hand and the company on the other hand, and generally may decide any question necessary or expedient to be decided for rectification of the register.

(4) In the case of a company required by this Act to send a list of its members to the registrar of companies, the court, when making an order for rectification of the register, shall by its order direct notice of the rectification to be given to the registrar.

Trusts not to
be entered
on register in
England and
Wales.

360. No notice of any trust, expressed, implied or constructive, shall be entered on the register, or be receivable by the registrar, in the case of companies registered in England and Wales.

Register to be
evidence.

361. The register of members is prima facie evidence of any matters which are by this Act directed or authorised to be inserted in it.

Overseas
branch
registers.

362.—(1) A company having a share capital whose objects comprise the transaction of business in any of the countries or territories specified in Part I of Schedule 14 to this Act may cause to be kept in any such country or territory in which it transacts business a branch register of members resident in that country or territory.

(2) Such a branch register is to be known as an " overseas branch register " ; and—

   (a) any dominion register kept by a company under section 119 of the Companies Act 1948 is to become known as an overseas branch register of the company ;

   (b) where any Act or instrument (including in particular a company's articles) refers to a company's dominion register, that reference is to be read (unless the context otherwise requires) as being to an overseas branch register kept under this section ; and

   (c) references to a colonial register occurring in articles registered before 1st November 1929 are to be read as referring to an overseas branch register.

(3) Part II of Schedule 14 has effect with respect to overseas branch registers kept under this section ; and Part III of the Schedule enables corresponding facilities in Great Britain to be accorded to companies incorporated in other parts of the world.

(4) The Foreign Jurisdiction Act 1890 has effect as if subsection (1) of this section, and Part II of Schedule 14, were included among the enactments which by virtue of section 5 of that Act may be applied by Order in Council to foreign countries in which for the time being Her Majesty has jurisdiction.

(5) Her Majesty may by Order in Council direct that subsection (1) above and Part II of Schedule 14 shall extend, with such exceptions, modifications or adaptations (if any) as may be specified in the Order, to any territories under Her Majesty's protection to which those provisions cannot be extended under the Foreign Jurisdiction Act 1890.

CHAPTER III

ANNUAL RETURN

363.—(1) Subject to the provisions of this section, every company having a share capital shall, at least once in every year, make a return containing with respect to the company's registered office, registers of members and debenture holders, shares and debentures, indebtedness, past and present members and directors and secretary, the matters specified in Schedule 15.

Annual return (company having a share capital).

(2) The annual return shall be in the prescribed form.

(3) A company need not make a return under subsection (1) either in the year of its incorporation or, if it is not required by this Act to hold an annual general meeting during the following year, in that year.

(4) Where the company has converted any of its shares into stock and given notice of the conversion to the registrar

of companies, the list referred to in paragraph 5 of Schedule 15 must state the amount of stock held by each of the existing members instead of the amount of shares and the particulars relating to shares required by that paragraph.

(5) The return may, in any year, if the return for either of the two immediately preceding years has given (as at the date of that return) the full particulars required by that paragraph of the Schedule, give only such of those particulars as relate to persons ceasing to be or becoming members since the date of the last return and to shares transferred since that date or to changes as compared with that date in the amount of stock held by a member.

(6) The following applies to a company keeping an overseas branch register—

(a) references in subsection (5) to the particulars required by paragraph 5 are to be taken as not including any such particulars contained in the overseas branch register, in so far as copies of the entries containing those particulars are not received at the company's registered office before the date when the return in question is made ;

(b) if an annual return is made between the date when entries are made in the overseas branch register and the date when copies of those entries are received at the company's registered office, the particulars contained in those entries (so far as relevant to an annual return) shall be included in the next or a subsequent annual return, as may be appropriate having regard to the particulars included in that return with respect to the company's register of members.

(7) If a company fails to comply with this section, the company and every officer of it who is in default is liable to a fine and, for continued contravention, to a daily default fine.

(8) For purposes of this section and Schedule 15, a shadow director is deemed a director and officer.

Annual return (company not having a share capital). **364.**—(1) Every company not having a share capital shall once at least in every calendar year make a return in the prescribed form stating—

(a) the address of the company's registered office ;

(b) if the register of members is under provisions of this Act kept elsewhere than at that office, the address of the place where it is kept ;

(c) if any register of holders of debentures of the company or any duplicate of any such register or part of it is under provisions of this Act kept elsewhere than at the company's registered office, the address of the place where it is kept;

(d) all such particulars with respect to the persons who at the date of the return are the directors of the company, and any person who at that date is its secretary, as are by this Act required to be contained (with respect to directors and the secretary respectively) in the company's register of directors and secretaries.

(2) A company need not make a return under subsection (1) either in the year of its incorporation or, if it is not required by this Act to hold an annual general meeting during the following year, in that year.

(3) There shall be included in the return a statement containing particulars of the total amount of the company's indebtedness in respect of all mortgages and charges (whenever created) of any description specified in section 396(1) or, in the case of a company registered in Scotland, section 410(4).

(4) If a company fails to comply with this section, the company and every officer of it who is in default is liable to a fine and, for continued contravention, to a daily default fine.

(5) For purposes of this section, a shadow director is deemed a director and officer.

365.—(1) A company's annual return must be completed within 42 days after the annual general meeting for the year, whether or not that meeting is the first or only ordinary general meeting, or the first or only general meeting of the company in that year. *Time for completion of annual return.*

(2) The company must forthwith forward to the registrar of companies a copy of the return signed both by a director and by the secretary of the company.

(3) If a company fails to comply with this section, the company and every officer of it who is in default is liable to a fine and, for continued contravention, to a daily default fine; and for this purpose a shadow director is deemed an officer.

Chapter IV

Meetings and Resolutions

Meetings

366.—(1) Every company shall in each year hold a general meeting as its annual general meeting in addition to any other meetings in that year, and shall specify the meeting as such in the notices calling it. *Annual general meeting.*

(2) However, so long as a company holds its first annual general meeting within 18 months of its incorporation, it need not hold it in the year of its incorporation or in the following year.

(3) Not more than 15 months shall elapse between the date of one annual general meeting of a company and that of the next.

(4) If default is made in holding a meeting in accordance with this section, the company and every officer of it who is in default is liable to a fine.

Secretary of
State's power
to call
meeting in
default.

367.—(1) If default is made in holding a meeting in accordance with section 366, the Secretary of State may, on the application of any member of the company, call, or direct the calling of, a general meeting of the company and give such ancillary or consequential directions as he thinks expedient, including directions modifying or supplementing, in relation to the calling, holding and conduct of the meeting, the operation of the company's articles.

(2) The directions that may be given under subsection (1) include a direction that one member of the company present in person or by proxy shall be deemed to constitute a meeting.

(3) If default is made in complying with directions of the Secretary of State under subsection (1), the company and every officer of it who is in default is liable to a fine.

(4) A general meeting held under this section shall, subject to any directions of the Secretary of State, be deemed to be an annual general meeting of the company; but, where a meeting so held is not held in the year in which the default in holding the company's annual general meeting occurred, the meeting so held shall not be treated as the annual general meeting for the year in which it is held unless at that meeting the company resolves that it be so treated.

(5) Where a company so resolves, a copy of the resolution shall, within 15 days after its passing, be forwarded to the registrar of companies and recorded by him; and if default is made in complying with this subsection, the company and every officer of it who is in default is liable to a fine and, for continued contravention, to a daily default fine.

Extraordinary
general
meeting on
members'
requisition.

368.—(1) The directors of a company shall, on a members' requisition, forthwith proceed duly to convene an extraordinary general meeting of the company.

This applies notwithstanding anything in the company's articles.

(2) A members' requisition is a requisition of—

(a) members of the company holding at the date of the deposit of the requisition not less than one-tenth of such of the paid-up capital of the company as at that date carries the right of voting at general meetings of the company ; or

(b) in the case of a company not having a share capital, members of it representing not less than one-tenth of the total voting rights of all the members having at the date of deposit of the requisition a right to vote at general meetings.

(3) The requisition must state the objects of the meeting, and must be signed by the requisitionists and deposited at the registered office of the company, and may consist of several documents in like form each signed by one or more requisitionists.

(4) If the directors do not within 21 days from the date of the deposit of the requisition proceed duly to convene a meeting, the requisitionists, or any of them representing more than one half of the total voting rights of all of them, may themselves convene a meeting, but any meeting so convened shall not be held after the expiration of 3 months from that date.

(5) A meeting convened under this section by requisitionists shall be convened in the same manner, as nearly as possible, as that in which meetings are to be convened by directors.

(6) Any reasonable expenses incurred by the requisitionists by reason of the failure of the directors duly to convene a meeting shall be repaid to the requisitionists by the company, and any sum so repaid shall be retained by the company out of any sums due or to become due from the company by way of fees or other remuneration in respect of their services to such of the directors as were in default.

(7) In the case of a meeting at which a resolution is to be proposed as a special resolution, the directors are deemed not to have duly convened the meeting if they do not give the notice required for special resolutions by section 378(2).

369.—(1) A provision of a company's articles is void in so far as it provides for the calling of a meeting of the company (other than an adjourned meeting) by a shorter notice than— *Length of notice for calling meetings.*

(a) in the case of the annual general meeting, 21 days' notice in writing ; and

(b) in the case of a meeting other than an annual general meeting or a meeting for the passing of a special resolution—

> (i) 7 days' notice in writing in the case of an un-limited company, and
>
> (ii) otherwise, 14 days' notice in writing.

(2) Save in so far as the articles of a company make other provision in that behalf (not being a provision avoided by subsection (1)), a meeting of the company (other than an adjourned meeting) may be called—

> (a) in the case of the annual general meeting, by 21 days' notice in writing ; and
>
> (b) in the case of a meeting other than an annual general meeting or a meeting for the passing of a special resolution—
>
>> (i) by 7 days' notice in writing in the case of an unlimited company, and
>>
>> (ii) otherwise, 14 days' notice in writing.

(3) Notwithstanding that a meeting is called by shorter notice than that specified in subsection (2) or in the company's articles (as the case may be), it is deemed to have been duly called if it is so agreed—

> (a) in the case of a meeting called as the annual general meeting, by all the members entitled to attend and vote at it ; and
>
> (b) otherwise, by the requisite majority.

(4) The requisite majority for this purpose is a majority in number of the members having a right to attend and vote at the meeting, being a majority—

> (a) together holding not less than 95 per cent. in nominal value of the shares giving a right to attend and vote at the meeting ; or
>
> (b) in the case of a company not having a share capital, together representing not less than 95 per cent. of the total voting rights at that meeting of all the members.

General
provisions as
to meetings
and votes.

370.—(1) The following provisions have effect in so far as the articles of the company do not make other provision in that behalf.

(2) Notice of the meeting of a company shall be served on every member of it in the manner in which notices are required to be served by Table A (as for the time being in force).

(3) Two or more members holding not less than one-tenth of the issued share capital or, if the company does not have a share capital, not less than 5 per cent. in number of the members of the company may call a meeting.

(4) Two members personally present are a quorum.

(5) Any member elected by the members present at a meeting may be chairman of it.

(6) In the case of a company originally having a share capital, every member has one vote in respect of each share or each £10 of stock held by him ; and in any other case every member has one vote.

371.—(1) If for any reason it is impracticable to call a meeting Power of court of a company in any manner in which meetings of that company to order may be called, or to conduct the meeting in manner prescribed meeting. by the articles or this Act, the court may, either of its own motion or on the application—

    (*a*) of any director of the company, or

    (*b*) of any member of the company who would be entitled to vote at the meeting,

order a meeting to be called, held and conducted in any manner the court thinks fit.

(2) Where such an order is made, the court may give such ancillary or consequential directions as it thinks expedient ; and these may include a direction that one member of the company present in person or by proxy be deemed to constitute a meeting.

(3) A meeting called, held and conducted in accordance with an order under subsection (1) is deemed for all purposes a meeting of the company duly called, held and conducted.

372.—(1) Any member of a company entitled to attend and Proxies. vote at a meeting of it is entitled to appoint another person (whether a member or not) as his proxy to attend and vote instead of him ; and in the case of a private company a proxy appointed to attend and vote instead of a member has also the same right as the member to speak at the meeting.

(2) But, unless the articles otherwise provide—

    (*a*) subsection (1) does not apply in the case of a company not having a share capital; and

    (*b*) a member of a private company is not entitled to appoint more than one proxy to attend on the same occasion ; and

    (*c*) a proxy is not entitled to vote except on a poll.

(3) In the case of a company having a share capital, in every notice calling a meeting of the company there shall appear with reasonable prominence a statement that a member entitled to attend and vote is entitled to appoint a proxy or, where that is

allowed, one or more proxies to attend and vote instead of him, and that a proxy need not also be a member.

(4) If default is made in complying with subsection (3) as respects any meeting, every officer of the company who is in default is liable to a fine.

(5) A provision contained in a company's articles is void in so far as it would have the effect of requiring the instrument appointing a proxy, or any other document necessary to show the validity of, or otherwise relating to, the appointment of a proxy, to be received by the company or any other person more than 48 hours before a meeting or adjourned meeting in order that the appointment may be effective.

(6) If for the purpose of any meeting of a company invitations to appoint as proxy a person or one of a number of persons specified in the invitations are issued at the company's expense to some only of the members entitled to be sent a notice of the meeting and to vote at it by proxy, then every officer of the company who knowingly and wilfully authorises or permits their issue in that manner is liable to a fine.

However, an officer is not so liable by reason only of the issue to a member at his request in writing of a form of appointment naming the proxy, or of a list of persons willing to act as proxy, if the form or list is available on request in writing to every member entitled to vote at the meeting by proxy.

(7) This section applies to meetings of any class of members of a company as it applies to general meetings of the company.

Right to
demand a poll.
373.—(1) A provision contained in a company's articles is void in so far as it would have the effect either—

    (*a*) of excluding the right to demand a poll at a general meeting on any question other than the election of the chairman of the meeting or the adjournment of the meeting ; or

    (*b*) of making ineffective a demand for a poll on any such question which is made either—

        (i) by not less than 5 members having the right to vote at the meeting ; or

        (ii) by a member or members representing not less than one-tenth of the total voting rights of all

the members having the right to vote at the
meeting; or

(iii) by a member or members holding shares in
the company conferring a right to vote at the
meeting, being shares on which an aggregate sum
has been paid up equal to not less than one-tenth
of the total sum paid up on all the shares conferring that right.

(2) The instrument appointing a proxy to vote at a meeting
of a company is deemed also to confer authority to demand
or join in demanding a poll; and for the purposes of subsection
(1) a demand by a person as proxy for a member is the same
as a demand by the member.

374. On a poll taken at a meeting of a company or a meeting
of any class of members of a company, a member entitled to
more than one vote need not, if he votes, use all his votes or
cast all the votes he uses in the same way.

Voting on a
poll.

375.—(1) A corporation, whether or not a company within
the meaning of this Act, may—

Representation
of corpora-
tions at
meetings.

(a) if it is a member of another corporation, being such a
company, by resolution of its directors or other governing body authorise such person as it thinks fit to act as
its representative at any meeting of the company or at
any meeting of any class of members of the company;

(b) if it is a creditor (including a holder of debentures) of
another corporation, being such a company, by resolution of its directors or other governing body authorise
such person as it thinks fit to act as its representative at
any meeting of creditors of the company held in pursuance of this Act or of rules made under it, or in
pursuance of the provisions contained in any debenture
or trust deed, as the case may be.

(2) A person so authorised is entitled to exercise the same
powers on behalf of the corporation which he represents as
that corporation could exercise if it were an individual shareholder, creditor or debenture-holder of the other company.

Resolutions

376.—(1) Subject to the section next following, it is the duty of a company, on the requisition in writing of such number of members as is specified below and (unless the company otherwise resolves) at the expense of the requisitionists—

    (a) to give to members of the company entitled to receive notice of the next annual general meeting notice of any resolution which may properly be moved and is intended to be moved at that meeting ;

    (b) to circulate to members entitled to have notice of any general meeting sent to them any statement of not more than 1,000 words with respect to the matter referred to in any proposed resolution or the business to be dealt with at that meeting.

(2) The number of members necessary for a requisition under subsection (1) is—

    (a) any number representing not less than one-twentieth of the total voting rights of all the members having at the date of the requisition a right to vote at the meeting to which the requisition relates ; or

    (b) not less than 100 members holding shares in the company on which there has been paid up an average sum, per member, of not less than £100.

(3) Notice of any such resolution shall be given, and any such statement shall be circulated, to members of the company entitled to have notice of the meeting sent to them, by serving a copy of the resolution or statement on each such member in any manner permitted for service of notice of the meeting.

(4) Notice of any such resolution shall be given to any other member of the company by giving notice of the general effect of the resolution in any manner permitted for giving him notice of meetings of the company.

(5) For compliance with subsections (3) and (4), the copy must be served, or notice of the effect of the resolution be given (as the case may be), in the same manner and (so far as practicable) at the same time as notice of the meeting ; and, where it is not practicable for it to be served or given at the same time, it must be served or given as soon as practicable thereafter.

(6) The business which may be dealt with at an annual general meeting includes any resolution of which notice is given in accordance with this section ; and for purposes of this subsection notice is deemed to have been so given notwithstanding the accidental omission, in giving it, of one or more members. This has effect notwithstanding anything in the company's articles.

(7) In the event of default in complying with this section, every officer of the company who is in default is liable to a fine.

377.—(1) A company is not bound under section 376 to give notice of a resolution or to circulate a statement unless—

(a) a copy of the requisition signed by the requisitionists (or two or more copies which between them contain the signatures of all the requisitionists) is deposited at the registered office of the company—

(i) in the case of a requisition requiring notice of a resolution, not less than 6 weeks before the meeting, and

(ii) otherwise, not less than one week before the meeting ; and

(b) there is deposited or tendered with the requisition a sum reasonably sufficient to meet the company's expenses in giving effect to it.

(2) But if, after a copy of a requisition requiring notice of a resolution has been deposited at the company's registered office, an annual general meeting is called for a date 6 weeks or less after the copy has been deposited, the copy (though not deposited within the time required by subsection (1)) is deemed properly deposited for the purposes of that subsection.

(3) The company is also not bound under section 376 to circulate a statement if, on the application either of the company or of any other person who claims to be aggrieved, the court is satisfied that the rights conferred by that section are being abused to secure needless publicity for defamatory matter ; and the court may order the company's costs on such an application to be paid in whole or in part by the requisitionists, notwithstanding that they are not parties to the application.

378.—(1) A resolution is an extraordinary resolution when it has been passed by a majority of not less than three-fourths of such members as (being entitled to do so) vote in person or, where proxies are allowed, by proxy, at a general meeting of which notice specifying the intention to propose the resolution as an extraordinary resolution has been duly given.

(2) A resolution is a special resolution when it has been passed by such a majority as is required for the passing of an extraordinary resolution and at a general meeting of which not less than 21 days' notice, specifying the intention to propose the resolution as a special resolution, has been duly given.

(3) If it is so agreed by a majority in number of the members having the right to attend and vote at such a meeting, being a majority—

(a) together holding not less than 95 per cent. in nominal value of the shares giving that right ; or (*b*) in the case of a company not having a share capital, together representing not less than 95 per cent. of the total voting rights at that meeting of all the members,

a resolution may be proposed and passed as a special resolution at a meeting of which less than 21 days' notice has been given.

(4) At any meeting at which an extraordinary resolution or a special resolution is submitted to be passed, a declaration by the chairman that the resolution is carried is, unless a poll is demanded, conclusive evidence of the fact without proof of the number or proportion of the votes recorded in favour of or against the resolution.

(5) In computing the majority on a poll demanded on the question that an extraordinary resolution or a special resolution be passed, reference is to be had to the number of votes cast for and against the resolution.

(6) For purposes of this section, notice of a meeting is deemed duly given, and the meeting duly held, when the notice is given and the meeting held in the manner provided by this Act or the company's articles.

Resolution
requiring
special notice.

379.—(1) Where by any provision of this Act special notice is required of a resolution, the resolution is not effective unless notice of the intention to move it has been given to the company at least 28 days before the meeting at which it is moved.

(2) The company shall give its members notice of any such resolution at the same time and in the same manner as it gives notice of the meeting or, if that is not practicable, shall give them notice either by advertisement in a newspaper having an appropriate circulation or in any other mode allowed by the company's articles, at least 21 days before the meeting.

(3) If, after notice of the intention to move such a resolution has been given to the company, a meeting is called for a date 28 days or less after the notice has been given, the notice is deemed properly given, though not given within the time required.

Registration,
etc. of
resolutions and
agreements.

380.—(1) A copy of every resolution or agreement to which this section applies shall, within 15 days after it is passed or made, be forwarded to the registrar of companies and recorded by him ; and it must be either a printed copy or else a copy in some other form approved by the registrar.

(2) Where articles have been registered, a copy of every such resolution or agreement for the time being in force shall be embodied in or annexed to every copy of the articles issued after the passing of the resolution or the making of the agreement.

(3) Where articles have not been registered, a printed copy of every such resolution or agreement shall be forwarded to any member at his request on payment of 5 pence or such less sum as the company may direct.

(4) This section applies to—

    (a) special resolutions ;

    (b) extraordinary resolutions ;

    (c) resolutions or agreements which have been agreed to by all the members of a company but which, if not so agreed to, would not have been effective for their purpose unless (as the case may be) they had been passed as special resolutions or as extraordinary resolutions ;

    (d) resolutions or agreements which have been agreed to by all the members of some class of shareholders but which, if not so agreed to, would not have been effective for their purpose unless they had been passed by some particular majority or otherwise in some particular manner, and all resolutions or agreements which effectively bind all the members of any class of shareholders though not agreed to by all those members ;

    (e) a resolution passed by the directors of a company in compliance with a direction under section 31(2) (change of name on Secretary of State's direction) ;

    (f) a resolution of a company to give, vary, revoke or renew an authority to the directors for the purposes of section 80 (allotment of relevant securities) ;

    (g) a resolution of the directors passed under section 147(2) (alteration of memorandum on company ceasing to be a public company, following acquisition of its own shares) ;

    (h) a resolution conferring, varying, revoking or renewing authority under section 166 (market purchase of company's own shares) ;

    (j) a resolution for voluntary winding up, passed under section 572(1)(a) ;

    (k) a resolution passed by the directors of an old public company, under section 2(1) of the Consequential Provisions Act, that the company should be re-registered as a public company.

(5) If a company fails to comply with subsection (1), the company and every officer of it who is in default is liable to a fine and, for continued contravention, to a daily default fine.

(6) If a company fails to comply with subsection (2) or (3), the company and every officer of it who is in default is liable to a fine.

(7) For purposes of subsections (5) and (6), a liquidator of a company is deemed an officer of it.

Resolution
passed at
adjourned
meeting.

381. Where a resolution is passed at an adjourned meeting of—

(a) a company ;

(b) the holders of any class of shares in a company ;

(c) the directors of a company ;

the resolution is for all purposes to be treated as having been passed on the date on which it was in fact passed, and is not to be deemed passed on any earlier date.

Records of proceedings

Minutes of
meetings.

382.—(1) Every company shall cause minutes of all proceedings of general meetings, all proceedings at meetings of its directors and, where there are managers, all proceedings at meetings of its managers to be entered in books kept for that purpose.

(2) Any such minute, if purporting to be signed by the chairman of the meeting at which the proceedings were had, or by the chairman of the next succeeding meeting, is evidence of the proceedings.

(3) Where a shadow director by means of a notice required by section 317(8) declares an interest in a contract or proposed contract, this section applies—

(a) if it is a specific notice under paragraph (a) of that subsection, as if the declaration had been made at the meeting there referred to, and

(b) otherwise, as if it had been made at the meeting of the directors next following the giving of the notice ;

and the making of the declaration is in either case deemed to form part of the proceedings at the meeting.

(4) Where minutes have been made in accordance with this section of the proceedings at any general meeting of the company or meeting of directors or managers, then, until the contrary is proved, the meeting is deemed duly held and convened, and all proceedings had at the meeting to have been duly had ; and all appointments of directors, managers or liquidators are deemed valid.

(5) If a company fails to comply with subsection (1), the company and every officer of it who is in default is liable to a fine and, for continued contravention, to a daily default fine.

Inspection of
minute books.

383.—(1) The books containing the minutes of proceedings of any general meeting of a company held on or after 1st November 1929 shall be kept at the company's registered office, and shall during business hours be open to the inspection of any member without charge.

(2) The reference to business hours is subject to such reasonable restrictions as the company may by its articles or in general meeting impose, but so that not less than 2 hours in each day be allowed for inspection.

(3) Any member shall be entitled to be furnished, within 7 days after he has made a request in that behalf to the company, with a copy of any such minutes as are referred to above, at a charge of not more than 2½ pence for every 100 words.

(4) If an inspection required under this section is refused or if a copy required under this section is not sent within the proper time, the company and every officer of it who is in default is liable in respect of each offence to a fine.

(5) In the case of any such refusal or default, the court may by order compel an immediate inspection of the books in respect of all proceedings of general meetings, or direct that the copies required be sent to the persons requiring them.

CHAPTER V

AUDITORS

384.—(1) Every company shall, at each general meeting of the company at which accounts are laid in accordance with section 241, appoint an auditor or auditors to hold office from the conclusion of that meeting until the conclusion of the next general meeting at which the requirements of section 241 are complied with.

This is subject to section 252 (exemption for dormant companies).

Annual appointment of auditors.

(2) The first auditors of a company may be appointed by the directors at any time before the first general meeting of the company at which accounts are laid ; and auditors so appointed shall hold office until the conclusion of that meeting.

(3) If the directors fail to exercise their powers under subsection (2), those powers may be exercised by the company in general meeting.

(4) The directors, or the company in general meeting, may fill any casual vacancy in the office of auditor ; but while any such vacancy continues, the surviving or continuing auditor or auditors (if any) may act.

K

(5) If at any general meeting of a company at which accounts are laid as required by section 241 no auditors are appointed or reappointed, the Secretary of State may appoint a person to fill the vacancy ; and the company shall, within one week of that power of the Secretary of State becoming exercisable, give to him notice of that fact.

If a company fails to give the notice required by this subsection, the company and every officer of it who is in default is guilty of an offence and liable to a fine and, for continued contravention, to a daily default fine.

Remuneration of auditors.

385.—(1) The remuneration of a company's auditors shall be fixed by the company in general meeting, or in such manner as the company in general meeting may determine.

(2) This does not apply in the case of auditors appointed by the directors or by the Secretary of State ; and in that case their remuneration may be fixed by the directors or by the Secretary of State (as the case may be).

(3) For the purpose of this section, " remuneration " includes any sums paid by the company in respect of the auditor's expenses.

Removal of auditors.

386.—(1) A company may by ordinary resolution remove an auditor before the expiration of his term of office, notwithstanding anything in any agreement between it and him.

(2) Where a resolution removing an auditor is passed at a general meeting of a company, the company shall within 14 days give notice of that fact in the prescribed form to the registrar of companies.

If a company fails to give the notice required by this subsection, the company and every officer of it who is in default is guilty of an offence and liable to a fine and, for continued contravention, to a daily default fine.

(3) Nothing in this section is to be taken as depriving a person removed under it of compensation or damages payable to him in respect of the termination of his appointment as auditor or of any appointment terminating with that as auditor.

Auditors' right to attend company meetings.

387.—(1) A company's auditors are entitled to attend any general meeting of the company and to receive all notices of, and other communications relating to, any general meeting which a member of the company is entitled to receive, and to be heard at any general meeting which they attend on any part of the business of the meeting which concerns them as auditors.

(2) An auditor of a company who has been removed is entitled to attend—

(a) the general meeting at which his term of office would otherwise have expired, and

(b) any general meeting at which it is proposed to fill the vacancy caused by his removal,

and to receive all notices of, and other communications relating to, any such meeting which any member of the company is entitled to receive, and to be heard at any such meeting which he attends on any part of the business of the meeting which concerns him as former auditor of the company.

388.—(1) Special notice is required for a resolution at a general meeting of a company—

(a) appointing as auditor a person other than a retiring auditor ; or

(b) filling a casual vacancy in the office of auditor ; or

(c) reappointing as auditor a retiring auditor who was appointed by the directors to fill a casual vacancy ; or

(d) removing an auditor before the expiration of his term of office.

(2) On receipt of notice of such an intended resolution as is mentioned above the company shall forthwith send a copy of it—

(a) to the person proposed to be appointed or removed, as the case may be ;

(b) in a case within subsection (1)(a), to the retiring auditor ; and

(c) where, in a case within subsection (1)(b) or (c), the casual vacancy was caused by the resignation of an auditor, to the auditor who resigned.

(3) Where notice is given of such a resolution as is mentioned in subsection (1) (a) or (d), and the retiring auditor or (as the case may be) the auditor proposed to be removed makes with respect to the intended resolution representations in writing to the company (not exceeding a reasonable length) and requests their notification to members of the company, the company shall (unless the representations are received by it too late for it to do so)—

(a) in any notice of the resolution given to members of the company state the fact of the representations having been made, and

K 2

(*b*) send a copy of the representations to every member of the company to whom notice of the meeting is or has been sent.

(4) If a copy of any such representations is not sent out as required by subsection (3) because received too late or because of the company's default, the auditor may (without prejudice to his right to be heard orally) require that the representations shall be read out at the meeting.

(5) Copies of the representations need not be sent out and the representations need not be read out at the meeting if, on the application either of the company or of any other person claiming to be aggrieved, the court is satisfied that the rights conferred by this section are being abused to secure needless publicity for defamatory matter ; and the court may order the company's costs on the application to be paid in whole or in part by the auditor, notwithstanding that he is not a party to the application.

389.—(1) Subject to the next subsection, a person is not qualified for appointment as auditor of a company unless either—

(*a*) he is a member of a body of accountants established in the United Kingdom and for the time being recognised for the purposes of this provision by the Secretary of State ; or

(*b*) he is for the time being authorised by the Secretary of State to be so appointed, as having similar qualifications obtained outside the United Kingdom or else he retains an authorisation formerly granted by the Board of Trade or the Secretary of State under section 161(1) (*b*) of the Companies Act 1948 (adequate knowledge and experience, or pre-1947 practice).

(2) Subject to subsections (6) to (8) below, a person is qualified for appointment as auditor of an unquoted company if he retains an authorisation granted by the Board of Trade or the Secretary of State under section 13(1) of the Companies Act 1967.

In this subsection—

(*a*) " unquoted company " means a company in the case of which, at the time of the person's appointment, the following condition is satisfied, namely, that no shares or debentures of the company, or of a body corporate of which it is the subsidiary, have been quoted on a stock exchange (whether in Great Britain or elsewhere) to the public for subscription or purchase, and

(b) "company" does not include a company that carries on business as the promoter of a trading stamp scheme within the meaning of the Trading Stamps Act 1964.

(3) Subject to the next subsection, the bodies of accountants recognised for the purposes of subsection (1)(a) are—

(a) the Institute of Chartered Accountants in England and Wales,

(b) the Institute of Chartered Accountants of Scotland,

(c) the Chartered Association of Certified Accountants, and

(d) the Institute of Chartered Accountants in Ireland.

(4) The Secretary of State may by regulations in a statutory instrument amend subsection (3) by adding or deleting any body, but shall not make regulations—

(a) adding any body, or

(b) deleting any body which has not consented in writing to its deletion,

unless he has published notice of his intention to do so in the London and Edinburgh Gazettes at least 4 months before making the regulations.

(5) The Secretary of State may refuse an authorisation under subsection (1)(b) to a person as having qualifications obtained outside the United Kingdom if it appears to him that the country in which the qualifications were obtained does not confer on persons qualified in the United Kingdom privileges corresponding to those conferred by that subsection.

(6) None of the following persons is qualified for appointment as auditor of a company—

(a) an officer or servant of the company ;

(b) a person who is a partner of or in the employment of an officer or servant of the company ;

(c) a body corporate ;

and for this purpose an auditor of a company is not to be regarded as either officer or servant of it.

(7) A person is also not qualified for appointment as auditor of a company if he is, under subsection (6), disqualified for appointment as auditor of any other body corporate which is that company's subsidiary or holding company or a subsidiary of that company's holding company, or would be so disqualified if the body corporate were a company.

(8) Notwithstanding subsections (1), (6) and (7), a Scottish firm is qualified for appointment as auditor of a company if, but only if, all the partners are qualified for appointment as auditors of it.

(9) No person shall act as auditor of a company at a time when he knows that he is disqualified for appointment to that office ; and if an auditor of a company to his knowledge becomes so disqualified during his term of office he shall thereupon vacate his office and give notice in writing to the company that he has vacated it by reason of that disqualification.

(10) A person who acts as auditor in contravention of subsection (9), or fails without reasonable excuse to give notice of vacating his office as required by that subsection, is guilty of an offence and liable to a fine and, for continued contravention, to a daily default fine.

Resignation of
auditors.
390.—(1) An auditor of a company may resign his office by depositing a notice in writing to that effect at the company's registered office ; and any such notice operates to bring his term of office to an end on the date on which the notice is deposited, or on such later date as may be specified in it.

(2) An auditor's notice of resignation is not effective unless it contains either—

(a) a statement to the effect that there are no circumstances connected with his resignation which he considers should be brought to the notice of the members or creditors of the company ; or

(b) a statement of any such circumstances as are mentioned above.

(3) Where a notice under this section is deposited at a company's registered office, the company shall within 14 days send a copy of the notice—

(a) to the registrar of companies ; and

(b) if the notice contained a statement under subsection (2)(b), to every person who under section 240 is entitled to be sent copies of the accounts.

(4) The company or any person claiming to be aggrieved may, within 14 days of the receipt by the company of a notice containing a statement under subsection (2)(b), apply to the court for an order under the next subsection.

(5) If on such an application the court is satisfied that the auditor is using the notice to secure needless publicity for defamatory matter, it may by order direct that copies of the notice need not be sent out; and the court may further order the company's costs on the application to be paid in whole or in part by the auditor, notwithstanding that he is not a party to the application.

(6) The company shall, within 14 days of the court's decision, send to the persons mentioned in subsection (3)—

> (*a*) if the court makes an order under subsection (5), a statement setting out the effect of the order ;
>
> (*b*) if not, a copy of the notice containing the statement under subsection (2)(*b*).

(7) If default is made in complying with subsection (3) or (6), the company and every officer of it who is in default is liable to a fine and, for continued contravention, to a daily default fine.

391.—(1) Where an auditor's notice of resignation contains a statement under section 390(2)(*b*) there may be deposited with the notice a requisition signed by the auditor calling on the directors of the company forthwith duly to convene an extraordinary general meeting of the company for the purpose of receiving and considering such explanation of the circumstances connected with his resignation as he may wish to place before the meeting.

(2) Where an auditor's notice of resignation contains such a statement, the auditor may request the company to circulate to its members—

> (*a*) before the general meeting at which his term of office would otherwise have expired ; or
>
> (*b*) before any general meeting at which it is proposed to fill the vacancy caused by his resignation or convened on his requisition,

a statement in writing (not exceeding a reasonable length) of the circumstances connected with his resignation.

(3) The company shall in that case (unless the statement is received by it too late for it to comply)—

> (*a*) in any notice of the meeting given to members of the company state the fact of the statement having been made, and
>
> (*b*) send a copy of the statement to every member of the company to whom notice of the meeting is or has been sent.

(4) If the directors do not within 21 days from the date of the deposit of a requisition under this section proceed duly to convene a meeting for a day not more than 28 days after the date on which the notice convening the meeting is given, every director who failed to take all reasonable steps to secure that a meeting was convened as mentioned above is guilty of an offence and liable to a fine.

(5) If a copy of the statement mentioned in subsection (2) is not sent out as required by subsection (3) because received too late or because of the company's default, the auditor may (without prejudice to his right to be heard orally) require that the statement shall be read out at the meeting.

(6) Copies of a statement need not be sent out and the statement need not be read out at the meeting if, on the application either of the company or of any other person who claims to be aggrieved, the court is satisfied that the rights conferred by this section are being abused to secure needless publicity for defamatory matter; and the court may order the company's costs on such an application to be paid in whole or in part by the auditor, notwithstanding that he is not a party to the application.

(7) An auditor who has resigned his office is entitled to attend any such meeting as is mentioned in subsection (2)(a) or (b) and to receive all notices of, and other communications relating to, any such meeting which any member of the company is entitled to receive, and to be heard at any such meeting which he attends on any part of the business of the meeting which concerns him as former auditor of the company.

Powers of
auditors in
relation to
subsidiaries.

392.—(1) Where a company (" the holding company ") has a subsidiary, then—

(a) if the subsidiary is a body corporate incorporated in Great Britain, it is the duty of the subsidiary and its auditors to give to the auditors of the holding company such information and explanation as those auditors may reasonably require for the purposes of their duties as auditors of the holding company;

(b) in any other case, it is the duty of the holding company, if required by its auditors to do so, to take all such steps as are reasonably open to it to obtain from the subsidiary such information and explanation as are mentioned above.

(2) If a subsidiary or holding company fails to comply with subsection (1), the subsidiary or holding company and every officer of it who is in default is guilty of an offence and liable to a fine; and if an auditor fails without reasonable excuse to comply with paragraph (a) of the subsection, he is guilty of an offence and so liable.

False
statements
to auditors.

393. An officer of a company commits an offence if he knowingly or recklessly makes to a company's auditors a statement (whether written or oral) which—

(a) conveys or purports to convey any information or explanation which the auditors require, or are entitled to require, as auditors of the company, and (*b*) is misleading, false or deceptive in a material particular.

A person guilty of an offence under this section is liable to imprisonment or a fine, or both.

394.—(1) Subject as follows, this section applies to every body which is both a company and a trade union or an employers' association to which section 11 of the Trade Union and Labour Relations Act 1974 applies.

(2) Section 11(3) of the Act of 1974 and paragraphs 6 to 15 of Schedule 2 to that Act (qualifications, appointment and removal of auditors) do not have effect in relation to bodies to which this section applies.

(3) The rights and powers conferred, and the duties imposed, by paragraphs 16 to 21 of that Schedule on the auditors of a body to which this section applies belong to the auditors from time to time appointed by or on behalf of that body under section 384 of this Act.

PART XII

REGISTRATION OF CHARGES

CHAPTER I

REGISTRATION OF CHARGES (ENGLAND AND WALES)

395.—(1) Subject to the provisions of this Chapter, a charge created by a company registered in England and Wales and being a charge to which this section applies is, so far as any security on the company's property or undertaking is conferred by the charge, void against the liquidator and any creditor of the company, unless the prescribed particulars of the charge together with the instrument (if any) by which the charge is created or evidenced, are delivered to or received by the registrar of companies for registration in the manner required by this Chapter within 21 days after the date of the charge's creation.

(2) Subsection (1) is without prejudice to any contract or obligation for repayment of the money secured by the charge; and when a charge becomes void under this section, the money secured by it immediately becomes payable.

PART XII
CHAPTER I
Charges
which have
to be
registered.

396.—(1) Section 395 applies to the following charges—

(*a*) a charge for the purpose of securing any issue of debentures,

(*b*) a charge on uncalled share capital of the company,

(*c*) a charge created or evidenced by an instrument which, if executed by an individual, would require registration as a bill of sale,

(*d*) a charge on land (wherever situated) or any interest in it, but not including a charge for any rent or other periodical sum issuing out of the land,

(*e*) a charge on book debts of the company,

(*f*) a floating charge on the company's undertaking or property,

(*g*) a charge on calls made but not paid,

(*h*) a charge on a ship or aircraft, or any share in a ship,

(*j*) a charge on goodwill, on a patent or a licence under a patent, on a trademark or on a copyright or a licence under a copyright.

(2) Where a negotiable instrument has been given to secure the payment of any book debts of a company, the deposit of the instrument for the purpose of securing an advance to the company is not, for purposes of section 395, to be treated as a charge on those book debts.

(3) The holding of debentures entitling the holder to a charge on land is not for purposes of this section deemed to be an interest in land.

(4) In this Chapter, " charge " includes mortgage.

397.—(1) Where a series of debentures containing, or giving by reference to another instrument, any charge to the benefit of which the debenture holders of that series are entitled pari passu is created by a company, it is for purposes of section 395 sufficient if there are delivered to or received by the registrar, within 21 days after the execution of the deed containing the charge (or, if there is no such deed, after the execution of any debentures of the series), the following particulars in the prescribed form—

(*a*) the total amount secured by the whole series, and

(*b*) the dates of the resolutions authorising the issue of the series and the date of the covering deed (if any) by which the security is created or defined, and

(*c*) a general description of the property charged, and

(*d*) the names of the trustees (if any) for the debenture holders,

together with the deed containing the charge or, if there is no such deed, one of the debentures of the series:

Provided that there shall be sent to the registrar of companies, for entry in the register, particulars in the prescribed form of the date and amount of each issue of debentures of the series, but any omission to do this does not affect the validity of any of those debentures.

(2) Where any commission, allowance or discount has been paid or made either directly or indirectly by a company to a person in consideration of his—

(*a*) subscribing or agreeing to subscribe, whether absolutely or conditionally, for debentures of the company, or

(*b*) procuring or agreeing to procure subscriptions, whether absolute or conditional, for such debentures,

the particulars required to be sent for registration under section 395 shall include particulars as to the amount or rate per cent. of the commission, discount or allowance so paid or made, but omission to do this does not affect the validity of the debentures issued.

(3) The deposit of debentures as security for a debt of the company is not, for the purposes of subsection (2), treated as the issue of the debentures at a discount.

398.—(1) In the case of a charge created out of the United Kingdom comprising property situated outside the United Kingdom, the delivery to and the receipt by the registrar of companies of a copy (verified in the prescribed manner) of the instrument by which the charge is created or evidenced has the same effect for purposes of sections 395 to 398 as the delivery and receipt of the instrument itself.

Verification of charge on property outside United Kingdom.

(2) In that case, 21 days after the date on which the instrument or copy could, in due course of post (and if despatched with due diligence), have been received in the United Kingdom are substituted for the 21 days mentioned in section 395(1) (or as the case may be, section 397(1)) as the time within which the particulars and instrument or copy are to be delivered to the registrar.

(3) Where a charge is created in the United Kingdom but comprises property outside the United Kingdom, the instrument creating or purporting to create the charge may be sent for registration under section 395 notwithstanding that further proceedings may be necessary to make the charge valid or effectual according to the law of the country in which the property is situated.

(4) Where a charge comprises property situated in Scotland or Northern Ireland and registration in the country where the property is situated is necessary to make the charge valid or effectual according to the law of that country, the delivery to and the receipt by the registrar of a copy (verified in the prescribed manner) of the instrument by which the charge is created or evidenced, together with a certificate in the prescribed form stating that the charge was presented for registration in Scotland or Northern Ireland (as the case may be) on the date on which it was so presented has, for purposes of sections 395 to 398, the same effect as the delivery and receipt of the instrument itself.

Company's
duty to
register
charges it
creates.

399.—(1) It is a company's duty to send to the registrar of companies for registration the particulars of every charge created by the company and of the issues of debentures of a series requiring registration under sections 395 to 398 ; but registration of any such charge may be effected on the application of any person interested in it.

(2) Where registration is effected on the application of some person other than the company, that person is entitled to recover from the company the amount of any fees properly paid by him to the registrar on the registration.

(3) If a company fails to comply with subsection (1), then, unless the registration has been effected on the application of some other person, the company and every officer of it who is in default is liable to a fine and, for continued contravention, to a daily default fine.

Charges
existing on
property
acquired.

400.—(1) This section applies where a company registered in England and Wales acquires property which is subject to a charge of any such kind as would, if it had been created by the company after the acquisition of the property, have been required to be registered under this Chapter.

(2) The company shall cause the prescribed particulars of the charge, together with a copy (certified in the prescribed manner to be a correct copy) of the instrument (if any) by which the charge was created or is evidenced, to be delivered to the

registrar of companies for registration in manner required by this Chapter within 21 days after the date on which the acquisition is completed.

(3) However, if the property is situated and the charge was created outside Great Britain, 21 days after the date on which the copy of the instrument could in due course of post, and if despatched with due diligence, have been received in the United Kingdom is substituted for the 21 days above-mentioned as the time within which the particulars and copy of the instrument are to be delivered to the registrar.

(4) If default is made in complying with this section, the company and every officer of it who is in default is liable to a fine and, for continued contravention, to a daily default fine.

401.—(1) The registrar of companies shall keep, with respect to each company, a register in the prescribed form of all the charges requiring registration under this Chapter; and he shall enter in the register with respect to such charges the following particulars—

Register of charges to be kept by registrar of companies.

(*a*) in the case of a charge to the benefit of which the holders of a series of debentures are entitled, the particulars specified in section 397(1),

(*b*) in the case of any other charge—

(i) if it is a charge created by the company, the date of its creation, and if it is a charge which was existing on property acquired by the company, the date of the acquisition of the property, and

(ii) the amount secured by the charge, and

(iii) short particulars of the property charged, and

(iv) the persons entitled to the charge.

(2) The registrar shall give a certificate of the registration of any charge registered in pursuance of this Chapter, stating the amount secured by the charge.

The certificate—

(*a*) shall be either signed by the registrar, or authenticated by his official seal, and

(*b*) is conclusive evidence that the requirements of this Chapter as to registration have been satisfied.

(3) The register kept in pursuance of this section shall be open to inspection by any person.

402.—(1) The company shall cause a copy of every certificate of registration given under section 401 to be endorsed on every debenture or certificate of debenture stock which is issued by the company, and the payment of which is secured by the charge so registered.

(2) But this does not require a company to cause a certificate of registration of any charge so given to be endorsed on any debenture or certificate of debenture stock issued by the company before the charge was created.

(3) If a person knowingly and wilfully authorises or permits the delivery of a debenture or certificate of debenture stock which under this section is required to have endorsed on it a copy of a certificate of registration, without the copy being so endorsed upon it, he is liable (without prejudice to any other liability) to a fine.

403.—(1) The registrar of companies, on receipt of a statutory declaration in the prescribed form verifying, with respect to a registered charge,—

> (*a*) that the debt for which the charge was given has been paid or satisfied in whole or in part, or
>
> (*b*) that part of the property or undertaking charged has been released from the charge or has ceased to form part of the company's property or undertaking,

may enter on the register a memorandum of satisfaction in whole or in part, or of the fact that part of the property or undertaking has been released from the charge or has ceased to form part of the company's property or undertaking (as the case may be).

(2) Where the registrar enters a memorandum of satisfaction in whole, he shall if required furnish the company with a copy of it.

404.—(1) The following applies if the court is satisfied that the omission to register a charge within the time required by this Chapter or that the omission or mis-statement of any particular with respect to any such charge or in a memorandum of satisfaction was accidental, or due to inadvertence or to some other sufficient cause, or is not of a nature to prejudice the position of creditors or shareholders of the company, or that on other grounds it is just and equitable to grant relief.

(2) The court may, on the application of the company or a person interested, and on such terms and conditions as seem to the court just and expedient, order that the time for registration shall be extended or, as the case may be, that the omission or mis-statement shall be rectified.

405.—(1) If a person obtains an order for the appointment of a receiver or manager of a company's property, or appoints such a receiver or manager under powers contained in an instrument, he shall within 7 days of the order or of the appointment under those powers, give notice of the fact to the registrar of companies; and the registrar shall enter the fact in the register of charges.

PART XII
CHAPTER I
Registration of enforcement of security.

(2) Where a person appointed receiver or manager of a company's property under powers contained in an instrument ceases to act as such receiver or manager, he shall, on so ceasing, give the registrar notice to that effect, and the registrar shall enter the fact in the register of charges.

(3) A notice under this section shall be in the prescribed form.

(4) If a person makes default in complying with the requirements of this section, he is liable to a fine and, for continued contravention, to a daily default fine.

406.—(1) Every company shall cause a copy of every instrument creating a charge requiring registration under this Chapter to be kept at its registered office.

Companies to keep copies of instruments creating charges.

(2) In the case of a series of uniform debentures, a copy of one debenture of the series is sufficient.

407.—(1) Every limited company shall keep at its registered office a register of charges and enter in it all charges specifically affecting property of the company and all floating charges on the company's undertaking or any of its property.

Company's register of charges.

(2) The entry shall in each case give a short description of the property charged, the amount of the charge and, except in the case of securities to bearer, the names of the persons entitled to it.

(3) If an officer of the company knowingly and wilfully authorises or permits the omission of an entry required to be made in pursuance of this section, he is liable to a fine.

408.—(1) The copies of instruments creating any charge requiring registration under this Chapter with the registrar of companies, and the register of charges kept in pursuance of section 407, shall be open during business hours (but subject to such reasonable restrictions as the company in general meeting may impose, so that not less than 2 hours in each day be allowed

Right to inspect instruments which create charges, etc.

PART XII
CHAPTER I

for inspection) to the inspection of any creditor or member of the company without fee.

(2) The register of charges shall also be open to the inspection of any other person on payment of such fee, not exceeding 5 pence, for each inspection, as the company may prescribe.

(3) If inspection of the copies referred to, or of the register, is refused, every officer of the company who is in default is liable to a fine and, for continued contravention, to a daily default fine.

(4) If such a refusal occurs in relation to a company registered in England and Wales, the court may by order compel an immediate inspection of the copies or register.

Charges on
property in
England and
Wales created
by oversea
company.

409.—(1) This Chapter extends to charges on property in England and Wales which are created, and to charges on property in England and Wales which is acquired, by a company (whether a company within the meaning of this Act or not) incorporated outside Great Britain which has an established place of business in England and Wales.

(2) In relation to such a company, sections 406 and 407 apply with the substitution, for the reference to the company's registered office, of a reference to its principal place of business in England and Wales.

CHAPTER II

REGISTRATION OF CHARGES (SCOTLAND)

Charges void
unless
registered.

410.—(1) The following provisions of this Chapter have effect for the purpose of securing the registration in Scotland of charges created by companies.

(2) Every charge created by a company, being a charge to which this section applies, is, so far as any security on the company's property or any part of it is conferred by the charge, void against the liquidator and any creditor of the company unless the prescribed particulars of the charge, together with a copy (certified in the prescribed manner to be a correct copy) of the instrument (if any) by which the charge is created or evidenced, are delivered to or received by the registrar of companies for registration in the manner required by this Chapter within 21 days after the date of the creation of the charge.

(3) Subsection (2) is without prejudice to any contract or
obligation for repayment of the money secured by the charge; and when a charge becomes void under this section the money secured by it immediately becomes payable.

(4) This section applies to the following charges—

   (*a*) a charge on land wherever situated, or any interest in such land (not including a charge for any rent, ground annual or other periodical sum payable in respect of the land, but including a charge created by a heritable security within the meaning of section 9(8) of the Conveyancing and Feudal Reform (Scotland) Act 1970),   1970 c. 35.

   (*b*) a security over the uncalled share capital of the company,

   (*c*) a security over incorporeal moveable property of any of the following categories—

      (i) the book debts of the company,

      (ii) calls made but not paid,

      (iii) goodwill,

      (iv) a patent or a licence under a patent,

      (v) a trademark,

      (vi) a copyright or a licence under a copyright,

   (*d*) a security over a ship or aircraft or any share in a ship, and

   (*e*) a floating charge.

(5) In this Chapter " company " (except in section 424) means an incorporated company registered in Scotland ; " registrar of companies " means the registrar or other officer performing under this Act the duty of registration of companies in Scotland ; and references to the date of creation of a charge are—

   (*a*) in the case of a floating charge, the date on which the instrument creating the floating charge was executed by the company creating the charge, and

   (*b*) in any other case, the date on which the right of the person entitled to the benefit of the charge was constituted as a real right.

411.—(1) In the case of a charge created out of the United Kingdom comprising property situated outside the United Kingdom, the period of 21 days after the date on which the copy of the instrument creating it could (in due course of post, and if despatched with due diligence) have been received in the United Kingdom is substituted for the period of 21 days after the date of the creation of the charge as the time within which, under section 410(2), the particulars and copy are to be delivered to the registrar.

PART XII
CHAPTER II

(2) Where a charge is created in the United Kingdom but comprises property outside the United Kingdom, the copy of the instrument creating or purporting to create the charge may be sent for registration under section 410 notwithstanding that further proceedings may be necessary to make the charge valid or effectual according to the law of the country in which the property is situated.

Negotiable instrument to secure book debts.

412. Where a negotiable instrument has been given to secure the payment of any book debts of a company, the deposit of the instrument for the purpose of securing an advance to the company is not, for purposes of section 410, to be treated as a charge on those book debts.

Charges associated with debentures.

413.—(1) The holding of debentures entitling the holder to a charge on land is not, for the purposes of section 410, deemed to be an interest in land.

(2) Where a series of debentures containing, or giving by reference to any other instrument, any charge to the benefit of which the debenture-holders of that series are entitled pari passu, is created by a company, it is sufficient for purposes of section 410 if there are delivered to or received by the registrar of companies within 21 days after the execution of the deed containing the charge or, if there is no such deed, after the execution of any debentures of the series, the following particulars in the prescribed form—

(a) the total amount secured by the whole series,

(b) the dates of the resolutions authorising the issue of the series and the date of the covering deed (if any) by which the security is created or defined,

(c) a general description of the property charged,

(d) the names of the trustees (if any) for the debenture holders, and

(e) in the case of a floating charge, a statement of any provisions of the charge and of any instrument relating to it which prohibit or restrict or regulate the power of the company to grant further securities ranking in priority to, or pari passu with, the floating charge, or which vary or otherwise regulate the order of ranking of the floating charge in relation to subsisting securities,

together with a copy of the deed containing the charge or, if there is no such deed, of one of the debentures of the series:

Provided that, where more than one issue is made of debentures in the series, there shall be sent to the registrar of companies for entry in the register particulars (in the prescribed form) of the date and amount of each issue of debentures of the series, but any omission to do this does not affect the validity of any of those debentures.

(3) Where any commission, allowance or discount has been paid or made, either directly or indirectly, by a company to any person in consideration of his subscribing or agreeing to subscribe, whether absolutely or conditionally, for any debentures of the company, or procuring or agreeing to procure subscriptions (whether absolute or conditional) for any such debentures, the particulars required to be sent for registration under section 410 include particulars as to the amount or rate per cent. of the commission, discount or allowance so paid or made ; but any omission to do this does not affect the validity of the debentures issued.

The deposit of any debentures as security for any debt of the company is not, for purposes of this subsection, treated as the issue of the debentures at a discount.

414.—(1) For the avoidance of doubt, it is hereby declared that, in the case of a charge created by way of an ex facie absolute disposition or assignation qualified by a back letter or other agreement, or by a standard security qualified by an agreement, compliance with section 410(2) does not of itself render the charge unavailable as security for indebtedness incurred after the date of compliance.

Charge by way of ex facie absolute disposition, etc.

(2) Where the amount secured by a charge so created is purported to be increased by a further back letter or agreement, a further charge is held to have been created by the ex facie absolute disposition or assignation or (as the case may be) by the standard security, as qualified by the further back letter or agreement ; and the provisions of this Chapter apply to the further charge as if—

(*a*) references in this Chapter (other than in this section) to the charge were references to the further charge, and

(*b*) references to the date of the creation of the charge were references to the date on which the further back letter or agreement was executed.

415.—(1) It is a company's duty to send to the registrar of companies for registration the particulars of every charge created by the company and of the issues of debentures of a series requiring registration under sections 410 to 414 ; but registration of any such charge may be effected on the application of any person interested in it.

Company's duty to register charges created by it.

(2) Where registration is effected on the application of some person other than the company, that person is entitled to recover

from the company the amount of any fees properly paid by him to the registrar on the registration.

(3) If a company makes default in sending to the registrar for registration the particulars of any charge created by the company or of the issues of debentures of a series requiring registration as above mentioned, then, unless the registration has been effected on the application of some other person, the company and every officer of it who is in default is liable to a fine and, for continued contravention, to a daily default fine.

Duty to register charges existing on property acquired.

416.—(1) Where a company acquires any property which is subject to a charge of any kind as would, if it had been created by the company after the acquisition of the property, have been required to be registered under this Chapter, the company shall cause the prescribed particulars of the charge, together with a copy (certified in the prescribed manner to be a correct copy) of the instrument (if any) by which the charge was created or is evidenced, to be delivered to the registrar of companies for registration in the manner required by this Chapter within 21 days after the date on which the transaction was settled.

(2) If, however, the property is situated and the charge was created outside Great Britain, 21 days after the date on which the copy of the instrument could (in due course of post, and if despatched with due diligence) have been received in the United Kingdom are substituted for 21 days after the settlement of the transaction as the time within which the particulars and the copy of the instrument are to be delivered to the registrar.

(3) If default is made in complying with this section, the company and every officer of it who is in default is liable to a fine and, for continued contravention, to a daily default fine.

Register of charges to be kept by registrar of companies.

417.—(1) The registrar of companies shall keep, with respect to each company, a register in the prescribed form of all the charges requiring registration under this Chapter, and shall enter in the register with respect to such charges the particulars specified below.

(2) In the case of a charge to the benefit of which the holders of a series of debentures are entitled, there shall be entered in the register the particulars specified in section 413(2).

(3) In the case of any other charge, there shall be entered—

    (a) if it is a charge created by the company, the date of its creation, and if it was a charge existing on property acquired by the company, the date of the acquisition of the property,

    (b) the amount secured by the charge,

(c) short particulars of the property charged,

(d) the persons entitled to the charge, and

(e) in the case of a floating charge, a statement of any of the provisions of the charge and of any instrument relating to it which prohibit or restrict or regulate the company's power to grant further securities ranking in priority to, or pari passu with, the floating charge, or which vary or otherwise regulate the order of ranking of the floating charge in relation to subsisting securities.

PART XII
CHAPTER II

(4) The register kept in pursuance of this section shall be open to inspection by any person.

418.—(1) The registrar of companies shall give a certificate of the registration of any charge registered in pursuance of this Chapter.

Certificate of registration to be issued.

(2) The certificate—

(a) shall be either signed by the registrar, or authenticated by his official seal,

(b) shall state the name of the company and the person first-named in the charge among those entitled to the benefit of the charge (or, in the case of a series of debentures, the name of the holder of the first such debenture to be issued) and the amount secured by the charge, and

(c) is conclusive evidence that the requirements of this Chapter as to registration have been complied with.

419—(1) The registrar of companies, on application being made to him in the prescribed form, and on receipt of a statutory declaration in the prescribed form verifying, with respect to any registered charge,—

Entries of satisfaction and relief.

(a) that the debt for which the charge was given has been paid or satisfied in whole or in part, or

(b) that part of the property charged has been released from the charge or has ceased to form part of the company's property,

may enter on the register a memorandum of satisfaction (in whole or in part) regarding that fact.

(2) Where the registrar enters a memorandum of satisfaction in whole, he shall, if required, furnish the company with a copy of the memorandum.

(3) Without prejudice to the registrar's duty under this section to require to be satisfied as above mentioned, he shall not be so satisfied unless—

(a) the creditor entitled to the benefit of the floating charge, or a person authorised to do so on his behalf, certifies as correct the particulars submitted to the registrar with respect to the entry on the register of a memorandum under this section, or

(*b*) the court, on being satisfied that such certification cannot readily be obtained, directs him accordingly.

(4) Nothing in this section requires the company to submit particulars with respect to the entry in the register of a memorandum of satisfaction where the company, having created a floating charge over all or any part of its property, disposes of part of the property subject to the floating charge.

(5) A memorandum or certification required for the purposes of this section shall be in such form as may be prescribed.

Rectification of register.

420. The court, on being satisfied that the omission to register a charge within the time required by this Act or that the omission or mis-statement of any particular with respect to any such charge or in a memorandum of satisfaction was accidental, or due to inadvertence or to some other sufficient cause, or is not of a nature to prejudice the position of creditors or shareholders of the company, or that it is on other grounds just and equitable to grant relief, may, on the application of the company or any person interested, and on such terms and conditions as seem to the court just and expedient, order that the time for registration shall be extended or (as the case may be) that the omission or mis-statement shall be rectified.

Copies of instruments creating charges to be kept by company.

421.—(1) Every company shall cause a copy of every instrument creating a charge requiring registration under this Chapter to be kept at the company's registered office.

(2) In the case of a series of uniform debentures, a copy of one debenture of the series is sufficient.

Company's register of charges.

422.—(1) Every company shall keep at its registered office a register of charges and enter in it all charges specifically affecting property of the company, and all floating charges on any property of the company.

(2) There shall be given in each case a short description of the property charged, the amount of the charge and, except in the case of securities to bearer, the names of the persons entitled to it.

(3) If an officer of the company knowingly and wilfully authorises or permits the omission of an entry required to be made in pursuance of this section, he is liable to a fine.

423.—(1) The copies of instruments creating charges requir- ing registration under this Chapter with the registrar of com- panies, and the register of charges kept in pursuance of section 422, shall be open during business hours (but subject to such reasonable restrictions as the company in general meeting may impose, so that not less than 2 hours in each day be allowed for inspection) to the inspection of any creditor or member of the company without fee.

(2) The register of charges shall be open to the inspection of any other person on payment of such fee, not exceeding 5 pence for each inspection, as the company may prescribe.

(3) If inspection of the copies or register is refused, every officer of the company who is in default is liable to a fine and, for continued contravention, to a daily default fine.

(4) If such a refusal occurs in relation to a company, the court may by order compel an immediate inspection of the copies or register.

424.—(1) This Chapter extends to charges on property in Scot- land which are created, and to charges on property in Scotland which is acquired, by a company incorporated outside Great Britain which has a place of business in Scotland.

(2) In relation to such a company, sections 421 and 422 apply with the substitution, for the reference to the company's registered office, of a reference to its principal place of business in Scotland.

PART XIII

ARRANGEMENTS AND RECONSTRUCTIONS

425.—(1) Where a compromise or arrangement is proposed between a company and its creditors, or any class of them, or between the company and its members, or any class of them, the court may on the application of the company or any creditor or member of it or, in the case of a company being wound up, of the liquidator, order a meeting of the creditors or class of creditors, or of the members of the company or class of members (as the case may be), to be summoned in such manner as the court directs.

(2) If a majority in number representing three-fourths in value of the creditors or class of creditors or members or class of members (as the case may be), present and voting either in person or by proxy at the meeting, agree to any compromise or arrangement, the compromise or arrangement, if sanctioned by the court, is binding on all creditors or the class of creditors or on the members or class of members (as the case may be), and

also on the company or, in the case of a company in the course of being wound up, on the liquidator and contributories of the company.

(3) The court's order under subsection (2) has no effect until an office copy of it has been delivered to the registrar of companies for registration ; and a copy of every such order shall be annexed to every copy of the company's memorandum issued after the order has been made or, in the case of a company not having a memorandum, of every copy so issued of the instrument constituting the company or defining its constitution.

(4) If a company makes default in complying with subsection (3), the company and every officer of it who is in default is liable to a fine.

(5) An order under subsection (1) pronounced in Scotland by the judge acting as vacation judge in pursuance of section 4 of the Administration of Justice (Scotland) Act 1933 is not subject to review, reduction, suspension or stay of execution.

(6) In this section and the next—

 (a) " company " means any company liable to be wound up under this Act, and

 (b) " arrangement " includes a reorganisation of the company's share capital by the consolidation of shares of different classes or by the division of shares into shares of different classes, or by both of those methods.

Information
as to
compromise
to be
circulated.
426.—(1) The following applies where a meeting of creditors or any class of creditors, or of members or any class of members, is summoned under section 425.

(2) With every notice summoning the meeting which is sent to a creditor or member there shall be sent also a statement explaining the effect of the compromise or arrangement and in particular stating any material interests of the directors of the company (whether as directors or as members or as creditors of the company or otherwise) and the effect on those interests of the compromise or arrangement, in so far as it is different from the effect on the like interests of other persons.

(3) In every notice summoning the meeting which is given by advertisement there shall be included either such a statement as above-mentioned or a notification of the place at which, and the manner in which, creditors or members entitled to attend the meeting may obtain copies of the statement.

(4) Where the compromise or arrangement affects the rights of debenture holders of the company, the statement shall give the like explanation as respects the trustees of any deed for

securing the issue of the debentures as it is required to give as respects the company's directors.

(5) Where a notice given by advertisement includes a notification that copies of a statement explaining the effect of the compromise or arrangement proposed can be obtained by creditors or members entitled to attend the meeting, every such creditor or member shall, on making application in the manner indicated by the notice, be furnished by the company free of charge with a copy of the statement.

(6) If a company makes default in complying with any requirement of this section, the company and every officer of it who is in default is liable to a fine ; and for this purpose a liquidator of the company and a trustee of a deed for securing the issue of debentures of the company is deemed an officer of it.

However, a person is not liable under this subsection if he shows that the default was due to the refusal of another person, being a director or trustee for debenture holders, to supply the necessary particulars of his interests.

(7) It is the duty of any director of the company, and of any trustee for its debenture holders, to give notice to the company of such matters relating to himself as may be necessary for purposes of this section ; and any person who makes default in complying with this subsection is liable to a fine.

427.—(1) The following applies where application is made to the court under section 425 for the sanctioning of a compromise or arrangement proposed between a company and any such persons as are mentioned in that section.

Provisions for facilitating company reconstruction or amalgamation.

(2) If it is shown—

(a) that the compromise or arrangement has been proposed for the purposes of, or in connection with, a scheme for the reconstruction of any company or companies, or the amalgamation of any two or more companies, and

(b) that under the scheme the whole or any part of the undertaking or the property of any company concerned in the scheme (" a transferor company ") is to be transferred to another company (" the transferee company "),

the court may, either by the order sanctioning the compromise or arrangement or by any subsequent order, make provision for all or any of the following matters.

(3) The matters for which the court's order may make provision are—

(a) the transfer to the transferee company of the whole or any part of the undertaking and of the property or liabilities of any transferor company, (*b*) the allotting or appropriation by the transferee company of any shares, debentures, policies or other like interests in that company which under the compromise or arrangement are to be allotted or appropriated by that company to or for any person,

(*c*) the continuation by or against the transferee company of any legal proceedings pending by or against any transferor company,

(*d*) the dissolution, without winding up, of any transferor company,

(*e*) the provision to be made for any persons who, within such time and in such manner as the court directs, dissent from the compromise or arrangement,

(*f*) such incidental, consequential and supplemental matters as are necessary to secure that the reconstruction or amalgamation is fully and effectively carried out.

(4) If an order under this section provides for the transfer of property or liabilities, then—

(*a*) that property is by virtue of the order transferred to, and vests in, the transferee company, and

(*b*) those liabilities are, by virtue of the order, transferred to and become liabilities of that company ;

and property (if the order so directs) vests freed from any charge which is by virtue of the compromise or arrangement to cease to have effect.

(5) Where an order is made under this section, every company in relation to which the order is made shall cause an office copy of the order to be delivered to the registrar of companies for registration within 7 days after its making ; and if default is made in complying with this subsection, the company and every officer of it who is in default is liable to a fine and, for continued contravention, to a daily default fine.

(6) In this section the expression " property " includes property, rights and powers of every description ; the expression " liabilities " includes duties and " company " includes only a company as defined in section 735(1).

Power to acquire shares of dissenting minority.

428.—(1) This section applies where a scheme or contract involving the transfer of shares or any class of shares in a company (" the transferor company ") to another company, whether or not a company as defined in section 735(1) (" the transferee company ") has, within 4 months after the making of the offer in that behalf by the transferee company, been approved by the holders of not less than nine-tenths in value of the shares whose transfer is involved (other than shares

already held at the date of the offer by, or by a nominee for,
the transferee company or its subsidiary).

(2) In those circumstances, the transferee company may, at
any time within 2 months after the expiration of the 4 months
mentioned above, give notice in the prescribed manner to any
dissenting shareholder that it desires to acquire his shares.

(3) The expression " dissenting shareholder " includes a shareholder who has not assented to the scheme or contract, and any
shareholder who has failed or refused to transfer his shares
to the transferee company in accordance with the scheme or
contract.

(4) If such a notice is given, the transferee company is then
(unless on an application made by the dissenting shareholder
within one month from the date on which the notice was given,
the court thinks fit to order otherwise) entitled and bound to
acquire those shares on the terms on which, under the scheme
or contract, the shares of the approving shareholders are to be
transferred to the transferee company.

(5) But where shares in the transferor company of the same
class or classes as the shares whose transfer is involved are
already held (at the date of the offer) by, or by a nominee for,
the transferee company or its subsidiary to a value greater than
one-tenth of the aggregate of their value and that of the shares
(other than those already so held) whose transfer is involved,
subsections (2) and (4) do not apply unless—

  (*a*) the transferee company offers the same terms to all
        holders of the shares (other than those already so held)
        whose transfer is involved or, where those shares
        include shares of different classes, of each class of
        them, and

  (*b*) the holders who approve the scheme or contract, be-
        sides holding not less than nine-tenths in value of the
        shares (other than those so held) whose transfer is
        involved, are not less than three-fourths in number of
        the holders of those shares.

429.—(1) This section applies where, in pursuance of such a Dissentient's
scheme or contract as is mentioned in section 428(1), shares right to compel
in a company are transferred to another company or its nominee, acquisition of
and those shares (together with any other shares in the first- his shares.
mentioned company held by, or by a nominee for, the transferee
company or its subsidiary at the date of the transfer) comprise
or include nine-tenths in value of the shares in the first-mentioned company or of any class of those shares.

(2) The transferee company shall within one month from the
date of the transfer (unless on a previous transfer in pursuance

PART XIII
of the scheme or contract it has already complied with this requirement), give notice of that fact in the prescribed manner to the holders of the remaining shares or of the remaining shares of that class (as the case may be) who have not assented to the scheme or contract.

(3) Any such holder may, within 3 months from the giving of that notice to him, himself give notice (in the prescribed form) requiring the transferee company to acquire the shares in question.

(4) If a shareholder gives notice under subsection (3) with respect to any shares, the transferee company is then entitled and bound to acquire those shares on the terms on which under the scheme or contract the shares of the approving shareholders were transferred to it, or on such other terms as may be agreed or as the court on the application of either the transferee company or the shareholder thinks fit to order.

Provisions supplementing ss. 428, 429.
430.—(1) Where notice has been given by the transferee company under section 428(2) and the court has not, on an application made by the dissenting shareholder, ordered to the contrary, the two following subsections apply.

(2) The transferee company shall, on expiration of one month from the date on which the notice has been given (or, if an application to the court by the dissenting shareholder is then pending, after that application has been disposed of) transmit a copy of the notice to the transferor company together with an instrument of transfer executed on behalf of the shareholder by any person appointed by the transferee company and on its own behalf by the transferee company.

An instrument of transfer is not required for any share for which a share warrant is for the time being outstanding.

(3) The transferee company shall also pay or transfer to the transferor company the amount or other consideration representing the price payable by the transferee company for the shares which by virtue of section 428(4) that company is entitled to acquire ; and the transferor company shall thereupon register the transferee company as the holder of those shares.

(4) Any sums received by the transferor company under this section shall be paid into a separate bank account, and any such sums and any other consideration so received shall be held by that company on trust for the several persons entitled to the shares in respect of which those sums, or that other consideration, were respectively received.

PART XIV

INVESTIGATION OF COMPANIES AND THEIR AFFAIRS ; REQUISITION
OF DOCUMENTS

Appointment and functions of inspectors

431.—(1) The Secretary of State may appoint one or more Investigation competent inspectors to investigate the affairs of a company of a company and to report on them in such manner as he may direct. on its own application or

(2) The appointment may be made— that of its members.

> (*a*) in the case of a company having a share capital, on the
> application either of not less than 200 members or of
> members holding not less than one-tenth of the shares
> issued,
>
> (*b*) in the case of a company not having a share capital,
> on the application of not less than one-fifth in number
> of the persons on the company's register of members,
> and
>
> (*c*) in any case, on application of the company.

(3) The application shall be supported by such evidence as the Secretary of State may require for the purpose of showing that the applicant or applicants have good reason for requiring the investigation.

(4) The Secretary of State may, before appointing inspectors, require the applicant or applicants to give security, to an amount not exceeding £5,000, or such other sum as he may by order specify, for payment of the costs of the investigation.

An order under this subsection shall be made by statutory instrument subject to annulment in pursuance of a resolution of either House of Parliament.

432.—(1) The Secretary of State shall appoint one or more Other company competent inspectors to investigate the affairs of a company investigations. and report on them in such manner as he directs, if the court by order declares that its affairs ought to be so investigated.

(2) The Secretary of State may make such an appointment if it appears to him that there are circumstances suggesting—

> (*a*) that the company's affairs are being or have been con-
> ducted with intent to defraud its creditors or the cred-
> itors of any other person, or otherwise for a fraudulent
> or unlawful purpose, or in a manner which is unfairly
> prejudicial to some part of its members, or
>
> (*b*) that any actual or proposed act or omission of the com-
> pany (including an act or omission on its behalf) is
> or would be so prejudicial, or that the company was
> formed for any fraudulent or unlawful purpose, or

(c) that persons concerned with the company's formation or the management of its affairs have in connection therewith been guilty of fraud, misfeasance or other misconduct towards it or towards its members, or

(d) that the company's members have not been given all the information with respect to its affairs which they might reasonably expect.

(3) Subsections (1) and (2) are without prejudice to the powers of the Secretary of State under section 431 ; and the power conferred by subsection (2) is exercisable with respect to a body corporate notwithstanding that it is in course of being voluntarily wound up.

(4) The reference in subsection (2)(a) to a company's members includes any person who is not a member but to whom shares in the company have been transferred or transmitted by operation of law.

Inspectors' powers during investigation.

433.—(1) If inspectors appointed under section 431 or 432 to investigate the affairs of a company think it necessary for the purposes of their investigation to investigate also the affairs of another body corporate which is or at any relevant time has been the company's subsidiary or holding company, or a subsidiary of its holding company or a holding company of its subsidiary, they have power to do so ; and they shall report on the affairs of the other body corporate so far as they think that the results of their investigation of its affairs are relevant to the investigation of the affairs of the company first mentioned above.

(2) Inspectors appointed under either section may at any time in the course of their investigation, without the necessity of making an interim report, inform the Secretary of State of matters coming to their knowledge as a result of the investigation tending to show that an offence has been committed.

Production of documents and evidence to inspectors.

434.—(1) When inspectors are appointed under section 431 or 432, it is the duty of all officers and agents of the company, and of all officers and agents of any other body corporate whose affairs are investigated under section 433(1)—

(a) to produce to the inspectors all books and documents of or relating to the company or, as the case may be, the other body corporate which are in their custody or power,

(b) to attend before the inspectors when required to do so, and

(c) otherwise to give the inspectors all assistance in connection with the investigation which they are reasonably able to give.

(2) If the inspectors consider that a person other than an officer or agent of the company or other body corporate is or may be in possession of information concerning its affairs, they may require that person to produce to them any books or documents in his custody or power relating to the company or other body corporate, to attend before them and otherwise to give them all assistance in connection with the investigation which he is reasonably able to give ; and it is that person's duty to comply with the requirement.

(3) An inspector may examine on oath the officers and agents of the company or other body corporate, and any such person as is mentioned in subsection (2), in relation to the affairs of the company or other body, and may administer an oath accordingly.

(4) In this section a reference to officers or to agents includes past, as well as present, officers or agents (as the case may be) ; and " agents ", in relation to a company or other body corporate, includes its bankers and solicitors and persons employed by it as auditors, whether these persons are or are not officers of the company or other body corporate.

(5) An answer given by a person to a question put to him in exercise of powers conferred by this section (whether as it has effect in relation to an investigation under any of sections 431 to 433, or as applied by any other section in this Part) may be used in evidence against him.

435.—(1) If an inspector has reasonable grounds for believing that a director, or past director, of the company or other body corporate whose affairs he is investigating maintains or has maintained a bank account of any description (whether alone or jointly with another person and whether in Great Britain or elsewhere), into or out of which there has been paid— *Power of inspector to call for directors' bank accounts.*

    (*a*) the emoluments or part of the emoluments of his office as such director particulars of which have not been disclosed in the accounts of the company or other body corporate for any financial year, contrary to paragraphs 24 to 26 of Schedule 5, or

    (*b*) any money which has resulted from or been used in the financing of an undisclosed transaction, arrangement or agreement, or

    (*c*) any money which has been in any way connected with an act or omission, or series of acts or omissions, which on the part of that director constituted misconduct (whether fraudulent or not) towards the company or body corporate or its members, the inspector may require the director to produce to him all documents in the director's possession, or under his control, relating to that bank account.

(2) For purposes of subsection (1)(*b*), an " undisclosed " transaction, arrangement or agreement is one—

(*a*) particulars of which have not been disclosed in the notes to the accounts of any company for any financial year, contrary to section 232 and Part I of Schedule 6 (disclosure of contracts between companies and their directors, etc.), or

(*b*) in respect of which an amount outstanding was not included in the aggregate amounts required to be disclosed in the notes to the accounts of any company for any financial year by section 234 and Part III of Schedule 6, contrary to that section (transactions between banks and their directors), or

(*c*) particulars of which were not included in the register of transactions, arrangements and agreements required to be maintained by section 343, contrary to that section.

Obstruction of inspectors treated as contempt of court.

436.—(1) When inspectors are appointed under section 431 or 432 to investigate the affairs of a company, the following applies in the case of—

(*a*) any officer or agent of the company,

(*b*) any officer or agent of another body corporate whose affairs are investigated under section 433, and

(*c*) any such person as is mentioned in section 434(2).

Section 434(4) applies with regard to references in this subsection to an officer or agent.

(2) If that person—

(*a*) refuses to produce any book or document which it is his duty under section 434 or 435 to produce, or

(*b*) refuses to attend before the inspectors when required to do so, or

(*c*) refuses to answer any question put to him by the inspectors with respect to the affairs of the company or other body corporate (as the case may be),

the inspectors may certify the refusal in writing to the court.

(3) The court may thereupon enquire into the case ; and, after hearing any witnesses who may be produced against or on behalf of the alleged offender and after hearing any statement which may be offered in defence, the court may punish the offender in like manner as if he had been guilty of contempt of the court.

437.—(1) The inspectors may, and if so directed by the Secretary of State shall, make interim reports to the Secretary of State, and on the conclusion of their investigation shall make a final report to him.

Any such report shall be written or printed, as the Secretary of State directs.

(2) If the inspectors were appointed under section 432 in pursuance of an order of the court, the Secretary of State shall furnish a copy of any report of theirs to the court.

(3) In any case the Secretary of State may, if he thinks fit—

(a) forward a copy of any report made by the inspectors to the company's registered office,

(b) furnish a copy on request and on payment of the prescribed fee to—

(i) any member of the company or other body corporate which is the subject of the report,

(ii) any person whose conduct is referred to in the report,

(iii) the auditors of that company or body corporate,

(iv) the applicants for the investigation,

(v) any other person whose financial interests appear to the Secretary of State to be affected by the matters dealt with in the report, whether as a creditor of the company or body corporate, or otherwise, and

(c) cause any such report to be printed and published.

438.—(1) If, from any report made under section 437 or from information or documents obtained under section 447 or 448 below, it appears to the Secretary of State that any civil proceedings ought in the public interest to be brought by any body corporate, he may himself bring such proceedings in the name and on behalf of the body corporate.

(2) The Secretary of State shall indemnify the body corporate against any costs or expenses incurred by it in or in connection with proceedings brought under this section.

439.—(1) The expenses of and incidental to an investigation by inspectors appointed by the Secretary of State shall be defrayed in the first instance by him ; but the persons mentioned in the following 4 subsections are, to the extent there specified, liable to make repayment to the Secretary of State.

(2) A person who is convicted on a prosecution instituted as a result of the investigation, or is ordered to pay the whole or any part of the costs of proceedings brought under section 438, may in the same proceedings be ordered to pay those expenses to such extent as may be specified in the order.

(3) A body corporate in whose name proceedings are brought under that section is liable to the amount or value of any sums or property recovered by it as a result of those proceedings ; and any amount for which a body corporate is liable under this subsection is a first charge on the sums or property recovered.

(4) A body corporate dealt with by the inspectors' report, where the inspectors were appointed otherwise than of the Secretary of State's own motion, is liable except where it was the applicant for the investigation, and except so far as the Secretary of State otherwise directs.

(5) The applicant or applicants for the investigation, where the inspectors were appointed under section 431, is or are liable to such extent (if any) as the Secretary of State may direct.

(6) The report of inspectors appointed otherwise than of the Secretary of State's own motion may, if they think fit, and shall if the Secretary of State so directs, include a recommendation as to the directions (if any) which they think appropriate, in the light of their investigation, to be given under subsection (4) or (5) of this section.

(7) For purposes of this section, any costs or expenses incurred by the Secretary of State in or in connection with proceedings brought under section 438 (including expenses incurred under subsection (2) of it) are to be treated as expenses of the investigation giving rise to the proceedings.

(8) Any liability to repay the Secretary of State imposed by subsections (2) and (3) above is (subject to satisfaction of his right to repayment) a liability also to indemnify all persons against liability under subsections (4) and (5) ; and any such liability imposed by subsection (2) is (subject as mentioned above) a liability also to indemnify all persons against liability under subsection (3).

(9) A person liable under any one of those subsections is entitled to contribution from any other person liable under the same subsection, according to the amount of their respective liabilities under it.

(10) Expenses to be defrayed by the Secretary of State under this section shall, so far as not recovered under it, be paid out of money provided by Parliament.

440. If in the case of a body corporate liable to be wound up under this Act it appears to the Secretary of State from a report made by inspectors under section 437, or from information or documents obtained under section 447 or 448 below, that it is expedient in the public interest that the body should be wound up, he may (unless the body is already being wound up by the court) present a petition for it to be so wound up if the court thinks it just and equitable for it to be so.

441.—(1) A copy of any report of inspectors appointed under section 431 or 432, certified by the Secretary of State to be a true copy, is admissible in any legal proceedings as evidence of the opinion of the inspectors in relation to any matter contained in the report.

(2) A document purporting to be such a certificate as is mentioned above shall be received in evidence and be deemed to be such a certificate, unless the contrary is proved.

Other powers of investigation available to the Secretary of State

442.—(1) Where it appears to the Secretary of State that there is good reason to do so, he may appoint one or more competent inspectors to investigate and report on the membership of any company, and otherwise with respect to the company, for the purpose of determining the true persons who are or have been financially interested in the success or failure (real or apparent) of the company or able to control or materially to influence its policy.

(2) The appointment of inspectors under this section may define the scope of their investigation (whether as respects the matter or the period to which it is to extend or otherwise) and in particular may limit the investigation to matters connected with particular shares or debentures.

(3) If application for an investigation under this section with respect to particular shares or debentures of a company is made to the Secretary of State by members of the company, and the number of applicants or the amount of the shares held by them is not less than that required for an application for the appointment of inspectors under section 431(2)(*a*) and (*b*)—

   (*a*) the Secretary of State shall appoint inspectors to conduct the investigation (unless he is satisfied that the application is vexatious), and

   (*b*) the inspectors' appointment shall not exclude from the scope of their investigation any matter which the application seeks to have included, except in so far as the

Secretary of State is satisfied that it is unreasonable for that matter to be investigated.

(4) Subject to the terms of their appointment, the inspectors' powers extend to the investigation of any circumstances suggesting the existence of an arrangement or understanding which, though not legally binding, is or was observed or likely to be observed in practice and which is relevant to the purposes of the investigation.

Provisions applicable on investigation under s. 442.

443.—(1) For purposes of an investigation under section 442, sections 433(1), 434, 436 and 437 apply with the necessary modifications of references to the affairs of the company or to those of any other body corporate, subject however to the following subsections.

(2) Those sections apply to—

(a) all persons who are or have been, or whom the inspector has reasonable cause to believe to be or have been, financially interested in the success or failure or the apparent success or failure of the company or any other body corporate whose membership is investigated with that of the company, or able to control or materially influence its policy (including persons concerned only on behalf of others), and

(b) any other person whom the inspector has reasonable cause to believe possesses information relevant to the investigation,

as they apply in relation to officers and agents of the company or the other body corporate (as the case may be).

(3) If the Secretary of State is of opinion that there is good reason for not divulging any part of a report made by virtue of section 442 and this section, he may under section 437 disclose the report with the omission of that part; and he may cause to be kept by the registrar of companies a copy of the report with that part omitted or, in the case of any other such report, a copy of the whole report.

(4) The expenses of an investigation under section 442 shall be defrayed by the Secretary of State out of money provided by Parliament.

Power to obtain information as to those interested in shares, etc.

444.—(1) If it appears to the Secretary of State that there is good reason to investigate the ownership of any shares in or debentures of a company and that it is unnecessary to appoint inspectors for the purpose, he may require any person whom he has reasonable cause to believe to have or to be able to obtain any information as to the present and past interests in those shares or debentures and the names and addresses of the persons interested and of any persons who act or have acted on their behalf in relation to the shares or debentures to give any such information to the Secretary of State.

(2) For this purpose a person is deemed to have an interest in shares or debentures if he has any right to acquire or dispose of them or of any interest in them, or to vote in respect of them, or if his consent is necessary for the exercise of any of the rights of other persons interested in them, or if other persons interested in them can be required, or are accustomed, to exercise their rights in accordance with his instructions.

(3) A person who fails to give information required of him under this section, or who in giving such information makes any statement which he knows to be false in a material particular, or recklessly makes any statement which is false in a material particular, is liable to imprisonment or a fine, or both.

445.—(1) If in connection with an investigation under either section 442 or 444 it appears to the Secretary of State that there is difficulty in finding out the relevant facts about any shares (whether issued or to be issued), he may by order direct that the shares shall until further order be subject to the restrictions of Part XV of this Act.

Power to impose restrictions on shares and debentures.

(2) This section, and Part XV in its application to orders under it, apply in relation to debentures as in relation to shares.

446.—(1) If it appears to the Secretary of State that there are circumstances suggesting that contraventions may have occurred, in relation to a company's shares or debentures, of section 323 or 324 (taken with Schedule 13), or of subsections (3) to (5) of section 328 (restrictions on share dealings by directors and their families ; obligation of director to disclose shareholding in his own company), he may appoint one or more competent inspectors to carry out such investigations as are requisite to establish whether or not such contraventions have occurred and to report the result of their investigations to him.

Investigation of share dealings.

(2) The appointment of inspectors under this section may limit the period to which their investigation is to extend or confine it to shares or debentures of a particular class, or both.

(3) For purposes of an investigation under this section, sections 434 to 436 apply—

    (*a*) with the substitution, for references to any other body corporate whose affairs are investigated under section 433(1), of a reference to any other body corporate which is, or has at any relevant time been, the company's subsidiary or holding company, or a subsidiary of its holding company, and

    (*b*) with the necessary modification of references in section 436 to the affairs of the company or other body corporate.

(4) Sections 434 to 436 apply under the preceding subsection—

    (*a*) to members of a recognised stock exchange or of a recognised association of dealers in securities who are individuals and to officers (past as well as present) of members of such an exchange or association being bodies corporate,

1958 c. 45.   (*b*) to holders of licences granted under section 3 of the Prevention of Fraud (Investments) Act 1958 who are individuals and to officers (past as well as present) of holders of licences so granted being bodies corporate, and

    (*c*) to any individual declared by an order of the Secretary of State for the time being in force to be an exempted dealer for purposes of that Act, and to officers (past as well as present) of any body corporate declared by an order of the Secretary of State for the time being in force to be such a dealer,

as they apply to officers of the company or of the other body corporate.

(5) The inspectors may, and if so directed by the Secretary of State shall, make interim reports to him ; and, on conclusion of the investigation, they shall make to him a final report.

Any such report shall be written or printed, as the Secretary of State may direct ; and he may cause it to be published.

(6) " Recognised association of dealers in securities " means any body of persons which is for the time being such an association for purposes of the Prevention of Fraud (Investments) Act 1958.

(7) The expenses of an investigation under this section shall be defrayed by the Secretary of State out of money provided by **Parliament.**

Requisition and seizure of books and papers

PART XIV
Secretary of
State's power
to require
production of
documents.

447.—(1) The powers of this section are exercisable in relation to the following bodies—

(a) a company, as defined by section 735(1);

(b) a company to which this Act applies by virtue of section 676 or which is registered under section 680;

(c) a body corporate incorporated in, and having a principal place of business in, Great Britain, being a body to which any of the provisions of this Act with respect to prospectuses and allotments apply by virtue of section 718 (unregistered companies); and

(d) a body corporate incorporated outside Great Britain which is carrying on business in Great Britain or has at any time carried on business there.

(2) The Secretary of State may at any time, if he thinks there is good reason to do so, give directions to any such body requiring it, at such time and place as may be specified in the directions, to produce such books or papers as may be so specified.

(3) The Secretary of State may at any time, if he thinks there is good reason to do so, authorise an officer of his, on producing (if so required) evidence of his authority, to require any such body to produce to him (the officer) forthwith any books or papers which the officer may specify.

(4) Where by virtue of subsection (2) or (3) the Secretary of State or an officer of his has power to require the production of books or papers from any body, he or the officer has the like power to require production of those books or papers from any person who appears to him or the officer to be in possession of them; but where any such person claims a lien on books or papers produced by him, the production is without prejudice to the lien.

(5) The power under this section to require a body or other person to produce books or papers includes power—

(a) if the books or papers are produced—

(i) to take copies of them or extracts from them, and

(ii) to require that person, or any other person who is a present or past officer of, or is or was at any time employed by, the body in question, to provide an explanation of any of them;

(b) if the books or papers are not produced, to require the person who was required to produce them to state, to the best of his knowledge and belief, where they are.

(6) If the requirement to produce books or papers or provide an explanation or make a statement is not complied with, the body or other person on whom the requirement was so imposed is guilty of an offence and liable to a fine.

Sections 732 (restriction on prosecutions) and 733(2) and (4) (liability of individuals for corporate default) apply to this offence.

(7) However, where a person is charged with an offence under subsection (6) in respect of a requirement to produce any books or papers, it is a defence to prove that they were not in his possession or under his control and that it was not reasonably practicable for him to comply with the requirement.

(8) A statement made by a person in compliance with such a requirement may be used in evidence against him.

Entry and search of premises.
448.—(1) The following applies if a justice of the peace is satisfied on information on oath laid by an officer of the Secretary of State, or laid under the Secretary of State's authority, that there are reasonable grounds for suspecting that there are on any premises any books or papers of which production has been required under section 447 and which have not been produced in compliance with that requirement.

(2) The justice may issue a warrant authorising any constable, together with any other persons named in the warrant and any other constables, to enter the premises specified in the information (using such force as is reasonably necessary for the purpose) and to search the premises and take possession of any books or papers appearing to be such books or papers as are mentioned above, or to take, in relation to any books or papers so appearing, any other steps which may appear to be necessary for preserving them and preventing interference with them.

(3) A warrant so issued continues in force until the end of one month after the date on which it is issued.

(4) Any books or papers of which possession is taken under this section may be retained—

    (a) for a period of 3 months, or

    (b) if within that period there are commenced any such criminal proceedings as are mentioned in subsection (1)(a) or (b) of the next following section (being pro-

ceedings to which the books or papers are relevant), PART XIV
until the conclusion of those proceedings.

(5) A person who obstructs the exercise of a right of entry
or search conferred by a warrant issued under this section, or
who obstructs the exercise of a right so conferred to take
possession of any books or papers, is guilty of an offence and
liable to a fine.

Sections 732 (restriction on prosecutions) and 733(2) and (4)
(liability of individuals for corporate default) apply to this offence.

(6) In the application of this section to Scotland, the reference
to a justice of the peace includes the sheriff and a magistrate.

449.—(1) No information or document relating to a body Provision for
which has been obtained under section 447 or 448 shall, without security of
the previous consent in writing of that body, be published or information
disclosed, except to a competent authority, unless the publication obtained.
or disclosure is required—

(*a*) with a view to the institution of, or otherwise for the
purposes of, any criminal proceedings pursuant to,
or arising out of, this Act, the Insider Dealing Act or
the Insurance Companies Act 1982, or any criminal pro- 1982 c. 50,
ceedings for an offence entailing misconduct in connection with the management of the body's affairs or
misapplication or wrongful retainer of its property ;

(*b*) with a view to the institution of, or otherwise for the
purposes of, any criminal proceedings pursuant to, or
arising out of, the Exchange Control Act 1947, 1947 c. 14.

(*c*) for the purposes of the examination of any person by
inspectors appointed under section 431, 432, 442 or
446 in the course of their investigation,

(*d*) for the purpose of enabling the Secretary of State to
exercise, in relation to that or any other body, any of
his functions under this Act, the Insider Dealing Act,
the Prevention of Fraud (Investments) Act 1958 and 1958 c. 45.
the Insurance Companies Act 1982,

(*e*) for the purposes of proceedings under section 448.

(2) A person who publishes or discloses any information or
document in contravention of this section is guilty of an offence
and liable to imprisonment or a fine, or both.

Sections 732 (restriction on prosecutions) and 733(2) and (4)
(liability of individuals for corporate default) apply to this
offence.

(3) For purposes of this section—

(a) in relation to information or a document relating to a body other than one carrying on industrial assurance business (as defined by section 1(2) of the Industrial Assurance Act 1923), each of the following is a competent authority—

(i) the Secretary of State for Trade and Industry, and any officer of his,

(ii) an inspector appointed under this Part by the Secretary of State,

(iii) the Treasury, and any officer of the Treasury,

(iv) the Lord Advocate,

(v) the Director of Public Prosecutions,

(vi) any constable, and

(vii) any procurator fiscal;

(b) in relation to information or a document relating to a body carrying on industrial assurance business (as so defined), all the same persons as above specified are competent authorities, and also the Industrial Assurance Commissioner and any officer of his.

Punishment for destroying, mutilating etc. company documents.

1982 c. 50.

450.—(1) A person, being an officer of any such body as is mentioned in paragraphs (a) to (d) of section 447(1) or a body other than as there mentioned, being an insurance company to which Part II of the Insurance Companies Act 1982 applies, who—

(a) destroys, mutilates or falsifies, or is privy to the destruction, mutilation or falsification of a document affecting or relating to the body's property or affairs, or

(b) makes, or is privy to the making of, a false entry in such a document,

is guilty of an offence, unless he proves that he had no intention to conceal the state of affairs of the body or to defeat the law.

(2) Such a person as above mentioned who fraudulently either parts with, alters or makes an omission in any such document or is privy to fraudulent parting with, fraudulent altering or fraudulent making of an omission in, any such document, is guilty of an offence.

(3) A person guilty of an offence under this section is liable to imprisonment or a fine, or both.

(4) Sections 732 (restriction on prosecutions) and 733(2) and (4) (liability of individuals for corporate default) apply to an offence under this section.

451. A person who, in purported compliance with a require- PART XIV
ment imposed under section 447 to provide an explanation or Punishment for
make a statement, provides or makes an explanation or statement furnishing
which he knows to be false in a material particular or recklessly false
provides or makes an explanation or statement which is so false, information.
is guilty of an offence and liable to imprisonment or a fine, or
both.

Sections 732 (restriction on prosecutions) and 733(2) and (4)
(liability of individuals for corporate default) apply to this offence.

Supplementary

452.—(1) Nothing in sections 431 to 446 requires the dis- Privileged
closure to the Secretary of State or to an inspector appointed by information.
him—

(a) by any person of information which he would in an
action in the High Court or the Court of Session be
entitled to refuse to disclose on grounds of legal professional privilege except, if he is a lawyer, the name
and address of his client,

(b) by a company's bankers (as such) of information as to
the affairs of any of their customers other than the
company.

(2) Nothing in sections 447 to 451 compels the production by
any person of a document which he would in an action in the
High Court or the Court of Session be entitled to refuse to
produce on grounds of legal professional privilege, or authorises
the taking of possession of any such document which is in the
person's possession.

(3) The Secretary of State shall not under section 447 require,
or authorise an officer of his to require, the production by a person carrying on the business of banking of a document relating
to the affairs of a customer of his unless either it appears to the
Secretary of State that it is necessary to do so for the purpose of
investigating the affairs of the first-mentioned person, or the
customer is a person on whom a requirement has been imposed
under that section, or under section 44(2) to (4) of the Insurance
Companies Act 1982 (provision corresponding to section 447). 1982 c. 50.

453.—(1) Sections 432 to 437, 439, 441 and 452(1) apply to Investigation
all bodies corporate incorporated outside Great Britain which of oversea
are carrying on business in Great Britain or have at any time companies.
carried on business there as if they were companies under this
Act, but subject to such (if any) adaptations and modifications
as may be specified by regulations made by the Secretary of
State.

PART XIV

(2) Regulations under this section shall be made by statutory instrument subject to annulment in pursuance of a resolution of either House of Parliament.

PART XV

ORDERS IMPOSING RESTRICTIONS ON SHARES (SECTIONS 210, 216, 445)

Consequence of order imposing restrictions.

454.—(1) So long as any shares are directed to be subject to the restrictions of this Part—

(a) any transfer of those shares or, in the case of unissued shares, any transfer of the right to be issued with them, and any issue of them, is void ;

(b) no voting rights are exercisable in respect of the shares ;

(c) no further shares shall be issued in right of them or in pursuance of any offer made to their holder ; and

(d) except in a liquidation, no payment shall be made of any sums due from the company on the shares, whether in respect of capital or otherwise.

(2) Where shares are subject to the restrictions of subsection (1)(a), any agreement to transfer the shares or, in the case of unissued shares, the right to be issued with them is void (except an agreement to sell the shares on the making of an order under section 456(3)(b) below).

(3) Where shares are subject to the restrictions of subsection (1)(c) or (d), an agreement to transfer any right to be issued with other shares in right of those shares, or to receive any payment on them (otherwise than in a liquidation) is void (except an agreement to transfer any such right on the sale of the shares on the making of an order under section 456(3)(b) below).

Punishment for attempted evasion of restrictions.

455.—(1) A person is liable to a fine if he—

(a) exercises or purports to exercise any right to dispose of any shares which, to his knowledge, are for the time being subject to the restrictions of this Part or of any right to be issued with any such shares, or

(b) votes in respect of any such shares (whether as holder or proxy), or appoints a proxy to vote in respect of them, or

(c) being the holder of any such shares, fails to notify of
their being subject to those restrictions any person
whom he does not know to be aware of that fact but
does know to be entitled (apart from the restrictions)
to vote in respect of those shares whether as holder
or as proxy, or

(d) being the holder of any such shares, or being entitled to
any right to be issued with other shares in right of
them, or to receive any payment on them (otherwise
than in a liquidation), enters into any agreement which
is void under section 454(2) or (3).

(2) If shares in a company are issued in contravention of
the restrictions, the company and every officer of it who is in
default is liable to a fine.

(3) Section 732 (restriction on prosecutions) applies to an
offence under this section.

456.—(1) Where shares in a company are by order made Relaxation and
subject to the restrictions of this Part, application may be made removal of
to the court for an order directing that the shares be no longer restrictions.
so subject.

(2) If the order applying the restrictions was made by the
Secretary of State, or he has refused to make an order disapplying
them, the application may be made by any person aggrieved ;
and if the order was made by the court under section 216 (non-
disclosure of share holding), it may be made by any such person
or by the company.

(3) Subject as follows, an order of the court or the Secretary
of State directing that shares shall cease to be subject to the
restrictions may be made only if—

(a) the court or (as the case may be) the Secretary of State
is satisfied that the relevant facts about the shares have
been disclosed to the company and no unfair advantage
has accrued to any person as a result of the earlier
failure to make that disclosure, or

(b) the shares are to be sold and the court (in any case) or
the Secretary of State (if the order was made under
section 210 or 445) approves the sale.

(4) Where shares in a company are subject to the restrictions,
the court may on application order the shares to be sold, subject
to the court's approval as to the sale, and may also direct that
the shares shall cease to be subject to the restrictions.

An application to the court under this subsection may be made by the Secretary of State (unless the restrictions were imposed by court order under section 216), or by the company.

(5) Where an order has been made under subsection (4), the court may on application make such further order relating to the sale or transfer of the shares as it thinks fit.

An application to the court under this subsection may be made—

(*a*) by the Secretary of State (unless the restrictions on the shares were imposed by court order under section 216), or

(*b*) by the company, or

(*c*) by the person appointed by or in pursuance of the order to effect the sale, or

(*d*) by any person interested in the shares.

(6) An order (whether of the Secretary of State or the court) directing that shares shall cease to be subject to the restrictions of this Part, if it is—

(*a*) expressed to be made with a view to permitting a transfer of the shares, or

(*b*) made under subsection (4) of this section,

may continue the restrictions mentioned in paragraphs (*c*) and (*d*) of section 454(1), either in whole or in part, so far as they relate to any right acquired or offer made before the transfer.

(7) Subsection (3) does not apply to an order directing that shares shall cease to be subject to any restrictions which have been continued in force in relation to those shares under subsection (6).

Further provisions on sale by court order of restricted shares.   **457.**—(1) Where shares are sold in pursuance of an order of the court under section 456(4) the proceeds of sale, less the costs of the sale, shall be paid into court for the benefit of the persons who are beneficially interested in the shares; and any such person may apply to the court for the whole or part of those proceeds to be paid to him.

(2) On application under subsection (1) the court shall (subject as provided below) order the payment to the applicant of the whole of the proceeds of sale together with any interest thereon or, if any other person had a beneficial interest in the shares at the time of their sale, such proportion of those proceeds and interest as is equal to the proportion which the value of the applicant's interest in the shares bears to the total value of the shares.

(3) On granting an application for an order under section 456(4) or (5) the court may order that the applicant's costs be paid out of the proceeds of sale ; and if that order is made, the applicant is entitled to payment of his costs out of those proceeds before any person interested in the shares in question receives any part of those proceeds.

PART XVI

FRAUDULENT TRADING BY A COMPANY

458. If any business of a company is carried on with intent to defraud creditors of the company or creditors of any other person, or for any fraudulent purpose, every person who was knowingly a party to the carrying on of the business in that manner is liable to imprisonment or a fine, or both.

Punishment for fraudulent trading.

This applies whether or not the company has been, or is in the course of being, wound up.

PART XVII

PROTECTION OF COMPANY'S MEMBERS AGAINST UNFAIR PREJUDICE

459.—(1) A member of a company may apply to the court by petition for an order under this Part on the ground that the company's affairs are being or have been conducted in a manner which is unfairly prejudicial to the interests of some part of the members (including at least himself) or that any actual or proposed act or omission of the company (including an act or omission on its behalf) is or would be so prejudicial.

Order on application of company member.

(2) The provisions of this Part apply to a person who is not a member of a company but to whom shares in the company have been transferred or transmitted by operation of law, as those provisions apply to a member of the company ; and references to a member or members are to be construed accordingly.

460.—(1) If in the case of any company—

Order on application of Secretary of State.
1982 c. 50.

    (a) the Secretary of State has received a report under section 437, or exercised his powers under section 447 or 448 of this Act or section 44(2) to (6) of the Insurance Companies Act 1982 (inspection of company's books and papers), and

    (b) it appears to him that the company's affairs are being or have been conducted in a manner which is unfairly prejudicial to the interests of some part of the members, or that any actual or proposed act or omission of the company (including an act or omission on its behalf) is or would be so prejudicial, he may himself (in addition to or instead of presenting a petition under section 440 for the winding up of the company) apply to the court by petition for an order under this Part.

(2) In this section (and, so far as applicable for its purposes, in the section next following) "company" means any body corporate which is liable to be wound up under this Act.

Provisions as to petitions and orders under this Part.

461.—(1) If the court is satisfied that a petition under this Part is well founded, it may make such order as it thinks fit for giving relief in respect of the matters complained of.

(2) Without prejudice to the generality of subsection (1), the court's order may—

(a) regulate the conduct of the company's affairs in the future,

(b) require the company to refrain from doing or continuing an act complained of by the petitioner or to do an act which the petitioner has complained it has omitted to do,

(c) authorise civil proceedings to be brought in the name and on behalf of the company by such person or persons and on such terms as the court may direct,

(d) provide for the purchase of the shares of any members of the company by other members or by the company itself and, in the case of a purchase by the company itself, the reduction of the company's capital accordingly.

(3) If an order under this Part requires the company not to make any, or any specified, alteration in the memorandum or articles, the company does not then have power without leave of the court to make any such alteration in breach of that requirement.

(4) Any alteration in the company's memorandum or articles made by virtue of an order under this Part is of the same effect as if duly made by resolution of the company, and the provisions of this Act apply to the memorandum or articles as so altered accordingly.

(5) An office copy of an order under this Part altering, or giving leave to alter, a company's memorandum or articles shall, within 14 days from the making of the order or such longer period as the court may allow, be delivered by the company to the registrar of companies for registration; and if a company makes default in complying with this subsection, the company and every officer of it who is in default is liable to a fine and, for continued contravention, to a daily default fine.

(6) Section 663 (winding-up rules) applies in relation to a petition under this Part as in relation to a winding-up petition.

Part XVIII

Floating Charges and Receivers (Scotland)

Chapter I

Floating Charges

462.—(1) It is competent under the law of Scotland for an incorporated company (whether a company within the meaning of this Act or not), for the purpose of securing any debt or other obligation (including a cautionary obligation) incurred or to be incurred by, or binding upon, the company or any other person, to create in favour of the creditor in the debt or obligation a charge, in this Part referred to as a floating charge, over all or any part of the property (including uncalled capital) which may from time to time be comprised in its property and undertaking. Power of incorporated company to create floating charge.

(2) A floating charge may be created, in the case of a company which the Court of Session has jurisdiction to wind up, only by the execution, under the seal of the company, of an instrument or bond or other written acknowledgment of debt or obligation which purports to create such a charge.

(3) Execution in accordance with this section includes execution by an attorney authorised for such purpose by the company by writing under its common seal; and any such execution on behalf of the company binds the company.

(4) References in this Part to the instrument by which a floating charge was created are, in the case of a floating charge created by words in a bond or other written acknowledgment, references to the bond or, as the case may be, the other written acknowledgment.

(5) Subject to this Act, a floating charge has effect in accordance with this Part in relation to any heritable property in Scotland to which it relates, notwithstanding that the instrument creating it is not recorded in the Register of Sasines or, as appropriate, registered in accordance with the Land Registration (Scotland) Act 1979. 1979 c. 33.

463.—(1) On the commencement of the winding up of a company, a floating charge created by the company attaches to the property then comprised in the company's property and undertaking or, as the case may be, in part of that property and undertaking, but does so subject to the rights of any person who— Effect of floating charge on winding up.

    (a) has effectually executed diligence on the property or any part of it; or

M

(b) holds a fixed security over the property or any part of it ranking in priority to the floating charge ; or

(c) holds over the property or any part of it another floating charge so ranking.

(2) The provisions of Part XX (except section 623(4)) have effect in relation to a floating charge, subject to subsection (1), as if the charge were a fixed security over the property to which it has attached in respect of the principal of the debt or obligation to which it relates and any interest due or to become due thereon.

(3) Nothing in this section—

(a) prejudices the operation of section 614(2) ;

(b) derogates from the provisions of sections 469(7) and 470(6) in this Part.

(4) Subject to section 617, interest accrues, in respect of a floating charge which after 16th November 1972 attaches to the property of the company, until payment of the sum due under the charge is made.

Ranking of floating charges.

464.—(1) Subject to subsection (2), the instrument creating a floating charge over all or any part of the company's property under section 462 may contain—

(a) provisions prohibiting or restricting the creation of any fixed security or any other floating charge having priority over, or ranking pari passu with, the floating charge ; or

(b) provisions regulating the order in which the floating charge shall rank with any other subsisting or future floating charges or fixed securities over that property or any part of it.

(2) Where all or any part of the property of a company is subject both to a floating charge and to a fixed security arising by operation of law, the fixed security has priority over the floating charge.

(3) Where the order of ranking of the floating charge with any other subsisting or future floating charges or fixed securities over all or any part of the company's property is not regulated

by provisions contained in the instrument creating the floating PART XVIII
charge, the order of ranking is determined in accordance with CHAPTER I
the following provisions of this section.

(4) Subject to the provisions of this section—

   (*a*) a fixed security, the right to which has been constituted
as a real right before a floating charge has attached to
all or any part of the property of the company, has
priority of ranking over the floating charge;

   (*b*) floating charges rank with one another according to the
time of registration in accordance with Chapter II of
Part XII;

   (*c*) floating charges which have been received by the registrar for registration by the same postal delivery rank
with one another equally.

(5) Where the holder of a floating charge over all or any part
of the company's property which has been registered in accordance with Chapter II of Part XII has received intimation in
writing of the subsequent registration in accordance with that
Chapter of another floating charge over the same property or any
part thereof, the preference in ranking of the first-mentioned
floating charge is restricted to security for—

   (*a*) the holder's present advances;

   (*b*) future advances which he may be required to make
under the instrument creating the floating charge or
under any ancillary document;

   (*c*) interest due or to become due on all such advances;
and

   (*d*) any expenses or outlays which may reasonably be
incurred by the holder.

(6) This section is subject to section 614(2) (preferential debts
in winding up).

465.—(1) Any floating charge which—   Continued

   (*a*) purported to subsist as a floating charge on 17th Novem- effect of
ber 1972, and   certain charges
  validated by

   (*b*) if it had been created on or after that date, would Act of 1972.
have been validly created by virtue of the Companies
(Floating Charges and Receivers) (Scotland) Act 1972, 1972 c. 67.

is deemed to have subsisted as a valid floating charge as from
the date of its creation.

M 2

(2) Any provision which—

(a) is contained in an instrument creating a floating charge or in any ancillary document executed prior to, and still subsisting at, the commencement of that Act,

(b) relates to the ranking of charges, and

(c) if it had been made after the commencement of that Act, would have been a valid provision,

is deemed to have been a valid provision as from the date of its making.

Alteration of
floating
charges.

466.—(1) The instrument creating a floating charge under section 462 or any ancillary document may be altered by the execution of an instrument of alteration by the company, the holder of the charge and the holder of any other charge (including a fixed security) which would be adversely affected by the alteration.

(2) Such an instrument of alteration is validly executed if it is executed—

(a) in the case of a company, under its common seal or by an attorney authorised for such purpose by the company by a writing under its common seal;

(b) where trustees for debenture-holders are acting under and in accordance with a trust deed, by those trustees;

(c) where, in the case of a series of secured debentures, no such trustees are acting, by or on behalf of—

(i) a majority in nominal value of those present or represented by proxy and voting at a meeting of debenture-holders at which the holders of at least one-third in nominal value of the outstanding debentures of the series are present or so represented; or

(ii) where no such meeting is held, the holders of at least one-half in nominal value of the outstanding debentures of the series; or

(d) in such manner as may be provided for in the instrument creating the floating charge or any ancillary document.

(3) Section 464 applies to an instrument of alteration under this section as it applies to an instrument creating a floating charge.

(4) Subject to the next subsection, section 410(2) and (3) and section 420 apply to an instrument of alteration under this

section which—

 (*a*) prohibits or restricts the creation of any fixed security or any other floating charge having priority over, or ranking pari passu with, the floating charge ; or

 (*b*) varies, or otherwise regulates the order of, the ranking of the floating charge in relation to fixed securities or to other floating charges ; or

 (*c*) releases property from the floating charge ; or

 (*d*) increases the amount secured by the floating charge.

(5) Section 410(2) and (3) and section 420 apply to an instrument of alteration falling under subsection (4) of this section as if references in the said sections to a charge were references to an alteration to a floating charge, and as if in section 410(2) and (3)—

 (*a*) references to the creation of a charge were references to the execution of such alteration ; and

 (*b*) for the words from the beginning of subsection (2) to the word " applies " there were substituted the words " Every alteration to a floating charge created by a company ".

(6) Any reference (however expressed) in any enactment, including this Act, to a floating charge is, for the purposes of this section and unless the context otherwise requires, to be construed as including a reference to the floating charge as altered by an instrument of alteration falling under subsection (4) of this section.

CHAPTER II

RECEIVERS

467.—(1) It is competent under the law of Scotland for the holder of a floating charge over all or any part of the property (including uncalled capital), which may from time to time be comprised in the property and undertaking of an incorporated company (whether a company within the meaning of this Act or not) which the Court of Session has jurisdiction to wind up, to appoint a receiver of such part of the property of the company as is subject to the charge.

Power to appoint receiver.

(2) It is competent under the law of Scotland for the court, on the application of the holder of such a floating charge, to

appoint a receiver of such part of the property of the company as is subject to the charge.

(3) The following are disqualified from being appointed as receiver—

  (a) a body corporate;

  (b) an undischarged bankrupt; and

  (c) a firm according to the law of Scotland.

(4) A body corporate or a firm according to the law of Scotland which acts as a receiver is liable to a fine.

(5) An undischarged bankrupt who so acts is liable to imprisonment or a fine, or both.

(6) In this section, " receiver " includes joint receivers.

Circumstances
justifying
appointment.
468.—(1) A receiver may be appointed under section 467(1) by the holder of the floating charge on the occurrence of any event which, by the provisions of the instrument creating the charge, entitles the holder of the charge to make that appointment and, in so far as not otherwise provided for by the instrument, on the occurrence of any of the following events, namely—

  (a) the expiry of a period of 21 days after the making of a demand for payment of the whole or any part of the principal sum secured by the charge, without payment having been made;

  (b) the expiry of a period of two months during the whole of which interest due and payable under the charge has been in arrears;

  (c) the making of an order or the passing of a resolution to wind up the company;

  (d) the appointment of a receiver by virtue of any other floating charge created by the company.

(2) A receiver may be appointed by the court under section 467(2) on the occurrence of any event which, by the provisions of the instrument creating the floating charge, entitles the holder of the charge to make that appointment and, in so far as not otherwise provided for by the instrument, on the occurrence of any of the following events, namely—

  (a) where the court, on the application of the holder of the charge, pronounces itself satisfied that the position of the holder of the charge is likely to be prejudiced if no such appointment is made;

(*b*) any of the events referred to in paragraphs (*a*) to (*c*) of   PART XVIII
    subsection (1) above.   CHAPTER II

469.—(1) The appointment of a receiver by the holder of the Mode of
floating charge under section 467(1) shall be by means of a appointment
validly executed instrument in writing (referred to as the " in- by holder
strument of appointment "), a copy (certified in the prescribed of charge.
manner to be a correct copy) whereof shall be delivered by or
on behalf of the person making the appointment to the registrar
of companies for registration within 7 days of its execution and
shall be accompanied by a notice in the prescribed form.

(2) If any person without reasonable excuse makes default in
complying with the requirements of subsection (1), he is liable
to a fine and, for continued contravention, to a daily default
fine.

(3) The instrument of appointment is validly executed—
    (*a*) by a company, if it is executed in accordance with the
       provisions of section 36 of this Act as if it were a
       contract ; and
    (*b*) by any other person, if it is executed in the manner
       required or permitted by the law of Scotland in the
       case of an attested deed.

(4) The instrument may be executed on behalf of the holder
of the floating charge by virtue of which the receiver is to be
appointed—
    (*a*) by any person duly authorised in writing by the holder
       to execute the instrument ; and
    (*b*) in the case of an appointment of a receiver by the
       holders of a series of secured debentures, by any
       person authorised by resolution of the debenture-
       holders to execute the instrument.

(5) On receipt of the certified copy of the instrument of
appointment in accordance with subsection (1) of this section,
the registrar shall, on payment of the prescribed fee, enter the
particulars of the appointment in the register of charges.

(6) The receiver is to be regarded as having been appointed
on the date of the execution of the instrument of his appointment.

(7) On the appointment of a receiver under this section, the
floating charge by virtue of which he was appointed attaches to

the property then subject to the charge ; and such attachment has effect as if the charge was a fixed security over the property to which it has attached.

Appointment
by court.

470.—(1) Application for the appointment of a receiver by the court under section 467(2) shall be by petition to the court, which shall be served on the company.

(2) On such application, the court shall, if it thinks fit, issue an interlocutor making the appointment of the receiver on such terms as to caution as it may think fit.

(3) A copy (certified by the clerk of the court to be a correct copy) of the court's interlocutor making the appointment shall be delivered by or on behalf of the petitioner to the registrar of companies for registration, accompanied by a notice in the prescribed form, within 7 days of the date of the interlocutor or such longer period as the court may allow.

If any person without reasonable excuse makes default in complying with the requirements of this subsection he is liable to a fine and, for continued contravention, to a daily default fine.

(4) On receipt of the certified copy interlocutor in accordance with subsection (3), and on receipt of a certificate by the appropriate officer of the court that caution as ordered by the court has been found, the registrar shall, on payment of the prescribed fee, enter the particulars of the appointment in the register of charges.

(5) The receiver is to be regarded as having been appointed on the date of his being appointed by the court.

(6) On the appointment of a receiver under this section, the floating charge by virtue of which he was appointed attaches to the property then subject to the charge ; and such attachment has effect as if the charge were a fixed security over the property to which it has attached.

(7) In making rules of court for the purposes of this section, the Court of Session shall have regard to the need for special provision for cases which appear to the court to require to be dealt with as a matter of urgency.

Powers of
receiver.

471.—(1) Subject to subsection (2) below, a receiver has in relation to such part of the property of the company as is attached by the floating charge by virtue of which he was appointed, the powers, if any, given to him by the instrument creating that charge and, in addition, he has under this Part the following powers as respects that property, in so far as these are not inconsistent with any provision contained in that instrument, namely—

(a) power to take possession of, collect and get in the property from the company or a liquidator thereof or any other person, and for that purpose, to take such proceedings as may seem to him expedient;

(b) power to sell, feu, hire out or otherwise dispose of the property by public roup or private bargain and with or without advertisement;

(c) power to borrow money and grant security therefor over the property;

(d) power to appoint a solicitor or accountant or other professionally qualified person to assist him in the performance of his functions;

(e) power to apply to the court for directions in connection with the performance of his functions;

(f) power to bring or defend any action or other legal proceedings in the name and on behalf of the company;

(g) power to refer to arbitration all questions affecting the company;

(h) power to effect and maintain insurances in respect of the business and property of the company;

(i) power to use the company's seal;

(j) power to do all acts and to execute in the name and on behalf of the company any deed, receipt or other document;

(k) power to draw, accept, make and endorse any bill of exchange or promissory note in the name and on behalf of the company;

(l) power to appoint any agent to do any business which he is unable to do himself or which can more conveniently be done by an agent and power to employ and discharge servants;

(m) power to have carried out to the best advantage any work on the property of the company and in general to do all such other things as may be necessary for the realisation of the property;

(n) power to make any payment which is necessary or incidental to the performance of his functions;

(o) power to carry on the business of the company so far as he thinks it desirable to do so;

(*p*) power to grant any lease of the property, and to input and output tenants, and to take on lease any property required or convenient for the business of the company ;

(*q*) power to rank and claim in the bankruptcy, insolvency, sequestration or liquidation of any person or company indebted to the company and to receive dividends, and to accede to trust deeds for creditors of any such person ;

(*r*) power to present or defend a petition for the winding up of the company ; and

(*s*) power to do all other things incidental to the exercise of the powers mentioned in this subsection.

(2) Subsection (1) applies—

(*a*) subject to the rights of any person who has effectually executed diligence on all or any part of the property of the company prior to the appointment of the receiver ; and

(*b*) subject to the rights of any person who holds over all or any part of the property of the company a fixed security or floating charge having priority over, or ranking pari passu with, the floating charge by virtue of which the receiver was appointed.

(3) A person transacting with a receiver shall not be concerned to inquire whether any event has happened to authorise the receiver to act.

Precedence
among
receivers.

472.—(1) Where there are two or more floating charges subsisting over all or any part of the property of the company, a receiver may be appointed under this Chapter by virtue of each such charge, but a receiver appointed by, or on the application of, the holder of a floating charge having priority of ranking over any other floating charge by virtue of which a receiver has been appointed has the powers given to a receiver by section 471 to the exclusion of any other receiver.

(2) Where two or more floating charges rank with one another equally, and two or more receivers have been appointed by virtue of such charges, the receivers so appointed are deemed to have been appointed as joint receivers.

(3) Receivers appointed, or deemed to have been appointed, as joint receivers shall act jointly unless the instrument of appointment or respective instruments of appointment otherwise provide.

(4) Subject to subsection (5) below, the powers of a receiver appointed by, or on the application of, the holder of a floating charge are suspended by, and as from the date of, the appointment of a receiver by, or on the application of, the holder of a floating charge having priority of ranking over that charge to such extent as may be necessary to enable the receiver second mentioned to exercise his powers under section 471 ; and any powers so suspended take effect again when the floating charge having priority of ranking ceases to attach to the property then subject to the charge, whether such cessation is by virtue of section 478(6) or otherwise.

(5) The suspension of the powers of a receiver under subsection (4) does not have the effect of requiring him to release any part of the property (including any letters or documents) of the company from his control until he receives from the receiver superseding him a valid indemnity (subject to the limit of the value of such part of the property of the company as is subject to the charge by virtue of which he was appointed) in respect of any expenses, charges and liabilities he may have incurred in the performance of his functions as receiver.

(6) The suspension of the powers of a receiver under subsection (4) does not cause the floating charge by virtue of which he was appointed to cease to attach to the property to which it attached by virtue of section 469(7) or 470(6).

(7) Nothing in this section prevents the same receiver being appointed by virtue of two or more floating charges.

473.—(1) A receiver is deemed to be the agent of the company in relation to such property of the company as is attached by the floating charge by virtue of which he was appointed. Agency and liability of receiver for contracts.

(2) Subject to subsection (1), a receiver (including a receiver whose powers are subsequently suspended under section 472) is personally liable on any contract entered into by him in the performance of his functions, except in so far as the contract otherwise provides.

(3) A receiver who is personally liable by virtue of subsection (2) is entitled to be indemnified out of the property in respect of which he was appointed.

(4) Any contract entered into by or on behalf of the company prior to the appointment of a receiver continues in force (subject to its terms) notwithstanding that appointment, but the receiver does not by virtue only of his appointment incur any personal liability on any such contract.

(5) Any contract entered into by a receiver in the performance of his functions continues in force (subject to its terms) although the powers of the receiver are subsequently suspended under section 472.

Remuneration of receiver. **474.**—(1) The remuneration to be paid to a receiver is to be determined by agreement between the receiver and the holder of the floating charge by virtue of which he was appointed.

(2) Where the remuneration to be paid to the receiver has not been determined under subsection (1) or where it has been so determined but is disputed by any of the persons mentioned in paragraphs (a) to (d), it may be fixed instead by the Auditor of the Court of Session on application made to him by—

(a) the receiver ;

(b) the holder of any floating charge or fixed security over all or any part of the property of the company ;

(c) the company ; or

(d) the liquidator of the company.

(3) Application to the Auditor of the Court of Session under subsection (2) shall be made in writing not later than one month after the sending of the abstract of receipts and payments of the receiver mentioned below in this Chapter which discloses the remuneration, if any, payable to the receiver.

(4) Where the receiver has been paid or has retained for his remuneration for any period before the remuneration has been fixed by the Auditor of the Court of Session under subsection (2) any amount in excess of the remuneration so fixed for that period, the receiver or his personal representatives shall account for the excess.

Priority of debts. **475.**—(1) Where a receiver is appointed and the company is not at the time of the appointment in course of being wound up, the debts which fall under subsection (2) of this section shall be paid out of any assets coming to the hands of the receiver in priority to any claim for principal or interest by the holder of the floating charge by virtue of which the receiver was appointed.

(2) Debts falling under this subsection are debts which satisfy the conditions of this subsection, that is to say, they are debts—

(*a*) which in every winding up are, under the provisions of Part XX relating to preferential payments, to be paid in priority to all other debts; and

(*b*) which, by the end of a period of six months after advertisement by the receiver for claims in the Edinburgh Gazette and in a newspaper circulating in the district where the company carries on business, either—

(i) have been intimated to him; or

(ii) have become known to him.

(3) In the application of Part XX, section 614 and Schedule 19 are to be read as if the provision for payment of accrued holiday remuneration becoming payable on the termination of employment before or by the effect of the winding-up order or resolution were a provision for payment of such remuneration becoming payable on the termination of employment before or by the effect of the appointment of the receiver.

(4) The periods of time mentioned in Schedule 19 are to be reckoned from the date of the appointment of the receiver under section 469(6) or 470(5).

(5) Any payments made under this section shall be recouped as far as may be out of the assets of the company available for payment of ordinary creditors.

476.—(1) Subject to section 477, and to the rights of any of the following categories of persons, namely—

Distribution of monies.

(*a*) the holder of any fixed security which is over property subject to the floating charge and which ranks prior to, or pari passu with, the floating charge;

(*b*) all persons who have effectually executed diligence on any part of the property of the company which is subject to the charge by virtue of which the receiver was appointed;

(*c*) creditors in respect of all liabilities, charges and expenses incurred by or on behalf of the receiver;

(*d*) the receiver in respect of his liabilities, expenses and remuneration; and

(*e*) the preferential creditors entitled to payment under section 475,

the receiver shall pay monies received by him to the holder of the floating charge by virtue of which the receiver was appointed in or towards satisfaction of the debt secured by the floating charge.

(2) Any balance of monies remaining after the provisions of subsection (1) of this section and section 477 have been satisfied shall be paid in accordance with their respective rights and interests to the following persons, as the case may require, namely—

(*a*) any other receiver ;

(*b*) the holder of a fixed security which is over property subject to the floating charge ;

(*c*) the company or its liquidator, as the case may be.

(3) Where any question arises as to the person entitled to a payment under this section, or where a receipt or a discharge of a security cannot be obtained in respect of any such payment, the receiver shall consign the amount of such payment in any joint stock bank of issue in Scotland in name of the Accountant of Court for behoof of the person or persons entitled thereto.

Disposal of interest in property.
477.—(1) Where the receiver sells or disposes, or is desirous of selling or disposing, of any property or interest in property of the company which is subject to the floating charge by virtue of which the receiver was appointed and which is—

(*a*) subject to any security or interest of, or burden or encumbrance in favour of, a creditor the ranking of which is prior to, pari passu with, or postponed to the floating charge ; or

(*b*) property or an interest in property affected or attached by effectual diligence executed by any person ;

and the receiver is unable to obtain the consent of such creditor or, as the case may be, such person to such a sale or disposal, the receiver may apply to the court for authority to sell or dispose of the property or interest in property free of such security, interest, burden, encumbrance or diligence.

(2) On such an application, the court may, if it thinks fit, authorise the sale or disposal of the property or interest in question free of such security, interest, burden, encumbrance or diligence, and such authorisation may be on such terms or conditions as the court thinks fit:

But that authorisation shall not be given where a fixed security over the property or interest in question which ranks prior to the floating charge has not been met or provided for in full.

(3) Where any sale or disposal is effected in accordance with the authorisation of the court under subsection (2) of this section, the receiver shall grant to the purchaser or disponee an appro-

priate document of transfer or conveyance of the property or interest in question, and that document has the effect, or, where recording, intimation or registration of that document is a legal requirement for completion of title to the property or interest, then that recording, intimation or registration, as the case may be, has the effect, of—

> (a) disencumbering the property or interest of the security, interest, burden or encumbrance affecting it ; and
>
> (b) freeing the property or interest from the diligence executed upon it.

(4) Nothing in this section prejudices the right of any creditor of the company to rank for his debt in the winding up of the company.

478.—(1) A receiver appointed by the holder of a floating charge under section 467(1) may resign on giving one month's notice thereof to—

> (a) the holders of floating charges over all or any part of the property of the company ;
>
> (b) the company or its liquidator ; and
>
> (c) the holders of any fixed security over property of the company which is subject to the floating charge by virtue of which the receiver was appointed.

(2) A receiver appointed by the court under section 467(2) may resign only with the authority of the court and on such terms and conditions, if any, as may be laid down by the court.

(3) Subject to subsection (4) below, a receiver may, on application to the court by the holder of the floating charge by virtue of which he was appointed, be removed by the court on cause shown.

(4) Where a receiver ceases to act as such, then, in respect of any expenses, charges or other liabilities he may have incurred in the performance of his functions as receiver, he is entitled to be indemnified out of the property which is subject to the floating charge by virtue of which he was appointed.

(5) When a receiver ceases to act as such otherwise than by death he shall, and, when a receiver is removed by the court, the holder of the floating charge by virtue of which he was appointed shall, within 7 days of the cessation or removal, as the case may be, give the registrar of companies notice to that effect, and the registrar shall enter the notice in the register of charges.

If the receiver or the holder of the floating charge, as the case may require, makes default in complying with the requirements of this subsection, he is liable to a fine and, for continued contravention, to a daily default fine.

(6) If by the expiry of a period of one month following upon the removal of the receiver or his ceasing to act as such no other receiver has been appointed, the floating charge by virtue of which the receiver was appointed—

> (a) thereupon ceases to attach to the property then subject to the charge ; and

> (b) again subsists as a floating charge.

Powers of court.

479.—(1) A holder of a floating charge by virtue of which a receiver was appointed may apply to the court for directions in any matter arising in connection with the performance by the receiver of his functions.

(2) Where a floating charge by virtue of which a person is purported to have been appointed receiver is discovered to be invalid, the court may, if it thinks fit, in whole or in part relieve that person from personal liability in respect of anything done or omitted to be done which, had he been validly appointed, would have been properly done or omitted.

(3) The court may, if it thinks fit, make the person by whom the invalid appointment was made personally liable in respect of anything done or omitted to be done to the extent to which the person purported to have been appointed receiver has been relieved of personal liability.

Notification that receiver appointed.

480.—(1) Where a receiver has been appointed, every invoice, order for goods or business letter issued by or on behalf of the company or the receiver or the liquidator of the company, being a document on or in which the name of the company appears, shall contain a statement that a receiver has been appointed.

(2) If default is made in complying with the requirements of this section, the company and any of the following persons who knowingly and wilfully authorises or permits the default, namely, any officer of the company, any liquidator of the company and any receiver, is liable to a fine.

Provisions as to information where receiver appointed.

481.—(1) Where a receiver is appointed then, subject to the provisions of this section and the section next following—

> (a) he shall forthwith send notice to the company of his appointment ; and

(*b*) there shall, within 14 days after receipt of the notice, or such longer period as may be allowed by the court or in writing by the receiver, be made out and submitted to the receiver in accordance with section 482 a statement in the prescribed form as to the affairs of the company ; and

(*c*) the receiver shall, within 2 months after receipt of the statement, send—

(i) to the registrar of companies and to the court, a copy of the statement and of any comments he sees fit to make thereon and, in the case of the registrar of companies, also a summary of the statement and of his comments (if any) thereon ; and

(ii) to the company, a copy of any such comments or, if he does not see fit to make any comment, a notice to that effect ; and

(iii) to the holder of the floating charge by virtue of which he was appointed, to any trustees for the debenture-holders on whose behalf he was appointed and, so far as he is aware of their addresses, to all such debenture-holders, a copy of the said summary.

(2) The receiver shall, within two months, or such longer period as the court may allow, after the expiration of the period of 12 months from the date of his appointment and of every subsequent period of twelve months, and within two months, or such longer period as the court may allow, after he ceases to act as receiver, send to—

(*a*) the registrar of companies ;

(*b*) the company ;

(*c*) the holder of the floating charge by virtue of which he was appointed ;

(*d*) any trustees for the debenture-holders of the company on whose behalf he was appointed ;

(*e*) all such debenture-holders (so far as he is aware of their addresses) ; and

(*f*) the holders of all other floating charges or fixed securities over property of the company,

an abstract in the prescribed form showing his receipts and payments during that period of twelve months, or, where he ceases to act as receiver, during the period from the end of the period to which the last preceding abstract related (or, if no preceding abstract has been sent under this section, from the date of his appointment) up to the date of his so ceasing, and the aggregate amounts of his receipts and of his payments during all preceding periods since his appointment.

(3) Where the receiver is appointed by the holder of the floating charge under section 467, this section has effect—

(a) with the omission of the references to the court in subsection (1) ; and

(b) with the substitution for the references to the court in subsection (2) of references to the Secretary of State ;

and, in any other case, references to the court shall be taken as referring to the court by which the receiver was appointed.

(4) Subsection (1) does not apply in relation to the appointment of a receiver to act with an existing receiver or in place of a receiver dying or ceasing to act, except that, where that subsection applies to a receiver who dies or ceases to act before it has been fully complied with, the references in paragraphs (b) and (c) of the subsection include (subject to subsection (5)) reference to his successor and to any continuing receiver.

Nothing in this subsection shall be taken as limiting the meaning of the expression " the receiver " where used in, or in relation to, subsection (2).

(5) Where the company is being wound up, this section and section 482 shall apply notwithstanding that the receiver and the liquidator are the same person, but with any necessary modifications arising from that fact.

(6) Nothing in subsection (2) above prejudices the duty of the receiver to render proper accounts of his receipts and payments to the persons to whom, and at the times at which, he may be required to do so apart from that subsection.

(7) If the receiver makes default in complying with the requirements of this section, he is liable to a fine and, for continued contravention, to a daily default fine.

Special
provisions as
to statement
submitted to
receiver. **482.**—(1) The statement as to the affairs of a company required by section 481 to be submitted to the receiver (or his successor) shall show as at the date of the receiver's appointment the particulars of the company's assets, debts and liabilities, the names, residences and occupations of its creditors, the securities held by them respectively, the dates when the securities were respectively given and such further or other information as may be prescribed.

(2) The statement shall be submitted by, and be verified by the statutory declaration of, one or more of the persons who

are at the date of the receiver's appointment the directors, and by the person who is at that date the secretary, of the company, or by such of the persons mentioned below in this subsection as the receiver (or his successor), subject to the direction of the court, may require to submit and verify the statement, that is to say, persons—

(a) who are or have been officers of the company ;

(b) who have taken part in the formation of the company at any time within one year before the date of the receiver's appointment ;

(c) who are in the employment of the company, or have been in its employment within that year, and are, in the opinion of the receiver, capable of giving the information required ;

(d) who are, or have been within that year, officers of, or in the employment of, a company which is, or within that year was, an officer of the company to which the statement relates.

(3) Any person making the statement and statutory declaration shall be allowed, and shall be paid by the receiver (or his successor) out of his receipts, such costs and expenses incurred in the preparation and making of the statement and statutory declaration as the receiver (or his successor) may consider reasonable, subject to an appeal to the court.

(4) Where the receiver is appointed by the holder of the floating charge under section 467(1), this section has effect with the substitution for the references to the court in subsections (2) and (3) of references to the Secretary of State ; and in any other case references to the court are to be taken as referring to the court by which the receiver was appointed.

(5) If any person without reasonable excuse makes default in complying with the requirements of this section, he is liable to a fine and, for continued contravention, to a daily default fine.

(6) References in this section to the receiver's successor include a continuing receiver.

483.—(1) If any receiver—

Enforcement of receiver's duty to make returns, etc.

(a) having made default in filing, delivering or making any return, account or other document, or in giving any notice, which a receiver is by law required to file, deliver, make or give, fails to make good the default within 14 days after the service on him of a notice requiring him to do so ; or

(b) has, after being required at any time by the liquidator of the company so to do, failed to render proper accounts of his receipts and payments and to vouch the same and to pay over to the liquidator the amount properly payable to him,

the court may, on an application made for the purpose, make an order directing the receiver to make good the default within such time as may be specified in the order.

(2) In the case of any such default as is mentioned in subsection (1)(*a*), an application for the purposes of this section may be made by any member or creditor of the company or by the registrar of companies, and, in the case of any such default as is mentioned in subsection (1)(*b*) the application shall be made by the liquidator, and, in either case, the order may provide that all expenses of and incidental to the application shall be borne by the receiver.

(3) Nothing in this section prejudices the operation of any enactments imposing penalties on receivers in respect of any such default as is mentioned in subsection (1).

Interpretation for Chapter II.

484.—(1) In this Chapter, unless the contrary intention appears, the following expressions have the following meanings respectively assigned to them, that is to say—

" company " means an incorporated company (whether a company within the meaning of this Act or not) which the Court of Session has jurisdiction to wind up ;

" secured debenture " means a bond, debenture, debenture stock or other security which, either itself or by reference to any other instrument, creates a floating charge over all or any part of the property of the company, but does not include a security which creates no charge other than a fixed security ;

" series of secured debentures " means two or more secured debentures created as a series by the company in such a manner that the holders thereof are entitled pari passu to the benefit of the floating charge.

(2) Where a floating charge, secured debenture or series of secured debentures has been created by the company, then, except where the context otherwise requires, any reference in this Chapter to the holder of the floating charge shall—

(a) where the floating charge, secured debenture or series of secured debentures provides for a receiver to be appointed by any person or body, be construed as a reference to that person or body ;

(b) where, in the case of a series of secured debentures, no such provision has been made therein but—

    (i) there are trustees acting for the debenture-holders under and in accordance with a trust deed, be construed as a reference to those trustees ; and

    (ii) where no such trustees are acting, be construed as a reference to—

        (aa) a majority in nominal value of those present or represented by proxy and voting at a meeting of debenture-holders at which the holders of at least one-third in nominal value of the outstanding debentures of the series are present or so represented ; or

        (bb) where no such meeting is held, the holders of at least one-half in nominal value of the outstanding debentures of the series.

(3) Any reference in this Chapter to a floating charge, secured debenture, series of secured debentures or instrument creating a charge includes, except where the context otherwise requires, a reference to that floating charge, debenture, series of debentures or instrument as varied by any instrument.

485.—(1) The notice referred to in section 478(5) and the notice referred to in section 481(1)(a) and the statutory declaration referred to in section 482(2) shall be in such form as may be prescribed.

(2) Any power conferred by this Part on the Secretary of State to make regulations is exercisable by statutory instrument ; and a statutory instrument made in the exercise of any power so conferred to prescribe a fee is subject to annulment in pursuance of a resolution of either House of Parliament.

CHAPTER III

GENERAL

486.—(1) In this Part, unless the context otherwise requires, the following expressions have the following meanings respectively assigned to them, that is to say—

" ancillary document " means—

    (a) a document which relates to the floating charge

and which was executed by the debtor or creditor in the charge before the registration of the charge in accordance with Chapter II of Part XII ; or

    (*b*) an instrument of alteration such as is mentioned in section 466 in this Part ;

" company ", other than in Chapter II of this Part, means an incorporated company (whether a company within the meaning of this Act or not) ;

" fixed security ", in relation to any property of a company, means any security, other than a floating charge or a charge having the nature of a floating charge, which on the winding up of the company in Scotland would be treated as an effective security over that property, and (without prejudice to that generality) includes a security over that property, being a heritable security within the meaning of section 9(8) of the Conveyancing and Feudal Reform (Scotland) Act 1970 ;

1970 c. 35.

" instrument of appointment " has the meaning given by section 469(1) ;

" prescribed " means prescribed by regulations made under this Part by the Secretary of State ;

" receiver " means a receiver of such part of the property of the company as is subject to the floating charge by virtue of which he has been appointed under section 467 ;

" register of charges " means the register kept by the registrar of companies for the purposes of Chapter II of Part XII ;

" Register of Sasines " means the appropriate division of the General Register of Sasines.

Extent of Part XVIII.

487. This Part extends to Scotland only.

Part XIX

Receivers and Managers

(England and Wales)

Extent of this Part.

488. This Part does not apply to receivers under Part XVIII.

Disqualification of body corporate from acting as receiver.

489. A body corporate is not qualified for appointment as receiver of the property of a company, and any body corporate which acts as such a receiver is liable to a fine.

490. If a person being an undischarged bankrupt acts as receiver or manager of the property of a company on behalf of debenture holders, he is liable to imprisonment or a fine, or both.

This does not apply to a receiver or manager acting under an appointment made by the court.

PART XIX
Disqualification of undischarged bankrupt.

491. Where application is made to the court to appoint a receiver on behalf of the debenture holders or other creditors of a company which is being wound up by the court, the official receiver may be appointed.

Power for court to appoint official receiver.

492.—(1) A receiver or manager of the property of a company appointed under powers contained in an instrument may apply to the court for directions in relation to any particular matter arising in connection with the performance of his functions.

Receivers and managers appointed out of court.

(2) On such an application, the court may give such directions, or may make such order declaring the rights of persons before the court or otherwise, as it thinks just.

(3) A receiver or manager so appointed is, to the same extent as if he had been appointed by order of a court—

 (a) personally liable on any contract entered into by him in the performance of his functions (except in so far as the contract otherwise provides), and

 (b) entitled in respect of that liability to indemnity out of the assets ;

but this subsection does not limit any right to indemnity which the receiver or manager would have apart from it, nor limit his liability on contracts entered into without authority, nor confer any right to indemnity in respect of that liability.

493.—(1) When a receiver or manager of the property of a company has been appointed, every invoice, order for goods or business letter issued by or on behalf of the company or the receiver or manager or the liquidator of the company, being a document on or in which the company's name appears, shall contain a statement that a receiver or manager has been appointed.

Notification that receiver or manager appointed.

(2) If default is made in complying with this section, the company and any of the following persons, who knowingly and wilfully authorises or permits the default, namely, any officer of the company, any liquidator of the company and any receiver or manager, is liable to a fine.

PART XIX
Court's
power to fix
remuneration
of receiver
or manager.

494.—(1) The court may, on an application made by the liquidator of a company, by order fix the amount to be paid by way of remuneration to a person who, under powers contained in an instrument, has been appointed receiver or manager of the company's property.

(2) The court's power under subsection (1), where no previous order has been made with respect thereto under the subsection—

(a) extends to fixing the remuneration for any period before the making of the order or the application for it, and

(b) is exercisable notwithstanding that the receiver or manager has died or ceased to act before the making of the order or the application, and

(c) where the receiver or manager has been paid or has retained for his remuneration for any period before the making of the order any amount in excess of that so fixed for that period, extends to requiring him or his personal representatives to account for the excess or such part of it as may be specified in the order.

But the power conferred by paragraph (c) shall not be exercised as respects any period before the making of the application for the order under this section, unless in the court's opinion there are special circumstances making it proper for the power to be exercised.

(3) The court may from time to time on an application made either by the liquidator or by the receiver or manager, vary or amend an order made under subsection (1).

Information
to be given
by and to
receiver on
appointment.

495.—(1) The following applies where, in the case of a company registered in England and Wales, a receiver or manager of the whole (or substantially the whole) of the company's property is appointed on behalf of the holders of any debentures of the company secured by a floating charge.

In this and the following two sections, he is referred to as " the receiver ".

(2) Subject to the following provisions of this section, and to sections 496 and 497—

(a) the receiver shall forthwith send to the company notice of his appointment in the prescribed form, and

(b) there shall within 14 days after receipt of the notice (or such longer period as may be allowed by the court or by the receiver) be made out and submitted to the receiver in accordance with section 496 a statement in the prescribed form as to the affairs of the company.

(3) The receiver shall, within 2 months after receipt of the statement, send—

    (*a*) to the registrar of companies and to the court, a copy of the statement and of any comments he sees fit to make on it and, in the case of the registrar of companies, also a summary of the statement and of his comments (if any) on it ; and

    (*b*) to the company, a copy of any such comments as above-mentioned or, if he does not see fit to make any comments, a notice to that effect ; and

    (*c*) to any trustees for the debenture holders on whose behalf he was appointed and, so far as he is aware of their addresses, to all such debenture holders a copy of the summary.

(4) If the receiver is appointed under powers contained in an instrument, subsections (2) and (3) have effect with the omission of references to the court ; and in any other case references to the court are to the court by which the receiver was appointed.

(5) This section does not apply in relation to the appointment of a receiver or manager to act—

    (*a*) with an existing receiver or manager, or

    (*b*) in place of a receiver or manager dying or ceasing to act,

except that, where it applies to a receiver or manager who dies or ceases to act before it has been fully complied with, the references in subsection (2)(*b*) and (3) to the receiver include (subject to the next subsection) his successor and any continuing receiver or manager.

(6) If the company is being wound up, this section and section 496 apply notwithstanding that the receiver or manager and the liquidator are the same person, but with any necessary modifications arising from that fact.

(7) If the receiver makes default in complying with this section, he is liable to a fine and, for continued contravention, to a daily default fine.

496.—(1) The company's statement of affairs required by sec- Company's tion 495 to be submitted to the receiver (or his successor) shall statement show as at the date of the receiver's appointment— of affairs.

    (*a*) the particulars of the company's assets, debts and liabilities,

    (*b*) the names, residences and occupations of its creditors,

(c) the securities held by them respectively,

(d) the dates when the securities were respectively given, and

(e) such further or other information as may be prescribed.

(2) The statement shall be submitted by, and be verified by affidavit of, one or more of the persons who are at the date of the receiver's appointment the directors and by the person who is at that date the secretary of the company, or by such of the persons mentioned in the next subsection as the receiver (or his successor), subject to the direction of the court, may require to submit and verify the statement.

(3) The persons referred to above are those—

(a) who are or have been officers of the company,

(b) who have taken part in the company's formation at any time within one year before the date of the receiver's appointment,

(c) who are in the company's employment, or have been in its employment during that year and are in the receiver's opinion capable of giving the information required,

(d) who are or have been during that year officers of or in the employment of a company which is, or within that year was, an officer of the company to which the statement relates.

(4) A person making the statement and affidavit shall be allowed, and shall be paid by the receiver (or his successor) out of his receipts, such costs and expenses incurred in and about the preparation and making of the statement and affidavit as the receiver (or his successor) may consider reasonable, subject to an appeal to the court.

(5) Where the receiver is appointed under powers contained in an instrument, this section applies with the substitution for references to the court of references to the Secretary of State, and for references to an affidavit of references to a statutory declaration ; and in any other case references to the court are to the court by which the receiver was appointed.

(6) If a person without reasonable excuse makes default in complying with the requirements of this section, he is liable to a fine and, for continued contravention, to a daily default fine.

(7) References in this section to the receiver's successor include a continuing receiver or manager.

497.—(1) In the case mentioned in section 495(1), the receiver shall—

(*a*) within 2 months (or such longer period as the court may allow) after the expiration of 12 months from the date of his appointment and of every subsequent period of 12 months, and

(*b*) within 2 months (or such longer period as the court may allow) after he ceases to act as receiver or manager of the company's property,

send the requisite accounts of his receipts and payments to the registrar of companies, to any trustees for the debenture holders on whose behalf he was appointed, to the company and (so far as he is aware of their addresses) to all such debenture holders.

(2) The requisite accounts shall be an abstract in the prescribed form showing—

(*a*) receipts and payments during the relevant period of 12 months, or

(*b*) where the receiver ceases to act, receipts and payments during the period from the end of the period of 12 months to which the last preceding abstract related (or, if no preceding abstract has been sent under this section, from the date of his appointment) up to the date of his so ceasing, and the aggregate amount of receipts and payments during all preceding periods since his appointment.

(3) Nothing in section 495(5) is to be taken as limiting the meaning of the expression " the receiver " where used in, or in relation to, subsection (1) or (2) above.

(4) Where the receiver is appointed under powers contained in an instrument, this section has effect with the substitution of the Secretary of State for the court; and in any other case references to the court are to the court by which the receiver was appointed.

(5) This section applies, where the company is being wound up, notwithstanding that the receiver or manager and the liquidator are the same person, but with any necessary modifications arising from that fact.

(6) This section does not prejudice the receiver's duty to render proper accounts of his receipts and payments to the persons to whom, and at the times at which, he may be required to do so apart from this section.

(7) If the receiver makes default in complying with the requirements of this section, he is liable to a fine and, for continued contravention, to a daily default fine.

Receivership accounts to be delivered to registrar.

498.—(1) Except where section 497 applies, every receiver or manager of a company's property who has been appointed under powers contained in an instrument shall deliver to the registrar of companies for registration the requisite accounts of his receipts and payments.

(2) The accounts shall be delivered within one month (or such longer period as the registrar may allow) after the expiration of 6 months from the date of his appointment and of every subsequent period of 6 months, and also within one month after he ceases to act as receiver or manager.

(3) The requisite accounts shall be an abstract in the prescribed form showing—

(a) receipts and payments during the relevant period of 6 months, or

(b) where the receiver or manager ceases to act, receipts and payments during the period from the end of the period of 6 months to which the last preceding abstract related (or, if no preceding abstract has been delivered under this section, from the date of his appointment) up to the date of his so ceasing, and the aggregate amount of receipts and payments during all preceding periods since his appointment.

(4) A receiver or manager who makes default in complying with this section is liable to a fine and, for continued contravention, to a daily default fine.

Enforcement of duty of receivers to make returns.

499.—(1) If a receiver or manager of a company's property—

(a) having made default in filing, delivering or making any return, account or other document, or in giving any notice, which a receiver or manager is by law required to file, deliver, make or give, fails to make good the default within 14 days after the service on him of a notice requiring him to do so, or

(*b*) having been appointed under powers contained in an instrument, has, after being required at any time by the liquidator of the company to do so, failed to render proper accounts of his receipts and payments and to vouch them and pay over to the liquidator the amount properly payable to him,

the court may, on an application made for the purpose, make an order directing the receiver or manager (as the case may be) to make good the default within such time as may be specified in the order.

(2) In the case of the default mentioned in subsection (1)(*a*), application to the court may be made by any member or creditor of the company or by the registrar of companies ; and in the case of the default mentioned in subsection (1)(*b*), the application shall be made by the liquidator.

In either case the court's order may provide that all costs of and incidental to the application shall be borne by the receiver or manager, as the case may be.

(3) Nothing in this section prejudices the operation of any enactment imposing penalties on receivers in respect of any such default as is mentioned in subsection (1).

500. It is hereby declared that, except where the context other- Construction wise requires— of references to receivers

(*a*) any reference in this Act to a receiver or manager of and managers. the property of a company, or to a receiver of it, includes a reference to a receiver or manager, or (as the case may be) to a receiver of part only of that property and to a receiver only of the income arising from the property or from part of it, and

(*b*) any reference in this Act to the appointment of a receiver or manager under powers contained in an instrument includes a reference to an appointment made under powers which, by virtue of any enactment, are implied in and have effect as if contained in an instrument.

PART XX

WINDING UP OF COMPANIES REGISTERED
UNDER THIS ACT OR THE FORMER COMPANIES ACTS

CHAPTER I

PRELIMINARY

Modes of winding up

The three
modes in
which a
company may
be wound up.

501.—(1) The winding up of a company may be either—

(a) by the court, or

(b) voluntary, or

(c) subject to the supervision of the court.

(2) This Part applies, unless the contrary appears, to the winding up of a company in any of those modes.

Contributories

Liability as
contributories
of present
and past
members.

502.—(1) When a company is wound up, every present and past member is liable to contribute to its assets to any amount sufficient for payment of its debts and liabilities, and the costs, charges and expenses of the winding up, and for the adjustment of the rights of the contributories among themselves.

(2) This is subject as follows—

(a) a past member is not liable to contribute if he has ceased to be a member for one year or more before the commencement of the winding up;

(b) a past member is not liable to contribute in respect of any debt or liability of the company contracted after he ceased to be a member;

(c) a past member is not liable to contribute unless it appears to the court that the existing members are unable to satisfy the contributions required to be made by them in pursuance of this Act;

(d) in the case of a company limited by shares, no contribution is required from any member exceeding the amount (if any) unpaid on the shares in respect of which he is liable as a present or past member;

(e) nothing in this Act invalidates any provision contained in a policy of insurance or other contract whereby the liability of individual members on the policy or contract is restricted, or whereby the funds of the company are alone made liable in respect of the policy or contract;

(f) a sum due to any member of the company (in his character of a member) by way of dividends, profits or otherwise is not deemed to be a debt of the company, payable to that member in a case of competition between himself and any other creditor not a member of the company, but any such sum may be taken into account for the purpose of the final adjustment of the rights of the contributories among themselves.

(3) In the case of a company limited by guarantee, no contribution is required from any member exceeding the amount undertaken to be contributed by him to the company's assets in the event of its being wound up; but if it is a company with a share capital, every member of it is liable (in addition to the amount so undertaken to be contributed to the assets), to contribute to the extent of any sums unpaid on shares held by him.

503.—(1) In the winding up of a limited company, any director or manager (whether past or present) whose liability is under this Act unlimited is liable, in addition to his liability (if any) to contribute as an ordinary member, to make a further contribution as if he were at the commencement of the winding up a member of an unlimited company.

Directors, etc., with unlimited liability.

(2) However—

(a) a past director or manager is not liable to make such further contribution if he has ceased to hold office for a year or more before the commencement of the winding up;

(b) a past director or manager is not liable to make such further contribution in respect of any debt or liability of the company contracted after he ceased to hold office;

(c) subject to the company's articles, a director or manager is not liable to make such further contribution unless the court deems it necessary to require that contribution in order to satisfy the company's debts and liabilities and the costs, charges and expenses of the winding up.

PART XX
CHAPTER I
Liability of
past directors
and share-
holders.

504.—(1) This section applies where a company is being wound up and—

    (a) it has under Chapter VII of Part V made a payment out of capital in respect of the redemption or purchase of any of its own shares (the payment being referred to below as " the relevant payment "), and

    (b) the aggregate amount of the company's assets and the amounts paid by way of contribution to its assets (apart from this section) is not sufficient for payment of its debts and liabilities and the costs, charges and expenses of the winding up.

(2) If the winding up commenced within one year of the date on which the relevant payment was made, then—

    (a) the person from whom the shares were redeemed or purchased, and

    (b) the directors who signed the statutory declaration made in accordance with section 173(3) for purposes of the redemption or purchase (except a director who shows that he had reasonable grounds for forming the opinion set out in the declaration),

are, so as to enable that insufficiency to be met, liable to contribute to the following extent to the company's assets.

(3) A person from whom any of the shares were redeemed or purchased is liable to contribute an amount not exceeding so much of the relevant payment as was made by the company in respect of his shares ; and the directors are jointly and severally liable with that person to contribute that amount.

(4) A person who has contributed any amount to the assets in pursuance of this section may apply to the court for an order directing any other person jointly and severally liable in respect of that amount to pay him such amount as the court thinks just and equitable.

(5) Sections 502 and 503 above do not apply in relation to liability accruing by virtue of this section.

(6) This section is deemed included in Chapter VII of Part V for the purposes of the Secretary of State's power to make regulations under section 179.

505.—(1) This section applies in the case of a company being wound up which was at some former time registered as unlimited but has re-registered— PART XX
CHAPTER I
Limited
company
formerly
unlimited.

  (*a*) as a public company under section 43 of this Act (or the former corresponding provision, section 5 of the Companies Act 1980), or

  (*b*) as a limited company under section 51 of this Act (or the former corresponding provision, section 44 of the Companies Act 1967).

(2) Notwithstanding section 502(2)(*a*) above, a past member of the company who was a member of it at the time of re-registration, if the winding up commences within the period of 3 years beginning with the day on which the company was re-registered, is liable to contribute to the assets of the company in respect of debts and liabilities contracted before that time.

(3) If no persons who were members of the company at that time are existing members of it, a person who at that time was a present or past member is liable to contribute as above notwithstanding that the existing members have satisfied the contributions required to be made by them under this Act.

This applies subject to section 502(2)(*a*) above and to subsection (2) of this section, but notwithstanding section 502(2)(*c*).

(4) Notwithstanding section 502(2)(*d*) and (3), there is no limit on the amount which a person who, at that time, was a past or present member of the company is liable to contribute as above.

506.—(1) This section applies in the case of a company being wound up which was at some former time registered as limited but has been re-registered as unlimited under section 49 (or the former corresponding provision, section 43 of the Companies Act 1967).

(2) A person who, at the time when the application for the company to be re-registered was lodged, was a past member of the company and did not after that again become a member of it is not liable to contribute to the assets of the company more than he would have been liable to contribute had the company not been re-registered.

507.—(1) In this Act, the expression " contributory " means every person liable to contribute to the assets of a company in the event of its being wound up, and for the purposes of all proceedings for determining, and all proceedings prior to the final determination of, the persons who are to be deemed contributories, includes any person alleged to be a contributory.

(2) A reference in a company's articles to a contributory does not (unless the context requires) include a person who is a contributory only by virtue of section 504.

This subsection is deemed included in Chapter VII of Part V for the purposes of the Secretary of State's power to make regulations under section 179.

Nature of contributory's liability.

508. The liability of a contributory creates a debt (in England and Wales in the nature of a specialty) accruing due from him at the time when his liability commenced, but payable at the times when calls are made for enforcing the liability.

Contributories in case of death of a member.

509.—(1) If a contributory dies either before or after he has been placed on the list of contributories, his personal representatives, and the heirs and legatees of heritage of his heritable estate in Scotland, are liable in a due course of administration to contribute to the assets of the company in discharge of his liability and are contributories accordingly.

(2) Where the personal representatives are placed on the list of contributories, the heirs or legatees of heritage need not be added, but they may be added as and when the court thinks fit.

(3) If in England and Wales the personal representatives make default in paying any money ordered to be paid by them, proceedings may be taken for administering the estate of the deceased contributory and for compelling payment out of it of the money due.

Effect of contributory's bankruptcy.

510.—(1) The following applies if a contributory becomes bankrupt, either before or after he has been placed on the list of contributories.

(2) His trustee in bankruptcy represents him for all purposes of the winding up, and is a contributory accordingly.

(3) The trustee may be called on to admit to proof against the bankrupt's estate, or otherwise allow to be paid out of the

bankrupt's assets in due course of law, any money due from the bankrupt in respect of his liability to contribute to the company's assets.

(4) There may be proved against the bankrupt's estate the estimated value of his liability to future calls as well as calls already made.

511.—(1) The following applies in the event of a company being wound up which has been registered under section 680 (or the previous corresponding provision).

(2) Every person is a contributory, in respect of the company's debts and liabilities contracted before registration, who is liable—

(*a*) to pay, or contribute to the payment of, any debt or liability so contracted, or

(*b*) to pay, or contribute to the payment of, any sum for the adjustment of the rights of the members among themselves in respect of any such debt or liability, or

(*c*) to pay, or contribute to the payment of, the costs and expenses of winding up the company, so far as relates to the debts or liabilities above-mentioned.

(3) Every contributory is liable to contribute to the assets of the company, in the course of the winding up, all sums due from him in respect of any such liability.

(4) In the event of the death, bankruptcy or insolvency of any contributory, provisions of this Act with respect to the personal representatives, to the heirs and legatees of heritage of the heritable estate in Scotland of deceased contributories and to the trustees of bankrupt or insolvent contributories respectively, apply.

CHAPTER II

WINDING UP BY THE COURT

Jurisdiction (England and Wales)

512.—(1) The High Court has jurisdiction to wind up any company registered in England and Wales.

(2) Where the amount of a company's share capital paid up or credited as paid up does not exceed £120,000, then (subject to the provisions of this section) the county court of the district in

which the company's registered office is situated has concurrent jurisdiction with the High Court to wind up the company.

(3) The money sum for the time being specified in subsection (2) is subject to increase or reduction by regulations under section 664; but no reduction of it affects any case in which proceedings were begun before the coming into force of the reduction.

(4) The Lord Chancellor may by order in a statutory instrument exclude a county court from having winding-up jurisdiction, and for the purposes of that jurisdiction may attach its district, or any part thereof, to any other county court, and may by statutory instrument revoke or vary any such order.

In exercising the powers of this section, the Lord Chancellor shall provide that a county court is not to have winding-up jurisdiction unless it has for the time being jurisdiction in bankruptcy.

(5) Every court in England and Wales having winding-up jurisdiction has for the purposes of that jurisdiction all the powers of the High Court; and every prescribed officer of the court shall perform any duties which an officer of the High Court may discharge by order of a judge of that court or otherwise in relation to winding up.

(6) For purposes of this section, a company's " registered office " is the place which has longest been its registered office during the 6 months immediately preceding the presentation of the petition for winding up.

Proceedings
taken in
wrong court.
513.—(1) Nothing in section 512 invalidates a proceeding by reason of its being taken in the wrong court.

(2) The winding up of a company by the court in England and Wales, or any procedings in the winding up, may be retained in the court in which the proceedings were commenced, although it may not be the court in which they ought to have been commenced.

Proceedings
in county
court: case
stated for
High Court.
514. If any question arises in any winding up proceedings in a county court which all the parties to the proceeding, or which one of them and the judge of the court, desire to have determined in the first instance in the High Court, the judge shall state the facts in the form of a special case for the opinion of the High Court; and thereupon the special case and the proceedings (or such of them as may be required) shall be transmitted to the High Court for the purposes of the determination.

Jurisdiction (Scotland)

PART XX
CHAPTER II
Court of
Session and
sheriff's court
jurisdiction.

515.—(1) The Court of Session has jurisdiction to wind up any company registered in Scotland.

(2) When the Court of Session is in vacation, the jurisdiction conferred on that court by this section may (subject to the provisions of this Part) be exercised by the judge acting as vacation judge in pursuance of section 4 of the Administration of Justice (Scotland) Act 1933.

(3) Where the amount of a company's share capital paid up or credited as paid up does not exceed £120,000, the sheriff court of the sheriffdom in which the company's registered office is situated has concurrent jurisdiction with the Court of Session to wind up the company ; but—

> (*a*) the Court of Session may, if it thinks expedient having regard to the amount of the company's assets to do so—
>
>> (i) remit to a sheriff court any petition presented to the Court of Session for winding up such a company, or
>>
>> (ii) require such a petition presented to a sheriff court to be remitted to the Court of Session ; and
>
> (*b*) the Court of Session may require any such petition as above-mentioned presented to one sheriff court to be remitted to another sheriff court ; and
>
> (*c*) in a winding up in the sheriff court it is lawful for the sheriff to submit a stated case for the opinion of the Court of Session on any question of law arising in that winding up.

(4) For the purposes of this section, the expression " registered office " means the place which has longest been the company's registered office during the 6 months immediately preceding the presentation of the petition for winding up.

(5) The money sum for the time being specified in subsection (3) is subject to increase or reduction by regulations under section 664 ; but no reduction of it affects any case in which proceedings were begun before the coming into force of the reduction.

516.—(1) The Court of Session may, by Act of Sederunt, make provision for the taking of proceedings in a winding up before one of the Lords Ordinary ; and, where provision is so made, the Lord Ordinary has, for the purposes of the winding up, all the powers and jurisdiction of the court.

(2) However, the Lord Ordinary may report to the Inner House any matter which may arise in the course of a winding up.

Grounds and effect of winding-up petition

Circumstances
in which
company may
be wound up
by the court.

517.—(1) A company may be wound up by the court if—

 (*a*) the company has by special resolution resolved that the company be wound up by the court,

 (*b*) being a public company which was registered as such on its original incorporation, the company has not been issued with a certificate under section 117 (public company share capital requirements) and more than a year has expired since it was so registered,

 (*c*) it is an old public company, within the meaning of section 1 of the Consequential Provisions Act,

 (*d*) the company does not commence its business within a year from its incorporation or suspends its business for a whole year,

 (*e*) the number of members is reduced below 2,

 (*f*) the company is unable to pay its debts,

 (*g*) the court is of the opinion that it is just and equitable that the company should be wound up.

(2) In Scotland, a company which the Court of Session has jurisdiction to wind up may be wound up by the Court if there is subsisting a floating charge over property comprised in the company's property and undertaking, and the court is satisfied that the security of the creditor entitled to the benefit of the floating charge is in jeopardy.

For this purpose a creditor's security is deemed to be in jeopardy if the Court is satisfied that events have occurred or are about to occur which render it unreasonable in the creditor's interests that the company should retain power to dispose of the property which is subject to the floating charge.

518.—(1) A company is deemed unable to pay its debts—

 (*a*) if a creditor (by assignment or otherwise) to whom the company is indebted in a sum exceeding £750 then due has served on the company, by leaving it at the company's registered office, a written demand requiring the company to pay the sum so due and the company has for 3 weeks thereafter neglected to pay the sum or to secure or compound for it to the reasonable satisfaction of the creditor, or

 (*b*) if, in England and Wales, execution or other process issued on a judgment, decree or order of any court in favour of a creditor of the company is returned unsatisfied in whole or in part, or

 (*c*) if, in Scotland, the induciae of a charge for payment on an extract decree, or an extract registered bond, or an extract registered protest, have expired without payment being made, or

(d) if, in Northern Ireland, a certificate of unenforceability has been granted in respect of a judgment against the company, or

(e) if it is proved to the satisfaction of the court that the company is unable to pay its debts (and, in determining that question, the court shall take into account the company's contingent and prospective liabilities).

(2) The money sum for the time being specified in subsection (1)(*a*) is subject to increase or reduction by regulations under section 664; but no increase of it affects any case in which the winding-up petition was presented before the coming into force of the increase.

519.—(1) Subject to the provisions of this section, an application to the court for the winding up of a company shall be by petition presented either by the company or by any creditor or creditors (including any contingent or prospective creditor or creditors), contributory or contributories, or by all or any of those parties, together or separately.

Application for winding up.

(2) Except as mentioned below, a contributory is not entitled to present a winding-up petition unless either—

(*a*) the number of members is reduced below 2, or

(*b*) the shares in respect of which he is a contributory, or some of them, either were originally allotted to him, or have been held by him, and registered in his name, for at least 6 months during the 18 months before the commencement of the winding up, or have devolved on him through the death of a former holder.

(3) A person who is liable under section 504 to contribute to a company's assets in the event of its being wound up may petition on either of the grounds set out in section 517(1)(*f*) and (*g*), and subsection (2) above does not then apply; but unless the person is a contributory otherwise than under section 504 he may not in his character as contributory petition on any other ground.

This subsection is deemed included in Chapter VII of Part V for the purposes of the Secretary of State's power to make regulations under section 179.

(4) If the ground of the petition is that in section 517(1)(*b*) or (*c*), a winding-up petition may be presented by the Secretary of State.

(5) The court shall not hear a petition presented by a contingent or prospective creditor until such security for costs has been given as the court thinks reasonable (or until caution is found, if so ordered by a Scottish court) and until a prima facie case for winding up has been established to the satisfaction of the court.

(6) In a case falling within section 440 (expedient in the public interest, following report of inspectors, etc.) a winding-up petition may be presented by the Secretary of State.

(7) Where a company is being wound up voluntarily or subject to supervision in England and Wales, a winding-up petition may be presented by the official receiver attached to the court as well as by any other person authorised in that behalf under the other provisions of this section ; but the court shall not make a winding-up order on the petition unless it is satisfied that the voluntary winding up or winding up subject to supervision cannot be continued with due regard to the interests of the creditors or contributories.

Powers of
court on
hearing of
petition.
520.—(1) On hearing a winding-up petition the court may dismiss it, or adjourn the hearing conditionally or unconditionally, or make an interim order, or any other order that it thinks fit ; but the court shall not refuse to make a winding-up order on the ground only that the company's assets have been mortgaged to an amount equal to or in excess of those assets or that the company has no assets.

(2) If the petition is presented by members of the company as contributories on the ground that it is just and equitable that the company should be wound up, the court, if it is of opinion—

(a) that the petitioners are entitled to relief either by winding up the company or by some other means, and

(b) that in the absence of any other remedy it would be just and equitable that the company should be wound up,

shall make a winding-up order ; but this does not apply if the court is also of the opinion both that some other remedy is available to the petitioners and that they are acting unreasonably in seeking to have the company wound up instead of pursuing that other remedy.

Power to
stay or
restrain
proceedings
against
company.
521.—(1) At any time after the presentation of a winding-up petition, and before a winding-up order has been made, the company, or any creditor or contributory, may—

(a) where any action or proceeding against the company is pending in the High Court or Court of Appeal in England and Wales or Northern Ireland, apply to the court in which the action or proceeding is pending for a stay of proceedings therein, and

(b) where any other action or proceeding is pending against the company, apply to the court having jurisdiction to wind up the company to restrain further proceedings in the action or proceeding,

and the court to which application is so made may (as the case
may be) stay, sist or restrain the proceedings accordingly on such
terms as it thinks fit.

(2) In the case of a company registered under section 680,
where the application to stay, sist or restrain is by a creditor,
this section extends to actions and proceedings against any contributory of the company.

522. In a winding up by the court, any disposition of the *Avoidance of*
company's property, and any transfer of shares, or alteration in *property*
the status of the company's members, made after the commence- *dispositions,*
ment of the winding up is, unless the court otherwise orders, void. *etc.*

523.—(1) Where a company registered in England and Wales *Avoidance of*
is being wound up by the court, any attachment, sequestration, *attachments,*
distress or execution put in force against the estate or effects of *etc.*
the company after the commencement of the winding up is void.

(2) This section, so far as relates to any estate or effects of the
company situated in England and Wales, applies in the case of a
company registered in Scotland as it applies in the case of a
company registered in England and Wales.

Commencement of winding up

524.—(1) If, before the presentation of a petition for the *Commence-*
winding up of a company by the court, a resolution has been *ment of*
passed by the company for voluntary winding up, the winding up *winding up by*
of the company is deemed to have commenced at the time of the *the court.*
passing of the resolution ; and unless the court, on proof of fraud
or mistake, directs otherwise, all proceedings taken in the voluntary winding up are deemed to have been validly taken.

(2) In any other case, the winding up of a company by the
court is deemed to commence at the time of the presentation
of the petition for winding up.

525.—(1) On the making of a winding-up order, a copy of the *Consequences*
order must forthwith be forwarded by the company (or otherwise *of winding-up*
as may be prescribed) to the registrar of companies, who shall *order.*
enter it in his records relating to the company.

(2) When a winding-up order has been made or a provisional
liquidator has been appointed, no action or proceeding shall
be proceeded with or commenced against the company except
by leave of the court and subject to such terms as the court
may impose.

(3) When an order has been made for winding up a company
registered under section 680, no action or proceeding shall be
commenced or proceeded with against the company or any con-

PART XX
CHAPTER II
tributory of the company, in respect of any debt of the company, except by leave of the court, and subject to such terms as the court may impose.

(4) An order for winding up a company operates in favour of all the creditors and of all contributories of the company as if made on the joint petition of a creditor and of a contributory.

The official receiver (England and Wales only)

The official receiver.
526.—(1) For the purposes of this Act as it relates to the winding up of companies by the court in England and Wales, the term "official receiver" means the official receiver (if any) attached to the court for bankruptcy purposes or, if there is more than one such official receiver, then such one of them as the Secretary of State may appoint or, if there is no such official receiver, then an officer appointed for the purpose by the Secretary of State.

(2) Any such officer shall, for the purpose of his duties under this Act, be styled "the official receiver".

Appointment of official receiver by court in certain cases.
527.—(1) If in the case of the winding up of a company by the court in England and Wales it appears to the court desirable, with a view to securing the more convenient and economical conduct of the winding up, that some officer other than the person who would under section 526 be the official receiver should be the official receiver for the purposes of that winding up, the court may appoint that other officer to act.

(2) The officer so appointed is then deemed, for all purposes of this Act, to be the official receiver in that winding up.

Statement of company's affairs.
528.—(1) Where the court in England and Wales has made a winding-up order or appointed a provisional liquidator, there shall (unless the court otherwise orders) be made out and submitted to the official receiver a statement as to the affairs of the company in the prescribed form.

(2) The statement shall be verified by affidavit and show particulars of the company's assets, its debts and liabilities, the names, residences and occupations of its creditors, the securities held by them respectively, the dates when the securities were respectively given, and such further or other information as may be prescribed or as the official receiver may require.

(3) The statement shall be submitted and verified by one or more of the persons who are at the relevant date the directors and by the person who at that date is the secretary of the company, or by such of the persons mentioned in the following subsection as the official receiver (subject to the direction of the court) may require to submit and verify the statement.

(4) The persons referred to above are—

    (*a*) those who are or have been officers of the company,

    (*b*) those who have taken part in the formation of the company at any time within one year before the relevant date,

    (*c*) those who are in the employment of the company, or have been in its employment within the year just mentioned, and are in the opinion of the official receiver capable of giving the information required, and

    (*d*) those who are or have been within that year officers of or in the employment of a company which is, or within that year was, an officer of the company to which the statement relates.

(5) For purposes of this section, " the relevant date " is—

    (*a*) in a case where a provisional liquidator is appointed the date of his appointment, and

    (*b*) in a case where no such appointment is made, the date of the winding-up order.

(6) The statement of affairs required by this section shall be submitted within 14 days from the relevant date, or within such extended time as the official receiver or the court may for special reasons appoint.

(7) If a person, without reasonable excuse, makes default in complying with the requirements of this section, he is liable to a fine and, for continued contravention, to a daily default fine.

529.—(1) A person making or concurring in the making of the statement and affidavit required by section 528 shall be allowed, and shall be paid by the official receiver or provisional liquidator (as the case may be) out of the company's assets such costs and expenses incurred in and about the preparation and making of the statement and affidavit as the official receiver may consider reasonable, subject to an appeal to the court.

(2) A person stating himself in writing to be a creditor or contributory of the company is entitled by himself or by his agent at all reasonable times, on payment of the prescribed fee, to inspect the statement submitted under section 528, and to a copy of or extract from it.

(3) A person untruthfully so stating himself to be a creditor or contributory is guilty of a contempt of court and, on the application of the official receiver or the liquidator, punishable accordingly.

PART XX
CHAPTER II

(4) The statement required by section 528 may be used in evidence against any person making or concurring in making it.

Report by
official
receiver.

530.—(1) When a winding-up order is made, the official receiver shall, as soon as practicable after the receipt of the statement to be submitted under section 528 (or, in a case where the court orders that no statement shall be submitted, as soon as practicable after the date of the order) submit a preliminary report to the court—

   (a) as to the amount of capital issued, subscribed and paid up, and the estimated amount of assets and liabilities, and

   (b) if the company has failed, as to the causes of the failure, and

   (c) whether in his opinion further enquiry is desirable as to any matter relating to the promotion, formation or failure of the company or the conduct of its business.

(2) The official receiver may also, if he thinks fit, make further reports (one or more) stating the manner in which the company was formed and whether in his opinion any fraud has been committed by any person in its promotion or formation, or by any officer of the company in relation to it since its formation, and any other matter which in his opinion it is desirable to bring to the notice of the court.

(3) If the official receiver states in any such further report that in his opinion a fraud has been committed as above-mentioned, the court has the further powers provided in sections 563 and 564 (public examination of promoters and officers).

Liquidators

Power of
court to
appoint
liquidators.

531. For the purpose of conducting the proceedings in winding up a company and performing such duties in reference thereto as the court may impose, the court may appoint a liquidator or liquidators.

Appointment
and powers
of provisional
liquidator.

532.—(1) Subject to the provisions of this section, the court may, at any time after the presentation of a winding-up petition, appoint a liquidator provisionally.

(2) In England and Wales, the appointment of a provisional liquidator may be made at any time before the making of a winding-up order, and either the official receiver or any other fit person may be appointed.

(3) In Scotland, such an appointment may be made at any time before the first appointment of liquidators.

(4) When a liquidator is provisionally appointed by the court, his powers may be limited by the order appointing him.

533.—(1) The following provisions with respect to liquidators have effect on a winding-up order being made in England and Wales.

(2) The official receiver by virtue of his office becomes the provisional liquidator and shall continue to act as such until he or another person becomes liquidator and is capable of acting as such.

(3) The official receiver shall summon separate meetings of the company's creditors and contributories for the purpose of determining whether or not an application is to be made to the court for appointing a liquidator in the place of the official receiver.

(4) The court may make any appointment and order required to give effect to that determination ; and, if there is a difference between the determinations of the meetings of the creditors and contributories in respect of the matter in question, the court shall decide the difference and make such order thereon as it may think fit.

(5) If a liquidator is not appointed by the court, the official receiver shall be the liquidator of the company.

(6) The official receiver is, ex officio, the liquidator during any vacancy.

(7) A liquidator shall be described, where a person other than the official receiver is liquidator, by the style of " the liquidator " and, where the official receiver is liquidator, by the style of " the official receiver and liquidator ", of the particular company in respect of which he is appointed (and not by his individual name).

534. If in the winding up of a company by the court in England and Wales a person other than the official receiver is appointed liquidator, that person—

    (*a*) cannot act as liquidator until he has notified his appointment to the registrar of companies and given security in the prescribed manner to the satisfaction of the Secretary of State,

    (*b*) shall give the official receiver such information, and such access to and facilities for inspecting the company's books and documents, and generally such aid as may be requisite for enabling that officer to perform his duties under this Act.

535.—(1) The following provisions with respect to liquidators have effect in a winding up by the court in Scotland.

(2) The court may determine whether any and what caution is to be found by a liquidator on his appointment.

(3) A liquidator shall be described by the style of " the official liquidator " of the particular company in respect of which he is appointed (and not by his individual name).

(4) Where an order has been made for winding up a company subject to supervision and an order is afterwards made for winding up by the court, the court may by the last-mentioned or by a subsequent order appoint any person who is then liquidator, either provisionally or permanently, and either with or without any other person, to be liquidator in the winding up by the court.

536.—(1) A liquidator appointed by the court may resign or, on cause shown, be removed by the court.

(2) Where a person other than the official receiver is appointed liquidator, he shall receive such salary or remuneration by way of percentage or otherwise as the court may direct ; and, if more such persons than one are appointed liquidators, their remuneration shall be distributed among them in such proportions as the court directs.

(3) A vacancy in the office of a liquidator appointed by the court shall be filled by the court.

(4) If more than one liquidator is appointed by the court, the court shall declare whether any act required or authorised by this Act to be done by the liquidator is to be done by all or any one or more of the persons appointed.

(5) Subject to section 634 (disqualification of bodies corporate for appointment as liquidator), the acts of a liquidator are valid notwithstanding any defects that may afterwards be discovered in his appointment or qualification.

537.—(1) When a winding-up order has been made, or where a provisional liquidator has been appointed, the liquidator or the provisional liquidator (as the case may be) shall take into his custody or under his control all the property and things in action to which the company is or appears to be entitled.

(2) In a winding up by the court in Scotland, if and so long as there is no liquidator, all the property of the company is deemed to be in the custody of the court.

538.—(1) When a company is being wound up by the court, the court may on the application of the liquidator by order direct that all or any part of the property of whatsoever description belonging to the company or held by trustees on its behalf shall vest in the liquidator by his official name ; and thereupon the property to which the order relates vests accordingly.

(2) The liquidator may, after giving such indemnity (if any) as the court may direct, bring or defend in his official name any action or other legal proceeding which relates to that property or which it is necessary to bring or defend for the purpose of effectually winding up the company and recovering its property.

539.—(1) The liquidator in a winding up by the court has power, with the sanction either of the court or of the committee of inspection—

Powers of liquidator.

(a) to bring or defend any action or other legal proceeding in the name and on behalf of the company,

(b) to carry on the business of the company so far as may be necessary for its beneficial winding up,

(c) to appoint a solicitor to assist him in the performance of his duties,

(d) to pay any class of creditors in full,

(e) to make any compromise or arrangement with creditors or persons claiming to be creditors, or having or alleging themselves to have any claim (present or future, certain or contingent, ascertained or sounding only in damages) against the company, or whereby the company may be rendered liable,

(f) to compromise all calls and liabilities to calls, debts and liabilities capable of resulting in debts, and all claims (present or future, certain or contingent, ascertained or sounding only in damages) subsisting or supposed to subsist between the company and a contributory or alleged contributory or other debtor or person apprehending liability to the company, and all questions in any way relating to or affecting the assets or the winding up of the company, on such terms as may be agreed, and take any security for the discharge of any such call, debt, liability or claim and give a complete discharge in respect of it.

(2) The liquidator in a winding up by the court has the power—

(a) to sell any of the company's property by public auction or private contract, with power to transfer the whole thereof to any person or to sell the same in parcels,

(b) to do all acts and to execute, in the name and on behalf of the company, all deeds, receipts and other documents and for that purpose to use, when necessary, the company's seal,

(c) to prove, rank and claim in the bankruptcy, insolvency or sequestration of any contributory for any balance against his estate, and to receive dividends in the bankruptcy, insolvency or sequestration in respect of that balance, as a separate debt due from the bankrupt or insolvent, and rateably with the other separate creditors,

(d) to draw, accept, make and indorse any bill of exchange or promissory note in the name and on behalf of the company, with the same effect with respect to the company's liability as if the bill or note had been drawn, accepted, made or indorsed by or on behalf of the company in the course of its business,

(e) to raise on the security of the assets of the company any money requisite,

(f) to take out in his official name letters of administration to any deceased contributory, and to do in his official name any other act necessary for obtaining payment of any money due from a contributory or his estate which cannot conveniently be done in the name of the company (and in all such cases the money due is deemed, for the purpose of enabling the liquidator to take out the letters of administration or recover the money, to be due to the liquidator himself),

(g) to appoint an agent to do any business which the liquidator is unable to do himself,

(h) to do all such other things as may be necessary for winding up the company's affairs and distributing its assets.

(3) The exercise by the liquidator in a winding up by the court of the powers conferred by this section is subject to the control of the court, and any creditor or contributory may apply to the court with respect to any exercise or proposed exercise of any of those powers.

(4) In the case of a winding up in Scotland, the court may provide by order that the liquidator may, where there is no committee of inspection, exercise any of the powers mentioned in subsection (1)(a) or (b) without the sanction or intervention of the court.

(5) In a winding up by the court in Scotland, the liquidator has (subject to general rules), the same powers as a trustee on a bankrupt estate.

Provisions about liquidators applying in England and Wales only

Exercise and control of liquidator's powers.

540.—(1) Subject to the provisions of this Act, the liquidator of a company which is being wound up by the court in England and Wales shall, in the administration of the company's assets and their distribution among its creditors, have regard to any directions that may be given by resolution of the creditors or

contributories at any general meeting or by the committee of
inspection.

(2) Directions given by the creditors or contributories at any general meeting are, in case of conflict, deemed to override any directions given by the committee of inspection.

(3) The liquidator may summon general meetings of the creditors or contributories for the purpose of ascertaining their wishes; and it is his duty to summon meetings at such times as the creditors or contributories by resolution (either at the meeting appointing the liquidator or otherwise) may direct, or whenever requested in writing to do so by one-tenth in value of the creditors or contributories (as the case may be).

(4) The liquidator may apply to the court (in the prescribed manner) for directions in relation to any particular matter arising in the winding up.

(5) Subject to the provisions of this Act, the liquidator shall use his own discretion in the management of the estate and its distribution among the creditors.

(6) If any person is aggrieved by any act or decision of the liquidator, that person may apply to the court; and the court may confirm, reverse or modify the act or decision complained of, and make such order in the case as it thinks just.

541.—(1) Every liquidator of a company which is being wound   Books to be
up by the court in England and Wales shall keep, in the pre-   kept by
scribed manner, proper books in which he shall cause to be   liquidator.
made entries or minutes of proceedings at meetings, and of
such other matters as may be prescribed.

(2) Any creditor or contributory may, subject to the control of the court, personally or by his agent inspect any such books.

542.—(1) The following applies to a liquidator of a company   Payments by
which is being wound up by the court in England and Wales.   liquidator into
bank.

(2) Subject to the next subsection, the liquidator shall, in such manner and at such times as the Secretary of State (with the concurrence of the Treasury) directs, pay the money received by him to the Insolvency Services Account at the Bank of England; and the Secretary of State shall furnish him with a certificate of receipt of the money so paid.

(3) However, if the committee of inspection satisfies the Secretary of State that for the purpose of carrying on the company's business or of obtaining advances, or for any other reason, it is for the advantage of the creditors or contributories that the liquidator should have an account at any other bank, the Secretary of State shall, on the application of the committee

PART XX
CHAPTER II

of inspection, authorise the liquidator to make his payments into and out of such other bank as the committee may select, and thereupon those payments shall be made in the prescribed manner.

(4) If the liquidator at any time retains for more than 10 days a sum exceeding £100 or such other amount as the Secretary of State in any particular case authorises him to retain, then unless he explains the retention to the Secretary of State's satisfaction, he shall pay interest on the amount so retained in excess at the rate of 20 per cent. per annum, and is liable to disallowance of all or such part of his remuneration as the Secretary of State thinks just, and to be removed from his office by the Secretary of State, and is liable to pay any expenses occasioned by reason of his default.

(5) The liquidator shall not pay any sums received by him as liquidator into his private banking account.

(6) The money sum for the time being specified in subsection (4) is subject to increase or reduction by regulations under section 664.

Submission of
liquidator's
accounts for
audit.

543.—(1) The following applies in the case of a company which is being wound up by the court in England and Wales.

(2) The liquidator shall, at such times as may be prescribed but not less than twice in each year during his tenure of office, send to the Secretary of State (or as he directs) an account of his receipts and payments as liquidator.

(3) The account shall be in the prescribed form, shall be made in duplicate, and shall be verified by a statutory declaration in the prescribed form; and the Secretary of State may cause the account to be audited.

(4) The liquidator shall furnish the Secretary of State with such vouchers and information as he requires, and the Secretary of State may at any time require the production of, and inspect, any books or accounts kept by the liquidator.

This applies whether or not the Secretary of State decides to cause the account to be audited, and extends to production and inspection at the liquidator's premises.

(5) After the account has been audited (or, as the case may be, forthwith if the Secretary of State decides not to have an audit) one copy of the account shall be filed by the Secretary of State, to be retained by him, and the other copy shall be delivered to the court for filing, each copy when filed to be open to inspection by any person on payment of the prescribed fee.

(6) The liquidator shall, when the account has been audited (alternatively, when he has been notified of the Secretary of

State's decision not to have an audit), cause the account, or a summary of it, to be printed, and shall send a printed copy by post to every creditor or contributory.

The Secretary of State may in any case dispense with compliance with this subsection.

544.—(1) The Secretary of State shall take cognizance of the Control of conduct of liquidators of companies which are being wound up liquidators by by the court in England and Wales ; and— Secretary of State.

(a) if a liquidator does not faithfully perform his duties and duly observe all the requirements imposed on him by statute, rules or otherwise with respect to the performance of his duties, or

(b) if any complaint is made to the Secretary of State by any creditor or contributory in regard thereto,

the Secretary of State shall inquire into the matter, and take such action on it as he thinks expedient.

(2) The Secretary of State may at any time require the liquidator to answer any inquiry in relation to a winding up in which he is engaged and may, if the Secretary of State thinks fit, apply to the court to examine him or any other person on oath concerning the winding up.

(3) The Secretary of State may also direct a local investigation to be made of the liquidator's books and vouchers.

545.—(1) The following applies to the liquidator of a company Release of which is being wound up by the court in England and Wales. liquidators.

(2) When the liquidator has realised all the company's property, or so much of it as can (in his opinion) be realised without needlessly protracting the liquidation, and has distributed a final dividend (if any) to the creditors, and adjusted the rights of the contributories among themselves, and made a final return (if any) to the contributories, or has resigned, or has been removed from his office, the following subsection has effect.

(3) The Secretary of State shall, on the liquidator's application, cause a report on the latter's accounts to be prepared and, on his complying with all the Secretary of State's requirements, shall take into consideration the report and any objection which may be urged by any creditor or contributory or person interested against the release of the liquidator, and shall either grant or withhold the release accordingly, subject nevertheless to an appeal to the High Court.

(4) If the release of the liquidator is withheld, the court may, on the application of any creditor or contributory or person interested, make such order as it thinks just, charging the

PART XX
CHAPTER II

liquidator with the consequences of any act or default which he may have done or made contrary to his duty.

(5) An order of the Secretary of State releasing the liquidator discharges him from all liability in respect of any act done or default made by him in the administration of the company's affairs or otherwise in relation to his conduct as liquidator ; but any such order may be revoked on proof that it was obtained by fraud or by suppression or concealment of any material fact.

(6) If the liquidator has not previously resigned or been removed, his release operates as removal of him from his office.

Committees of inspection

Decision whether committee of inspection to be appointed.

546.—(1) When a winding-up order has been made by the court in England and Wales, and separate meetings of creditors and contributories have been summoned for the purpose of determining whether an application should be made to the court for the appointment of a liquidator in place of the official receiver, it is the business of those meetings to determine further whether or not an application is to be made to the court for the appointment of a committee of inspection to act with the liquidator, and who are to be members of the committee if appointed.

(2) In Scotland, when a winding-up order has been made by the court, the liquidator shall summon separate meetings of the company's creditors and contributories for the purpose of determining whether or not an application is to be made to the court for the appointment of a committee of inspection and who are to be the members of the committee if appointed.

However, if the winding-up order has been made on the ground that the company is unable to pay its debts, it is not necessary for the liquidator to summon a meeting of the contributories.

(3) The court may make the appointment and order required to give effect to such determination ; and if there is a difference between the determinations of the meetings of the creditors and contributories in respect of the matters referred to above, the court shall decide the difference and make such order on those matters as the court may think fit.

Constitution and proceedings of committee of inspection.

547.—(1) Subject as follows, the committee of inspection (if appointed) shall consist of creditors and contributories of the company or persons holding general powers of attorney from creditors or contributories in such proportions as may be agreed on by the meetings of creditors and contributories or as, in case of difference, may be determined by the court.

(2) In Scotland—

    (*a*) if a winding-up order has been made on the ground that the company is unable to pay its debts, the committee shall consist of creditors or persons holding general powers of attorney from creditors, and

    (*b*) the committee has, in addition to the powers and duties conferred and imposed on it by this Act, such of the powers and duties of commissioners on a bankrupt estate as may be conferred and imposed on committees of inspection by general rules.

(3) Schedule 17 has effect with respect to the committee of inspection and its proceedings.

548. If in the case of a winding up in England and Wales there is no committee of inspection, the Secretary of State may, on the application of the liquidator, do any act or thing or give any direction or permission which is by this Act authorised or required to be done or given by the committee.

General powers of court in case of winding up by the court

549.—(1) The court may at any time after an order for winding up, on the application either of the liquidator or the official receiver or any creditor or contributory, and on proof to the satisfaction of the court that all proceedings in the winding up ought to be stayed or sisted, make an order staying or sisting the proceedings, either altogether or for a limited time, on such terms and conditions as the court thinks fit.

(2) The court may, before making an order, require the official receiver to furnish to the court a report with respect to any facts or matters which are in his opinion relevant to the application.

(3) A copy of every order made under this section shall forthwith be forwarded by the company, or otherwise as may be prescribed, to the registrar of companies, who shall enter it in his records relating to the company.

550.—(1) As soon as may be after making a winding-up order, the court shall settle a list of contributories, with power to rectify the register of members in all cases where rectification is required in pursuance of this Act, and shall cause the company's assets to be collected, and applied in discharge of its liabilities.

(2) If it appears to the court that it will not be necessary to make calls on or adjust the rights of contributories, the court may dispense with the settlement of a list of contributories.

(3) In settling the list, the court shall distinguish between persons who are contributories in their own right and persons

PART XX
CHAPTER II

who are contributories as being representatives of or liable for the debts of others.

Delivery of property to liquidator.

551. The court may, at any time after making a winding-up order, require any contributory for the time being on the list of contributories and any trustee, receiver, banker, agent or officer of the company to pay, deliver, convey, surrender or transfer forthwith (or within such time as the court directs) to the liquidator any money, property or books and papers in his hands to which the company is prima facie entitled.

Debts due from contributory to company.

552.—(1) The court may, at any time after making a winding-up order, make an order on any contributory for the time being on the list of contributories to pay, in manner directed by the order, any money due from him (or from the estate of the person whom he represents) to the company, exclusive of any money payable by him or the estate by virtue of any call in pursuance of this Act.

(2) The court in making such an order may—

    (*a*) in the case of an unlimited company, allow to the contributory by way of set-off any money due to him or the estate which he represents from the company on any independent dealing or contract with the company, but not any money due to him as a member of the company in respect of any dividend or profit, and

    (*b*) in the case of a limited company, make to any director or manager whose liability is unlimited or to his estate the like allowance.

(3) In the case of any company, whether limited or unlimited, when all the creditors are paid in full, any money due on any account whatever to a contributory from the company may be allowed to him by way of set-off against any subsequent call.

Power to make calls.

553.—(1) The court may, at any time after making a winding-up order, and either before or after it has ascertained the sufficiency of the company's assets, make calls on all or any of the contributories for the time being settled on the list of the contributories to the extent of their liability, for payment of any money which the court considers necessary to satisfy the company's debts and liabilities, and the costs, charges and expenses of winding up, and for the adjustment of the rights of the contributories among themselves, and make an order for payment of any calls so made.

(2) In making a call the court may take into consideration the probability that some of the contributories may partly or wholly fail to pay it.

554.—(1) The court may order any contributory, purchaser or other person from whom money is due to the company to pay the amount due into the Bank of England (or any branch of it) to the account of the liquidator instead of to the liquidator, and any such order may be enforced in the same manner as if it had directed payment to the liquidator.

(2) All money and securities paid or delivered into the Bank of England (or branch) in the event of a winding up by the court are subject in all respects to the orders of the court.

555.—(1) An order made by the court on a contributory is conclusive evidence that the money (if any) thereby appearing to be due or ordered to be paid is due, but subject to any right of appeal.

(2) All other pertinent matters stated in the order are to be taken as truly stated as against all persons and in all proceedings, except proceedings in Scotland against the heritable estate of a deceased contributory; and in that case the order is only prima facie evidence for the purpose of charging his heritable estate, unless his heirs or legatees of heritage were on the list of contributories at the time of the order being made.

556.—(1) Where in proceedings in England and Wales the official receiver becomes the liquidator of a company, whether provisionally or otherwise, he may, if satisfied that the nature of the company's estate or business, or the interests of the creditors or contributories generally, require the appointment of a special manager of the estate or business other than himself, apply to the court.

(2) The court may on the application appoint a special manager of the company's estate or business to act during such time as the court may direct, with such powers (including any of the powers of a receiver or manager) as may be entrusted to him by the court.

(3) The special manager shall give such security and account in such manner as the Secretary of State directs, and shall receive such remuneration as may be fixed by the court.

557. The court may fix a time or times within which creditors are to prove their debts or claims or to be excluded from the benefit of any distribution made before those debts are proved.

558. The court shall adjust the rights of the contributories among themselves and distribute any surplus among the persons entitled to it.

PART XX
CHAPTER II
Inspection of
books by
creditors and
contributories.

559.—(1) The court may, at any time after making a winding-up order, make such order for inspection of the company's books and papers by creditors and contributories as the court thinks just; and any books and papers in the company's possession may be inspected by creditors and contributories accordingly, but not further or otherwise.

(2) Nothing in this section excludes or restricts any statutory rights of a government department or person acting under the authority of a government department.

Costs of
winding up
may be made
payable out of
assets.

560. The court may, in the event of the assets being insufficient to satisfy the liabilities, make an order as to the payment out of the assets of the costs, charges and expenses incurred in the winding up in such order of priority as the court thinks just.

Summoning of
persons
suspected of
having
company
property, etc.

561.—(1) The court may, at any time after the appointment of a provisional liquidator or the making of a winding-up order, summon before it any officer of the company or any person known or suspected to have in his possession any property of the company or supposed to be indebted to the company, or any person whom the court deems capable of giving information concerning the promotion, formation, trade, dealings, affairs or property of the company.

(2) The court may examine the officer or other person summoned on oath concerning those matters either by word of mouth or on written interrogatories, and may reduce his answers to writing and require him to sign them.

(3) The court may require him to produce any books and papers in his custody or power relating to the company; but if he claims any lien on books or papers produced by him, the production is without prejudice to that lien, and the court has jurisdiction in the winding up to determine all questions relating to that lien.

(4) If a person so summoned, after being tendered a reasonable sum for his expenses, refuses to come before the court at the time appointed, not having a lawful impediment (made known to the court at the time of its sitting and allowed by it), the court may cause him to be apprehended and brought before the court for examination.

Attendance at
company
meetings
(Scotland).

562. In the winding up by the court of a company registered in Scotland, the court has power to require the attendance of any officer of the company at any meeting of creditors or of contributories, or of a committee of inspection, for the purpose of giving information as to the trade, dealings, affairs or property of the company.

563.—(1) Where an order has been made in England and Wales for winding up a company by the court, and the official receiver has made a further report under this Act stating that in his opinion a fraud has been committed by any person in the promotion or formation of the company, or by any officer of the company in relation to it since its formation, the following applies.

PART XX
CHAPTER II
Public
examination
of promoters
and officers
(England and
Wales).

(2) The court may, after consideration of the report, direct that that person or officer shall attend before the court on a day appointed by the court for that purpose and be publicly examined as to the promotion or formation of the company, or the conduct of its business, or as to the conduct or dealings of that person as an officer of it.

(3) The official receiver shall take part in the examination and for that purpose may, if specially authorised by the Secretary of State in that behalf, employ a solicitor with or without counsel.

(4) The liquidator (where the official receiver is not the liquidator) and any creditor or contributory may also take part in the examination either personally or by solicitor or counsel.

564.—(1) On a public examination ordered by the court under section 563, the court may put such questions to the person examined as it thinks fit.

(2) The person examined shall be examined on oath and shall answer all such questions as the court may put or allow to be put to him.

(3) The person shall at his own cost, before his examination, be furnished with a copy of the official receiver's report, and may at his own cost employ a solicitor with or without counsel, who is at liberty to put to him such questions as the court may deem just for the purpose of enabling him to explain or qualify any answers given by him.

(4) If the person applies to the court to be exculpated from any charges made or suggested against him, it is the duty of the official receiver to appear on the hearing of the application and call the court's attention to any matters which appear to him to be relevant; and if the court, after hearing evidence given or witnesses called by the official receiver, grants the application, the court may allow the applicant such costs as in its discretion it thinks fit.

(5) Notes of a person's public examination shall be taken down in writing, and shall be read over to or by, and signed by, him and may thereafter be used in evidence against him, and

PART XX
CHAPTER II

shall be open to the inspection of any creditor or contributory at all reasonable times.

(6) The court may, if it thinks fit, adjourn the examination from time to time.

(7) The examination may, if the court so directs (and subject to general rules) be held before any Circuit judge, or before any officer of the Supreme Court being an official referee, master or registrar in bankruptcy, or before a district registrar of the High Court named for the purpose by the Lord Chancellor; and the powers of the court under this section may be exercised by the person before whom the examination is held.

Power to arrest absconding contributory.

565. The court, at any time either before or after making a winding-up order, on proof of probable cause for believing that a contributory is about to quit the United Kingdom or otherwise to abscond or to remove or conceal any of his property for the purpose of evading payment of calls or of avoiding examination respecting the company's affairs, may cause the contributory to be arrested and his books and papers and movable personal property to be seized and him and them to be kept safely until such time as the court may order.

Powers of court to be cumulative.

566. Powers conferred by this Act on the court are in addition to and not in restriction of any existing powers of instituting proceedings against a contributory or debtor of the company, or the estate of any contributory or debtor, for the recovery of any call or other sums.

Delegation of powers to liquidator (England and Wales).

567.—(1) Provision may be made by general rules for enabling or requiring all or any of the powers and duties conferred and imposed on the court in England and Wales by this Act in respect of the following matters—

(a) the holding and conducting of meetings to ascertain the wishes of creditors and contributories,

(b) the settling of lists of contributories and the rectifying of the register of members where required, and the collection and application of the assets,

(c) the payment, delivery, conveyance, surrender or transfer of money, property, books or papers to the liquidator,

(d) the making of calls,

(e) the fixing of a time within which debts and claims must be proved,

to be exercised or performed by the liquidator as an officer of the court, and subject to the court's control.

(2) But the liquidator shall not, without the special leave of the court, rectify the register of members, and shall not make

any call without either that special leave or the sanction of the committee of inspection.

568.—(1) When the company's affairs have been completely wound up, the court (if the liquidator makes an application in that behalf) shall make an order that the company be dissolved from the date of the order, and the company is then dissolved accordingly.

Dissolution of company.

(2) A copy of the order shall within 14 days from its date be forwarded by the liquidator to the registrar of companies who shall record the company's dissolution.

(3) If the liquidator makes default in complying with the requirements of subsection (2), he is liable to a fine and, for continued contravention, to a daily default fine.

Enforcement of, and appeal from, orders

569.—(1) In Scotland, where an order, interlocutor or decree has been made for winding up a company by the court, it is competent to the court, on production by the liquidators of a list certified by them of the names of the contributories liable in payment of any calls, and of the amount due by each contributory, and of the date when that amount became due, to pronounce forthwith a decree against those contributories for payment of the sums so certified to be due, with interest from that date until payment (at 5 per cent. per annum) in the same way and to the same effect as if they had severally consented to registration for execution, on a charge of 6 days, of a legal obligation to pay those calls and interest.

Orders for calls on contributories (Scotland).

(2) The decree may be extracted immediately, and no suspension of it is competent, except on caution or consignation, unless with special leave of the court.

570.—(1) An order made by the court in England and Wales for or in the course of winding up a company shall be enforced in Scotland and Northern Ireland in the courts that would respectively have jurisdiction in respect of that company if registered in Scotland or Northern Ireland and in the same manner in all respects as if the order had been made by those courts.

Enforcement throughout United Kingdom of orders made in winding up.

(2) Orders, interlocutors and decrees made by the court in Scotland for or in the course of winding up a company shall in like manner be enforced in England and Wales and Northern Ireland by any court which would respectively have jurisdiction in respect of that company if registered in that part of the United Kingdom where the order is required to be enforced, and in the same manner in all respects as if the order had been made by that court.

(3) Where an order, interlocutor or decree made by one court is required to be enforced by another court, an office copy of it shall be produced to the proper officer of the court required to enforce it.

(4) The production of an office copy is sufficient evidence of the order, interlocutor or decree ; and thereupon the last-mentioned court shall take the requisite steps in the matter for enforcing it, in the same manner as if it had been made by that court.

(5) This section extends to Northern Ireland.

Appeals from
orders in
Scotland.

571.—(1) Subject to the provisions of this section and to rules of court, an appeal from any order or decision made or given in the winding up of a company by the court in Scotland under this Act lies in the same manner and subject to the same conditions as an appeal from an order or decision of the court in cases within its ordinary jurisdiction.

(2) In regard to orders or judgments pronounced by the judge acting as vacation judge in pursuance of section 4 of the Administration of Justice (Scotland) Act 1933—

1933 c. 41.

    (*a*) none of the orders specified in Part I of Schedule 16 to this Act are subject to review, reduction, suspension or stay of execution, and

    (*b*) every other order or judgment (except as mentioned below) may be submitted to review by the Inner House by reclaiming motion enrolled within 14 days from the date of the order or judgment.

(3) However, an order being one of those specified in Part II of the Schedule shall, from the date of the order and notwithstanding that it has been submitted to review as above, be carried out and receive effect until the Inner House have disposed of the matter.

(4) In regard to orders or judgments pronounced in Scotland by a Lord Ordinary before whom proceedings in a winding up are being taken, any such order or judgment may be submitted to review by the Inner House by reclaiming motion enrolled within 14 days from its date ; but should it not be so submitted to review during session, the provisions of this section in regard to orders or judgments pronounced by the judge acting as vacation judge apply.

(5) Nothing in this section affects provisions of this Act in reference to decrees in Scotland for payment of calls in the winding up of companies, whether voluntary or by, or subject to the supervision of, the court.

CHAPTER III

PART XX

VOLUNTARY WINDING UP

Resolutions for, and commencement of, voluntary winding up

572.—(1) A company may be wound up voluntarily— Circumstances in which company may be wound up voluntarily.

(a) when the period (if any) fixed for the duration of the company by the articles expires, or the event (if any) occurs, on the occurrence of which the articles provide that the company is to be dissolved, and the company in general meeting has passed a resolution requiring it to be wound up voluntarily ;

(b) if the company resolves by special resolution that it be wound up voluntarily ;

(c) if the company resolves by extraordinary resolution to the effect that it cannot by reason of its liabilities continue its business, and that it is advisable to wind up.

(2) In this Act the expression " a resolution for voluntary winding up " means a resolution passed under any of the paragraphs of subsection (1).

(3) A resolution passed under paragraph (a) of subsection (1), as well as a special resolution under paragraph (b) and an extraordinary resolution under paragraph (c), is subject to section 380 (copy of resolution to be forwarded to registrar of companies within 15 days).

573.—(1) When a company has passed a resolution for voluntary winding up, it shall, within 14 days after the passing of the resolution, give notice of the resolution by advertisement in the Gazette. Notice of resolution to wind up voluntarily.

(2) If default is made in complying with this section, the company and every officer of it who is in default is liable to a fine and, for continued contravention, to a daily default fine.

For purposes of this subsection the liquidator is deemed an officer of the company.

574. A voluntary winding up is deemed to commence at the time of the passing of the resolution for voluntary winding up. Commencement of voluntary winding up.

PART XX
CHAPTER III
Effect on
business and
status of
company.

Consequences of voluntary winding up

575.—(1) In case of a voluntary winding up, the company shall from the commencement of the winding up cease to carry on its business, except so far as may be required for its beneficial winding up.

(2) However, the corporate state and corporate powers of the company, notwithstanding anything to the contrary in its articles, continue until the company is dissolved.

576. Any transfer of shares, not being a transfer made to or with the sanction of the liquidator, and any alteration in the status of the company's members, made after the commencement of a voluntary winding up is void.

Declaration of solvency

577.—(1) Where it is proposed to wind up a company voluntarily, the directors (or, in the case of a company having more than two directors, the majority of them) may at a directors' meeting make a statutory declaration to the effect that they have made a full inquiry into the company's affairs and that, having done so, they have formed the opinion that the company will be able to pay its debts in full within such period, not exceeding 12 months from the commencement of the winding up, as may be specified in the declaration.

(2) Such a declaration by the directors has no effect for purposes of this Act unless—

(a) it is made within the 5 weeks immediately preceding the date of the passing of the resolution for winding up, or on that date but before the passing of the resolution, and

(b) it embodies a statement of the company's assets and liabilities as at the latest practicable date before the making of the declaration.

(3) The declaration shall be delivered to the registrar of companies before the expiration of 15 days immediately following the date on which the resolution for winding up is passed.

(4) A director making a declaration under this section without having reasonable grounds for the opinion that the company will be able to pay its debts in full within the period specified is liable to imprisonment or a fine, or both.

(5) If the company is wound up in pursuance of a resolution passed within 5 weeks after the making of the declaration, and its debts are not paid or provided for in full within the period

specified, it is to be presumed (unless the contrary is shown) that the director did not have reasonable grounds for his opinion.

(6) If a declaration required by subsection (3) to be delivered to the registrar is not so delivered within the time prescribed by that subsection, the company and every officer in default is liable to a fine and, for continued contravention, to a daily default fine.

578. A winding up in the case of which a directors' statutory declaration under section 577 has been made is a " members' voluntary winding up " ; and a winding up in the case of which such a declaration has not been made is a " creditors' voluntary winding up ".

Provisions applicable to a members' voluntary winding up

579. The provisions contained in sections 580 to 586 apply in relation to a members' voluntary winding up.

580.—(1) The company in general meeting shall appoint one or more liquidators for the purpose of winding up the company's affairs and distributing its assets, and may fix the remuneration to be paid to him or them.

(2) On the appointment of a liquidator all the powers of the directors cease, except so far as the company in general meeting or the liquidator sanctions their continuance.

581.—(1) If a vacancy occurs by death, resignation or otherwise in the office of liquidator appointed by the company, the company in general meeting may, subject to any arrangement with its creditors, fill the vacancy.

(2) For that purpose a general meeting may be convened by any contributory or, if there were more liquidators than one, by the continuing liquidators.

(3) The meeting shall be held in manner provided by this Act or by the articles, or in such manner as may, on application by any contributory or by the continuing liquidators, be determined by the court.

582.—(1) The following applies where a company is proposed to be, or is being, wound up altogether voluntarily, and the whole or part of its business or property is proposed to be transferred or sold to another company (" the transferee company "), whether or not this latter is a company within the meaning of this Act.

(2) The liquidator of the company to be, or being, wound up (" the transferor company ") may, with the sanction of a special resolution of that company, conferring either a general authority on himself or an authority in respect of any particular arrangement, receive, in compensation or part compensation for the transfer or sale, shares, policies or other like interests in the transferee company for distribution among the members of the transferor company.

(3) Alternatively, the liquidator may (with that sanction) enter into any other arrangement whereby the members of the transferor company may, in lieu of receiving cash, shares, policies or other like interests (or in addition thereto), participate in the profits of, or receive any other benefit from, the transferee company.

(4) A sale or arrangement in pursuance of this section is binding on members of the transferor company.

(5) If a member of the transferor company who did not vote in favour of the special resolution expresses his dissent from it in writing addressed to the liquidator, and left at the company's registered office within 7 days after the passing of the resolution, he may require the liquidator either to abstain from carrying the resolution into effect or to purchase his interest at a price to be determined by agreement or by arbitration in manner provided by this section.

(6) If the liquidator elects to purchase the member's interest, the purchase money must be paid before the company is dissolved and be raised by the liquidator in such manner as may be determined by special resolution.

(7) A special resolution is not invalid for purposes of this section by reason that it is passed before or concurrently with a resolution for voluntary winding up or for appointing liquidators ; but, if an order is made within a year for winding up the company by or subject to the supervision of the court, the special resolution is not valid unless sanctioned by the court.

(8) For purposes of an arbitration under this section, the provisions of the Companies Clauses Consolidation Act 1845 or, in the case of a winding up in Scotland, the Companies Clauses Consolidation (Scotland) Act 1845 with respect to the settlement of disputes by arbitration are incorporated with this Act, and—

8 & 9 Vict.
c. 16.

8 & 9 Vict.
c. 17.

    (*a*) in the construction of those provisions this Act is deemed the special Act and " the company " means the transferor company, and

    (*b*) any appointment by the incorporated provisions directed to be made under the hand of the secretary or any two of the directors may be made in writing by the liquidator (or, if there is more than one liquidator, then any two or more of them).

583.—(1) If the liquidator is at any time of opinion that the company will not be able to pay its debts in full within the period stated in the directors' declaration under section 577, he shall forthwith summon a meeting of the creditors, and shall lay before the meeting a statement of the company's assets and liabilities.

(2) If the liquidator fails to comply with this section, he is liable to a fine.

584.—(1) Subject to section 586, in the event of the winding up continuing for more than one year, the liquidator shall summon a general meeting of the company at the end of the first year from the commencement of the winding up, and of each succeeding year, or at the first convenient date within 3 months from the end of the year or such longer period as the Secretary of State may allow, and shall lay before the meeting an account of his acts and dealings and of the conduct of the winding up during the preceding year.

(2) If the liquidator fails to comply with this section, he is liable to a fine.

585.—(1) As soon as the company's affairs are fully wound up, the liquidator shall make up an account of the winding up, showing how it has been conducted and the company's property has been disposed of, and thereupon shall call a general meeting of the company for the purpose of laying before it the account, and giving an explanation of it.

(2) The meeting shall be called by advertisement in the Gazette, specifying its time, place and object and published at least one month before the meeting.

(3) Within one week after the meeting, the liquidator shall send to the registrar of companies a copy of the account, and shall make a return to him of the holding of the meeting and of its date; and if the copy is not sent or the return is not made in accordance with this subsection the liquidator is liable to a fine and, for continued contravention, to a daily default fine.

(4) If a quorum is not present at the meeting, the liquidator shall, in lieu of the return mentioned above, make a return that the meeting was duly summoned and that no quorum was present; and upon such a return being made, the provisions of subsection (3) as to the making of the return are deemed complied with.

(5) The registrar on receiving the account and either of these returns shall forthwith register them, and on the expiration of 3 months from the registration of the return the company is deemed to be dissolved ; but the court may, on the application of the liquidator or of any other person who appears to the court to be interested, make an order deferring the date at which the dissolution of the company is to take effect for such time as the court thinks fit.

(6) It is the duty of the person on whose application an order of the court under this section is made within 7 days after the making of the order to deliver to the registrar an office copy of the order for registration ; and if that person fails to do so he is liable to a fine and, for continued contravention, to a daily default fine.

(7) If the liquidator fails to call a general meeting of the company as required by subsection (1), he is liable to a fine.

Alternative provision as to company meetings in case of insolvency.
586.—(1) Where section 583 has effect, sections 594 and 595 apply to the winding up to the exclusion of sections 584 and 585, as if the winding up were a creditors' voluntary winding up and not a members' voluntary winding up.

(2) However, the liquidator is not required to summon a meeting of creditors under section 594 at the end of the first year from the commencement of the winding up, unless the meeting held under section 583 is held more than 3 months before the end of that year.

*Provisions applicable to a creditors'
voluntary winding up*

Introduction to next 8 sections.
587. The provisions contained in sections 588 to 595 apply in relation to a creditors' voluntary winding up.

Meeting of creditors.
588.—(1) The company shall give at least 7 days' notice of the company meeting at which the resolution for voluntary winding up is to be proposed.

This applies notwithstanding any power of the members, or of any particular majority of the members, to exclude or waive any other requirement of this Act or the company's articles with respect to the period of notice to be given of any company meeting.

(2) The company shall in addition—
(a) cause a meeting of its creditors to be summoned for the day, or the day next following the day, on which the company meeting is to be held,

(*b*) cause the notices of the creditors' meeting to be sent by post to the creditors simultaneously with the sending of the notices of the company meeting, and

(*c*) cause notice of the creditors' meeting to be advertised once in the Gazette and once at least in two local newspapers circulating in the district in which the company's registered office or its principal place of business is situated.

(3) The directors of the company shall—

(*a*) cause a full statement of the position of the company's affairs, together with a list of its creditors and the estimated amount of their claims, to be laid before the creditors' meeting, and

(*b*) appoint one of their number to preside at the meeting ;

and it is the duty of the director so appointed to attend the meeting and preside at it.

(4) If the company meeting at which the resolution for voluntary winding up is to be proposed is adjourned and the resolution is passed at an adjourned meeting, any resolution passed at the creditors' meeting held under subsection (2) has effect as if it had been passed immediately after the passing of the resolution for voluntary winding up.

(5) If default is made—

(*a*) by the company in complying with subsections (1) and (2),

(*b*) by the directors in complying with subsection (3),

(*c*) by any director in complying with that subsection, so far as requiring him to attend and preside at the creditors' meeting,

the company, the directors or the director (as the case may be) is or are liable to a fine ; and, in the case of default by the company, every officer of the company who is in default is also so liable.

(6) Failure to give notice of the company meeting as required by subsection (1) does not affect the validity of any resolution passed or other thing done at that meeting which would be valid apart from that subsection.

589.—(1) The creditors and the company at their respective meetings mentioned in section 588 may nominate a person to be liquidator for the purpose of winding up the company's affairs and distributing its assets.

Appointment of liquidator

(2) If the creditors and the company nominate different persons, the person nominated by the creditors shall be liquidator ;

and if no person is nominated by the creditors the person (if any) nominated by the company shall be liquidator.

(3) In the case of different persons being nominated, any director, member or creditor of the company may, within 7 days after the date on which the nomination was made by the creditors, apply to the court for an order either—

> (*a*) directing that the person nominated as liquidator by the company shall be liquidator instead of or jointly with the person nominated by the creditors, or
>
> (*b*) appointing some other person to be liquidator instead of the person nominated by the creditors.

Appointment
of committee
of inspection.

590.—(1) The creditors at the meeting to be held under section 588 or at any subsequent meeting may, if they think fit, appoint a committee of inspection consisting of not more than 5 persons.

(2) If such a committee is appointed, the company may, either at the meeting at which the resolution for voluntary winding up is passed or at any time subsequently in general meeting, appoint such number of persons as they think fit to act as members of the committee, not exceeding 5.

(3) However, the creditors may, if they think fit, resolve that all or any of the persons so appointed by the company ought not to be members of the committee of inspection ; and if the creditors so resolve—

> (*a*) the persons mentioned in the resolution are not then, unless the court otherwise directs, qualified to act as members of the committee, and
>
> (*b*) on any application to the court under this provision the court may, if it thinks fit, appoint other persons to act as such members in place of the persons mentioned in the resolution.

(4) Schedule 17 has effect with respect to a committee of inspection appointed under this section and its proceedings.

(5) In Scotland, such a committee has, in addition to the powers and duties conferred and imposed on it by this Act, such of the powers and duties of commissioners on a bankrupt estate as may be conferred and imposed on committees of inspection by general rules.

Remuneration
of liquidator;
cesser of
directors'
powers.

591.—(1) The committee of inspection or, if there is no such committee, the creditors may fix the remuneration to be paid to the liquidator or liquidators.

(2) On the appointment of a liquidator, all the powers of the directors cease, except so far as the committee of inspection (or,

if there is no such committee, the creditors) sanction their continuance.

PART XX
CHAPTER III

592. If a vacancy occurs, by death, resignation or otherwise, in the office of a liquidator (other than a liquidator appointed by, or by the direction of, the court), the creditors may fill the vacancy.

Vacancy in office of liquidator.

593. Section 582 applies in the case of a creditors' voluntary winding up as in the case of a members' voluntary winding up, with the modification that the liquidator's powers under that section are not to be exercised except with the sanction either of the court or of the committee of inspection.

Application of s. 582 to creditors' voluntary winding up.

594.—(1) If the winding up continues for more than one year, the liquidator shall summon a general meeting of the company and a meeting of the creditors at the end of the first year from the commencement of the winding up, and of each succeeding year, or at the first convenient date within 3 months from the end of the year or such longer period as the Secretary of State may allow, and shall lay before the meetings an account of his acts and dealings and of the conduct of the winding up during the preceding year.

Meetings of company and creditors at end of each year.

(2) If the liquidator fails to comply with this section, he is liable to a fine.

595.—(1) As soon as the company's affairs are fully wound up, the liquidator shall make up an account of the winding up, showing how it has been conducted and the company's property has been disposed of, and thereupon shall call a general meeting of the company and a meeting of the creditors for the purpose of laying the account before the meetings and giving an explanation of it.

Final meeting and dissolution.

(2) Each such meeting shall be called by advertisement in the Gazette specifying the time, place and object of the meeting, and published at least one month before it.

(3) Within one week after the date of the meetings (or, if they are not held on the same date, after the date of the later one) the liquidator shall send to the registrar of companies a copy of the account, and shall make a return to him of the holding of the meetings and of their dates.

(4) If the copy is not sent or the return is not made in accordance with subsection (3), the liquidator is liable to a fine and, for continued contravention, to a daily default fine.

(5) However, if a quorum is not present at either such meeting, the liquidator shall, in lieu of the return required by subsection (3), make a return that the meeting was duly summoned and that no quorum was present ; and upon such return being made the provisions of that subsection as to the making of the return are, in respect of that meeting, deemed complied with.

(6) The registrar on receiving the account and, in respect of each such meeting, either of the returns mentioned above, shall forthwith register them, and on the expiration of 3 months from their registration the company is deemed to be dissolved ; but the court may, on the application of the liquidator or of any other person who appears to the court to be interested, make an order deferring the date at which the dissolution of the company is to take effect for such time as the court thinks fit.

(7) It is the duty of the person on whose application an order of the court under this section is made, within 7 days after the making of the order, to deliver to the registrar an office copy of the order for registration ; and if that person fails to do so he is liable to a fine and, for continued contravention, to a daily default fine.

(8) If the liquidator fails to call a general meeting of the company or a meeting of the creditors as required by this section, he is liable to a fine.

Provisions applicable to every voluntary winding up

Introduction to next 9 sections.

596. The provisions of sections 597 to 605 apply to every voluntary winding up, whether a members' or a creditors' winding up.

Distribution of company's property.

597. Subject to the provisions of this Act as to preferential payments, the company's property shall on the winding up be applied in satisfaction of the company's liabilities pari passu and, subject to that application, shall (unless the articles otherwise provide) be distributed among the members according to their rights and interests in the company.

Powers and duties of liquidator in voluntary winding up.

598.—(1) The liquidator may—

  (a) in the case of a members' voluntary winding up, with the sanction of an extraordinary resolution of the company, and

  (b) in the case of a creditors' voluntary winding up, with the sanction of the court or the committee of inspection (or, if there is no such committee, a meeting of the creditors),

exercise any of the powers given by paragraphs (d), (e) and (f) of section 539(1) to a liquidator in a winding up by the court.

(2) The liquidator may, without sanction, exercise any of the other powers given by this Act to the liquidator in a winding up by the court.

PART XX CHAPTER III

(3) The liquidator may—

(a) exercise the court's power of settling a list of contributories (and the list of contributories is prima facie evidence of the liability of the persons named in it to be contributories),

(b) exercise the court's power of making calls,

(c) summon general meetings of the company for the purpose of obtaining its sanction by special or extraordinary resolution or for any other purpose he may think fit.

(4) The liquidator shall pay the company's debts and adjust the rights of the contributories among themselves.

(5) When several liquidators are appointed, any power given by this Act may be exercised by such one or more of them as may be determined at the time of their appointment or, in default of such determination, by any number not less than two.

599.—(1) If from any cause whatever there is no liquidator acting, the court may appoint a liquidator.

Appointment or removal of liquidator by the court.

(2) The court may, on cause shown, remove a liquidator and appoint another.

600.—(1) The liquidator shall, within 14 days after his appointment, publish in the Gazette and deliver to the registrar of companies for registration a notice of his appointment in the form prescribed by statutory instrument made by the Secretary of State.

Notice by liquidator of his appointment.

(2) If the liquidator fails to comply with this section he is liable to a fine and, for continued contravention, to a daily default fine.

601.—(1) Any arrangement entered into between a company about to be, or in the course of being, wound up and its creditors is (subject to the right of appeal under this section) binding—

Arrangement when binding on creditors.

(a) on the company, if sanctioned by an extraordinary resolution, and

(b) on the creditors, if acceded to by three-fourths in number and value of them.

(2) Any creditor or contributory may, within 3 weeks from the completion of the arrangement, appeal to the court against it; and the court may thereupon, as it thinks just, amend, vary or confirm the arrangement.

PART XX
CHAPTER III
Reference of
questions and
powers to
court.

602.—(1) The liquidator or any contributory or creditor may apply to the court to determine any question arising in the winding up of a company, or to exercise, as respects the enforcing of calls or any other matter, all or any of the powers which the court might exercise if the company were being wound up by the court.

(2) The court, if satisfied that the determination of the question or the required exercise of power will be just and beneficial, may accede wholly or partially to the application on such terms and conditions as it thinks fit or may make such other order on the application as it thinks just.

(3) A copy of an order made by virtue of this section staying the proceedings in the winding up shall forthwith be forwarded by the company, or otherwise as may be prescribed, to the registrar of companies, who shall enter it in his records relating to the company.

Court's power
to control
proceedings
(Scotland).

603. If the court, on the application of the liquidator in the winding up of a company registered in Scotland, so directs, no action or proceeding shall be proceeded with or commenced against the company except by leave of the court and subject to such terms as the court may impose.

Costs of
voluntary
winding up.

604. All costs, charges and expenses properly incurred in the winding up, including the remuneration of the liquidator, are payable out of the company's assets in priority to all other claims.

Saving for
rights of
creditors and
contributories.

605. The winding up of a company under this Chapter does not bar the right of any creditor or contributory to have it wound up by the court; but in the case of an application by a contributory the court must be satisfied that the rights of the contributories will be prejudiced by a voluntary winding up.

CHAPTER IV

WINDING UP SUBJECT TO SUPERVISION OF COURT

Power to
order winding
up under
supervision.

606. When a company has passed a resolution for voluntary winding up, the court may make an order that the voluntary winding up shall continue but subject to such supervision of the court, and with such liberty for creditors, contributories or others to apply to the court, and generally on such terms and conditions, as the court thinks just.

Effect of
petition for
court
supervision.

607. A petition for the continuance of a voluntary winding up subject to the supervision of the court is deemed, for the purpose of giving jurisdiction to the court over actions, to be a petition for winding up by the court.

608. A winding up subject to the supervision of the court is deemed for the purposes of sections 522 and 523 (avoidance of dispositions of property, etc.) to be a winding up by the court.

609.—(1) Where an order is made for a winding up subject to supervision, the court may by that or any subsequent order appoint an additional liquidator.

(2) A liquidator so appointed has the same powers, is subject to the same obligations, and in all respects stands in the same position, as if he had been duly appointed in accordance with provisions of this Act with respect to the appointment of liquidators in a voluntary winding up.

(3) The court may remove a liquidator so appointed by the court, or any liquidator continued under the supervision order, and fill any vacancy occasioned by the removal, or by death or resignation.

610.—(1) Where an order is made for a winding up subject to supervision, the liquidator may (subject to any restrictions imposed by the court) exercise all his powers, without the court's sanction or intervention, in the same manner as if the company were being wound up altogether voluntarily.

(2) However, the powers specified in paragraphs (*d*), (*e*) and (*f*) of section 539(1) shall not be exercised by the liquidator except with the sanction of the court or, in a case where before the order the winding up was a creditors' voluntary winding up, with the sanction of the court or the committee of inspection or (if there is no such committee) a meeting of the creditors.

(3) A winding up subject to the supervision of the court is not a winding up by the court for the purposes of the provisions of this Act specified in Schedule 18, nor for those of section 491 (power in England and Wales to appoint official receiver as receiver for debenture holders or creditors) ; but, subject to this, an order for a winding up subject to supervision is deemed to be for all purposes an order for winding up by the court.

(4) But where the order for winding up subject to supervision was made in relation to a creditors' voluntary winding up in which a committee of inspection had been appointed, the order is deemed an order for winding up by the court for the purposes of section 547(2)(*b*) and Schedule 17, except in so far as the operation of those provisions is excluded in a voluntary winding up by general rules.

CHAPTER V

PROVISIONS APPLICABLE TO EVERY MODE OF
WINDING UP

Proof and ranking of claims

Debts of all
descriptions
may be proved.

611.—(1) In every winding up (subject, in the case of insolvent companies, to the application in accordance with this Act of the law of bankruptcy) all debts payable on a contingency, and all claims against the company, present or future, certain or contingent, ascertained or sounding only in damages, are admissible to proof against the company.

(2) A just estimate is to be made (so far as possible) of the value of such debts or claims as may be subject to any contingency or sound only in damages, or for some other reason do not bear a certain value.

Application
of bankruptcy
rules (England
and Wales).

612.—(1) In the winding up of an insolvent company registered in England and Wales the same rules prevail and are to be observed with regard to the respective rights of secured and unsecured creditors, and to debts provable and to the valuation of annuities and future and contingent liabilities, as are in force for the time being under the law of bankruptcy in England and Wales with respect to the estates of persons adjudged bankrupt.

(2) All those who in any such case would be entitled to prove for and receive dividends out of the company's assets may come in under the winding up and make such claims against the company as they respectively are entitled to by virtue of this section.

Ranking of
claims
(Scotland).

1913 c. 20.

613.—(1) In the winding up of a company registered in Scotland, the following provisions of the Bankruptcy (Scotland) Act 1913—

(a) sections 45 to 62 regarding voting and ranking for payment of dividends,

(b) section 96 (reckoning of majorities), and

(c) section 105 (interruption of prescription),

apply, so far as is consistent with this Act, in like manner as they apply in the sequestration of a bankrupt's estate, with the substitutions specified below, and with any other necessary modifications.

(2) The substitutions to be made in those sections of the Act of 1913 are as follows—

(a) for references to sequestration, substitute references to winding up,

(b) for references to the sheriff, substitute references to the court, (*c*) for references to the trustee, substitute references to the liquidator, and

(*d*) for references to the bankrupt, substitute references to the company.

614.—(1) In a winding up the preferential debts listed in Schedule 19 shall be paid in priority to all other debts, but with the exceptions and reservations specified in that Schedule.

Preferential payments.

(2) The preferential debts shall—

(*a*) rank equally among themselves and be paid in full, unless the assets are insufficient to meet them, in which case they shall abate in equal proportions, and

(*b*) so far as the assets of the company available for payment of general creditors are insufficient to meet them, have priority over the claims of holders of debentures under any floating charge created by the company, and be paid accordingly out of any property comprised in or subject to that charge.

(3) Subject to the retention of such sums as may be necessary for the costs and expenses of the winding up, the preferential debts shall be discharged forthwith so far as the assets are sufficient to meet them; and in the case of the debts to which priority is given by paragraph 8 of Schedule 19 (social security payments), formal proof of them is not required except in so far as is otherwise provided by general rules.

(4) In the event of a landlord or other person distraining or having distrained on any goods or effects of the company within 3 months next before the date of a winding-up order, the preferential debts are a first charge on the goods or effects so distrained on, or the proceeds of their sale; but in respect of any money paid under such a charge, the landlord or other person has the same rights of priority as the person to whom the payment is made.

Effect of winding up on antecedent and other transactions

615.—(1) Any conveyance, mortgage, delivery of goods, payment, execution or other act relating to property made or done by or against a company within 6 months before the commencement of its winding up which, had it been made or done by or against an individual within 6 months before the presentation of a bankruptcy petition on which he is adjudged bankrupt, would be deemed in his bankruptcy a fraudulent preference, is in the event of the company being wound up deemed a fraudulent preference of its creditors and invalid accordingly.

Fraudulent preference.

(2) Any conveyance or assignment by a company of all its property to trustees for the benefit of all its creditors is void to all intents.

(3) In the application of this section to Scotland, " bankruptcy petition " means petition for sequestration.

Liabilities
and rights
of those
fraudulently
preferred
(England
and Wales).

616.—(1) Where in the case of a company wound up in England and Wales anything made or done is void under section 615 as a fraudulent preference of a person interested in property mortgaged or charged to secure the company's debt, then (without prejudice to any rights or liabilities arising apart from this provision) the person preferred is subject to the same liabilities, and has the same rights, as if he had undertaken to be personally liable as surety for the debt to the extent of the charge on the property or the value of his interest, whichever is the less.

(2) The value of the person's interest is determined as at the date of the transaction constituting the fraudulent preference, and as if the interest were free of all incumbrances other than those to which the charge for the company's debt was then subject.

(3) On an application made to the court with respect to any payment on the ground that the payment was a fraudulent preference of a surety or guarantor, the court has jurisdiction to determine any question with respect to the payment arising between the person to whom the payment was made and the surety or guarantor, and to grant relief in respect of it.

(4) The court's jurisdiction under subsection (3) is exercisable notwithstanding that the determination of the question is not necessary for the purposes of the winding up; and the court may for the purposes of that subsection give leave to bring in the surety or guarantor as a third party as in the case of an action for the recovery of the sum paid.

(5) Subsections (3) and (4) apply, with the necessary modifications, in relation to transactions other than the payment of money as they apply in relation to payments.

Effect of
floating
charge.

617.—(1) Where a company is being wound up, a floating charge on its undertaking or property created within 12 months of the commencement of the winding up is invalid (unless it is proved that the company immediately after the creation of the charge was solvent), except to the amount of any cash paid to the company at the time of or subsequently to the creation of, and in consideration for, the charge, together with interest on that amount.

(2) Interest under this section is at the rate of 5 per cent. per annum or such other rate as may for the time being be prescribed by order of the Treasury in a statutory instrument subject to annulment in pursuance of a resolution of either House of Parliament.

(3) Where a company is being wound up in Scotland, a floating charge over all or any part of its property is not to be held an alienation or preference voidable by statute (other than by the provisions of this section) or at common law on the ground of insolvency or notour bankruptcy.

618.—(1) Where any part of the property of a company which is being wound up consists of land (of any tenure) burdened with onerous covenants, of shares or stock in companies, of unprofitable contracts, or of any other property that is unsaleable, or not readily saleable, by reason of its binding its possessor to the performance of any onerous act or to the payment of any sum of money, the liquidator may, with the leave of the court and subject to the provisions of this section and the next, disclaim the property.

Disclaimer of onerous property (England and Wales).

(2) The power to disclaim is exercisable notwithstanding that the liquidator has endeavoured to sell or has taken possession of the property or exercised any act of ownership in relation to it ; and the disclaimer must be in writing signed by him.

(3) The power is exercisable at any time within 12 months after the commencement of the winding up or such extended period as may be allowed by the court ; but where any such property has not come to the liquidator's knowledge within one month after the commencement of the winding up, he may disclaim at any time within 12 months after he has become aware of it or such extended period as may be so allowed.

(4) The disclaimer operates to determine, as from the date of disclaimer, the rights, interests and liabilities of the company, and the company's property, in or in respect of the property disclaimed ; but it does not (except so far as is necessary for the purpose of releasing the company and its property from liability) affect the rights or liabilities of any other person.

(5) This section does not apply in the case of a winding up in Scotland.

619.—(1) The court, before or on granting leave to disclaim under section 618, may require such notices to be given to persons interested, and impose such terms as a condition of granting leave, and make such other order in the matter, as the court thinks just.

Further provisions about disclaimer under s. 618.

(2) The liquidator is not entitled to disclaim property under section 618 in a case where application in writing has been made to him by persons interested in the property requiring

him to decide whether he will or will not disclaim and he has not within 28 days after the receipt of the application (or such further period as may be allowed by the court) given notice to the applicant that he intends to apply to the court for leave to disclaim.

(3) In the case of a contract, if the liquidator after such an application does not within that period or further period disclaim the contract, the company is deemed to have adopted it.

(4) The court may, on the application of a person who is, as against the liquidator, entitled to the benefit or subject to the burden of a contract made with the company, make an order rescinding the contract on such terms as to payment by or to either party of damages for the non-performance of the contract, or otherwise as the court thinks just; and any damages payable under the order to such a person may be proved by him as a debt in the winding up.

(5) The court may, on an application by a person who either claims an interest in disclaimed property or is under a liability not discharged by this Act in respect of disclaimed property, and on hearing any such persons as it thinks fit, make an order for the vesting of the property in or its delivery to any persons entitled to it, or to whom it may seem just that the property should be delivered by way of compensation for such liability, or a trustee for him, and on such terms as the court thinks just.

(6) On such a vesting order being made, the property comprised in it vests accordingly in the person named in that behalf in the order, without conveyance or assignment for that purpose.

(7) Part I of Schedule 20 has effect for the protection of third parties where the property disclaimed is of a leasehold nature.

(8) A person injured by the operation of a disclaimer under section 618 and this section is deemed a creditor of the company to the amount of the injury, and may accordingly prove the debt in the winding up.

620.—(1) Where on a disclaimer under section 618 land in England and Wales vests subject to a rentcharge in the Crown or any other person, that does not impose on the Crown or that other person, or on its or his successors in title, any personal liability in respect of the rentcharge.

(2) But this section does not affect any liability in respect of sums accruing due after the Crown or other person, or some person claiming through or under it or him, has taken possession or control of the land or has entered into occupation of it.

(3) This section applies to land whenever vesting, and to sums whenever accrued.

621.—(1) Where a creditor has issued execution against the goods or land of a company or has attached any debt due to it, and the company is subsequently wound up, he is not entitled to retain the benefit of the execution or attachment against the liquidator in the winding up unless he has completed the execution or attachment before the commencement of the winding up.

PART XX
CHAPTER V
Effect of execution or attachment (England and Wales).

(2) However—

(a) if a creditor has had notice of a meeting having been called at which a resolution for voluntary winding up is to be proposed, the date on which he had notice is substituted, for the purpose of subsection (1), for the date of commencement of the winding up,

(b) a person who purchases in good faith under a sale by the sheriff any goods of a company on which execution has been levied in all cases acquires a good title to them against the liquidator, and

(c) the rights conferred by subsection (1) on the liquidator may be set aside by the court in favour of the creditor to such extent and subject to such terms as the court thinks fit.

(3) For purposes of this Act—

(a) an execution against goods is completed by seizure and sale, or by the making of a charging order under section 1 of the Charging Orders Act 1979 ;

1979 c. 53.

(b) an attachment of a debt is completed by receipt of the debt ; and

(c) an execution against land is completed by seizure, by the appointment of a receiver, or by the making of a charging order under section 1 of the Act above-mentioned.

(4) In this section, " goods " includes all chattels personal ; and " the sheriff " includes any officer charged with the execution of a writ or other process.

(5) This section does not apply in the case of a winding up in Scotland.

622.—(1) The following applies where a company's goods are taken in execution and, before their sale or the completion of the execution (by the receipt or recovery of the full amount of the levy), notice is served on the sheriff that a provisional liquidator has been appointed or that a winding-up order has been made, or that a resolution for voluntary winding up has been passed.

Duties of sheriff where goods seized in execution (England and Wales).

(2) The sheriff shall, on being so required, deliver the goods and any money seized or received in part satisfaction of the execution to the liquidator ; but the costs of execution are a first charge on the goods or money so delivered, and the liquidator

may sell the goods, or a sufficient part of them, for the purpose of satisfying the charge.

(3) If under an execution in respect of a judgment for a sum exceeding £250 a company's goods are sold or money is paid in order to avoid sale, the sheriff shall deduct the costs of the execution from the proceeds of sale or the money paid and retain the balance for 14 days.

(4) If within that time notice is served on the sheriff of a petition for the winding up of the company having been presented, or of a meeting having been called at which there is to be proposed a resolution for voluntary winding up, and an order is made or a resolution passed (as the case may be), the sheriff shall pay the balance to the liquidator, who is entitled to retain it as against the execution creditor.

(5) The rights conferred by this section on the liquidator may be set aside by the court in favour of the creditor to such extent and subject to such terms as the court thinks fit.

(6) In this section, " goods " includes all chattels personal; and " the sheriff " includes any officer charged with the execution of a writ or other process.

(7) The money sum for the time being specified in subsection (3) is subject to increase or reduction by regulations under section 664; but no increase or reduction of it affects any case where the goods are sold, or the payment to avoid sale is made, before the coming into force of the increase or reduction.

(8) This section does not apply in the case of a winding up in Scotland.

Effect of
diligence
within 60 days
of winding up.

623.—(1) The following applies in the case of the winding up of a company registered in Scotland.

(2) The winding up is equivalent, as at the date of its commencement, to an arrestment in execution and decree of forthcoming, and to an executed or completed poinding; and—

    (*a*) no arrestment or poinding of the funds or effects of the company executed on or after the 60th day prior to that date is effectual, and

    (*b*) those funds or effects (or their proceeds if sold) shall be made forthcoming to the liquidator:

But any arrester or poinder before that date who is thus deprived of the benefit of his diligence has preference out of those funds or effects for the expense bona fide incurred by him in the diligence.

(3) As at the date of its commencement, the winding up is equivalent to a decree of adjudication of the heritable estates of the company for the payment of its whole debts, principal and interest, accumulated at that date, subject to such preferable heritable rights and securities as existed at that date and are

valid and unchallengeable, and the right to poind the ground
provided below in this section.

(4) Sections 108 to 113 and 116 of the Bankruptcy (Scotland)
Act 1913 apply (so far as is consistent with this Act) to the
realisation of heritable estates affected by such heritable rights
and securities as are mentioned above ; and for the purposes of
this Act those sections are modified as follows—

  (a) " sequestration " and " trustee " mean respectively
      " winding up " and " liquidator ", and

  (b) " the Lord Ordinary or the court " means " the court "
      as defined by this Act with respect to Scotland.

(5) No poinding of the ground which has not been carried
into execution by sale of the effects 60 days before the date of
commencement of the winding up is available (except to the
extent provided below) in any question with the liquidator.

However, no creditor who holds a security over the heritable
estate preferable to the right of the liquidator is prevented from
executing a poinding of the ground after that date ; but that
poinding is, in competition with the liquidator, available only
for interest on the debt for the current half-yearly term, and for
arrears of interest for one year immediately before the commencement of that term.

(6) This section, so far as relating to any estate or effects of
the company situated in Scotland, applies in the case of a company registered in England as in the case of one registered in
Scotland.

*Offences of fraud, deception, etc., before and in course of
winding up ; fraudulent trading and its consequences*

624.—(1) When a company is ordered to be wound up by Fraud, etc. in
the court, or passes a resolution for voluntary winding up, any anticipation of
person, being a past or present officer of the company, is deemed winding up.
to have committed an offence if, within the 12 months immediately preceding the commencement of the winding up, he has—

  (a) concealed any part of the company's property to the
      value of £120 or more, or concealed any debt due to
      or from the company,

  (b) fraudulently removed any part of the company's pro-
      perty to the value of £120 or more, or

  (c) concealed, destroyed, mutilated or falsified any book
      or paper affecting or relating to the company's property
      or affairs, or

  (d) made any false entry in any book or paper affecting or
      relating to the company's property or affairs, or

  (e) fraudulently parted with, altered or made any omission
      in any document affecting or relating to the company's
      property or affairs, or

(*f*) pawned, pledged or disposed of any property of the company which has been obtained on credit and has not been paid for (unless the pawning, pledging or disposal was in the ordinary way of the company's business).

(2) Such a person is deemed to have committed an offence if within the period above mentioned he has been privy to the doing by others of any of the things mentioned in paragraphs (*c*), (*d*) and (*e*) of subsection (1); and he commits an offence if, at any time after the commencement of the winding up, he does any of the things mentioned in paragraphs (*a*) to (*f*) of that subsection, or is privy to the doing by others of any of the things mentioned in paragraphs (*c*) to (*e*) of it.

(3) For purposes of this section, " officer " includes a shadow director.

(4) It is a defence—

(*a*) for a person charged under paragraph (*a*) or (*f*) of subsection (1) (or under subsection (2) in respect of the things mentioned in either of those paragraphs) to prove that he had no intent to defraud, and

(*b*) for a person charged under paragraph (*c*) or (*d*) of subsection (1) (or under subsection (2) in respect of the things mentioned in either of those two paragraphs) to prove that he had no intent to conceal the state of affairs of the company or to defeat the law.

(5) Where a person pawns, pledges or disposes of any property in circumstances which amount to an offence under subsection (1)(*f*), every person who takes in pawn or pledge, or otherwise receives the property knowing it to be pawned, pledged or disposed of in such circumstances, is guilty of an offence.

(6) A person guilty of an offence under this section is liable to imprisonment or a fine, or both.

(7) The money sums specified in paragraphs (*a*) and (*b*) of subsection (1) are subject to increase or reduction by regulations under section 664.

Transactions
in fraud of
creditors.

625.—(1) When a company is ordered to be wound up by the court or passes a resolution for voluntary winding up, a person is deemed to have committed an offence if he, being at the time an officer of the company—

(*a*) with intent to defraud creditors of the company, has made or caused to be made any gift or transfer of, or charge on, or has caused or connived at the levying of any execution against, the company's property, **or**

(*b*) with that intent, has concealed or removed any part of
the company's property since, or within 2 months before, the date of any unsatisfied judgment or order
for the payment of money obtained against the company.

(2) A person guilty of an offence under this section is liable
to imprisonment or a fine, or both.

626.—(1) When a company is being wound up, whether by or
under the supervision ot the court or voluntarily, any person,
being a past or present officer of the company, commits an offence
if he—

(*a*) does not to the best of his knowledge and belief fully and
truly discover to the liquidator all the company's property, and how and to whom and for what consideration and when the company disposed of any part of
that property (except such part as has been disposed of
in the ordinary way of the company's business), or

(*b*) does not deliver up to the liquidator (or as he directs)
all such part of the company's property as is in his
custody or under his control, and which he is required
by law to deliver up, or

(*c*) does not deliver up to the liquidator (or as he directs)
all books and papers in his custody or under his control
belonging to the company and which he is required by
law to deliver up, or

(*d*) knowing or believing that a false debt has been proved
by any person in the winding up, fails for the period
of a month to inform the liquidator of it, or

(*e*) after the commencement of the winding up, prevents the
production of any book or paper affecting or relating to
the company's property or affairs.

(2) Such a person commits an offence if after the commencement of the winding up he attempts to account for any part of
the company's property by fictitious losses or expenses ; and he
is deemed to have committed that offence if he has so attempted
at any meeting of the company's creditors within the 12 months
immediately preceding the commencement of the winding up.

(3) For purposes of this section, " officer " includes a shadow
director.

(4) It is a defence—

(*a*) for a person charged under paragraph (*a*), (*b*) or (*c*) of
subsection (1) to prove that he had no intent to defraud,
and

(*b*) for a person charged under paragraph (*e*) of that sub-section to prove that he had no intent to conceal the state of affairs of the company or to defeat the law.

(5) A person guilty of an offence under this section is liable to imprisonment or a fine, or both.

Falsification of company's books.

627.—(1) When a company is being wound up, an officer or contributory of the company commits an offence if he destroys, mutilates, alters or falsifies any books, papers or securities, or makes or is privy to the making of any false or fraudulent entry in any register, book of account or document belonging to the company with intent to defraud or deceive any person.

(2) A person guilty of an offence under this section is liable to imprisonment or a fine, or both.

Material omissions from statements relating to company affairs.

628.—(1) When a company is being wound up, whether by or under the supervision of the court or voluntarily, any person, being a past or present officer of the company, commits an offence if he makes any material omission in any statement relating to the company's affairs.

(2) When a company has been ordered to be wound up by the court, or has passed a resolution for voluntary winding up, any such person is deemed to have committed that offence if, prior to the winding up, he has made any material omission in any such statement.

(3) For purposes of this section, " officer " includes a shadow director.

(4) It is a defence for a person charged under this section to prove that he had no intent to defraud.

(5) A person guilty of an offence under this section is liable to imprisonment or a fine, or both.

False representations to creditors.

629.—(1) When a company is being wound up, whether by or under the supervision of the court or voluntarily, any person, being a past or present officer of the company—

(*a*) commits an offence if he makes any false representation or commits any other fraud for the purpose of obtaining the consent of the company's creditors or any of them to an agreement with reference to the company's affairs or to the winding up, and

(*b*) is deemed to have committed that offence if, prior to the winding up, he has made any false representation, or committed any other fraud, for that purpose.

(2) For purposes of this section, " officer " includes a shadow director.

(3) A person guilty of an offence under this section is liable to imprisonment or a fine, or both.

630.—(1) If in the course of the winding up of a company it appears that any business of the company has been carried on with intent to defraud creditors of the company or creditors of any other person, or for any fraudulent purpose, the following has effect.

(2) The court, on the application of the official receiver, or the liquidator or any creditor or contributory of the company, may, if it thinks proper to do so, declare that any persons who were knowingly parties to the carrying on of the business in the manner above mentioned are to be personally responsible, without any limitation of liability, for all or any of the debts or other liabilities of the company as the court may direct.

(3) On the hearing of the application, the official receiver or the liquidator (as the case may be) may himself give evidence or call witnesses.

(4) Where the court makes such a declaration, it may give such further directions as it thinks proper for giving effect to the declaration ; and in particular, the court may—

    (a) provide for the liability of any person under the declaration to be a charge on any debt or obligation due from the company to him, or on any mortgage or charge or any interest in a mortgage or charge on assets of the company held by or vested in him, or any person on his behalf, or any person claiming as assignee from or through the person liable or any person acting on his behalf, and

    (b) from time to time make such further order as may be necessary for enforcing any charge imposed under this subsection.

(5) For purposes of subsection (4), " assignee "—

    (a) includes a person to whom or in whose favour, by the directions of the person made liable, the debt, obligation, mortgage or charge was created, issued or transferred or the interest created, but

    (b) does not include an assignee for valuable consideration (not including consideration by way of marriage) given in good faith and without notice of any of the matters on the ground of which the declaration is made.

(6) This section has effect notwithstanding that the person concerned may be criminally liable in respect of matters on the ground of which the declaration under subsection (2) is to be made ; and where the declaration is made in the case of a

winding up in England and Wales, it is deemed a final judgment within section 1(1)(*g*) of the Bankruptcy Act 1914.

Assessment of
damages
against
delinquent
directors, etc.

631.—(1) The following applies if in the course of winding up a company it appears that a person who has taken part in its formation or promotion, or any past or present director, manager or liquidator, or an officer of the company, has misapplied or retained or become liable or accountable for any money or property of the company, or been guilty of any misfeasance or breach of trust in relation to the company.

(2) The court may, on the application of the official receiver or the liquidator, or of any creditor or contributory, examine into the conduct of the promoter, director, manager, liquidator or officer and compel him—

(*a*) to repay or restore the money or property, or any part of it, respectively with interest at such rate as the court thinks just, or

(*b*) to contribute such sum to the company's assets by way of compensation in respect of the misapplication, retainer, misfeasance or breach of trust as the court thinks just.

(3) This section has effect notwithstanding that the offence is one for which the offender may be criminally liable.

(4) If in the case of a winding up in England and Wales an order for payment of money is made under this section, the order is deemed a final judgment within section 1(1)(*g*) of the Bankruptcy Act 1914.

Prosecution
of delinquent
officers and
members of
company.

632.—(1) If it appears to the court in the course of a winding up by, or subject to the supervision of, the court that any past or present officer, or any member, of the company has been guilty of any offence in relation to the company for which he is criminally liable, the court may (either on the application of a person interested in the winding up or of its own motion) direct the liquidator to refer the matter to the prosecuting authority.

(2) " The prosecuting authority " means—

(*a*) in the case of a winding up in England and Wales, the Director of Public Prosecutions, and

(*b*) in the case of a winding up in Scotland, the Lord Advocate.

(3) If it appears to the liquidator in the course of a voluntary winding up that any past or present officer of the company, or

any member of it, has been guilty of any offence in relation to the company for which he is criminally liable, he shall—

    (*a*) forthwith report the matter to the prosecuting authority, and

    (*b*) furnish to that authority such information and give to him such access to and facilities for inspecting and taking copies of documents (being information or documents in the possession or under the control of the liquidator and relating to the matter in question) as the authority requires.

(4) Where a report is made to him under subsection (3), the prosecuting authority may, if he thinks fit, refer the matter to the Secretary of State for further enquiry; and the Secretary of State—

    (*a*) shall thereupon investigate the matter, and

    (*b*) for the purpose of his investigation may exercise any of the powers which are exercisable by inspectors appointed under section 431 or 432 to investigate a company's affairs.

(5) If it appears to the court in the course of a voluntary winding up that any past or present officer of the company, or any member of it, has been guilty as above-mentioned, and that no report with respect to the matter has been made by the liquidator to the prosecuting authority under subsection (3), the court may (on the application of any person interested in the winding up or of its own motion) direct the liquidator to make such a report; and on a report being made accordingly this section has effect as though the report had been made in pursuance of subsection (3).

633.—(1) For the purpose of an investigation by the Secretary of State under section 632(4), any obligation imposed on a person by any provision of this Act to produce documents or give information to, or otherwise to assist, inspectors appointed as mentioned in that subsection is to be regarded as an obligation similarly to assist the Secretary of State in his investigation.

(2) An answer given by a person to a question put to him in exercise of the powers conferred by section 632(4) may be used in evidence against him.

(3) Where criminal proceedings are instituted by the prosecuting authority or the Secretary of State following any report or reference under section 632, it is the duty of the liquidator and every officer and agent of the company past and present (other than the defendant or defender) to give to that authority

or the Secretary of State (as the case may be) all assistance in connection with the prosecution which he is reasonably able to give.

For this purpose "agent" includes any banker or solicitor of the company and any person employed by the company as auditor, whether that person is or is not an officer of the company.

(4) If a person fails or neglects to give assistance in the manner required by subsection (3), the court may, on the application of the prosecuting authority or the Secretary of State (as the case may be) direct the person to comply with that subsection; and if the application is made with respect to a liquidator, the court may (unless it appears that the failure or neglect to comply was due to the liquidator not having in his hands sufficient assets of the company to enable him to do so) direct that the costs shall be borne by the liquidator personally.

Supplementary provisions as to winding up

Disqualification for appointment as liquidator. **634.**—(1) A body corporate is not qualified for appointment as liquidator of a company, whether in a winding up by or under the supervision of the court or in a voluntary winding up.

(2) Any appointment made in contravention of this section is void; and a body corporate which acts as liquidator of a company is liable to a fine.

Corrupt inducement affecting appointment as liquidator. **635.** A person who gives or agrees or offers to give to any member or creditor of a company any valuable consideration with a view to securing his own appointment or nomination, or to securing or preventing the appointment or nomination of some person other than himself, as the company's liquidator is liable to a fine.

Enforcement of liquidator's duty to make returns, etc. **636.**—(1) If a liquidator who has made any default—

    (a) in filing, delivering or making any return, account or other document, or

    (b) in giving any notice which he is by law required to file, deliver, make or give,

fails to make good the default within 14 days after the service on him of a notice requiring him to do so, the court has the following powers.

(2) On an application made by any creditor or contributory of the company, or by the registrar of companies, the court may make an order directing the liquidator to make good the default within such time as may be specified in the order.

(3) The court's order may provide that all costs of and incidental to the application shall be borne by the liquidator.

(4) Nothing in this section prejudices the operation of any enactment imposing penalties on a liquidator in respect of any such default as is mentioned above.

PART XX
CHAPTER V

637.—(1) When a company is being wound up, whether by or under supervision of the court or voluntarily, every invoice, order for goods or business letter issued by or on behalf of the company, or a liquidator of the company, or a receiver or manager of the company's property, being a document on or in which the name of the company appears, shall contain a statement that the company is being wound up.

Notification that company is in liquidation.

(2) If default is made in complying with this section, the company and any of the following persons who knowingly and wilfully authorises or permits the default, namely, any officer of the company, any liquidator of the company and any receiver or manager, is liable to a fine.

638.—(1) In the case of a winding up by the court, or of a creditors' voluntary winding up, the following has effect as regards exemption from duties chargeable under the enactments relating to stamp duties.

In a winding up, certain documents exempt from stamp duty.

(2) If the company is registered in England and Wales, the following documents are exempt from stamp duty—

(a) every assurance relating solely to freehold or leasehold property, or to any estate, right or interest in, any real or personal property, which forms part of the company's assets and which, after the execution of the assurance, either at law or in equity, is or remains part of those assets, and

(b) every power of attorney, proxy paper, writ, order, certificate, or other instrument or writing relating solely to the property of any company which is being wound up as mentioned in subsection (1), or to any proceeding under such a winding up.

" Assurance " here includes deed, conveyance, assignment and surrender.

(3) If the company is registered in Scotland, the following documents are exempt from stamp duty—

(a) every conveyance relating solely to property which forms part of the company's assets and which, after the execution of the conveyance, is or remains the company's property for the benefit of its creditors,

(b) every power of attorney, commission, factory, articles of roup or sale, submission and every other instrument and writing whatsoever relating solely to the company's property, and

(c) every deed or writing forming part of the proceedings in the winding up.

" Conveyance " here includes assignation, instrument, discharge, writing and deed.

Company's books to be evidence.

639. Where a company is being wound up, all books and papers of the company and of the liquidators are, as between the contributories of the company, prima facie evidence of the truth of all matters purporting to be recorded in them.

Disposal of books and papers.

640.—(1) When a company has been wound up and is about to be dissolved, its books and papers and those of the liquidators may be disposed of as follows—

(a) in the case of a winding up by or subject to the supervision of the court, in such way as the court directs ;

(b) in the case of a members' voluntary winding up, in such way as the company by extraordinary resolution directs, and

(c) in the case of a creditors' voluntary winding up, in such way as the committee of inspection or, if there is no such committee, the company's creditors may direct.

(2) After 5 years from the company's dissolution no responsibility rests on the company, the liquidators, or any person to whom the custody of the books and papers has been committed, by reason of any book or paper not being forthcoming to a person claiming to be interested in it.

(3) Provision may be made by general rules—

(a) for enabling the Secretary of State to prevent, for such period as he thinks proper (but not exceeding 5 years from the company's dissolution), the destruction of the books and papers of a company which has been wound up, and

(b) for enabling any creditor or contributory of the company to make representations to the Secretary of State and to appeal to the court from any direction which may be given by the Secretary of State in the matter.

(4) If a person acts in contravention of general rules made for the purposes of this section, or of any direction of the Secretary of State under them, he is liable to a fine.

Information as to pending liquidations.

641.—(1) If the winding up of a company is not concluded within one year after its commencement, the liquidator shall, at such intervals as may be prescribed, until the winding up is concluded, send to the registrar of companies a statement in the prescribed form and containing the prescribed particulars with respect to the proceedings in, and position of, the liquidation.

(2) If a liquidator fails to comply with this section, he is   PART XX liable to a fine and, for continued contravention, to a daily   CHAPTER V default fine.

642.—(1) This section applies if, where a company is being Unclaimed wound up in England and Wales, it appears (either from any assets statement sent to the registrar under section 641 or otherwise) (England and that a liquidator has in his hands or under his control any Wales). money—

(a) representing unclaimed or undistributed assets of the company which have remained unclaimed or undistributed for 6 months after the date of their receipt, or

(b) held by the company in trust in respect of dividends or other sums due to any person as a member of the company.

(2) The liquidator shall forthwith pay the money in question to the Insolvency Services Account at the Bank of England, and is entitled to the prescribed certificate of receipt for the money so paid, and that certificate is an effectual discharge to him in respect of it.

(3) For the purpose of ascertaining and getting in any money payable into the Bank of England in pursuance of this section, the like powers may be exercised, and by the like authority, as are exercisable under section 153 of the Bankruptcy Act 1914 c. 59. 1914 for the purpose of ascertaining and getting in the sums, funds and dividends referred to in that section.

(4) Any person claiming to be entitled to money paid into the Bank of England under this section may apply to the Secretary of State for payment ; and the Secretary of State may, on a certificate by the liquidator that the person claiming is entitled, make an order for payment to that person of the sum due.

(5) Any person dissatisfied with a decision of the Secretary of State in respect of a claim made under this section may appeal to the High Court.

643.—(1) The following applies where a company registered Unclaimed in Scotland has been wound up, and is about to be dissolved. dividends, etc. (Scotland).

(2) The liquidator shall lodge in a joint stock bank of issue in Scotland (not being a bank in or of which the liquidator is acting partner, manager, agent or cashier) in the name of the Accountant of Court the whole unclaimed dividends and un-applied or undistributable balances, and the deposit receipts shall be transmitted to the Accountant of Court.

PART XX
CHAPTER V
1913 c. 20.

(3) The provisions of section 153 of the Bankruptcy (Scotland) Act 1913 (so far as consistent with this Act) apply with any necessary modifications to sums lodged in a bank under this section as they apply to sums deposited under that section.

Resolutions passed at adjourned meetings.

644. Where a resolution is passed at an adjourned meeting of a company's creditors or contributories, the resolution is treated for all purposes as having been passed on the date on which it was in fact passed, and not as having been passed on any earlier date.

Supplementary powers of court

Meetings to ascertain wishes of creditors or contributories.

645.—(1) The court may—

(a) as to all matters relating to the winding up of a company, have regard to the wishes of the creditors or contributories (as proved to it by any sufficient evidence), and

(b) if it thinks fit, for the purpose of ascertaining those wishes, direct meetings of the creditors or contributories to be called, held and conducted in such manner as the court directs, and appoint a person to act as chairman of any such meeting and report the result of it to the court.

(2) In the case of creditors, regard shall be had to the value of each creditor's debt.

(3) In the case of contributories, regard shall be had to the number of votes conferred on each contributory by this Act ~~of each creditor's debt~~. *or the articles.*

Judicial notice of signature of court officers.

646. In all proceedings under this Part, all courts, judges and persons judicially acting, and all officers, judicial or ministerial, of any court, or employed in enforcing the process of any court shall take judicial notice—

(a) of the signature of any officer of the High Court or of a county court in England and Wales, or of the Court of Session or a sheriff court in Scotland, or of the High Court in Northern Ireland, and also

(b) of the official seal or stamp of the several offices of the High Court in England and Wales or Northern Ireland, or of the Court of Session, appended to or impressed on any document made, issued or signed under the provisions of this Act, or any official copy of such a document.

Commission for receiving evidence.

647.—(1) When a company is wound up in England and Wales or in Scotland, the court may refer the whole or any part of the examination of witnesses—

(a) to a specified county court in England and Wales, or

Companies Act

PGA 1985 c. 6

ISBN 0 10 540685 6

CORRECTION (No. 3)

On page 400, in section 645(3) the last line should read—
" or the articles."

PRINTED IN ENGLAND BY J A DOLE
Controller and Chief Executive of Her Majesty's Stationery Office and
Queen's Printer of Acts of Parliament.

June 1986

(572961)

(*b*) to the sheriff principal for a specified sheriffdom in Scotland, or

(*c*) to the High Court in Northern Ireland or a specified Northern Ireland County Court,

(" specified " meaning specified in the order of the winding-up court).

(2) Any person exercising jurisdiction as a judge of the court to which the reference is made (or, in Scotland, the sheriff principal to whom it is made) shall then, by virtue of this section, be a commissioner for the purpose of taking the evidence of those witnesses.

(3) The judge or sheriff principal has in the matter referred the same power of summoning and examining witnesses, of requiring the production and delivery of documents, of punishing defaults by witnesses, and of allowing costs and expenses to witnesses, as the court which made the winding-up order.

These powers are in addition to any which the judge or sheriff principal might lawfully exercise apart from this section.

(4) The examination so taken shall be returned or reported to the court which made the order in such manner as that court requests.

(5) This section extends to Northern Ireland.

648.—(1) The court may direct the examination in Scotland of any person for the time being in Scotland (whether a contributory of the company or not), in regard to the trade, dealings, affairs or property of any company in course of being wound up, or of any person being a contributory of the company, so far as the company may be interested by reason of his being a contributory.

Court order for examination of persons in Scotland.

(2) The order or commission to take the examination shall be directed to the sheriff principal of the sheriffdom in which the person to be examined is residing or happens to be for the time ; and the sheriff principal shall summon the person to appear before him at a time and place to be specified in the summons for examination on oath as a witness or as a haver, and to produce any books or papers called for which are in his possession or power.

(3) The sheriff principal may take the examination either orally or on written interrogatories, and shall report the same in writing in the usual form to the court, and shall transmit with the report the books and papers produced, if the originals are required and specified by the order or commission, or otherwise copies or extracts authenticated by the sheriff.

(4) If a person so summoned fails to appear at the time and place specified, or refuses to be examined or to make the production required, the sheriff principal shall proceed against him

PART XX
CHAPTER V

as a witness or haver duly cited ; and failing to appear or refusing to give evidence or make production may be proceeded against by the law of Scotland.

(5) The sheriff principal is entitled to such fees, and the witness is entitled to such allowances, as sheriffs principal when acting as commissioners under appointment from the Court of Session and as witnesses and havers are entitled to in the like cases according to the law and practice of Scotland.

(6) If any objection is stated to the sheriff principal by the witness, either on the ground of his incompetency as a witness, or as to the production required, or on any other ground, the sheriff principal may, if he thinks fit, report the objection to the court, and suspend the examination of the witness until it has been disposed of by the court.

Costs of application for leave to proceed (Scottish companies).

649. Where a petition or application for leave to proceed with an action or proceeding against a company which is being wound up in Scotland is unopposed and is granted by the court, the costs of the petition or application shall, unless the court otherwise directs, be added to the amount of the petitioner's or applicant's claim against the company.

Affidavits, etc., in United Kingdom and overseas.

650.—(1) An affidavit required to be sworn under or for the purposes of this Part may be sworn in the United Kingdom or elsewhere in Her Majesty's dominions, before any court, judge or person lawfully authorised to take and receive affidavits, or before any of Her Majesty's consuls or vice-consuls in any place outside Her dominions.

(2) All courts, judges, justices, commissioners and persons acting judicially shall take judicial notice of the seal or stamp or signature (as the case may be) of any such court, judge, person, consul or vice-consul attached, appended or subscribed to any such affidavit, or to any other document to be used for the purposes of this Part.

CHAPTER VI

MATTERS ARISING SUBSEQUENT TO WINDING UP

Power of court to declare dissolution of company void.

651.—(1) Where a company has been dissolved, the court may at any time within 2 years of the date of the dissolution, on an application made for the purpose by the liquidator of the company or by any other person appearing to the court to be interested, make an order, on such terms as the court thinks fit, declaring the dissolution to have been void.

(2) Thereupon such proceedings may be taken as might have been taken if the company had not been dissolved.

(3) It is the duty of the person on whose application the order was made, within 7 days after its making (or such further time as the court may allow), to deliver to the registrar of companies for registration an office copy of the order.

If the person fails to do so, he is liable to a fine and, for continued contravention, to a daily default fine.

652.—(1) If the registrar of companies has reasonable cause to believe that a company is not carrying on business or in operation, he may send to the company by post a letter inquiring whether the company is carrying on business or in operation.

(2) If the registrar does not within one month of sending the letter receive any answer to it, he shall within 14 days after the expiration of that month send to the company by post a registered letter referring to the first letter, and stating that no answer to it has been received, and that if an answer is not received to the second letter within one month from its date, a notice will be published in the Gazette with a view to striking the company's name off the register.

(3) If the registrar either receives an answer to the effect that the company is not carrying on business or in operation, or does not within one month after sending the second letter receive any answer, he may publish in the Gazette, and send to the company by post, a notice that at the expiration of 3 months from the date of that notice the name of the company mentioned in it will, unless cause is shown to the contrary, be struck off the register and the company will be dissolved.

(4) If, in a case where a company is being wound up, the registrar has reasonable cause to believe either that no liquidator is acting, or that the affairs of the company are fully wound up, and the returns required to be made by the liquidator have not been made for a period of 6 consecutive months, the registrar shall publish in the Gazette and send to the company or the liquidator (if any) a like notice as is provided in subsection (3).

(5) At the expiration of the time mentioned in the notice the registrar may, unless cause to the contrary is previously shown by the company, strike its name off the register, and shall publish notice of this in the Gazette ; and on the publication of that notice in the Gazette the company is dissolved.

(6) However—

    (*a*) the liability (if any) of every director, managing officer and member of the company continues and may be enforced as if the company had not been dissolved, and (*b*) nothing in subsection (5) affects the power of the court to wind up a company the name of which has been struck off the register.

(7) A notice to be sent to a liquidator under this section may be addressed to him at his last known place of business; and a letter or notice to be sent under this section to a company may be addressed to the company at its registered office or, if no office has been registered, to the care of some officer of the company.

If there is no officer of the company whose name and address are known to the registrar of companies, the letter or notice may be sent to each of the persons who subscribed the memorandum, addressed to him at the address mentioned in the memorandum.

Objection to
striking off by
person
aggrieved.

653.—(1) The following applies if a company or any member or creditor of it feels aggrieved by the company having been struck off the register.

(2) The court, on an application by the company or the member or creditor made before the expiration of 20 years from publication in the Gazette of notice under section 652, may, if satisfied that the company was at the time of the striking off carrying on business or in operation, or otherwise that it is just that the company be restored to the register, order the company's name to be restored.

(3) On an office copy of the order being delivered to the registrar of companies for registration the company is deemed to have continued in existence as if its name had not been struck off; and the court may by the order give such directions and make such provisions as seem just for placing the company and all other persons in the same position (as nearly as may be) as if the company's name had not been struck off.

Property of
dissolved
company to
be bona
vacantia.

654.—(1) When a company is dissolved, all property and rights whatsoever vested in or held on trust for the company immediately before its dissolution (including leasehold property, but not including property held by the company on trust for any other person) are deemed to be bona vacantia and—

(*a*) accordingly belong to the Crown, or to the Duchy of Lancaster or to the Duke of Cornwall for the time being (as the case may be), and

(*b*) vest and may be dealt with in the same manner as other bona vacantia accruing to the Crown, to the Duchy of Lancaster or to the Duke of Cornwall.

(2) Except as provided by the section next following, the above has effect subject and without prejudice to any order made by the court under section 651 or 653.

655.—(1) The person in whom any property or right is vested by section 654 may dispose of, or of an interest in, that property or right notwithstanding that an order may be made under section 651 or 653.

PART XX
CHAPTER VI
Effect on s.
654 of
company's
revival after
dissolution.

(2) Where such an order is made—

 (a) it does not affect the disposition (but without prejudice to the order so far as it relates to any other property or right previously vested in or held on trust for the company), and

 (b) the Crown or, as the case may be, the Duke of Cornwall shall pay to the company an amount equal to—

  (i) the amount of any consideration received for the property or right, or interest therein, or

  (ii) the value of any such consideration at the time of the disposition,

or, if no consideration was received, an amount equal to the value of the property, right or interest disposed of, as at the date of the disposition.

(3) Where a liability accrues under subsection (2) in respect of any property or right which, before the order under section 651 or 653 was made, had accrued as bona vacantia to the Duchy of Lancaster, the Attorney General of the Duchy shall represent Her Majesty in any proceedings arising in connection with that liability.

(4) Where a liability accrues under subsection (2) in respect of any property or right which, before the order under section 651 or 653 was made, had accrued as bona vacantia to the Duchy of Cornwall, such persons as the Duke of Cornwall (or other possessor for the time being of the Duchy) may appoint shall represent the Duke (or other possessor) in any proceedings arising out of that liability.

(5) This section applies in relation to the disposition of any property, right or interest on or after 22nd December 1981, whether the company concerned was dissolved before, on or after that day.

656.—(1) Where property vests in the Crown under section 654, the Crown's title to it under that section may be disclaimed by a notice signed by the Crown representative, that is to say the Treasury Solicitor, or, in relation to property in Scotland, the Queen's and Lord Treasurer's Remembrancer.

(2) The right to execute a notice of disclaimer under this section may be waived by or on behalf of the Crown either expressly or by taking possession or other act evincing that intention.

(3) A notice of disclaimer under this section is of no effect unless it is executed—

(*a*) within 12 months of the date on which the vesting of the property under section 654 came to the notice of the Crown representative, or

(*b*) if an application in writing is made to the Crown representative by any person interested in the property requiring him to decide whether he will or will not disclaim, within a period of 3 months after the receipt of the application or such further period as may be allowed by the court which would have had jurisdiction to wind up the company if it had not been dissolved.

(4) A statement in a notice of disclaimer of any property under this section that the vesting of it came to the notice of the Crown representative on a specified date, or that no such application as above mentioned was received by him with respect to the property before a specified date, is sufficient evidence of the fact stated, until the contrary is proved.

(5) A notice of disclaimer under this section shall be delivered to the registrar of companies and retained and registered by him; and copies of it shall be published in the Gazette and sent to any persons who have given the Crown representative notice that they claim to be interested in the property.

(6) This section applies to property vested in the Duchy of Lancaster or the Duke of Cornwall under section 654 as if for references to the Crown and the Crown representative there were respectively substituted references to the Duchy of Lancaster and to the Solicitor to that Duchy, or to the Duke of Cornwall and to the Solicitor to the Duchy of Cornwall, as the case may be.

Effect of Crown disclaimer under s. 656.
657.—(1) Where notice of disclaimer is executed under section 656 as respects any property, that property is deemed not to have vested in the Crown under section 654.

(2) As regards property in England and Wales, the following provisions above in this Chapter—

(*a*) section 618(4) (effect of disclaimer by liquidator),

(*b*) section 619(1) to (7) (court's power to vest property in the person entitled), with Part I of Schedule 20 (protection of third parties where property is leasehold), and

(*c*) section 620 (liability for rentcharge following disclaimer), apply as if the property had been disclaimed by the liquidator under section 618(1) immediately before the dissolution of the company.

(3) As regards property in Scotland, the following 4 subsec- PART XX
CHAPTER VI
tions apply.

(4) The Crown's disclaimer operates to determine, as from the
date of the disclaimer, the rights, interests and liabilities of the
company, and the property of the company, in or in respect of
the property disclaimed; but it does not (except so far as is
necessary for the purpose of releasing the company and its property from liability) affect the rights or liabilities of any other
person.

(5) The court may, on application by a person who either
claims an interest in disclaimed property or is under a liability
not discharged by this Act in respect of disclaimed property, and
on hearing such persons as it thinks fit, make an order for the
vesting of the property in or its delivery to any persons entitled
to it, or to whom it may seem just that the property should be
delivered by way of compensation for such liability, or a trustee
for him, and on such terms as the court thinks just.

(6) On such a vesting order being made, the property comprised in it vests accordingly in the person named in that behalf
in the order, without conveyance or assignation for that purpose.

(7) Part II of Schedule 20 has effect for the protection of
third parties where the property disclaimed is held under a lease.

658.—(1) Section 620 applies to land in England and Wales Liability for rentcharge on company's land after dissolution.
which by operation of law vests subject to a rentcharge in the
Crown or any other person on the dissolution of a company
as it applies to land so vesting on a disclaimer under section 618.

(2) In this section "company" includes any body corporate.

CHAPTER VII
MISCELLANEOUS PROVISIONS ABOUT WINDING UP

659.—(1) On the winding up of a company (whether by the Power to make over assets to employees.
court or voluntarily), the liquidator may, subject to the following
provisions of this section, make any payment which the company has, before the commencement of the winding up, decided
to make under section 719 (power to provide for employees or
former employees on cessation or transfer of business).

(2) The power which a company may exercise by virtue only
of that section may be exercised by the liquidator after the
winding up has commenced if, after the company's liabilities
have been fully satisfied and provision has been made for the
costs of the winding up, the exercise of that power has been
sanctioned by such a resolution of the company as would be
required of the company itself by section 719(3) before that commencement, if paragraph (b) of that subsection were omitted
and any other requirement applicable to its exercise by the
company had been met.

(3) Any payment which may be made by a company under this section (that is, a payment after the commencement of its winding up) may be made out of the company's assets which are available to the members on the winding up.

(4) On a winding up by the court, the exercise by the liquidator of his powers under this section is subject to the court's control, and any creditor or contributory may apply to the court with respect to any exercise or proposed exercise of the power.

(5) Subsections (1) and (2) above have effect notwithstanding anything in any rule of law or in section 597 of this Act (property of company after satisfaction of liabilities to be distributed among members).

Separate
accounts of
particular
estates
(England
and Wales).
660.—(1) An account shall be kept by the Secretary of State of the receipts and payments in the winding up of each company in England and Wales.

(2) When the cash balance standing to the credit of the account of any company is in excess of the amount which, in the opinion of the committee of inspection, is required for the time being to answer demands in respect of the company's estate, the Secretary of State shall on the request of the committee invest the amount not so required in Government securities, to be placed to the credit of that account for the company's benefit.

(3) When any part of the money so invested is, in the opinion of the committee of inspection, required to answer any demands in respect of the company's estate, the Secretary of State shall, on the committee's request, raise such sum as may be required by the sale of such part of those securities as may be necessary.

(4) The dividends on investments under this section shall be paid to the credit of the company.

(5) When the balance at the credit of a company's account in the hands of the Secretary of State exceeds £2,000, and the liquidator gives notice to him that the excess is not required for the purposes of the liquidation, the company is entitled to interest on the excess at such rate as may for the time being be prescribed by order of the Treasury.

(6) The Treasury's power to make orders under this section is exercisable by statutory instrument subject to annulment in pursuance of a resolution of either House of Parliament.

Officers and
remuneration
(England
and Wales).
661.—(1) The Secretary of State may, with the approval of the Treasury, appoint such additional officers as may be required by him for the execution of this Part as respects England and Wales, and may remove any person so appointed.

(2) The Secretary of State, with the concurrence of the Treasury, shall direct whether any and what remuneration is to

be allowed to any officer of, or person attached to, his depart- PART XX
ment performing any duties under this Part in relation to the CHAPTER VII
winding up of companies in England and Wales, and may vary,
increase or diminish that remuneration as he (the Secretary of
State) thinks fit.

662. The officers of the courts acting in the winding up of Returns by
companies in England and Wales shall make to the Secretary of officers in
State such returns of the business of their respective courts and (England
offices at such times, and in such manner and form, as may be and Wales).
prescribed ; and from these returns the Secretary of State shall
cause books to be prepared which shall (under regulations made
by him) be open for public information and searches.

663.—(1) The Lord Chancellor may, with the concurrence of Rules and fees.
the Secretary of State, make general rules for carrying into effect
the objects of this Act so far as relates to the winding up of
companies in England and Wales.

(2) The Court of Session may by Act of Sederunt make general
rules for carrying into effect the objects of this Act so far as
relates to the winding up of companies in Scotland.

(3) An answer given by a person to a question put to him in
exercise of powers conferred by general rules may be used in
evidence against him.

(4) There shall be paid in respect of proceedings under this
Act in relation to the winding up of companies in England and
Wales such fees as the Lord Chancellor may, with the sanction
of the Treasury, direct ; and the Treasury may direct by whom
and in what manner the fees are to be collected and accounted
for.

(5) The powers conferred by this section on the Lord
Chancellor, the Court of Session and the Treasury are exercisable by statutory instrument ; and a statutory instrument containing general rules shall be laid before Parliament after being
made.

(6) Fees in respect of proceedings under this Act in relation
to the winding up of companies shall be paid into the Consolidated Fund.

664.—(1) The Secretary of State may by regulations in a Power to
statutory instrument increase or reduce any of the money sums alter
for the time being specified in the following provisions of this limits.
Part—

    section 512(2),
    section 515(3),
    section 518(1)(*a*),
    section 542(4),
    section 622(3),
    section 624(1)(*a*) and (*b*), and
    paragraph 12 of Schedule 19.

(2) Regulations shall not be made under this section unless a draft of the statutory instrument containing them has been approved by resolution of each House of Parliament.

Part XXI

Winding Up of Unregistered Companies

Meaning of
" unregistered
company ".
665. For the purposes of this Part, the expression " unregistered company " includes any trustee savings bank certified under the enactments relating to such banks and any partnership (whether limited or not), any association and any company, with the following exceptions—

 (a) a railway company incorporated by Act of Parliament,

 (b) a company registered in any part of the United Kingdom under the Joint Stock Companies Acts or under the legislation (past or present) relating to companies in Great Britain,

 (c) a partnership, association or company which consists of less than 8 members and is not a foreign partnership, association or company,

 (d) a limited partnership registered in England and Wales or Northern Ireland.

Winding up
of unregistered
companies.
666.—(1) Subject to the provisions of this Part, any unregistered company may be wound up under this Act ; and all the provisions of this Act about winding up apply to an unregistered company, with the exceptions and additions mentioned in the following subsections.

(2) If an unregistered company has a principal place of business situated in Northern Ireland, it shall not be wound up under this Part unless it has a principal place of business situated in England and Wales or Scotland, or in both England and Wales and Scotland.

(3) For the purpose of determining a court's winding-up jurisdiction, an unregistered company is deemed—

 (a) to be registered in England and Wales or Scotland, according as its principal place of business is situated in England and Wales or Scotland, or

 (b) if it has a principal place of business situated in both countries, to be registered in both countries ;

and the principal place of business situated in that part of Great Britain in which proceedings are being instituted is, for all purposes of the winding up, deemed to be the registered office of the company.

(4) No unregistered company shall be wound up under this
Act voluntarily or subject to supervision.

(5) The circumstances in which an unregistered company may
be wound up are as follows—

    (*a*) if the company is dissolved, or has ceased to carry on
        business, or is carrying on business only for the pur-
        pose of winding up its affairs ;

    (*b*) if the company is unable to pay its debts ;

    (*c*) if the court is of opinion that it is just and equitable that
        the company should be wound up.

(6) A petition for winding up a trustee savings bank may be
presented by the Trustee Savings Banks Central Board or by a
commissioner appointed under section 35 of the Trustee Savings 1981 c. 65.
Banks Act 1981 as well as by any person authorised under Part
XX to present a petition for winding up a company.

(7) In the case of a limited partnership, the provisions of this
Act about winding up apply with such modifications (if any)
as may be provided by rules made by statutory instrument by the
Lord Chancellor with the concurrence of the Secretary of State,
and with the substitution of general partners for directors.

(8) In Scotland, an unregistered company which the Court of
Session has jurisdiction to wind up may be wound up by the
court if there is subsisting a floating charge over property comprised in the company's property and undertaking, and the court
is satisfied that the security of the creditor entitled to the benefit
of the floating charge is in jeopardy.

For this purpose a creditor's security is deemed to be in
jeopardy if the court is satisfied that events have occurred or are
about to occur which render it unreasonable in the creditor's
interests that the company should retain power to dispose of
the property which is subject to the floating charge.

667.—(1) An unregistered company is deemed (for purposes of Inability to
section 666) unable to pay its debts if there is a creditor, by pay debts:
assignment or otherwise, to whom the company is indebted in unpaid
a sum exceeding £750 then due and— creditor for
£750 or more.

    (*a*) the creditor has served on the company, by leaving at
        its principal place of business, or by delivering to the
        secretary or some director, manager or principal officer
        of the company, or by otherwise serving in such manner
        as the court may approve or direct, a written demand
        requiring the company to pay the sum due, and

    (*b*) the company has for 3 weeks after the service of the
        demand neglected to pay the sum or to secure or
        compound for it to the creditor's satisfaction.

(2) The Secretary of State may by regulations in a statutory instrument increase or reduce the money sum for the time being specified in subsection (1); but—

(a) such regulations shall not be made unless a draft of the statutory instrument containing them has been approved by resolution of each House of Parliament, and

(b) no increase in the sum so specified affects any case in which the winding-up petition was presented before the coming into force of the increase.

Inability to pay debts: debt remaining unsatisfied after action brought.

668. An unregistered company is deemed (for purposes of section 666) unable to pay its debts if an action or other proceeding has been instituted against any member for any debt or demand due, or claimed to be due, from the company, or from him in his character of member, and—

(a) notice in writing of the institution of the action or proceeding has been served on the company by leaving it at the company's principal place of business (or by delivering it to the secretary, or some director, manager or principal officer of the company, or by otherwise serving it in such manner as the court may approve or direct), and

(b) the company has not within 10 days after service of the notice paid, secured or compounded for the debt or demand, or procured the action or proceeding to be stayed or sisted, or indemnified the defendant or defender to his reasonable satisfaction against the action or proceeding, and against all costs, damages and expenses to be incurred by him because of it.

Inability to pay debts: other cases.

669. An unregistered company is deemed (for purposes of section 666) unable to pay its debts—

(a) if in England and Wales execution or other process issued on a judgment, decree or order obtained in any court in favour of a creditor against the company, or any member of it as such, or any person authorised to be sued as nominal defendant on behalf of the company, is returned unsatisfied;

(b) if in Scotland the induciae of a charge for payment on an extract decree, or an extract registered bond, or an extract registered protest, have expired without payment being made;

(c) if in Northern Ireland a certificate of unenforceability has been granted in respect of any judgment, decree or order obtained as mentioned in paragraph (a);

(d) if it is otherwise proved to the satisfaction of the court that the company is unable to pay its debts.

670. Where a company incorporated outside Great Britain which has been carrying on business in Great Britain ceases to carry on business in Great Britain, it may be wound up as an unregistered company under this Act, notwithstanding that it has been dissolved or otherwise ceased to exist as a company under or by virtue of the laws of the country under which it was incorporated.

PART XXI

Oversea company may be wound up though dissolved.

671.—(1) In the event of an unregistered company being wound up, every person is deemed a contributory who is liable to pay or contribute to the payment of any debt or liability of the company, or to pay or contribute to the payment of any sum for the adjustment of the rights of members among themselves, or to pay or contribute to the payment of the costs and expenses of winding up the company.

Contributories in winding up of unregistered company.

(2) Every contributory is liable to contribute to the company's assets all sums due from him in respect of any such liability as is mentioned above.

(3) In the case of an unregistered company engaged in or formed for working mines within the stannaries, a past member is not liable to contribute to the assets if he has ceased to be a member for 2 years or more either before the mine ceased to be worked or before the date of the winding up order.

(4) In the event of the death, bankruptcy or insolvency of any contributory, the provisions of this Act with respect to the personal representatives, to the heirs and legatees of heritage of the heritable estate in Scotland of deceased contributories, and to the trustees of bankrupt or insolvent contributories, respectively apply.

672. The provisions of this Part with respect to staying, sisting or restraining actions and proceedings against a company at any time after the presentation of a petition for winding up and before the making of a winding up order extend, in the case of an unregistered company, where the application to stay, sist or restrain is presented by a creditor, to actions and proceedings against any contributory of the company.

Power of court to stay, sist or restrain proceedings.

673. Where an order has been made for winding up an unregistered company, no action or proceeding shall be proceeded with or commenced against any contributory of the company in respect of any debt of the company, except by leave of the court, and subject to such terms as the court may impose.

Actions stayed on winding up order.

674.—(1) The provisions of this Part with respect to unregistered companies are in addition to and not in restriction of

Provisions of this Part to be cumulative.

any provisions in Part XX with respect to winding up companies by the court ; and the court or liquidator may exercise any powers or do any act in the case of unregistered companies which might be exercised or done by it or him in winding up companies formed and registered under this Act.

(2) However, an unregistered company is not, except in the event of its being wound up, deemed to be a company under this Act, and then only to the extent provided by this Part.

PART XXII

BODIES CORPORATE SUBJECT, OR BECOMING SUBJECT, TO THIS ACT (OTHERWISE THAN BY ORIGINAL FORMATION UNDER PART I)

CHAPTER I

COMPANIES FORMED OR REGISTERED UNDER FORMER COMPANIES ACTS

Companies formed and registered under former Companies Acts.

675.—(1) In its application to existing companies, this Act applies in the same manner—

(a) in the case of a limited company (other than a company limited by guarantee), as if the company had been formed and registered under Part I of this Act as a company limited by shares,

(b) in the case of a company limited by guarantee, as if the company had been formed and registered under that Part as a company limited by guarantee, and

(c) in the case of a company other than a limited company, as if the company had been formed and registered under that Part as an unlimited company.

25 & 26 Vict.
c. 89.
8 Edw. 7 c. 69.
1929 c. 23.
1948 c. 38.

(2) But reference, express or implied, to the date of registration is to be read as the date at which the company was registered under the Joint Stock Companies Acts, the Companies Act 1862, the Companies (Consolidation) Act 1908, the Companies Act 1929, or the Companies Act 1948.

Companies registered but not formed under former Companies Acts.

676.—(1) This Act applies to every company registered but not formed under the Joint Stock Companies Acts, the Companies Act 1862, the Companies (Consolidation) Act 1908, the Companies Act 1929, or the Companies Act 1948, in the same manner as it is in Chapter II of this Part declared to apply to companies registered but not formed under this Act.

(2) But reference, express or implied, to the date of registration is to be read as referring to the date at which the company was registered under the Joint Stock Companies Acts, the Companies Act 1862, the Companies (Consolidation) Act 1908, the Companies Act 1929, or the Companies Act 1948.

677.—(1) This Act applies to every unlimited company registered or re-registered as limited in pursuance of the Companies Act 1879, section 57 of the Companies (Consolidation) Act 1908, section 16 of the Companies Act 1929, section 16 of the Companies Act 1948 or section 44 of the Companies Act 1967 as it (this Act) applies to an unlimited company re-registered as limited in pursuance of Part II of this Act.

(2) But reference, express or implied, to the date of registration or re-registration is to be read as referring to the date at which the company was registered or re-registered as a limited company under the relevant enactment.

PART XXII
CHAPTER I
Companies re-registered with altered status under former Companies Acts.
42 & 43 Vict. c. 76.
8 Edw. 7 c. 69.
1929 c. 23.
1948 c. 38.
1967 c. 81.

678.—(1) A company registered under the Joint Stock Companies Acts may cause its shares to be transferred in manner hitherto in use, or in such other manner as the company may direct.

(2) The power of altering articles under section 9 of this Act extends, in the case of an unlimited company formed and registered under the Joint Stock Companies Acts, to altering any regulations relating to the amount of capital or to its distribution into shares, notwithstanding that those regulations are contained in the memorandum.

Companies registered under Joint Stock Companies Acts.

679. Nothing in sections 675 to 678 applies to companies registered in Northern Ireland or the Republic of Ireland.

Northern Ireland and Irish companies.

CHAPTER II

COMPANIES NOT FORMED UNDER COMPANIES LEGISLATION, BUT AUTHORISED TO REGISTER

680.—(1) With the exceptions and subject to the provisions contained in this section and the next—

(*a*) any company consisting of two or more members, which was in existence on 2nd November 1862, including any company registered under the Joint Stock Companies Acts, and

(*b*) any company formed after that date (whether before or after the commencement of this Act), in pursuance of any Act of Parliament (other than this Act), or of letters patent, or being otherwise duly constituted according to law, and consisting of two or more members,

may at any time, on making application in the prescribed form, register under this Act as an unlimited company, or as a com-

Companies capable of being registered under this Chapter.

PART XXII
CHAPTER II

25 & 26 Vict.
c. 89.
8 Edw. 7 c. 69.
1929 c. 23.
1948 c. 38.

Procedural
requirements
for
registration.

pany limited by shares, or as a company limited by guarantee; and the registration is not invalid by reason that it has taken place with a view to the company's being wound up.

(2) A company registered in any part of the United Kingdom under the Companies Act 1862, the Companies (Consolidation) Act 1908, the Companies Act 1929 or the Companies Act 1948 shall not register under this section.

(3) A company having the liability of its members limited by Act of Parliament or letters patent, and not being a joint stock company, shall not register under this section.

(4) A company having the liability of its members limited by Act of Parliament or letters patent shall not register in pursuance of this section as an unlimited company or as a company limited by guarantee.

(5) A company that is not a joint stock company shall not register under this section as a company limited by shares.

681.—(1) A company shall not register under section 680 without the assent of a majority of such of its members as are present in person or by proxy (in cases where proxies are allowed) at a general meeting summoned for the purpose.

(2) Where a company not having the liability of its members limited by Act of Parliament or letters patent is about to register as a limited company, the majority required to assent as required by subsection (1) shall consist of not less than three-fourths of the members present in person or by proxy at the meeting.

(3) In computing any majority under this section when a poll is demanded, regard is to be had to the number of votes to which each member is entitled according to the company's regulations.

(4) Where a company is about to register (under section 680) as a company limited by guarantee, the assent to its being so registered shall be accompanied by a resolution declaring that each member undertakes to contribute to the company's assets, in the event of its being wound up while he is a member, or within one year after he ceases to be a member, for payment of the company's debts and liabilities contracted before he ceased to be a member, and of the costs and expenses of winding up and for the adjustment of the rights of the contributories among themselves, such amount as may be required, not exceeding a specified amount.

(5) Before a company is registered under section 680, it shall deliver to the registrar of companies—

    (a) a statement that the registered office of the company is to be situated in England and Wales, or in Wales, or in Scotland (as the case may be), (*b*) a statement specifying the intended situation of the company's registered office after registration, and

(*c*) in an appropriate case, if the company wishes to be registered with the Welsh equivalent of " public limited company " or, as the case may be, " limited " as the last words or word of its name, a statement to that effect.

(6) Any statement delivered to the registrar under subsection (5) shall be made in the prescribed form.

682.—(1) Where the name of a company seeking registration under section 680 is a name by which it is precluded from registration by section 26 of this Act, either because it falls within subsection (1) of that section or, if it falls within subsection (2), because the Secretary of State would not approve the company's being registered with that name, the company may change its name with effect from the date on which it is registered under this Chapter.

Change of name on registration.

(2) A change of name under this section requires the like assent of the company's members as is required by section 681 for registration.

683.—(1) For purposes of this Chapter, as far as relates to registration of companies as companies limited by shares, " joint stock company " means a company—

Definition of " joint stock company ".

(*a*) having a permanent paid-up or nominal share capital of fixed amount divided into shares, also of fixed amount, or held and transferable as stock, or divided and held partly in one way and partly in the other, and

(*b*) formed on the principle of having for its members the holders of those shares or that stock, and no other persons.

(2) Such a company when registered with limited liability under this Act is deemed a company limited by shares.

684.—(1) Before the registration under section 680 of a joint stock company, there shall be delivered to the registrar of companies the following documents—

Requirements for registration by joint stock companies.

(*a*) a statement in the prescribed form specifying the name with which the company is proposed to be registered,

(*b*) a list in the prescribed form showing the names and addresses of all persons who on a day named in the list (not more than 6 clear days before the day of registration) were members of the company, with the addition of the shares or stock held by them respectively (distinguishing, in cases where the shares are numbered, each share by its number), and (*c*) a copy of any Act of Parliament, royal charter, letters patent, deed of settlement, contract of copartnery or other instrument constituting or regulating the company.

(2) If the company is intended to be registered as a limited company, there shall also be delivered to the registrar of companies a statement in the prescribed form specifying the following particulars—

    (*a*) the nominal share capital of the company and the number of shares into which it is divided, or the amount of stock of which it consists, and

    (*b*) the number of shares taken and the amount paid on each share.

Registration
of joint stock
company as
public
company.

685.—(1) A joint stock company applying to be registered under section 680 as a company limited by shares may, subject to—

    (*a*) satisfying the conditions set out in section 44(2)(*a*) and (*b*) (where applicable) and section 45(2) to (4) as applied by this section, and

    (*b*) complying with subsection (4) below,

apply to be so registered as a public company.

(2) Sections 44 and 45 apply for this purpose as in the case of a private company applying to be re-registered under section 43, but as if a reference to the special resolution required by section 43 were to the joint stock company's resolution that it be a public company.

(3) The resolution may change the company's name by deleting the word " company " or the words " and company ", or its or their equivalent in Welsh (" cwmni ", " a'r cwmni "), including any abbreviation of them.

(4) The joint stock company's application shall be made in the form prescribed for the purpose, and shall be delivered to the registrar of companies together with the following documents (as well as those required by section 684), namely—

    (*a*) a copy of the resolution that the company be a public company,

    (*b*) a copy of a written statement by an accountant with the appropriate qualifications that in his opinion a relevant balance sheet shows that at the balance sheet date the amount of the company's net assets was not less than the aggregate of its called up share capital and undistributable reserves,

    (*c*) a copy of the relevant balance sheet, together with a copy of an unqualified report (by an accountant with such qualifications) in relation to that balance sheet, (*d*) a copy of any valuation report prepared under section 44(2)(*b*) as applied by this section, and

(*e*) a statutory declaration in the prescribed form by a director or secretary of the company—

(i) that the conditions set out in section 44(2)(*a*) and (*b*) (where applicable) and section 45(2) to (4) have been satisfied, and

(ii) that, between the balance sheet date referred to in paragraph (*b*) of this subsection and the joint stock company's application, there has been no change in the company's financial position that has resulted in the amount of its net assets becoming less than the aggregate of its called up share capital and undistributable reserves.

(5) The registrar may accept a declaration under subsection (4)(*e*) as sufficient evidence that the conditions referred to in that paragraph have been satisfied.

(6) In this section—

" accountant with the appropriate qualifications " means a person who would be qualified under section 389(1) for appointment as the company's auditor, if it were a company registered under this Act,

" relevant balance sheet " means a balance sheet prepared as at a date not more than 7 months before the joint stock company's application to be registered as a public company limited by shares, and

"undistributable reserves " has the meaning given by section 264(3);

and section 46 applies (with necessary modifications) for the interpretation of the reference in subsection (4)(*c*) above to an unqualified report by the accountant.

686.—(1) Before the registration in pursuance of this Chapter Other of any company (not being a joint stock company), there shall be requirements delivered to the registrar of companies— for registration.

(*a*) a statement in the prescribed form specifying the name with which the company is proposed to be registered,

(*b*) a list showing the names, addresses and occupations of the directors or other managers (if any) of the company,

(*c*) a copy of any Act of Parliament, letters patent, deed of settlement, contract of copartnery or other instrument constituting or regulating the company, and

(*d*) in the case of a company intended to be registered as a company limited by guarantee, a copy of the resolution declaring the amount of the guarantee.

PART XXII
CHAPTER II

(2) The lists of members and directors and any other particulars relating to the company which are required by this Chapter to be delivered to the registrar shall be verified by a statutory declaration in the prescribed form made by any two or more directors or other principal officers of the company.

(3) The registrar may require such evidence as he thinks necessary for the purpose of satisfying himself whether a company proposing to be registered is or is not a joint stock company as defined by section 683.

Name of company registering.

687.—(1) The following applies with respect to the name of a company registering under this Chapter (whether a joint stock company or not).

(2) If the company is to be registered as a public company, its name must end with the words " public limited company " or, if it is stated that the company's registered office is to be situated in Wales, with those words or their equivalent in Welsh (" cwmni cyfyngedig cyhoeddus ") ; and those words or that equivalent may not be preceded by the word " limited " or its equivalent in Welsh (" cyfyngedig ").

(3) In the case of a company limited by shares or by guarantee (not being a public company), the name must have " limited " as its last word (or, if the company's registered office is to be situated in Wales, " cyfyngedig ") ; but this is subject to section 30 (exempting a company, in certain circumstances, from having " limited " as part of the name).

(4) If the company is registered with limited liability, then any additions to the company's name set out in the statements delivered under section 684(1)(*a*) or 686(1)(*a*) shall form and be registered as the last part of the company's name.

Certificate of registration under this Chapter.

688.—(1) On compliance with the requirements of this Chapter with respect to registration, the registrar of companies shall give a certificate (which may be signed by him, or authenticated by his official seal) that the company applying for registration is incorporated as a company under this Act and, in the case of a limited company, that it is limited.

(2) On the issue of the certificate, the company shall be so incorporated ; and a banking company in Scotland so incorporated is deemed a bank incorporated, constituted or established by or under Act of Parliament.

(3) The certificate is conclusive evidence that the requirements of this Chapter in respect of registration, and of matters precedent and incidental to it, have been complied with.

(4) Where on an application by a joint stock company to register as a public company limited by shares the registrar of
companies is satisfied that the company may be registered as
a public company so limited, the certificate of incorporation
given under this section shall state that the company is a public
company ; and that statement is conclusive evidence that the
requirements of section 685 have been complied with and that
the company is a public company so limited.

689. Schedule 21 to this Act has effect with respect to the Effect of
consequences of registration under this Chapter, the vesting of registration.
property, savings for existing liabilities, continuation of existing
actions, status of the company following registration, and other
connected matters.

690.—(1) Subject as follows, a company registered in pur- Power to
suance of this Chapter may by special resolution alter the form substitute
of its constitution by substituting a memorandum and articles memorandum
for a deed of settlement. and articles
for deed of
(2) The provisions of sections 4 to 6 of this Act with respect settlement.
to applications to the court for cancellation of alterations of
the objects of a company and matters consequential on the
passing of resolutions for such alterations (so far as applicable)
apply, but with the following modifications—

    (*a*) there is substituted for the printed copy of the altered
        memorandum required to be delivered to the registrar
        of companies a printed copy of the substituted memor-
        andum and articles, and

    (*b*) on the delivery to the registrar of the substituted
        memorandum and articles or the date when the alter-
        ation is no longer liable to be cancelled by order of the
        court (whichever is the later)—

           (i) the substituted memorandum and articles apply
        to the company in the same manner as if it were a
        company registered under Part I with that memor-
        andum and those articles, and

           (ii) the company's deed of settlement ceases to
        apply to the company.

(3) An alteration under this section may be made either with
or without alteration of the company's objects.

(4) In this section " deed of settlement " includes any contract
of copartnery or other instrument constituting or regulating the
company, not being an Act of Parliament, a royal charter or
letters patent.

Part XXIII

Oversea Companies

Chapter I

Registration, Etc.

Documents
to be delivered
to registrar.

691.—(1) When a company incorporated outside Great Britain establishes a place of business in Great Britain, it shall within one month of doing so deliver to the registrar of companies for registration—

(*a*) a certified copy of the charter, statutes or memorandum and articles of the company or other instrument constituting or defining the company's constitution, and, if the instrument is not written in the English language, a certified translation of it ; and

(*b*) a return in the prescribed form containing—

(i) a list of the company's directors and secretary, containing the particulars specified in the next subsection,

(ii) a list of the names and addresses of some one or more persons resident in Great Britain authorised to accept on the company's behalf service of process and any notices required to be served on it,

(iii) a list of the documents delivered in compliance with paragraph (*a*) of this subsection, and

(iv) a statutory declaration (made by a director or secretary of the company or by any person whose name and address are given in the list required by sub-paragraph (ii)), stating the date on which the company's place of business in Great Britain was established.

(2) The list referred to in subsection (1)(*b*)(i) shall contain the following particulars—

(*a*) with respect to each director—

(i) in the case of an individual, his present Christian name and surname and any former Christian name or surname, his usual residential address, his nationality and his business occupation (if any), or, if he has no business occupation but holds other directorships, particulars of any of them,

(ii) in the case of a corporation, its corporate name and registered or principal office ;

(b) with respect to the secretary (or, where there are joint secretaries, with respect to each of them)—

    (i) in the case of an individual, his present Christian name and surname, any former Christian name and surname and his usual residential address,

    (ii) in the case of a corporation or a Scottish firm, its corporate or firm name and registered or principal office.

Where all the partners in a firm are joint secretaries of the company, the name and principal office of the firm may be stated instead of the particulars mentioned in paragraph (b).

Section 289(2) applies for the purposes of the construction of references above to present and former Christian names and surnames.

692.—(1) If any alteration is made in—

    (a) the charter, statutes, or memorandum and articles of an oversea company or any such instrument as is mentioned above, or

    (b) the directors or secretary of an oversea company or the particulars contained in the list of the directors and secretary, or

    (c) the names or addresses of the persons authorised to accept service on behalf of an oversea company,

the company shall, within the time specified below, deliver to the registrar of companies for registration a return containing the prescribed particulars of the alteration.

Registration of altered particulars.

(2) If any change is made in the corporate name of an oversea company, the company shall, within the time specified below, deliver to the registrar of companies for registration a return containing the prescribed particulars of the change.

(3) The time for delivery of the returns required by subsections (1) and (2) is—

    (a) in the case of an alteration to which subsection (1)(c) applies, 21 days after the making of the alteration, and

    (b) otherwise, 21 days after the date on which notice of the alteration or change in question could have been received in Great Britain in due course of post (if despatched with due diligence).

693. Every oversea company shall—

    (a) in every prospectus inviting subscriptions for its shares or debentures in Great Britain, state the country in which the company is incorporated,

    (b) conspicuously exhibit on every place where it carries on business in Great Britain the company's name and the country in which it is incorporated,

Obligation to state name and other particulars.

(c) cause the company's name and the country in which it is incorporated to be stated in legible characters in all bill-heads and letter paper, and in all notices and other official publications of the company, and

(d) if the liability of the members of the company is limited, cause notice of that fact to be stated in legible characters in every such prospectus as above mentioned and in all bill-heads, letter paper, notices and other official publications of the company in Great Britain, and to be affixed on every place where it carries on its business.

Regulation of oversea companies in respect of their names.

694.—(1) If it appears to the Secretary of State that the corporate name of an oversea company is a name by which the company, had it been formed under this Act, would on the relevant date (defined below in subsection (3)) have been precluded from being registered by section 26 either—

(a) because it falls within subsection (1) of that section, or

(b) if it falls within subsection (2) of that section, because the Secretary of State would not approve the company's being registered with that name,

the Secretary of State may serve a notice on the company, stating why the name would not have been registered.

(2) If the corporate name of an oversea company is in the Secretary of State's opinion too like a name appearing on the relevant date in the index of names kept by the registrar of companies under section 714 or which should have appeared in that index on that date, or is the same as a name which should have so appeared, the Secretary of State may serve a notice on the company specifying the name in the index which the company's name is too like or which is the same as the company's name.

(3) No notice shall be served on a company under subsection (1) or (2) later than 12 months after the relevant date, being the date on which the company has complied with—

(a) section 691 in this Part, or

(b) if there has been a change in the company's corporate name, section 692(2).

(4) An oversea company on which a notice is served under subsection (1) or (2)—

(a) may deliver to the registrar of companies for registration a statement in the prescribed form specifying a name approved by the Secretary of State other than its corporate name under which it proposes to carry on business in Great Britain, and

(b) may, after that name has been registered, at any time deliver to the registrar for registration a statement in the prescribed form specifying a name approved by the Secretary of State (other than its corporate name) in substitution for the name previously registered.

(5) The name by which an oversea company is for the time being registered under subsection (4) is, for all purposes of the law applying in Great Britain (including this Act and the Busi- 1985 c. 7. ness Names Act 1985), deemed to be the company's corporate name ; but—

> (a) this does not affect references to the corporate name in this section, or any rights or obligations of the company, or render defective any legal proceedings by or against the company, and

> (b) any legal proceedings that might have been continued or commenced against the company by its corporate name or its name previously registered under this section may be continued or commenced against it by its name for the time being so registered.

(6) An oversea company on which a notice is served under subsection (1) or (2) shall not at any time after the expiration of 2 months from the service of that notice (or such longer period as may be specified in that notice carry on business in Great Britain under its corporate name.

Nothing in this subsection, or in section 697(2) (which imposes penalties for its contravention) invalidates any transaction entered into by the company.

(7) The Secretary of State may withdraw a notice served under subsection (1) or (2) at any time before the end of the period mentioned in subsection (6) ; and that subsection does not apply to a company served with a notice which has been withdrawn.

695.—(1) Any process or notice required to be served on an Service of oversea company is sufficiently served if addressed to any person documents on whose name has been delivered to the registrar under preceding oversea sections in this Part and left at or sent by post to the address company. which has been so delivered.

(2) However—

> (a) where such a company makes default in delivering to the registrar the name and address of a person resident in Great Britain who is authorised to accept on behalf of the company service of process or notices, or

> (b) if at any time all the persons whose names and addresses have been so delivered are dead or have ceased so to reside, or refuse to accept service on the company's behalf, or for any reason cannot be served,

a document may be served on the company by leaving it at, or sending it by post to, any place of business established by the company in Great Britain.

Office where
documents to
be filed.
696.—(1) Any document which an oversea company is required to deliver to the registrar of companies shall be delivered to the registrar at the registration office in England and Wales or Scotland, according to where the company has established a place of business.

(2) If the company has established a place of business both in England and Wales and in Scotland, the document shall be delivered at the registration office both in England and Wales and in Scotland.

(3) References in this Part to the registrar of companies are to be construed in accordance with the above subsections.

(4) If an oversea company ceases to have a place of business in either part of Great Britain, it shall forthwith give notice of that fact to the registrar of companies for that part ; and as from the date on which notice is so given the obligation of the company to deliver any document to the registrar ceases.

Penalties for
non-
compliance.
697.—(1) If an oversea company fails to comply with any of sections 691 to 693 and 696, the company, and every officer or agent of the company who knowingly and wilfully authorises or permits the default, is liable to a fine and, in the case of a continuing offence, to a daily default fine for continued contravention.

(2) If an oversea company contravenes section 694(6), the company and every officer or agent of it who knowingly and wilfully authorises or permits the contravention is guilty of an offence and liable to a fine and, for continued contravention, to a daily default fine.

Definitions for
this Chapter
698. For purposes of this Chapter—
" certified " means certified in the prescribed manner to be a true copy or a correct translation ;
" director ", in relation to an oversea company, includes shadow director ; and
" secretary " includes any person occupying the position of secretary by whatever name called.

Channel
Islands and
Isle of Man
companies.
699.—(1) With the exceptions specified in subsection (3) below, the provisions of this Act requiring documents to be forwarded or delivered to or filed with the registrar of companies and applying to companies formed and registered under Part I

apply also (if they would not otherwise) to an oversea company
incorporated in the Channel Islands or the Isle of Man.

(2) Those provisions apply to such a company—

  (*a*) if it has established a place of business in En_land and
Wales, as if it were registered in England and Wales,

  (*b*) if it has established a place of business in Scotland, as
if it were registered in Scotland, and

  (*c*) if it has established a place of business both in England
and Wales and in Scotland, as if it were registered
in both England and Wales and Scotland,

with such modifications as may be necessary and, in particular,
apply in a similar way to documents relating to things done
outside Great Britain as if they had been done in Great Britain.

(3) The exceptions are—

section 6(1) (resolution altering company's objects),

section 18 (alteration of memorandum or articles by statute
or statutory instrument),

section 241(3) (directors' duty to file accounts),

section 288(2) (notice to registrar of change of directors or
secretary), and

section 380 (copies of certain resolutions and agreements
to be sent to registrar within 15 days), so far as applicable to a resolution altering a company's memorandum
or articles.

CHAPTER II

DELIVERY OF ACCOUNTS

700.—(1) Every oversea company shall in respect of each
accounting reference period of the company prepare such
accounts, made up by reference to such date or dates, and in
such form, containing such particulars and having annexed to
them such documents, as would have been required if it were
a company formed and registered under this Act.

Preparation
and delivery
of accounts
by oversea
companies.

(2) An oversea company shall, in respect of each accounting
reference period of the company, deliver to the registrar of
companies copies of the accounts and other documents required
by subsection (1); and, if such an account or other document is
in a language other than English, there shall be annexed to the
copy so delivered a translation of it into English certified in the
prescribed manner to be a correct translation.

(3) If in relation to an accounting reference period the company's directors would be exempt under section 241(4) from compliance with subsection (3) of that section (independent company with unlimited liability), if the company were otherwise subject to that section, compliance with this section is not required in respect of that accounting reference period.

(4) The Secretary of State may by order in a statutory instrument—

(a) modify the requirements referred to in subsection (1) for the purpose of their application to oversea companies,

(b) exempt an oversea company from those requirements or from such of them as may be specified in the order.

(5) An order under subsection (4) may make different provision in relation to different cases or classes of case and may contain such incidental and supplementary provisions as the Secretary of State thinks fit; and a statutory instrument containing an order so made is subject to annulment in pursuance of a resolution of either House of Parliament.

Oversea
company's
accounting
reference
period and
date.
701.—(1) An oversea company's accounting reference periods are determined according to its accounting reference date.

(2) The company may give notice in the prescribed form to the registrar of companies specifying a date in the calendar year as being the date on which in each successive calendar year an accounting reference period of the company is to be treated as coming to an end; and the date specified in the notice is then the company's accounting reference date.

(3) No such notice has effect unless it is given before the end of 6 months beginning with the date on which a place of business in Great Britain is or was established by the company; and, failing such a notice, the company's accounting reference date is 31st March.

(4) The company's first accounting reference period is such period ending with its accounting reference date as—

(a) begins or began on a date determined by the company, but not later than that on which a place of business is or was established in Great Britain, and

(b) is a period exceeding 6 months and not exceeding 18 months.

(5) Each successive period of 12 months beginning after the end of the first accounting reference period and ending with the company's accounting reference date is also an accounting reference period of the company.

(6) Subsections (2) to (5) are subject to section 225 of this Act, under which in certain circumstances a company's accounting reference period may be altered, and which applies to oversea companies as well as to companies subject to Part VII, but omitting subsections (6) and (7).

702.—(1) In the case of an oversea company, the period *Period* allowed for delivering accounts in relation to an accounting *allowed for* reference period is 13 months after the end of the period. *delivering accounts.*

(2) Where the company's first accounting reference period—

(*a*) begins or began on the date determined by the company for the purposes of section 701(4)(*a*) and

(*b*) is or was a period of more than 12 months,

the period which would otherwise be allowed for delivering accounts in relation to that accounting reference period is treated as reduced by the number of days by which the accounting reference period is or was longer than 12 months.

(3) But the period allowed in relation to a company's first accounting reference period is not by subsection (2) reduced to less than 3 months after the end of that accounting reference period.

(4) In relation to an accounting reference period of an oversea company as respects which notice is given by the company under section 225 (as applied) and which by virtue of that section is treated as shortened in accordance with the notice, the period allowed for delivering accounts is—

(*a*) the period allowed in relation to that accounting reference period in accordance with the preceding subsections, or

(*b*) the period of 3 months beginning with the date of the notice,

whichever of those periods last expires.

(5) If for any special reason the Secretary of State thinks fit to do so, he may by notice in writing to an oversea company extend, by such further period as may be specified in the notice, the period which in accordance with the preceding subsections is the period allowed for delivering accounts in relation to any accounting reference period of the company.

703.—(1) If in respect of an accounting reference period of *Penalty for* an oversea company any of the requirements of section 700(2) *non-* is not complied with before the end of the period allowed for *compliance.* delivering accounts, the company and every officer or agent of it who knowingly and wilfully authorises or permits the default is, in respect of the company's failure to comply with the requirements in question, guilty of an offence and liable to a fine and, for continued contravention, to a daily default fine.

(2) For purposes of any proceedings under this section with respect to a requirement to deliver a copy of a document to the registrar of companies, it is not a defence to prove that the document in question was not in fact prepared as required by section 700.

PART XXIV

THE REGISTRAR OF COMPANIES, HIS FUNCTIONS AND OFFICES

Registration
offices.
704.—(1) For the purposes of the registration of companies under the Companies Acts, there shall continue to be offices in England and Wales and in Scotland, at such places as the Secretary of State thinks fit.

(2) The Secretary of State may appoint such registrars, assistant registrars, clerks and servants as he thinks necessary for that purpose, and may make regulations with respect to their duties, and may remove any persons so appointed.

(3) The salaries of the persons so appointed continue to be fixed by the Secretary of State, with the concurrence of the Treasury, and shall be paid out of money provided by Parliament.

(4) The Secretary of State may direct a seal or seals to be prepared for the authentication of documents required for or in connection with the registration of companies ; and any seal so prepared is referred to in this Act as the registrar's official seal.

(5) Wherever any act is by the Companies Acts directed to be done to or by the registrar of companies, it shall (until the Secretary of State otherwise directs) be done to or by the existing registrar of companies in England and Wales or in Scotland (as the case may be), or to or by such person as the Secretary of State may for the time being authorise.

(6) In the event of the Secretary of State altering the constitution of the existing registration offices or any of them, any such act shall be done to or by such officer and at such place with reference to the local situation of the registered offices of the companies to be registered as the Secretary of State may appoint.

705.—(1) The registrar of companies shall allocate to every company a number, which shall be known as the company's registered number ; and he may in addition allocate to any such company a letter, which is then deemed for all purposes to be part of the registered number.

(2) " Company " here includes—

(a) an oversea company which has complied with section 691 (delivery of statutes to registrar of companies, etc.) and which does not appear to the registrar not to have a place of business in Great Britain, and

(b) any incorporated or unincorporated body to which any provision of this Act applies by virtue of section 718 (unregistered companies).

706.—(1) For the purpose of securing that documents de- livered to the registrar of companies under the Companies Acts are of standard size, durable and easily legible, regulations made by the Secretary of State by statutory instrument may pre- scribe such requirements (whether as to size, weight, quality or colour of paper, size, type or colouring of lettering, or other- wise) as he may consider appropriate ; and different requirements may be so prescribed for different documents or classes of documents.

(2) If under any such provision there is delivered to the registrar a document (whether an original document or a copy) which in the registrar's opinion does not comply with such requirements prescribed under this section as are applicable to it, the registrar may serve on any person by whom under that provision the document was required to be delivered (or, if there are two or more such persons, may serve on any of them) a notice stating his opinion to that effect and indicating the requirements so prescribed with which in his opinion the document does not comply.

(3) Where the registrar serves such a notice with respect to a document delivered under any such provision, then, for the purposes of any enactment which enables a penalty to be imposed in respect of any omission to deliver to the registrar of companies a document required to be delivered under that provision (and, in particular, for the purposes of any such enactment whereby such a penalty may be imposed by reference to each day during which the omission continues)—

(a) any duty imposed by that provision to deliver such a document to the registrar is to be treated as not having been discharged by the delivery of that document, but

PART XXIV

(*b*) no account is to be taken of any days falling within the period mentioned in the following subsection.

(4) That period begins with the day on which the document was delivered to the registrar as mentioned in subsection (2) and ends with the 14th day after the date of service of the notice under subsection (2) by virtue of which subsection (3) applies.

(5) In this section any reference to delivering a document includes sending, forwarding, producing or (in the case of a notice) giving it.

Power of registrar to accept information on microfilm, etc.

707.—(1) The registrar of companies may, if he thinks fit, accept under any provision of the Companies Acts requiring a document to be delivered to him any material other than a document which contains the information in question and is of a kind approved by him.

(2) The delivery to the registrar of material so accepted is sufficient compliance with the provision in question.

(3) In this section any reference to delivering a document includes sending, forwarding, producing or (in the case of a notice) giving it.

Fees payable to registrar.

708.—(1) The Secretary of State may by regulations made by statutory instrument require the payment to the registrar of companies of such fees as may be specified in the regulations in respect of—

(*a*) the performance by the registrar of such functions under the Companies Acts as may be so specified, including the receipt by him of any notice or other document which under those Acts is required to be given, delivered, sent or forwarded to him.

(*b*) the inspection of documents or other material kept by him under those Acts.

(2) A statutory instrument containing regulations under this section requiring the payment of a fee in respect of a matter for which no fee was previously payable, or increasing a fee, shall be laid before Parliament after being made and shall cease to have effect at the end of the period of 28 days beginning with the day on which the regulations were made (but without prejudice to anything previously done under the regulations or to the making of further regulations) unless in that period the regulations are approved by resolution of each House of Parliament.

In reckoning that period of 28 days no account is to be taken of any time during which Parliament is dissolved or prorogued or during which both Houses are adjourned for more than 4 days.

(3) A statutory instrument containing regulations under this section, where subsection (2) does not apply, is subject to annulment in pursuance of a resolution of either House of Parliament.

(4) Fees paid to the registrar under the Companies Acts shall be paid into the Consolidated Fund.

(5) It is hereby declared that the registrar may charge a fee for any services provided by him otherwise than in pursuance of an obligation on him by law.

709.—(1) Subject to the provisions of this section, any person may—

  (a) inspect a copy of any document kept by the registrar of companies or, if the copy is illegible or unavailable, the document itself,

  (b) require a certificate of the incorporation of any company, or a certified copy or extract of any other document or any part of any other document.

A certificate given under paragraph (b) may be signed by the registrar, or authenticated by his official seal.

(2) In relation to documents delivered to the registrar with a prospectus in pursuance of section 65(2), the rights conferred by subsection (1) of this section are exercisable only during the 14 days beginning with the date of publication of the prospectus, or with the permission of the Secretary of State.

(3) In relation to documents so delivered in pursuance of section 77(3)(b) and (4) (prospectus of oversea company), those rights are exercisable only during the 14 days beginning with the date of the prospectus, or with that permission.

(4) The right conferred by subsection (1) (a) of this section does not extend to any copy sent to the registrar under section 495 (information to be given by receiver or manager following his appointment) of a statement as to the affairs of a company, or of any comments of the receiver or his successor, or a continuing receiver or manager, on the statement, but only to the summary of it, except where the person claiming the right either is or is the agent of a person stating himself in writing to be a member or creditor of the company to which the statement relates.

The rights conferred by subsection (1)(b) are similarly limited.

710.—(1) No process for compelling the production of any document kept by the registrar shall issue from any court except with the leave of that court; and any such process if issued shall bear on it a statement that it is issued with leave of the court.

(2) A copy of, or extract from, any document kept and registered at any of the offices for the registration of companies in England and Wales or Scotland, certified in writing by the registrar (whose official position it is unnecessary to prove) to be a true copy, is in all legal proceedings admissible in evidence as of equal validity with the original document.

(3) Copies or extracts of documents or parts of documents furnished by the registrar under section 709 may, instead of being certified by him in writing to be true copies, be sealed with his official seal.

(4) Any person untruthfully stating himself in writing for the purposes of section 709(4) to be a member or creditor of a company is liable to a fine.

(5) For purposes of section 709 and this section, a copy is to be taken to be the copy of a document notwithstanding that it is taken from a copy or other reproduction of the original; and in both sections " document " includes any material which contains information kept by the registrar of companies for purposes of the Companies Acts.

Public notice
by registrar
of receipt and
issue of
certain
documents.

711.—(1) The registrar of companies shall cause to be published in the Gazette notice of the issue or receipt by him of documents of any of the following descriptions (stating in the notice the name of the company, the description of document and the date of issue or receipt)—

(a) any certificate of incorporation of a company,

(b) any document making or evidencing an alteration in a company's memorandum or articles,

(c) any notification of a change among the directors of a company,

(d) any copy of a resolution of a public company which gives, varies, revokes or renews an authority for the purposes of section 80 (allotment of relevant securities),

(e) any copy of a special resolution of a public company passed under section 95(1), (2) or (3) (disapplication of pre-emption rights),

(f) any report under section 103 or 104 as to the value of a non-cash asset,

(g) any statutory declaration delivered under section 117 PART XXIV
(public company share capital requirements),

(h) any notification (given under section 122) of the redemption of shares,

(j) any statement or notice delivered by a public company under section 128 (registration of particulars of special rights),

(k) any documents delivered by a company under section 241 (annual accounts),

(l) a copy of any resolution or agreement to which section 380 applies and which—

> (i) states the rights attached to any shares in a public company, other than shares which are in all respects uniform (for purposes of section 128) with shares previously allotted, or

> (ii) varies rights attached to any shares in a public company, or

> (iii) assigns a name or other designation, or a new name or designation, to any class of shares in a public company,

(m) any return of allotments of a public company,

(n) any notice of a change in the situation of a company's registered office,

(p) any copy of a winding-up order in respect of a company,

(q) any order for the dissolution of a company on a winding up,

(r) any return by a liquidator of the final meeting of a company on a winding up.

(2) In section 42 " official notification " means—

(a) in relation to anything stated in a document of any of the above descriptions, the notification of that document in the Gazette under this section, and

(b) in relation to the appointment of a liquidator in a voluntary winding up, the notification of it in the Gazette under section 600 ;

and " officially notified " is to be construed accordingly.

712.—(1) Where a company has been dissolved, whether Removal of under this Act or otherwise, the registrar may, at any time documents to after the expiration of 2 years from the date of the dissolution, Public Record direct that any documents in his custody relating to that com- Office. pany may be removed to the Public Record Office ; and documents in respect of which such a direction is given shall be

PART XXIV   disposed of in accordance with the enactments relating to that Office and the rules made under them.

(2) In this section " company " includes a company pro-
7 & 8 Vict. c. 110.   visionally or completely registered under the Joint Stock Companies Act 1844.

(3) This section does not extend to Scotland.

Enforcement of company's duty to make returns.   **713.**—(1) If a company, having made default in complying with any provision of the Companies Acts which requires it to file with, deliver or send to the registrar of companies any return, account or other document, or to give notice to him of any matter, fails to make good the default within 14 days after the service of a notice on the company requiring it to do so, the court may, on an application made to it by any member or creditor of the company or by the registrar of companies, make an order directing the company and any officer of it to make good the default within such time as may be specified in the order.

(2) The court's order may provide that all costs of and incidental to the application shall be borne by the company or by any officers of it responsible for the default.

(3) Nothing in this section prejudices the operation of any enactment imposing penalties on a company or its officers in respect of any such default as is mentioned above.

Registrar's index of company and corporate names.   **714.**—(1) The registrar of companies shall keep an index of the names of the following bodies—

(a) companies as defined by this Act,

(b) companies incorporated outside Great Britain which have complied with section 691 and which do not appear to the registrar of companies not to have a place of business in Great Britain,

(c) incorporated and unincorporated bodies to which any provision of this Act applies by virtue of section 718 (unregistered companies),

7 Edw. 7 c. 24.   (d) limited partnerships registered under the Limited Partnerships Act 1907,

1960 c. 22 (N.I.).   (e) companies within the meaning of the Companies Act (Northern Ireland) 1960,

(f) companies incorporated outside Northern Ireland which have complied with section 356 of that Act (which corresponds with section 691 of this Act), and which do not appear to the registrar not to have a place of business in Northern Ireland, and

(g) societies registered under the Industrial and Provident
Societies Act 1965 or the Industrial and Provident 1965 c. 12.
Societies Act (Northern Ireland) 1969. 1969 c. 24
(N.I.).

(2) The Secretary of State may by order in a statutory instrument vary subsection (1) by the addition or deletion of any class of body, except any within paragraph (a) or (b) of the subsection, whether incorporated or unincorporated; and any such statutory instrument is subject to annulment in pursuance of a resolution of either House of Parliament.

715.—(1) The registrar of companies may destroy any documents or other material which he has kept for over 10 years and which were, or were comprised in or annexed or attached to, the accounts or annual returns of any company. Destruction of old records.

(2) The registrar shall retain a copy of any document or other material destroyed in pursuance of subsection (1); and sections 709 and 710 apply in relation to any such copy as if it were the original.

PART XXV

MISCELLANEOUS AND SUPPLEMENTARY PROVISIONS

716.—(1) No company, association or partnership consisting of more than 20 persons shall be formed for the purpose of carrying on any business that has for its object the acquisition of gain by the company, association or partnership, or by its individual members, unless it is registered as a company under this Act, or is formed in pursuance of some other Act of Parliament, or of letters patent. Prohibition of partnerships with more than 20 members.

(2) However, this does not prohibit the formation—

    (a) for the purpose of carrying on practice as solicitors, of a partnership consisting of persons each of whom is a solicitor;

    (b) for the purpose of carrying on practice as accountants, of a partnership consisting of persons each of whom falls within either paragraph (a) or (b) of section 389(1) (qualifications of company auditors);

    (c) for the purpose of carrying on business as members of a recognised stock exchange, of a partnership consisting of persons each of whom is a member of that stock exchange.

(3) The Secretary of State may by regulations in a statutory instrument provide that subsection (1) shall not apply to the formation (otherwise than as permitted by subsection (2)), for a

PART XXV   purpose specified in the regulations, of a partnership of a description so specified.

(4) In this section " solicitor "—

(a) in relation to England and Wales, means solicitor of the Supreme Court, and

1980 c. 46.

(b) in relation to Scotland, means a person enrolled or deemed enrolled as a solicitor in pursuance of the Solicitors (Scotland) Act 1980.

(5) Subsection (1) does not apply in relation to any body of persons for the time being approved for the purposes of the

1952 c. 57.   Marine and Aviation Insurance (War Risks) Act 1952 by the Secretary of State, being a body the objects of which are or include the carrying on of business by way of the re-insurance of risks which may be re-insured under any agreement for the purpose mentioned in section 1(1)(b) of that Act.

Limited
partnerships:
limit on
number of
members.

717.—(1) So much of the Limited Partnerships Act 1907 as provides that a limited partnership shall not consist of more than 20 persons does not apply—

(a) to a partnership carrying on practice as solicitors and consisting of persons each of whom is a solicitor,

7 Edw. 7 c. 24.

(b) to a partnership carrying on practice as accountants and consisting of persons each of whom falls within either paragraph (a) or (b) of section 389(1) of this Act (qualification of company auditors),

(c) to a partnership carrying on business as members of a recognised stock exchange and consisting of persons each of whom is a member of that exchange.

(2) The Secretary of State may by regulations in a statutory instrument provide that so much of section 4(2) of the Act of 1907 as provides that a limited partnership shall not consist of more than 20 persons shall not apply to a partnership (other than one permitted by subsection (1) of this section) carrying on business of a description specified in the regulations, being a partnership of a description so specified.

(3) In this section " solicitor " means the same as in section 716.

Unregistered
companies.

718.—(1) The provisions of this Act specified in the first column of Schedule 22 (relating respectively to the matters specified in the second column of the Schedule) apply to all bodies corporate incorporated in and having a principal place of business in Great Britain, other than those mentioned in subsection (2) below, as if they were companies registered under this Act, but subject to any limitations mentioned in relation to those provisions respectively in the third column and to such adaptations and modifications (if any) as may be specified by regulations made by the Secretary of State.

(2) Those provisions of this Act do not apply by virtue of this section to any of the following—

> (a) any body incorporated by or registered under any public general Act of Parliament,
>
> (b) any body not formed for the purpose of carrying on a business which has for its object the acquisition of gain by the body or its individual members,
>
> (c) any body for the time being exempted by direction of the Secretary of State (or before him by the Board of Trade).

(3) Where against any provision of this Act specified in the first column of Schedule 22 there appears in the third column the entry " Subject to section 718(3) ", it means that the provision is to apply by virtue of this section so far only as may be specified by regulations made by the Secretary of State and to such bodies corporate as may be so specified.

(4) The provisions specified in the first column of the Schedule also apply in like manner in relation to any unincorporated body of persons entitled by virtue of letters patent to any of the privileges conferred by the Chartered Companies Act 1837 and 1837 c. 73. not registered under any other public general Act of Parliament, but subject to the like exceptions as are provided for in the case of bodies corporate by paragraphs (b) and (c) of subsection (2).

(5) This section does not repeal or revoke in whole or in part any enactment, royal charter or other instrument constituting or regulating any body in relation to which those provisions are applied by virtue of this section, or restrict the power of Her Majesty to grant a charter in lieu of or supplementary to any such charter as above mentioned ; but, in relation to any such body, the operation of any such enactment, charter or instrument is suspended in so far as it is inconsistent with any of those provisions as they apply for the time being to that body.

(6) The power to make regulations conferred by this section (whether regulations under subsection (1) or subsection (3)) is exercisable by statutory instrument subject to annulment in pursuance of a resolution of either House of Parliament.

719.—(1) The powers of a company include (if they would not Power of otherwise do so apart from this section) power to make the company to following provision for the benefit of persons employed or for- provide for merly employed by the company or any of its subsidiaries, that employees on is to say, provision in connection with the cessation or the transfer of business.

PART XXV   transfer to any person of the whole or part of the undertaking of the company or that subsidiary.

(2) The power conferred by subsection (1) is exercisable notwithstanding that its exercise is not in the best interests of the company.

(3) The power which a company may exercise by virtue only of subsection (1) shall only be exercised by the company if sanctioned—

(a) in a case not falling within paragraph (b) or (c) below, by an ordinary resolution of the company, or

(b) if so authorised by the memorandum or articles, a resolution of the directors, or

(c) if the memorandum or articles require the exercise of the power to be sanctioned by a resolution of the company of some other description for which more than a simple majority of the members voting is necessary, with the sanction of a resolution of that description ;

and in any case after compliance with any other requirements of the memorandum or articles applicable to its exercise.

(4) Any payment which may be made by a company under this section may, if made before the commencement of any winding up of the company, be made out of profits of the company which are available for dividend.

Certain
companies
to publish
periodical
statement.

720.—(1) Every company, being an insurance company or a deposit, provident or benefit society, shall before it commences business, and also on the first Monday in February and the first Tuesday in August in every year during which it carries on business, make a statement in the form set out in Schedule 23, or as near to it as circumstances admit.

(2) A copy of the statement shall be put up in a conspicuous place in the company's registered office, and in every branch office or place where the business of the company is carried on.

(3) Every member and every creditor of the company is entitled to a copy of the statement, on payment of a sum not exceeding 2½ pence.

(4) If default is made in complying with this section, the company and every officer of it who is in default is liable to a fine and, for continued contravention, to a daily default fine.

(5) For purposes of this Act, a company which carries on the business of insurance in common with any other business or businesses is deemed an insurance company.

1982 c. 50.

(6) In the case of an insurance company to which Part II of the Insurance Companies Act 1982 applies, this section does not apply if the company complies with provisions of that Act as to the accounts and balance sheet to be prepared annually and deposited by such a company.

(7) The Secretary of State may, by regulations in a statutory PART XXV instrument (subject to annulment in pursuance of a resolution of either House of Parliament), alter the form in Schedule 23.

721.—(1) The following applies if on an application made— Production
  (a) in England and Wales, to a judge of the High Court and inspection of books
      by the Director of Public Prosecutions, the Secretary where offence
      of State or a chief officer of police, or suspected.
  (b) in Scotland, to one of the Lords Commissioners of
      Justiciary by the Lord Advocate,
there is shown to be reasonable cause to believe that any person has, while an officer of a company, committed an offence in connection with the management of the company's affairs and that evidence of the commission of the offence is to be found in any books or papers of or under the control of the company.

(2) An order may be made—
  (a) authorising any person named in it to inspect the books
      or papers in question, or any of them, for the purpose
      of investigating and obtaining evidence of the offence,
      or
  (b) requiring the secretary of the company or such other
      officer of it as may be named in the order to produce
      the books or papers (or any of them) to a person
      named in the order at a place so named.

(3) The above applies also in relation to any books or papers of a person carrying on the business of banking so far as they relate to the company's affairs, as it applies to any books or papers of or under the control of the company, except that no such order as is referred to in subsection (2)(b) shall be made by virtue of this subsection.

(4) The decision of a judge of the High Court or of any of the Lords Commissioners of Justiciary on an application under this section is not appealable.

722.—(1) Any register, index, minute book or accounting Form of records required by the Companies Acts to be kept by a com- company pany may be kept either by making entries in bound books or registers, etc. by recording the matters in question in any other manner.

(2) Where any such register, index, minute book or account-ing record is not kept by making entries in a bound book, but by some other means, adequate precautions shall be taken for guarding against falsification and facilitating its discovery.

(3) If default is made in complying with subsection (2), the company and every officer of it who is in default is liable to a fine and, for continued contravention, to a daily default fine.

R

PART XXV
Use of
computers for
company
records.

723.—(1) The power conferred on a company by section 722(1) to keep a register or other record by recording the matters in question otherwise than by making entries in bound books includes power to keep the register or other record by recording those matters otherwise than in a legible form, so long as the recording is capable of being reproduced in a legible form.

(2) Any provision of an instrument made by a company before 12th February 1979 which requires a register of holders of the company's debentures to be kept in a legible form is to be read as requiring the register to be kept in a legible or non-legible form.

(3) If any such register or other record of a company as is mentioned in section 722(1), or a register of holders of a company's debentures, is kept by the company by recording the matters in question otherwise than in a legible form, any duty imposed on the company by this Act to allow inspection of, or to furnish a copy of, the register or other record or any part of it is to be treated as a duty to allow inspection of, or to furnish, a reproduction of the recording or of the relevant part of it in a legible form.

(4) The Secretary of State may by regulations in a statutory instrument make such provision in addition to subsection (3) as he considers appropriate in connection with such registers or other records as are mentioned in that subsection, and are kept as so mentioned ; and the regulations may make modifications of provisions of this Act relating to such registers or other records.

(5) A statutory instrument under subsection (4) is subject to annulment in pursuance of a resolution of either House of Parliament.

Cross-border
operation of
receivership
provisions.

724.—(1) A receiver appointed under the law of either part of Great Britain in respect of the whole or any part of any property or undertaking of a company and in consequence of the company having created a charge which, as created, was a floating charge may exercise his powers in the other part of Great Britain so far as their exercise is not inconsistent with the law applicable there.

(2) In subsection (1) " receiver " includes a manager and a person who is appointed both receiver and manager.

Service of
documents.

725.—(1) A document may be served on a company by leaving it at, or sending it by post to, the company's registered office.

(2) Where a company registered in Scotland carries on business in England and Wales, the process of any court in England

and Wales may be served on the company by leaving it at, or sending it by post to, the company's principal place of business in England and Wales, addressed to the manager or other head officer in England and Wales of the company.

(3) Where process is served on a company under subsection (2), the person issuing out the process shall send a copy of it by post to the company's registered office.

726.—(1) Where in England and Wales a limited company is plaintiff in an action or other legal proceeding, the court having jurisdiction in the matter may, if it appears by credible testimony that there is reason to believe that the company will be unable to pay the defendant's costs if successful in his defence, require sufficient security to be given for those costs, and may stay all proceedings until the security is given.

(2) Where in Scotland a limited company is pursuer in an action or other legal proceeding, the court having jurisdiction in the matter may, if it appears by credible testimony that there is reason to believe that the company will be unable to pay the defender's expenses if successful in his defence, order the company to find caution and sist the proceedings until caution is found.

727.—(1) If in any proceedings for negligence, default, breach of duty or breach of trust against an officer of a company or a person employed by a company as auditor (whether he is or is not an officer of the company) it appears to the court hearing the case that that officer or person is or may be liable in respect of the negligence, default, breach of duty or breach of trust, but that he has acted honestly and reasonably, and that having regard to all the circumstances of the case (including those connected with his appointment) he ought fairly to be excused for the negligence, default, breach of duty or breach of trust, that court may relieve him, either wholly or partly, from his liability on such terms as it thinks fit.

(2) If any such officer or person as above-mentioned has reason to apprehend that any claim will or might be made against him in respect of any negligence, default, breach of duty or breach of trust, he may apply to the court for relief; and the court on the application has the same power to relieve him as under this section it would have had if it had been a court before which proceedings against that person for negligence, default, breach of duty or breach of trust had been brought.

(3) Where a case to which subsection (1) applies is being tried by a judge with a jury, the judge, after hearing the evidence, may, if he is satisfied that the defendant or defender ought in pursuance of that subsection to be relieved either in whole or in part

PART XXV

Costs and expenses in actions by certain limited companies.

Power of court to grant relief in certain cases.

R 2

PART XXV   from the liability sought to be enforced against him, withdraw the case in whole or in part from the jury and forthwith direct judgment to be entered for the defendant or defender on such terms as to costs or otherwise as the judge may think proper.

Enforcement of High Court orders.

728. Orders made by the High Court under this Act may be enforced in the same manner as orders made in an action pending in that court.

Annual report by Secretary of State.

729. The Secretary of State shall cause a general annual report of matters within the Companies Acts to be prepared and laid before both Houses of Parliament.

Punishment of offences.

730.—(1) Schedule 24 to this Act has effect with respect to the way in which offences under this Act are punishable on conviction.

(2) In relation to an offence under a provision of this Act specified in the first column of the Schedule (the general nature of the offence being described in the second column), the third column shows whether the offence is punishable on conviction on indictment, or on summary conviction, or either in the one way or the other.

(3) The fourth column of the Schedule shows, in relation to an offence, the maximum punishment by way of fine or imprisonment under this Act which may be imposed on a person convicted of the offence in the way specified in relation to it in the third column (that is to say, on indictment or summarily), a reference to a period of years or months being to a term of imprisonment of that duration.

(4) The fifth column shows (in relation to an offence for which there is an entry in that column) that a person convicted of the offence after continued contravention is liable to a daily default fine ; that is to say, he is liable on a second or subsequent summary conviction of the offence to the fine specified in that column for each day on which the contravention is continued (instead of the penalty specified for the offence in the fourth column of the Schedule).

(5) For the purpose of any enactment in the Companies Acts which provides that an officer of a company who is in default is liable to a fine or penalty, the expression " officer who is in default " means any officer of the company who knowingly and wilfully authorises or permits the default, refusal or contravention mentioned in the enactment.

731.—(1) Summary proceedings for any offence under the Companies Acts may (without prejudice to any jurisdiction exercisable apart from this subsection) be taken against a body corporate at any place at which the body has a place of business, and against any other person at any place at which he is for the time being.

PART XXV
Summary
proceedings.

(2) Notwithstanding anything in section 127(1) of the Magistrates' Courts Act 1980, an information relating to an offence under the Companies Acts which is triable by a magistrates' court in England and Wales may be so tried if it is laid at any time within 3 years after the commission of the offence and within 12 months after the date on which evidence sufficient in the opinion of the Director of Public Prosecutions or the Secretary of State (as the case may be) to justify the proceedings comes to his knowledge.

1980 c. 43.

(3) Summary proceedings in Scotland for an offence under the Companies Acts shall not be commenced after the expiration of 3 years from the commission of the offence.

Subject to this (and notwithstanding anything in section 331 of the Criminal Procedure (Scotland) Act 1975), such proceedings may (in Scotland) be commenced at any time within 12 months after the date on which evidence sufficient in the Lord Advocate's opinion to justify the proceedings came to his knowledge or, where such evidence was reported to him by the Secretary of State, within 12 months after the date on which it came to the knowledge of the latter ; and subsection (3) of that section applies for the purpose of this subsection as it applies for the purpose of that section.

1975 c. 21.

(4) For purposes of this section, a certificate of the Director of Public Prosecutions, the Lord Advocate or the Secretary of State (as the case may be) as to the date on which such evidence as is referred to above came to his knowledge is conclusive evidence.

732.—(1) In respect of an offence under any of sections 210, 324, 329, 447 to 451 and 455, proceedings shall not, in England and Wales, be instituted except by or with the consent of the appropriate authority.

Prosecution
by public
authorities.

(2) That authority is—

   (a) for an offence under any of sections 210, 324 and 329, the Secretary of State or the Director of Public Prosecutions,

   (b) for an offence under any of sections 447 to 451, either one of those two persons or the Industrial Assurance Commissioner, and

   (c) for an offence under section 455, the Secretary of State.

R 3

(3) Where proceedings are instituted under the Companies Acts against any person by the Director of Public Prosecutions or by or on behalf of the Secretary of State or the Lord Advocate, nothing in those Acts is to be taken to require any person to disclose any information which he is entitled to refuse to disclose on grounds of legal professional privilege.

Offences by
bodies
corporate.

733.—(1) The following applies to offences under any of sections 210, 216(3) and 447 to 451.

(2) Where a body corporate is guilty of such an offence and it is proved that the offence occurred with the consent or connivance of, or was attributable to any neglect on the part of any director, manager, secretary or other similar officer of the body, or any person who was purporting to act in any such capacity, he as well as the body corporate is guilty of that offence and is liable to be proceeded against and punished accordingly.

(3) Where the affairs of a body corporate are managed by its members, then in the case of an offence under section 210 or 216(3), subsection (2) above applies in relation to the acts and defaults of a member in connection with his functions of management as if he were a director of the body corporate.

(4) In this section " director ", in relation to an offence under any of sections 447 to 451, includes a shadow director.

Criminal
proceedings
against
unincorpora-
ted bodies.

734.—(1) Proceedings for an offence alleged to have been committed under any of sections 447 to 451 by an unincorporated body shall be brought in the name of that body (and not in that of any of its members), and for the purposes of any such proceedings, any rules of court relating to the service of documents apply as if that body were a corporation.

(2) A fine imposed on an unincorporated body on its conviction of such an offence shall be paid out of the funds of that body.

(3) In a case in which an unincorporated body is charged in England and Wales with such an offence, section 33 of the 1925 c. 86.
1980 c. 43. Criminal Justice Act 1925 and Schedule 3 to the Magistrates' Courts Act 1980 (procedure on charge of an offence against a corporation) have effect in like manner as in the case of a corporation so charged.

(4) In relation to proceedings on indictment in Scotland for such an offence alleged to have been committed by an unin-
1975 c. 21. corporated body, section 74 of the Criminal Procedure (Scotland) Act 1975 (proceedings on indictment against bodies corporate) has effect as if that body were a body corporate.

PART XXVI

INTERPRETATION

735.—(1) In this Act—   " Company ",

   (*a*) " company " means a company formed and registered etc.
under this Act, or an existing company ;

   (*b*) " existing company " means a company formed and
registered under the former Companies Acts, but does
not include a company registered under the Joint Stock 25 & 26 Vict. c.
Companies Acts, the Companies Act 1862 or the Com- 89.
panies (Consolidation) Act 1908 in what was then Ire- 8 Edw. 7 c. 69.
land ;

   (*c*) " the former Companies Acts " means the Joint Stock
Companies Acts, the Companies Act 1862, the Companies (Consolidation) Act 1908, the Companies Act 1929 c. 23.
1929 and the Companies Acts 1948 to 1983.

(2) " Public company " and " private company " have the meanings given by section 1(3).

(3) " The Joint Stock Companies Acts " means the Joint Stock 20 & 21 Vict.
Companies Act 1856, the Joint Stock Companies Acts 1856, c. 14.
1857, the Joint Stock Banking Companies Act 1857 and the Act 20 & 21 Vict.
to enable Joint Stock Banking Companies to be formed on the c. 49.
principle of limited liability, or any one or more of those Acts 21 & 22 Vict.
(as the case may require), but does not include the Joint Stock c. 91.
Companies Act 1844. 7 & 8 Vict.
                                                         c. 110.

(4) The definitions in this section apply unless the contrary
intention appears.

736.—(1) For the purposes of this Act, a company is deemed " Holding
to be a subsidiary of another if (but only if)— company ",
                                                     " subsidiary "

   (*a*) that other either— and " wholly-
                                                  owned

      (i) is a member of it and controls the composition subsidiary".
      of its board of directors, or

      (ii) holds more than half in nominal value of its
      equity share capital, or

   (*b*) the first-mentioned company is a subsidiary of any
company which is that other's subsidiary.

The above is subject to subsection (4) below in this section.

(2) For purposes of subsection (1), the composition of a
company's board of directors is deemed to be controlled by
another company if (but only if) that other company by the
exercise of some power exercisable by it without the consent
or concurrence of any other person can appoint or remove the
holders of all or a majority of the directorships.

(3) For purposes of this last provision, the other company is
deemed to have power to appoint to a directorship with respect

PART XXVI to which any of the following conditions is satisfied—

> (*a*) that a person cannot be appointed to it without the exercise in his favour by the other company of such a power as is mentioned above, or
>
> (*b*) that a person's appointment to the directorship follows necessarily from his appointment as director of the other company, or
>
> (*c*) that the directorship is held by the other company itself or by a subsidiary of it.

(4) In determining whether one company is a subsidiary of another—

> (*a*) any shares held or power exercisable by the other in a fiduciary capacity are to be treated as not held or exercisable by it,
>
> (*b*) subject to the two following paragraphs, any shares held or power exercisable—
>
> > (i) by any person as nominee for the other (except where the other is concerned only in a fiduciary capacity), or
> >
> > (ii) by, or by a nominee for, a subsidiary of the other (not being a subsidiary which is concerned only in a fiduciary capacity),
>
> are to be treated as held or exercisable by the other,
>
> (*c*) any shares held or power exercisable by any person by virtue of the provisions of any debentures of the first-mentioned company or of a trust deed for securing any issue of such debentures are to be disregarded,
>
> (*d*) any shares held or power exercisable by, or by a nominee for, the other or its subsidiary (not being held or exercisable as mentioned in paragraph (*c*)) are to be treated as not held or exercisable by the other if the ordinary business of the other or its subsidiary (as the case may be) includes the lending of money and the shares are held or the power is exercisable as above mentioned by way of security only for the purposes of a transaction entered into in the ordinary course of that business.

(5) For purposes of this Act—

> (*a*) a company is deemed to be another's holding company if (but only if) the other is its subsidiary, and
>
> (*b*) a body corporate is deemed the wholly-owned subsidiary of another if it has no members except that other and that other's wholly-owned subsidiaries and its or their nominees.

(6) In this section " company " includes any body corporate.

737.—(1) In this Act, " called-up share capital ", in relation to   PART XXVI
a company, means so much of its share capital as equals the   " Called-up
aggregate amount of the calls made on its shares (whether or   share
not those calls have been paid), together with any share capital   capital ".
paid up without being called and any share capital to be paid
on a specified future date under the articles, the terms of allotment of the relevant shares or any other arrangements for payment of those shares.

(2) " Uncalled share capital " is to be construed accordingly.

(3) The definitions in this section apply unless the contrary
intention appears.

738.—(1) In relation to an allotment of shares in a company,   "Allotment "
the shares are to be taken for the purposes of this Act to be   and " paid
allotted when a person acquires the unconditional right to be   up ".
included in the company's register of members in respect of
those shares.

(2) For purposes of this Act, a share in a company is deemed
paid up (as to its nominal value or any premium on it) in cash,
or allotted for cash, if the consideration for the allotment or
payment up is cash received by the company, or is a cheque
received by it in good faith which the directors have no reason
for suspecting will not be paid, or is a release of a liability of the
company for a liquidated sum, or is an undertaking to pay cash
to the company at a future date.

(3) In relation to the allotment or payment up of any shares
in a company, references in this Act (except sections 89 to 94)
to consideration other than cash and to the payment up of
shares and premiums on shares otherwise than in cash include
the payment of, or any undertaking to pay, cash to any person
other than the company.

(4) For the purpose of determining whether a share is or is to
be allotted for cash, or paid up in cash, " cash " includes
foreign currency.

739.—(1) In this Act " non-cash asset " means any property   " Non-cash
or interest in property other than cash ; and for this purpose   asset ".
" cash " includes foreign currency.

(2) A reference to the transfer or acquisition of a non-cash
asset includes the creation or extinction of an estate or interest in,
or a right over, any property and also the discharge of any
person's liability, other than a liability for a liquidated sum.

740. References in this Act to a body corporate or to a   "Body
corporation do not include a corporation sole, but include a   corporate "
company incorporated elsewhere than in Great Britain.   and
                                                          " corpora-
                                                          tion ".

Such references to a body corporate do not include a Scottish firm.

741.—(1) In this Act, " director " includes any person occupying the position of director, by whatever name called.

(2) In relation to a company, " shadow director " means a person in accordance with whose directions or instructions the directors of the company are accustomed to act.

However, a person is not deemed a shadow director by reason only that the directors act on advice given by him in a professional capacity.

(3) For the purposes of the following provisions of this Act, namely—

> section 309 (directors' duty to have regard to interests of employees),
>
> section 319 (directors' long-term contracts of employment),
>
> sections 320 to 322 (substantial property transactions involving directors), and
>
> sections 330 to 346 (general restrictions on power of companies to make loans, etc., to directors and others connected with them),

(being provisions under which shadow directors are treated as directors), a body corporate is not to be treated as a shadow director of any of its subsidiary companies by reason only that the directors of the subsidiary are accustomed to act in accordance with its directions or instructions.

742.—(1) In this Act, unless the contrary intention appears—

> (*a*) " accounting reference period " has the meaning given by sections 224 to 226 ;
>
> (*b*) " accounts " includes a company's group accounts (within the meaning of section 229), whether prepared in the form of accounts or not ;
>
> (*c*) " balance sheet date ", in relation to a balance sheet, means the date as at which the balance sheet was prepared ;
>
> (*d*) " financial year "—
>
> > (i) in relation to a body corporate to which Part VII applies, means a period in respect of which a profit and loss account under section 227 in that Part is made up, and
> >
> > (ii) in relation to any other body corporate, means a period in respect of which a profit and loss account of the body laid before it in general meeting is made up,
>
> (whether, in either case, that period is a year or not) ;

(*e*) any reference to a profit and loss account, in the case of a company not trading for profit, is to its income and expenditure account, and references to profit or loss and, if the company has subsidiaries, references to a consolidated profit and loss account are to be construed accordingly. Part **XXVI**

(2) Except in relation to special category accounts, any reference to a balance sheet or profit and loss account includes any notes to the account in question giving information which is required by any provision of this Act, and required or allowed by any such provision to be given in a note to company accounts.

(3) In relation to special category accounts, any reference to a balance sheet or profit and loss account includes any notes thereon or document annexed thereto giving information which is required by this Act and is thereby allowed to be so given.

(4) References to special category companies and special category accounts are to be construed in accordance with Chapter II of Part VII.

(5) For the purposes of Part VII, a body corporate is to be regarded as publishing any balance sheet or other account if it publishes, issues or circulates it or otherwise makes it available for public inspection in a manner calculated to invite members of the public generally, or any class of members of the public, to read it.

(6) Expressions which, when used in Schedule 4, fall to be construed in accordance with any provision of Part VII of that Schedule have the same meaning (unless the contrary intention appears) when used in any provision of this Act.

743. For purposes of this Act, an employees' share scheme is a scheme for encouraging or facilitating the holding of shares or debentures in a company by or for the benefit of— " Employees' share scheme ".

(*a*) the bona fide employees or former employees of the company, the company's subsidiary or holding company or a subsidiary of the company's holding company, or

(*b*) the wives, husbands, widows, widowers or children or step-children under the age of 18 of such employees or former employees.

744. In this Act, unless the contrary intention appears, the following definitions apply— Expressions used generally in this Act.

" agent " does not include a person's counsel acting as such ;

" annual return " means the return to be made by a company under section 363 or 364 (as the case may be) ;

PART XXVI

" articles " means, in relation to a company, its articles of association, as originally framed or as altered by resolution, including (so far as applicable to the company) regulations contained in or annexed to any enactment relating to companies passed before this Act, as altered by or under any such enactment ;

" authorised minimum " has the meaning given by section 118 ;

1971 c. 80.

" bank holiday " means a holiday under the Banking and Financial Dealings Act 1971 ;

" books and papers " and " books or papers " include accounts, deeds, writings and documents ;

" the Companies Acts " means this Act, the Insider Dealing Act and the Consequential Provisions Act ;

1985 c. 9.

" the Consequential Provisions Act " means the Companies Consolidation (Consequential Provisions) Act 1985 ;

" the court ", in relation to a company, means the court having jurisdiction to wind up the company ;

" debenture " includes debenture stock, bonds and any other securities of a company, whether constituting a charge on the assets of the company or not ;

" document " includes summons, notice, order, and other legal process, and registers ;

" equity share capital " means, in relation to a company, its issued share capital excluding any part of that capital which, neither as respects dividends nor as respects capital, carries any right to participate beyond a specified amount in a distribution ;

" expert " has the meaning given by section 62 ;

" floating charge " includes a floating charge within the meaning given by section 462 ;

" the Gazette " means, as respects companies registered in England and Wales, the London Gazette and, as respects companies registered in Scotland, the Edinburgh Gazette ;

" general rules " means general rules made under section 663, and includes forms ;

1974 c. 39.

" hire-purchase agreement " has the same meaning as in the Consumer Credit Act 1974 ;

1985 c. 8.

" the Insider Dealing Act " means the Company Securities (Insider Dealing) Act 1985 ;

1982 c. 50.

" insurance company " means the same as in the Insurance Companies Act 1982 ;

" joint stock company " has the meaning given by section 683 ;

" memorandum ", in relation to a company, means its memorandum of association, as originally framed or as altered in pursuance of any enactment ;

" number ", in relation to shares, includes amount, where the context admits of the reference to shares being construed to include stock ;

" officer ", in relation to a body corporate, includes a director, manager or secretary ;

" official seal ", in relation to the registrar of companies, means a seal prepared under section 704(4) for the authentication of documents required for or in connection with the registration of companies ;

" oversea company " means—

    (a) a company incorporated elsewhere than in Great Britain which, after the commencement of this Act, establishes a place of business in Great Britain, and

    (b) a company so incorporated which has, before that commencement, established a place of business and continues to have an established place of business in Great Britain at that commencement ;

" place of business " includes a share transfer or share registration office ;

" prescribed " means—

    (a) as respects provisions of this Act relating to winding up, prescribed by general rules under section 663, and

    (b) otherwise, prescribed by statutory instrument made by the Secretary of State ;

" prospectus " means any prospectus, notice, circular, advertisement, or other invitation, offering to the public for subscription or purchase any shares in or debentures of a company ;

" prospectus issued generally " means a prospectus issued to persons who are not existing members of the company or holders of its debentures ;

" recognised bank " means a company which is recognised as a bank for the purposes of the Banking Act 1979 ;   1979 c. 37.

" recognised stock exchange " means any body of persons which is for the time being a recognised stock exchange for the purposes of the Prevention of Fraud (Invest- 1958 c. 45. ments) Act 1958 ;

" the registrar of companies " and " the registrar " mean the registrar or other officer performing under this Act

PART XXVI
the duty of registration of companies in England and Wales or in Scotland, as the case may require;

" share " means share in the share capital of a company, and includes stock (except where a distinction between shares and stock is express or implied); and

" undistributable reserves " has the meaning given by section 264(3).

PART XXVII

FINAL PROVISIONS

Northern
Ireland.

745.—(1) Except where otherwise expressly provided, nothing in this Act (except provisions relating expressly to companies registered or incorporated in Northern Ireland or outside Great Britain) applies to or in relation to companies so registered or incorporated.

(2) Subject to any such provision, and to any express provision as to extent, this Act does not extend to Northern Ireland.

Commence-
ment.

746. Except as provided by section 243(6), this Act comes into force on 1st July 1985.

Citation.

747. This Act may be cited as the Companies Act 1985.

SCHEDULES

SCHEDULE 1

PARTICULARS OF DIRECTORS ETC. TO BE CONTAINED IN STATEMENT UNDER SECTION 10

Directors

1.—Subject as provided below, the statement under section 10(2) shall contain the following particulars with respect to each person named as director —

(a) in the case of an individual, his present Christian name and surname, any former Christian name or surname, his usual residential address, his nationality, his business occupation (if any), particulars of any other directorships held by him, or which have been held by him and, in the case of a company subject to section 293, the date of his birth ;

(b) in the case of a corporation, its corporate name and registered or principal office.

2.—(1) It is not necessary for the statement to contain particulars of a directorship—

(a) which has not been held by a director at any time during the 5 years preceding the date on which the statement is delivered to the registrar,

(b) which is held by a director in a company which—

(i) is dormant or grouped with the company delivering the statement, and

(ii) if he also held that directorship for any period during those 5 years, was for the whole of that period either dormant or so grouped,

(c) which was held by a director for any period during those 5 years in a company which for the whole of that period was either dormant or grouped with the company delivering the statement.

(2) For these purposes, " company " includes any body corporate incorporated in Great Britain ; and—

(a) section 252(5) applies as regards whether and when a company is or has been " dormant ", and

(b) a company is treated as being or having been at any time grouped with another company if at that time it is or was a company of which that other is or was a wholly-owned subsidiary, or if it is or was a wholly-owned subsidiary of the other or of another company of which that other is or was a wholly-owned subsidiary.

Secretaries

3.—(1) The statement shall contain the following particulars with respect to the person named as secretary or, where there are to be joint secretaries, with respect to each person named as one of them—

(a) in the case of an individual, his present Christian name and surname, any former Christian name or surname and his usual residential address,

Sch. 1

(*b*) in the case of a corporation or a Scottish firm, its corporate or firm name and registered or principal office.

(2) However, if all the partners in a firm are joint secretaries, the name and principal office of the firm may be stated instead of the particulars otherwise required by this paragraph.

Interpretation

4. In paragraphs 1 and 3 above—

(*a*) " Christian name " includes a forename,

(*b*) " surname ", in the case of a peer or a person usually known by a title different from his surname, means that title,

(*c*) the reference to a former Christian name or surname does not include—

(i) in the case of a peer or a person usually known by a British title different from his surname, the name by which he was known previous to the adoption of or succession to the title, or

(ii) in the case of any person, a former Christian name or surname where that name or surname was changed or disused before the person bearing the name attained the age of 18 or has been changed or disused for a period of not less than 20 years, or

(iii) in the case of a married woman, the name or surname by which she was known previous to the marriage.

Sections 23,
145, 146, 148.

SCHEDULE 2

Interpretation of References to " Beneficial Interest "

Residual interests under pension and employees' share schemes

1.—(1) Where shares in a company are held on trust for the purposes of a pension scheme or an employees' share scheme, there is to be disregarded any residual interest which has not vested in possession, being an interest of the company or, as respects—

section 23(4),
paragraph 60(2) of Schedule 4, or
paragraph 19(3) of Schedule 9,

of any subsidiary of the company.

(2) In this paragraph, " a residual interest " means a right of the company or subsidiary in question (" the residual beneficiary ") to receive any of the trust property in the event of—

(*a*) all the liabilities arising under the scheme having been satisfied or provided for, or

(*b*) the residual beneficiary ceasing to participate in the scheme, or

(*c*) the trust property at any time exceeding what is necessary for satisfying the liabilities arising or expected to arise under the scheme.

(3) In sub-paragraph (2), references to a right include a right dependent on the exercise of a discretion vested by the scheme in the trustee or any other person ; and references to liabilities arising under a scheme include liabilities that have resulted or may result from the exercise of any such discretion.

(4) For purposes of this paragraph, a residual interest vests in possession—

> (a) in a case within (a) of sub-paragraph (2), on the occurrence of the event there mentioned, whether or not the amount of the property receivable pursuant to the right mentioned in that sub-paragraph is then ascertained, and
>
> (b) in a case within (b) or (c) of that sub-paragraph, when the residual beneficiary becomes entitled to require the trustee to transfer to that beneficiary any of the property receivable pursuant to that right.

(5) As respects paragraph 60(2) of Schedule 4 and paragraph 19(3) of Schedule 9, sub-paragraph (1) has effect as if references to shares included debentures.

2.—(1) The following has effect as regards the operation of sections 23, 144, 145 and 146 to 149 in cases where a residual interest vests in possession.

(2) Where by virtue of the vesting in possession of a residual interest a subsidiary ceases to be exempt from section 23, that section does not prevent the subsidiary from continuing to be a member of its holding company ; but subject to subsection (4) of that section, the subsidiary has no right from the date of vesting to vote at meetings of the holding company or any class of its members.

(3) Where by virtue of paragraph 1 of this Schedule any shares are exempt from section 144 or 145 at the time when they are issued or acquired but the residual interest in question vests in possession before they are disposed of or fully paid up, those sections apply to the shares as if they had been issued or acquired on the date on which that interest vests in possession.

(4) Where by virtue of paragraph 1 any shares are exempt from sections 146 to 149 at the time when they are acquired but the residual interest in question vests in possession before they are disposed of, those sections apply to the shares as if they had been acquired on the date on which that interest vests in possession.

(5) The above sub-paragraphs apply irrespective of the date on which the residual interest vests or vested in possession ; but where the date on which it vested was before 26th July 1983 (the passing of the Companies (Beneficial Interests) Act 1983), they have effect as if the vesting had occurred on that date.

1983 c. 50.

Employer's charges and other rights of recovery

3.—(1) Where shares in a company are held on trust, there are to be disregarded—

> (a) if the trust is for the purposes of a pension scheme, any such rights as are mentioned in the following sub-paragraph, and

　　　　　　(*b*) if the trust is for the purposes of an employees' share scheme,
　　　　　　　　any such rights as are mentioned in (*a*) of the sub-paragraph,
being rights of the company or, as respects section 23(4), paragraph
60(2) of Schedule 4 or paragraph 19(3) of Schedule 9 of any subsidiary of the company.

　　(2) The rights referred to are—

　　　　(*a*) any charge or lien on, or set-off against, any benefit or other
　　　　　　right or interest under the scheme for the purpose of
　　　　　　enabling the employer or former employer of a member
　　　　　　of the scheme to obtain the discharge of a monetary obliga-
　　　　　　tion due to him from the member, and

　　　　(*b*) any right to receive from the trustee of the scheme, or as
　　　　　　trustee of the scheme to retain, an amount that can be
　　　　　　recovered or retained under section 47 of the Social Security
　　　　　　Pensions Act 1975 (deduction of premium from refund of
　　　　　　contributions) or otherwise as reimbursement or partial
　　　　　　reimbursement for any state scheme premium paid in con-
　　　　　　nection with the scheme under Part III of that Act.

　　(3) As respects paragraph 60(2) of Schedule 4 and paragraph 19(3)
of Schedule 9, sub-paragraph (1) has effect as if references to shares
included debentures.

Trustee's right to expenses, remuneration, indemnity, etc.

　　4.—(1) Where a company is a trustee (whether as personal representative or otherwise), there are to be disregarded any rights
which the company has in its capacity as trustee including, in particular, any right to recover its expenses or be remunerated out of the
trust property and any right to be indemnified out of that property for
any liability incurred by reason of any act or omission of the company in the performance of its duties as trustee.

　　(2) As respects section 23(4), paragraph 60(2) of Schedule 4 and
paragraph 19(3) of Schedule 9, sub-paragraph (1) has effect as if
references to a company included any body corporate which is a
subsidiary of a company.

Supplementary

　　5.—(1) The following applies for the interpretation of this Schedule.

　　(2) " Pension scheme " means any scheme for the provision of benefits consisting of or including relevant benefits for or in respect of
employees or former employees ; and " relevant benefits " means any
pension, lump sum, gratuity or other like benefit given or to be
given on retirement or on death or in anticipation of retirement or,
in connection with past service, after retirement or death.

　　(3) In sub-paragraph (2) of this paragraph, and in paragraph
3(2)(*a*), " employer " and " employee " are to be read as if a director
of a company were employed by it.

SCHEDULE 3

MANDATORY CONTENTS OF PROSPECTUS

PART I

MATTERS TO BE STATED

The company's proprietorship, management and its capital requirement

1.—(1) The prospectus must state—

(*a*) the number of founders or management or deferred shares (if any) and the nature and extent of the interest of the holders in the property and profits of the company ;

(*b*) the number of shares (if any) fixed by the company's articles as the qualification of a director, and any provision in the articles as to the remuneration of directors ; and

(*c*) the names, descriptions and addresses of the directors or proposed directors.

(2) As this paragraph applies for the purposes of section 72(3), sub-paragraph (1)(*b*) is to be read with the substitution for the reference to the company's articles of a reference to its constitution.

(3) Sub-paragraphs (1)(*b*) and (1)(*c*) do not apply in the case of a prospectus issued more than 2 years after the date at which the company is entitled to commence business.

2. Where shares are offered to the public for subscription, the prospectus must give particulars as to—

(*a*) the minimum amount which, in the opinion of the directors, must be raised by the issue of those shares in order to provide the sums (or, if any part of them is to be defrayed in any other manner, the balance of the sums) required to be provided in respect of each of the following—

(i) the purchase price of any property purchased or to be purchased which is to be defrayed in whole or in part out of the proceeds of the issue,

(ii) any preliminary expenses payable by the company, and any commission so payable to any person in consideration of his agreeing to subscribe for, or of his procuring or agreeing to procure subscriptions for, any shares in the company,

(iii) the repayment of any money borrowed by the company in respect of any of the foregoing matters,

(iv) working capital, and

(*b*) the amounts to be provided in respect of the matters above mentioned otherwise than out of the proceeds of the issue and the sources out of which those amounts are to be provided.

Details relating to the offer

3.—(1) The prospectus must state—

    (*a*) the time of the opening of the subscription lists, and

    (*b*) the amount payable on application and allotment on each share (including the amount, if any, payable by way of premium).

(2) In the case of a second or subsequent offer of shares, there must also be stated the amount offered for subscription on each previous allotment made within the 2 preceding years, the amount actually allotted and the amount (if any) paid on the shares so allotted, including the amount (if any) paid by way of premium.

4.—(1) There must be stated the number, description and amount of any shares in or debentures of the company which any person has, or is entitled to be given, an option to subscribe for.

(2) The following particulars of the option must be given—

    (*a*) the period during which it is exercisable,

    (*b*) the price to be paid for shares or debentures subscribed for under it,

    (*c*) the consideration (if any) given or to be given for it or the right to it,

    (*d*) the names and addresses of the persons to whom it or the right to it was given or, if given to existing shareholders or debenture holders as such, the relevant shares or debentures.

(3) References in this paragraph to subscribing for shares or debentures include acquiring them from a person to whom they have been allotted or agreed to be allotted with a view to his offering them for sale.

5. The prospectus must state the number and amount of shares and debentures which within the 2 preceding years have been issued, or agreed to be issued, as fully or partly paid up otherwise than in cash ; and—

    (*a*) in the latter case the extent to which they are so paid up, and

    (*b*) in either case the consideration for which those shares or debentures have been issued or are proposed or intended to be issued.

Property acquired or to be acquired by the company

6.—(1) For purposes of the following two paragraphs, " relevant property " is property purchased or acquired by the company, or proposed so to be purchased or acquired,

    (*a*) which is to be paid for wholly or partly out of the proceeds of the issue offered for subscription by the prospectus, or

    (*b*) the purchase or acquisition of which has not been completed at the date of the issue of the prospectus.

(2) But those two paragraphs do not apply to property—

(*a*) the contract for whose purchase or acquisition was entered into in the ordinary course of the company's business, the contract not being made in contemplation of the issue nor the issue in consequence of the contract, or

(*b*) as respects which the amount of the purchase money is not material.

7. As respects any relevant property, the prospectus must state—

(*a*) the names and addresses of the vendors,

(*b*) the amount payable in cash, shares or debentures to the vendor and, where there is more than one separate vendor, or the company is a sub-purchaser, the amount so payable to each vendor,

(*c*) short particulars of any transaction relating to the property completed within the 2 preceding years in which any vendor of the property to the company or any person who is, or was at the time of the transaction, a promoter or a director or proposed director of the company had any interest direct or indirect.

8. There must be stated the amount (if any) paid or payable as purchase money in cash, shares or debentures for any relevant property, specifying the amount (if any) payable for goodwill.

9.—(1) The following applies for the interpretation of paragraphs 6, 7 and 8.

(2) Every person is deemed a vendor who has entered into any contract (absolute or conditional) for the sale or purchase, or for any option of purchase, of any property to be acquired by the company, in any case where—

(*a*) the purchase money is not fully paid at the date of the issue of the prospectus,

(*b*) the purchase money is to be paid or satisfied wholly or in part out of the proceeds of the issue offered for subscription by the prospectus,

(*c*) the contract depends for its validity or fulfilment on the result of that issue.

(3) Where any property to be acquired by the company is to be taken on lease, paragraphs 6, 7 and 8 apply as if " vendor " included the lessor, " purchase money " included the consideration for the lease, and " sub-purchaser " included a sub-lessee.

(4) For purposes of paragraph 7, where the vendors or any of them are a firm, the members of the firm are not to be treated as separate vendors.

Commissions, preliminary expenses, etc.

10.—(1) The prospectus must state—

(a) the amount (if any) paid within the 2 preceding years, or payable, as commission (but not including commission to sub-underwriters) for subscribing or agreeing to subscribe, or procuring or agreeing to procure subscriptions, for any shares in or debentures of the company, or the rate of any such commission,

(b) the amount or estimated amount of any preliminary expenses and the persons by whom any of those expenses have been paid or are payable, and the amount or estimated amount of the expenses of the issue and the persons by whom any of those expenses have been paid or are payable,

(c) any amount or benefit paid or given within the 2 preceding years or intended to be paid or given to any promoter, and the consideration for the payment or the giving of the benefit.

(2) Sub-paragraph (1)(b) above, so far as it relates to preliminary expenses, does not apply in the case of a prospectus issued more than 2 years after the date at which the company is entitled to commence business.

Contracts

11.—(1) The prospectus must give the dates of, parties to and general nature of every material contract.

(2) This does not apply to a contract entered into in the ordinary course of the business carried on or intended to be carried on by the company, or a contract entered into more than 2 years before the date of issue of the prospectus.

Auditors

12. The prospectus must state the names and addresses of the company's auditors (if any).

Interests of directors

13.—(1) The prospectus must give full particulars of—

(a) the nature and extent of the interest (if any) of every director in the promotion of, or in the property proposed to be acquired by, the company, or

(b) where the interest of such a director consists in being a partner in a firm, the nature and extent of the interest of the firm.

(2) With the particulars under sub-paragraph (1)(b) must be provided a statement of all sums paid or agreed to be paid to the director or the firm in cash or shares or otherwise by any person either to induce him to become, or to qualify him as, a director, or otherwise for services rendered by him or the firm in connection with the promotion or formation of the company.

(3) This paragraph does not apply in the case of a prospectus issued more than 2 years after the date at which the company is entitled to commence business.

Other matters

14. If the prospectus invites the public to subscribe for shares in the company and the company's share capital is divided into different classes of shares, the prospectus must state the right of voting at meetings of the company conferred by, and the rights in respect of capital and dividends attached to, the several classes of shares respectively.

15. In the case of a company which has been carrying on business, or of a business which has been carried on for less than 3 years, the prospectus must state the length of time during which the business of the company (or the business to be acquired, as the case may be) has been carried on.

PART II

AUDITORS' AND ACCOUNTANTS' REPORTS TO BE SET OUT IN PROSPECTUS

Auditors' report

16.—(1) The prospectus shall set out a report by the company's auditors with respect to—

    (*a*) profits and losses and assets and liabilities, in accordance with sub-paragraphs (2) and (3) below, as the case requires, and

    (*b*) the rates of the dividends (if any) paid by the company in respect of each class of shares in respect of each of the 5 financial years immediately preceding the issue of the prospectus, giving particulars of each such class of shares on which such dividends have been paid and particulars of the cases in which no dividends have been paid in respect of any class of shares in respect of any of those years.

If no accounts have been made up in respect of any part of the 5 years ending on a date 3 months before the issue of the prospectus, the report shall contain a statement of that fact.

(2) If the company has no subsidiaries, the report shall—

    (*a*) deal with profits and losses of the company in respect of each of the 5 financial years immediately preceding the issue of the prospectus, and

    (*b*) deal with the assets and liabilities of the company at the last date to which the company's accounts were made up.

(3) If the company has subsidiaries, the report shall—

    (*a*) deal separately with the company's profits or losses as provided by sub-paragraph (2), and in addition deal either—

        (i) as a whole with the combined profits or losses

of its subsidiaries, so far as they concern members of the company, or

    (ii) individually with the profits or losses of each subsidiary, so far as they concern members of the company,

or, instead of dealing separately with the company's profits or losses, deal as a whole with the profits or losses of the company and (so far as they concern members of the company) with the combined profits and losses of its subsidiaries ; and

    (*b*) deal separately with the company's assets and liabilities as provided by sub-paragraph (2), and in addition deal either—

        (i) as a whole with the combined assets and liabilities of its subsidiaries, with or without the company's assets and liabilities, or

        (ii) individually with the assets and liabilities of each subsidiary,

indicating, as respects the assets and liabilities of the subsidiaries, the allowance to be made for persons other than members of the company.

Accountants' reports

17. If the proceeds of the issue of the shares or debentures are to be applied directly or indirectly in the purchase of any business, or any part of the proceeds of the issue is to be so applied, there shall be set out in the prospectus a report made by accountants upon—

    (*a*) the profits or losses of the business in respect of each of the 5 financial years immediately preceding the issue of the prospectus, and

    (*b*) the assets and liabilities of the business at the last date to which the accounts of the business were made up.

18.—(1) The following applies if—

    (*a*) the proceeds of the issue are to be applied directly or indirectly in any manner resulting in the acquisition by the company of shares in any other body corporate, or any part of the proceeds is to be so applied, and

    (*b*) by reason of that acquisition or anything to be done in consequence of or in connection with it, that body corporate will become a subsidiary of the company.

(2) There shall be set out in the prospectus a report made by accountants upon—

    (*a*) the profits or losses of the other body corporate in respect of each of the 5 financial years immediately preceding the issue of the prospectus, and (*b*) the assets and liabilities of the other body corporate at the last date to which its accounts were made up.

(3) The accountants' report required by this paragraph shall—

(*a*) indicate how the profits or losses of the other body corporate dealt with by the report would, in respect of the shares to be acquired, have concerned members of the company and what allowance would have fallen to be made, in relation to assets and liabilities so dealt with, for holders of other shares, if the company had at all material times held the shares to be acquired, and

(*b*) where the other body corporate has subsidiaries, deal with the profits or losses and the assets and liabilities of the body corporate and its subsidiaries in the manner provided by paragraph 16(3) above in relation to the company and its subsidiaries.

Provisions interpreting preceding paragraphs, and modifying them in certain cases

19. If in the case of a company which has been carrying on business, or of a business which has been carried on for less than 5 years, the accounts of the company or business have only been made up in respect of 4 years, 3 years, 2 years or one year, the preceding paragraphs of this Part have effect as if references to 4 years, 3 years, 2 years or one year (as the case may be) were substituted for references to 5 years.

20. The expression " financial year " in this Part means the year in respect of which the accounts of the company or of the business (as the case may be) are made up ; and where by reason of any alteration of the date on which the financial year of the company or business terminates the accounts have been made up for a period greater or less than one year, that greater or less period is for purposes of this Part deemed to be a financial year.

21. Any report required by this Part shall either indicate by way of note any adjustments as respects the figures of any profits or losses or assets and liabilities dealt with by the report which appear to the persons making the report necessary, or shall make those adjustments and indicate that adjustments have been made.

22.—(1) A report required by paragraph 17 or 18 shall be made by accountants qualified under this Act for appointment as auditors of a company.

(2) Such a report shall not be made by any accountant who is an officer or servant, or a partner of or in the employment of an officer or servant, of the company or the company's subsidiary or holding company or of a subsidiary of the company's holding company.

In this paragraph, " officer " includes a proposed director, but not an auditor.

(3) The accountants making any report required for purposes of paragraph 17 or 18 shall be named in the prospectus.

c. 6   *Companies Act 1985*

SCHEDULE 4

FORM AND CONTENT OF COMPANY ACCOUNTS

PART I

GENERAL RULES AND FORMATS

SECTION A

GENERAL RULES

1.—(1) Subject to the following provisions of this Schedule—

(*a*) every balance sheet of a company shall show the items listed in either of the balance sheet formats set out below in section B of this Part ; and

(*b*) every profit and loss account of a company shall show the items listed in any one of the profit and loss account formats so set out ;

in either case in the order and under the headings and sub-headings given in the format adopted.

(2) Sub-paragraph (1) above is not to be read as requiring the heading or sub-heading for any item to be distinguished by any letter or number assigned to that item in the format adopted.

2.—(1) Where in accordance with paragraph 1 a company's balance sheet or profit and loss account for any financial year has been prepared by reference to one of the formats set out in section B below, the directors of the company shall adopt the same format in preparing the accounts for subsequent financial years of the company unless in their opinion there are special reasons for a change.

(2) Particulars of any change in the format adopted in preparing a company's balance sheet or profit and loss account in accordance with paragraph 1 shall be disclosed, and the reasons for the change shall be explained, in a note to the accounts in which the new format is first adopted.

3.—(1) Any item required in accordance with paragraph 1 to be shown in a company's balance sheet or profit and loss account may be shown in greater detail than required by the format adopted.

(2) A company's balance sheet or profit and loss account may include an item representing or covering the amount of any asset or liability, income or expenditure not otherwise covered by any of the items listed in the format adopted, but the following shall not be treated as assets in any company's balance sheet—

(*a*) preliminary expenses ;

(*b*) expenses of and commission on any issue of shares or debentures ; and

(*c*) costs of research.

(3) In preparing a company's balance sheet or profit and loss account the directors of the company shall adapt the arrangement and headings and sub-headings otherwise required by paragraph 1 in respect of items to which an Arabic number is assigned in the format adopted, in any case where the special nature of the company's business requires such adaptation.

(4) Items to which Arabic numbers are assigned in any of the formats set out in section B below may be combined in a company's accounts for any financial year if either—

(*a*) their individual amounts are not material to assessing the state of affairs or profit or loss of the company for that year ; or

(*b*) the combination facilitates that assessment ;

but in a case within paragraph (*b*) the individual amounts of any items so combined shall be disclosed in a note to the accounts.

(5) Subject to paragraph 4(3) below, a heading or sub-heading corresponding to an item listed in the format adopted in preparing a company's balance sheet or profit and loss account shall not be included if there is no amount to be shown for that item in respect of the financial year to which the balance sheet or profit and loss account relates.

(6) Every profit and loss account of a company shall show the amount of the company's profit or loss on ordinary activities before taxation.

(7) Every profit and loss account of a company shall show separately as additional items—

(*a*) any amount set aside or proposed to be set aside to, or withdrawn or proposed to be withdrawn from, reserves ; and

(*b*) the aggregate amount of any dividends paid and proposed.

4.—(1) In respect of every item shown in a company's balance sheet or profit and loss account the corresponding amount for the financial year immediately preceding that to which the balance sheet or profit and loss account relates shall also be shown.

(2) Where that corresponding amount is not comparable with the amount to be shown for the item in question in respect of the financial year to which the balance sheet or profit and loss account relates, the former amount shall be adjusted and particulars of the adjustment and the reasons for it shall be disclosed in a note to the accounts.

(3) Paragraph 3(5) does not apply in any case where an amount can be shown for the item in question in respect of the financial year immediately preceding that to which the balance sheet or profit and loss account relates, and that amount shall be shown under the heading or sub-heading required by paragraph 1 for that item.

5. Amounts in respect of items representing assets or income may not be set off against amounts in respect of items representing liabilities or expenditure (as the case may be), or vice versa.

Section B

The Required Formats for Accounts

Preliminary

6. References in this Part of this Schedule to the items listed in any of the formats set out below are to those items read together with any of the notes following the formats which apply to any of those items, and the requirement imposed by paragraph 1 to show the items listed in any such format in the order adopted in the format is subject to any provision in those notes for alternative positions for any particular items.

7. A number in brackets following any item in any of the formats set out below is a reference to the note of that number in the notes following the formats.

8. In the notes following the formats—

(*a*) the heading of each note gives the required heading or sub-heading for the item to which it applies and a reference to any letters and numbers assigned to that item in the formats set out below (taking a reference in the case of Format 2 of the balance sheet formats to the item listed under " Assets " or under " Liabilities " as the case may require) ; and

(*b*) references to a numbered format are to the balance sheet format or (as the case may require) to the profit and loss account format of that number set out below.

Balance Sheet Formats

Format 1

A. Called up share capital not paid (*1*)

B. Fixed assets
    I   Intangible assets
        1. Development costs
        2. Concessions, patents, licences, trade marks and similar rights and assets (*2*)
        3. Goodwill (*3*)
        4. Payments on account

    II Tangible assets
        1. Land and buildings
        2. Plant and machinery
        3. Fixtures, fittings, tools and equipment
        4. Payments on account and assets in course of construction

    III Investments
        1. Shares in group companies
        2. Loans to group companies
        3. Shares in related companies
        4. Loans to related companies
        5. Other investments other than loans
        6. Other loans
        7. Own shares (*4*)

C. Current assets
    I   Stocks
        1. Raw materials and consumables
        2. Work in progress
        3. Finished goods and goods for resale
        4. Payments on account

    II Debtors (*5*)
        1. Trade debtors
        2. Amounts owed by group companies
        3. Amounts owed by related companies
        4. Other debtors
        5. Called up share capital not paid (*1*)
        6. Prepayments and accrued income (*6*)

    III Investments
        1. Shares in group companies
        2. Own shares (*4*)
        3. Other investments

    IV Cash at bank and in hand

D. Prepayments and accrued income (*6*).

E. Creditors: amounts falling due within one year
        1. Debenture loans (*7*)
        2. Bank loans and overdrafts
        3. Payments received on account (*8*)

4. Trade creditors
5. Bills of exchange payable
6. Amounts owed to group companies
7. Amounts owed to related companies
8. Other creditors including taxation and social security (*9*)
9. Accruals and deferred income (*10*)

F. Net current assets (liabilities) (*11*)

G. Total assets less current liabilities

H.   Creditors: amounts falling due after more than one year
1. Debenture loans (*7*)
2. Bank loans and overdrafts
3. Payments received on account (*8*)
4. Trade creditors
5. Bills of exchange payable
6. Amounts owed to group companies
7. Amounts owed to related companies
8. Other creditors including taxation and social security (*9*)
9. Accruals and deferred income (*10*)

I. Provisions for liabilities and charges
1. Pensions and similar obligations
2. Taxation, including deferred taxation
3. Other provisions

J. Accruals and deferred income (*10*)

K. Capital and reserves

I   Called up share capital (*12*)

II   Share premium account

III   Revaluation reserve

IV   Other reserves
1. Capital redemption reserve
2. Reserve for own shares
3. Reserves provided for by the articles of association
4. Other reserves

V   Profit and loss account

Balance Sheet Formats

Format 2

ASSETS

  A. Called up share capital not paid (*1*)

  B. Fixed assets

    I Intangible assets
      1. Development costs
      2. Concessions, patents, licences, trade marks and similar rights and assets (*2*)
      3. Goodwill (*3*)
      4. Payments on account

    II Tangible assets
      1. Land and buildings
      2. Plant and machinery
      3. Fixtures, fittings, tools and equipment
      4. Payments on account and assets in course of construction

    III Investments
      1. Shares in group companies
      2. Loans to group companies
      3. Shares in related companies
      4. Loans to related companies
      5. Other investments other than loans
      6. Other loans
      7. Own shares (*4*)

  C. Current assets

    I Stocks
      1. Raw materials and consumables
      2. Work in progress
      3. Finished goods and goods for resale
      4. Payments on account

    II Debtors (*5*)
      1. Trade debtors
      2. Amounts owed by group companies
      3. Amounts owed by related companies
      4. Other debtors
      5. Called up share capital not paid (*1*)
      6. Prepayments and accrued income (*6*)

    III Investments
      1. Shares in group companies
      2. Own shares (*4*)
      3. Other investments

    IV Cash at bank and in hand

  D. Prepayments and accrued income (*6*)

LIABILITIES

A. Capital and reserves

    I   Called up share capital (*12*)

    II   Share premium account

    III Revaluation reserve

    IV Other reserves
        1. Capital redemption reserve
        2. Reserve for own shares
        3. Reserves provided for by the articles of association
        4. Other reserves

    V   Profit and loss account

B. Provisions for liabilities and charges
        1. Pensions and similar obligations
        2. Taxation including deferred taxation
        3. Other provisions

C. Creditors (*13*)
        1. Debenture loans (*7*)
        2. Bank loans and overdrafts
        3. Payments received on account (*8*)
        4. Trade creditors
        5. Bills of exchange payable
        6. Amounts owed to group companies
        7. Amounts owed to related companies
        8. Other creditors including taxation and social security (*9*)
        9. Accruals and deferred income (*10*)

D. Accruals and deferred income (*10*)

Notes on the balance sheet formats

(*1*) *Called up share capital not paid*

(Formats 1 and 2, items A and C.II.5.)

This item may be shown in either of the two positions given in Formats 1 and 2.

(*2*) *Concessions, patents, licences, trade marks and similar rights and assets*

(Formats 1 and 2, item B.I.2.)

Amounts in respect of assets shall only be included in a company's balance sheet under this item if either—

(*a*) the assets were acquired for valuable consideration and are not required to be shown under goodwill ; or

(*b*) the assets in question were created by the company itself.

(*3*) *Goodwill*

(Formats 1 and 2, item B.I.3.)

Amounts representing goodwill shall only be included to the extent that the goodwill was acquired for valuable consideration.

(*4*) *Own shares*

(Formats 1 and 2, items B.III.7 and C.III.2.)

The nominal value of the shares held shall be shown separately.

(*5*) *Debtors*

(Formats 1 and 2, items C.II.1 to 6.)

The amount falling due after more than one year shall be shown separately for each item included under debtors.

(*6*) *Prepayments and accrued income*

(Formats 1 and 2, items C.II.6 and D.)

This item may be shown in either of the two positions given in Formats 1 and 2.

(*7*) *Debenture loans*

(Format 1, items E.1 and H.1 and Format 2, item C.1.)

The amount of any convertible loans shall be shown separately.

(*8*) *Payments received on account*

(Format 1, items E.3 and H.3 and Format 2, item C.3.)

Payments received on account of orders shall be shown for each of these items in so far as they are not shown as deductions from stocks.

S

(9) Other creditors including taxation and social security

(Format 1, items E.8 and H.8 and Format 2, item C.8.)

> The amount for creditors in respect of taxation and social security shall be shown separately from the amount for other creditors.

(10) Accruals and deferred income

(Format 1, items E.9, H.9 and J and Format 2, items C.9 and D.)

> The two positions given for this item in Format 1 at E.9 and H.9 are an alternative to the position at J, but if the item is not shown in a position corresponding to that at J it may be shown in either or both of the other two positions (as the case may require).

> The two positions given for this item in Format 2 are alternatives.

(11) Net current assets (liabilities)

(Format 1, item F.)

> In determining the amount to be shown for this item any amounts shown under " prepayments and accrued income " shall be taken into account wherever shown.

(12) Called up share capital

(Format 1, item K.I and Format 2, item A.I.)

> The amount of allotted share capital and the amount of called up share capital which has been paid up shall be shown separately.

(13) Creditors

(Format 2, items C.1 to 9.)

> Amounts falling due within one year and after one year shall be shown separately for each of these items and their aggregate shall be shown separately for all of these items.

Profit and loss account formats

Format 1

(see note (*17*) below)

1. Turnover
2. Cost of sales (*14*)
3. Gross profit or loss
4. Distribution costs (*14*)
5. Administrative expenses (*14*)
6. Other operating income
7. Income from shares in group companies
8. Income from shares in related companies
9. Income from other fixed asset investments (*15*)
10. Other interest receivable and similar income (*15*)
11. Amounts written off investments
12. Interest payable and similar charges (*16*)
13. Tax on profit or loss on ordinary activities
14. Profit or loss on ordinary activities after taxation
15. Extraordinary income
16. Extraordinary charges
17. Extraordinary profit or loss
18. Tax on extraordinary profit or loss
19. Other taxes not shown under the above items
20. Profit or loss for the financial year

Profit and loss account formats

Format 2

1. Turnover
2. Change in stocks of finished goods and in work in progress
3. Own work capitalised
4. Other operating income
5. (*a*) Raw materials and consumables
   (*b*) Other external charges
6. Staff costs:
   (*a*) wages and salaries
   (*b*) social security costs
   (*c*) other pension costs
7. (*a*) Depreciation and other amounts written off tangible and intangible fixed assets
   (*b*) Exceptional amounts written off current assets
8. Other operating charges
9. Income from shares in group companies
10. Income from shares in related companies
11. Income from other fixed asset investments (*15*)
12. Other interest receivable and similar income (*15*)
13. Amounts written off investments
14. Interest payable and similar charges (*16*)
15. Tax on profit or loss on ordinary activities
16. Profit or loss on ordinary activities after taxation
17. Extraordinary income
18. Extraordinary charges
19. Extraordinary profit or loss
20. Tax on extraordinary profit or loss
21. Other taxes not shown under the above items
22. Profit or loss for the financial year

Profit and loss account formats

Format 3

(see note (*17*) below)

A. Charges
1. Cost of sales (*14*)
2. Distribution costs (*14*)
3. Administrative expenses (*14*)
4. Amounts written off investments
5. Interest payable and similar charges (*16*)
6. Tax on profit or loss on ordinary activities
7. Profit or loss on ordinary activities after taxation
8. Extraordinary charges
9. Tax on extraordinary profit or loss
10. Other taxes not shown under the above items
11. Profit or loss for the financial year

B. Income
1. Turnover
2. Other operating income
3. Income from shares in group companies
4. Income from shares in related companies
5. Income from other fixed asset investments (*15*)
6. Other interest receivable and similar income (*15*)
7. Profit or loss on ordinary activities after taxation
8. Extraordinary income
9. Profit or loss for the financial year

Profit and loss account formats

Format 4

A. Charges

1. Reduction in stocks of finished goods and in work in progress
2. (*a*) Raw materials and consumables
   (*b*) Other external charges
3. Staff costs:
   (*a*) wages and salaries
   (*b*) social security costs
   (*c*) other pension costs
4. (*a*) Depreciation and other amounts written off tangible and intangible fixed assets
   (*b*) Exceptional amounts written off current assets
5. Other operating charges
6. Amounts written off investments
7. Interest payable and similar charges (*16*)
8. Tax on profit or loss on ordinary activities
9. Profit or loss on ordinary activities after taxation
10. Extraordinary charges
11. Tax on extraordinary profit or loss
12. Other taxes not shown under the above items
13. Profit or loss for the financial year

B. Income

1. Turnover
2. Increase in stocks of finished goods and in work in progress
3. Own work capitalised
4. Other operating income
5. Income from shares in group companies
6. Income from shares in related companies
7. Income from other fixed asset investments (*15*)
8. Other interest receivable and similar income (*15*)
9. Profit or loss on ordinary activities after taxation
10. Extraordinary income
11. Profit or loss for the financial year

Notes on the profit and loss account formats

(14) Cost of sales: distribution costs: administrative expenses

(Format 1, items 2, 4 and 5 and Format 3, items A.1, 2 and 3.)

These items shall be stated after taking into account any necessary provisions for depreciation or diminution in value of assets.

(15) Income from other fixed asset investments: other interest receivable and similar income

(Format 1, items 9 and 10: Format 2, items 11 and 12: Format 3, items B.5 and 6: Format 4, items B.7 and 8.)

Income and interest derived from group companies shall be shown separately from income and interest derived from other sources.

(16) Interest payable and similar charges

(Format 1, item 12: Format 2, item 14: Format 3, item A.5: Format 4, item A.7.)

The amount payable to group companies shall be shown separately.

(17) Formats 1 and 3

The amount of any provisions for depreciation and diminution in value of tangible and intangible fixed assets falling to be shown under items 7(*a*) and A.4(*a*) respectively in Formats 2 and 4 shall be disclosed in a note to the accounts in any case where the profit and loss account is prepared by reference to Format 1 or Format 3.

PART II

ACCOUNTING PRINCIPLES AND RULES

SECTION A

ACCOUNTING PRINCIPLES

Preliminary

9. Subject to paragraph 15 below, the amounts to be included in respect of all items shown in a company's accounts shall be determined in accordance with the principles set out in paragraphs 10 to 14.

Accounting principles

10. The company shall be presumed to be carrying on business as a going concern.

11. Accounting policies shall be applied consistently from one financial year to the next.

12. The amount of any item shall be determined on a prudent basis, and in particular—

    (*a*) only profits realised at the balance sheet date shall be included in the profit and loss account ; and

    (*b*) all liabilities and losses which have arisen or are likely to arise in respect of the financial year to which the accounts relate or a previous financial year shall be taken into account, including those which only become apparent between the balance sheet date and the date on which it is signed on behalf of the board of directors in pursuance of section 238 of this Act.

13. All income and charges relating to the financial year to which the accounts relate shall be taken into account, without regard to the date of receipt or payment.

14. In determining the aggregate amount of any item the amount of each individual asset or liability that falls to be taken into account shall be determined separately.

Departure from the accounting principles

15. If it appears to the directors of a company that there are special reasons for departing from any of the principles stated above in preparing the company's accounts in respect of any financial year they may do so, but particulars of the departure, the reasons for it and its effect shall be given in a note to the accounts.

SECTION B

HISTORICAL COST ACCOUNTING RULES

Preliminary

16. Subject to section C of this Part of this Schedule, the amounts to be included in respect of all items shown in a company's accounts shall be determined in accordance with the rules set out in paragraphs 17 to 28.

Fixed assets

General rules

17. Subject to any provision for depreciation or diminution in value made in accordance with paragraph 18 or 19 the amount to be included in respect of any fixed asset shall be its purchase price or production cost.

18. In the case of any fixed asset which has a limited useful economic life, the amount of—

(*a*) its purchase price or production cost ; or

(*b*) where it is estimated that any such asset will have a residual value at the end of the period of its useful economic life, its purchase price or production cost less that estimated residual value ;

shall be reduced by provisions for depreciation calculated to write off that amount systematically over the period of the asset's useful economic life.

19.—(1) Where a fixed asset investment of a description falling to be included under item B.III of either of the balance sheet formats set out in Part I of this Schedule has diminished in value provisions for diminution in value may be made in respect of it and the amount to be included in respect of it may be reduced accordingly ; and any such provisions which are not shown in the profit and loss account shall be disclosed (either separately or in aggregate) in a note to the accounts.

(2) Provisions for diminution in value shall be made in respect of any fixed asset which has diminished in value if the reduction in its value is expected to be permanent (whether its useful economic life is limited or not), and the amount to be included in respect of it shall be reduced accordingly ; and any such provisions which are not shown in the profit and loss account shall be disclosed (either separately or in aggregate) in a note to the accounts.

(3) Where the reasons for which any provision was made in accordance with sub-paragraph (1) or (2) have ceased to apply to any extent, that provision shall be written back to the extent that it is no longer necessary ; and any amounts written back in accordance with this sub-paragraph which are not shown in the profit and loss account shall be disclosed (either separately or in aggregate) in a note to the accounts.

Rules for determining particular fixed asset items

20.—(1) Notwithstanding that an item in respect of " development costs " is included under " fixed assets " in the balance sheet formats set out in Part I of this Schedule, an amount may only be included in a company's balance sheet in respect of development costs in special circumstances.

(2) If any amount is included in a company's balance sheet in respect of development costs the following information shall be given in a note to the accounts—

(a) the period over which the amount of those costs originally capitalised is being or is to be written off ; and

(b) the reasons for capitalising the development costs in question.

21.—(1) The application of paragraphs 17 to 19 in relation to goodwill (in any case where goodwill is treated as an asset) is subject to the following provisions of this paragraph.

(2) Subject to sub-paragraph (3) below, the amount of the consideration for any goodwill acquired by a company shall be reduced by provisions for depreciation calculated to write off that amount systematically over a period chosen by the directors of the company.

(3) The period chosen shall not exceed the useful economic life of the goodwill in question.

(4) In any case where any goodwill acquired by a company is shown or included as an asset in the company's balance sheet the period chosen for writing off the consideration for that goodwill and the reasons for choosing that period shall be disclosed in a note to the accounts.

Current assets

22. Subject to paragraph 23, the amount to be included in respect of any current asset shall be its purchase price or production cost.

23.—(1) If the net realisable value of any current asset is lower than its purchase price or production cost the amount to be included in respect of that asset shall be the net realisable value.

(2) Where the reasons for which any provision for diminution in value was made in accordance with sub-paragraph (1) have ceased to apply to any extent, that provision shall be written back to the extent that it is no longer necessary.

Miscellaneous and supplementary provisions

Excess of money owed over value received as an asset item

24.—(1) Where the amount repayable on any debt owed by a company is greater than the value of the consideration received in the transaction giving rise to the debt, the amount of the difference may be treated as an asset.

(2) Where any such amount is so treated—

(a) it shall be written off by reasonable amounts each year and must be completely written off before repayment of the debt ; and

(b) if the current amount is not shown as a separate item in the company's balance sheet it must be disclosed in a note to the accounts.

Assets included at a fixed amount

25.—(1) Subject to the following sub-paragraph, assets which fall to be included—

    (a) amongst the fixed assets of a company under the item " tangible assets " ; or

    (b) amongst the current assets of a company under the item " raw materials and consumables " ;

may be included at a fixed quantity and value.

(2) Sub-paragraph (1) applies to assets of a kind which are constantly being replaced, where—

    (a) their overall value is not material to assessing the company's state of affairs ; and

    (b) their quantity, value and composition are not subject to material variation.

Determination of purchase price or production cost

26.—(1) The purchase price of an asset shall be determined by adding to the actual price paid any expenses incidental to its acquisition.

(2) The production cost of an asset shall be determined by adding to the purchase price of the raw materials and consumables used the amount of the costs incurred by the company which are directly attributable to the production of that asset.

(3) In addition, there may be included in the production cost of an asset—

    (a) a reasonable proportion of the costs incurred by the company which are only indirectly attributable to the production of that asset, but only to the extent that they relate to the period of production ; and

    (b) interest on capital borrowed to finance the production of that asset, to the extent that it accrues in respect of the period of production ;

provided, however, in a case within paragraph (b) above, that the inclusion of the interest in determining the cost of that asset and the amount of the interest so included is disclosed in a note to the accounts.

(4) In the case of current assets distribution costs may not be included in production costs.

27.—(1) Subject to the qualification mentioned below, the purchase price or production cost of—

    (a) any assets which fall to be included under any item shown in a company's balance sheet under the general item " stocks " ; and

    (b) any assets which are fungible assets (including investments) ;

may be determined by the application of any of the methods mentioned in sub-paragraph (2) below in relation to any such assets of the same class.

The method chosen must be one which appears to the directors to be appropriate in the circumstances of the company.

(2) Those methods are—

   (*a*) the method known as "first in, first out" (FIFO) ;

   (*b*) the method known as "last in, first out" (LIFO) ;

   (*c*) a weighted average price ; and

   (*d*) any other method similar to any of the methods mentioned above.

(3) Where in the case of any company—

   (*a*) the purchase price or production cost of assets falling to be included under any item shown in the company's balance sheet has been determined by the application of any method permitted by this paragraph ; and

   (*b*) the amount shown in respect of that item differs materially from the relevant alternative amount given below in this paragraph ;

the amount of that difference shall be disclosed in a note to the accounts.

(4) Subject to sub-paragraph (5) below, for the purposes of sub-paragraph (3)(*b*) above, the relevant alternative amount, in relation to any item shown in a company's balance sheet, is the amount which would have been shown in respect of that item if assets of any class included under that item at an amount determined by any method permitted by this paragraph had instead been included at their replacement cost as at the balance sheet date.

(5) The relevant alternative amount may be determined by reference to the most recent actual purchase price or production cost before the balance sheet date of assets of any class included under the item in question instead of by reference to their replacement cost as at that date, but only if the former appears to the directors of the company to constitute the more appropriate standard of comparison in the case of assets of that class.

(6) For the purposes of this paragraph, assets of any description shall be regarded as fungible if assets of that description are substantially indistinguishable one from another.

Substitution of original stated amount where price or cost unknown

28. Where there is no record of the purchase price or production cost of any asset of a company or of any price, expenses or costs relevant for determining its purchase price or production cost in accordance with paragraph 26, or any such record cannot be obtained without unreasonable expense or delay, its purchase price or production cost shall be taken for the purposes of paragraphs 17 to 23 to be the value ascribed to it in the earliest available record of its value made on or after its acquisition or production by the company.

SECTION C

ALTERNATIVE ACCOUNTING RULES

Preliminary

29.—(1) The rules set out in section B are referred to below in this Schedule as the historical cost accounting rules.

(2) Those rules, with the omission of paragraphs 16, 21 and 25 to 28, are referred to below in this Part of this Schedule as the depreciation rules ; and references below in this Schedule to the historical cost accounting rules do not include the depreciation rules as they apply by virtue of paragraph 32.

30. Subject to paragraphs 32 to 34, the amounts to be included in respect of assets of any description mentioned in paragraph 31 may be determined on any basis so mentioned.

Alternative accounting rules

31.—(1) Intangible fixed assets, other than goodwill, may be included at their current cost.

(2) Tangible fixed assets may be included at a market value determined as at the date of their last valuation or at their current cost.

(3) Investments of any description falling to be included under item B.III of either of the balance sheet formats set out in Part I of this Schedule may be included either—

(a) at a market value determined as at the date of their last valuation ; or

(b) at a value determined on any basis which appears to the directors to be appropriate in the circumstances of the company ;

but in the latter case particulars of the method of valuation adopted and of the reasons for adopting it shall be disclosed in a note to the accounts.

(4) Investments of any description falling to be included under item C.III of either of the balance sheet formats set out in Part 1 of this Schedule may be included at their current cost.

(5) Stocks may be included at their current cost.

Application of the depreciation rules

32.—(1) Where the value of any asset of a company is determined on any basis mentioned in paragraph 31, that value shall be, or (as the case may require) be the starting point for determining, the amount to be included in respect of that asset in the company's accounts, instead of its purchase price or production cost or any value previously so determined for that asset ; and the depreciation rules shall apply accordingly in relation to any such asset with the substitution for any reference to its purchase price or production cost of a reference to the value most recently determined for that asset on any basis mentioned in paragraph 31.

(2) The amount of any provision for depreciation required in the case of any fixed asset by paragraph 18 or 19 as it applies by virtue of sub-paragraph (1) is referred to below in this paragraph as the adjusted amount, and the amount of any provision which would be required by that paragraph in the case of that asset according to the historical cost accounting rules is referred to as the historical cost amount.

(3) Where sub-paragraph (1) applies in the case of any fixed asset the amount of any provision for depreciation in respect of that asset—

    (a) included in any item shown in the profit and loss account in respect of amounts written off assets of the description in question ; or

    (b) taken into account in stating any item so shown which is required by note (*14*) of the notes on the profit and loss account formats set out in Part I of this Schedule to be stated after taking into account any necessary provisions for depreciation or diminution in value of assets included under it ;

may be the historical cost amount instead of the adjusted amount, provided that the amount of any difference between the two is shown separately in the profit and loss account or in a note to the accounts.

Additional information to be provided in case of departure from historical cost accounting rules

33.—(1) This paragraph applies where the amounts to be included in respect of assets covered by any items shown in a company's accounts have been determined on any basis mentioned in paragraph 31.

(2) The items affected and the basis of valuation adopted in determining the amounts of the assets in question in the case of each such item shall be disclosed in a note to the accounts.

(3) In the case of each balance sheet item affected (except stocks) either—

    (a) the comparable amounts determined according to the historical cost accounting rules ; or

    (b) the differences between those amounts and the corresponding amounts actually shown in the balance sheet in respect of that item ;

shall be shown separately in the balance sheet or in a note to the accounts.

(4) In sub-paragraph (3) above, references in relation to any item to the comparable amounts determined as there mentioned are references to—

    (a) the aggregate amount which would be required to be shown in respect of that item if the amounts to be included in respect of all the assets covered by that item were determined according to the historical cost accounting rules ; and

    (b) the aggregate amount of the cumulative provisions for depreciation or diminution in value which would be permitted or required in determining those amounts according to those rules.

Revaluation reserve

34.—(1) With respect to any determination of the value of an asset of a company on any basis mentioned in paragraph 31, the amount of any profit or loss arising from that determination (after allowing, where appropriate, for any provisions for depreciation or diminution in value made otherwise than by reference to the value so determined and any adjustments of any such provisions made in the light of that determination) shall be credited or (as the case may be) debited to a separate reserve (" the revaluation reserve ").

(2) The amount of the revaluation reserve shall be shown in the company's balance sheet under a separate sub-heading in the position given for the item "revaluation reserve" in Format 1 or 2 of the balance sheet formats set out in Part I of this Schedule, but need not be shown under that name.

(3) The revaluation reserve shall be reduced to the extent that the amounts standing to the credit of the reserve are in the opinion of the directors of the company no longer necessary for the purpose of the accounting policies adopted by the company ; but an amount may only be transferred from the reserve to the profit and loss account if either—

(*a*) the amount in question was previously charged to that account ; or

(*b*) it represents realised profit.

(4) The treatment for taxation purposes of amounts credited or debited to the revaluation reserve shall be disclosed in a note to the accounts.

PART III

NOTES TO THE ACCOUNTS

Preliminary

35. Any information required in the case of any company by the following provisions of this Part of this Schedule shall (if not given in the company's accounts) be given by way of a note to those accounts.

Disclosure of accounting policies

36. The accounting policies adopted by the company in determining the amounts to be included in respect of items shown in the balance sheet and in determining the profit or loss of the company shall be stated (including such policies with respect to the depreciation and diminution in value of assets).

Information supplementing the balance sheet

37. Paragraphs 38 to 51 require information which either supplements the information given with respect to any particular items shown in the balance sheet or is otherwise relevant to assessing the company's state of affairs in the light of the information so given.

Share capital and debentures

38.—(1) The following information shall be given with respect to the company's share capital—

(a) the authorised share capital ; and

(b) where shares of more than one class have been allotted, the number and aggregate nominal value of shares of each class allotted.

(2) In the case of any part of the allotted share capital that consists of redeemable shares, the following information shall be given—

(a) the earliest and latest dates on which the company has power to redeem those shares ;

(b) whether those shares must be redeemed in any event or are liable to be redeemed at the option of the company or of the shareholder ; and

(c) whether any (and, if so, what) premium is payable on redemption.

39. If the company has allotted any shares during the financial year, the following information shall be given—

(a) the reason for making the allotment ;

(b) the classes of shares allotted ; and

(c) as respects each class of shares, the number allotted, their aggregate nominal value, and the consideration received by the company for the allotment.

40.—(1) With respect to any contingent right to the allotment of shares in the company the following particulars shall be given—

(a) the number, description and amount of the shares in relation to which the right is exercisable ;

(b) the period during which it is exercisable ; and

(c) the price to be paid for the shares allotted.

(2) In sub-paragraph (1) above " contingent right to the allotment of shares " means any option to subscribe for shares and any other right to require the allotment of shares to any person whether arising on the conversion into shares of securities of any other description or otherwise.

41.—(1) If the company has issued any debentures during the financial year to which the accounts relate, the following information shall be given—

(a) the reason for making the issue ;

(b) the classes of debentures issued ; and

(c) as respects each class of debentures, the amount issued and the consideration received by the company for the issue.

(2) Particulars of any redeemed debentures which the company has power to reissue shall also be given.

(3) Where any of the company's debentures are held by a nominee of or trustee for the company, the nominal amount of the debentures and the amount at which they are stated in the accounting records kept by the company in accordance with section 221 of this Act shall be stated.

Fixed assets

42.—(1) In respect of each item which is or would but for paragraph 3(4)(*b*) be shown under the general item " fixed assets " in the company's balance sheet the following information shall be given—

(*a*) the appropriate amounts in respect of that item as at the date of the beginning of the financial year and as at the balance sheet date respectively ;

(*b*) the effect on any amount shown in the balance sheet in respect of that item of—

(i) any revision of the amount in respect of any assets included under that item made during that year on any basis mentioned in paragraph 31 ;

(ii) acquisitions during that year of any assets ;

(iii) disposals during that year of any assets ; and

(iv) any transfers of assets of the company to and from that item during that year.

(2) The reference in sub-paragraph (1)(*a*) to the appropriate amounts in respect of any item as at any date there mentioned is a reference to amounts representing the aggregate amounts determined, as at that date, in respect of assets falling to be included under that item on either of the following bases, that is to say—

(*a*) on the basis of purchase price or production cost (determined in accordance with paragraphs 26 and 27) ; or

(*b*) on any basis mentioned in paragraph 31,

(leaving out of account in either case any provisions for depreciation or diminution in value).

(3) In respect of each item within sub-paragraph (1)—

(*a*) the cumulative amount of provisions for depreciation or diminution in value of assets included under that item as at each date mentioned in sub-paragraph (1)(*a*) ;

(*b*) the amount of any such provisions made in respect of the financial year ;

(*c*) the amount of any adjustments made in respect of any such provisions during that year in consequence of the disposal of any assets ; and

(*d*) the amount of any other adjustments made in respect of any such provisions during that year ;

shall also be stated.

43. Where any fixed assets of the company (other than listed investments) are included under any item shown in the company's balance sheet at an amount determined on any basis mentioned in paragraph 31, the following information shall be given—

   (a) the years (so far as they are known to the directors) in which the assets were severally valued and the several values ; and

   (b) in the case of assets that have been valued during the financial year, the names of the persons who valued them or particulars of their qualifications for doing so and (whichever is stated) the bases of valuation used by them.

44. In relation to any amount which is or would but for paragraph 3(4)(b) be shown in respect of the item " land and buildings " in the company's balance sheet there shall be stated—

   (a) how much of that amount is ascribable to land of freehold tenure and how much to land of leasehold tenure ; and

   (b) how much of the amount ascribable to land of leasehold tenure is ascribable to land held on long lease and how much to land held on short lease.

Investments

45.—(1) In respect of the amount of each item which is or would but for paragraph 3(4)(b) be shown in the company's balance sheet under the general item " investments " (whether as fixed assets or as current assets) there shall be stated—

   (a) how much of that amount is ascribable to listed investments ; and

   (b) how much of any amount so ascribable is ascribable to investments as respects which there has been granted a listing on a recognised stock exchange and how much to other listed investments.

(2) Where the amount of any listed investments is stated for any item in accordance with sub-paragraph (1)(a), the following amounts shall also be stated—

   (a) the aggregate market value of those investments where it differs from the amount so stated ; and

   (b) both the market value and the stock exchange value of any investments of which the former value is, for the purposes of the accounts, taken as being higher than the latter.

Reserves and provisions

46.—(1) Where any amount is transferred—

   (a) to or from any reserves ; or

   (b) to any provisions for liabilities and charges ; or

   (c) from any provision for liabilities and charges otherwise than for the purpose for which the provision was established ;

and the reserves or provisions are or would but for paragraph 3(4)(b) be shown as separate items in the company's balance sheet, the information mentioned in the following sub-paragraph shall be given in respect of the aggregate of reserves or provisions included in the same item.

(2) That information is—

(a) the amount of the reserves or provisions as at the date of the beginning of the financial year and as at the balance sheet date respectively ;

(b) any amounts transferred to or from the reserves or provisions during that year ; and

(c) the source and application respectively of any amounts so transferred.

(3) Particulars shall be given of each provision included in the item " other provisions " in the company's balance sheet in any case where the amount of that provision is material.

Provision for taxation

47. The amount of any provisions for taxation other than deferred taxation shall be stated.

Details of indebtedness

48.—(1) In respect of each item shown under " creditors " in the company's balance sheet there shall be stated—

(a) the aggregate amount of any debts included under that item which are payable or repayable otherwise than by instalments and fall due for payment or repayment after the end of the period of five years beginning with the day next following the end of the financial year ; and

(b) the aggregate amount of any debts so included which are payable or repayable by instalments any of which fall due for payment after the end of that period ;

and in the case of debts within paragraph (b) above the aggregate amount of instalments falling due after the end of that period shall also be disclosed for each such item.

(2) Subject to sub-paragraph (3), in relation to each debt falling to be taken into account under sub-paragraph (1), the terms of payment or repayment and the rate of any interest payable on the debt shall be stated.

(3) If the number of debts is such that, in the opinion of the directors, compliance with sub-paragraph (2) would result in a statement of excessive length, it shall be sufficient to give a general indication of the terms of payment or repayment and the rates of any interest payable on the debts.

(4) In respect of each item shown under " creditors " in the company's balance sheet there shall be stated—

(a) the aggregate amount of any debts included under that item in respect of which any security has been given by the company ; and

(b) an indication of the nature of the securities so given.

(5) References above in this paragraph to an item shown under " creditors " in the company's balance sheet include references.

where amounts falling due to creditors within one year and after more than one year are distinguished in the balance sheet—

(*a*) in a case within sub-paragraph (1), to an item shown under the latter of those categories ; and

(*b*) in a case within sub-paragraph (4), to an item shown under either of those categories ;

and references to items shown under " creditors " include references to items which would but for paragraph 3(4)(*b*) be shown under that heading.

49. If any fixed cumulative dividends on the company's shares are in arrear, there shall be stated—

(*a*) the amount of the arrears ; and

(*b*) the period for which the dividends or, if there is more than one class, each class of them are in arrear.

Guarantees and other financial commitments

50.—(1) Particulars shall be given of any charge on the assets of the company to secure the liabilities of any other person, including, where practicable, the amount secured.

(2) The following information shall be given with respect to any other contingent liability not provided for—

(*a*) the amount or estimated amount of that liability ;

(*b*) its legal nature ; and

(*c*) whether any valuable security has been provided by the company in connection with that liability and if so, what.

(3) There shall be stated, where practicable—

(*a*) the aggregate amount or estimated amount of contracts for capital expenditure, so far as not provided for ; and

(*b*) the aggregate amount or estimated amount of capital expenditure authorised by the directors which has not been contracted for.

(4) Particulars shall be given of—

(*a*) any pension commitments included under any provision shown in the company's balance sheet ; and

(*b*) any such commitments for which no provision has been made ;

and where any such commitment relates wholly or partly to pensions payable to past directors of the company separate particulars shall be given of that commitment so far as it relates to such pensions.

(5) Particulars shall also be given of any other financial commitments which—

(*a*) have not been provided for ; and

(*b*) are relevant to assessing the company's state of affairs.

(6) Commitments within any of the preceding sub-paragraphs undertaken on behalf of or for the benefit of—

(*a*) any holding company or fellow subsidiary of the company ; or

(*b*) any subsidiary of the company ;

shall be stated separately from the other commitments within that sub-paragraph (and commitments within paragraph (*a*) shall also be stated separately from those within paragraph (*b*)).

Miscellaneous matters

51.—(1) Particulars shall be given of any case where the purchase price or production cost of any asset is for the first time determined under paragraph 28.

(2) Where any outstanding loans made under the authority of section 153(4)(*b*) or (*c*) or section 155 of this Act (various cases of financial assistance by a company for purchase of its own shares) are included under any item shown in the company's balance sheet, the aggregate amount of those loans shall be disclosed for each item in question.

(3) The aggregate amount which is recommended for distribution by way of dividend shall be stated.

Information supplementing the profit and loss account

52. Paragraphs 53 to 57 require information which either supplements the information given with respect to any particular items shown in the profit and loss account or otherwise provides particulars of income or expenditure of the company or of circumstances affecting the items shown in the profit and loss account.

Separate statement of certain items of income and expenditure

53.—(1) Subject to the following provisions of this paragraph, each of the amounts mentioned below shall be stated.

(2) The amount of the interest on or any similar charges in respect of—

(*a*) bank loans and overdrafts, and loans made to the company (other than bank loans and overdrafts) which—

(i) are repayable otherwise than by instalments and fall due for repayment before the end of the period of five years beginning with the day next following the end of the financial year ; or

(ii) are repayable by instalments the last of which falls due for payment before the end of that period ; and

(*b*) loans of any other kind made to the company.

This sub-paragraph does not apply to interest or charges on loans to the company from group companies, but, with that exception, it applies to interest or charges on all loans, whether made on the security of debentures or not.

(3) The amounts respectively set aside for redemption of share capital and for redemption of loans.

(4) The amount of income from listed investments.

(5) The amount of rents from land (after deduction of ground rents, rates and other outgoings).

This amount need only be stated if a substantial part of the company's revenue for the financial year consists of rents from land.

(6) The amount charged to revenue in respect of sums payable in respect of the hire of plant and machinery.

(7) The amount of the remuneration of the auditors (taking "remuneration", for the purposes of this sub-paragraph, as including any sums paid by the company in respect of the auditors' expenses).

Particulars of tax

54.—(1) The basis on which the charge for United Kingdom corporation tax and United Kingdom income tax is computed shall be stated.

(2) Particulars shall be given of any special circumstances which affect liability in respect of taxation of profits, income or capital gains for the financial year or liability in respect of taxation of profits, income or capital gains for succeeding financial years.

(3) The following amounts shall be stated—

(*a*) the amount of the charge for United Kingdom corporation tax ;

(*b*) if that amount would have been greater but for relief from double taxation, the amount which it would have been but for such relief ;

(*c*) the amount of the charge for United Kingdom income tax ; and

(*d*) the amount of the charge for taxation imposed outside the United Kingdom of profits, income and (so far as charged to revenue) capital gains.

These amounts shall be stated separately in respect of each of the amounts which is or would but for paragraph 3(4)(*b*) be shown under the following items in the profit and loss account, that is to say "tax on profit or loss on ordinary activities" and "tax on extraordinary profit or loss".

Particulars of turnover

55.—(1) If in the course of the financial year the company has carried on business of two or more classes that, in the opinion of the directors, differ substantially from each other, there shall be stated in respect of each class (describing it)—

(*a*) the amount of the turnover attributable to that class ; and

(*b*) the amount of the profit or loss of the company before taxation which is in the opinion of the directors attributable to that class.

(2) If in the course of the financial year the company has supplied markets that, in the opinion of the directors, differ substantially from each other, the amount of the turnover attributable to each such market shall also be stated.

In this paragraph "market" means a market delimited by geographical bounds.

(3) In analysing for the purposes of this paragraph the source (in terms of business or in terms of market) of turnover or (as the case may be) of profit or loss, the directors of the company shall have regard to the manner in which the company's activities are organised.

(4) For the purposes of this paragraph—

(a) classes of business which, in the opinion of the directors, do not differ substantially from each other shall be treated as one class ; and

(b) markets which, in the opinion of the directors, do not differ substantially from each other shall be treated as one market ;

and any amounts properly attributable to one class of business or (as the case may be) to one market which are not material may be included in the amount stated in respect of another.

(5) Where in the opinion of the directors the disclosure of any information required by this paragraph would be seriously prejudicial to the interests of the company, that information need not be disclosed, but the fact that any such information has not been disclosed must be stated.

Particulars of staff

56.—(1) The following information shall be given with respect to the employees of the company—

(a) the average number of persons employed by the company in the financial year ; and

(b) the average number of persons so employed within each category of persons employed by the company.

(2) The average number required by sub-paragraph (1)(a) or (b) shall be determined by dividing the relevant annual number by the number of weeks in the financial year.

(3) The relevant annual number shall be determined by ascertaining for each week in the financial year—

(a) for the purposes of sub-paragraph (1)(a), the number of persons employed under contracts of service by the company in that week (whether throughout the week or not) ;

(b) for the purposes of sub-paragraph (1)(b), the number of persons in the category in question of persons so employed ;

and, in either case, adding together all the weekly numbers.

(4) In respect of all persons employed by the company during the financial year who are taken into account in determining the relevant annual number for the purposes of sub-paragraph (1)(*a*) there shall also be stated the aggregate amounts respectively of—

(*a*) wages and salaries paid or payable in respect of that year to those persons ;

(*b*) social security costs incurred by the company on their behalf ; and

(*c*) other pension costs so incurred ;

save in so far as those amounts or any of them are stated in the profit and loss account.

(5) The categories of persons employed by the company by reference to which the number required to be disclosed by sub-paragraph (1)(*b*) is to be determined shall be such as the directors may select, having regard to the manner in which the company's activities are organised.

Miscellaneous matters

57.—(1) Where any amount relating to any preceding financial year is included in any item in the profit and loss account, the effect shall be stated.

(2) Particulars shall be given of any extraordinary income or charges arising in the financial year.

(3) The effect shall be stated of any transactions that are exceptional by virtue of size or incidence though they fall within the ordinary activities of the company.

General

58.—(1) Where sums originally denominated in foreign currencies have been brought into account under any items shown in the balance sheet or profit and loss account, the basis on which those sums have been translated into sterling shall be stated.

(2) Subject to the following sub-paragraph, in respect of every item stated in a note to the accounts the corresponding amount for the financial year immediately preceding that to which the accounts relate shall also be stated and where the corresponding amount is not comparable, it shall be adjusted and particulars of the adjustment and the reasons for it shall be given.

(3) Sub-paragraph (2) does not apply in relation to any amounts stated by virtue of any of the following provisions of this Act—

(*a*) section 231 as applying Parts I and II of Schedule 5 (proportion of share capital of subsidiaries and other bodies corporate held by the company, etc.),

(*b*) sections 232 to 234 and Schedule 6 (particulars of loans to directors, etc.), and

(*c*) paragraphs 42 and 46 above.

PART IV

SPECIAL PROVISIONS WHERE THE COMPANY IS A HOLDING OR
SUBSIDIARY COMPANY

Company's own accounts

59. Where a company is a holding company or a subsidiary of
another body corporate and any item required by Part I of this
Schedule to be shown in the company's balance sheet in relation to
group companies includes—

(*a*) amounts attributable to dealings with or interests in any
holding company or fellow subsidiary of the company;
or

(*b*) amounts attributable to dealings with or interests in any
subsidiary of the company;

the aggregate amounts within paragraphs (*a*) and (*b*) respectively
shall be shown as separate items, either by way of subdivision of
the relevant item in the balance sheet or in a note to the company's
accounts.

60.—(1) Subject to the following sub-paragraph, where the company
is a holding company, the number, description and amount of the
shares in and debentures of the company held by its subsidiaries or
their nominees shall be disclosed in a note to the company's accounts.

(2) Sub-paragraph (1) does not apply in relation to any shares
or debentures—

(*a*) in the case of which the subsidiary is concerned as personal
representative; or

(*b*) in the case of which it is concerned as trustee;

provided that in the latter case neither the company nor any subsidiary of the company is beneficially interested under the trust,
otherwise than by way of security only for the purposes of a transaction entered into by it in the ordinary course of a business which
includes the lending of money.

Schedule 2 to this Act has effect for the interpretation of the
reference in this sub-paragraph to a beneficial interest under a trust.

**Consolidated accounts of holding company
and subsidiaries**

61. Subject to paragraphs 63 and 66, the consolidated balance
sheet and profit and loss account shall combine the information
contained in the separate balance sheets and profit and loss
accounts of the holding company and of the subsidiaries dealt with
by the consolidated accounts, but with such adjustments (if any) as
the directors of the holding company think necessary.

62. Subject to paragraphs 63 to 66, and to Part V of this
Schedule, the consolidated accounts shall, in giving the information
required by paragraph 61, comply so far as practicable with the
requirements of this Schedule and with the other requirements of
this Act as if they were the accounts of an actual company.

63. The following provisions of this Act, namely—

(a) section 231 as applying Schedule 5, but only Parts II, III, V and VI of that Schedule, and

(b) sections 232 to 234 and Schedule 6, so far as relating to accounts other than group accounts,

do not, by virtue of paragraphs 61 and 62, apply for the purposes of the consolidated accounts.

64. Paragraph 62 is without prejudice to any requirement of this Act which applies (otherwise than by virtue of paragraph 61 or 62) to group accounts.

65.—(1) Notwithstanding paragraph 62, the consolidated accounts prepared by a holding company may deal with an investment of any member of the group in the shares of any other body corporate by way of the equity method of accounting in any case where it appears to the directors of the holding company that that body corporate is so closely associated with any member of the group as to justify the use of that method in dealing with investments by that or any other member of the group in the shares of that body corporate.

(2) In this paragraph, references to the group, in relation to consolidated accounts prepared by a holding company, are references to the holding company and the subsidiaries dealt with by the accounts.

66. Notwithstanding paragraphs 61 and 62, paragraphs 17 to 19 and 21 do not apply to any amount shown in the consolidated balance sheet in respect of goodwill arising on consolidation.

67. In relation to any subsidiaries of the holding company not dealt with by the consolidated accounts paragraphs 59 and 60 apply for the purpose of those accounts as if those accounts were the accounts of an actual company of which they were subsidiaries.

Group accounts not prepared as consolidated accounts

68. Group accounts which are not prepared as consolidated accounts, together with any notes to those accounts, shall give the same or equivalent information as that required to be given by consolidated accounts by virtue of paragraphs 61 to 67.

Provisions of general application

69.—(1) This paragraph applies where the company is a holding company and either—

(a) does not prepare group accounts ; or

(b) prepares group accounts which do not deal with one or more of its subsidiaries ;

and references below in this paragraph to the company's subsidiaries shall be read in a case within paragraph (b) as references to such of the company's subsidiaries as are excluded from the group accounts.

(2) Subject to the following provisions of this paragraph—

(a) the reasons why the subsidiaries are not dealt with in group accounts ; and

(b) a statement showing any qualifications contained in the reports of the auditors of the subsidiaries on their accounts for their respective financial years ending with or during the financial year of the company, and any note or saving contained in those accounts to call attention to a matter which, apart from the note or saving, would properly have been referred to in such a qualification, in so far as the matter which is the subject of the qualification or note is not covered by the company's own accounts and is material from the point of view of its members,

shall be given in a note to the company's accounts.

(3) Subject to the following provisions of this paragraph, the aggregate amount of the total investment of the holding company in the shares of the subsidiaries shall be stated in a note to the company's accounts by way of the equity method of valuation.

(4) Sub-paragraph (3) does not apply where the company is a wholly-owned subsidiary of another body corporate incorporated in Great Britain if there is included in a note to the company's accounts a statement that in the opinion of the directors of the company the aggregate value of the assets of the company consisting of shares in, or amounts owing (whether on account of a loan or otherwise) from, the company's subsidiaries is not less than the aggregate of the amounts at which those assets are stated or included in the company's balance sheet.

(5) In so far as information required by any of the preceding provisions of this paragraph to be stated in a note to the company's accounts is not obtainable, a statement to that effect shall be given instead in a note to those accounts.

(6) The Secretary of State may, on the application or with the consent of the company's directors, direct that in relation to any subsidiary sub-paragraphs (2) and (3) shall not apply, or shall apply only to such extent as may be provided by the direction.

(7) Where in any case within sub-paragraph (1)(b) the group accounts are consolidated accounts, references above in this paragraph to the company's accounts and the company's balance sheet respectively shall be read as references to the consolidated accounts and the consolidated balance sheet.

70. Where a company has subsidiaries whose financial years did not end with that of the company, the following information shall be given in relation to each such subsidiary (whether or not dealt with in any group accounts prepared by the company) by way of

a note to the company's accounts or (where group accounts are prepared) to the group accounts, that is to say—

    (*a*) the reasons why the company's directors consider that the subsidiaries' financial years should not end with that of the company ; and

    (*b*) the dates on which the subsidiaries' financial years ending last before that of the company respectively ended or the earliest and latest of those dates.

Part V

Special Provisions where the Company is an Investment Company

71.—(1) Paragraph 34 does not apply to the amount of any profit or loss arising from a determination of the value of any investments of an investment company on any basis mentioned in paragraph 31(3).

(2) Any provisions made by virtue of paragraph 19(1) or (2) in the case of an investment company in respect of any fixed asset investments need not be charged to the company's profit and loss account provided they are either—

    (*a*) charged against any reserve account to which any amount excluded by sub-paragraph (1) from the requirements of paragraph 34 has been credited ; or

    (*b*) shown as a separate item in the company's balance sheet under the sub-heading " other reserves ".

(3) For the purposes of this paragraph, as it applies in relation to any company, "fixed asset investment" means any asset falling to be included under any item shown in the company's balance sheet under the subdivision " investments " under the general item " fixed assets ".

72.—(1) Any distribution made by an investment company which reduces the amount of its net assets to less than the aggregate of its called-up share capital and undistributable reserves shall be disclosed in a note to the company's accounts.

(2) For purposes of this paragraph, a company's net assets are the aggregate of its assets less the aggregate of its liabilities (including any provision for liabilities or charges within paragraph 89) ; and " undistributable reserves " has the meaning given by section 264 (3) of this Act.

73. A company shall be treated as an investment company for the purposes of this Part of this Schedule in relation to any financial year of the company if—

    (*a*) during the whole of that year it was an investment company as defined by section 266 of this Act, and

    (*b*) it was not at any time during that year prohibited under section 265(4) of this Act (no distribution where capital profits have been distributed, etc.) from making a distribution by virtue of that section.

74. Where a company entitled to the benefit of any provision contained in this Part of this Schedule is a holding company, the reference in paragraph 62 to consolidated accounts complying with the requirements of this Act shall, in relation to consolidated accounts of that company, be construed as referring to those requirements in so far only—

    (*a*) as they apply to the individual accounts of that company; and

    (*b*) as they apply otherwise than by virtue of paragraphs 61 and 62 to any group accounts prepared by that company.

PART VI

SPECIAL PROVISIONS WHERE THE COMPANY HAS ENTERED INTO ARRANGEMENTS SUBJECT TO MERGER RELIEF

75.—(1) Where during the financial year the company has allotted shares in consideration for the issue, transfer or cancellation of shares in another body corporate (" the other company ") in circumstances where by virtue of section 131(2) of this Act (merger relief) section 130 did not apply to the premiums on those shares, the following information shall be given by way of a note to the company's accounts—

    (*a*) the name of the other company;

    (*b*) the number, nominal value and class of shares so allotted;

    (*c*) the number, nominal value and class of shares in the other company so issued, transferred or cancelled;

    (*d*) particulars of the accounting treatment adopted in the company's accounts (including any group accounts) in respect of such issue, transfer or cancellation; and

    (*e*) where the company prepares group accounts, particulars of the extent to which and manner in which the profit or loss for the year of the group which appears in those accounts is affected by any profit or loss of the other company or any of its subsidiaries which arose at any time before the allotment.

(2) Where the company has during the financial year or during either of the two financial years immediately preceding it made such an allotment of shares as is mentioned in sub-paragraph (1) above and there is included in the company's consolidated profit and loss account or, if it has no such account, in its individual profit and loss account, any profit or loss (or part thereof) to which this sub-paragraph applies then the net amount of any such profit or loss (or part thereof) shall be shown in a note to the accounts together with an explanation of the transactions to which that information relates.

(3) Sub-paragraph (2) applies—

    (*a*) to any profit or loss realised during the financial year by the company, or any of its subsidiaries, on the disposal of any shares in the other company or of any assets which were

fixed assets of the other company, or of any of its subsidiaries, at the time of the allotment ; and

(*b*) to any part of any profit or loss realised during the financial
year by the company, or any of its subsidiaries, on the
disposal of any shares (not being shares in the other company), which was attributable to the fact that at the time of
the disposal there were amongst the assets of the company
which issued those shares, or any of its subsidiaries, such
shares or assets as are described in sub-paragraph (*a*) above.

(4) Where in pursuance of the arrangement in question shares
are allotted on different dates, the time of allotment for the purposes of sub-paragraphs (1)(*e*) and (3)(*a*) above is taken to be—

(*a*) if the other company becomes a subsidiary of the company
as a result of the arrangement—

(i) if the arrangement becomes binding only upon
the fulfilment of a condition, the date on which that
condition is fulfilled, and

(ii) in any other case, the date on which the other
company becomes a subsidiary of the company ;

(*b*) if the other company is a subsidiary of the company when
the arrangement is proposed, the date of the first allotment
pursuant to that arrangement.

PART VII

INTERPRETATION OF SCHEDULE

76. The following paragraphs apply for the purposes of this Schedule and its interpretation.

Assets : fixed or current

77. Assets of a company are taken to be fixed assets if they are
intended for use on a continuing basis in the company's activities,
and any assets not intended for such use shall be taken to be current
assets.

Balance sheet date

78. " Balance sheet date ", in relation to a balance sheet, means the
date as at which the balance sheet was prepared.

Capitalisation

79. References to capitalising any work or costs are to treating
that work or those costs as a fixed asset.

Fellow subsidiary

80. A body corporate is treated as a fellow subsidiary of another
body corporate if both are subsidiaries of the same body corporate
but neither is the other's.

Group companies

81. " Group company ", in relation to any company, means any
body corporate which is that company's subsidiary or holding company, or a subsidiary of that company's holding company.

Historical cost accounting rules

82. References to the historical cost accounting rules shall be read in accordance with paragraph 29.

Leases

83.—(1) " Long lease " means a lease in the case of which the portion of the term for which it was granted remaining unexpired at the end of the financial year is not less than 50 years.

(2) " Short lease " means a lease which is not a long lease.

(3) " Lease " includes an agreement for a lease.

Listed investments

84. " Listed investment " means an investment as respects which there has been granted a listing on a recognised stock exchange, or on any stock exchange of repute (other than a recognised stock exchange) outside Great Britain.

Loans

85. A loan is treated as falling due for repayment, and an instalment of a loan is treated as falling due for payment, on the earliest date on which the lender could require repayment or (as the case may be) payment, if he exercised all options and rights available to him.

Materiality

86. Amounts which in the particular context of any provision of this Schedule are not material may be disregarded for the purposes of that provision.

Notes to the accounts

87. Notes to a company's accounts may be contained in the accounts or in a separate document annexed to the accounts.

Provisions

88.—(1) References to provisions for depreciation or diminution in value of assets are to any amount written off by way of providing for depreciation or diminution in value of assets.

(2) Any reference in the profit and loss account formats set out in Part I of this Schedule to the depreciation of, or amounts written off, assets of any description is to any provision for depreciation or diminution in value of assets of that description.

89. References to provisions for liabilities or charges are to any amount retained as reasonably necessary for the purpose of providing for any liability or loss which is either likely to be incurred, or certain to be incurred but uncertain as to amount or as to the date on which it will arise.

Purchase price

90. References (however expressed) to the purchase price of any asset of a company or of any raw materials or consumables used in the production of any such asset include any consideration (whether in cash or otherwise) given by the company in respect of that asset or in respect of those materials or consumables (as the case may require).

Realised profits

91. Without prejudice to—

    (*a*) the construction of any other expression (where appropriate) by reference to accepted accounting principles or practice, or

    (*b*) any specific provision for the treatment of profits of any description as realised,

it is hereby declared for the avoidance of doubt that references in this Schedule to realised profits, in relation to a company's accounts, are to such profits of the company as fall to be treated as realised profits for the purposes of those accounts in accordance with principles generally accepted with respect to the determination for accounting purposes of realised profits at the time when those accounts are prepared.

Related companies

92.—(1) " Related company ", in relation to any company, means any body corporate (other than one which is a group company in relation to that company) in which that company holds on a long-term basis a qualifying capital interest for the purpose of securing a contribution to that company's own activities by the exercise of any control or influence arising from that interest.

(2) In this paragraph " qualifying capital interest " means, in relation to any body corporate, an interest in shares comprised in the equity share capital of that body corporate of a class carrying rights to vote in all circumstances at general meetings of that body corporate.

(3) Where—

    (*a*) a company holds a qualifying capital interest in a body corporate ; and

    (*b*) the nominal value of any relevant shares in that body corporate held by that company is equal to twenty per cent. or more of the nominal value of all relevant shares in that body corporate ;

it shall be presumed to hold that interest on the basis and for the purpose mentioned in sub-paragraph (1), unless the contrary is shown.

In this sub-paragraph " relevant shares " means, in relation to any body corporate, any such shares in that body corporate as are mentioned in sub-paragraph (2).

Scots land tenure

93. In the application of this Schedule to Scotland, " land of free-hold tenure " means land in respect of which the company is the proprietor of the *dominium utile* or, in the case of land not held on feudal tenure, is the owner ; " land of leasehold tenure " means land of which the company is the tenant under a lease ; and the reference to ground-rents, rates and other outgoings includes feu-duty and ground annual.

Staff costs

94.—(1) " Social security costs " means any contributions by the company to any state social security or pension scheme, fund or arrangement.

(2) " Pension costs " includes any other contributions by the company for the purposes of any pension scheme established for the purpose of providing pensions for persons employed by the company, any sums set aside for that purpose and any amounts paid by the company in respect of pensions without first being so set aside.

(3) Any amount stated in respect of either of the above items or in respect of the item " wages and salaries " in the company's profit and loss account shall be determined by reference to payments made or costs incurred in respect of all persons employed by the company during the financial year who are taken into account in determining the relevant annual number for the purposes of paragraph 56(1)(*a*).

Turnover

95. " Turnover ", in relation to a company, means the amounts derived from the provision of goods and services falling within the company's ordinary activities, after deduction of—

(*a*) trade discounts,

(*b*) value added tax, and

(*c*) any other taxes based on the amounts so derived.

SCHEDULE 5

Section 231.

MISCELLANEOUS MATTERS TO BE DISCLOSED
IN NOTES TO COMPANY ACCOUNTS

PART I

PARTICULARS OF SUBSIDIARIES

1. If at the end of the financial year the company has subsidiaries, there shall in the case of each subsidiary be stated—

(*a*) the name of the subsidiary and—

(i) if it is incorporated in Great Britain and if it is registered in England and Wales and the company is registered in Scotland (or vice versa), the part of Great Britain in which it is registered, and

(ii) if it is incorporated outside Great Britain, the country in which it is incorporated ; and

T

(*b*) in relation to shares of each class of the subsidiary held by the company, the identity of the class and the proportion of the nominal value of the allotted shares of that class represented by the shares held.

2. The particulars required by paragraph 1 include, with reference to the proportion of the nominal value of the allotted shares of a class represented by shares held by the company, a statement of the extent (if any) to which it consists in shares held by, or by a nominee for, a subsidiary of the company and the extent (if any) to which it consists in shares held by, or by a nominee for, the company itself.

3. Paragraph 1 does not require the disclosure of information with respect to a body corporate which is the subsidiary of another and is incorporated outside the United Kingdom or, being incorporated in the United Kingdom, carries on business outside it if the disclosure would, in the opinion of the directors of that other, be harmful to the business of that other or of any of its subsidiaries and the Secretary of State agrees that the information need not be disclosed.

4. If at the end of its financial year the company has subsidiaries and the directors are of the opinion that the number of them is such that compliance with paragraph 1 would result in particulars of excessive length being given, compliance with that paragraph is required only in the case of the subsidiaries carrying on the businesses the results of the carrying on of which (in the opinion of the directors) principally affected the amount of the profit or loss of the company and its subsidiaries or the amount of the assets of the company and its subsidiaries.

5. If advantage is taken of paragraph 4, there must be included in the statement required by this Part the information that it deals only with the subsidiaries carrying on such businesses as are referred to in that paragraph; and in that case section 231(3) (subsequent disclosure with annual return) applies to the particulars given in compliance with paragraph 1, together with those which (but for the fact that advantage is so taken) would have to be so given.

6. For purposes of this Part, shares of a body corporate are treated as held, or not held, by another such body if they would, by virtue of section 736(4) of this Act, be treated as being held or (as the case may be) not held by that other body for the purpose of determining whether the first-mentioned body is its subsidiary.

PART II

SHAREHOLDINGS IN COMPANIES ETC. OTHER THAN SUBSIDIARIES

7. If at the end of its financial year the company holds shares of any class comprised in the equity share capital of another body corporate (not being its subsidiary) exceeding in nominal value one-tenth of the nominal value of the allotted shares of that class, there shall be stated—

(*a*) the name of that other body corporate and—

(i) if it is incorporated in Great Britain and if it is

registered in England and Wales and the company is registered in Scotland (or vice versa), the part of Great Britain in which it is registered, and

(ii) if it is incorporated outside Great Britain, the country in which it is incorporated ;

(b) the identity of the class and the proportion of the nominal value of the allotted shares of that class represented by the shares held ; and

(c) if the company also holds shares in that other body corporate of another class (whether or not comprised in its equity share capital), or of other classes (whether or not so comprised), the like particulars as respects that other class or (as the case may be) those other classes.

8. If at the end of its financial year the company holds shares comprised in the share capital of another body corporate (not being its subsidiary) exceeding in nominal value one-tenth of the allotted share capital of that other body, there shall be stated—

(a) with respect to that other body corporate, the same information as is required by paragraph 7(a), and

(b) the identity of each class of such shares held and the proportion of the nominal value of the allotted shares of that class represented by the shares of that class held by the company.

9. If at the end of its financial year the company holds shares in another body corporate (not being its subsidiary) and the amount of all shares in it which the company holds (as stated or included in the company's accounts) exceeds one-tenth of the amount of the company's assets (as so stated), there shall be stated—

(a) with respect to the other body corporate, the same information as is required by paragraph 7(a), and

(b) in relation to shares in that other body corporate of each class held, the identity of the class and the proportion of the nominal value of the allotted shares of that class represented by the shares held.

10. None of the foregoing provisions of this Part requires the disclosure by a company of information with respect to another body corporate if that other is incorporated outside the United Kingdom or, being incorporated in the United Kingdom, carries on business outside it if the disclosure would, in the opinion of the company's directors, be harmful to the business of the company or of that other body and the Secretary of State agrees that the information need not be disclosed.

11. If at the end of its financial year the company falls within paragraph 7 or 8 in relation to more bodies corporate than one, and the number of them is such that, in the directors' opinion, compliance with either or both of those paragraphs would result in particulars of excessive length being given, compliance with paragraph 7 or (as the case may be) paragraph 8 is not required except in the case of the bodies carrying on the businesses the results of the

carrying on of which (in the directors' opinion) principally affected the amount of the profit or loss of the company or the amount of its assets.

12. If advantage is taken of paragraph 11, there must be included in the statement dealing with the bodies last mentioned in that paragraph the information that it deals only with them ; and section 231(3) of this Act (subsequent disclosure in annual return) applies to the particulars given in compliance with paragraph 7 or 8 (as the case may be), together with those which, but for the fact that advantage is so taken, would have to be so given.

13. For purposes of this Part, shares of a body corporate are treated as held, or not held, by another such body if they would, by virtue of section 736(4) of this Act (but on the assumption that paragraph (b)(ii) were omitted from that subsection) be treated as being held or (as the case may be), not held by that other body for the purpose of determining whether the first-mentioned body is its subsidiary.

PART III

FINANCIAL INFORMATION ABOUT SUBSIDIARIES

14. If—
   (a) at the end of its financial year the company has subsidiaries, and
   (b) it is required by paragraph 1 in Part I above to disclose particulars with respect to any of those subsidiaries,

the additional information specified below shall be given with respect to each subsidiary to which the requirement under paragraph 1 applies.

15. If—
   (a) at the end of the financial year the company holds shares in another body corporate, and
   (b) it is required by paragraph 8 in Part II above to disclose particulars with respect to that body corporate, and
   (c) the shares held by the company in that body corporate exceed in nominal value one-fifth of the allotted share capital of that body,

the additional information specified below shall be given with respect to that body corporate.

16. The information required by paragraphs 14 and 15 is, in relation to any body corporate (whether a subsidiary of the company or not) the aggregate amount of the capital and reserves of that body corporate as at the end of its relevant financial year, and its profit or loss for that year ; and for this purpose the relevant financial year is—
   (a) if the financial year of the body corporate ends with that of the company giving the information in a note to its accounts, that financial year, and

(*b*) if not, the body corporate's financial year ending last before the end of the financial year of the company giving that information.

This is subject to the exceptions and other provisions in the next paragraph.

17.—(1) The information otherwise required by paragraph 16 need not be given in respect of a subsidiary of a company if either—

(*a*) the company is exempt under this Act from the requirement to prepare group accounts, as being at the end of its financial year the wholly-owned subsidiary of another body corporate incorporated in Great Britain, or

(*b*) the company prepares group accounts and—

(i) the accounts of the subsidiary are included in the group accounts, or

(ii) the investment of the company in the shares of the subsidiary is included in, or in a note to, the company's accounts by way of the equity method of valuation.

(2) That information need not be given in respect of another body corporate in which the company holds shares if the company's investment in those shares is included in, or in a note to, the accounts by way of the equity method of valuation.

(3) That information need not be given in respect of any body corporate if—

(*a*) that body is not required by any provision of this Act to deliver a copy of its balance sheet for its relevant financial year mentioned in paragraph 16, and does not otherwise publish that balance sheet in Great Britain or elsewhere, and

(*b*) the shares held by the company in that body do not amount to at least one half in nominal value of the body's allotted share capital.

(4) Information otherwise required by paragraph 16 need not be given if it is not material.

18. Where, with respect to any subsidiary of the company or any other body corporate, particulars which would otherwise be required by paragraph 1 in Part I or paragraph 8 in Part II of this Schedule to be stated in a note to the company's accounts are omitted by virtue of paragraph 4 or (as the case may be) paragraph 11, section 231(3) of this Act (subsequent disclosure in next annual return) applies—

(*a*) to any information with respect to any other subsidiary or body corporate which is given in or in a note to the company's accounts in accordance with this Part, and

(*b*) to any information which would have been required by this Part to be given in relation to a subsidiary or other body corporate but for the exemption under paragraph 4 or 11.

19. For purposes of this Part, shares of a body corporate are treated as held, or not held, by the company if they would, by

T 3

virtue of section 736(4) of this Act (but on the assumption that paragraph (*b*)(ii) were omitted from that subsection), be treated as being held or (as the case may be) not held by the company for the purpose of determining whether that body corporate is the company's subsidiary.

PART IV
IDENTIFICATION OF ULTIMATE HOLDING COMPANY

20. If at the end of its financial year the company is the subsidiary of another body corporate, there shall be stated the name of the body corporate regarded by the directors as being the company's ultimate holding company and, if known to them, the country in which it is incorporated.

21. Paragraph 20 does not require the disclosure by a company which carries on business outside the United Kingdom of information with respect to the body corporate regarded by the directors as being its ultimate holding company if the disclosure would, in their opinion, be harmful to the business of that holding company or of the first-mentioned company, or any other of that holding company's subsidiaries, and the Secretary of State agrees that the information need not be disclosed.

PART V
CHAIRMAN'S AND DIRECTORS' EMOLUMENTS, PENSIONS AND COMPENSATION FOR LOSS OF OFFICE
Emoluments

22.—(1) There shall be shown the aggregate amount of the directors' emoluments.

(2) This amount—

    (*a*) includes any emoluments paid to or receivable by a person in respect of his services as director of the company or in respect of his services, while director of the company, as director of any subsidiary of it or otherwise in connection with the management of the affairs of the company or any subsidiary of it ; and

    (*b*) shall distinguish between emoluments in respect of services as director, whether of the company or its subsidiary, and other emoluments.

(3) For purposes of this paragraph " emoluments ", in relation to a director, includes fees and percentages, any sums paid by way of expenses allowance (insofar as those sums are charged to United Kingdom income tax), any contributions paid in respect of him under any pension scheme and the estimated money value of any other benefits received by him otherwise than in cash.

23. A company which is neither a holding company nor a subsidiary of another body corporate need not comply with paragraphs 24 to 27 below as respects a financial year in the case of which the amount shown in compliance with paragraph 22 above does not exceed £60,000.

24.—(1) The following applies as respects the emoluments of the company's chairman ; and for this purpose " chairman " means the person elected by the directors to be chairman of their meetings and includes a person who, though not so elected, holds any office (however designated) which in accordance with the company's constitution carries with it functions substantially similar to those discharged by a person so elected.

(2) If one person has been chairman throughout the financial year, there shall be shown his emoluments, unless his duties as chairman were wholly or mainly discharged outside the United Kingdom.

(3) Otherwise, there shall be shown with respect to each person who has been chairman during the year his emoluments so far as attributable to the period during which he was chairman, unless his duties as chairman were wholly or mainly discharged outside the United Kingdom.

25.—(1) The following applies as respects the emoluments of directors.

(2) With respect to all the directors (other than any who discharged their duties as such wholly or mainly outside the United Kingdom), there shall be shown—

(a) the number (if any) who had no emoluments or whose several emoluments amounted to not more than £5,000 ; and

(b) by reference to each pair of adjacent points on a scale whereon the lowest point is £5,000 and the succeeding ones are successive integral multiples of £5,000, the number (if any) whose several emoluments exceeded the lower point but did not exceed the higher.

(3) If, of the directors (other than any who discharged their duties as such wholly or mainly outside the United Kingdom), the emoluments of one only exceed the relevant amount, his emoluments (so far as so ascertainable) shall also be shown.

(4) If, of the directors (other than any who discharged their duties as such wholly or mainly outside the United Kingdom), the emoluments of each of two or more exceed the relevant amount, the emoluments of him (or them, in the case of equality) who had the greater or, as the case may be, the greatest shall also be shown.

(5) " The relevant amount "—

(a) if one person has been chairman throughout the year, means the amount of his emoluments ; and

(b) otherwise, means an amount equal to the aggregate of the emoluments, so far as attributable to the period during which he was chairman, of each person who has been chairman during the year.

26. There shall under paragraphs 24 and 25 be brought into account as emoluments of a person all such amounts (other than

T 4

contributions paid in respect of him under a pension scheme) as in his case are to be included in the amount shown under paragraph 22.

Emoluments waived

27.—(1) There shall be shown—

(a) the number of directors who have waived rights to receive emoluments which, but for the waiver, would have fallen to be included in the amount shown under paragraph 22, and

(b) the aggregate amount of those emoluments.

(2) For these purposes—

(a) it is assumed that a sum not receivable in respect of a period would have been paid at the time at which it was due to be paid,

(b) a sum not so receivable that was payable only on demand, being a sum the right to receive which has been waived, is deemed to have been due to be paid at the time of the waiver.

Pensions of directors and past directors

28.—(1) There shall be shown the aggregate amount of directors' or past directors' pensions.

(2) This amount does not include any pension paid or receivable under a pension scheme if the scheme is such that the contributions under it are substantially adequate for the maintenance of the scheme ; but, subject to this, it includes any pension paid or receivable in respect of any such services of a director or past director as are mentioned in paragraph 22(2), whether to or by him or, on his nomination or by virtue of dependence on or other connection with him, to or by any other person.

(3) The amount shown shall distinguish between pensions in respect of services as director, whether of the company or its subsidiary, and other pensions.

Compensation to directors for loss of office

29.—(1) There shall be shown the aggregate amount of any compensation to directors or past directors in respect of loss of office.

(2) This amount—

(a) includes any sums paid to or receivable by a director or past director by way of compensation for the loss of office as director of the company or for the loss, while director of the company or on or in connection with his ceasing to be a director of it, of any other office in connection with the management of the company's affairs or of any office as director or otherwise in connection with the management of the affairs of any subsidiary of the company ; and

(b) shall distinguish between compensation in respect of the

office of director, whether of the company or its subsidiary,
and compensation in respect of other offices.

(3) References to compensation for loss of office include sums
paid as consideration for or in connection with a person's retirement from office.

Supplementary

30.—(1) The following applies with respect to the amounts to
be shown under paragraphs 22, 28 and 29.

(2) The amount in each case includes all relevant sums paid by
or receivable from—

(*a*) the company ; and

(*b*) the company's subsidiaries ; and

(*c*) any other person,

except sums to be accounted for to the company or any of its
subsidiaries or, by virtue of sections 314 and 315 of this Act (duty
of directors to make disclosure on company takeover ; consequence
of non-compliance), to past or present members of the company or
any of its subsidiaries or any class of those members.

(3) The amount to be shown under paragraph 29 shall distinguish
between the sums respectively paid by or receivable from the
company, the company's subsidiaries and persons other than the
company and its subsidiaries.

31.—(1) The amounts to be shown for any financial year under
paragraphs 22, 28 and 29 are the sums receivable in respect of that
year (whenever paid) or, in the case of sums not receivable in respect of a period, the sums paid during that year.

(2) But where—

(*a*) any sums are not shown in a note to the accounts for the
relevant financial year on the ground that the person
receiving them is liable to account for them as mentioned
in paragraph 30(2), but the liability is thereafter wholly or
partly released or is not enforced within a period of 2
years ; or

(*b*) any sums paid by way of expenses allowance are charged
to United Kingdom income tax after the end of the
relevant financial year,

those sums shall, to the extent to which the liability is released
or not enforced or they are charged as mentioned above (as the
case may be), be shown in a note to the first accounts in which
it is practicable to show them and shall be distinguished from the
amounts to be shown apart from this provision.

32. Where it is necessary to do so for the purpose of making
any distinction required by the preceding paragraphs in an amount
to be shown in compliance with this Part, the directors may
apportion any payments between the matters in respect of which
these have been paid or are receivable in such manner as they think
appropriate.

Interpretation

33.—(1) The following applies for the interpretation of paragraphs 22 to 32.

(2) A reference to the company's subsidiary—

(*a*) in relation to a person who is or was, while a director of the
company, a director also, by virtue of the company's nomination (direct or indirect) of any other body corporate,
includes (subject to the following sub-paragraph) that body
corporate, whether or not it is or was in fact the company's
subsidiary, and

(*b*) for purposes of paragraphs 22 to 28 (including any provision
of this Part referring to paragraph 22) is to a subsidiary at
the time the services were rendered, and for purposes of
paragraph 29 to a subsidiary immediately before the loss
of office as director.

(3) The following definitions apply—

(*a*) " pension " includes any superannuation allowance, superannuation gratuity or similar payment,

(*b*) " pension scheme " means a scheme for the provision of
pensions in respect of services as director or otherwise
which is maintained in whole or in part by means of
contributions, and

(*c*) " contribution ", in relation to a pension scheme, means any
payment (including an insurance premium) paid for the
purposes of the scheme by or in respect of persons rendering services in respect of which pensions will or may
become payable under the scheme, except that it does not
include any payment in respect of two or more persons
if the amount paid in respect of each of them is not ascertainable.

Supplementary

34. This Part of this Schedule requires information to be given
only so far as it is contained in the company's books and papers or
the company has the right to obtain it from the persons concerned.

PART VI

PARTICULARS RELATING TO NUMBER OF EMPLOYEES REMUNERATED
AT HIGHER RATES

35.—(1) There shall be shown by reference to each pair of adjacent
points on a scale whereon the lowest point is £30,000 and the
succeeding ones are successive integral multiples of £5,000 beginning
with that in the case of which the multiplier is 7, the number (if any)
of persons in the company's employment whose several emoluments
exceeded the lower point but did not exceed the higher.

(2) The persons whose emoluments are to be taken into account
for this purpose do not include—

(*a*) directors of the company ; or

(*b*) persons (other than directors of the company) who—

(i) if employed by the company throughout the financial year, worked wholly or mainly during that year
outside the United Kingdom, or

(ii) if employed by the company for part only of that year, worked wholly or mainly during that part outside the United Kingdom.

36.—(1) For these purposes, a person's emoluments include any paid to or receivable by him from the company, the company's subsidiaries and any other person in respect of his services as a person in the employment of the company or a subsidiary of it or as a director of a subsidiary of the company (except sums to be accounted for to the company or any of its subsidiaries).

(2) " Emoluments " here includes fees and percentages, any sums paid by way of expenses allowance in so far as those sums are charged to United Kingdom income tax, and the estimated money value of any other benefits received by a person otherwise than in cash.

(3) The amounts to be brought into account for the purpose of complying with paragraph 35 are the sums receivable in respect of the financial year (whenever paid) or, in the case of sums not receivable in respect of a period, the sums paid during that year.

(4) But where—

(a) any sums are not brought into account for the financial year on the ground that the person receiving them is liable to account for them as mentioned in sub-paragraph (1), but the liability is wholly or partly released or is not enforced within a period of 2 years ; or

(b) any sums paid to a person by way of expenses allowance are charged to United Kingdom income tax after the end of the financial year,

those sums shall, to the extent to which the liability is released or not enforced or they are charged as above mentioned (as the case may be), be brought into account for the purpose of complying with paragraph 35 on the first occasion on which it is practicable to do so.

37. References in paragraph 36 to a company's subsidiary—

(a) in relation to a person who is or was, while employed by the company a director, by virtue of the company's nomination (direct or indirect), of any other body corporate, include that body corporate (but subject to the following sub-paragraph), whether or not it is or was in fact the company's subsidiary ; and

(b) are to be taken as referring to a subsidiary at the time the services were rendered.

SCHEDULE 6

PARTICULARS IN COMPANY ACCOUNTS OF LOAN AND OTHER TRANSACTIONS FAVOURING DIRECTORS AND OFFICERS

PART I

MATTERS TO BE DISCLOSED UNDER SECTION 232

1. Group accounts shall contain the particulars required by this Schedule of—

(a) any transaction or arrangement of a kind described in

section 330 entered into by the company or by a subsidiary
of the company for a person who at any time during the
financial year was a director of the company or its holding
company, or was connected with such a director ;

(b) an agreement by the company or by a subsidiary of the
company to enter into any such transaction or arrangement
for a person who was at any time during the financial year
a director of the company or its holding company, or was
connected with such a director ; and

(c) any other transaction or arrangement with the company
or a subsidiary of it in which a person who at any time
during the financial year was a director of the company or
its holding company had, directly or indirectly, a material
interest.

2. The accounts prepared by a company other than a holding
company shall contain the particulars required by this Schedule of—

(a) any transaction or arrangement of a kind described in section
330 entered into by the company for a person who at any
time during the financial year was a director of it or of its
holding company or was connected with such a director ;

(b) an agreement by the company to enter into any such
transaction or arrangement for a person who at any time
during the financial year was a director of the company or
its holding company or was connected with such a director ;
and

(c) any other transaction or arrangement with the company in
which a person who at any time during the financial year
was a director of the company or of its holding company
had, directly or indirectly, a material interest.

3.—(1) For purposes of paragraphs 1(c) and 2(c), a transaction or
arrangement between a company and a director of it or of its holding
company, or a person connected with such a director, is to be treated
(if it would not otherwise be so) as a transaction, arrangement or
agreement in which that director is interested.

(2) An interest in such a transaction or arrangement is not
" material " for purposes of those sub-paragraphs if in the board's
opinion it is not so ; but this is without prejudice to the question
whether or not such an interest is material in a case where the
board have not considered the matter.

" The board " here means the directors of the company preparing
the accounts, or a majority of those directors, but excluding in either
case the director whose interest it is.

4. Paragraphs 1 and 2 do not apply, for the purposes of accounts
prepared by a company which is, or is the holding company of, a
recognised bank, in relation to a transaction or arrangement of a
kind described in section 330 or an agreement to enter into such
a transaction or arrangement, to which that recognised bank is a
party.

5. Paragraphs 1 and 2 do not apply in relation to the following
transactions, arrangements and agreements—

  (a) a transaction, arrangement or agreement between one com-
      pany and another in which a director of the former or of
      its subsidiary or holding company is interested only by
      virtue of his being a director of the latter ;

  (b) a contract of service between a company and one of its
      directors or a director of its holding company, or between
      a director of a company and any of that company's sub-
      sidiaries ;

  (c) a transaction, arrangement or agreement which was not
      entered into during the financial year and which did not
      subsist at any time during that year.

6. Paragraphs 1 and 2 apply whether or not—

  (a) the transaction or arrangement was prohibited by section
      330 ;

  (b) the person for whom it was made was a director of the
      company or was connected with a director of it at the time
      it was made ;

  (c) in the case of a transaction or arrangement made by a
      company which at any time during a financial year is a
      subsidiary of another company, it was a subsidiary of that
      other company at the time the transaction or arrangement
      was made.

7. Neither paragraph 1(c) nor paragraph 2 (c) applies in relation
to any transaction or arrangement if—

  (a) each party to the transaction or arrangement which is a
      member of the same group of companies (meaning a hold-
      ing company and its subsidiaries) as the company entered
      into the transaction or arrangement in the ordinary course
      of business, and

  (b) the terms of the transaction or arrangement are not less
      favourable to any such party than it would be reasonable
      to expect if the interest mentioned in that sub-paragraph
      had not been an interest of a person who was a director
      of the company or of its holding company.

8. Neither paragraph 1(c) nor paragraph 2(c) applies in relation
to any transaction or arrangement if—

  (a) the company is a member of a group of companies (mean-
      ing a holding company and its subsidiaries), and

  (b) either the company is a wholly-owned subsidiary or no body
      corporate (other than the company or a subsidiary of the
      company) which is a member of the group of companies
      which includes the company's ultimate holding company was
      a party to the transaction or arrangement, and

  (c) the director in question was at some time during the rele-
      vant period associated with the company, and

(*d*) the material interest of the director in question in the transaction or arrangement would not have arisen if he had
not been associated with the company at any time during
the relevant period.

The particulars required by this Part

9.—(1) Subject to the next paragraph, the particulars required by
this Part are those of the principal terms of the transaction, arrangement or agreement.

(2) Without prejudice to the generality of sub-paragraph (1), the
following particulars are required—

(*a*) a statement of the fact either that the transaction, arrangement or agreement was made or subsisted (as the case
may be) during the financial year ;

(*b*) the name of the person for whom it was made and, where
that person is or was connected with a director of the
company or of its holding company, the name of that
director ;

(*c*) in a case where paragraph 1(*c*) or 2(*c*) applies, the name of
the director with the material interest and the nature of
that interest ;

(*d*) in the case of a loan or an agreement for a loan or an
arrangement within section 330(6) or (7) of this Act relating
to a loan—

(i) the amount of the liability of the person to whom
the loan was or was agreed to be made, in respect of
principal and interest, at the beginning and at the end
of the financial year ;

(ii) the maximum amount of that liability during that
year ;

(iii) the amount of any interest which, having fallen
due, has not been paid ; and

(iv) the amount of any provision (within the meaning
of Schedule 4 to this Act) made in respect of any failure
or anticipated failure by the borrower to repay the whole
or part of the loan or to pay the whole or part of any
interest on it ;

(*e*) in the case of a guarantee or security or an arrangement
within section 330(6) relating to a guarantee or security—

(i) the amount for which the company (or its subsidiary) was liable under the guarantee or in respect of
the security both at the beginning and at the end of the
financial year ;

(ii) the maximum amount for which the company (or
its subsidiary) may become so liable ; and

(iii) any amount paid and any liability incurred by the
company (or its subsidiary) for the purpose of fulfilling
the guarantee or discharging the security (including any
loss incurred by reason of the enforcement of the
guarantee or security) ; and

(f) in the case of any transaction, arrangement or agreement other than those mentioned in sub-paragraphs (d) and (e), the value of the transaction or arrangement or (as the case may be) the value of the transaction or arrangement to which the agreement relates.

10. In paragraph 9(2) above, sub-paragraphs (c) to (f) do not apply in the case of a loan or quasi-loan made or agreed to be made by a company to or for a body corporate which is either—

(a) a body corporate of which that company is a wholly-owned subsidiary, or

(b) a wholly-owned subsidiary of a body corporate of which that company is a wholly-owned subsidiary, or

(c) a wholly-owned subsidiary of that company,

if particulars of that loan, quasi-loan or agreement for it would not have been required to be included in that company's annual accounts if the first-mentioned body corporate had not been associated with a director of that company at any time during the relevant period.

Transactions excluded from section 232

11.—(1) In relation to a company's accounts for a financial year, compliance with this Part is not required in the case of transactions of a kind mentioned in the following sub-paragraph which are made by the company or a subsidiary of it for a person who at any time during that financial year was a director of the company or of its holding company, or was connected with such a director, if the aggregate of the values of each transaction, arrangement or agreement so made for that director or any person connected with him, less the amount (if any) by which the liabilities of the person for whom the transaction or arrangement was made has been reduced, did not at any time during the financial year exceed £5,000.

(2) The transactions in question are—

(a) credit transactions,

(b) guarantees provided or securities entered into in connection with credit transactions,

(c) arrangements within subsection (6) or (7) of section 330 relating to credit transactions,

(d) agreements to enter into credit transactions.

12. In relation to a company's accounts for a financial year, compliance with this Part is not required by virtue of paragraph 1(c) or 2(c) in the case of any transaction or arrangement with a company or any of its subsidiaries in which a director of the company or its holding company had, directly or indirectly, a material interest if—

(a) the value of each transaction or arrangement within paragraph 1(c) or 2(c) (as the case may be) in which that director had (directly or indirectly) a material interest and which was made after the commencement of the financial year with the company or any of its subsidiaries, and

(b) the value of each such transaction or arrangement which was made before the commencement of the financial year less the amount (if any) by which the liabilities of the person for whom the transaction or arrangement was made have been reduced,

did not at any time during the financial year exceed in the aggregate £1,000 or, if more, did not exceed £5,000 or 1 per cent. of the value of the net assets of the company preparing the accounts in question as at the end of the financial year, whichever is the less.

For this purpose a company's net assets are the aggregate of its assets, less the aggregate of its liabilities (" liabilities " to include any provision for liabilities or charges within paragraph 89 of Schedule 4).

13. Section 345 of this Act (power of Secretary of State to alter sums by statutory instrument subject to negative resolution in Parliament) applies as if the money sums specified in paragraph 11 or 12 above were specified in Part X.

Interpretation

14. The following provisions of this Act apply for purposes of this Part of this Schedule—

> (*a*) section 331(2), (5) and (7), as regards the meaning of " guarantee ", " recognised bank " and " credit transaction ";
>
> (*b*) section 331(9), as to the interpretation of references to a transaction or arrangement being made " for " a person ;
>
> (*c*) section 340, in assigning values to transactions and arrangements, and
>
> (*d*) section 346, as to the interpretation of references to a person being " connected with " a director of a company.

PART II

MATTERS TO BE DISCLOSED UNDER SECTION 233

15. This Part of this Schedule applies in relation to the following classes of transactions, arrangements and agreements—

> (*a*) loans, guarantees and securities relating to loans, arrangements of a kind described in subsection (6) or (7) of section 330 of this Act relating to loans and agreements to enter into any of the foregoing transactions and arrangements ;
>
> (*b*) quasi-loans, guarantees and securities relating to quasi-loans arrangements of a kind described in either of those subsections relating to quasi-loans and agreements to enter into any of the foregoing transactions and arrangements ;
>
> (*c*) credit transactions, guarantees and securities relating to credit transactions, arrangements of a kind described in either of those subsections relating to credit transactions and agreements to enter into any of the foregoing transactions and arrangements.

16.—(1) To comply with this Part of this Schedule, the accounts must contain a statement, in relation to transactions, arrangements and agreements made as mentioned in section 233(1), of—

> (*a*) the aggregate amounts outstanding at the end of the financial year under transactions, arrangements and agreements

within sub-paragraphs (*a*), (*b*) and (*c*) respectively of paragraph 15 above, and

(*b*) the numbers of officers for whom the transactions, arrangements and agreements falling within each of those sub-paragraphs were made.

(2) This paragraph does not apply to transactions, arrangements and agreements made by the company or any of its subsidiaries for an officer of the company if the aggregate amount outstanding at the end of the financial year under the transactions, arrangements and agreements so made for that officer does not exceed £2,500.

(3) Section 345 of this Act (power of Secretary of State to alter money sums by statutory instrument subject to negative resolution in Parliament) applies as if the money sum specified above in this paragraph were specified in Part X.

17. The following provisions of this Act apply for purposes of this Part—

(*a*) section 331(2), (3), (5) and (7), as regards the meaning of " guarantee ", " quasi-loan ", " recognised bank " and " credit transaction ", and

(*b*) section 331(9), as to the interpretation of references to a transaction or arrangement being made " for " a person ;

and " amount outstanding " means the amount of the outstanding liabilities of the person for whom the transaction, arrangement or agreement was made or, in the case of a guarantee or security, the amount guaranteed or secured.

Part III

MATTERS TO BE DISCLOSED UNDER SECTION 234 (RECOGNISED BANKS)

18. This Part of this Schedule applies in relation to the same classes of transactions, arrangements and agreements as does Part II.

19. To comply with this Part, the accounts must contain a statement, in relation to such transactions, arrangements and agreements made as mentioned in section 234(1), of—

(*a*) the aggregate amounts outstanding at the end of the financial year under transactions, arrangements and agreements within sub-paragraphs (*a*), (*b*) and (*c*) respectively of paragraph 15 of this Schedule, and

(*b*) the numbers of persons for whom the transactions, arrangements and agreements falling within each of those sub-paragraphs were made.

20. For the purposes of the application of paragraph 19 in relation to loans and quasi-loans made by a company to persons connected with a person who at any time is a director of the company or of its holding company, a company which a person does not control is not connected with him.

21. The following provisions of this Act apply for purposes of this Part—

>   (*a*) section 331(3), as regards the meaning of " quasi-loan " ;

>   (*b*) section 331(9), as to the interpretation of references to a transaction or arrangement being made "for" a person ; and

>   (*c*) section 346, as to the interpretation of references to a person being connected with a director, or to a director controlling a company ;

and " amount outstanding " means the amount of the outstanding liabilities of the person for whom the transaction, arrangement or agreement was made or, in the case of a guarantee or security, the amount guaranteed or secured.

SCHEDULE 7

Matters to be Dealt With in Directors' Report

Part I

Matters of a General Nature

Asset values

1.—(1) If significant changes in the fixed assets of the company or of any of its subsidiaries have occurred in the financial year, the report shall contain particulars of the changes.

(2) If, in the case of such of those assets as consist in interests in land, their market value (as at the end of the financial year) differs substantially from the amount at which they are included in the balance sheet, and the difference is, in the directors' opinion, of such significance as to require that the attention of members of the company or of holders of its debentures should be drawn to it, the report shall indicate the difference with such degree of precision as is practicable.

Directors' interests

2.—(1) The report shall state the following, with respect to each person who, at the end of the financial year, was a director of the company—

>   (*a*) whether or not, according to the register kept by the company for the purposes of sections 324 to 328 of this Act (director's obligation to notify his interests in the company and companies in the same group), he was at the end of that year interested in shares in, or debentures of, the company or any other body corporate, being the company's subsidiary or holding company or a subsidiary of the company's holding company ;

>   (*b*) if he was so interested—

>>   (i) the number and amount of shares in, and debentures of, each body (specifying it) in which, according to that register, he was then interested,

(ii) whether or not (according to that register) he was, at the beginning of that year (or, if he was not then a director, when he became one), interested in shares in, or debentures of, the company or any other such body corporate, and

(iii) if he was, the number and amount of shares in, and debentures of, each body (specifying it) in which, according to that register, he was interested at the beginning of the financial year or (as the case may be) when he became a director.

(2) An interest in shares or debentures which, under sections 324 to 328, falls to be treated as being the interest of a director is so treated for the purposes of this paragraph; and the references above to the time when a person became a director, in the case of a person who became a director on more than one occasion, is to the time when he first became a director.

(3) The particulars required by this paragraph may be given by way of notes to the company's accounts in respect of the financial year, instead of being stated in the directors' report.

Political and charitable gifts

3.—(1) The following applies if the company (not being the wholly-owned subsidiary of a company incorporated in Great Britain) has in the financial year given money for political purposes or charitable purposes or both.

(2) If the money given exceeded £200 in amount, there shall be contained in the directors' report for the year—

(*a*) in the case of each of the purposes for which money has been given, a statement of the amount of money given for that purpose, and

(*b*) in the case of political purposes for which money has been given, the following particulars (so far as applicable)—

(i) the name of each person to whom money has been given for those purposes exceeding £200 in amount and the amount of money given,

(ii) if money exceeding £200 in amount has been given by way of donation or subscription to a political party, the identity of the party and the amount of money given.

4.—(1) Paragraph 3 does not apply to a company which, at the end of the financial year, has subsidiaries which have, in that year, given money as mentioned above, but is not itself the wholly-owned subsidiary of a company incorporated in Great Britain.

(2) But in such a case there shall (if the amount of money so given in that year by the company and the subsidiaries between them exceeds £200) be contained in the directors' report for the year—

(*a*) in the case of each of the purposes for which money has been given by the company and the subsidiaries between them, a statement of the amount of money given for that purpose, and (*b*) in the case of political purposes for which money has been given, the like particulars (so far as applicable) as are required by paragraph 3.

5.—(1) The following applies for the interpretation of paragraphs 3 and 4.

(2) A company is to be treated as giving money for political purposes if, directly or indirectly—

(*a*) it gives a donation or subscription to a political party of the United Kingdom or any part of it ; or

(*b*) it gives a donation or subscription to a person who, to the company's knowledge, is carrying on, or proposing to carry on, any activities which can, at the time at which the donation or subscription was given, reasonably be regarded as likely to affect public support for such a political party as is mentioned above.

(3) Money given for charitable purposes to a person who, when it was given, was ordinarily resident outside the United Kingdom is to be left out of account.

(4) " Charitable purposes " means purposes which are exclusively charitable ; and, as respects Scotland, " charitable " is to be construed as if it were contained in the Income Tax Acts.

Miscellaneous

6. The directors' report shall contain—

(*a*) particulars of any important events affecting the company or any of its subsidiaries which have occurred since the end of the financial year,

(*b*) an indication of likely future developments in the business of the company and of its subsidiaries, and

(*c*) an indication of the activities (if any) of the company and its subsidiaries in the field of research and development.

PART II

DISCLOSURE REQUIRED BY COMPANY ACQUIRING ITS OWN SHARES, ETC.

7. This Part of this Schedule applies where shares in a company—

(*a*) are purchased by the company or are acquired by it by forfeiture or surrender in lieu of forfeiture, or in pursuance of section 143(3) of this Act (acquisition of own shares by company limited by shares), or

(*b*) are acquired by another person in circumstances where paragraph (*c*) or (*d*) of section 146(1) applies (acquisition by company's nominee, or by another with company financial assistance, the company having a beneficial interest), or

(c) are made subject to a lien or other charge taken (whether expressly or otherwise) by the company and permitted by section 150(2) or (4), or section 6(3) of the Consequential Provisions Act (exceptions from general rule against a company having a lien or charge on its own shares).

8. The directors' report with respect to a financial year shall state—

    (a) the number and nominal value of the shares so purchased, the aggregate amount of the consideration paid by the company for such shares and the reasons for their purchase ;

    (b) the number and nominal value of the shares so acquired by the company, acquired by another person in such circumstances and so charged respectively during the financial year ;

    (c) the maximum number and nominal value of shares which, having been so acquired by the company, acquired by another person in such circumstances or so charged (whether or not during that year) are held at any time by the company or that other person during that year ;

    (d) the number and nominal value of the shares so acquired by the company, acquired by another person in such circumstances or so charged (whether or not during that year) which are disposed of by the company or that other person or cancelled by the company during that year ;

    (e) where the number and nominal value of the shares of any particular description are stated in pursuance of any of the preceding sub-paragraphs, the percentage of the called-up share capital which shares of that description represent ;

    (f) where any of the shares have been so charged the amount of the charge in each case ; and

    (g) where any of the shares have been disposed of by the company or the person who acquired them in such circumstances for money or money's worth the amount or value of the consideration in each case.

PART III

DISCLOSURE CONCERNING EMPLOYMENT, ETC, OF DISABLED PERSONS

9.—(1) This Part of this Schedule applies to the directors' report where the average number of persons employed by the company in each week during the financial year exceeded 250.

(2) That average number is the quotient derived by dividing, by the number of weeks in the financial year, the number derived by ascertaining, in relation to each of those weeks, the number of persons who, under contracts of service, were employed in the week (whether throughout it or not) by the company, and adding up the numbers ascertained.

(3) The directors' report shall in that case contain a statement describing such policy as the company has applied during the financial year—

(*a*) for giving full and fair consideration to applications for employment by the company made by disabled persons, having regard to their particular aptitudes and abilities,

(*b*) for continuing the employment of, and for arranging appropriate training for, employees of the company who have become disabled persons during the period when they were employed by the company, and

(*c*) otherwise for the training, career development and promotion of disabled persons employed by the company.

(4) In this Part—

(*a*) " employment " means employment other than employment to work wholly or mainly outside the United Kingdom, and " employed " and " employee " shall be construed accordingly ; and

1944 c. 10.

(*b*) " disabled person " means the same as in the Disabled Persons (Employment) Act 1944.

PART IV

HEALTH, SAFETY AND WELFARE AT WORK OF COMPANY'S EMPLOYEES

10.—(1) In the case of companies of such classes as may be prescribed by regulations made by the Secretary of State, the directors' report shall contain such information as may be so prescribed about the arrangements in force in the financial year for securing the health, safety and welfare at work of employees of the company and its subsidiaries, and for protecting other persons against risks to health or safety arising out of or in connection with the activities at work of those employees.

(2) Regulations under this Part may—

(*a*) make different provision in relation to companies of different classes,

(*b*) enable any requirements of the regulations to be dispensed with or modified in particular cases by any specified person or by any person authorised in that behalf by a specified authority,

(*c*) contain such transitional provisions as the Secretary of State thinks necessary or expedient in connection with any provision made by the regulations.

(3) The power to make regulations under this paragraph is exercisable by statutory instrument subject to annulment in pursuance of a resolution of either House of Parliament.

(4) Any expression used in sub-paragraph (1) above and in Part I of the Health and Safety at Work etc. Act 1974 has the same meaning

1974 c. 37.

here as it has in that Part of that Act ; section 1(3) of that Act
applies for interpreting that sub-paragraph ; and in sub-paragraph (2)
" specified " means specified in regulations made under that sub-
paragraph.

PART V

EMPLOYEE INVOLVEMENT

11.—(1) This Part of this Schedule applies to the directors' report
where the average number of persons employed by the company in
each week during the financial year exceeded 250.

(2) That average number is the quotient derived by dividing by the
number of weeks in the financial year the number derived by ascertaining, in relation to each of those weeks, the number of persons who,
under contracts of service, were employed in the week (whether
throughout it or not) by the company, and adding up the numbers
ascertained.

(3) The directors' report shall in that case contain a statement describing the action that has been taken during the financial year to
introduce, maintain or develop arrangements aimed at—

(a) providing employees systematically with information on
matters of concern to them as employees,

(b) consulting employees or their representatives on a regular
basis so that the views of employees can be taken into
account in making decisions which are likely to affect their
interests,

(c) encouraging the involvement of employees in the company's
performance through an employees' share scheme or by
some other means,

(d) achieving a common awareness on the part of all employees
of the financial and economic factors affecting the performance of the company.

(4) In sub-paragraph (3) " employee " does not include a person
employed to work wholly or mainly outside the United Kingdom ;
and for the purposes of sub-paragraph (2) no regard is to be had to
such a person.

SCHEDULE 8

MODIFIED ACCOUNTS OF COMPANIES QUALIFYING AS SMALL OR MEDIUM SIZED

PART I

MODIFIED INDIVIDUAL ACCOUNTS

Introductory

1. In this Part of this Schedule—

(a) paragraphs 2 to 6 relate to a company's individual accounts
modified as for a small company,

(*b*) paragraphs 7 and 8 relate to a company's individual accounts modified as for a medium-sized company, and

(*c*) paragraphs 9 to 11 relate to both cases.

Accounts modified as for a small company

2.—(1) In respect of the relevant financial year, there may be delivered a copy of a modified balance sheet, instead of the full balance sheet.

(2) The modified balance sheet shall be an abbreviated version of the full balance sheet, showing only those items to which a letter or Roman number is assigned in the balance sheet format adopted under Schedule 4, Part I, but in other respects corresponding to the full balance sheet.

(3) The copy of the modified balance sheet shall be signed as required by section 238.

3. A copy of the company's profit and loss account need not be delivered, nor a copy of the directors' report otherwise required by section 241.

4. The information required by Parts V and VI of Schedule 5 need not be given.

5. The information required by Schedule 4 to be given in notes to the accounts need not be given, with the exception of any information required by the following provisions of that Schedule—

　　paragraph 36 (accounting policies),

　　paragraph 38 (share capital),

　　paragraph 39 (particulars of allotments),

　　paragraph 48(1) and (4) (particulars of debts),

　　paragraph 58(1) (basis of translation of foreign currency amounts into sterling), and

　　paragraph 58(2) (corresponding amounts for preceding financial year) ;

and the reference here to paragraph 58(2) includes that sub-paragraph as applied to any item stated in a note to the company's accounts, whether by virtue of a requirement of Schedule 4 or under any other provision of this Act.

6. If a modified balance sheet is delivered, there shall be disclosed in it (or in a note to the company's accounts delivered)—

(*a*) the aggregate of the amounts required by note (*5*) of the notes on the balance sheet formats set out in Schedule 4 Part I to be shown separately for each item included under debtors (amounts falling due after one year), and

(*b*) the aggregate of the amounts required by note (*13*) of those notes to be shown separately for each item included under creditors in Format 2 (amounts falling due within one year or after more than one year).

Accounts modified as for a medium-sized company

7.—(1) There may be delivered a copy of a modified profit and loss account, instead of the company's full profit and loss account (that is, the profit and loss account prepared as under section 227).

(2) The modified profit and loss account shall, save for one exception, correspond to the full profit and loss account ; and that exception is the combination as one item, under the heading "gross profit or loss", of the following items listed in the profit and loss account formats set out in Schedule 4 Part I—

Items 1, 2, 3 and 6 in Format 1 ;

Items 1 to 5 in Format 2 ;

Items A.1, B.1 and B.2 in Format 3 ; and

Items A.1, A.2 and B.1 to B.4 in Format 4.

8. The information required by paragraph 55 of Schedule 4 (particulars of turnover) need not be given.

Both cases

9. The company's balance sheet shall contain a statement by the directors that—

(*a*) they rely on sections 247 to 249 of this Act as entitling them to deliver modified accounts, and

(*b*) they do so on the ground that the company is entitled to the benefit of those sections as a small or (as the case may be) a medium-sized company ;

and the statement shall appear in the balance sheet immediately above the signatures of the directors.

10.—(1) The accounts delivered shall be accompanied by a special report of the auditors stating that in their opinion—

(*a*) the directors are entitled to deliver modified accounts in respect of the financial year, as claimed in the directors' statement, and

(*b*) any accounts comprised in the documents delivered as modified accounts are properly prepared as such in accordance with this Schedule.

(2) A copy of the auditors' report under section 236 need not be delivered ; but the full text of it shall be reproduced in the special report under this paragraph.

(3) If the directors propose to rely on sections 247 to 249 as entitling them to deliver modified accounts, it is the auditors' duty to provide them with a report stating whether in their opinion the directors are so entitled, and whether the documents to be delivered as modified accounts are properly prepared in accordance with this Act.

11. Subject as above, where the directors rely on sections 247 to 249 in delivering any documents, and—

(*a*) the company is entitled to the benefit of those sections on the ground claimed by the directors in their statement under paragraph 9, and (*b*) the accounts comprised in the documents delivered as modified accounts are properly prepared in accordance with this Schedule,

then section 241(3) has effect as if any document which by virtue of this Part of this Schedule is included in or omitted from the documents delivered as modified accounts were (or, as the case may be, were not) required by this Act to be comprised in the company's accounts in respect of the financial year.

PART II

MODIFIED GROUP ACCOUNTS (IN CONSOLIDATED FORM)

Introductory

12. In this Part of this Schedule—

   (*a*) paragraphs 13 to 17 relate to modified accounts for a small group, and

   (*b*) paragraphs 18 and 19 relate to modified accounts for a medium-sized group.

Small groups

13.—(1) In respect of the relevant financial year, there may be delivered a copy of a modified balance sheet, instead of the full consolidated balance sheet.

(2) The modified balance sheet shall be an abbreviated version of the full consolidated balance sheet, showing only those items to which a letter or Roman numeral is assigned in the balance sheet format adopted under Schedule 4 Part I, but in other respects corresponding to the full consolidated balance sheet.

14. A copy of the profit and loss account need not be delivered, nor a copy of the directors' report otherwise required by section 241.

15. The information required by Schedule 4 to be given in notes to group accounts need not be given, with the exception of any information required by provisions of that Schedule listed in paragraph 5 above.

16. There shall be disclosed in the modified balance sheet, or in a note to the group accounts delivered, aggregate amounts corresponding to those specified in paragraph 6 above.

17. The information required by Parts V and VI of Schedule 5 need not be given.

Medium-sized groups

18.—(1) There may be delivered a copy of a modified profit and loss account, instead of a full consolidated profit and loss account prepared as under section 229.

(2) The modified profit and loss account shall, save for one exception, correspond to the full consolidated profit and loss

account ; and that exception is the combination as one item, under the heading " gross profit or loss ", of the items listed in the profit and loss account formats set out in Schedule 4 Part I which are specified in paragraph 7(2) above.

19. The information required by paragraph 55 of Schedule 4 (particulars of turnover) need not be given.

PART III

MODIFIED GROUP ACCOUNTS (CONSOLIDATED OR OTHER)

20. If modified group accounts are delivered, the following paragraphs apply.

21. The directors' statement required by paragraph 9 to be contained in the balance sheet shall include a statement that the documents delivered include modified group accounts, in reliance on section 250.

22.—(1) The auditors' special report under paragraph 10 shall include a statement that in their opinion—

     (a) the directors are entitled to deliver modified group accounts, as claimed in their statement in the balance sheet, and

     (b) any accounts comprised in the documents delivered as modified group accounts are properly prepared as such in accordance with this Schedule.

(2) A copy of the auditors' report under section 236 need not be delivered ; but the full text of it shall be reproduced in the special report under paragraph 10.

(3) If the directors propose to rely on section 250 as entitling them to deliver modified group accounts, it is the auditors' duty to provide them with a report stating whether in their opinion the directors are so entitled, and whether the documents to be delivered as modified group accounts are properly prepared in accordance with this Schedule.

23. Subject as above, where the directors rely on section 250 in delivering any documents, and

     (a) the company is entitled to the benefit of that section on the ground claimed by the directors in their statement in the balance sheet, and

     (b) the accounts comprised in the documents delivered as modified accounts are properly prepared in accordance with this Schedule,

then section 241(3) has effect as if any document which by virtue of this Schedule is included in or omitted from the documents delivered as modified group accounts were (or, as the case may be, were not) required by this Act to be comprised in the company's accounts in respect of the financial year.

SCHEDULE 9

FORM AND CONTENT OF SPECIAL CATEGORY ACCOUNTS

Preliminary

1. Paragraphs 2 to 13 of this Schedule apply to the balance sheet and 14 to 18 to the profit and loss account, and are subject to the exceptions and modifications provided for by Part II of this Schedule in the case of a holding or subsidiary company and by Part III thereof in the case of companies of the classes there mentioned.

PART I

GENERAL PROVISIONS AS TO BALANCE SHEET AND PROFIT AND LOSS ACCOUNT

Balance sheet

2. The authorised share capital, issued share capital, liabilities and assets shall be summarised, with such particulars as are necessary to disclose the general nature of the assets and liabilities, and there shall be specified—

    (a) any part of the issued capital that consists of redeemable shares, the earliest and latest dates on which the company has power to redeem those shares, whether those shares must be redeemed in any event or are liable to be redeemed at the option of the company or of the shareholder and whether any (and, if so, what) premium is payable on redemption ;

    (b) so far as the information is not given in the profit and loss account, any share capital on which interest has been paid out of capital during the financial year, and the rate at which interest has been so paid ;

    (c) the amount of the share premium account ;

    (d) particulars of any redeemed debentures which the company has power to re-issue.

3. There shall be stated under separate headings, so far as they are not written off,—

    (a) the preliminary expenses ;

    (b) any expenses incurred in connection with any issue of share capital or debentures ;

    (c) any sums paid by way of commission in respect of any shares or debentures;

    (d) any sums allowed by way of discount in respect of any debentures ; and

    (e) the amount of the discount allowed on any issue of shares at a discount.

4.—(1) The reserves, provisions, liabilities and assets shall be
classified under headings appropriate to the company's business:

Provided that—

(a) where the amount of any class is not material, it may be included under the same heading as some other class ; and

(b) where any assets of one class are not separable from assets of another class, those assets may be included under the same heading.

(2) Fixed assets, current assets and assets that are neither fixed nor current shall be separately identified.

(3) The method or methods used to arrive at the amount of the fixed assets under each heading shall be stated.

5.—(1) The method of arriving at the amount of any fixed asset shall, subject to the next following sub-paragraph, be to take the difference between—

(a) its cost or, if it stands in the company's books at a valuation, the amount of the valuation ; and

(b) the aggregate amount provided or written off since the date of acquisition or valuation, as the case may be, for depreciation or diminution in value ;

and for the purposes of this paragraph the net amount at which any assets stood in the company's books on 1st July 1948 (after deduction of the amounts previously provided or written off for depreciation or diminution in value) shall, if the figures relating to the period before that date cannot be obtained without unreasonable expense or delay, be treated as if it were the amount of a valuation of those assets made at that date and, where any of those assets are sold, the said net amount less the amount of the sales shall be treated as if it were the amount of a valuation so made of the remaining assets.

(2) The foregoing sub-paragraph shall not apply—

(a) to assets for which the figures relating to the period beginning with 1st July 1948 cannot be obtained without unreasonable expense or delay ; or

(b) to assets the replacement of which is provided for wholly or partly—

(i) by making provision for renewals and charging the cost of replacement against the provision so made ; or

(ii) by charging the cost of replacement direct to revenue ; or

(c) to any listed investments or to any unlisted investments of which the value as estimated by the directors is shown either as the amount of the investments or by way of note ; or

(d) to goodwill, patents or trade marks.

(3) For the assets under each heading whose amount is arrived at in accordance with sub-paragraph (1) of this paragraph, there shall be shown—

   (a) the aggregate of the amounts referred to in paragraph (a) of that sub-paragraph ; and

   (b) the aggregate of the amounts referred to in paragraph (b) thereof.

(4) As respects the assets under each heading whose amount is not arrived at in accordance with the said sub-paragraph (1) because their replacement is provided for as mentioned in sub-paragraph (2)(b) of this paragraph, there shall be stated—

   (a) the means by which their replacement is provided for ; and

   (b) the aggregate amount of the provision (if any) made for renewals and not used.

6. In the case of unlisted investments consisting in equity share capital of other bodies corporate (other than any whose values as estimated by the directors are separately shown, either individually or collectively or as to some individually and as to the rest collectively, and are so shown either as the amount thereof, or by way of note), the matters referred to in the following heads shall, if not otherwise shown, be stated by way of note or in a statement or report annexed :—

   (a) the aggregate amount of the company's income for the financial year that is ascribable to the investments ;

   (b) the amount of the company's share before taxation, and the amount of that share after taxation, of the net aggregate amount of the profits of the bodies in which the investments are held, being profits for the several periods to which accounts sent by them during the financial year to the company related, after deducting those bodies' losses for those periods (or vice versa) ;

   (c) the amount of the company's share of the net aggregate amount of the undistributed profits accumulated by the bodies in which the investments are held since the time when the investments were acquired after deducting the losses accumulated by them since that time (or vice versa) ;

   (d) the manner in which any losses incurred by the said bodies have been dealt with in the company's accounts.

7. The aggregate amounts respectively of reserves and provisions (other than provisions for depreciation, renewals or diminution in value of assets) shall be stated under separate headings ;

Provided that—

   (a) this paragraph shall not require a separate statement of either of the said amounts which is not material ; and

   (b) the Secretary of State may direct that a separate statement shall not be required of the amount of provisions where he is satisfied that that is not required in the public interest

and would prejudice the company, but subject to the condition that any heading stating an amount arrived at after
taking into account a provision (other than as aforesaid)
shall be so framed or marked as to indicate that fact.

8.—(1) There shall also be shown (unless it is shown in the profit
and loss account or a statement or report annexed thereto, or the
amount involved is not material)—

(a) where the amount of the reserves or of the provisions (other
than provisions for depreciation, renewals or diminution in
value of assets) shows an increase as compared with the
amount at the end of the immediately preceding financial
year, the source from which the amount of the increase has
been derived ; and

(b) where—

(i) the amount of the reserves shows a decrease as
compared with the amount at the end of the immediately
preceding financial year ; or

(ii) the amount at the end of the immediately preceding
financial year of the provisions (other than provisions
for depreciation, renewals or diminution in value of assets)
exceeded the aggregate of the sums since applied and
amounts still retained for the purposes thereof ;

the application of the amounts derived from the difference.

(2) Where the heading showing the reserves or any of the provisions aforesaid is divided into sub-headings, this paragraph shall
apply to each of the separate amounts shown in the sub-headings
instead of applying to the aggregate amount thereof.

9. If an amount is set aside for the purpose of its being used
to prevent undue fluctuations in charges for taxation, it shall be
stated.

10.—(1) There shall be shown under separate headings—

(a) the aggregate amounts respectively of the company's listed
investments and unlisted investments ;

(b) if the amount of the goodwill and of any patents and trade
marks or part of that amount is shown as a separate item
in or is otherwise ascertainable from the books of the company, or from any contract for the sale or purchase of any
property to be acquired by the company, or from any documents in the possession of the company relating to the stamp
duty payable in respect of any such contract or the conveyance of any such property, the said amount so shown
or ascertained as far as not written off or, as the case may
be, the said amount so far as it is so shown or ascertainable
and as so shown or ascertained, as the case may be ;

(c) the aggregate amount of any outstanding loans made under
the authority of section 153(4)(b) or (c) or 155 of this Act ;

(*d*) the aggregate amount of bank loans and overdrafts and the aggregate amount of loans made to the company which—

> (i) are repayable otherwise than by instalments and fall due for repayment after the expiration of the period of five years beginning with the day next following the expiration of the financial year ; or
>
> (ii) are repayable by instalments any of which fall due for payment after the expiration of that period ;
>
> not being, in either case, bank loans or overdrafts ;

(*e*) the aggregate amount which is recommended for distribution by way of dividend.

(2) Nothing in head (*b*) of the foregoing sub-paragraph shall be taken as requiring the amount of the goodwill, patents and trade marks to be stated otherwise than as a single item.

(3) The heading showing the amount of the listed investments shall be subdivided, where necessary, to distinguish the investments as respects which there has, and those as respects which there has not, been granted a listing on a recognised stock exchange.

(4) In relation to each loan falling within head (*d*) of sub-paragraph (1) of this paragraph (other than a bank loan or overdraft), there shall be stated by way of note (if not otherwise stated) the terms on which it is repayable and the rate at which interest is payable thereon:

Provided that if the number of loans is such that, in the opinion of the directors, compliance with the foregoing requirement would result in a statement of excessive length, it shall be sufficient to give a general indication of the terms on which the loans are repayable and the rates at which interest is payable thereon.

11. Where any liability of the company is secured otherwise than by operation of law on any assets of the company, the fact that that liability is so secured shall be stated, but it shall not be necessary to specify the assets on which the liability is secured.

12. Where any of the company's debentures are held by a nominee of or trustee for the company, the nominal amount of the debentures and the amount at which they are stated in the books of the company shall be stated.

13.—(1) The matters referred to in the following sub-paragraphs shall be stated by way of note, or in a statement or report annexed, if not otherwise shown.

(2) The number, description and amount of any shares in the company which any person has an option to subscribe for, together with the following particulars of the option, that is to say—

(*a*) the period during which it is exercisable ;

(*b*) the price to be paid for shares subscribed for under it.

(3) Where shares in a public company (other than an old public company within the meaning of section 1 of the Consequential

Provisions Act) are purchased or are acquired by the company by
forfeiture or surrender in lieu of forfeiture, or as expressly permitted
by section 143(3) of this Act, or are acquired by another person in
circumstances where paragraph (c) or (d) of section 146(1) applies
or are made subject to a lien or charge taken (whether expressly or
otherwise) by the company and permitted by section 150(2) or (4),
or section 6(3) of the Consequential Provisions Act—

    (a) the number and nominal value of the shares so purchased,
the aggregate amount of the consideration paid by the
company for such shares and the reasons for their purchase ;

    (b) the number and nominal value of the shares so acquired
by the company, acquired by another person in such
circumstances and so charged respectively during the
financial year ;

    (c) the maximum number and nominal value of shares which,
having been so acquired by the company, acquired by
another person in such circumstances or so charged
(whether or not during the financial year) are held at any
time by the company or that other person during that year ;

    (d) the number and nominal value of shares so acquired by the
company, acquired by another person in such circumstances
or so charged (whether or not during that year) which are
disposed of by the company or that other person or cancelled by the company during that year ;

    (e) where the number and nominal value of the shares of any
particular description are stated in pursuance of any of the
preceding paragraphs, the percentage of the called-up share
capital which shares of that description represent ;

    (f) where any of the shares have been so charged, the amount
of the charge in each case ;

    (g) where any of the shares have been disposed of by the com-
pany or the person who acquired them in such circumstances for money or money's worth, the amount or value
of the consideration in each case.

(4) Any distribution made by an investment company within
the meaning of Part VIII of this Act which reduces the amount of
its net assets to less than the aggregate of its called-up share capital
and undistributable reserves.

For purposes of this sub-paragraph, a company's net assets are the
aggregate of its assets less the aggregate of its liabilities ; and " undistributable reserves " has the meaning given by section 264(3).

(5) The amount of any arrears of fixed cumulative dividends on
the company's shares and the period for which the dividends or, if
there is more than one class, each class of them are in arrear.

(6) Particulars of any charge on the assets of the company to
secure the liabilities of any other person, including, where practicable,
the amount secured.

U

(7) The general nature of any other contingent liabilities not provided for and, where practicable, the aggregate amount or estimated amount of those liabilities, if it is material.

(8) Where practicable the aggregate amount or estimated amount, if it is material, of contracts for capital expenditure, so far as not provided for and, where practicable, the aggregate amount or estimated amount, if it is material, of capital expenditure authorised by the directors which has not been contracted for.

(9) In the case of fixed assets under any heading whose amount is required to be arrived at in accordance with paragraph 5(1) of this Schedule (other than unlisted investments) and is so arrived at by reference to a valuation, the years (so far as they are known to the directors) in which the assets were severally valued and the several values, and, in the case of assets that have been valued during the financial year, the names of the persons who valued them or particulars of their qualifications for doing so and (whichever is stated) the bases of valuation used by them.

(10) If there are included amongst fixed assets under any heading (other than investments) assets that have been acquired during the financial year, the aggregate amount of the assets acquired as determined for the purpose of making up the balance sheet, and if during that year any fixed assets included under a heading in the balance sheet made up with respect to the immediately preceding financial year (other than investments) have been disposed of or destroyed, the aggregate amount thereof as determined for the purpose of making up that balance sheet.

(11) Of the amount of fixed assets consisting of land, how much is ascribable to land of freehold tenure and how much to land of leasehold tenure, and, of the latter, how much is ascribable to land held on long lease and how much to land held on short lease.

(12) If in the opinion of the directors any of the current assets have not a value, on realisation in the ordinary course of the company's business, at least equal to the amount at which they are stated, the fact that the directors are of that opinion.

(13) The aggregate market value of the company's listed investments where it differs from the amount of the investments as stated and the stock exchange value of any investments of which the market value is shown (whether separately or not) and is taken as being higher than their stock exchange value.

(14) If a sum set aside for the purpose of its being used to prevent undue fluctuations in charges for taxation has been used during the financial year for another purpose, the amount thereof and the fact that it has been so used.

(15) If the amount carried forward for stock in trade or work in progress is material for the appreciation by its members of the company's state of affairs or of its profit or loss for the financial year, the manner in which that amount has been computed.

(16) The basis on which foreign currencies have been converted into sterling, where the amount of the assets or liabilities affected is material.

(17) The basis on which the amount, if any, set aside for United Kingdom corporation tax is computed.

(18) The corresponding amounts at the end of the immediately preceding financial year for all items shown in the balance sheet other than any item the amount for which is shown—

(a) in pursuance of sub-paragraph (10) of this paragraph, or

(b) as an amount the source or application of which is required by paragraph 8 to be shown.

Profit and loss account

14.—(1) There shall be shown—

(a) the amount charged to revenue by way of provision for depreciation, renewals or diminution in value of fixed assets ;

(b) the amount of the interest on loans of the following kinds made to the company (whether on the security of debentures or not), namely, bank loans, overdrafts and loans which, not being bank loans or overdrafts,—

(i) are repayable otherwise than by instalments and fall due for repayment before the expiration of the period of five years beginning with the day next following the expiration of the financial year ; or

(ii) are repayable by instalments the last of which falls due for payment before the expiration of that period ;

and the amount of the interest on loans of other kinds so made (whether on the security of debentures or not) ;

(c) the amount of the charge to revenue for United Kingdom corporation tax and, if that amount would have been greater but for relief from double taxation, the amount which it would have been but for such relief, the amount of the charge for United Kingdom income tax, and the amount of the charge for taxation imposed outside the United Kingdom of profits, income and (so far as charged to revenue) capital gains ;

(d) the amounts respectively set aside for redemption of share capital and for redemption of loans ;

(e) the amount, if material, set aside or proposed to be set aside to, or withdrawn from, reserves ;

(f) subject to sub-paragraph (2) of this paragraph, the amount, if material, set aside to provisions other than provisions for depreciation, renewals, or diminution in value of assets or, as the case may be, the amount, if material, withdrawn from such provisions and not applied for the purposes thereof ;

(g) the amounts respectively of income from listed investments and income from unlisted investments ;

U 2

(*h*) if a substantial part of the company's revenue for the financial year consists in rents from land, the amount thereof (after deduction of ground-rents, rates and other outgoings) ;

(*j*) the amount, if material, charged to revenue in respect of sums payable in respect of the hire of plant and machinery ;

(*k*) the aggregate amount of the dividends paid and proposed.

(2) The Secretary of State may direct that a company shall not be obliged to show an amount set aside to provisions in accordance with sub-paragraph (1)(*f*) of this paragraph, if he is satisfied that that is not required in the public interest and would prejudice the company, but subject to the condition that any heading stating an amount arrived at after taking into account the amount set aside as aforesaid shall be so framed or marked as to indicate that fact.

(3) If, in the case of any assets in whose case an amount is charged to revenue by way of provision for depreciation or diminution in value, an amount is also so charged by way of provision for renewal thereof, the last-mentioned amount shall be shown separately.

(4) If the amount charged to revenue by way of provision for depreciation or diminution in value of any fixed assets (other than investments) has been determined otherwise than by reference to the amount of those assets as determined for the purpose of making up the balance sheet, that fact shall be stated.

15. The amount of any charge arising in consequence of the occurrence of an event in a preceding financial year and of any credit so arising shall, if not included in a heading relating to other matters, be stated under a separate heading.

16. The amount of the remuneration of the auditors shall be shown under a separate heading, and for the purposes of this paragraph, any sums paid by the company in respect of the auditors' expenses shall be deemed to be included in the expression " remuneration ".

17.—(1) The following matters shall be stated by way of note, if not otherwise shown.

(2) The turnover for the financial year, except in so far as it is attributable to the business of banking or discounting or to business of such other class as may be prescribed for the purposes of this sub-paragraph.

(3) If some or all of the turnover is omitted by reason of its being attributable as aforesaid, the fact that it is so omitted.

(4) The method by which turnover stated is arrived at.

(5) A company shall not be subject to the requirements of this paragraph if it is neither a holding company nor a subsidiary of another body corporate and the turnover which, apart from this sub-paragraph, would be required to be stated does not exceed £1 million.

18.—(1) The following matters shall be stated by way of note, if not otherwise shown.

(2) If depreciation or replacement of fixed assets is provided for
by some method other than a depreciation charge or provision for
renewals, or is not provided for, the method by which it is provided
for or the fact that it is not provided for, as the case may be.

(3) The basis on which the charge for United Kingdom corporation tax and United Kingdom income tax is computed.

(4) Any special circumstances which affect liability in respect of
taxation of profits, income or capital gains for the financial year or
liability in respect of taxation of profits, income or capital gains
for succeeding financial years.

(5) The corresponding amounts for the immediately preceding
financial year for all items shown in the profit and loss account.

(6) Any material respects in which items shown in the profit and
loss account are affected—

  (a) by transactions of a sort not usually undertaken by the
      company or otherwise by circumstances of an exceptional
      or non-recurrent nature ; or

  (b) by any change in the basis of accounting.

PART II

SPECIAL PROVISIONS WHERE THE COMPANY IS A HOLDING OR SUBSIDIARY COMPANY

Modifications of and additions to requirements as to company's own accounts

19.—(1) This paragraph applies where the company is a holding company, whether or not it is itself a subsidiary of another
body corporate.

(2) The aggregate amount of assets consisting of shares in, or
amounts owing (whether on account of a loan or otherwise) from,
the company's subsidiaries, distinguishing shares from indebtedness,
shall be set out in the balance sheet separately from all the other
assets of the company, and the aggregate amount of indebtedness
(whether on account of a loan or otherwise) to the company's subsidiaries shall be so set out separately from all its other liabilities
and—

  (a) the references in Part I of this Schedule to the company's
      investments (except those in paragraphs 13(10) and 14(4))
      shall not include investments in its subsidiaries required by
      this paragraph to be separately set out ; and

  (b) paragraph 5, sub-paragraph (1)(a) of paragraph 14, and sub-
      paragraph (2) of paragraph 18 of this Schedule shall not
      apply in relation to fixed assets consisting of interests in
      the company's subsidiaries.

(3) There shall be shown by way of note on the balance sheet
or in a statement or report annexed thereto the number, description
and amount of the shares in and debentures of the company held

by its subsidiaries or their nominees, but excluding any of those shares or debentures in the case of which the subsidiary is concerned as personal representative or in the case of which it is concerned as trustee and neither the company nor any subsidiary thereof is beneficially interested under the trust, otherwise than by way of security only for the purposes of a transaction entered into by it in the ordinary course of a business which includes the lending of money.

Schedule 2 has effect for the interpretation of the reference in this sub-paragraph to a beneficial interest under a trust.

(4) Where group accounts are not submitted, there shall be annexed to the balance sheet a statement showing—

 (*a*) the reasons why subsidiaries are not dealt with in group accounts ;

 (*b*) the net aggregate amount, so far as it concerns members of the holding company and is not dealt with in the company's accounts, of the subsidiaries' profits after deducting the subsidiaries' losses (or vice versa)—

  (i) for the respective financial years of the subsidiaries ending with or during the financial year of the company ; and

  (ii) for their previous financial years since they respectively became the holding company's subsidiary ;

 (*c*) the net aggregate amount of the subsidiaries' profits after deducting the subsidiaries' losses (or vice versa)—

  (i) for the respective financial years of the subsidiaries ending with or during the financial year of the company ; and

  (ii) for their other financial years since they respectively became the holding company's subsidiary ;

 so far as those profits are dealt with, or provision is made for those losses, in the company's accounts ;

 (*d*) any qualifications contained in the report of the auditors of the subsidiaries on their accounts for their respective financial years ending as aforesaid, and any note or saving contained in those accounts to call attention to a matter which, apart from the note or saving, would properly have been referred to in such a qualification, in so far as the matter which is the subject of the qualification or note is not covered by the company's own accounts and is material from the point of view of its members ;

or, in so far as the information required by this sub-paragraph is not obtainable, a statement that it is not obtainable:

Provided that the Secretary of State may, on the application or with the consent of the company's directors, direct that in relation to any subsidiary this sub-paragraph shall not apply or shall apply only to such extent as may be provided by the direction.

(5) Paragraphs (*b*) and (*c*) of the last foregoing sub-paragraph shall apply only to profits and losses of a subsidiary which may properly be treated in the holding company's accounts as revenue profits or

losses, and the profits or losses attributable to any shares in a subsidiary for the time being held by the holding company or any other
of its subsidiaries shall not (for the purposes of those paragraphs) be
treated as aforesaid so far as they are profits or losses for the period
before the date on or as from which the shares were acquired by
the company or any of its subsidiaries, except that they may in a
proper case be so treated where—

 (a) the company is itself the subsidiary of another body corporate ; and

 (b) the shares were acquired from that body corporate or a
   subsidiary of it ;

and for the purpose of determining whether any profits or losses are
to be treated as profits or losses for the said period the profit or loss
for any financial year of the subsidiary may, if it is not practicable
to apportion it with reasonable accuracy by reference to the facts, be
treated as accruing from day to day during that year and be ap-
portioned accordingly.

 The amendment of the previous corresponding provision by section
40(3) of the Companies Act 1981 (substituting " (for the purposes of
those paragraphs) " for " (for that or any other purpose) ") is without
prejudice to any other restriction with respect to the manner in which
a holding company may treat pre-acquisition profits or losses of a
subsidiary in its accounts.

 (6) Paragraphs (b) and (c) of sub-paragraph (4) above shall not
apply where the company is a wholly-owned subsidiary of another
body corporate incorporated in Great Britain if there is annexed
to the balance sheet a statement that in the opinion of the directors
of the company the aggregate value of the assets of the company
consisting of shares in, or amounts owing (whether on account of a
loan or otherwise) from, the company's subsidiaries is not less than
the aggregate of the amounts at which those assets are stated or
included in the balance sheet.

 (7) Where group accounts are not submitted, there shall be annexed
to the balance sheet a statement showing, in relation to the subsidiaries (if any) whose financial years did not end with that of the
company—

 (a) the reasons why the company's directors consider that the
   subsidiaries' financial years should not end with that of the
   company ; and

 (b) the dates on which the subsidiaries' financial years ending
   last before that of the company respectively ended or the
   earliest and latest of those dates.

 20.—(1) The balance sheet of a company which is a subsidiary
of another body corporate, whether or not it is itself a holding company, shall show the aggregate amount of its indebtedness to all
bodies corporate of which it is a subsidiary or a fellow subsidiary
and the aggregate amount of indebtedness of all such bodies corporate
to it, distinguishing in each case between indebtedness in respect of
debentures and otherwise, and the aggregate amount of assets consisting of shares in fellow subsidiaries.

(2) For the purposes of this paragraph a company shall be deemed to be a fellow subsidiary of another body corporate if both are subsidiaries of the same body corporate but neither is the other's.

Consolidated accounts of holding company and subsidiaries

21. Subject to the following paragraphs of this Part of this Schedule the consolidated balance sheet and profit and loss account shall combine the information contained in the separate balance sheets and profit and loss accounts of the holding company and of the subsidiaries dealt with by the consolidated accounts, but with such adjustments (if any) as the directors of the holding company think necessary.

22. Subject as aforesaid and to Part III of this Schedule, the consolidated accounts shall, in giving the said information, comply so far as practicable, with the requirements of this Act as if they were the accounts of an actual company.

23. The following provisions of this Act, namely—

(a) section 231 as applying Schedule 5, but only Parts II, V and VI of that Schedule, and

(b) sections 232 to 234 and Schedule 6, so far as relating to accounts other than group accounts,

do not by virtue of the two last foregoing paragraphs apply for the purpose of the consolidated accounts.

24. Paragraph 22 above is without prejudice to any requirement of this Act which applies (otherwise than by virtue of paragraph 21 or 22) to group accounts.

25. In relation to any subsidiaries of the holding company not dealt with by the consolidated accounts—

(a) sub-paragraphs (2) and (3) of paragraph 19 of this Schedule shall apply for the purpose of those accounts as if those accounts were the accounts of an actual company of which they were subsidiaries ; and

(b) there shall be annexed the like statement as is required by sub-paragraph (4) of that paragraph where there are no group accounts, but as if references therein to the holding company's accounts were references to the consolidated accounts.

26. In relation to any subsidiary (whether or not dealt with by the consolidated accounts), whose financial year did not end with that of the company, there shall be annexed the like statement as is required by sub-paragraph (7) of paragraph 19 of this Schedule where there are no group accounts.

Part III

Exceptions for Certain Special Category Companies

S.I. 1970/327.

27.—(1) The following applies to a banking company (if not subject to the Banking Companies (Accounts) Regulations 1970) which satisfies the Secretary of State that it ought to have the benefit of this paragraph.

(2) The company shall not be subject to the requirements of Part I
of this Schedule other than—

    (*a*) as respects its balance sheet, those of paragraphs 2 and 3, paragraph 4 (so far as it relates to assets), paragraph 10 (except sub-paragraphs (1)(*d*) and (4)), paragraphs 11 and 12 and paragraph 13 (except sub-paragraphs (9), (10), (11), (13) and (14)) ; and

    (*b*) as respects its profit and loss account, those of sub-paragraph (1)(*h*) and (*k*) of paragraph 14, paragraphs 15 and 16 and sub-paragraphs (1) and (5) of paragraph 18.

(3) But, where in the company's balance sheet reserves or provisions (other than provisions for depreciation, renewals or diminution in value of assets) are not stated separately, any heading stating an amount arrived at after taking into account a reserve or such a provision shall be so framed or marked as to indicate that fact, and its profit and loss account shall indicate by appropriate words the manner in which the amount stated for the company's profit or loss has been arrived at.

(4) The company's accounts shall not be deemed, by reason only of the fact that they do not comply with any requirements of the said Part I from which the company is exempt by virtue of this paragraph, not to give the true and fair view required by this Act.

28.—(1) An insurance company to which Part II of the Insurance 1982 c. 50. Companies Act 1982 applies shall not be subject to the following requirements of Part I of this Schedule, that is to say—

    (*a*) as respects its balance sheet, those of paragraphs 4 to 8 (both inclusive), sub-paragraphs (1)(*a*) and (3) of paragraph 10 and sub-paragraphs (6), (7) and (9) to (13) (both inclusive) of paragraph 13 ;

    (*b*) as respects its profit and loss account, those of paragraph 14 (except sub-paragraph (1)(*b*), (*c*), (*d*) and (*k*)) and paragraph 18(2) ;

but, where in its balance sheet reserves or provisions (other than provisions for depreciation, renewals or diminution in value of assets) are not stated separately, any heading stating an amount arrived at after taking into account a reserve or such a provision shall be so framed or marked as to indicate that fact, and its profit and loss account shall indicate by appropriate words the manner in which the amount stated for the company's profit or loss has been arrived at:

Provided that the Secretary of State may direct that any such insurance company whose business includes to a substantial extent business other than insurance business shall comply with all the requirements of the said Part I or such of them as may be specified in the direction and shall comply therewith as respects either the whole of its business or such part thereof as may be so specified.

(2) The accounts of a company shall not be deemed, by reason only of the fact that they do not comply with any requirement of Part I of this Schedule from which the company is exempt by virtue

of this paragraph, not to give the true and fair view required by this Act.

29.—(1) A shipping company shall not be subject to the following requirements of Part I of this Schedule, that is to say—

    (*a*) as respects its balance sheet, those of paragraph 4 (except so far as it relates to assets), paragraphs 5, 7 and 8 and sub-paragraphs (9) and (10) of paragraph 13 ;

    (*b*) as respects its profit and loss account, those of sub-paragraph (1)(*a*), (*e*) and (*f*) and sub-paragraphs (3) and (4) of paragraph 14 and paragraph 17.

(2) The accounts of a company shall not be deemed, by reason only of the fact that they do not comply with any requirements of Part I of this Schedule from which the company is exempt by virtue of this paragraph, not to give the true and fair view required by this Act.

30. Where a company entitled to the benefit of any provision contained in this Part of this Schedule is a holding company, the reference in Part II of this Schedule to consolidated accounts complying with the requirements of this Act shall, in relation to consolidated accounts of that company, be construed as referring to those requirements in so far only—

    (*a*) as they apply to the individual accounts of that company, and

    (*b*) as they apply (otherwise than by virtue of paragraphs 21 and 22) to the group accounts prepared by that company.

PART IV

SPECIAL PROVISIONS WHERE THE COMPANY HAS ENTERED INTO ARRANGEMENTS SUBJECT TO MERGER RELIEF

31.—(1) Where during the financial year the company has allotted shares in consideration for the issue, transfer or cancellation of shares in another body corporate (" the other company ") in circumstances where by virtue of section 131(2) (merger relief) section 130 did not apply to the premiums on those shares, the following information shall be given by way of a note to the company's accounts—

    (*a*) the name of the other company ;

    (*b*) the number, nominal value and class of shares so allotted ;

    (*c*) the number, nominal value and class of shares in the other company so issued, transferred or cancelled ;

    (*d*) particulars of the accounting treatment adopted in the company's accounts (including any group accounts) in respect of such issue, transfer or cancellation ; and

    (*e*) where the company prepares group accounts, particulars of the extent to which and manner in which the profit or loss for the year of the group which appears in those accounts is affected by any profit or loss of the other company or any of its subsidiaries which arose at any time before the allotment.

(2) Where the company has during the financial year or during
either of the two financial years immediately preceding it made such an allotment of shares as is mentioned in sub-paragraph (1) above and there is included in the company's consolidated profit and loss account, or if it has no such account, in its individual profit and loss account, any profit or loss (or part thereof) to which this sub-paragraph applies then the net amount of any such profit or loss (or part thereof) shall be shown in a note to the accounts together with an explanation of the transactions to which that information relates.

(3) Sub-paragraph (2) applies—

> (*a*) to any profit or loss realised during the financial year by the company, or any of its subsidiaries, on the disposal of any shares in the other company or of any assets which were fixed assets of the other company, or of any of its subsidiaries, at the time of the allotment; and

> (*b*) to any part of any profit or loss realised during the financial year by the company, or any of its subsidiaries, on the disposal of any shares (not being shares in the other company), which was attributable to the fact that at the time of the disposal there were amongst the assets of the company which issued those shares, or any of its subsidiaries, such shares or assets as are described in paragraph (*a*) above.

(4) Where in pursuance of the arrangement in question shares are allotted on different dates, the time of allotment for the purposes of sub-paragraphs (1)(*e*) and (3)(*a*) above is taken to be—

> (*a*) if the other company becomes a subsidiary of the company as a result of the arrangement—

>> (i) if the arrangement becomes binding only upon the fulfilment of a condition, the date on which that condition is fulfilled, and

>> (ii) in any other case, the date on which the other company becomes a subsidiary of the company;

> (*b*) if the other company is a subsidiary of the company when the arrangement is proposed, the date of the first allotment pursuant to that arrangement.

PART V

INTERPRETATION OF SCHEDULE

32.—(1) For the purposes of this Schedule, unless the context otherwise requires,—

> (*a*) the expression " provision " shall, subject to sub-paragraph (2) of this paragraph, mean any amount written off or retained by way of providing for depreciation, renewals or diminution in value of assets or retained by way of providing for any known liability of which the amount cannot be determined with substantial accuracy;

> (*b*) the expression " reserve " shall not, subject as aforesaid, include any amount written off or retained by way of providing for depreciation, renewals or diminution in value

of assets or retained by way of providing for any known liability or any sum set aside for the purpose of its being used to prevent undue fluctuations in charges for taxation ;

and in this paragraph the expression " liability " shall include all liabilities in respect of expenditure contracted for and all disputed or contingent liabilities.

(2) Where—

(a) any amount written off or retained by way of providing for depreciation, renewals or diminution in value of assets ; or

(b) any amount retained by way of providing for any known liability ;

is in excess of that which in the opinion of the directors is reasonably necessary for the purpose, the excess shall be treated for the purposes of this Schedule as a reserve and not as a provision.

33. For the purposes aforesaid, the expression " listed investment " means an investment as respects which there has been granted a listing on a recognised stock exchange, or on any stock exchange of repute outside Great Britain and the expression " unlisted investment " shall be construed accordingly.

34. For the purposes aforesaid, the expression " long lease " means a lease in the case of which the portion of the term for which it was granted remaining unexpired at the end of the financial year is not less than fifty years, the expression " short lease " means a lease which is not a long lease and the expression " lease " includes an agreement for a lease.

35. For the purposes aforesaid, a loan shall be deemed to fall due for repayment, and an instalment of a loan shall be deemed to fall due for payment, on the earliest date on which the lender could require repayment or, as the case may be, payment if he exercised all options and rights available to him.

36. In the application of this Schedule to Scotland, " land of freehold tenure " means land in respect of which the company is the proprietor of the *dominium utile* or, in the case of land not held on feudal tenure, is the owner ; " land of leasehold tenure " means land of which the company is the tenant under a lease ; and the reference to ground-rents, rates and other outgoings includes a reference to feu-duty and ground annual.

Sections 235(6), 261.

SCHEDULE 10

ADDITIONAL MATTERS TO BE DEALT WITH IN DIRECTORS' REPORT ATTACHED TO SPECIAL CATEGORY ACCOUNTS

Recent issues

1.—(1) If in the financial year to which the accounts relate the company has issued any shares, the directors' report shall state the reason for making the issue, the classes of shares issued and, as respects each class of shares, the number issued and the consideration received by the company for the issue.

(2) If in that year the company has issued any debentures, the report shall state the reason for making the issue, the classes of debentures issued, and, as respects each class of debentures, the amount issued and the consideration received by the company for the issue.

Turnover and profitability

2. If in the course of the financial year the company (being one subject to the requirements of paragraph 17 of Schedule 9, but not one that has subsidiaries at the end of the year and submits in respect of that year group accounts prepared as consolidated accounts) has carried on business of two or more classes (other than banking or discounting or a class prescribed for the purpose of paragraph 17(2) of that Schedule) that, in the opinion of the directors, differ substantially from each other, there shall be contained in the directors' report a statement of—

(*a*) the proportions in which the turnover for the year (so far as stated in the accounts in respect of the year in pursuance of that Schedule) is divided amongst those classes (describing them), and

(*b*) as regards business of each class, the extent or approximate extent (expressed, in either case, in monetary terms) to which, in the opinion of the directors, the carrying on of business of that class contributed to, or restricted, the profit or loss of the company for that year before taxation.

3.—(1) This paragraph applies if—

(*a*) the company has subsidiaries at the end of the financial year and submits in respect of that year group accounts prepared as consolidated accounts, and

(*b*) the company and the subsidiaries dealt with by the accounts carried on between them in the course of the year business of two or more classes (other than banking or discounting or a class prescribed for the purposes of paragraph 17(2) of Schedule 9) that, in the opinion of the directors, differ substantially from each other.

(2) There shall be contained in the directors' report a statement of—

(*a*) the proportions in which the turnover for the financial year (so far as stated in the accounts for that year in pursuance of Schedule 9) is divided amongst those classes (describing them), and

(*b*) as regards business of each class, the extent or approximate extent (expressed, in either case, in monetary terms) to which, in the opinion of the directors of the company, the carrying on of business of that class contributed to, or restricted, the profit or loss for that year (before taxation) of the company and the subsidiaries dealt with by the accounts.

4. For the purposes of the preceding two paragraphs, classes of business which, in the opinion of the directors, do not differ substantially from each other, are to be treated as one class.

Labour force and wages paid

5.—(1) If at the end of the financial year the company does not have subsidiaries, there shall be contained in the directors' report a statement of—

> (a) the average number of persons employed by the company in each week in the year, and

> (b) the aggregate remuneration paid or payable in respect of the year to the persons by reference to whom the number stated under sub-paragraph (a) is ascertained.

(2) The number to be stated under that sub-paragraph is the quotient derived by dividing, by the number of weeks in the financial year, the number derived by ascertaining, in relation to each of those weeks, the number of persons who, under contracts of service, were employed in the week (whether throughout it or not) by the company and adding up the numbers ascertained.

6.—(1) If at the end of the financial year the company has subsidiaries, there shall be contained in the directors' report a statement of—

> (a) the average number of persons employed between them in each week in that year by the company and the subsidiaries, and

> (b) the aggregate remuneration paid or payable in respect of that year to the persons by reference to whom the number stated under sub-paragraph (a) is ascertained.

(2) The number to be stated under that sub-paragraph is the quotient derived by dividing, by the number of weeks in the financial year, the number derived by ascertaining, in relation to each of those weeks, the number of persons who, under contracts of service, were employed between them in the week (whether throughout it or not) by the company and its subsidiaries and adding up the numbers ascertained.

7. The remuneration to be taken into account under paragraphs 5(1)(b) and 6(1)(b) is the gross remuneration paid or payable in respect of the financial year; and for this purpose " remuneration " includes bonuses (whether payable under contract or not).

8.—(1) Paragraphs 5 and 6 are qualified as follows.

(2) Neither paragraph applies if the number that, apart from this sub-paragraph, would fall to be stated under paragraph 5(1)(a) or 6(1)(a) is less than 100.

(3) Neither paragraph applies to a company which is a wholly-
owned subsidiary of a company incorporated in Great Britain.

(4) For purposes of both paragraphs, no regard is to be had to any
person who worked wholly or mainly outside the United Kingdom.

General matters

9. The directors' report shall contain particulars of any matters
(other than those required to be dealt with in it by section 261(5) and
the preceding provisions of this Schedule) so far as they are material
for the appreciation of the state of the company's affairs by its
members, being matters the disclosure of which will not, in the
opinion of the directors, be harmful to the business of the company
or of any of its subsidiaries.

SCHEDULE 11   Section 279.

MODIFICATIONS OF PART VIII WHERE COMPANY'S RELEVANT ACCOUNTS ARE SPECIAL CATEGORY

1. Section 264 applies as if in subsection (2) for the words following "the aggregate of its liabilities" there were substituted
"("liabilities" to include any provision within the meaning of
Schedule 9, except to the extent that that provision is taken into
account in calculating the value of any asset of the company)".

2. Section 265 applies as if—

(a) for subsection (2) there were substituted—

"(2) In subsection (1)(a), "liabilities" includes any
provision (within the meaning of Schedule 9) except
to the extent that that provision is taken into account for
the purposes of that subsection in calculating the value
of any asset of the company", and

(b) there were added at the end of the section—

"(7) In determining capital and revenue profits and
losses, an asset which is not a fixed asset or a current
asset is treated as a fixed asset".

3. Section 269 does not apply.

4. Section 270 applies as if—

(a) in subsection (2) the following were substituted for paragraph
(b)—

"(b) provisions (within the meaning of Schedule 9)";

(b) in subsection (3), for the words from "which were laid"
onwards there were substituted—

"which were laid or filed in respect of the last preceding accounting reference period in respect of which

accounts so prepared were laid or filed ; and for this purpose accounts are laid or filed if section 241(1) or (as the case may be) (3) has been complied with in relation to them " ; and

(c) in subsection (4)(b) the words " or filed " were inserted after " laid ".

5. Section 271 applies as if—

(a) in subsection (2), immediately before paragraph (a) there were inserted " except where the company is entitled to avail itself, and has availed itself, of any of the provisions of Part III of Schedule 9 ", and

(b) at the end of subsection (4) there were added the words " or delivered to the registrar of companies according as those accounts have been laid or filed ".

6. Sections 272 and 273 apply as if in section 272(3)—

(a) for the references to section 228 and Schedule 4 there were substituted references to section 258 and Schedule 9, and

(b) immediately before paragraph (a) there were inserted " except where the company is entitled to avail itself, and has availed itself, of any of the provisions of Part III of Schedule 9 ".

7. Section 275 applies as if—

(a) for subsection (1) there were substituted—

" (1) For purposes of section 263, any provision (within the meaning of Schedule 9), other than one in respect of any diminution of value of a fixed asset appearing on a revaluation of all the fixed assets of the company, or of all its fixed assets other than goodwill, is to be treated as a realised loss " ; and

(b) " fixed assets " were defined to include any other asset which is not a current asset.

SCHEDULE 12

Supplementary Provisions in Connection with Disqualification Orders

Part I

Orders under Sections 296 to 299

Application for order

1. A person intending to apply for the making of an order under any of sections 296 to 299 by the court having jurisdiction to wind up a company shall give not less than 10 days' notice of his intention to the person against whom the order is sought ; and on the hearing of the application the last-mentioned person may appear and himself give evidence or call witnesses.

2. An application to a court with jurisdiction to wind up com- panies for the making of such an order against any person may be made by the Secretary of State or the official receiver, or by the liquidator or any past or present member or creditor of any company in relation to which that person has committed or is alleged to have committed an offence or other default.

Hearing of application

3. On the hearing of an application made by the Secretary of State or the official receiver or the liquidator the applicant shall appear and call the attention of the court to any matters which seem to him to be relevant, and may himself give evidence or call witnesses.

Application for leave under an order

4.—(1) As regards the court to which application must be made for leave under a disqualification order made under any of sections 296 to 299, the following applies.

(2) Where the application is for leave to promote or form a company, it is any court with jurisdiction to wind up companies.

(3) Where the application is for leave to be a liquidator or director of, or otherwise to take part in the management of a company, or to be a receiver or manager of a company's property, it is any court having jurisdiction to wind up that company.

5. On the hearing of an application for leave made by a person against whom a disqualification order has been made on the application of the Secretary of State, the official receiver or the liquidator, the Secretary of State, official receiver or liquidator shall appear and call the attention of the court to any matters which seem to him to be relevant, and may himself give evidence or call witnesses.

Part II

Orders under Section 300

Application for order

6.—(1) In the case of a person who is or has been a director of a company which has gone into liquidation as mentioned in section 300(1) and is being wound up by the court, any application under that section shall be made by the official receiver or, in Scotland, the Secretary of State.

(2) In any other case an application shall be made by the Secretary of State.

7. Where the official receiver or the Secretary of State intends to make an application under the section in respect of any person, he shall give not less than 10 days' notice of his intention to that person.

Hearing of application

8. On the hearing of an application under section 300 by the official receiver or the Secretary of State, or of an application for

X

SCH. 12
PART II

leave by a person against whom an order has been made on the application of the official receiver or Secretary of State—

  (a) the official receiver or Secretary of State shall appear and call the attention of the court to any matters which seem to him to be relevant, and may himself give evidence or call witnesses, and

  (b) the person against whom the order is sought may appear and himself give evidence or call witnesses.

PART III

TRANSITIONAL PROVISIONS AND SAVINGS FROM COMPANIES ACT 1981, ss. 93, 94

9. Sections 296 and 298 (1)(b) do not apply in relation to anything done before 15th June 1982 by a person in his capacity as liquidator of a company or as receiver or manager of a company's property.

10. Subject to paragraph 9—

  (a) section 296 applies in a case where a person is convicted on indictment of an offence which he committed (and, in the case of a continuing offence, has ceased to commit) before 15th June 1982 ; but in such a case a disqualification order under that section shall not be made for a period in excess of 5 years ;

  (b) that section does not apply in a case where a person is convicted summarily—

      (i) in England and Wales, if he had consented so to be tried before that date, or

      (ii) in Scotland, if the summary proceedings commenced before that date.

11. Subject to paragraph 9, section 298 applies in relation to an offence committed or other thing done before 15th June 1982 ; but a disqualification order made on the grounds of such an offence or other thing done shall not be made for a period in excess of 5 years.

12. The powers of a court under section 299 are not exercisable in a case where a person is convicted of an offence which he committed (and, in the case of a continuing offence, had ceased to commit) before 15th June 1982.

13. For purposes of section 297(1) and section 299, no account is to be taken of any offence which was committed, or any default order which was made, before 1st June 1977.

1976 c. 69.

14. An order made under section 28 of the Companies Act 1976 has effect as if made under section 297 of this Act ; and an application made before 15th June 1982 for such an order is to be treated as an application for an order under the section last mentioned.

15. The period which may be specified as the period of disqualification in an order under section 300 may not exceed 5 years if

none of the conduct to which the court has regard under subsection (1) of the section occurred after 15th June 1982.

16. Section 300(1) does not apply unless at least one of the companies there mentioned has gone into liquidation after 1st October 1977 ; and the conduct to which regard may be had under that subsection does not include conduct as director of a company that has gone into liquidation before that date.

SCHEDULE 13

PROVISIONS SUPPLEMENTING AND INTERPRETING SECTIONS 324 TO 328

PART I

RULES FOR INTERPRETATION OF THE SECTIONS
AND ALSO SECTION 346(4) AND (5)

1.—(1) A reference to an interest in shares or debentures is to be read as including any interest of any kind whatsoever in shares or debentures.

(2) Accordingly, there are to be disregarded any restraints or restrictions to which the exercise of any right attached to the interest is or may be subject.

2. Where property is held on trust and any interest in shares or debentures is comprised in the property, any beneficiary of the trust who (apart from this paragraph) does not have an interest in the shares or debentures is to be taken as having such an interest ; but this paragraph is without prejudice to the following provisions of this Part of this Schedule.

3.—(1) A person is taken to have an interest in shares or debentures if—

 (*a*) he enters into a contract for their purchase by him (whether for cash or other consideration), or

 (*b*) not being the registered holder, he is entitled to exercise any right conferred by the holding of the shares or debentures, or is entitled to control the exercise of any such right.

(2) For purposes of sub-paragraph (1)(*b*), a person is taken to be entitled to exercise or control the exercise of a right conferred by the holding of shares or debentures if he—

 (*a*) has a right (whether subject to conditions or not) the exercise of which would make him so entitled, or

 (*b*) is under an obligation (whether or not so subject) the fulfilment of which would make him so entitled.

(3) A person is not by virtue of sub-paragraph (1)(*b*) taken to be interested in shares or debentures by reason only that he—

 (*a*) has been appointed a proxy to vote at a specified meeting of a company or of any class of its members and at any adjournment of that meeting, or

X 2

(*b*) has been appointed by a corporation to act as its representative at any meeting of a company or of any class of its members.

4. A person is taken to be interested in shares or debentures if a body corporate is interested in them and—

(*a*) that body corporate or its directors are accustomed to act in accordance with his directions or instructions, or

(*b*) he is entitled to exercise or control the exercise of one-third or more of the voting power at general meetings of that body corporate.

As this paragraph applies for the purposes of section 346(4) and (5), " more than one-half " is substituted for " one-third or more ".

5. Where a person is entitled to exercise or control the exercise of one-third or more of the voting power at general meetings of a body corporate, and that body corporate is entitled to exercise or control the exercise of any of the voting power at general meetings of another body corporate (" the effective voting power "), then, for purposes of paragraph 4(*b*), the effective voting power is taken to be exercisable by that person.

As this paragraph applies for the purposes of section 346(4) and (5), " more than one-half " is substituted for " one-third or more ".

6.—(1) A person is taken to have an interest in shares or debentures if, otherwise than by virtue of having an interest under a trust—

(*a*) he has a right to call for delivery of the shares or debentures to himself or to his order, or

(*b*) he has a right to acquire an interest in shares or debentures or is under an obligation to take an interest in shares or debentures ;

whether in any case the right or obligation is conditional or absolute.

(2) Rights or obligations to subscribe for shares or debentures are not to be taken, for purposes of sub-paragraph (1), to be rights to acquire, or obligations to take, an interest in shares or debentures.

This is without prejudice to paragraph 1.

7. Persons having a joint interest are deemed each of them to have that interest.

8. It is immaterial that shares or debentures in which a person has an interest are unidentifiable.

9. So long as a person is entitled to receive, during the lifetime of himself or another, income from trust property comprising shares or debentures, an interest in the shares or debentures in reversion or remainder or (as regards Scotland) in fee, are to be disregarded.

10. A person is to be treated as uninterested in shares or debentures if, and so long as, he holds them under the law in force in England and Wales as a bare trustee or as a custodian trustee, or under the law in force in Scotland, as a simple trustee. Sch. 13
Part I

11. There is to be disregarded an interest of a person subsisting by virtue of—

    (*a*) any unit trust scheme declared by an order of the Secretary of State (or any predecessor of his) for the time being in force under the Prevention of Fraud (Investments) Act 1958 to be an authorised unit trust scheme for the purposes of that Act; 1958 c. 45.

    (*b*) a scheme made under section 22 of the Charities Act 1960, section 11 of the Trustee Investments Act 1961 or section 1 of the Administration of Justice Act 1965; or 1960 c. 58.
1961 c. 62.
1965 c. 2.

    (*c*) the scheme set out in the Schedule to the Church Funds Investment Measure 1958. 1958 No. 1.

12. There is to be disregarded any interest—

    (*a*) of the Church of Scotland General Trustees or of the Church of Scotland Trust in shares or debentures held by them;

    (*b*) of any other person in shares or debentures held by those Trustees or that Trust otherwise than as simple trustees.

" The Church of Scotland General Trustees " are the body incorporated by the order confirmed by the Church of Scotland (General Trustees) Order Confirmation Act 1921; and " the Church of Scotland Trust " is the body incorporated by the order confirmed by the Church of Scotland Trust Order Confirmation Act 1932. 1921 c. xxv.

1932 c. xxi.

13. Delivery to a person's order of shares or debentures in fulfilment of a contract for the purchase of them by him or in satisfaction of a right of his to call for their delivery, or failure to deliver shares or debentures in accordance with the terms of such a contract or on which such a right falls to be satisfied, is deemed to constitute an event in consequence of the occurrence of which he ceases to be interested in them, and so is the lapse of a person's right to call for delivery of shares or debentures.

Part II

Periods Within Which Obligations Imposed By Section 324 Must Be Fulfilled

14.—(1) An obligation imposed on a person by section 324(1) to notify an interest must, if he knows of the existence of the interest on the day on which he becomes a director, be fulfilled before the expiration of the period of 5 days beginning with the day following that day.

(2) Otherwise, the obligation must be fulfilled before the expiration of the period of 5 days beginning with the day following that on which the existence of the interest comes to his knowledge.

15.—(1) An obligation imposed on a person by section 324(2) to notify the occurrence of an event must, if at the time at which the event occurs he knows of its occurrence and of the fact that its occurrence gives rise to the obligation, be fulfilled before the expiration of the period of 5 days beginning with the day following that on which the event occurs.

(2) Otherwise, the obligation must be fulfilled before the expiration of a period of 5 days beginning with the day following that on which the fact that the occurrence of the event gives rise to the obligation comes to his knowledge.

16. In reckoning, for purposes of paragraphs 14 and 15, any period of days, a day that is a Saturday or Sunday, or a bank holiday in any part of Great Britain, is to be disregarded.

PART III

CIRCUMSTANCES IN WHICH OBLIGATION IMPOSED BY SECTION 324 IS NOT DISCHARGED

17.—(1) Where an event of whose occurrence a director is, by virtue of section 324(2)(*a*), under obligation to notify a company consists of his entering into a contract for the purchase by him of shares or debentures, the obligation is not discharged in the absence of inclusion in the notice of a statement of the price to be paid by him under the contract.

(2) An obligation imposed on a director by section 324(2)(*b*) is not discharged in the absence of inclusion in the notice of the price to be received by him under the contract.

18.—(1) An obligation imposed on a director by virtue of section 324(2)(*c*) to notify a company is not discharged in the absence of inclusion in the notice of a statement of the consideration for the assignment (or, if it be the case that there is no consideration, that fact).

(2) Where an event of whose occurrence a director is, by virtue of section 324(2)(*d*), under obligation to notify a company consists in his assigning a right, the obligation is not discharged in the absence of inclusion in the notice of a similar statement.

19.—(1) Where an event of whose occurrence a director is, by virtue of section 324(2)(*d*), under obligation to notify a company consists in the grant to him of a right to subscribe for shares or debentures, the obligation is not discharged in the absence of inclusion in the notice of a statement of—

  (*a*) the date on which the right was granted,
  (*b*) the period during which or the time at which the right is exercisable.

(*c*) the consideration for the grant (or, if it be the case that there is no consideration, that fact), and

(*d*) the price to be paid for the shares or debentures.

(2) Where an event of whose occurrence a director is, by section 324(2)(*d*), under obligation to notify a company consists in the exercise of a right granted to him to subscribe for shares or debentures, the obligation is not discharged in the absence of inclusion in the notice of a statement of—

(*a*) the number of shares or amount of debentures in respect of which the right was exercised, and

(*b*) if it be the case that they were registered in his name, that fact, and, if not, the name or names of the person or persons in whose name or names they were registered, together (if they were registered in the names of 2 persons or more) with the number or amount registered in the name of each of them.

20. In this Part, a reference to price paid or received includes any consideration other than money.

PART IV

PROVISIONS WITH RESPECT TO REGISTER OF DIRECTORS' INTERESTS TO BE KEPT UNDER SECTION 325

21. The register must be so made up that the entries in it against the several names appear in chronological order.

22. An obligation imposed by section 325(2) to (4) must be fulfilled before the expiration of the period of 3 days beginning with the day after that on which the obligation arises ; but in reckoning that period, a day which is a Saturday or Sunday or a bank holiday in any part of Great Britain is to be disregarded.

23. The nature and extent of an interest recorded in the register of a director in any shares or debentures shall, if he so requires, be recorded in the register.

24. The company is not, by virtue of anything done for the purposes of section 325 or this Part of this Schedule, affected with notice of, or put upon enquiry as to, the rights of any person in relation to any shares or debentures.

25. The register shall—

(*a*) if the company's register of members is kept at its registered office, be kept there ;

(*b*) if the company's register of members is not so kept, be kept at the company's registered office or at the place where its register of members is kept ;

and shall during business hours (subject to such reasonable restrictions as the company in general meeting may impose, so that not less than 2 hours in each day be allowed for inspection) be open to the inspection of any member of the company without charge and of any other person on payment of 5 pence, or such less sum as the company may prescribe, for each inspection.

26.—(1) Any member of the company or other person may require a copy of the register, or of any part of it, on payment of 10 pence, or such less sum as the company may prescribe, for every 100 words or fractional part of 100 words required to be copied.

(2) The company shall cause any copy so required by a person to be sent to him within the period of 10 days beginning with the day after that on which the requirement is received by the company.

27. The company shall send notice in the prescribed form to the registrar of companies of the place where the register is kept and of any change in that place, save in a case in which it has at all times been kept at its registered office.

28. Unless the register is in such a form as to constitute in itself an index, the company shall keep an index of the names inscribed in it, which shall—

   (a) in respect of each name, contain a sufficient indication to enable the information entered against it to be readily found ; and

   (b) be kept at the same place as the register ;

and the company shall, within 14 days after the date on which a name is entered in the register, make any necessary alteration in the index.

29. The register shall be produced at the commencement of the company's annual general meeting and remain open and accessible during the continuance of the meeting to any person attending the meeting.

SCHEDULE 14

OVERSEAS BRANCH REGISTERS

PART I

COUNTRIES AND TERRITORIES IN WHICH OVERSEAS BRANCH
REGISTER MAY BE KEPT

Northern Ireland

Any part of Her Majesty's dominions outside the United
Kingdom, the Channel Islands or the Isle of Man

> Bangladesh
> Cyprus
> Dominica
> The Gambia
> Ghana
> Guyana
> India
> Kenya
> Kiribati
> Lesotho
> Malawi
> Malaysia
> Malta
> Nigeria
> Pakistan
> Republic of Ireland
> Seychelles
> Sierra Leone
> Singapore
> South Africa
> Sri Lanka
> Swaziland
> Trinidad and Tobago
> Uganda
> Zimbabwe

PART II

GENERAL PROVISIONS WITH RESPECT TO OVERSEAS BRANCH
REGISTERS

1.—(1) A company keeping an overseas branch register shall give
to the registrar of companies notice in the prescribed form of the
situation of the office where any overseas branch register is kept
and of any change in its situation, and, if it is discontinued, of its
discontinuance.

(2) Any such notice shall be given within 14 days of the opening
of the office or of the change or discontinuance, as the case may be.

(3) If default is made in complying with this paragraph, the company and every officer of it who is in default is liable to a fine and,
for continued contravention, to a daily default fine.

2.—(1) An overseas branch register is deemed to be part of the company's register of members (" the principal register ").

(2) It shall be kept in the same manner in which the principal register is by this Act required to be kept, except that the advertisement before closing the register shall be inserted in a newspaper circulating in the district where the overseas branch register is kept.

3.—(1) A competent court in a country or territory where an overseas branch register is kept may exercise the same jurisdiction of rectifying the register as is under this Act exercisable by the court in Great Britain ; and the offences of refusing inspection or copies of the register, and of authorising or permitting the refusal, may be prosecuted summarily before any tribunal having summary criminal jurisdiction.

(2) This paragraph extends only to those countries and territories where, immediately before the coming into force of this Act, provision to the same effect made by section 120(2) of the Companies Act 1948 had effect as part of the local law.

4.—(1) The company shall—

(a) transmit to its registered office a copy of every entry in its overseas branch register as soon as may be after the entry is made, and

(b) cause to be kept at the place where the company's principal register is kept a duplicate of its overseas branch register duly entered up from time to time.

Every such duplicate is deemed for all purposes of this Act to be part of the principal register.

(2) If default is made in complying with sub-paragraph (1), the company and every officer of it who is in default is liable to a fine and, for continued contravention, to a daily default fine.

(3) Where, by virtue of section 353(1)(b), the principal register is kept at the office of some person other than the company, and by reason of any default of his the company fails to comply with sub-paragraph (1)(b) above he is liable to the same penalty as if he were an officer of the company who was in default.

5. Subject to the above provisions with respect to the duplicate register, the shares registered in an overseas branch register shall be distinguished from those registered in the principal register ; and no transaction with respect to any shares registered in an overseas branch register shall, during the continuance of that registration, be registered in any other register.

6. A company may discontinue to keep an overseas branch register, and thereupon all entries in that register shall be transferred to some other overseas branch register kept by the company in the same country or territory, or to the principal register.

7. Subject to the provisions of this Act, any company may, by its articles, make such provisions as it thinks fit respecting the keeping of overseas branch registers.

8. An instrument of transfer of a share registered in an overseas branch register (other than such a register kept in Northern Ireland) is deemed a transfer of property situated outside the United Kingdom and, unless executed in a part of the United Kingdom, is exempt from stamp duty chargeable in Great Britain.

PART III

PROVISIONS FOR BRANCH REGISTERS OF OVERSEA COMPANIES TO BE KEPT IN GREAT BRITAIN

9.—(1) If by virtue of the law in force in any country or territory to which this paragraph applies companies incorporated under that law have power to keep in Great Britain branch registers of their members resident in Great Britain, Her Majesty may by Order in Council direct that—

   (a) so much of section 353 as requires a company's register of members to be kept at its registered office,

   (b) section 356 (register to be open to inspection by members), and

   (c) section 359 (power of court to rectify),

shall, subject to any modifications and adaptations specified in the Order, apply to and in relation to any such branch registers kept in Great Britain as they apply to and in relation to the registers of companies subject to those sections.

(2) The countries and territories to which this paragraph applies are—

   (a) all those specified in Part I of this Schedule, plus the Channel Islands and the Isle of Man,

   (b) Botswana, Zambia and Tonga, and

   (c) any territory for the time being under Her Majesty's protection or administered by the Government of the United Kingdom under the Trusteeship System of the United Nations.

SCHEDULE 15

Section 363.

CONTENTS OF ANNUAL RETURN OF A COMPANY HAVING A SHARE CAPITAL

1. The address of the registered office of the company.

2.—(1) If the register of members is, under the provisions of this Act, kept elsewhere than at the registered office of the company, the address of the place where it is kept.

(2) If any register of holders of debentures of the company or any duplicate of any such register or part of any such register is, under the provisions of this Act, kept, in England and Wales in the case of a company registered in England and Wales or in Scotland in the

SCH. 15   case of a company registered in Scotland, elsewhere than at the registered office of the company, the address of the place where it is kept.

3. A summary, distinguishing between shares issued for cash and shares issued as fully or partly paid up otherwise than in cash, specifying the following particulars—

(a) the amount of the share capital of the company and the number of shares into which it is divided ;

(b) the number of shares taken from the commencement of the company up to the date of the return ;

(c) the amount called up on each share ;

(d) the total amount of calls received ;

(e) the total amount of calls unpaid ;

(f) the total amount of the sums (if any) paid by way of commission in respect of any shares or debentures ;

(g) the discount allowed on the issue of any shares issued at a discount or so much of that discount as has not been written off at the date on which the return is made ;

(h) the total amount of the sums (if any) allowed by way of discount in respect of any debentures since the date of the last return ;

(i) the total number of shares forfeited ;

(j) the total number of shares for which share warrants are outstanding at the date of the return and of share warrants issued and surrendered respectively since the date of the last return, and the number of shares comprised in each warrant.

4. Particulars of the total amount of the company's indebtedness in respect of all mortgages and charges (whenever created) of any description specified in section 396(1) or, in the case of a company registered in Scotland, section 410(4).

5. A list—

(a) containing the names and addresses of all persons who, on the fourteenth day after the company's annual general meeting for the year, are members of the company, and of persons who have ceased to be members since the date of the last return or, in the case of the first return, since the incorporation of the company ;

(b) stating the number of shares held by each of the existing members at the date of the return, specifying shares transferred since the date of the last return (or, in the case of the first return, since the incorporation of the company) by persons who are still members and have ceased to be members respectively and the dates of registration of the transfers ;

(c) if the names are not arranged in alphabetical order, having annexed to it an index sufficient to enable the name of any person in the list to be easily found.

6. All such particulars with respect to the persons who at the date of the return are the directors of the company and any person who at that date is the secretary of the company as are by this Act required to be contained with respect to directors and the secretary respectively in the register of the directors and secretaries of a company.

Sch. 15

SCHEDULE 16

Section 571.

Orders in Course of Winding Up Pronounced in Vacation (Scotland)

Part I

Orders Which are to be Final

Order under section 557, as to the time for proving debts and claims.

Orders under section 561, as to the attendance of, and production of documents by, persons indebted to, or having property of, or information as to the affairs or property of, a company.

Orders under section 645 as to meetings for ascertaining wishes of creditors or contributories.

Orders under section 648, as to the examination of witnesses in regard to the property or affairs of a company.

Part II

Orders Which are to take Effect Until Matter Disposed of by Inner House

Orders under section 521(1), 525(2) or (3), 549, 672 or 673, restraining or permitting the commencement or the continuance of legal proceedings.

Orders under section 532(4), limiting the powers of provisional liquidators.

Orders under section 536, 599 or 609, appointing a liquidator to fill a vacancy, or appointing (except to fill a vacancy caused by the removal of a liquidator by the court) a liquidator for a winding up voluntarily or subject to supervision.

Orders under section 539, sanctioning the exercise of any power by a liquidator, other than the powers specified in paragraphs (*c*), (*d*), (*e*) and (*f*) of subsection (1).

Orders under section 551, requiring the delivery of property or documents to the liquidator.

Orders under section 565, as to the arrest and detention of an absconding contributory and his property.

Orders under section 606, for continuance of winding up subject to supervision.

SCHEDULE 17

Proceedings of Committee
of Inspection

1. The committee shall meet at such times as it may from time to time appoint and, failing such appointment, at least once a month ; and the liquidator or any member of the committee may also call a meeting of the committee as and when he thinks necessary.

2. The committee may act by a majority of its members present at a meeting, but shall not act unless a majority of the committee are present.

3. A member of the committee may resign by notice in writing signed by him and delivered to the liquidator.

4. If a member of the committee becomes bankrupt or compounds or arranges with his creditors or is absent from five consecutive meetings of the committee without leave of those members who together with himself represent the creditors or contributories (as the case may be), his office thereupon becomes vacant.

5. A member of the committee may be removed by an ordinary resolution at a meeting of creditors (if he represents creditors) or of contributories (if he represents contributories) of which 7 days' notice has been given, stating the object of the meeting.

6.—(1) On a vacancy occurring in the committee the liquidator shall forthwith summon a meeting of creditors or of contributories (as the case may require) to fill the vacancy ; and the meeting may, by resolution, reappoint the same or appoint another creditor or contributory to fill the vacancy.

(2) However, if the liquidator, having regard to the position in the winding up, is of the opinion that it is unnecessary for the vacancy to be filled, he may apply to the court ; and the court may make an order that the vacancy be not filled, or be not filled except in circumstances specified by the order.

(3) The continuing members of the committee, if not less than two, may act notwithstanding any vacancy in the committee.

SCHEDULE 18

Section 610

PROVISIONS OF PART XX NOT APPLICABLE IN WINDING UP
SUBJECT TO SUPERVISION OF THE COURT

Section		*Subject matter*
528 529 }		Statement of company's affairs to be submitted to official receiver.
530		Report by official receiver.
531		Power of court to appoint liquidators.
532		Appointment and powers of provisional liquidator.
533		Appointment, style, etc. of liquidators in England and Wales.
534		Provisions where person other than official receiver is appointed liquidator.
535		Provision as to liquidators in Scotland.
536	(except subs. (5))	General provisions as to liquidators.
540		Exercise and control of liquidator's powers in England and Wales.
541		Books to be kept by liquidator (England and Wales).
542		Payments by liquidator into bank (England and Wales).
543		Audit of liquidator's accounts (England and Wales).
544		Control of Secretary of State over liquidators in England and Wales.
545		Release of liquidators (England and Wales).
546		Meetings of creditors and contributories to determine whether committee of inspection shall be appointed.
547 548 }	(with Sch. 17)	Constitution, proceedings, etc. of committee of inspection; powers of Secretary of State where no committee.
556		Appointment of special manager (England and Wales).
563 564 }		Power to order public examination of promoters and officers (England and Wales).
567		Delegation to liquidator of certain powers of the court (England and Wales).

SCHEDULE 19

PREFERENCE AMONG CREDITORS IN COMPANY WINDING UP

" The relevant date "

1. For the purposes of this Schedule, " the relevant date " is—

   (*a*) in the case of a company ordered to be wound up compulsorily, the date of the appointment (or first appointment) of a provisional liquidator or, if no such appointment has been made, the date of the winding-up order, unless in either case the company had commenced to be wound up voluntarily before that date, and

   (*b*) otherwise, the date of the passing of the resolution for winding up the company.

Debts to Inland Revenue

2. All income tax, corporation tax, capital gains tax and other assessed taxes, assessed on the company up to 5th April next before the relevant date, and not exceeding in the whole one year's assessment.

3. Any sums due at the relevant date from the company on account of tax deductions for the 12 months next before that date.

The sums here referred to—

   (*a*) are those due by way of deduction of income tax from emoluments during the relevant period, which the company was liable to make under section 204 of the Income and Corporation Taxes Act 1970, less the amount of the repayments of income tax which the company was liable to make during the same period, and

   (*b*) include amounts due from the company in respect of deductions required to be made by it under section 69 of the Finance (No. 2) Act 1975 (construction industry contract workers).

1970 c. 10.

1975 c. 45.

Debts due to Customs & Excise

4. Any value added tax due at the relevant date from the company and having become due within the 12 months next before that date.

For purposes of this paragraph, the tax having become due within those 12 months in respect of any prescribed accounting period falling partly within and partly outside those 12 months is taken to be such part of the tax due for the whole of that accounting reference period as is proportionate to the part of the period falling within the 12 months.

5. The amount of any car tax due at the relevant date from the company and having become due within the 12 months next before that date.

6. Any amount due—   Sᴄʜ. 19

    (*a*) by way of general betting duty or bingo duty, or

    (*b*) under section 12(1) of the Betting and Gaming Duties Act 1981 c. 63.
        1981 (general betting duty and pool betting duty recover-
        able from agent collecting stakes), or

    (*c*) under section 14 of, or Schedule 2 to, that Act (gaming
        licence duty),

from the company at the relevant date and which became due within
the 12 months next before that date.

Local rates

7. All local rates due from the company at the relevant date and
having become due and payable within 12 months next before
that date.

Social security debts

8. All the debts specified in section 153(2) of the Social Security 1975 c. 14.
Act 1975, Schedule 3 to the Social Security Pensions Act 1975, and 1975 c. 60.
any corresponding provisions in force in Northern Ireland.

(This does not apply if the company is being wound up voluntarily
merely for the purposes of reconstruction or amalgamation with
another company.)

Debts to and in respect of company's employees

9. All wages or salary (whether or not earned wholly or in part
by way of commission) of any clerk or servant in respect of services
rendered to the company during 4 months next before the relevant
date, and all wages (whether payable for time or for piece work)
of any workman or labourer in respect of services so rendered.

10. All accrued holiday remuneration becoming payable to any
clerk, servant, workman or labourer (or in the case of his death
to any other person in his right) on the termination of his employment before or by the effect of the winding-up order or resolution.

This includes, in relation to any person, all sums which, by virtue
either of his contract of employment or of any enactment (including
any order made or direction given under an Act), are payable on
account of the remuneration which would, in the ordinary course,
have become payable to him in respect of a period of holiday had
his employment with the company continued until he became entitled
to be allowed the holiday.

Y

11. The following amounts owed by the company to an employee are treated as wages payable by it to him in respect of the period for which they are payable—

    (*a*) a guarantee payment under section 12(1) of the Employment Protection (Consolidation) Act 1978 (employee without work to do for a day or part of a day),

    (*b*) remuneration on suspension on medical grounds under section 19 of that Act,

    (*c*) any payment for time off under section 27(3) (trade union duties), 31(3) (looking for work, etc.) or 31A(4) (ante-natal care) of that Act,

    (*d*) statutory sick pay under Part I of the Social Security and Housing Benefits Act 1982, and

    (*e*) remuneration under a protective award made by an industrial tribunal under section 101 of the Employment Protection Act 1975 (redundancy dismissal with compensation).

12.—(1) The remuneration to which priority is to be given under paragraph 9 shall not, in the case of any claimant, exceed £800:

Provided that where a claimant under paragraph 9 is a labourer in husbandry who has entered into a contract for the payment of a portion of his wages in a lump sum at the end of the year of hiring, he has priority in respect of the whole of that sum, or a part of it, as the court may decide to be due under the contract, proportionate to the time of service up to the relevant date.

(2) No increase or reduction of the money sum specified above in this paragraph affects any case where the relevant date (or, where provisions of this Schedule apply by virtue of section 196, the date referred to in subsection (4) of that section) occurred before the coming into force of the increase or reduction.

*Priority for third party advancing
funds for wage-payments, etc.*

13. Where any payment has been made—

    (*a*) to any clerk, servant, workman or labourer in the employment of the company on account of wages or salary, or

    (*b*) to any such clerk, servant, workman or labourer or, in case of his death, to any other person in his right, on account of accrued holiday remuneration,

out of money advanced by some person for that purpose, the person by whom the money was advanced has in the winding up a right of priority in respect of the money so advanced and paid up to the amount by which the sum in respect of which the clerk, servant, workman or labourer, or other person in his right, would have been entitled to priority in the winding up has been diminished by reason of the payment having been made.

Interpretation for the above paragraphs

14. For purposes of this Schedule—

(*a*) any remuneration in respect of a period of holiday or of absence from work through sickness or other good cause is deemed to be wages in respect of services rendered to the company in that period ; and

(*b*) references to remuneration in respect of a period of holiday include any sums which, if they had been paid, would have been treated for purposes of the enactments relating to social security as earnings in respect of that period.

SCHEDULE 20

Vesting of Disclaimed Property ; Protection of Third Parties

Part I

Disclaimer by Liquidator under sections 618, 619 ; Crown Disclaimer under section 656

(England and Wales Only)

1. The court shall not under section 619 (including that section as applied by section 657(2)) make a vesting order, where the property disclaimed is of a leasehold nature, in favour of a person claiming under the company, except on the following terms.

2. The person must by the order be made subject—

(*a*) to the same liabilities and obligations as those to which the company was subject under the lease in respect of the property at the commencement of the winding up, or

(*b*) (if the court thinks fit) only to the same liabilities and obligations as if the lease had been assigned to him at that date ;

and in either event (if the case so requires) the liabilities and obligations must be as if the lease had comprised only the property comprised in the vesting order.

3. A mortgagee or under-lessee declining to accept a vesting order on such terms is excluded from all interest in and security on the property.

4. If there is no person claiming under the company who is willing to accept an order on such terms, the court has power to vest the company's estate and interest in the property in any person liable (either personally or in a representative character, and either alone or jointly with the company) to perform the lessee's covenants in the lease, freed and discharged from all estates, incumbrances and interests created therein by the company.

PART II

CROWN DISCLAIMER UNDER SECTION 656
(SCOTLAND ONLY)

5. The court shall not under section 657 make a vesting order, where the property disclaimed is held under a lease, in favour of a person claiming under the company (whether as sub-lessee or as creditor in a duly registered or, as appropriate, recorded heritable security over a lease), except on the following terms.

6. The person must by the order be made subject—

  (a) to the same liabilities and obligations as those to which the company was subject under the lease in respect of the property at the commencement of the winding up, or

  (b) (if the court thinks fit) only to the same liabilities and obligations as if the lease had been assigned to him at that date ;

and in either event (if the case so requires) the liabilities and obligations must be as if the lease had comprised only the property comprised in the vesting order.

7. A creditor or sub-lessee declining to accept a vesting order on such terms is excluded from all interest in and security over the property.

8. If there is no person claiming under the company who is willing to accept an order on such terms, the court has power to vest the company's estate and interest in the property in any person liable (either personally or in a representative character, and either alone or jointly with the company) to perform the lessee's obligations under the lease, freed and discharged from all interests, rights and obligations created by the company in the lease or in relation to the lease.

1979 c. 33.

9. For the purposes of paragraph 5 above, a heritable security is duly recorded if it is recorded in the Register of Sasines and is duly registered if registered in accordance with the Land Registration (Scotland) Act 1979.

Section 689.

SCHEDULE 21

EFFECT OF REGISTRATION UNDER SECTION 680

Interpretation

1. In this Schedule—

  " registration " means registration in pursuance of section 680 in Chapter II of Part XXII of this Act, and " registered " has the corresponding meaning, and

  " instrument " includes deed of settlement, contract of copartnery and letters patent.

Vesting of property

2. All property belonging to or vested in the company at the date of its registration passes to and vests in the company on registration for all the estate and interest of the company in the property.

Existing liabilities

3. Registration does not affect the company's rights or liabilities in respect of any debt or obligation incurred, or contract entered into, by, to, with or on behalf of the company before registration.

Pending actions at law

4.—(1) All actions and other legal proceedings which at the time of the company's registration are pending by or against the company, or the public officer or any member of it, may be continued in the same manner as if the registration had not taken place.

(2) However, execution shall not issue against the effects of any individual member of the company on any judgment, decree or order obtained in such an action or proceeding; but in the event of the company's property and effects being insufficient to satisfy the judgment, decree or order, an order may be obtained for winding up the company.

The company's constitution

5.—(1) All provisions contained in any Act of Parliament or other instrument constituting or regulating the company are deemed to be conditions and regulations of the company, in the same manner and with the same incidents as if so much of them as would, if the company had been formed under this Act, have been required to be inserted in the memorandum, were contained in a registered memorandum, and the residue were contained in registered articles.

(2) The provisions brought in under this paragraph include, in the case of a company registered as a company limited by guarantee, those of the resolution declaring the amount of the guarantee; and they include also the statement under section 681(5)(*a*), and any statement under section 684(2).

6.—(1) All the provisions of this Act apply to the company, and to its members, contributories and creditors, in the same manner in all respects as if it had been formed under this Act, subject as follows.

(2) Table A does not apply unless adopted by special resolution.

(3) Provisions relating to the numbering of shares do not apply to any joint stock company whose shares are not numbered.

(4) Subject to the provisions of this Schedule, the company does not have power—

(*a*) to alter any provision contained in an Act of Parliament relating to the company,

(*b*) without the sanction of the Secretary of State, to alter any provision contained in letters patent relating to the company.

(5) The company does not have power to alter any provision contained in a royal charter or letters patent with respect to the company's objects.

Capital structure

7. Provisions of this Act with respect to—

(*a*) the registration of an unlimited company as limited,

(*b*) the powers of an unlimited company on registration as a limited company to increase the nominal amount of its share capital and to provide that a portion of its share capital shall not be capable of being called up except in the event of winding up, and

(*c*) the power of a limited company to determine that a portion of its share capital shall not be capable of being called up except in that event,

apply, notwithstanding any provisions contained in an Act of Parliament, royal charter or other instrument constituting or regulating the company.

Supplementary

8. Nothing in paragraphs 5 to 7 authorises a company to alter any such provisions contained in an instrument constituting or regulating the company as would, if the company had originally been formed under this Act, have been required to be contained in the memorandum and are not authorised to be altered by this Act.

9. None of the provisions of this Act (except section 461(3)) derogate from any power of altering the company's constitution or regulations which may, by virtue of any Act of Parliament or other instrument constituting or regulating it, be vested in the company.

Section 718.

SCHEDULE 22

PROVISIONS OF THIS ACT APPLYING TO UNREGISTERED COMPANIES

Provisions of this Act applied	Subject matter	Limitations and exceptions (if any)
In Part I—		
section 18	Statutory and other amendments of memorandum and articles to be registered.	Subject to section 718(3).
section 35	Company's capacity; power of directors to bind it.	Subject to section 718(3).
section 36(4)	Binding effect of contract made for company before its formation.	Subject to section 718(3).
section 40	Official seal for share certificates, etc.	Subject to section 718(3).
section 42	Events affecting a company's status to be officially notified.	Subject to section 718(3).
In Part III, Chapter I (with Schedule 3) ...	Prospectus and requirements in connection with it.	Subject to section 718(3).
In Part IV, sections 82, 86 and 87 ...	Allotments.	Subject to section 718(3).
In Part V—		
section 185(4)	Exemption from duty to prepare certificates where shares etc. issued to stock exchange nominee.	Subject to section 718(3).
section 186	Certificate as evidence of title.	Subject to section 718(3).
Part VII, with— Schedule 4 to 8 ... Schedule 9 (except sub-paragraphs (*a*) to (*d*) of paragraph 2, sub-paragraphs (*c*) (*d*) and (*e*) of paragraph 3 and sub-paragraph (1)(*c*) of paragraph 10), and Schedule 10	Accounts and audit.	Subject to section 718(3).
In Part IX—		
section 287	Registered office.	Subject to section 718(3).
sections 288 to 290	Register of directors and secretaries.	—

Provisions of this Act applied	Subject matter	Limitations and exceptions (if any)
In Part X, sections 343 to 347	Register to be kept of certain transactions not disclosed in accounts; other related matters.	Subject to section 718(3).
In Part XI—		
section 351(1), (2) and (5)(a)	Particulars of company to be given in correspondence.	Subject to section 718(3).
sections 363 (with Schedule 15) to 365 ...	Annual return.	Subject to section 718(3).
sections 384 to 393	Appointment, qualifications, etc., of auditors.	Subject to section 718(3).
In Part XIV, sections 431 to 445 and 452(1) ...	Investigation of companies and their affairs.	—
Part XV	Effect of order imposing restrictions on shares.	To apply so far only as relates to orders under section 445.
In Part XXIV—		
sections 706, 708 to 710, 712 and 713 ...	Miscellaneous provisions about registration.	—
section 711	Public notice by registrar of companies with respect to certain documents.	Subject to section 718(3).
In Part XXV—		
section 720	Companies to publish periodical statement.	Subject to section 718(3).
section 721	Production and inspection of company's books.	
section 722	Form of company registers, etc.	To apply so far only as these provisions have effect in relation to provisions applying by virtue of the foregoing provisions of this Schedule.
section 723	Use of computers for company records.	
section 725	Service of documents.	
section 730, with Schedule 24	Punishment of offences; meaning of " officer in default ".	
section 731	Summary proceedings.	
section 732	Prosecution by public authorities.	
Part XXVI	Interpretation.	To apply so far as requisite for the interpretation of other provisions applied by section 718 and this Schedule.

SCHEDULE 23 Section 720.

FORM OF STATEMENT TO BE PUBLISHED BY CERTAIN COMPANIES UNDER
SECTION 720

*The share capital of the company is   , divided into shares of   each.

The number of shares issued is

Calls to the amount of   pounds per share have been made, under which the sum of   pounds has been received.

The liabilities of the company on the first day of January (*or* July) were—

Debts owing to sundry persons by the company.

On judgment (in Scotland, in respect of which decree has been granted), £

On specialty, £

On notes or bills, £

On simple contracts, £

On estimated liabilities, £

The assets of the company on that day were—

Government securities [*stating them*]

Bills of exchange and promissory notes, £

Cash at the bankers, £

Other securities, £

---

* If the company has no share capital the portion of the statement relating to capital and shares must be omitted.

Section 730.

SCHEDULE 24

Punishment of Offences Under this Act

Note: In the fourth and fifth columns of this Schedule, " the statutory maximum " means—

(a) in England and Wales, the prescribed sum under section 32 of the Magistrates' Courts Act 1980 (c. 43), and

(b) in Scotland, the prescribed sum under section 289B of the Criminal Procedure (Scotland) Act 1975 (c. 21).

Section of Act creating offence		General nature of offence	Mode of prosecution	Punishment	Daily default fine (where applicable)
6(3)	...	Company failing to deliver to registrar notice or other document, following alteration of its objects.	Summary.	One-fifth of the statutory maximum.	One-fiftieth of the statutory maximum.
18(3)	...	Company failing to register change in memorandum or articles.	Summary.	One-fifth of the statutory maximum.	One-fiftieth of the statutory maximum.
19(2)	...	Company failing to send to one of its members a copy of the memorandum or articles, when so required by the member.	Summary.	One-fifth of the statutory maximum.	
20(2)	...	Where company's memorandum altered, company issuing copy of the memorandum without the alteration.	Summary.	One-fifth of the statutory maximum for each occasion on which copies are so issued after the date of the alteration.	
28(5)	...	Company failing to change name on direction of Secretary of State.	Summary.	One-fifth of the statutory maximum.	One-fiftieth of the statutory maximum.
31(5)	...	Company altering its memorandum or articles, so ceasing to be exempt from having " limited " as part of its name.	Summary.	The statutory maximum.	One-tenth of the statutory maximum.
31(6)	...	Company failing to change name, on Secretary of State's direction, so as to have " limited " (or Welsh equivalent) at the end.	Summary.	One-fifth of the statutory maximum.	One-fiftieth of the statutory maximum

Section of Act creating offence	General nature of offence	Mode of prosecution	Punishment	Daily default fine (where applicable)
32(4) ...	Company failing to comply with Secretary of State's direction to change its name, on grounds that the name is misleading.	Summary.	One-fifth of the statutory maximum.	One-fiftieth of the statutory maximum.
33 ...	Trading under misleading name (use of " public limited company" or Welsh equivalent when not so entitled); purporting to be a private company.	Summary.	One-fifth of the statutory maximum.	One-fiftieth of the statutory maximum.
34 ...	Trading or carrying on business with improper use of " limited " or " cyfyngedig ".	Summary.	One-fifth of the statutory maximum.	One-fiftieth of the statutory maximum.
54(10) ...	Public company failing to give notice, or copy of court order, to registrar, concerning application to re-register as private company.	Summary.	One-fifth of the statutory maximum.	One-fiftieth of the statutory maximum.
56(4) ...	Issuing form of application for shares or debentures without accompanying prospectus.	1. On indictment. 2. Summary.	A fine. The statutory maximum.	
61 ...	Issuing prospectus with expert's statement in it, he not having given his consent; omission to state in prospectus that expert has consented.	1. On indictment. 2. Summary.	A fine. The statutory maximum.	
64(5) ...	Issuing company prospectus without copy being delivered to registrar of companies, or without requisite documents endorsed or attached.	Summary.	One-fifth of the statutory maximum.	One-fiftieth of the statutory maximum.
70(1) ...	Authorising issue of prospectus with untrue statement.	1. On indictment. 2. Summary.	2 years or a fine; or both. 6 months or the statutory maximum; or both.	
78(1) ...	Being responsible for issue, circulation of prospectus, etc. contrary to Part III, Chapter II (oversea companies).	1. On indictment. 2. Summary.	A fine. The statutory maximum.	
80(9) ...	Directors exercising company's power of allotment without the authority required by section 80(1).	1. On indictment. 2. Summary.	A fine. The statutory maximum.	

Section of Act creating offence	General nature of offence	Mode of prosecution	Punishment	Daily default fine (where applicable)
81(2) ...	Private limited company offering shares to the public, or allotting shares with a view to their being so offered.	1. On indictment. 2. Summary.	A fine. The statutory maximum.	
82(5) ...	Allotting shares or debentures before third day after issue of prospectus.	1. On indictment. 2. Summary.	A fine. The statutory maximum.	
86(6) ...	Company failing to keep money in separate bank account, where received in pursuance of prospectus stating that stock exchange listing is to be applied for.	1. On indictment. 2. Summary.	A fine. The statutory maximum.	
87(4) ...	Offeror of shares for sale failing to keep proceeds in separate bank account.	1. On indictment. 2. Summary.	A fine. The statutory maximum.	
88(5) ...	Officer of company failing to deliver return of allotments, etc., to registrar.	1. On indictment. 2. Summary.	A fine. The statutory maximum.	One-tenth of the statutory maximum.
95(6) ...	Knowingly or recklessly authorising or permitting misleading, false or deceptive material in statement by directors under section 95(5).	1. On indictment. 2. Summary.	2 years or a fine; or both. 6 months or the statutory maximum; or both.	
97(4) ...	Company failing to deliver to registrar the prescribed form disclosing amount or rate of share commission.	Summary.	One-fifth of the statutory maximum.	
110(2) ...	Making misleading, false or deceptive statement in connection with valuation under section 103 or 104.	1. On indictment. 2. Summary.	2 years or a fine; or both. 6 months or the statutory maximum; or both.	
111(3) ...	Officer of company failing to deliver copy of asset valuation report to registrar.	1. On indictment. 2. Summary.	A fine. The statutory maximum.	One-tenth of the statutory maximum.

Section of Act creating offence	General nature of offence	Mode of prosecution	Punishment	Daily default fine (where applicable)
111(4) ...	Company failing to deliver to registrar copy of resolution under section 104(4), with respect to transfer of an asset as consideration for allotment.	Summary.	One-fifth of the statutory maximum.	One-fiftieth of the statutory maximum.
114 ...	Contravention of any of the provisions of sections 99 to 104, 106.	1. On indictment. 2. Summary.	A fine. The statutory maximum.	
117(7) ...	Company doing business or exercising borrowing powers contrary to section 117.	1. On indictment. 2. Summary.	A fine. The statutory maximum.	
122(2) ...	Company failing to give notice to registrar of re-organisation of share capital.	Summary.	One-fifth of the statutory maximum.	One-fiftieth of the statutory maximum.
123(4) ...	Company failing to give notice to registrar of increase of share capital.	Summary.	One-fifth of the statutory maximum.	One-fiftieth of the statutory maximum.
127(5) ...	Company failing to forward to registrar copy of court order, when application made to cancel resolution varying shareholders' rights.	Summary.	One-fifth of the statutory maximum.	One-fiftieth of the statutory maximum.
128(5) ...	Company failing to send to registrar statement or notice required by section 128 (particulars of shares carrying special rights).	Summary.	One-fifth of the statutory maximum.	One-fiftieth of the statutory maximum.
129(4) ...	Company failing to deliver to registrar statement or notice required by section 129 (registration of newly created class rights).	Summary.	One-fifth of the statutory maximum.	One-fiftieth of the statutory maximum.
141 ...	Officer of company concealing name of creditor entitled to object to reduction of capital, or wilfully misrepresenting nature or amount of debt or claim, etc.	1. On indictment. 2. Summary.	A fine. The statutory maximum.	
142(2)	Director authorising or permitting non-compliance with section 142 (requirement to convene company meeting to consider serious loss of capital).	1. On indictment. 2. Summary.	A fine. The statutory maximum.	

Section of Act creating offence	General nature of offence	Mode of prosecution	Punishment	Daily default fine (where applicable)
143(2) ...	Company acquiring its own shares in breach of section 143.	1. On indictment.	In the case of the company, a fine. In the case of an officer of the company who is in default, 2 years or a fine; or both.	
		2. Summary.	In the case of the company, the statutory maximum. In the case of an officer of the company who is in default, 6 months or the statutory maximum; or both.	
149(2) ...	Company failing to cancel its own shares, acquired by itself, as required by section 146(2); or failing to apply for re-registration as private company as so required in the case there mentioned.	Summary.	One-fifth of the statutory maximum.	One-fiftieth of the statutory maximum.
151(3) ...	Company giving financial assistance towards acquisition of its own shares.	1. On indictment.	Where the company is convicted, a fine. Where an officer of the company is convicted, 2 years or a fine; or both.	
		2. Summary.	Where the company is convicted, the statutory maximum. Where an officer of the company is convicted, 6 months or the statutory maximum; or both.	
156(6) ...	Company failing to register statutory declaration under section 155.	Summary.	The statutory maximum.	One-fiftieth of the statutory maximum.
156(7) ...	Director making statutory declaration under section 155, without having reasonable grounds for opinion expressed in it.	1. On indictment. 2. Summary.	2 years or a fine; or both. 6 months or the statutory maximum; or both.	

Section of Act creating offence	General nature of offence	Mode of prosecution	Punishment	Daily default fine (where applicable)
169(6)	Default by company's officer in delivering to registrar the return required by section 169 (disclosure by company of purchase of own shares).	1. On indictment. 2. Summary.	A fine. The statutory maximum.	One-tenth of the statutory maximum.
169(7)	Company failing to keep copy of contract, etc., at registered office; refusal of inspection to person demanding it.	Summary.	One-fifth of the statutory maximum.	One-fiftieth of the statutory maximum.
173(6)	Director making statutory declaration under section 173 without having reasonable grounds for the opinion expressed in the declaration.	1. On indictment. 2. Summary.	2 years or a fine; or both. 6 months or the statutory maximum; or both.	
175(7)	Refusal of inspection of statutory declaration and auditors' report under section 173, etc.	Summary.	One-fifth of the statutory maximum.	One-fiftieth of the statutory maximum.
176(4)	Company failing to give notice to registrar of application to court under section 176, or to register court order.	Summary.	One-fifth of the statutory maximum.	One-fiftieth of the statutory maximum.
183(6)	Company failing to send notice of refusal to register a transfer of shares or debentures.	Summary.	One-fifth of the statutory maximum.	One-fiftieth of the statutory maximum.
185(5)	Company default in compliance with section 185(1) (certificates to be made ready following allotment or transfer of shares, etc.).	Summary.	One-fifth of the statutory maximum.	One-fiftieth of the statutory maximum.
189(1)	Offences of fraud and forgery in connection with share warrants in Scotland.	1. On indictment. 2. Summary.	7 years or a fine; or both. 6 months or the statutory maximum; or both.	
189(2)	Unauthorised making of, or using or possessing apparatus for making, share warrants in Scotland.	1. On indictment. 2. Summary.	7 years or a fine; or both. 6 months or the statutory maximum; or both.	
191(4)	Refusal of inspection or copy of register of debenture-holders, etc.	Summary.	One-fifth of the statutory maximum.	One-fiftieth of the statutory maximum.

Section of Act creating offence	General nature of offence	Mode of prosecution	Punishment	Daily default fine (where applicable)
210(3) ...	Failure to discharge obligation of disclosure under Part VI; other forms of non-compliance with that Part.	1. On indictment. 2. Summary.	2 years or a fine; or both. 6 months or the statutory maximum; or both.	
211(10) ...	Company failing to keep register of interests disclosed under Part VI; other contraventions of section 211.	Summary.	One-fifth of the statutory maximum.	One-fiftieth of the statutory maximum.
214(5) ...	Company failing to exercise powers under section 212, when so required by the members.	1. On indictment. 2. Summary.	A fine. The statutory maximum.	
215(8) ...	Company default in compliance with section 215 (company report of investigation of shareholdings on members' requisition).	1. On indictment. 2. Summary.	A fine. The statutory maximum.	
216(3) ...	Failure to comply with company notice under section 212; making false statement in response, etc.	1. On indictment. 2. Summary.	2 years or a fine; or both. 6 months or the statutory maximum; or both.	
217(7) ...	Company failing to notify a person that he has been named as a shareholder; on removal of name from register, failing to alter associated index.	Summary.	One-fifth of the statutory maximum.	One-fiftieth of the statutory maximum.
218(3) ...	Improper removal of entry from register of interests disclosed; company failing to restore entry improperly removed.	Summary.	One-fifth of the statutory maximum.	For continued contravention of section 218(2) one-fiftieth of the statutory maximum.
219(3) ...	Refusal of inspection of register or report under Part VI; failure to send copy when required.	Summary.	One-fifth of the statutory maximum.	One-fiftieth of the statutory maximum.
223(1) ...	Company failing to keep accounting records (liability of officers).	1. On indictment. 2. Summary.	2 years or a fine; or both. 6 months or the statutory maximum; or both.	

Section of Act creating offence	General nature of offence	Mode of prosecution	Punishment	Daily default fine (where applicable)
223(2) ...	Officer of company failing to secure compliance with, or intentionally causing default under, section 222(4) (preservation of accounting records for requisite number of years).	1. On indictment. 2. Summary.	2 years or a fine; or both. 6 months or the statutory maximum; or both.	
231(3) ...	Company failing to annex to its annual return certain particulars required by Schedule 5 and not included in annual accounts.	Summary.	One-fifth of the statutory maximum.	One-fiftieth of the statutory maximum
231(4) ...	Default by director or officer of a company in giving notice of matters relating to himself for purposes of Schedule 5 Part V.	Summary.	One-fifth of the statutory maximum.	
235(7) ...	Non-compliance with the section, as to directors' report and its content; directors individually liable.	1. On indictment. 2. Summary.	A fine. The statutory maximum.	
238(2) ...	Laying or delivery of unsigned balance sheet; circulating copies of balance sheet without signatures.	Summary.	One-fifth of the statutory maximum.	
240(5) ...	Failing to send company balance sheet, directors' report and auditors' report to those entitled to receive them.	1. On indictment. 2. Summary.	A fine. The statutory maximum.	
243(1) ...	Director in default as regards duty to lay and deliver company accounts.	Summary.	The statutory maximum.	One-tenth of the statutory maximum.
245(1) ...	Company's individual accounts not in conformity with requirements of this Act; directors individually liable.	1. On indictment. 2. Summary.	A fine. The statutory maximum.	
245(2) ...	Holding company's group accounts not in conformity with sections 229 and 230 and other requirements of this Act; directors individually liable.	1. On indictment. 2. Summary.	A fine. The statutory maximum.	

Section of Act creating offence		General nature of offence	Mode of prosecution	Punishment	Daily default fine (where applicable)
246(2)	...	Company failing to supply copy of accounts to shareholder on his demand.	Summary.	One-fifth of the statutory maximum.	One-fiftieth of the statutory maximum.
254(6)	...	Company or officer in default contravening section 254 as regards publication of full individual or group accounts.	Summary.	One-fifth of the statutory maximum.	
255(5)	...	Company or officer in default contravening section 255 as regards publication of abridged accounts.	Summary.	One-fifth of the statutory maximum.	
260(3)	...	Director of special category company failing to secure compliance with special disclosure provision.	1. On indictment. 2. Summary.	A fine. The statutory maximum.	
287(3)	...	Company failing to have registered office; failing to notify change in its situation.	Summary.	One-fifth of the statutory maximum.	One-fiftieth of the statutory maximum.
288(4)	...	Default in complying with section 288 (keeping register of directors and secretaries, refusal of inspection).	Summary.	The statutory maximum.	One-tenth of the statutory maximum.
291(5)	...	Acting as director of a company without having the requisite share qualification.	Summary.	One-fifth of the statutory maximum.	One-fiftieth of the statutory maximum.
294(3)	...	Director failing to give notice of his attaining retirement age; acting as director under appointment invalid due to his attaining it.	Summary.	One-fifth of the statutory maximum.	One-fiftieth of the statutory maximum.
295(7)	...	Acting in contravention of a disqualification order under sections 295 to 300.	1. On indictment. 2. Summary.	2 years or a fine; or both. 6 months or the statutory maximum; or both.	

Section of Act creating offence	General nature of offence	Mode of prosecution	Punishment	Daily default fine (where applicable)
302(1) ...	Undischarged bankrupt acting as director, etc.	1. On indictment. 2. Summary.	2 years or a fine; or both. 6 months or the statutory maximum; or both.	
305(3) ...	Company default in complying with section 305 (directors' names to appear on company correspondence, etc.).	Summary.	One-fifth of the statutory maximum.	
306(4) ...	Failure to state that liability of proposed director or manager is unlimited; failure to give notice of that fact to person accepting office.	1. On indictment. 2. Summary.	A fine. The statutory maximum.	
314(3) ...	Director failing to comply with section 314 (duty to disclose compensation payable on takeover, etc.); a person's failure to include required particulars in a notice he has to give of such matters.	Summary.	One-fifth of the statutory maximum.	
317(7) ...	Director failing to disclose interest in contract.	1. On indictment. 2. Summary.	A fine. The statutory maximum.	
318(8) ...	Company default in complying with section 318(1) or (5) (directors' service contracts to be open to inspection); 14 days' default in complying with section 318(4) (notice to registrar as to where copies of contracts and memoranda are kept); refusal of inspection required under section 318(7).	Summary.	One-fifth of the statutory maximum.	One-fiftieth of the statutory maximum.
323(2) ...	Director dealing in options to buy or sell company's listed shares or debentures.	1. On indictment. 2. Summary.	2 years or a fine; or both. 6 months or the statutory maximum; or both.	
324(7) ...	Director failing to notify interest in company's shares; making false statement in purported notification.	1. On indictment. 2. Summary.	2 years or a fine; or both. 6 months or the statutory maximum; or both.	

Section of Act creating offence	General nature of offence	Mode of prosecution	Punishment	Daily default fine (where applicable)
326(2), (3), (4), (5).	Various defaults in connection with company register of directors' interests.	Summary.	One-fifth of the statutory maximum.	Except in the case of section 326(5), one-fiftieth of the statutory maximum.
328(6)	Director failing to notify company that members of his family have, or have exercised, options to buy shares or debentures; making false statement in purported notification.	1. On indictment. 2. Summary.	2 years or a fine; or both. 6 months or the statutory maximum; or both.	
329(3)	Company failing to notify stock exchange of acquisition of its securities by a director.	Summary.	One-fifth of the statutory maximum.	One-fiftieth of the statutory maximum.
342(1)	Director of relevant company authorising or permitting company to enter into transaction or arrangement, knowing or suspecting it to contravene section 330.	1. On indictment. 2. Summary.	2 years or a fine; or both. 6 months or the statutory maximum; or both.	
342(2)	Relevant company entering into transaction or arrangement for a director in contravention of section 330.	1. On indictment. 2. Summary.	2 years or a fine; or both. 6 months or the statutory maximum; or both.	
342(3)	Procuring a relevant company to enter into transaction or arrangement known to be contrary to section 330.	1. On indictment. 2. Summary.	2 years or a fine; or both. 6 months or the statutory maximum; or both.	
343(8)	Company failing to maintain register of transactions, etc., made with and for directors and not disclosed in company accounts; failing to make register available at registered office or at company meeting.	1. On indictment. 2. Summary.	A fine. The statutory maximum.	
348(2)	Company failing to paint or affix name; failing to keep it painted or affixed.	Summary.	One-fifth of the statutory maximum.	In the case of failure to keep the name painted or affixed, one-fiftieth of the statutory maximum.
349(2)	Company failing to have name on business correspondence, invoices, etc.	Summary.	One-fifth of the statutory maximum.	

Section of Act creating offence	General nature of offence	Mode of prosecution	Punishment	Daily default fine (where applicable)
349(3) ...	Officer of company issuing business letter or document not bearing company's name.	Summary.	One-fifth of the statutory maximum.	
349(4) ...	Officer of company signing cheque, bill of exchange, etc. on which company's name not mentioned.	Summary.	One-fifth of the statutory maximum.	
350(1) ...	Company failing to have its name engraved on company seal.	Summary.	One-fifth of the statutory maximum.	
350(2) ...	Officer of company, etc., using company seal without name engraved on it.	Summary.	One-fifth of the statutory maximum.	
351(5)(a) ...	Company failing to comply with section 351(1) or (2) (matters to be stated on business correspondence, etc.).	Summary.	One-fifth of the statutory maximum.	
351(5)(b) ...	Officer or agent of company issuing, or authorising issue of, business document not complying with those subsections.	Summary.	One-fifth of the statutory maximum.	
351(5)(c) ...	Contravention of section 351(3) or (4) (information in English to be stated on Welsh company's business correspondence, etc.).	Summary.	One-fifth of the statutory maximum.	For contravention of section 351(3), one-fiftieth of the statutory maximum.
352(5) ...	Company default in complying with section 352 (requirement to keep register of members and their particulars).	Summary.	One-fifth of the statutory maximum.	One-fiftieth of the statutory maximum.
353(4) ...	Company failing to send notice to registrar as to place where register of members is kept.	Summary.	One-fifth of the statutory maximum.	One-fiftieth of the statutory maximum.
354(4) ...	Company failing to keep index of members.	Summary.	One-fifth of the statutory maximum.	One-fiftieth of the statutory maximum.
356(5) ...	Refusal of inspection of members' register; failure to send copy on requisition.	Summary.	One-fifth of the statutory maximum.	

Section of Act creating offence	General nature of offence	Mode of prosecution	Punishment	Daily default fine (where applicable)
363(7) ...	Company with share capital failing to make annual return.	Summary.	The statutory maximum.	One-tenth of the statutory maximum.
364(4) ...	Company without share capital failing to complete and register annual return in due time.	Summary.	The statutory maximum.	One-tenth of the statutory maximum.
365(3) ...	Company failing to complete and send annual return to registrar in due time.	Summary.	The statutory maximum.	One-tenth of the statutory maximum.
366(4) ...	Company default in holding annual general meeting.	1. On indictment. 2. Summary.	A fine. The statutory maximum.	
367(3) ...	Company default in complying with Secretary of State's direction to hold company meeting.	1. On indictment. 2. Summary.	A fine. The statutory maximum.	
367(5) ...	Company failing to register resolution that meeting held under section 367 is to be its annual general meeting.	Summary.	One-fifth of the statutory maximum.	One-fiftieth of the statutory maximum.
372(4) ...	Failure to give notice, to member entitled to vote at company meeting, that he may do so by proxy.	Summary.	One-fifth of the statutory maximum.	
372(6) ...	Officer of company authorising or permitting issue of irregular invitations to appoint proxies.	Summary.	One-fifth of the statutory maximum.	
376(7) ...	Officer of company in default as to circulation of members' resolutions for company meeting.	1. On indictment. 2. Summary.	A fine. The statutory maximum.	
380(5) ...	Company failing to comply with section 380 (copies of certain resolutions etc. to be sent to registrar of companies).	Summary.	One-fifth of the statutory maximum.	One-fiftieth of the statutory maximum.

Section of Act creating offence	General nature of offence	Mode of prosecution	Punishment	Daily default fine (where applicable)
380(6) ...	Company failing to include copy of resolution to which section 380 applies in articles; failing to forward copy to member on request.	Summary.	One-fifth of the statutory maximum for each occasion on which copies are issued or, as the case may be, requested.	
382(5) ...	Company failing to keep minutes of proceedings at company and board meetings, etc.	Summary.	One-fifth of the statutory maximum.	One-fiftieth of the statutory maximum.
383(4) ...	Refusal of inspection of minutes of general meeting; failure to send copy of minutes on member's request.	Summary.	One-fifth of the statutory maximum.	
384(5) ...	Company failing to give Secretary of State notice of non-appointment of auditors.	Summary.	One-fifth of the statutory maximum.	One-fiftieth of the statutory maximum.
386(2) ...	Failing to give notice to registrar of removal of auditor.	Summary.	One-fifth of the statutory maximum.	One-fiftieth of the statutory maximum.
389(10) ...	Person acting as company auditor knowing himself to be disqualified; failing to give notice vacating office when he becomes disqualified.	1. On indictment. 2. Summary.	A fine. The statutory maximum.	One-tenth of the statutory maximum.
390(7) ...	Company failing to forward notice of auditor's resignation to registrar or persons entitled under section 240 in Part VII; failing to send to persons so entitled statement as to effect of court order or, if no such order, the auditor's resignation statement.	1. On indictment. 2. Summary.	A fine. The statutory maximum.	One-tenth of the statutory maximum.
391(4) ...	Directors failing to convene meeting requisitioned by resigning auditors.	1. On indictment. 2. Summary.	A fine. The statutory maximum.	

Section of Act creating offence	General nature of offence	Mode of prosecution	Punishment	Daily default fine (where applicable)
392(2)	...	Failure of subsidiary to give its holding company, and failure of holding company to obtain from its subsidiary, information needed for purposes of audit; failure of subsidiary's auditors to give information and explanation to holding company's auditors.	Summary.	One-fifth of the statutory maximum.	
393	...	Company officer making misleading, false or deceptive statement to auditors.	1. On indictment. 2. Summary.	2 years or a fine; or both. 6 months or the statutory maximum; or both.	
399(3)	...	Company failing to send to registrar particulars of charge created by it, or of issue of debentures which requires registration.	1. On indictment. 2. Summary.	A fine. The statutory maximum.	One-tenth of the statutory maximum.
400(4)	...	Company failing to send to registrar particulars of charge on property acquired.	1. On indictment. 2. Summary.	A fine. The statutory maximum.	One-tenth of the statutory maximum.
402(3)	...	Authorising or permitting delivery of debenture or certificate of debenture stock, without endorsement on it of certificate of registration of charge.	Summary.	One-fifth of the statutory maximum.	
405(4)	...	Failure to give notice to registrar of appointment of receiver or manager, or of his ceasing to act.	Summary.	One-fifth of the statutory maximum.	One-fiftieth of the statutory maximum.
407(3)	...	Authorising or permitting omission from company register of charges.	1. On indictment. 2. Summary.	A fine. The statutory maximum.	
408(3)	...	Officer of company refusing inspection of charging instrument, or of register of charges.	Summary.	One-fifth of the statutory maximum.	One-fiftieth of the statutory maximum.
415(3)	...	Scottish company failing to send to registrar particulars of charge created by it, or of issue of debentures which requires registration.	1. On indictment. 2. Summary.	A fine. The statutory maximum.	One-tenth of the statutory maximum.

Section of Act creating offence	General nature of offence	Mode of prosecution	Punishment	Daily default fine (where applicable)
416(3)	Scottish company failing to send to registrar particulars of charge on property acquired by it.	1. On indictment. 2. Summary.	A fine. The statutory maximum.	One-tenth of the statutory maximum.
422(3)	Scottish company authorising or permitting omission from its register of charges.	1. On indictment. 2. Summary.	A fine. The statutory maximum.	
423(3)	Officer of Scottish company refusing inspection of charging instrument, or of register of charges.	Summary.	One-fifth of the statutory maximum.	One-fiftieth of the statutory maximum.
425(4)	Company failing to annex to memorandum court order sanctioning compromise or arrangement with creditors.	Summary.	One-fifth of the statutory maximum.	
426(6)	Company failing to comply with requirements of section 426 (information to members and creditors about compromise or arrangement.)	1. On indictment. 2. Summary.	A fine. The statutory maximum.	
426(7)	Director or trustee for debenture holders failing to give notice to company of matters necessary for purposes of section 426.	Summary.	One-fifth of the statutory maximum.	
427(5)	Failure to deliver to registrar office copy of court order under section 427 (company reconstruction or amalgamation).	Summary.	One-fifth of the statutory maximum.	One-fiftieth of the statutory maximum.
444(3)	Failing to give Secretary of State, when required to do so, information about interests in shares, etc.; giving false information.	1. On indictment. 2. Summary.	2 years or a fine; or both. 6 months or the statutory maximum; or both.	
447(6)	Failure to comply with requirement to produce books and papers imposed by Secretary of State under section 447.	1. On indictment. 2. Summary.	A fine. The statutory maximum.	
48(5)	Obstructing the exercise of a right of entry or search, or a right to take possession of books or papers.	1. On indictment. 2. Summary.	A fine. The statutory maximum.	

Section of Act creating offence	General nature of offence	Mode of prosecution	Punishment	Daily default fine (where applicable)
449(2) ...	Wrongful disclosure of information or document obtained under section 447 or 448.	1. On indictment. 2. Summary.	2 years or a fine; or both. 6 months or the statutory maximum; or both.	
450 ...	Destroying or mutilating company documents; falsifying such documents or making false entries; parting with such documents or altering them or making omissions.	1. On indictment. 2. Summary.	7 years or a fine; or both. 6 months or the statutory maximum; or both.	
451 ...	Making false statement or explanation in purported compliance with section 447.	1. On indictment. 2. Summary.	2 years or a fine; or both. 6 months or the statutory maximum; or both.	
455(1) ...	Exercising a right to dispose of, or vote in respect of, shares which are subject to restrictions under Part XV; failing to give notice in respect of shares so subject; entering into agreement void under section 454(2), (3).	1. On indictment. 2. Summary.	A fine. The statutory maximum.	
455(2) ...	Issuing shares in contravention of restrictions of Part XV.	1. On indictment. 2. Summary.	A fine. The statutory maximum.	
458 ...	Being a party to carrying on company's business with intent to defraud creditors, or for any fraudulent purpose.	1. On indictment. 2. Summary.	7 years or a fine; or both. 6 months or the statutory maximum; or both.	
461(5) ...	Failure to register office copy of court order under Part XVII altering, or giving leave to alter, company's memorandum.	Summary.	One-fifth of the statutory maximum.	One-fiftieth of the statutory maximum.
467(4) ...	Body corporate or Scottish firm acting as receiver.	1. On indictment. 2. Summary.	A fine. The statutory maximum.	
467(5) ...	Undischarged bankrupt acting as receiver.	1. On indictment. 2. Summary.	2 years or a fine; or both. 6 months or the statutory maximum; or both.	

Section of Act creating offence	General nature of offence	Mode of prosecution	Punishment	Daily default fine (where applicable)
469(2) ...	Failing to deliver to registrar copy instrument of appointment of receiver.	Summary.	One-fifth of the statutory maximum.	One-fiftieth of the statutory maximum.
470(3) ...	Failing to deliver to registrar the court's interlocuter making the appointment of a receiver.	Summary.	One-fifth of the statutory maximum.	One-fiftieth of the statutory maximum.
478(5) ...	Failing to give notice to registrar of cessation or removal of receiver.	Summary.	One-fifth of the statutory maximum.	One-fiftieth of the statutory maximum.
480(2) ...	Not stating on company documents that receiver has been appointed.	Summary.	One-fifth of the statutory maximum.	One-fiftieth of the statutory maximum.
481(7) ...	Receiver making default in complying with provisions as to information where receiver appointed.	Summary.	One-fifth of the statutory maximum.	One-fiftieth of the statutory maximum.
482(5) ...	Default in relation to provisions as to statement to be submitted to receiver.	Summary.	One-fifth of the statutory maximum.	One-fiftieth of the statutory maximum.
489 ...	Body corporate acting as receiver.	1. On indictment. 2. Summary.	A fine. The statutory maximum.	
490 ...	Undischarged bankrupt acting as receiver or manager.	1. On indictment. 2. Summary.	2 years or a fine; or both. 6 months or the statutory maximum; or both.	
493(2) ...	Company failing to state in its correspondence, etc. that a receiver has been appointed.	Summary.	One-fifth of the statutory maximum.	One-fiftieth of the statutory maximum.
495(7) ...	Receiver failing to notify his appointment to the company; failing to send company's statement of affairs to registrar and others concerned.	Summary.	One-fifth of the statutory maximum.	One-fiftieth of the statutory maximum.
496(6) ...	Default in relation to statement of affairs to be given to receiver.	Summary.	One-fifth of the statutory maximum.	One-fiftieth of the statutory maximum.

Section of Act creating offence	General nature of offence	Mode of prosecution	Punishment	Daily default fine (where applicable)
497(7) ...	Receiver failing to send accounts of his receipts and payments to registrar and others concerned.	Summary.	One-fifth of the statutory maximum.	One-fiftieth of the statutory maximum.
498(4) ...	Receiver failing to send accounts to registrar for registration.	Summary	One-fifth of the statutory maximum.	One-fiftieth of the statutory maximum.
528(7) ...	Default in compliance with section 528 (submission of statement of company's affairs to official receiver).	1. On indictment. 2. Summary.	A fine. The statutory maximum.	One-tenth of the statutory maximum.
568(3) ...	Liquidator failing to send to registrar of companies copy of court order dissolving company.	Summary.	One-fifth of the statutory maximum.	One-fiftieth of the statutory maximum.
573(2) ...	Company failing to give notice in Gazette of resolution for voluntary winding up.	Summary.	One-fifth of the statutory maximum.	One-fiftieth of the statutory maximum.
577(4) ...	Director making statutory declaration of company's solvency without reasonable grounds for his opinion.	1. On indictment. 2. Summary.	2 years or a fine; or both. 6 months or the statutory maximum; or both.	
577(6) ...	Declaration under section 577 not delivered to registrar of companies within prescribed time.	Summary.	One-fifth of the statutory maximum.	One-fiftieth of the statutory maximum.
583(2) ...	Liquidator failing to summon creditors' meeting in case of insolvency.	Summary.	One-fifth of the statutory maximum.	
584(2) ...	Liquidator failing to summon general meeting of company at end of each year from commencement of winding up.	Summary.	One-fifth of the statutory maximum.	
585(3) ...	Liquidator failing to send to registrar a copy of the account of a winding up and return of final general meeting.	Summary.	One-fifth of the statutory maximum.	One-fiftieth of the statutory maximum.
585(6) ...	Failing to deliver to registrar office copy of court order for registration made under the section.	Summary.	One-fifth of the statutory maximum.	One-fiftieth of the statutory maximum.
585(7) ...	Liquidator failing to summon final meeting of company prior to dissolution.	Summary.	One-fifth of the statutory maximum.	

Section of Act creating offence	General nature of offence	Mode of prosecution	Punishment	Daily default fine (where applicable)
588(5) ...	Company or its directors or officers failing to comply with the section in relation to summoning or advertisement of creditors' meeting.	1. On indictment. 2. Summary.	A fine. The statutory maximum.	
594(2) ...	Liquidator failing to summon general meeting of company, and meeting of creditors, at end of each year.	Summary.	One-fifth of the statutory maximum.	
595(4) ...	Liquidator failing to send to registrar account of winding up and return of final company and creditors' meetings.	Summary.	One-fifth of the statutory maximum.	One-fiftieth of the statutory maximum.
595(7) ...	Failing to deliver to registrar office copy of court order for registration made under the section.	Summary.	One-fifth of the statutory maximum.	One-fiftieth of the statutory maximum.
595(8) ...	Liquidator failing to call final meeting of company or creditors.	Summary.	One-fifth of the statutory maximum.	
600(2) ...	Liquidator failing to publish notice of his appointment.	Summary.	One-fifth of the statutory maximum.	One-fiftieth of the statutory maximum.
624(2) ...	Fraud, etc., in anticipation of winding up (offence under subsection (1) or (2) of the section).	1. On indictment. 2. Summary.	7 years or a fine; or both. 6 months or the statutory maximum; or both.	
624(5) ...	Knowingly taking in pawn or pledge, or otherwise receiving, company property.	1. On indictment. 2. Summary.	7 years or a fine; or both. 6 months or the statutory maximum; or both.	
625 ...	Officer of company entering into transactions in fraud of company's creditors.	1. On indictment. 2. Summary.	2 years or a fine; or both. 6 months or the statutory maximum; or both.	
626 ...	Officer of company misconducting himself in course of winding up.	1. On indictment. 2. Summary.	7 years or a fine; or both. 6 months or the statutory maximum; or both.	

Section of Act creating offence	General nature of offence	Mode of prosecution	Punishment	Daily default fine (where applicable)
627 ...	Officer or contributory destroying, falsifying, etc., company's books.	1. On indictment. 2. Summary.	7 years or a fine; or both. 6 months or the statutory maximum; or both.	
628 ...	Officer of company making material omission from statement relating to company's affairs.	1. On indictment. 2. Summary.	7 years or a fine; or both. 6 months or the statutory maximum; or both.	
629 ...	False representation or fraud for purpose of obtaining creditors' consent to an agreement in connection with winding up.	1. On indictment. 2. Summary.	7 years or a fine; or both. 6 months or the statutory maximum; or both.	
634 ...	Body corporate acting as liquidator.	1. On indictment. 2. Summary.	A fine. The statutory maximum.	
635 ...	Giving, offering, etc, corrupt inducement affecting appointment of liquidator.	1. On indictment. 2. Summary.	A fine. The statutory maximum.	
637(2) ...	Default in compliance with the section, as to notification that company is being wound up.	Summary.	One-fifth of the statutory maximum.	One-fiftieth of the statutory maximum.
640(4) ...	Contravention of general rules as to disposal of company books and papers after winding up.	Summary.	One-fifth of the statutory maximum.	
641(2) ...	Liquidator failing to notify registrar as to progress of winding up.	Summary.	One-fifth of the statutory maximum.	One-fiftieth of the statutory maximum.
651(3) ...	Person obtaining court order to declare company's dissolution void, then failing to register the order.	Summary.	One-fifth of the statutory maximum.	One-fiftieth of the statutory maximum.
697(1) ...	Oversea company failing to comply with any of sections 691 to 693 or 696.	Summary.	For an offence which is not a continuing offence, one-fifth of the statutory maximum. For an offence which is a continuing offence, one-fifth of the statutory maximum.	One-fiftieth of the statutory maximum.

Section of Act creating offence	General nature of offence	Mode of prosecution	Punishment	Daily default fine (where applicable)
697(2) ...	Oversea company contravening section 694(6) (carrying on business under its corporate name after Secretary of State's direction).	1. On indictment. 2. Summary.	A fine. The statutory maximum.	One-tenth of the statutory maximum.
703(1) ...	Oversea company failing to comply with s. 700 as respects delivery of annual accounts.	1. On indictment. 2. Summary.	A fine. The statutory maximum.	One-tenth of the statutory maximum.
710(4) ...	Person untruthfully stating himself to be a member or creditor of company, for purpose of obtaining or inspecting company documents.	Summary.	One-fifth of the statutory maximum.	One-fiftieth of the statutory maximum.
720(4) ...	Insurance company etc. failing to send twice-yearly statement in form of Schedule 23.	Summary.	One-fifth of the statutory maximum.	One-fiftieth of the statutory maximum.
722(3) ...	Company failing to comply with section 722(2), as regards the manner of keeping registers, minute books and accounting records.	Summary.	One-fifth of the statutory maximum.	One-fiftieth of the statutory maximum.
Sch. 14, Pt. II, para. 1(3)	Company failing to give notice of location of overseas branch register, etc.	Summary.	One-fifth of the statutory maximum.	One-fiftieth of the statutory maximum.
Sch. 14, Pt. II, para. 4(2)	Company failing to transmit to its registered office in Great Britain copies of entries in overseas branch register, or to keep a duplicate of overseas branch register.	Summary.	One-fifth of the statutory maximum.	One-fiftieth of the statutory maximum.

Section 132(7).

SCHEDULE 25

COMPANIES ACT 1981, SECTION 38, AS ORIGINALLY ENACTED

Relief from
section 56 in
respect of group
reconstructions.

38.—(1) This section applies where the issuing company—

   (a) is a wholly-owned subsidiary of another company ("the holding company"); and

   (b) allots shares to the holding company or to another wholly-owned subsidiary of the holding company in consideration for the transfer to it of shares in another subsidiary (whether wholly-owned or not) of the holding company.

(2) Where the shares in the issuing company allotted in consideration for the transfer are issued at a premium, the issuing company shall not be required by section 56 of the 1948 Act to transfer any amount in excess of the minimum premium value to the share premium account.

(3) In subsection (2) above "the minimum premium value" means the amount (if any) by which the base value of the shares transferred exceeds the aggregate nominal value of the shares allotted in consideration for the transfer.

(4) For the purposes of subsection (3) above, the base value of the shares transferred shall be taken as—

   (a) the cost of those shares to the company transferring them; or

   (b) the amount at which those shares are stated in that company's accounting records immediately before the transfer;
whichever is the less.

(5) Section 37 of this Act shall not apply in a case to which this section applies.

TABLE OF DERIVATIONS

The following abbreviations are used in this Table:—

" 1948 "	=	Companies Act 1948 (c. 38).
" 1967 "	=	Companies Act 1967 (c. 81).
" 1972 Sc."	=	Companies (Floating Charges and Receivers) (Scotland) Act 1972 (c. 67).
" ECA 1972 "	=	European Communities Act 1972 (c. 68).
" SECOBA"	=	Stock Exchange (Completion of Bargains) Act 1976 (c. 47).
" 1976 c. 60 "	=	Insolvency Act 1976 (c. 60).
" 1976 "	=	Companies Act 1976 (c. 69).
" 1980 "	=	Companies Act 1980 (c. 22).
" 1981	=	Companies Act 1981 (c. 62).
" STA 1982 "	=	Stock Transfer Act 1982 (c. 41).
" 1983 (BI) "	=	Companies (Beneficial Interests) Act 1983 (c. 50).
" OinC–1 "	=	Companies Acts (Pre-Consolidation Amendments) Order 1984 (S.I. 1984/134).
" OinC–2 "	=	Companies Acts (Pre-Consolidation Amendments) (No. 2) Order 1984 (S.I. 1984/1169).

Provision	Derivation
1	1948 s. 1; 1980 ss. 1(1), (2), 2(1), Sch. 3 para. 2.
2	1948 ss. 2, 3, 4; 1976 s. 30(1), (2); OinC–1 No. 1.
3	1948 ss. 11(*a*)–(*d*), 454(2); 1980 s. 2(4), Sch 3 para. 34
4	1948 s. 5(1).
5	1948 s. 5(2)–(5); 1980 Sch. 3 para. 4.
6	1948 s. 5(7)–(9); 1976 Sch. 1.
7	1948 ss. 6, 7, 9; OinC–1 No. 2.
8	1948 ss. 8, 11(*b*)–(*d*), 454(2).
9	1948 s. 10; 1980 Sch. 3 para. 2.
10	1948 s. 12; 1976 ss. 21(1)–(5), 23(2), Sch. 2.
11	1980 s. 3(2).
12	1948 s. 12; 1980 s. 3(1), (5).
13	1948 s. 13; 1976 ss. 21(5), 38(2), Sch. 2; 1980 s. 3(3), (4,); 1981 s. 99.

Z

Provision	Derivation
14	1948 s. 20.
15	1948 s. 21; 1980 s. 1(3).
16	1948 s. 22.
17	1948 s. 23; 1980 Sch. 3 para. 6.
18	ECA 1972 s. 9(5).
19	1948 s. 24.
20	1948 s. 25.
21	1976 s. 30(6)–(9).
22	1948 s. 26.
23	1948 s. 27; 1983 (BI) s. 2.
24	1948 s. 31; 1980 Sch. 3 para. 7.
25	1948 s. 2(1)(a); 1976 s. 30(3); 1980 ss. 2(2), 78(4)(a), (d), Sch. 3 para. 3.
26	1980 s. 78(4)(a)–(e); 1981 ss. 22, 34, Sch. 3 para. 60.
27	1980 s. 78(1)–(3).
28	1981 s. 24; OinC–1 No. 53.
29	1981 ss. 31(1), (2), (4), (5), 32; OinC–1 No. 55.
30	1981 s. 25(1)–(4), (8).
31	1981 s. 25(5)–(10).
32	1967 s. 46; 1981 Sch. 3 para. 31; OinC–1 No. 33.
33	1980 s. 76(1), (2), (4).
34	1948 s. 439; 1976 Sch. 2.
35	ECA 1972 s. 9(1).
36	1948 s. 32; ECA 1972 s. 9(2).
37	1948 s. 33.
38	1948 s. 34.
39	1948 s. 35.
40	SECOBA s. 2(1).
41	1948 s. 36.
42	ECA 1972 s. 9(3) (in part), (4).
43	1980 ss. 2(3), 5(1)–(3), (10) (in part), 78(4); OinC–1 No. 39.

Provision	Derivation
44	1980 s. 5(5), as applying s. 24(2), (2A), (3), (11A), (12) (in part); 1980 s. 87(1); 1981 Sch. 3 para. 42; OinC–1 No. 40.
45	1980 s. 6.
46	1980 s. 5(10) (in part), (11), (12); 1981 Sch. 2 para. 6(1).
47	1980 s. 5(4), (6)–(9).
48	1980 s. 7(1)–(3).
49	1967 s. 43(1)–(3), (7); 1980 Sch. 3 para. 43; OinC–1 No. 31.
50	1967 s. 43(4), (5).
51	1967 s. 44(1)–(3); 1980 s. 7(4), Sch. 3 para. 44; OinC–1 No. 32.
52	1967 s. 44(4), (5).
53	1980 s. 10(1), (2); OinC–1 No. 41.
54	1980 s. 11.
55	1980 s. 10(3)–(5).
56	1948 s. 38(1), (3), (5); 1976 Sch. 2.
57	1948 s. 38(2).
58	1948 s. 45.
59	1948 s. 55(1).
60	1948 s. 55(2)–(4); 1980 Sch. 3 para. 11; SI 1984 No. 716. Art. 7(2).
61	1948 s. 40(1), (2).
62	1948 s. 40(3).
63	1948 s. 37.
64	1948 ss. 41(1)(*a*), (2)–(4), 45(3), (4).
65	1948 ss. 41(1)(*b*), etc., 455(1).
66	1948 s. 38(4), (6).
67	1948 s. 43(1), (5).
68	1948 s. 43(1) proviso, (2), (3).
69	1948 s. 43(4).
70	1948 s. 44.
71	1948 s. 46.
72	1948 s. 417(1), (3), (5); 1976 Sch. 2.
73	1948 s. 417(2).
74	1948 s. 419(1) (excl. para. (*b*)), (2).

Z 2

Provision	Derivation
75	1948 s. 419(1) (excl. para. (*a*)), (2).
76	1948 ss. 418, 455(1); 1976 Sch. 2.
77	1948 s. 420.
78	1948 ss. 417(4), (6), 421, 422.
79	1948 s. 423.
80	1980 s. 14; OinC–1 No. 42.
81	1980 s. 15(1), (3), (4).
82	1948 s. 50(1)–(6).
83	1948 s. 47.
84	1980 s. 16 (applying 1948 s. 47(4), (5)).
85	1948 s. 49; 1980 s. 16(2), Sch. 3 para. 8.
86	1948 ss. 50(6), 51(1)–(5), (6)(*a*); 1976 Sch. 2; OinC–1 No. 3.
87	1948 s. 51(7), inserted by OinC–1 No. 3.
88	1948 s. 52; 1976 Schs. 1, 2; OinC–1 No. 4.
89	1980 s. 17(1)–(5).
90	1980 s. 17(6)–(8); Table A Regs. 131–134.
91	1980 s. 17(9).
92	1980 s. 17(10).
93	1980 s. 17(12).
94	1980 s. 17(11), (13); 1981 Sch. 3 para. 40; OinC–1 No. 43.
95	1980 s. 18.
96	1980 s. 19(1)(*b*), (2)–(5).
97	1948 s. 53(1), (5); 1980 Sch. 3 para. 9.
98	1948 s. 53(2)–(4).
99	1980 s. 20(1)–(3), (5), (6).
100	1980 s. 21(1), (2); 1981 Sch. 3 para. 41.
101	1980 s. 22(1)–(4).
102	1980 s. 23(1)–(5), (7).
103	1980 s. 24(1)–(3), (8), (9), (11A), (12)(*aa*), (*a*); 1981 Sch. 3 para. 42; OinC–1 No. 44.
104	1980 s. 26(1)–(4).
105	1980 s. 26(7), (8) (in part).

Provision	Derivation
106	1980 s. 29.
107	1980 s. 87(1), (6).
108	1980 s. 24(4)–(7), (11), (12)(*b*).
109	1980 ss. 26(5), (6), 27(3).
110	1980 ss. 25(1), (3)–(5), 27(1).
111	1980 s. 25(2) (with 1948 s. 52(3) as applied); 1980 s. 27(2).
112	1980 ss. 20(4), (6), 21(3), 22(5), 23(6), 24(10), 26(8).
(2) (3) (4) (5)	1980 s. 26(8)(*b*), applying s. 20(4). 1980 s. 20(4), as applied. 1980 s. 20(6). 1980 s. 23(6), applying s. 20(4).
113	1980 s. 28.
114	1980 s. 30(1).
115	1980 s. 30(2).
116	1980 s. 31 (in part).
117	1980 s. 4.
118	1980 s. 85.
119	1948 s. 59.
120	1948 s. 60.
121	1948 s. 61.
122	1948 s. 62; 1976 Sch. 1.
123	1948 s. 63; 1967 s. 51(1).
124	1948 s. 64; 1967 s. 44(6); 1980 s. 7(4).
125	1980 s. 32(1)–(7) (excl. (6)(*a*),(*b*)), (9).
126	1980 s. 32(10).
127	1948 s. 72; 1980 s. 32(8).
128	1980 s. 33(1)–(4), (6).
129	1981 s. 102(1)–(3), (5).
130	1948 s. 56(1), (2); 1980 Sch. 3 para 12; 1981 s. 36.
131	1981 ss. 37, 40(6).
132	1981 s. 38; S.I. 1984/2007.
133	1981 s. 40(1), (4), (5), (7).
134	1981 s. 41.

Z 3

Provision	Derivation
135	1948 s. 66.
136	1948 s. 67.
137	1948 s. 68.
138	1948 s. 69; 1976 s. 38(2); 1981 s. 99.
139	1980 s. 12, with modified application of s. 10.
140	1948 s. 70.
141	1948 s. 71.
142	1980 s. 34.
143	1980 s. 35; 1981 Sch. 3 para. 43.
144	1980 s. 36(1)–(4).
145	1980 s. 36(5) (with s. 37(1)(*d*)), s. 36(6); 1983 (BI).
146	1980 s. 37(1)–(3), (11); 1981 Sch. 3 para. 44; 1983 (BI).
147	1980 s. 37(2) (in part), (4), (5), (8).
148	1980 s. 37(9), (10); 1983 (BI); OinC-1 Nos. 45, 59.
149	1980 s. 37(6), (7).
150	1980 s. 38.
151	1981 s. 42(1), (2), (12).
152	1981 ss. 42(8)–(10), 62(1).
153	1981 s. 42 (3)–(6), (11).
154	1981 s. 42(7), (11).
155	1981 ss. 43(1)–(6), 44(8), 62(1); OinC-1 No. 57.
156	1981 ss. 43(7), (8), 44(5)–(7).
157	1981 s. 44(1)–(4).
158	1981 s. 43(9).
159	1981 s. 45(1)–(4).
160	1981 s. 45(5)–(9).
161	1981 s. 45(10)–(12).
162	1981 s. 46.
163	1981 ss. 47(2), (3), 49(2).
164	1981 s. 47(4)–(12).
165	1981 s. 48.

Provision	Derivation
166	1981 s. 49(3)–(10).
167	1981 s. 50.
168	1981 s. 51.
169	1981 s. 52.
170	1981 ss. 53, 54(6)(*b*).
171	1981 s. 54(1)–(6).
172	1981 s. 54(7)–(10).
173	1981 s. 55(1)–(5), (9).
174	1981 s. 55(6)–(8), (10).
175	1981 s. 56.
176	1981 s. 57(1)–(3), (7).
177	1981 s. 57(4)–(6); 1980 s. 11(7)–(9) (as applied).
178	1981 s. 59.
179	1981 s. 61.
180	1981 s. 62(2)–(4).
181	1981 s. 62(1).
182	1948 ss. 73, 74.
183	1948 ss. 75–78; STA 1982 Sch. 2.
184	1948 s. 79.
185	1948 s. 80; SECOBA ss. 1, 7(2); STA 1982 Sch. 2.
186	1948 s. 81; SECOBA s. 2(3).
187	1948 s. 82.
188	1948 s. 83.
189	1948 s. 85.
190	1948 s. 86; 1976 Sch. 1.
191	1948 ss. 87, 110(6); 1967 s. 52(1); 1981 s. 101(2).
192	1948 s. 88.
193	1948 s. 89.
194	1948 s. 90.
195	1948 s. 92.
196	1948 s. 94; F.A. 1952 s. 30(3).

Provision	Derivation
197	1948 s. 93.
198	1981 ss. 63(1), (4), (9), (10), 82(2).
199	1981 s. 63(2), (3), (5), (6).
200	1981 s. 63(7).
201	1981 ss. 63(8), 64.
202	1981 s. 65.
203	1981 s. 66.
204	1981 s. 67(1)–(5), (10).
205	1981 s. 67(6)–(9).
206	1981 s. 68.
207	1981 s. 69.
208	1981 s. 70.
209	1981 s. 71.
210	1981 ss. 72(1)–(7), (9), 81.
211	1981 s. 73.
212	1981 s. 74.
213	1981 ss. 75, 83(8).
214	1981 s. 76(1)–(4), (12).
215	1981 s. 76(5)–(12).
216	1981 ss. 77(1), (2), (5)–(7); OinC–1 No. 58.
217	1981 s. 78.
218	1981 s. 79.
219	1981 s. 80.
220	1981 s. 82(1), (3).
221	1976 s. 12(1)–(5).
222	1976 s. 12(6)–(9).
223	1976 s. 12(10), (11).
224	1976 s. 2(1), (2), (4), (5).
225	1976 s. 3(1)–(7).
226	1976 s. 3(8)–(10).
227	1948 ss. 149(8) (*b*), 153(1); 1976 s. 1(1)–(4); 1981 s. 1.

Provision	Derivation
228	1948 s. 149(1)–(6) (inserted, 1981 s. 1(1)).
229	1948 ss. 150(1) (as substituted, 1976 s. 8(1)), 150(2), 151(1) (as am. 1976 Sch. 2), (2), (3).
230	1948 s. 152 (as inserted, 1981 s. 2); OinC-1 No. 12.
231	1948 s. 196(1); 1967 ss. 3(1), 4(1), 5(1), 6(1), 7(1), (2), 8(1); 1981 s. 4, Sch. 3 paras. 10, 23, 25, 26.
(3)	1967 ss. 3(5) (*b*), (6), 4(5) (*b*), (6); 1980 Sch. 3 para. 41; 1981 s. 4(8), (9).
(4)	1948 s. 198; 1967 ss. 6(5), 7(3).
232	1980 ss. 54(1), (2), (2A), (3), 63(1); 1981 Sch. 3 para. 51.
233	1980 s. 56(2), (3), (6); 1981 Sch. 3 para. 52.
234	1980 ss. 56(4), (4A), (6), 63(1); 1981 Sch. 3 para. 52.
235	1948 s. 157(1); 1967 ss. 16(1), 16A(1), 19(1), 23; 1976 Sch. 2; 1980 Sch. 3; 1981 ss. 13(1), 14, Sch. 3 para. 6.
(6)	1981 s. 16(1) (partially excluding 1967 ss. 17, 18).
236	1967 s. 14(1), (3) (*a*); 1976 Sch. 2; 1980 Sch. 3 para. 41(3); 1981 Sch. 3 para. 27.
237	1948 s. 196(8); 1967 ss. 6(4), 7(3), 8(4), 14(4)–(6), 23A; 1976 Sch. 2; 1980 s. 59; 1981 s. 15.
238	1948 ss. 155, 156; 1976 Sch. 2.
239	1948 s. 150(1) (as substituted, 1976 s. 8(1); 1976 s. 1(5)).
240	1948 s. 158(1), (3); 1967 s. 24; 1976 Sch. 2.
241	1967 s. 14(2); 1976 s. 1(6)–(8).
242	1976 s.6.
243	1976 ss. 4(1)–(5), 45(3).
244	1976 s. 5.
245	1948 ss. 149(5), (7) (as inserted, 1981 s. 1(1)), 149A(6), 150(3); 1976 s. 8; 1980 Sch. 3 para. 20; 1981 Sch. 3 para. 5.
246	1948 s. 158(2), (3); 1967 s. 24.
247	1981 ss. 5(1)–(5), 6(1), 12(7), (9).
248	1981 s. 8(1)–(3), (9)–(11).
249	1981 s. 8(1), (5), (6), (7).
250	1981 ss. 9(1)–(6), 10(1)–(3); OinC–2 No. 10.
251	1981 s. 5(7)–(9).
252	1981 s. 12(1)–(6), (12), (13); OinC–1 No. 52.
253	1981 s. 12(7), (8), (10). (11) (including s. 7(2) as applied).

Provision	Derivation
254	1981 s. 11(1)–(5), (9), (10).
255	1980 s. 43(8); 1981 s. 11(6)–(8), (10).
256	1948 s. 454(1), (1A), (2A), (3), (4); 1981 s. 18.
257	1981 Sch. 2 paras. 1–3, 5(7), 8.
258	1948 s. 149A(1)–(5), (7)(*a*); 1981 s. 1(1), Sch. 2 para. 4(1).
259	1948 s. 152A; 1976 Sch. 2; 1981 s. 2, Sch. 2 para. 4(1); OinC–2 No. 1.
260	1967 s. 11; 1981 Sch. 2 paras. 5(1), (2), 7(1).
261(2) (3) (4) (5) (6) (7)	1948 s. 157(1); 1981 Sch. 2 para. 4(2). 1948 s. 163, proviso; 1981 Sch. 2 para. 4(3). 1967 s. 22; 1981 Sch. 2 para. 5(6). 1967 s. 16; 1981 Sch. 2 para. 5(4), (5). 1967 ss. 17, 18. 1981 Sch. 2 para. 5(5) (excluding 1967 s. 23A).
262	1967 s. 14(3)(*b*); 1980 Sch. 3 para. 41(3)(*b*).
263	1980 ss. 39(1)–(3), 45(2); 1981 Sch. 3 para 48(*a*).
264	1980 ss. 40, 87(4).
265	1980 s. 41(1), (2), (5), (6); 1981 Sch. 3 para. 46.
266	1980 s. 41(3), (4), (7), (8).
267	1980 s. 41(9), (10).
268	1980 s. 42.
269	1980 s. 42A; 1981 s. 84.
270	1980 s. 43(1), (2), (8); 1981 Sch. 3 para. 47.
271	1980 s. 43(3), (4), (8).
272	1980 s. 43(5), (8), (9).
273	1980 s. 43(6), (8), (9).
274	1980 s. 43(7); 1981 ss. 60(1), (3), 61.
275	1980 ss. 39(4), (4A), (5)–(7), 40(4), 43(7A); 1981 Sch. 3 paras. 45(1), (2), 47.
276	1980 s. 43A; 1981 s. 85.
277	1980 s. 44; 1981 ss. 60(2), 61.
278	1980 s. 45(1).
279	1981 Sch. 2 para. 6.
280	1980 s. 45(3), (4); 1981 Sch. 3 para. 48(*b*).
281	1980 s. 45(5).

Provision	Derivation
282	1948 s. 176.
283	1948 ss. 177, 178.
284	1948 s. 179.
285	1948 ss. 180, 183(2)(*a*).
286	1980 s. 79.
287	1976 s. 23(1), (3), (4).
288	1948 s. 200(1), (4), (6)–(8), (9)(*a*); 1976 s. 22(1); 1981 s. 95(1)–(3).
289	1948 s. 200(2), (9)(*b*)–(*d*); 1981 s. 95(2).
290	1948 s. 200(3), (9)(*b*)–(*d*).
291	1948 s. 182.
292	1948 s. 183; 1980 Sch. 3 para. 22.
293	1948 s. 185; 1980 Sch. 3 para. 23.
294	1948 s. 186.
295	1948 s. 188(1B), (2D), (2F), (6), (7); 1976 c. 60 s. 9(1), (1A), (2), (5), (7A); 1981 ss. 93, 94.
296	1948 s. 188(1)(*a*), (2D), (2E); 1981 s. 93.
297	1948 s. 188(1)(*b*), (2C), (2D); 1981 s. 93.
298	1948 s. 188(1)(*c*), (2D); 1981 s. 93.
299	1948 s. 188(1A), (2D), (2E); 1981 s. 93.
300	1976 c. 60 s. 9(1), (2), (6), (7A); 1981 s. 94.
301	1976 s. 29; 1981 Sch. 3 para. 36; OinC–1 No. 38.
302	1948 s. 187; 1981 Sch. 3 para. 9; OinC–2 No. 2.
303	1948 s. 184(1), (2), (4)–(6).
304	1948 s. 184(2), (3).
305	1948 s. 201; 1981 Sch. 3 para. 11.
306	1948 s. 202.
307	1948 s. 203.
308	1948 s. 204.
309	1980 ss. 46, 63(1).
310	1948 s. 205; 1980 Sch. 3 para. 26.
311	1948 s. 189.
312	1948 s. 191.

Provision	Derivation
313	1948 s. 192.
314	1948 s. 193(1), (2).
315	1948 s. 193(3)–(5).
316	1948 s. 194.
317	1948 s. 199; 1980 ss. 60, 63(3), Sch. 3 para. 25.
318	1967 s. 26; 1976 Sch. 1; 1980 ss. 61, 63(4).
319	1980 ss. 47, 63(1).
320	1980 ss. 48(1), (2), 63(1); 1981 s. 110(2); OinC–1 No. 46.
321	1980 s. 48(6)–(8); 1981 s. 110(3).
322	1980 s. 48(3), (4), (5); OinC–1 No. 47.
323	1967 s. 25; 1976 Sch. 2; 1981 Sch. 3 para. 28.
324	1967 s. 27(1), (2), (4), (8)–(11), (13); 1976 Sch. 2.
325	1967 s. 29(1), (2), (14); 1981 Sch. 3 para. 28.
326	1967 s. 29(12), (13).
327	1967 s. 30.
328	1967 s. 31; 1976 s. 24.
329	1976 s. 25.
330	1980 ss. 49, 63(1).
331	1980 ss. 65(1), (2), (3), (6), 87(1); 1981 Sch. 3 para 56.
332	1980 s. 50(2).
333	1980 s. 50(1); 1981 Sch. 3 para. 49.
334	1980 s. 50(2A); 1981 s. 111(1).
335	1980 s. 50(3)(*a*), (*b*).
336	1980 s. 50(4)(*a*), (*b*).
337	1980 s. 50(4)(*c*), (5).
338	1980 ss. 50(4)(*d*), (6), (7), 65(1).
339	1980 s. 51; 1981 s. 111(2), Sch. 3 para. 50.
340	1980 s. 65(4), (5).
341	1980 s. 52.
342	1980 s. 53; OinC–2 No. 6.
343	1980 ss. 57(1)–(4), (6), (7), (8), 63(2); OinC–1 No. 49.

Provision	Derivation
344	1980 ss. 57(5), 58(4).
345	1980 s. 62.
346	1980 s. 64; 1981 Sch. 3 paras. 54, 55; OinC–2 No. 7.
347	1980 s. 65(8).
348	1948 s. 108(1)(*a*), (2).
349	1948 s. 108(1)(*c*), (3), (4)(*b*), (*c*).
350	1948 s. 108(1)(*b*), (3), (4)(*a*).
351	ECA 1972 s. 9(7) (as am. 1980 Sch. 3 para. 45(2)); 1976 s. 30(5); 1980 s. 77.
352	1948 s. 110(1), (4)–(6); 1981 s. 101(1), (2).
353	1948 s. 110(2)–(4); 1976 Sch. 1.
354	1948 s. 111.
355	1948 s. 112.
356	1948 s. 113; 1967 s. 52(2).
357	1948 s. 114.
358	1948 s. 115.
359	1948 s. 116.
360	1948 s. 117.
361	1948 s. 118.
362	1948 ss. 119(1), (4), 122.
363	1948 s. 124; 1981 Sch. 3 para. 4; OinC–1 No. 7.
364	1948 s. 125(1)–(4); 1976 Sch. 1; 1981 Sch. 3 para. 4; OinC–1 Nos. 8, 9.
365	1948 s. 126; OinC–1 No. 10.
366	1948 s. 131(1), (5).
367	1948 s. 131(2)–(4), (5).
368	1948 s. 132.
369	1948 s. 133.
370	1948 s. 134; 1980 Sch. 3 para. 16.
371	1948 s. 135.
372	1948 s. 136.
373	1948 s. 137.

Provision	Derivation
374	1948 s. 138.
375	1948 s. 139.
376	1948 s. 140(1)–(3), (6), (7).
377	1948 s. 140(4), (5).
378	1948 s. 141.
379	1948 s. 142.
380	1948 s. 143; 1967 s. 51(2); 1980 s. 14(6), Sch. 3 para. 17; 1981 ss. 25(6), 49(10); OinC–1 No. 11.
381	1948 s. 144.
382	1948 s. 145; 1980 s. 63(3); OinC–1 No. 50.
383	1948 s. 146.
384	1976 s. 14(1)–(5), (7).
385	1976 s. 14(8).
386	1976 s. 14(6), (7), (10).
387	1967 s. 14(7); 1976 s. 15(6).
388	1976 s. 15(1)–(5).
389	1948 s. 161; 1967 s. 13(1), (6); 1976 s. 13.
390	1976 s. 16(1)–(7).
391	1976 s. 17.
392	1976 s. 18.
393	1976 s. 19(1), (2).
394	1976 s. 20.
395	1948 s. 95(1).
396	1948 s. 95(2), (6), (7), (10)(*a*), (*b*); S.I. 1972/1268, Art. 16(2).
397	1948 s. 95(8), (9); 1976 Sch. 1; 1980 Sch. 3 paras. 15, 52.
398	1948 s. 95(3)–(5).
399	1948 s. 96.
400	1948 s. 97.
401	1948 s. 98; 1976 s. 38(2); 1981 s. 99.
402	1948 s. 99.
403	1948 s. 100; 1976 Sch. 1.
404	1948 s. 101.

Provision	Derivation
405	1948 s. 102; 1976 Sch. 1.
406	1948 s. 103.
407	1948 s. 104.
408	1948 s. 105.
409	1948 s. 106; 1981 Sch. 3 para. 3; OinC–1 No. 5.
410	1948 s. 106A(1), (2), (10); 1972 Sc. ss. 6, 32(2), Sch.; S.I. 1972/1268; OinC–2 No. 5.
411	1948 s. 106A(3), (4).
412	1948 s. 106A(5).
413	1948 s. 106A(6), (7), (8); 1976 Sch. 1; 1980 Sch. 3 paras. 15, 52.
414	1948 s. 106A(9).
415	1948 s. 106B.
416	1948 s. 106C.
417	1948 s. 106D.
418	1948 s. 106E; 1976 s. 38(2); 1981 s. 99.
419	1948 s. 106F; 1976 Sch. 1.
420	1948 s. 106G.
421	1948 s. 106H.
422	1948 s. 106I.
423	1948 s. 106J.
424	1948 s. 106K; OinC–1 No. 6.
425	1948 s. 206.
426	1948 s. 207.
427	1948 s. 208.
428	1948 s. 209(1), (5).
429	1948 s. 209(2); 1976 Sch. 1.
430	1948 s. 209(3), (4).
431	1948 s. 164; 1981 s. 86(1), (2).
432	1948 s. 165; 1980 Sch. 3 para. 21; 1981 s. 86(3).
433	1948 s. 166; 1967 s. 41.
434	1948 s. 167(1), (1A), (2), (5); 1967 ss. 39(*a*), (*b*), 50; 1981 s. 87, Sch. 3 para. 32; OinC–1 No. 13.

Provision	Derivation
435	1948 s. 167(1B); 1981 s. 87(1).
436	1948 s. 167(3); 1967 s. 39; 1981 s. 87(2).
437	1948 s. 168; 1981 s. 88(1).
438	1967 s. 37(1), (2).
439	1948 s. 170; 1967 ss. 37(3), 40(1)–(4); 1981 Sch. 3 para. 7.
440	1967 s. 35(1).
441	1948 s. 171; 1981 s. 88(2).
442	1948 s. 172(1)–(4); 1981 Sch. 3 para. 8.
443	1948 s. 172(5), (6); 1981 s. 89.
444	1948 s. 173; 1981 s. 90.
445	1948 s. 174(1), (8).
446	1967 s. 32.
447	1967 s. 109.
448	1967 s. 110.
449	1967 s. 111; 1973 c. 58 Sch. 1 para. 16; 1976 s. 39(2); 1980 s. 84(3); 1981 s. 104(1)–(3); OinC–1 No. 34.
450	1967 s. 113; 1974 c. 49 Sch. 1; 1982 c. 50.
451	1967 s. 114.
452	1948 s. 175; 1967 ss. 32(6), 116 (as am. 1974 c. 49 Sch. 1, 1982 c. 50 Sch. 5 para. 6); 1981 s. 103(1), (3).
453	1967 s. 42.
454	1948 s. 174(2), (2A), (2B).
455	1948 s. 174(5)–(7); 1981 ss. 72(8), 77(4), 91(7).
456	1948 s. 174(3), (3A), (3B), (3C), (4), (4A); 1981 ss. 72(8), 77(3), (4), 91(4)–(6).
457	1948 s. 174(3D), (3E), (3F); 1981 ss. 72(8), 77(4), 91(4).
458	1948 s. 332(3); 1981 s. 96.
459	1980 s. 75(1), (9).
460	1980 s. 75(2), (10).
461	1980 s. 75(3)–(8).
462	1972 Sc. ss. 1(1), 2, 3 1979 c. 33 s. 29(2).
463	1972 Sc. s. 1(2)–(4).
464	1972 Sc. s. 5.

Provision	Derivation
465	1972 Sc. s. 30(2), (3).
466	1972 Sc. ss. 5(1), 7.
467	1972 Sc. s. 11; OinC–2 No. 4.
468	1972 Sc. s. 12.
469	1972 Sc. s. 13.
470	1972 Sc. s. 14(1)–(6), (8).
471	1972 Sc. s. 15.
472	1972 Sc. s. 16.
473	1972 Sc. s. 17.
474	1972 Sc. s. 18.
475	1972 Sc. s. 19.
476	1972 Sc. s. 20.
477	1972 Sc. s. 21.
478	1972 Sc. s. 22.
479	1972 Sc. s. 23.
480	1972 Sc. s. 24.
481	1972 Sc. s. 25; OinC–1 No. 35.
482	1972 Sc. s. 26.
483	1972 Sc. s. 27.
484	1972 Sc. s. 28.
485	1972 Sc. s. 29.
486	1972 Sc. s. 31.
487	1972 Sc. s. 32.
488	1972 Sc. s. 31(5).
489	1948 s. 366.
490	1948 s. 367.
491	1948 s. 368.
492	1948 s. 369.
493	1948 s. 370.
494	1948 s. 371.
495	1948 s. 372(1), (3)–(5),(7); 1976 Sch. 1.

Provision	Derivation
496	1948 s. 373.
497	1948 s. 372(2), (3), (4), (5)–(7); OinC–1 No. 18.
498	1948 s. 374; OinC–1 No. 19.
499	1948 s. 375.
500	1948 s. 376.
501	1948 s. 211.
502	1948 s. 212(1), (3).
503	1948 s. 212(2); 1981 s. 58(5).
504	1981 ss. 58(1)–(5), 61.
505	1967 s. 44(7); 1980 s. 7(4).
506	1967 s. 43(6).
507	1948 s. 213; 1981 ss. 58(6), 61.
508	1948 s. 214.
509	1948 s .215.
510	1948 s. 216.
511	1948 s. 394(3)(f), (g).
512	1948 s. 218(1), (3), (5), (6), (8); 1976 c. 60 s. 1(1), Sch. 1 Parts I, II.
513	1948 ss. 218(7), 219(1).
514	1948 s. 219(3).
515	1948 s. 220; 1976 c. 60 s. 1(1), (2), Sch. 1 Pts. I, II.
516	1948 s. 221.
517	1948 s. 222; 1972 Sc. s. 4; 1980 Sch. 3 para. 27.
518	1948 s. 223; 1976 c. 60 s. 1(1), (2), Sch. 1 Pts. I, II; S.I. 1984/1199.
519	1948 s. 224; 1980 Sch. 3 para. 28; 1981 s. 58(7).
520	1948 s. 225.
521	1948 ss. 226, 396.
522	1948 s. 227.
523	1948 s. 228.
524	1948 s. 229.
525	1948 ss. 230, 231, 232, 397.
526	1948 s. 233.

Provision	Derivation
527	1948 s. 234.
528	1948 s. 235(1)–(3), (5), (8).
529	1948 s. 235(4), (6), (7); 1967 s. 50.
530	1948 s. 236.
531	1948 s. 237.
532	1948 s. 238.
533	1948 s. 239.
534	1948 s. 240.
535	1948 s. 241.
536	1948 s. 242.
537	1948 s. 243.
538	1948 s. 244.
539	1948 s. 245.
540	1948 s. 246.
541	1948 s. 247.
542	1948 s. 248; 1976 c. 60 ss. 1(1), (2), 3, Sch. 2 para. 3.
543	1948 s. 249; 1976 c. 60 s. 2; OinC–1 No. 14.
544	1948 s. 250.
545	1948 s. 251.
546	1948 s. 252.
547	1948 ss. 253(1), 255.
548	1948 s. 254.
549	1948 s. 256.
550	1948 s. 257.
551	1948 s. 258.
552	1948 s. 259.
553	1948 s. 260.
554	1948 s. 261.
555	1948 s. 262.
556	1948 s. 263.
557	1948 s. 264.

Provision	Derivation
558	1948 s. 265.
559	1948 s. 266.
560	1948 s. 267.
561	1948 s. 268.
562	1948 s. 269.
563	1948 s. 270(1)–(3).
564	1948 s. 270(4)–(9).
565	1948 s. 271.
566	1948 s. 272.
567	1948 s. 273.
568	1948 s. 274.
569	1948 s. 275.
570	1948 s. 276.
571	1948 s. 277.
572	1948 ss. 143(4)(*e*), 278.
573	1948 s. 279.
574	1948 s. 280.
575	1948 s. 281.
576	1948 s. 282.
577	1948 s. 283(1)–(3); 1981 s. 105(1).
578	1948 s. 283(4).
579	1948 s. 284.
580	1948 s. 285.
581	1948 s. 286.
582	1948 s. 287.
583	1948 s. 288.
584	1948 s. 289.
585	1948 s. 290.
586	1948 s. 291.
587	1948 s. 292.
588	1948 s. 293; 1981 s. 106.

Provision	Derivation
589	1948 s. 294.
590	1948 s. 295.
591	1948 s. 296.
592	1948 s. 297.
593	1948 s. 298.
594	1948 s. 299.
595	1948 s. 300.
596	1948 s. 301.
597	1948 s. 302.
598	1948 s. 303.
599	1948 s. 304.
600	1948 s. 305.
601	1948 s. 306.
602	1948 s. 307.
603	1948 s. 308(1).
604	1948 s. 309.
605	1948 s. 310.
606	1948 s. 311.
607	1948 s. 312.
608	1948 s. 313.
609	1948 s. 314.
610	1948 s. 315.
611	1948 s. 316.
612	1948 s. 317.
613	1948 s. 318.
614	1948 s. 319.
615	1948 s. 320; OinC–1 No. 15.
616	1948 s. 321.
617	1948 s. 322; 1972 Sc. s. 8; OinC–1 No. 16.
618	1948 s. 323(1), (2), (8).
619	1948 s. 323(3)–(7).

Provision	Derivation
620	1948 s. 324.
621	1948 s. 325; Charging Orders Act 1979 s. 4.
622	1948 s. 326; 1976 c. 60 s. 1(1), (2), Sch. 1 Pts. I, II.
623	1948 s. 327.
624	1948 s. 328(1)(*d*), (*e*), (*i*), (*j*), (*k*), (*o*), s. 328(2), (3); 1976 c. 60 s. 1, Sch. 1 Pt. I; OinC–2 No. 3.
625	1948 s. 330.
626	1948 s. 328(1)(*a*)—(*c*), (*g*), (*h*), (*l*), proviso, (3).
627	1948 s. 329.
628	1948 s. 328(1)(*f*), proviso, (3).
629	1948 s. 328(1)(*p*), (3).
630	1948 s. 332(1), (2), (4).
631	1948 s. 333.
632	1948 s. 334(1)–(3), (4); 1981 s. 92(1).
633	1948 s. 334(5), (6); 1981 s. 92(1)–(4).
634	1948 s. 335.
635	1948 s. 336.
636	1948 s. 337.
637	1948 s. 338.
638	1948 s. 339.
639	1948 s. 340.
640	1948 s. 341.
641	1948 s. 342.
642	1948 s. 343; 1976 c. 60 Sch. 2.
643	1948 s. 344.
644	1948 s. 345.
645	1948 s. 346.
646	1948 s. 347.
647	1948 s. 348; OinC–1 No. 17.
648	1948 s. 349.
649	1948 s. 350.
650	1948 s. 351.

Provision	Derivation
651	1948 s. 352.
652	1948 s. 353(1)–(5), (7).
653	1948 s. 353(6).
654	1948 s. 354; 1981 s. 108(5).
655	1981 s. 108(1)–(4).
656	1948 s. 355.
657	1948 s. 355(2), (9).
658	1948 s. 356.
659	1980 s. 74(4), (5), (6)(*b*), (7), (8).
660	1948 s. 362.
661	1948 s. 363.
662	1948 s. 364.
663	1948 s. 365(1), (3), (5); 1967 s. 50; 1970 c. 8 s. 1(3)(*c*).
664	1976 c. 60 s. 1(2), (4).
665	1948 s. 398; 1981 c. 65 Sch. 6.
666	1948 s. 399(1)–(5), (8), (9); 1972 Sc. s. 4; 1981 c. 65 Sch. 6.
667	1948 s. 399(6)(*a*); 1976 c. 60 s. 1(2), (4), Sch. 1 Pts. I, II; S.I. 1984/1199.
668	1948 s. 399(6)(*b*).
669	1948 s. 399(6)(*c*), (*d*), (*e*).
670	1948 s. 400.
671	1948 ss. 401, 455(1).
672	1948 s. 402.
673	1948 s. 403.
674	1948 s. 404.
675	1948 s. 377.
676	1948 s. 378.
677	1948 s. 379; 1967 s. 53(2).
678	1948 s. 380.
679	1948 s. 381.
680	1948 s. 382(1), excl. proviso (v)–(vii); 1976 Sch. 1; 1980 Sch. 3 para. 29.

Provision	Derivation
681	1948 s. 382(1) proviso (v)–(vii), (2)–(4); 1980 Sch. 3 para. 29; 1981 Sch. 3 para. 13.
682	1981 s. 26(1), (2).
683	1948 s. 383.
684	1948 s. 384; 1976 Sch. 1; 1981 Sch. 3 para 14; OinC–1 Nos. 20, 21, 24.
685	1980 ss. 2(3), 13(1)–(5), (7).
686	1948 ss. 385, 386, 387; 1976 Sch. 1; OinC–1 No. 22.
687	1981 s. 26(3); OinC–1 Nos. 23, 54.
688	1948 s. 390; 1976 s. 38(2), Sch. 2; 1980 s. 13(6), Sch. 3 para. 31; 1981 s. 99.
689	1948 ss. 391, 392, 393, 394.
690	1948 s. 395.
691	1948 s. 407(1), (2); 1976 Sch. 1; 1981 Sch. 3 para. 15; OinC–1 No. 25.
692	1948 s. 409(1), (2); 1976 Sch. 2; OinC–1 No. 26.
693	1948 s. 411.
694	1976 s. 31; 1981 s. 27.
695	1948 s. 412.
696	1948 s. 413.
697	1948 s. 414; 1976 s. 31(5).
698	1948 s. 415.
699	1948 s. 416; 1981 s. 109.
700	1976 s. 9(1)–(3), (3A), (3B); 1980 Sch. 3 para. 49; 1981 s. 19; OinC–1 No. 37.
701	1976 ss. 2, 3 (as applied by s. 10).
702	1976 s. 6 (as applied by s. 11(2), (3)).
703	1976 s. 11(1), (4).
704	1948 s. 424; 1981 Sch. 3 para. 16.
705	1981 ss. 23(2), 97.
706	1976 s. 35.
707	1976 s. 36.
708	1948 s. 425(2); 1976 s. 37; 1981 Sch. 3 para. 37.
709	1948 s. 426(1); 1976 Sch. 2; 1981 ss. 98(1), 99.

Provision	Derivation
710	1948 s. 426(2)–(6); 1976 s. 38(3); 1981 ss. 98(2), 99.
711	ECA 1972 s. 9(3); 1976 ss. 1(10), 22(3), 23(6); 1980 Sch. 3 para. 45(1); 1981 Sch. 3 para. 34.
712	1948 s. 427.
713	1948 s. 428; 1976 s. 16(8); 1980 s. 84(1); 1981 s. 115(1).
714	1981 s. 23; S.I. 1982/1654.
715	1981 s. 100.
716	1948 s. 434(1); 1967 s. 120; 1979 c. 37 Sch. 7.
717	1967 s. 121.
718	1948 s. 435.
719	1980 s. 74(1)–(3), (6)(*a*).
720	1948 ss. 433, 454(2)(*a*).
721	1948 s. 441.
722	1948 s. 436; 1967 s. 56(6), Sch. 4; 1976 Sch. 2.
723	SECOBA s. 3 1976 Sch. 2; 1980 Sch. 3 para. 48.
724	1977 c. 38 s. 7.
725	1948 s. 437.
726	1948 s. 447.
727	1948 s. 448.
728	1948 s. 449.
729	1948 s. 451; 1976 s. 38(1); 1980 Sch. 3 para. 33; 1981 Sch. 3 para. 18.
730(4) (5)	1980 s. 80(2). 1948 s. 440(2).
731	1967 ss. 49(2)–(5), 115(1); 1972 Sc. s. 28(4); 1980 s. 84(2); 1981 s. 115(2).
732	1948 ss. 174(7), 446; 1967 s. 27(10); 1967 s. 91, as applied ibid. s. 115(2); 1976 s. 25(4); 1981 s. 72(9).
733	1967 ss. 89, as applied ibid. s. 115(2), 102(3); 1981 s. 81.
734	1967 s. 88, as applied ibid. s. 115(2).
735	1948 s. 455.
736	1948 ss. 150(4), 154.
737	1980 s. 87(1).
738	1980 s. 87(2), (3).

Provision	Derivation
739	1980 s. 87(1), (4)(*b*).
740	1948 s. 455(3).
741	1948 s. 455(1), (2); 1980 s. 63(1), (5).
742	1948 ss. 149(8)(*a*), (*b*), 149A(7)(*a*), 455(1); 1967 s. 56(2); 1976 s. 1(9); 1980 s. 87(1); 1981 ss. 1, 21(1), (3), Sch. 2 para. 5(7), Sch. 3 para. 33.
743	1980 s. 87(1).
744	1948 ss. 154(5), 406, 455(1); 1976 s. 1(9); 1980 s. 87(1), Sch 3. para. 35; OinC–1 No. 27.
745	(Northern Ireland).
746	(Commencement).
747	(Citation).
Sch. 1	1948 s. 200(2), (3); 1976 s. 21(1), (2); 1981 s. 95(2).
Sch. 2	1983 (BI) ss. 2–5, Sch.
Sch. 3	1948 s. 417(1)(*b*), Sch. 4; 1976 s. 33.
para. 1	1948 Sch. 4 paras. 1–3, 22.
2	1948 Sch. 4 para. 4.
3	1948 Sch. 4 paras. 5, 6; 1976 s. 33.
4	1948 Sch. 4 paras. 7, 25.
5	1948 Sch. 4 para. 8.
6	1948 Sch. 4 para. 9(2).
7	1948 Sch. 4 para. 9(1).
8	1948 Sch. 4 para. 10.
9	1948 Sch. 4 paras. 23, 24, 26.
10	1948 Sch. 4 paras. 11–13, 22.
11	1948 Sch. 4 para. 14.
12	1948 Sch. 4 para. 15.
13	1948 Sch. 4 paras. 16, 22.
14	1948 Sch. 4 para. 17.
15	1948 Sch. 4 para. 18.
16	1948 Sch. 4 para. 19.
17	1948 Sch. 4 para. 20.
18	1948 Sch. 4 para. 21.
19	1948 Sch. 4 para. 27.
20	1948 Sch. 4 para. 28.
21	1948 Sch. 4 para. 29.
22(1)	1948 Sch. 4 para. 30.
(3)	1948 Sch. 4 paras. 20, 21(1).
Sch. 4	1948 Sch. 8, substituted by 1981 s. 1.
para. 38(2)	OinC–1 No. 29.
60	1983 (BI) s. 2.
75(4)	S.I. 1984/1859.
Part VI	1948 Sch. 8 Part VA, inserted by S.I. 1982/1092.
Sch. 5	
para. 1	1967 s. 3(1); 1980 Sch. 3 para. 41; 1981 Sch. 3 paras. 23, 24.
2	1967 s. 3(2); 1981 Sch. 3 para. 24.
3	1967 s. 3(3).
4	1967 s. 3(4).
5	1967 s. 3(5).
6	1967 s. 3(2).

Provision	Derivation
7	1967 s. 4(1); 1981 Sch. 3 paras. 23, 24.
8	1967 s. 4(1A); 1981 s. 3(1).
9	1967 s. 4(2); 1980 Sch. 3 para. 41; 1981 Sch. 3 para. 24.
10	1967 s. 4(3); 1981 s. 3(2)(*a*).
11	1967 s. 4(4); 1981 s. 3(2)(*b*).
12	1967 s. 4(5); 1981 s. 3(2)(*c*).
13	1967 s. 4(7).
14	1981 s. 4(1).
15	1981 s. 4(2).
16	1981 s. 4(3); OinC–2 No. 8.
17	1981 s. 4(4)–(7); OinC–2 No. 9.
18	1981 s. 4(8).
19	1981 s. 4(10).
20	1967 s. 5(1); 1980 Sch. 3 para. 41; 1981 Sch. 3 para. 23.
21	1967 s. 5(2).
22	1948 s. 196(1)(*a*), (2); 1981 Sch. 3 para. 10.
23	1967 s. 6(6); S.I. 1982/1698.
24	1967 s. 6(1)(*a*), (7)(*a*).
25	1967 s. 6(1)(*b*), (2), (7)(*b*); S.I. 1979/1618 para. 3; 1981 Sch. 3 para. 6.
26	1967 s. 6(3).
27	1967 s. 7(1)–(3); 1981 Sch. 3 para. 26.
28	1948 s. 196(1)(*b*), (3).
29	1948 s. 196(1)(*c*), (4).
30	1948 s. 196(5).
31	1948 s. 196(6); 1981 Sch. 3 para. 10.
32	1948 s. 196(7).
33	1948 s. 196(3), (9).
34	1948 s. 196(1); 1967 ss. 6(1), 7(1).
35	1967 s. 8(1); 1981 Sch. 3 para. 26; S.I. 1982/1698.
36	1967 s. 8(2), (3).
37	1967 s. 8(5).
Sch. 6	
para. 1	1980 s. 54(1); 1981 Sch. 3 para. 51.
2	1980 s. 54(2).
3	1980 s. 54(4).
4	1980 s. 54(5).
5	1980 s. 54(6); 1981 Sch. 3 para. 51.
6	1980 s. 54(7).
7	S.I. 1984/1860.
8	S.I. 1984/1860.
9	1980 s. 55; OinC–1 No. 48.
10	S.I. 1984/1860.
11	1980 s. 58(1), (2).
12	1980 ss. 58(3), 87(4); 1981 Sch. 3 paras. 53, 62.
13	1980 s. 62.
14	1980 ss. 64, 65(1), (3), (4), (6).
15	1980 s. 56(1).
16	1980 ss. 56(2), (2A), (3), 62; 1981 Sch. 3 para. 52.
17	1980 ss. 56(8), 64, 65(1), (2), (3).
18	1980 s. 56(1), (4).
19	1980 s. 56(4).
20	1980 s. 56(5).
21	1980 ss. 56(8), 64, 65(2), (6).
Sch. 7	
para. 1	1967 s. 16(1)(*a*).
2	1967 s. 16(1)(*e*), (4), (4A); 1981 s. 13(4).
3	1967 s. 19(1); S.I. 1980/1055.
4	1967 s. 19(2); S.I. 1980/1055.
5	1967 s. 19(3)–(5).

Provision	Derivation
6	1967 s. 16(1)(*f*); 1981 s. 13(3).
7	1967 s. 16A(1), inserted 1981 s. 14.
8	1967 s. 16A(2), inserted 1981 s. 14.
9	S.I. 1980/1160.
10	1967 s. 16(1)(*g*), (5)–(7); 1974 c. 37 s. 79(3).
11	1967 s. 16(1)(*h*), (1A), (8); 1982 c. 46 s. 1.
Sch. 8	
Part I	
para. 1	1981 ss. 6(2)–(8), 7(1)–(8).
2	1981 ss. 6(2)(*a*), (3), 7(1).
3	1981 s. 6(2)(*b*), (6).
4	1981 s. 6(2)(*d*).
5	1981 s. 6(2)(*c*), (5).
6	1981 s. 6(4).
7	1981 s. 6(7)(*a*), (8).
8	1981 s. 6(7)(*b*).
9	1981 s. 7(2), (3).
10	1981 s. 7(4)–(6), (8).
11	1981 s. 7(7).
Part II	1981 s. 10(4), (5).
Part III	1981 s. 10(3)–(5).
Sch. 9	1948 Sch. 8A (formerly Sch. 8, renumbered 8A by 1981 s. 1(2)), as amended by 1967 s. 9, Sch. 2.
para. 2	1948 Sch. 8A para. 2(*a*), as modified by 1981 Sch. 2 para. 4(4); OinC–1 No. 30.
5(2)	1948 Sch. 8A para. 5(2)(*c*), as amended by 1976 Sch. 2.
6	1948 Sch. 8A para. 5A, as amended by 1976 Sch. 2.
10	1948 Sch. 8A para. 8(1), (3), as amended by 1976 Sch. 2, and modified by 1981 Sch. 2 para. 4(4).
13	1948 Sch. 8A para. 11, with insertions by 1980 Sch. 3 para. 39(2), amendments by S.I. 1970/1333, 1976 Sch. 2 and 1980 Sch. 3 para. 39(2), and modification by 1981 Sch. 2 para. 4(4).
14	1948 Sch. 8A para. 12, with amendment by 1976 Sch. 2 and modification by 1981 Sch 2 para 4(4).
17	1948 Sch. 8A para. 13A(5), as amended by S.I. 1979/1618.
19	1948 Sch. 8A para. 15, with amendments by S.I. 1973/1150 and 1981 s. 40(3); 1983 (BI).
22	1948 Sch. 8A para. 18, as modified by 1981 Sch. 2 para. 4(4).
23	1948 Sch. 8A para. 19, as modified by 1981 Sch. 2 para. 4(4)(*f*).
24	1948 Sch. 8A para. 19A, inserted by 1981 Sch. 2 para. 4(4).
27	1948 Sch. 8A para. 23, as modified by 1981 Sch. 2 para. 4(5); S.I. 1970/327.
28	1948 Sch. 8A para. 24, as modified by 1981 Sch. 2 para. 4(5).
30	1948 Sch. 8A para. 26, as modified by 1981 Sch. 2 para. 4(4).
Part IV	1948 Sch. 8A Part IIIA, inserted by S.I. 1982/1092; as amended by S.I. 1984/1859.
para. 33	1948 Sch. 8A para. 28, as amended by 1976 Sch. 2.
Sch. 10	
para. 1	1967 s. 16(1)(*b*); 1981 Sch. 2 para. 5(4).
2	1967 s. 17(1); 1981 Sch. 2 para. 5(4).
3	1967 s. 17(2); 1981 Sch. 2 para. 5(4).
4	1967 s. 17(3).
5	1967 s. 18(1), (3).
6	1967 s. 18(2), (3).
7	1967 s. 18(4).
8	1967 s. 18(5), (6).
9	1967 s. 16(1)(*f*).
Sch. 11	1981 Sch. 2 para. 6(1)–(4).

Provision	Derivation
Sch. 12	
Part I	1948 s. 188(2D), (3), (4); 1981 s. 93.
Part II	1976 c. 60 s. 9(2), (3), (4).
Part III	1948 s. 188(1C), (2)(*a*), (*b*), (2A), (2B); 1976 c. 60 s. 9(1A), (9); 1981 s. 93(5).
Sch. 13	1967 ss. 27–29; 1981 Sch. 3 paras. 28, 29.
Sch. 14	
Part I	1948 s. 119(1).
Part II	1948 ss. 119(2), (3), 120, 121; 1976 Sch. 1.
Part III	1948 s. 123.
Sch. 15	1948 Sch. 6 Part I.
para. 4	1948 Sch. 6 para. 4, OinC–1 No. 28.
Sch. 16	1948 Sch. 10.
Sch. 17	1948 ss. 253(2)–(8), 295(2).
Sch. 18	1948 Sch. 11.
Sch. 19	
para. 1	1948 s. 319(8)(*d*).
2	1948 s. 319(1)(*a*)(ii); F.A. 1966 Sch. 6 para. 14.
3	F.A. 1952 s. 30(2), (4), (5); F.A. (No. 2) 1975 s. 69.
4	V.A.T. Act 1983 (c. 55) Sch. 7 para. 12(1)(*c*).
5	Car Tax Act 1983 (c. 53) Sch. 1 para. 4(1)(*c*).
6	1981 c. 63 s. 30(1), (2).
7	1948 s. 319(1)(*a*)(i).
8	1948 s. 319(1)(*e*), as amended by Social Security Act 1973 (c. 38 and Social Security Pensions Act 1975 (c. 60).
9	1948 s. 319(1)(*b*).
10	1948 s. 319(1)(*b*), (*d*), (8)(*b*).
11	1978 c. 44 s. 121(1)(*c*), (2); 1980 c. 42 Sch. 1 para. 15; 1982 c. 24 Sch. 2 para. 12.
12	1948 s. 319(1)(*c*).
13	1948 s. 319(2); 1976 c. 60 s. 1, Sch. 1 Parts I, II.
14	1948 s. 319(4).
15	1948 s. 319(8)(*a*), (*c*).
Sch. 20	
Part I	1948 s. 323(6) proviso.
Part II	1948 s. 355(9).
Sch. 21	
para. 1	1948 s. 394(7).
2	1948 s. 391.
3	1948 s. 392.
4	1948 s. 393.
5	1948 s. 394(2); 1980 Sch. 3 para. 32(*a*).
6	1948 s. 394(3)(*a*)–(*e*).
7	1948 s. 394(4).
8	1948 s. 394(5).
9	1948 s. 394(6).
Sch. 22	1948 Sch. 14, as amended by 1967 s. 54, ECA 1972 s. 9(8), 1976 s. 41, SECOBA s. 4, 1980 s. 67, 1981 s. 20; OinC–1 No. 36.
Sch. 23	1948 Sch. 13.

Provision	Derivation
Sch. 24	The derivation of any entry in this Schedule is the cumulative effect of the original provision of the Act of 1948, 1967, 1972 Sc., 1976, 1980 or 1981 in so far as it provided a penalty for contravention, with the effect (in certain cases) of section 80 of, and Schedule 2 to, the Act of 1980. The derivation may also include provisions of the general law relating to the trial and punishment of statutory offences of greater or lesser gravity. 1980 Sch. 2 was amended by OinC–1 No. 51. OinC–2 Nos. 2, 3 and 4 amended 1948 ss. 187 and 328 and 1972 Sc. s. 11 in respect of punishment of contraventions of those sections in Scotland.
Sch. 25	1981 s. 38.

PRODUCED IN THE UK FOR W.J. SHARP
Controller and Chief Executive of Her Majesty's Stationery Office
and Queen's Printer of Acts of Parliament
LONDON: PUBLISHED BY HER MAJESTY'S STATIONERY OFFICE

PS 6351439 Dd.905406 C100 6/86 CCP